Lecture Notes in Computer Science 8744

Commenced Publication in 1973
Founding and Former Series Editors:
Gerhard Goos, Juris Hartmanis, and Jan van Leeuwen

Josep Domingo-Ferrer (Ed.)

Privacy in Statistical Databases

UNESCO Chair in Data Privacy
International Conference, PSD 2014
Ibiza, Spain, September 17-19, 2014
Proceedings

 Springer

Volume Editor

Josep Domingo-Ferrer
Universitat Rovira i Virgili
Department of Computer Engineering
and Mathematics
UNESCO Chair in Data Privacy
Av. Països Catalans 26
43007 Tarragona, Spain
E-mail: josep.domingo@urv.cat

ISSN 0302-9743   e-ISSN 1611-3349
ISBN 978-3-319-11256-5   e-ISBN 978-3-319-11257-2
DOI 10.1007/978-3-319-11257-2
Springer Cham Heidelberg New York Dordrecht London

Library of Congress Control Number: 2014947979

LNCS Sublibrary: SL 3 – Information Systems and Application, incl. Internet/Web
and HCI

Typesetting: Camera-ready by author, data conversion by Scientific Publishing Services, Chennai, India

Printed on acid-free paper

Springer is part of Springer Science+Business Media (www.springer.com)

Preface

Privacy in statistical databases is a discipline whose purpose is to provide solutions to the tension between the social, political, economic, and corporate demand of accurate information, and the legal and ethical obligation to protect the privacy of the various parties involved. Those parties are the respondents (the individuals and enterprises to which the database records refer), the data owners (those organizations investing in data collection) and the users (the ones querying the database or the search engine, who would like their queries to stay confidential). Beyond law and ethics, there are also practical reasons for data-collecting agencies and corporations to invest in respondent privacy: if individual respondents feel their privacy is guaranteed, they are likely to provide more accurate responses. Data owner privacy is primarily motivated by practical considerations: if an enterprise collects data at its own expense, it may wish to minimize leakage of those data to other enterprises (even to those with whom joint data exploitation is planned). Finally, user privacy results in increased user satisfaction, even if it may curtail the ability of the database owner to profile users.

There are at least two traditions in statistical database privacy, both of which started in the 1970s: the first one stems from official statistics, where the discipline is also known as statistical disclosure control (SDC) or statistical disclosure limitation (SDL), and the second one originates from computer science and database technology. In official statistics, the basic concern is respondent privacy. In computer science, the initial motivation was also respondent privacy but, from 2000 onwards, growing attention has been devoted to owner privacy (privacy-preserving data mining) and user privacy (private information retrieval). In the last few years, the interest and the achievements of computer scientists in the topic have substantially increased, as reflected in the contents of this volume.

"Privacy in Statistical Databases 2014" (PSD 2014) is held under the sponsorship of the UNESCO Chair in Data Privacy, which has provided a stable umbrella for the PSD biennial conference series since 2008. Previous PSD conferences were PSD 2012, held in 2012 in Palermo; PSD 2010, held in 2010 in Corfu; PSD 2008, held in 2008 in Istanbul; PSD 2006, the final conference of the Eurostat-funded CENEX-SDC project, held in 2006 in Rome; and PSD 2004, the final conference of the European FP5 CASC project, held in 2004 in Barcelona. Proceedings of PSD 2012, PSD 2010, PSD 2008, PSD 2006 and PSD 2004 were published by Springer in LNCS 7556, LNCS 6344, LNCS 5262, LNCS 4302 and LNCS 3050, respectively. The six PSD conferences held so far are a follow-up of a series of high-quality technical conferences on SDC which started sixteen years ago with "Statistical Data Protection-SDP 1998", held in Lisbon in 1998 and with proceedings published by OPOCE, and continued with the AMRADS

project SDC Workshop, held in Luxemburg in 2001 and with proceedings published by Springer in LNCS 2316.

The PSD 2014 Program Committee accepted for publication in this volume
27 papers out of 41 submissions. Furthermore, 9 of the above submissions were
reviewed for short presentation at the conference and inclusion in the companion
CD proceedings. Papers came from 17 different countries in five different conti-
nents. Each submitted paper received at least two reviews. The revised versions
of the 27 accepted papers in this volume are a fine blend of contributions from
official statistics and computer science. Covered topics include tabular data protection, microdata masking, protection using privacy models (differential privacy,
k-anonymity), synthetic data, record linkage, remote access, privacy-preserving
protocols, and case studies.

We are indebted to many people. First, to the Universitat de les Illes Balears
for providing the conference venue and local support and to the Templeton World
Charity Foundation for financial help. Also, to the Organization Committee for
making the conference possible and especially to Jesús Manjón, who helped
prepare these proceedings. In evaluating the papers we were assisted by the
Program Committee and the following external reviewers: Montserrat Batet,
Vassilis Fotopoulos, Raymond Heatherly, Vishesh Karwa, Sergio Martínez, Fang-
Yu Rao, and Bharath Kumar Samanthula.

We also wish to thank all the authors of submitted papers and apologize for
possible omissions.

July 2014   Josep Domingo-Ferrer

Organization

Program Committee

Elisa Bertino	CERIAS, Purdue University, USA
Aleksandra Bujnowska	EUROSTAT, European Union
Jordi Castro	Polytechnical University of Catalonia, Spain
Lawrence Cox	National Institute of Statistical Sciences, USA
Josep Domingo-Ferrer	Universitat Rovira i Virgili, Spain
Jörg Drechsler	IAB, Germany
Khaled El Emam	University of Ottawa, Canada
Mark Elliot	Manchester University, UK
Stephen Fienberg	Carnegie Mellon University, USA
Luisa Franconi	ISTAT, Italy
Sarah Giessing	Destatis, Germany
Julia Hoeninger	Statistik Berlin, Germany
Llorenç Huguet	Universitat de les Illes Balears, Spain
Anco Hundepool	Statistics Netherlands, The Netherlands
Alan Karr	National Institute of Statistical Sciences, USA
Julia Lane	American Institutes for Research, USA
Bradley Malin	Vanderbilt University, USA
Josep M. Mateo-Sanz	Universitat Rovira i Virgili, Spain
Laura McKenna	Census Bureau, USA
Gerome Miklau	University of Massachusetts-Amherst, USA
Krishnamurty Muralidhar	University of Kentucky, USA
Anna Oganian	National Center for Health Statistics, USA
Christine O'Keefe	CSIRO, Australia
Yosef Rinott	Hebrew University, Israel
Gerd Ronning	University of Tübingen, Germany
Juan José Salazar	University of La Laguna, Spain
Pierangela Samarati	University of Milan, Italy
David Sánchez	Universitat Rovira i Virgili, Spain
Eric Schulte-Nordholt	Statistics Netherlands, The Netherlands
Natalie Shlomo	University of Southampton, UK
Aleksandra Slavković	Penn State University, UK
Jordi Soria-Comas	Universitat Rovira i Virgili, Spain
Tamir Tassa	The Open University, Israel
Vicenç Torra	IIIA-CSIC, Spain
Vassilios Verykios	University of Thessaly, Greece
William E. Winkler	Census Bureau, USA
Peter-Paul de Wolf	Statistics Netherlands, The Netherlands

Program and General Chair

Josep Domingo-Ferrer   Universitat Rovira i Virgili, Spain

Organization Committee

Joaquín García-Alfaro   Télécom SudParis, France
Jesús Manjón   Universitat Rovira i Virgili, Spain
Tamar Molina   Universitat Rovira i Virgili, Spain
Marilina Tur   Universitat de les Illes Balears, Spain

Table of Contents

Remote Access

Privacy-Preserving Protocols

Case Studies

Enabling Statistical Analysis of Suppressed Tabular Data

Lawrence H. Cox

National Institute of Statistical Sciences, Washington, DC, USA
cox@niss.org

Abstract. For decades, NSOs have used complementary cell suppression for disclosure limitation of tabular data, magnitude data in particular. Indications of its continued use abound, even though suppression thwarts statistical analysis of both the expert and the novice. We introduce methods for creating alternative tables that the NSO can release unsuppressed, while ensuring within statistical certainty that their analysis is conformal with analysis of the original.

Keywords: cell suppression, algebraic circuit, divergence.

1 Introduction

Since the 1940s, national statistical offices (NSO) have employed cell suppression for statistical disclosure limitation (SDL) of tabular data. Cell suppression "pokes holes" in tables, thwarting statistical analysis for the less sophisticated analyst, but also for the expert as cells are blanked not-at-random. This paper introduces methods usable by either analyst or NSO that enable statistical analysis of tabular data. These techniques are focused on identifying alternative tables to the original table that in most cases yield analytical outcomes comparable to those on the original. Using these methods, an unsuppressed alternative table may be released and analyzed; or a sample of alternatives combined into a surrogate table and analyzed or each analyzed separately and analyses combined.

Table deconstruction is defined here to include:

- estimating feasible values of suppressed entries
- identifying feasible alternative tables to the original
- ruling out otherwise feasible values or tables
- identifying alternative tables exchangeable with the original for inferential purposes (*surrogates*)

Table deconstruction can be a computationally demanding task, so we focus initial research on table structures arising regularly in survey statistics, including network tables. Most U.S. Economic Censuses tables are 2- or 3-way tables controlled to 1- or 2-way totals ([1], [2]).

Our investigation has and explores strong connections to SDL transparency ([3]) in terms of what NSOs should (or should not) reveal about disclosure and suppression rules and what constitutes safe release of a set of alternative tables. We introduce

J. Domingo-Ferrer (Ed.): PSD 2014, LNCS 8744, pp. 1–10, 2014.

methods for winnowing sets of alternative tables, table deconstruction, and identification or construction of alternative tables suitable as surrogates.

Sec. 2 discusses complementary cell suppression (CCS). Sec. 3 describes moves from one alternative table to another based on algebraic circuits among suppressed table entries. Sec. 4 presents techniques for winnowing the set of alternative tables and discusses interplay of these methods with transparency issues. Sec. 5 presents methods for identifying alternative tables expected (statistically) to produce comparable analytical results to the original table. Sec. 6 contrasts behaviors of analyst and intruder in the context of alternative tables. Sec. 7 examines our methods in relation to other SDL methods. Sec. 8 contains concluding comments and directions for future research. This paper has been shortened considerably from the original to meet publication requirements; the original is available from the author.

2   Complementary Cell Suppression

Tabular data are data exhibiting an additive structure between *tabular cells*. Tabular structure is expressed as a system of linear equations $\mathbf{A}\mathbf{x} = \mathbf{b}$. The constant right-hand side satisfies $\mathbf{b} \geq 0$ and entries of the coefficient matrix $\mathbf{A}$ are restricted to $\{-1, 0, +1\}$ with at most one -1 in each row. In official statistics, of interest are solutions $\mathbf{x} \geq \mathbf{0}$, and often only fully integer solutions (e.g., contingency tables) ([1], [4]). Entity data (e.g., person data) are often counts presented in contingency tables: each entity contributes 1 to a cell value if the entity's characteristics match those defining the cell, and 0 otherwise. Establishment data may be presented in tables as aggregates of a nonnegative quantity of interest, e.g., retail sales, over all entities in the cell-- *magnitude data* ([2]).

Aggregation defines a constraint system of a linear program (continuous data) or mixed integer linear program (integer data) ([5]). Cox ([1], [2], [5]) provides full discussion.

Release of any statistical information based on data pertaining to individual subjects poses some *risk of disclosure* of individual subject data ([6], [7], [8]). *Complementary cell suppression* is described in [1], [2].

Sufficient protection may be characterized in terms of alternative tables. For each sensitive cell $\mathbf{X}$, the NSO determines acceptable lower (l_x) and upper (u_x) protection levels based on the disclosure rule. If there does not exist an alternative table exhibiting a feasible value x for $\mathbf{X}$ satisfying $x \leq l_x$ and a second alternative table satisfying $x \geq u_x$, protection is **not** sufficient. Alternative notions of sufficient protection, e.g., sliding protection ([9]), result in analogous formulations.

Although there is compelling evidence against use of cell suppression on confidentiality and data usability grounds ([10], [11]), overwhelmingly cell suppression has been and continues to be used. Complementary cell suppression performed using modern methods and software ([1], [12], [13]) is consistent internally, meaning that it provides sufficient protection. Consistency relies upon weighted *circuits* between suppressed entries that enable movement from one alternative table to another (viz., between nonnegative solutions of $\mathbf{A}\mathbf{x} = \mathbf{b}$). However, CCS is vulnerable to intruder attack based on applying outside intruder knowledge to these circuits, demonstrated by Cox ([11]). The mathematical program for CCS is driven by *local* and *global* data loss criteria represented by constraints on individual cell values and by a linear cost function such as total value suppressed, respectively ([10]).

3   Mathematical Basis for CCS: Circuits

Disclosure limitation via CCS is based on circuits between sets of suppressed cells. A circuit corresponds to a solution of $A_z = 0$; when z is integer; this is called a move. In one important case (tables of network type [14]), a circuit admits a bounded (network) flow between its constituent suppressed entries. Consider the table of counts:

Table 1. Table with suppressions (D) containing 4 sensitive cells

D_{11} (1)	18	D_{13} (6)	25
13	D_{22} (5)	D_{23} (2)	20
D_{31} (4)	D_{32} (1)	10	15
18	24	18	60

Original values of suppressed cells (D) are in parentheses. Assume a (t=5)-threshold disclosure rule--the risk region is then $\{1, 2, 3, 4\}$. Table 1 contains 4 disclosure cells (bolded) and 2 complementary cells. This example was contrived so that the suppression pattern is optimal with respect to both minimum number of suppressions (6) and minimum total value of suppressions (19). Mathematically, this is equivalent to Table 2. Its single circuit is given by Table 3.

Table 2. Reduction of Table 1

D_{11} (1)	0	D_{13} (6)	7
0	D_{22} (5)	D_{23} (2)	7
D_{31} (4)	D_{32} (1)	0	5
5	6	8	19

Table 3. Circuit for Table 1 suppressions

+/-	0	-/+
0	-/+	+/-
-/+	+/-	0

Relative to D_{11}, up to 4 units can be moved in the + direction along this circuit (increasing the value of D_{11}) and up to 1 unit in the − direction, yielding 6 alternative integer values for D_{11} and 6 alternative integer tables, corresponding to $D_{11} = 0, 1, ...,$ 5. Among the alternative tables, each sensitive cell achieves a value outside the risk region (0, 5)—each receives sufficient protection. This simple circuit is: $(z_{ij}) = (1, 0, -1, 0, -1, 1, -1, 1, 0)$, viz., a move from D_{ij} to $D'_{ij} = D_{ij} + z_{ij}$.

A cell suppression pattern may comprise multiple independent or overlapping circuits. For higher-dimensional tables, circuits can be more complex than such simple +/- paths—referred to as square-free circuits. This involves algebraic statistics and circuits that are non-square-free. Many tables arising in official statistics are tables of network type, studied in [14]. These are the starting point here, and include:

- 2-way tables
- hierarchies of 2-way tables organized along one, but not both, dimensions
- "thin" multi-way tables: tables of size fxgx2x2x....x2
- contingency tables fit to a log-linear model with 2 configurations of minimal sufficient statistics

All network tables, three-way tables, k-dimensional tables subject to (k-1)-dimensional marginal totals, and tables characterized by complete independence models ([15]) are within our initial scope.

4   Alternative Tables

Table 1 offers 6 alternative tables of nonnegative counts consistent with the suppression pattern, corresponding to $D_{11} = 0, 1, ..., 5$. The true (original) table has $D_{11} = 1$. What is or is not a sensitive (primary) cell differs between tables as the value of D_{11} changes. Consider the 5 other alternative tables, with notation primary (P) and complementary (C). First, the $D_{11} = 0$ table:

Table 4. Alternative table ($D_{11} = 0$) and optimal suppression pattern

0	18	7	25		0	18	7	25
13	6	1(P)	20		13	D	D	20
5	0	10	15		5	D	D	15
18	24	18	60		18	24	18	60

The $D_{11} = 0$ table contains 1 sensitive cell (P). The pattern is optimal but fails to suppress D_{11} and differs from Table 1. Thus, the $D_{11} = 0$ table could not have been the original table, and may be excluded, reducing from 6 to 5 the number of alternative tables. This illustrates one method for winnowing the set of alternative tables.

For $D_{11} = 2$:

Table 5. Alternative table (D_{11} = 2) and optimal suppression pattern

2(P)	18	5	25
13	4(P)	3(P)	20
3(P)	2(P)	10	15
18	24	18	60

D	18	D	25
13	D	D	20
D	D	10	15
18	24	18	60

This table contains 5 primary and 1 complementary suppressions, and the pattern is identical to Table 1. So, D_{11} = 2 is not yet ruled out. However, if the NSO distinguishes primaries and complementaries—or if the intruder can do so--then the intruder/analyst would detect the difference, and could rule out the D_{11} = 2 table.

Table 6. Optimal pattern (D_{11} = 1) and optimal pattern (D_{11} = 2)

P	18	C	25
13	C	P	20
P	P	10	15
18	24	18	60

P	18	C	25
13	P	P	20
P	P	10	15
18	24	18	60

The same holds for D_{11} = 3, 4, 5 tables. Thus, if primaries are identified, all tables other than the original are ruled out as alternatives, and no disclosure protection is achieved. Magnitude cell with entity count 1 or 2 are de facto primaries and identified. This illustrates the interplay between protection, winnowing the set of alternative tables, and transparency issues ([3])—what, if any, auxiliary information should the NSO provide regarding its disclosure and/or suppression rules.

5 Table Deconstruction and Analysis of Suppressed Tables

To provide a working example for magnitude data, entries of Table 1 are multiplied by 100 and the suppression pattern is preserved, resulting in Table 7. To assess data quality, it is reasonable to compare cell-value distributions across alternative tables using standard measures of divergence (f-divergences) between distributions. We express divergence in a convenient form below for conditional chi-square.

Table 7. Table of magnitude data with suppressions (D)

D_{11} (100)	1800	D_{13} (600)	2500
1300	D_{22} (500)	D_{23} (200)	2000
D_{31} (400)	D_{32} (100)	1000	1500
1800	2400	1800	6000

The conditional chi-square statistic is used to compare distributions of alternative $\{c_i\}$ and original suppressed values $\{a_i\}$:

$$\chi^2_{(df)} = \Sigma_i \frac{(c_i - a_i)^2}{a_i} \quad \text{where } df = \text{degrees of freedom} \quad (1)$$

In Table 7, the suppression pattern comprises a single circuit, so $df = 1$, corresponding to a quantity d that can be moved around the circuit while preserving nonnegativity: $c_i = a_i \pm d$. For Table 7 ($D_{11} = 100$), $-100 \leq d \leq 400$. Thus, relative to any alternative table $\{a_i\}$:

$$\chi^2_{(1)} = \Sigma_i \frac{d^2}{a_i} = d^2 \Sigma_i \frac{1}{a_i} \quad (2)$$

For Table 7, the sum of reciprocals of suppressed entries is 0.03117. For $\alpha = 0.05$, the critical chi-square value is 3.84. For $d^2 > 123.2$, the chi-square statistic exceeds the critical value. Consequently, alternative tables corresponding to $|d| > 12$ are not reliable substitutes for Table 7 ($D_{11} = 100$) and are ruled out for inferential purposes. Surrogates for Table 7 are limited to: $88 < D_{11} < 112$. For integer tables, there are 23 suitable choices among 501 alternatives: $D_{11} = 0, \ldots, 500$. Thus, it is not necessary—nor desirable--to construct all alternative tables but rather a sample of tables that, for inferential purposes, are expected to be interchangeable with the original table. This analysis is from the perspective of the NSO which knows that $D_{11} = 100$ for (the true) Table 7. The NSO may or may not choose to provide analysts with information on selection of suitable alternative tables (a transparency issue). The NSO should avoid information that is symmetric about the true value as CCS is vulnerable to symmetric attack (see [11]).

The NSO knows which alternative is the original, but the analyst does not and requires more information. Below approaches for the analyst and the NSO are sketched, illustrated for conditional chi-square.

With standard methods, anyone can identify the 501 alternative tables to Table 7. Based on domain knowledge, analysts can often derive effective lower and/or upper bounds on particular suppressed cell value(s), thereby limiting the effective range of D_{11}. For example, if the analyst can determine that $D_{11} > 70$ and $D_{23} < 550$, only 81 choices remain, viz., $70 < D_{11} < 150$. Knowledge of the disclosure and suppression rules also can be brought to bear, particularly for magnitude data. For example, the analyst may infer D_{11} to within some percentage (5%,10%, 15%, ...) of the largest (primary) cell contributor because, based on a p-percent rule, a primary cell value is replaced by a safe value at a distance of at most p-percent of its original value. The analyst could compute all 501 sum-of-reciprocals and corresponding chi-square statistics, from which clusters of similar alternative tables could be identified and ranges for D_{11} narrowed. Or, (s)he could examine the behavior of the sum of reciprocals of suppressed entries for any alternative table in the current range and possibly develop bounds on this quantity to compare potential chi-square values with the critical value, leading to a "generic" d and a small range for it, as follows.

Consider the four alternative tables $D_{11} = 100, 200, 300, 400$. The respective sums of reciprocals are: 0.03117, 0.0211, 0.0199 and 0.0253. A conditional chi-square relative to these tables yields ranges for allowable displacements d of each table of

(-12, 12), (-14, 14), (-14, 14) and (-13, 13). The analyst could adopt the range -14 < d < 14 on a generic d centered on any alternative table and, next, by other means infer one or more clusters of (27) tables containing the original.

6   The Intruder and the Analyst

Is the net effect of this research to strengthen the hand of the intruder? No. The intruder's objective is to reconstruct or narrowly estimate selected original cell values. The analyst's objective is to deconstruct—or have the NSO deconstruct--the table to create a surrogate table or sample of surrogates for analysis. Analysis of circuits of suppressed cells is an important tool for both intruder and analyst/NSO. To limit the intruder's damage, the NSO must first understand the intruder's capabilities. Focused on discovering original "true" values, the intruder for the most part targets individual cell values using deterministic or averaging methods based on circuits. While these methods are intended to improve methods for deconstructing circuits, such methods are discoverable by an intruder ([11]). Other available tools include prior knowledge, which tends to be domain specific, and ancillary information on the data and disclosure and suppression rules, which the NSO may or may not share (SDL transparency).

By comparison, the analyst is focused on identifying interchangeable alternative tables. Circuit analysis is the first step in this process, but subsequent challenges— error, bias, dependencies—rely on statistical reasoning and methods. Disclosure of individual values sometimes may be a by-product of such procedures, but is not their objective.

7   Relationship to Other SDL Methods

All post-tabular SDL methods are supported by a common mathematical framework based on the algebra of tables, and there is much to be gained by other methods in studying suppression, and conversely ([7], [8], [16]). It is instructive here to consider the relationship of our methods to controlled tabular adjustment and multiple imputation.

Controlled tabular adjustment ([17], [18]) is an imputation method for tables designed to replace complementary cell suppression. Values for sensitive cells are imputed along with sufficiently many (usually a small number of) values to restore additivity to the table, using mathematical programming. The resulting table is devoid of suppressions and available for analysis. Quality effects of CTA are controlled through mathematical (QP-CTA [17]) or statistical (MDI-CTA [18]) constraints aimed at preserving distributional parameters or shape, respectively. A principal difference between CTA and methods here is emphasis on creating inference-based multiple surrogates or composites, with estimates of uncertainty. QP-CTA on the other hand controls key statistics but is not designed to create an analytical surrogate. Also, CTA is designed to change many values each by a small amount whereas our methods are applied to a fixed suppression pattern that, presumptively, is parsimonious. Nevertheless, it would be possible to increase the number of circuits and extend our methods to a CTA-like setting.

Imputing missing values and providing multiple imputed copies of a data file are at the center of synthetic data and multiple imputation methods. These methods rely upon statistical models based on original data to impute all or a subset of variables. Synthetic data files have been successfully created for various kinds of microdata ([19], [20], [21]) and have been proposed for contingency tables. Uncertainties for synthetic microdata are knowable. Methods presented here enable release of surrogate tables containing imputations which are not model-generated, but instead comprise alternative tables created using the algebra of tables. Analogous to synthetic microdata and multiple imputation methods, multiple surrogates can be released or combined using methods presented here.

The key difference between this method and other methods is that, instead of relying on a statistical or optimization model, changes to the original tables are based on the circuit structure of the suppressions. All unsuppressed values remain fixed, and a suitable set of alternative values and tables is identified and analyzed separately or through combination. Winnowing methods are a key ingredient.

An issue of importance in disclosure limitation of sets of tables is consistency—ensuring that that two logically identical cells exhibit the same value. Many SDL methods fail this criterion; a notable exception is Wooton and Fraser ([22]). Methods here assure that any unsuppressed value is consistent with any unsuppressed counterpart, and that suppressed values are represented by similar, narrowly clustered set of values—interchangeable values.

Regarding similar work, use of prior information but not formal methods for table deconstruction was reported at the 2012 NISS Workshop on Cell Suppression. Isserman and Westervelt ([23]) offer an approach for deconstruction of a large set of tables (U.S. County Business Patterns) based on exploiting weak suppression within and between tables. Their focus was on recovering or bounding original values, as opposed to identifying alternative tables, and relies on linear programming and considerable domain knowledge. Cox ([11]) is based on circuit analysis and strong suppression. The concept of alternative tables for SDL that are interchangeable for analytical purposes is new, and will benefit from work on multiple imputation for SDL ([21]).

Finally, there is the issue of computational complexity. For tables familiar to official statistics—tables of network type in particular—computation of alternative tables is easy for both the analyst and the NSO. The NSO knows the true table, but even if the analyst does not, they may solve the linear system defined by the suppressions for a continuous solution. From this, a first and ultimately many or all alternative tables can be identified based on the fact that the moves are square-free. For non square-free tables, however, this can be far from true ([24]) for reasons including the possibility of gaps in the sequence of integer solutions to the integer linear system ([25]).

8   Concluding Comments

We have introduced methods to enable statistical analysis of suppressed tabular data. These methods can be employed by either the analyst or the NSO. For best and most broadly useful results, NSOs should consider adopting these methods with the aim of releasing single or multiple alternative tables suitable as surrogates for the original table, or surrogates based on combining (a sample) of surrogates. We have demonstrated the interplay of these methods with SDL transparency issues.

Initial research focused on tabular structures arising regularly in official statistics, characterized by moves between alternative tables that are square-free. Further research will consider the utility of square-free (only) scenarios for more general classes of tables. A computational algebra for circuits will be developed to account for suppression patterns comprising multiple overlapping circuits, and formulations that render other f-divergences in a convenient form will be developed.

Presentation of this research was supported in part by NSF grant SES-11-31897.

References

1. Cox, L.H.: Suppression methodology and statistical disclosure control. Journal of the American Statistical Association 75(370), 377–385 (1980)
2. Cox, L.H.: Disclosure risk for tabular economic data. In: Doyle, P., Lane, J., Theeuwes, J., Zayatz, L. (eds.) Confidentiality, Disclosure and Data Access: Theory and Practical Applications for Statistical Agencies, ch. 8, pp. 167–183. Elsevier, New York (2001)
3. Cox, L.H., Karr, A.F., Kinney, S.: Risk-Utility paradigms for statistical disclosure limitation: How to think but not how to act (with discussion). International Statistical Review 2, 160–183 (2011) (with discussion)
4. Fellegi, I.P.: On the question of statistical confidentiality. Journal of the American Statistical Association 67, 7–18 (1972)
5. Cox, L.H.: Network models for complementary cell suppression. Journal of the American Statistical Association, 90(432), 1153–1162 (1995)
6. Dalenius, T.: Towards a methodology for statistical disclosure control. Statist Tidskrift 5, 429–444 (1977)
7. Federal Committee on Statistical Methodology. Report on Disclosure Limitation Methodology—Statistical Policy Working Paper 22. Office Management & Budget, Washington, DC (Rev: 2006) (1994)
8. U.S. Department of Commerce. Report on Statistical Disclosure and Disclosure Limitation—Statistical Policy Working Paper 2. Office of Statistical Policy and Standards Washington, DC (1978)
9. Kelly, J.P., Golden, B.L., Assad, A.A.: Cell suppression: Disclosure protection for sensitive tabular data. Networks 22, 397–417 (1992)
10. Cox, L.H.: A data quality and data confidentiality assessment of complementary cell suppression. In: Domingo-Ferrer, J., Saygın, Y. (eds.) PSD 2008. LNCS, vol. 5262, pp. 13–23. Springer, Heidelberg (2008)
11. Cox, L.H.: Vulnerability of complementary cell suppression to intruder attack. Journal of Privacy and Confidentiality 1(2), 235–251 (2009), http://jpc.stat.cmu.edu

12. Fischetti, M., Salazar, J.J.: Models and algorithnms for optimizing cell suppression in tabular data with linear constraints. Journal of the American Statistical Association 95, 916–928 (2000)
13. Fischetti, M., Salazar, J.J.: Solving the cell suppression problem in tabular data with linear constraints. Management Science 47(7), 1008–1026 (2001)
14. Cox, L.H.: Contingency tables of network type: Models, Markov basis and applications. Statistica Sinica 17(4), 1371–1393 (2007)
15. Dobra, A., Fienberg, S.E.: Bounds for cell entries in contingency tables given marginal totals and decomposable graphs. Proceedings of the National Academy of Sciences 97(22), 11885–11892 (2000)
16. Salazar, J.J.: Statistical confidentiality: Optimization techniques to protect tables. Computers & Operations Research 35, 1638–1651 (2008)
17. Cox, L.H., Kelly, J.P., Patil, R.: Balancing quality and confidentiality for multivariate tabular data. In: Domingo-Ferrer, J., Torra, V. (eds.) PSD 2004. LNCS, vol. 3050, pp. 87–98. Springer, Heidelberg (2004)
18. Cox, L.H., Orelien, J.G., Shah, B.V.: A method for preserving statistical distributions subject to controlled tabular adjustment. In: Domingo-Ferrer, J., Franconi, L. (eds.) PSD 2006. LNCS, vol. 4302, pp. 1–11. Springer, Heidelberg (2006)
19. Raghunathan, T.E., Reiter, J.P., Rubin, D.B.: Multiple imputation for statistical disclosure limitation. Journal of Official Statistics 19, 1–16 (2003)
20. Reiter, J.P.: Satisfying disclosure restrictions with synthetic data sets. Journal of Official Statistics 18, 531–544 (2002)
21. Reiter, J.P.: Releasing multiply-imputed, synthetic public use microdata: An illustration and empirical study. Journal of the Royal Statistical Society, Series A 168, 185–205 (2005)
22. Wooton, J., Fraser, B.: A review of confidentiality protections for statistical tables, with special reference to the differencing problem. Australian Bureau of Statistics Methodology Report 1352.0.55.072. Australian Bureau of Statistics, Canberra (2005)
23. Isserman, A.M., Westervelt, J.: 1.5 million missing numbers: overcoming employment suppression in County Business Patterns data. International Regional Science Review 29(3), 311–335 (2006)
24. Cox, L.H.: On properties of multi-dimensional statistical tables. Journal of Statistical Planning and Inference 17(2), 251–273 (2003)
25. Cox, L.H.: Inference control problems in statistical database query systems. In: Farkas, C., Samarati, P. (eds.) Research Directions in Data and Applications Security, pp. 1–13. Kluwer, Boston (2004)

Assessing the Information Loss of Controlled Adjustment Methods in Two-Way Tables*

Jordi Castro** and José A. González

Department of Statistics and Operations Research,
Universitat Politècnica de Catalunya,
Jordi Girona 1–3, 08034 Barcelona, Catalonia
{jordi.castro,jose.a.gonzalez}@upc.edu

Abstract. Minimum distance controlled tabular adjustment (CTA) is a perturbative technique of statistical disclosure control for tabular data. Given a table to be protected, CTA looks for the closest safe table by solving an optimization problem using some particular distance in the objective function. CTA has shown to exhibit a low disclosure risk. The purpose of this work is to show that CTA also provides a low information loss, focusing on two-way tables. Computational results on a set of midsize tables validate this statement.

Keywords: Statistical disclosure control, controlled tabular adjustment, information loss, data utility, mixed integer linear programming.

1 Introduction

Minimum-distance controlled tabular adjustment (CTA in short) was suggested in [2,12] as a post-tabular perturbation approach for statistical disclosure control. A description of the state-of-the-art in the statistical disclosure field can be found in the monograph [20] and the survey [3]. Briefly, given a table with sensitive information, the goal of CTA is to compute the closest safe table through the solution of an optimization problem using some particular distance in its objective function. CTA is being considered an emerging technology for tabular data protection [20]. CTA can be applied to both frequency and magnitude tables (i.e., tables providing, respectively, either cell counts or aggregated information for another variable). This work only considers frequency tables, i.e., cell values are integer. For two-way tables CTA will always provide integral values, such that integrality constraints are not needed, and the two information loss measures used in this paper (one of them requiring integrality of cell values) can be applied.

---

* Supported by grants MTM2012-31440 of the Spanish Ministry of Economy and Competitiveness, SGR-2014-542 of the Government of Catalonia, and DwB INFRA-2010-262608 of the FP7 European Union Program.
** Corresponding author.

J. Domingo-Ferrer (Ed.): PSD 2014, LNCS 8744, pp. 11–23, 2014.

Several recent papers have been devoted to CTA. Some of them focused on the solution of the optimization problem formulated [5,7,16], whereas others dealt with quality and confidentiality issues of the computed solution [6,10]. A tabular data protection method can be seen as a map F such that $F(T) = T'$, i.e., table T is transformed to another table T'. Two are the main requirements for F: (1) the output table T' should be "safe", and (2) the information loss should be small, i.e., T' should be a good replacement for T. The disclosure risk can be analyzed through the inverse map $T = F^{-1}(T')$: if not available or difficult to compute by any attacker, then we may guarantee that F is safe. It was empirically observed in [4] that estimates $\hat{T} = \hat{F}^{-1}(T')$, $\hat{F}^{-1}$ being an estimate of F^{-1} for CTA, were not close to T for some real tables, concluding that CTA was a safe method for these tables. However, a similar analysis regarding the utility of T' has not been performed for CTA (though it was for some microdata methods, as reported in [13]). Other methods (random record swapping and semi-controlled random rounding) have been compared using a table from the 2001 UK Census in [24]. The purpose of this work is then to fill this gap by performing a computational analysis on the data utility of two-way tables protected with CTA. The same procedure may be extended to multidimensional, hierarchical or linked tables but, due to its higher complexity, is out of the scope of this work and part of the further research to be done in this field.

The paper is organized as follows. Section 2 reviews the CTA formulation used in this work. Section 3 shows the methodology developed for analyzing the information loss. Finally, Section 4 reports computational results with some midsize two-way tables.

2   The CTA Formulation

Given (i) a set of cells $a_i, i = 1, \ldots, n$, that satisfy some linear relations $Aa = b$ (a being the vector of a_i's); (ii) a lower and upper bound for each cell $i = 1, \ldots, n$, respectively l_{a_i} and u_{a_i}, which are considered to be known by any attacker; (iii) positive cell weights $w_i, i = 1, \ldots, n$, associated to the cost of perturbing cell values; (iv) a set $\mathcal{S} = \{i_1, i_2, \ldots, i_s\} \subseteq \{1, \ldots, n\}$ of indices of sensitive cells; (v) and a lower and upper protection level for each sensitive cell $i \in \mathcal{S}$, respectively lpl_i and upl_i, such that the released values musty satisfy either $x_i \geq a_i + upl_i$ or $x_i \leq a_i - lpl_i$; the goal of CTA is to find the closest safe values $x_i, i = 1, \ldots, n$, according to some distance ℓ, that makes the released table safe. This is achieved by the solution of the following optimization problem:

$$\min_{x} \ \|x - a\|_{\ell}$$
$$\text{s. to } Ax = b$$
$$l_{a_i} \leq x_i \leq u_{a_i} \quad i = 1, \ldots, n \tag{1}$$
$$x_i \leq a_i - lpl_i \text{ or } x_i \geq a_i + upl_i \quad i \in \mathcal{S}.$$

Problem (1) can also be formulated in terms of deviations from the current cell values. Defining $z_i = x_i - a_i, \quad i = 1, \ldots, n$ —and similarly $l_{z_i} = l_{x_i} - a_i$ and $u_{z_i} = u_{x_i} - a_i$—, (1) can be recast as

$$\min_{z} \ \|z\|_{\ell}$$
$$\text{s. to} \ \ Az = 0$$
$$l_{z_i} \leq z_i \leq u_{z_i} \quad i = 1, \dots, n \tag{2}$$
$$z_i \leq -lpl_i \ \text{or} \ z_i \geq upl_i \quad i \in \mathcal{S},$$

$z \in \mathbb{R}^n$ being the vector of deviations. Using the ℓ_1 distance, considering the splitting $z = z^+ - z^-$, and after some manipulation, (2) can be written as

$$\min_{z^+, z^-, y} \ \sum_{i=1}^{n} w_i(z_i^+ + z_i^-)$$
$$\text{s. to} \ \ A(z^+ - z^-) = 0$$
$$0 \leq z_i^+ \leq \ u_{z_i} \quad i \notin \mathcal{S}$$
$$0 \leq z_i^- \leq -l_{z_i} \quad i \notin \mathcal{S} \tag{3}$$
$$upl_i \, y_i \leq z_i^+ \leq u_{zi} \, y_i \quad i \in \mathcal{S}$$
$$lpl_i(1 - y_i) \leq z_i^- \leq -l_{zi}(1 - y_i) \quad i \in \mathcal{S}$$
$$y_i \in \{0, 1\} \quad i \in \mathcal{S},$$

$w \in \mathbb{R}^n$ being the vector of positive cell weights, $z^+ \in \mathbb{R}^n$ and $z^- \in \mathbb{R}^n$ the vector of positive and negative deviations in absolute value, and $y \in \mathbb{R}^s$ being the vector of binary variables associated to protections directions. When $y_i = 1$ the constraints mean $upl_i \leq z_i^+ \leq u_{zi}$ and $z_i^- = 0$, thus the protection direction is "upper"; when $y_i = 0$ we get $z_i^+ = 0$ and $lpl_i \leq z_i^- \leq -l_{zi}$, thus protection direction is "lower". Model (3) is a (in general difficult) mixed integer linear optimization problem, but it may provide better quality solutions than other CTA variants without binary variables (e.g., [8,9]). In this work tables have been protected by solving (3) by the CTA package [17] recently improved within the Data without Boundaries INFRA-2010-262608 FP7 project.

3   Assessment of Information Loss

In [13] the information loss was measured by comparing several statistics on the original and protected microdata. We followed a similar approach, but restricting the analysis to a few available statistics for two-way tables to measure the association between the row and column variables. A simple statistic as the correlation between the values of the cells of the original and perturbed table a_i and $a_i + z_i$, $i = 1, \dots, n$, is avoided, since it is meaningless: in practice it is almost 1 and it does not capture the relationship between the row and column categories. The assessment methodology is outlined in next subsections.

3.1   Generation of Tables

The analysis was restricted to two-way tables, which were randomly generated by the following algorithm:

- Input: r, number of categories for row variable (rows of the table); c, number of categories for column variable (columns of the table); N: total number of observations or respondents; ρ: correlation between both variables (a number in $[-1, 1]$).

- Output: a contingency table of dimensions $r \times c$; table margins may also be provided.
- Step 1. We obtain a binormal random sample of N points, say $(x_i, y_i), i = 1 \ldots N$, with zero mean and covariance matrix

$$\begin{pmatrix} 1 & \rho \\ \rho & 1 \end{pmatrix}.$$

- Step 2. The variables are discretized into r and c categories, respectively. The cutpoints are randomly chosen so that very small frequencies are not possible; to be precise, at least 10 observations are required in the marginal cell of each row and column (though internal cells may be below 10).
- Step 3. A two-way table is created by cross-tabulation of both discretized variables. If required, a margin row and a margin column are created, as well as a grand-total cell (equal to N).

The software package used to produce the tables, obtain the measures described below and analyze the results was R, release 2.15 [23]. In order to get two samples with the given correlation and normal distribution we used the function rmvnorm from the R package 'mvtnorm' [14,15].

3.2 Measures

Contingency tables summarize the information coming from cross-tabulation of two or more categorical variables, and there are several analytical ways to represent them through numerical estimators. Although single measures are usually too simple to catch the dependence structure underlying the variables—especially in high dimensional tables—we have chosen a few of them to allow the comparison between the original and protected tables.

Some of the most used measures of association are based on the well-known Pearson's coefficient

$$\chi^2 = \sum_{i=1}^{n} \frac{(o_i - e_i)^2}{e_i},$$

where n is the number of cells in the table, o_i means an observed frequency, and e_i an expected frequency, normally under independence of the variables. The Pearson's chi-squared test is based on the assumption that it follows a χ^2 probability distribution, with known number of degrees of freedom ($(r-1)(c-1)$ in two-way tables), depending on some conditions and whenever the variables are independent.

We considered the coefficient known as Cramér's V [11], computed as

$$V = \sqrt{\frac{\chi^2}{N \cdot \min(r-1, c-1)}}.$$

Cramér's V ranges from 0 (in case of no association between the variables) to 1 (maximum association), being only 1 when the variables are identical. Cramér's V is invariable to changes in the order of the categories of the variables. This measure was computed using the function `assocstats` from the R package 'vcd' [21]. Cramér's V was one of the measures employed in [24].

The second technique considered in this work to explore the relationships between the two variables of the table is correspondence analysis (CA). CA is frequently employed as an exploratory tool, with the aim to identify more detailed ways of association between the variables, instead of a single measure of the strength of such a relationship. For our purposes, we used the variant for two-way contingency tables named Simple Correspondence Analysis (SCA).

SCA reduces the high dimensionality of the original data (given by the number of categories of our variables) to a low-dimensional space which retains as much information as possible. Briefly, SCA involves the generalized singular value decomposition [18] of a matrix M computed as follows. Denoting by T the matrix containing the $r \times c$ entries of the two-way contingency table, by e_t the column vector of 1's of dimension t, and by $\mathrm{diag}(v)$ a diagonal matrix containing the elements of vector v in its diagonal positions, M is computed as

$$M = R - e_r c^\top \quad \text{where} \quad R = \mathrm{diag}(Te_c)^{-1}T \quad \text{and} \quad c = (e_r^\top T e_c)^{-1}(e_r^\top T).$$

Denoting

$$W_r = \mathrm{diag}(e_r^\top T e_c)^{-1}(Te_c) \quad \text{and} \quad W_c = \mathrm{diag}(c)^{-1}$$

then M is decomposed by the generalized singular value decomposition as

$$M = U\Sigma V \quad \text{where} \quad U^\top W_r U = I_r \quad \text{and} \quad V^\top W_c V = I_c,$$

where I_t is the $t \times t$ identity matrix, U and V contain the row and column singular vectors, and $\Sigma \in \mathbb{R}^{r \times c}$ contains l nonzero singular values (where $l \leq \min(r, c)$) in its diagonal entries (see, for instance, [19] for a comprehensive description). The rows of the two-way table can be projected onto the singular vectors U, obtaining the factor scores. The variance of the factor scores for a given dimension is equal to the squared singular value of this dimension. The squared singular values of M are equal to the eigenvalues of $MM^\top$ [18]. It is worth to remind that the concept of *inertia* is equal to the χ^2 statistic divided by N, that the sum of all the eigenvalues of $MM^\top$, $\sum_{i=1}^{l} \lambda_i$, is equal to the inertia, and that a few dimensions (or directions, or eigenvectors) related to the largest eigenvalues may explain most of the information in the table.

In this work we focus on the larger eigenvalue (λ_1) from the SCA, and the contribution of λ_1 among all the eigenvalues, i.e., the ratio $\lambda_1 / \sum_{i=1}^{l} \lambda_i$ between λ_1 and the inertia as a percentage, denoted as π_1. The relation between V and the contribution of λ_1 is not straightforward, and much less between V and π_1. The singular values were computed with the function `ca`, from the R package of the same name [22].

3.3   Description of the Experiments

Two experiments have been designed. They are independent since different tables have been considered for them. Alternatively, the same tables could have been used in both experiments, but we decided to consider two different sets. The procedure is similar in both cases:

- Set the parameters of the instances: Percentage of sensitive cells in the tables, and correlation ρ; other factors have been fixed; 15 instances will be generated for each combination of percentage of sensitive cells and ρ.
- For each instance:
  - generate a table with random r, c and N;
  - compute the measures from the original table;
  - write the table in a format allowed by the CTA package;
  - run the CTA package, and write the protected table;
  - computed the measures from the protected table;
  - save the results;
- Read the results file, and compare the outcomes.

The optimality gap is a bound for the maximum relative difference allowed between the computed and the optimal solutions. The value considered for all the executions, 2.5%, was chosen after some exploration with different values. It became apparent that the CTA procedure was robust (i.e., there were no large deviations between the original and the protected tables) even with large gaps such as 50%. However, the number of sensitive cells protected upwards was significantly higher with those larger gaps, while smaller gaps produced tables with a good balance among the protection directions of their sensitive cells (i.e., the number of sensitive cells upper and lower protected was similar, which reduces the disclosure risk against an attacker). On the other hand, very small gaps may result in large CTA executions for the solution of (3). We set a limit time of 300 seconds for all the executions, which was enough for most of the cases. In particular, CTA took more than one minute in 78 tables (3.42% of the overall 2280 tables protected—720 tables for the first experiment with Cramér's V, and 1560 tables for the second experiment with SCA), and 25 (1.1% of tables) reached the maximum limit of five minutes. Median time to solution was 0.22 seconds.

Sensitive cells were chosen at random, and protection levels were 10% of the cell value, rounded to the nearest integer. The dimensions of the table were taken at random between 10 and 40. The table margins were included as cells for convenience, but we don't allow them to differ from the original value. The total number of observations N is dependent of r and c, so larger tables usually have more observations. The percentage of zero cells in the generated tables is approximately 5%; the percentage of cells with one respondent is also 5%. By construction a complete row or column cannot be empty. Zero cells are preserved in the protected table.

Table 1. Summary of dimensions and V for generated tables

	median	min	max
cells	600	121	1640
sensitive cells	57	2	309
N	29640	7050	94831
original V	0.0666	0.0181	0.1825

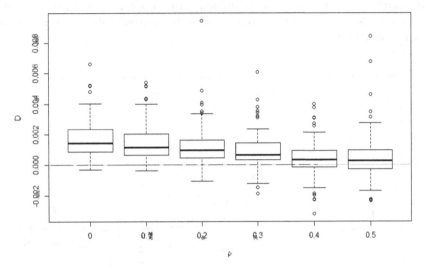

Fig. 1. Boxplots of D for different ρ values

4   Computational Results

4.1   Cramér's V

We generated 720 tables, with a percentage of sensitive cells between 5% and 19%, and values of $\rho \in \{0, 0.1, 0.2, 0.3, 0.4, 0.5\}$. A summary of the dimensions of these tables and their V values is reported in Table 1.

The median of V was 0.0680 in the protected tables, ranging between 0.0197 and 0.1839. Since V is highly correlated with ρ and moderately related to N, we studied the difference $D = V_{prot} - V_{orig}$. Relative differences were discarded because the original quantities can be close to zero, especially for uncorrelated variables, and V ranges from 0 to 1, thus absolute differences can be easily interpreted. Figure 1 reports boxplots of D for different ρ values, showing that D increases when ρ is close to 0. The change is small in magnitude, compared with its variability, as shown in Table 2.

The tables with larger deviations in the Cramér's V measure are small tables (300 cells in average) with a high percentage of sensitive cells (16%). The most significant factors by a general linear model for D are: the correlation ρ (coefficient $-3 \cdot 10^{-3}$), the percentage of sensitive cells (coefficient $8.3 \cdot 10^{-5}$), and the number of cells (coefficient $8 \cdot 10^{-7}$). However, these factors explain only 25.8% of the total variability observed in D.

4.2 Simple Correspondence Analysis

For this second experiment we generated 1560 tables, using values of $\rho \in \{-0.6, -0.5, \ldots, 0, \ldots, 0.5, 0.6\}$. Unlike for the Cramér's V, we considered negative correlations for if they might influence the results. For each original and protected table the measures λ_1 and π_1 were computed. Table 3 shows a summary of collected values.

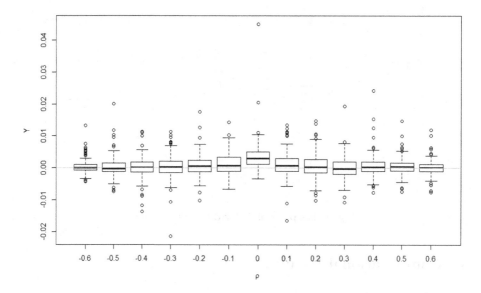

Fig. 2. Boxplots of Y for different ρ values

We studied the singular value $\sqrt{\lambda_1}$ instead of the eigenvalue because it appeared to be proportional to $|\rho|$ and it showed a greater stability in variance. As before, the effect observed after the protection performed by CTA is studied through the change $Y = \sqrt{\lambda_{1,prot}} - \sqrt{\lambda_{1,orig}}$. As for D, Y is defined as an absolute difference since the original eigenvalues $\lambda_{1,orig}$ are close to zero, especially with null ρ (relative differences are used below in Table 4). Figure 2 shows boxplots of Y for the different ρ values. The outlier at $\rho = 0$ appearing on top of

Table 2. Mean and standard deviation of D with respect to ρ

ρ	0	0.1	0.2	0.3	0.4	0.5
mean	0.0017	0.0015	0.0012	0.0009	0.0004	0.0004
std. dev.	0.0012	0.0012	0.0013	0.0011	0.0012	0.0014

Table 3. Summary of λ_1 and π_1 for original and protected tables

	median	min	max
orig. λ_1	0.0875	0.0011	0.3586
prot. λ_1	0.0881	0.0014	0.3587
orig. π_1	76.33%	9.5%	92.6%
prot. π_1	75.45%	9.6%	90.9%

Table 4. Bounds for the intervals containing 90% of relative changes in the singular value, expressed as $Y/\sqrt{\lambda_{1,orig}} \cdot 100$

$|\rho|$	0	0.1	0.2	0.3	0.4	0.5	0.6
Lower (%)	0.27	-4.30	-2.47	-1.33	-1.27	-0.86	-0.56
Upper (%)	24.23	7.64	3.86	2.20	1.43	1.27	0.80

the figure was produced by a table of 392 cells, whose eigenvalues λ_1 before and after protection were 0.001074 and 0.006043, respectively; it was the table with the smallest λ_1. Aside from this outlier, it can be seen that in general changes due to the protection were small.

Table 4 shows the intervals which include 90% of the relative changes, expressed as $Y/\sqrt{\lambda_{1,orig}} \cdot 100$, in the singular values, depending on ρ. The sign of ρ is not important for the analysis, so we considered only its absolute value. It is shown that relevant changes only appear for $\rho = 0$ (as large as, e.g. 25%). Indeed, the 95% confidence interval for the mean of Y when $\rho = 0$ was $(0.0032, 0.0046)$. For nonzero correlations there is no evidence of change. Moreover, from Table 4 it is clear that relative changes in $\sqrt{\lambda_1}$ are a decreasing function of $|\rho|$.

As for the percentage π_1 explained by the first dimension, we observed: a) a symmetrical pattern with respect to $\rho = 0$, b) small values of π_1 for $\rho = 0$ (about 16%), quickly increasing with $|\rho|$ until approximately $|\rho| = 0.4$ (about 83%), and decreasing slowly beyond that point, both before and after the table protection. Figure 3 shows the ratio $Z = \pi_{1,prot}/\pi_{1,orig}$. The outlier at $\rho = 0$ appearing on top of the Figure 2 was not drawn in Figure 3, since it modified π_1 from 18.6% to 53.4% ($Z \approx 3$ is out of the range of the vertical axis of Figure 3).

Changes in π_1 can be analyzed through Figure 3 and Table 5, which report the intervals with 90% of observed Z for different ρ. In general, the π_1 of the protected table tends to decrease for small $|\rho|$ values, though the trend in uncorrelated factors points to an increase; for large $|\rho|$ the change in π_1 can be negligible.

Table 5. Lower and upper bounds for the intervals containing 90% of the ratios Z

$|\rho|$	0	0.1	0.2	0.3	0.4	0.5	0.6
Lower	0.936	0.885	0.945	0.967	0.972	0.970	0.969
Upper	1.180	1.031	1.001	0.998	1.004	1.013	1.018

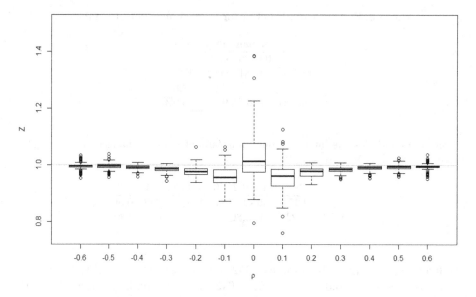

Fig. 3. Boxplots of Z for different ρ values

CTA provided solutions with well balanced sensitive cells with respect to the direction of the deviation. The percentage of sensitive cells protected upwards lied between 41.7% and 58.8% in 90% of the tables, which makes the procedure unpredictable, thus safer.

5   Conclusions

Through the measures considered in this work, we may conclude that a two-way table protected with CTA experiment a slight information loss. It was observed that only the tables from independent factors could suffer significant alteration in Cramér's V or in indicators related to SCA. For V, we have found that the chance of change is higher in small tables or tables with a high percentage of sensitive cells. Anyway, in absolute numbers V barely changed: an average increase of 0.0017 if uncorrelated factors were present.

With respect to SCA, relative changes in λ_1 were significant only when $\rho = 0$. However, we have found that the absolute change in $\sqrt{\lambda_1}$ is usually insignificant: while the average first singular value is 0.052, it increases at most (in 95% of cases) by 0.0093. Differences tend to increase for π_1: for $\rho = 0$ the variation of π_1 can be large, normally above the original value; for $\rho \neq 0$ the variation of π_1 is lesser though usually below the original value. It should be kept in mind that, even when $\rho = 0$, the absolute changes in π_1 were small: only two tables —1 out of 1000— modified by more than 10% the original π_1 value.

There is not a conclusive explanation of why the greatest information loss occurred for $\rho = 0$. One possible reason could be that, since for $\rho = 0$ cells values are evenly scattered through the table, the number of additional cells with deviations (aside from the sensitive ones) increases; whereas in two-way tables from correlated variables it might be easier to compensate deviations due to protection levels just using sensitive cells. However, a deeper analysis is part of the additional work to be done.

A more exhaustive study considering also real-world tables is needed, and part of the further work to be done. Some preliminary results with two standard two-way tables used in the literature (named "table8" and "dale") confirm that changes in measures increase with the size of the table and the percentage of sensitive cells. For instance, for the 40×30 "table8" instance with only 3 sensitive cells, the V statistic was almost the same before and after protection (0.09270563 vs 0.09280493). On the other hand, for the 358×45 "dale" instance with a 30% of sensitive cells the change in V was significant: from 0.0692391 to 0.1093475. However, for "dale", the information loss was small according to the other measure: $\lambda_{1,orig} = 0.09809$ and $\lambda_{1,prot} = 0.10264$.

Alternative measures could have been applied. One of them would be hypothesis testing on the independence of the two variables using Pearson's χ^2 test. However, even for original independent tables, it is likely that the null hypothesis is rejected for CTA-protected tables, since sensitive cells are forced to be "significantly" perturbed, and this perturbation affects quadratically to the Pearson's χ^2 statistic. This effect may increase with the percentage of sensitive cells. Some preliminary tests with synthetic independent tables confirmed this assertion. Anyway, hypothesis testing might not be a suitable measure in this context: data may not come from random sampling and, furthermore, there is considerable debate around the hypothesis testing nature and the use of p-values [1].

In summary, it can be concluded that the data utility of the CTA-protected tables used in this work is in general acceptable/high and comparable to that of the original tables. Among the further lines of work we find:

- Extension of the above measures to higher-dimensional, hierarchical and linked real-world tables.
- Extension to magnitude tables, using other information loss measures (e.g., generalized linear models).
- Joint analysis of the data utility and disclosure risk of CTA-protected tables, likely in the form of risk-utility plots.

References

1. Batanero, C.: Controversies around the role of statistical tests in experimental research. Mathematical Thinking and Learning 2, 75–97 (2000)
2. Castro, J.: Minimum-distance controlled perturbation methods for large-scale tabular data protection. European Journal of Operational Research 171, 39–52 (2006)
3. Castro, J.: Recent advances in optimization techniques for statistical tabular data protection. European Journal of Operational Research 216, 257–269 (2012)

4. Castro, J.: On assessing the disclosure risk of controlled adjustment methods for statistical tabular data. International Journal of Uncertainty, Fuzziness and Knowledge-Based Systems 20, 921–941 (2012)
5. Castro, J., Frangioni, A., Gentile, C.: Perspective reformulations of the CTA problem with L_2 distances. Operations Research (in press, 2014)
6. Castro, J., Giessing, S.: Testing variants of minimum distance controlled tabular adjustment. Monographs of Official Statistics, Eurostat-Office for Official Publications of the European Communities, Luxembourg, pp. 333–343 (2006)
7. Castro, J., González, J.A.: A tool for analyzing and fixing infeasible RCTA instances. In: Domingo-Ferrer, J., Magkos, E. (eds.) PSD 2010. LNCS, vol. 6344, pp. 17–28. Springer, Heidelberg (2010)
8. Castro, J., González, J.A.: A fast CTA method without the complicating binary decisions. In: Documents of the Joint UNECE/Eurostat Work Session on Statistical Data Confidentiality, Statistics Canada, Ottawa, pp. 1–7 (2013)
9. Castro, J., González, J.A.: A multiobjective LP approach for controlled tabular adjustment in statistical disclosure control. Working paper, Dept. of Statistics and Operations Research, Universitat Politècnica de Catalunya (2014)
10. Cox, L.H., Kelly, J.P., Patil, R.: Balancing quality and confidentiality for multivariate tabular data. In: Domingo-Ferrer, J., Torra, V. (eds.) PSD 2004. LNCS, vol. 3050, pp. 87–98. Springer, Heidelberg (2004)
11. Cramér, H.: Mathematical Methods of Statistics. Princeton University Press, Princeton (1946)
12. Dandekar, R.A., Cox, L.H.: Synthetic tabular Data: an alternative to complementary cell suppression, manuscript, Energy Information Administration, U.S. (2002)
13. Domingo-Ferrer, J., Mateo-Sanz, J.M., Torra, V.: Comparing SDC methods for microdata on the basis of information loss and disclosure risk. In: Proceedings of ETK-NTTS 2001, pp. 807–826. Eurostat, Luxemburg (2001)
14. Genz, A., Bretz, F.: Computation of Multivariate Normal and t Probabilities. Lecture Notes in Statistics, vol. 195. Springer, Heidelberg (2009)
15. Genz, A., Bretz, F., Miwa, T., Mi, X., Leisch, F., Scheipl, F., Hothorn, T.: mvtnorm: Multivariate Normal and t Distributions, R package version 0.9-9999 (2014), `http://CRAN.R-project.org/package=mvtnorm`
16. González, J.A., Castro, J.: A heuristic block coordinate descent approach for controlled tabular adjustment. Computers & Operations Research 38, 1826–1835 (2011)
17. Giessing, S., Hundepool, A., Castro, J.: Rounding methods for protecting EU-aggregates. In: Eurostat Methodologies and Working Papers. Worksession on Statistical Data Confidentiality, Eurostat-Office for Official Publications of the European Communities, Luxembourg, pp. 255–264 (2009) ISBN 978-92-79-12055-8.
18. Golub, G.H., Van Loan, C.F.: Matrix Computations, 3rd edn. Johns Hopkins Univ. Press, Baltimore (1996)
19. Greenacre, M. J.: Theory and applications of correspondence analysis. Academic Press, New York (1984)
20. Hundepool, A., Domingo-Ferrer, J., Franconi, L., Giessing, S., Schulte-Nordholt, E., Spicer, K., de Wolf, P.P.: Statistical Disclosure Control. Wiley, Chichester (2012)

21. Meyer, D., Zeileis, A., Hornik, K.: vcd: Visualizing Categorical Data. R package version 1.3-1 (2013), http://CRAN.R-project.org/package=vcd
22. Nenadic, O., Greenacre, M.: Correspondence Analysis in R, with two- and three-dimensional graphics: The ca package. Journal of Statistical Software 20, 1–13 (2007)
23. R Development Core Team: R: A language and environment for statistical computing. R Foundation for Statistical Computing, Vienna, Austria (2012), http://www.R-project.org/
24. Shlomo, N., Young, C.: Statistical disclosure control methods through a risk-utility framework. In: Domingo-Ferrer, J., Franconi, L. (eds.) PSD 2006. LNCS, vol. 4302, pp. 68–81. Springer, Heidelberg (2006)

Further Developments with Perturbation Techniques to Protect Tabular Data

María-Salomé Hernández-García and Juan-José Salazar-González

Universidad de La Laguna, Tenerife, Spain
{mshergar,jjsalaza}@ull.es

Abstract. Statistical agencies collect input data from individuals and deliver output information to the society based on these data. A fundamental feature of output information is the "protection" of sensitive information, since too many details could disseminate privacy information from individuals and therefore violate their rights. Another feature of output information is the "utility" to data users, as a scientific may use this output for research or a politician for making decisions. Clearly more details are in the output, more useful it is, but it is also less protected. There are several methodologies based on Mathematical Optimization to solve the problem of finding "good" protected and useful solutions. While the literature on algorithms to apply them is extensive, statisticians have major concerns to use them in practice because these algorithms may have numeral troubles on frequency tables and may produce biased solutions. This article discusses these observations and describes how to overcome them using a modern technique called Enhanced Controlled Tabular Adjustment. Computational experiments show the effectiveness of the approach on benchmark instances.

Keywords: Mixed Integer Linear Programming, Controlled Tabular Adjustment, Tabular Data Protection, Unbiased Methods.

1 Introduction

A statistical agency collects data from respondents, analyzes this data, and releases information to users. The released information is called output. In this process it is fundamental to maximize the utility of the output to the final users, but also to maximize the protection of the information provided by each respondent. Therefore, in general, publishing data aims solving a two-criteria optimization problem. Since the two criteria are in conflict, this optimization problem is very complex.

A widely accepted paradigm is that protection has priority over utility. This means that a minimum level of protection is a-priori decided and set in the optimization problem through constraints. Then an output maximizing the utility is searched among all solutions with an acceptable level of protection. This paradigm reduces the two-criterion problem to a single-criterion constrained problem, where it makes sense to find an optimal solution (the output to publish). The priority of protection versus utility justifies why the area is called "Statistical Confidentiality".

J. Domingo-Ferrer (Ed.): PSD 2014, LNCS 8744, pp. 24–35, 2014.
© Springer International Publishing Switzerland 2014

Still there is the issue of how to properly define the "utility" and "protection" of an output. Several methodologies have proposed in the literature. Two examples –used when publishing tabular data– are cell suppression and controlled rounding. All the methodologies replace the original table (with the true cell values) by another table where some cells contain a "range" of potential values (being the true value inside the range). This is a way of creating uncertainty to a data user, and hence protecting the information provided by each respondent. In most of the cases this range of values is not explicitly given in the output, but it may be anyway computed by the user after the output has been published. That is the case when using cell suppression, for example. The user will solve two optimization problems to detect the extreme values defining the range of a cell in the output. These two mathematical problems for a given cell in the output are called "attacker problems" and the range of values is called "protected interval". Before releasing a given output, the statistical agency may be interested in checking these ranges by solving all attacker problems in the so-called "auditing phase". When the extreme values of all ranges satisfy the required levels of protection then the output is said to be "protected". The utility is measured in general as a function of the difference between the extreme values of each range. Clearly the larger this difference is, the more protected is the cell, but less useful will be the output to a user. Following the above mentioned paradigm, among all protected outputs the statistical agency wish to find one with maximum utility. This implies the need to solve a Mathematical Programming model, either exactly or heuristically. We refer the reader to (for example) the book of Duncan, Elliot and Salazar (2011) for details.

This paper is concerned with a recent methodology in Statistical Confidentiality called Enhanced Controlled Tabular Adjustment (ECTA). It is based on a pioneer methodology introduced by Dandekar and Cox (2002), called CTA, and later developed by different authors. See Hernández-García and Salazar-González (2014) for a detailed description of ECTA and related methods. The current paper addresses the following three new issues.

A first criticism by statisticians when using the methods based on Linear Programming is that they generate solutions with a numerical precision that is not releasable in practice. For example, it makes sense to publish integer numbers, or fractional numbers with up to 2 or 3 decimals, but it is not desired to publish fractional numbers with 20 decimals even if computers can deal internally with them. This concern is very clear when dealing with frequency tables, i.e. tables where each cell must be an integer number (e.g. the number of responders within a group of categories). Then solutions based on fractional cell values must be rounded (or truncated) before being published. This task is far from trivial when one wants to preserve additivity. Cox and Kim (2006) analyzed rounding procedures to protect tables. In this paper we address the rounding procedure not to protect confidentiality (which is done by another method) but to make the output releasable with decimals of fixed length.

Another criticism concerns the statistical properties of optimization solutions coming from methodologies based on Mathematical Programming. Although solutions from basic implementations can be biased, this is not the case of ECTA. A procedure to achieve statistical unbiasedness in CTA, while preserving additivity of the output, is another contribution of this paper.

A third contribution in this paper regards computational comparison of our ECTA implementation when linked to a commercial Mathematical Programming library versus when linked to a free-and-open-source solver. This is of great interest to practitioners in statistical agencies dealing with statistical confidentiality.

This paper is organized as follows. Section 2 summarizes the main concepts in Statistical Confidentiality that will be used in the rest of this paper. Section 3 summarizes CTA and ECTA, two methodologies described in the literature to protect magnitude tables. The section discusses how to adapt them to deal with frequency tables and analyzes the problem of ensuring unbiased solutions. Finally Section 4 shows computational results based on using an ECTA code linked to different Mathematical Programming solvers, some commercial and others free-and-open-source. This section allows understanding the current limits of ECTA on tables with rounded values in practice.

2   Background

Let us assume that the statistical agency needs to deal with a table given by a vector a and a linear system of equations $My=b$. Each equation defines a marginal cell value, and the vector a satisfies all of them. The set of indices associated with cells is denoted by I and the set of indices associated with equations by J. A subset of I is assumed to be the sensitive cells that need to be protected, and it is denoted by P.

Although there are several types of tables, we emphasize here a classification depending on the values in a. A table is called *magnitude table* when the cell values are obtained by adding a feature in a microdata, typically a continuous number like (e.g.) money. A table is called *frequency table* when the cell values count number of contributors.

Let K denote the set of intruders. For each intruder $k \in K$ and each cell $i \in I$, values lb_i^k and ub_i^k represent bounds assumed by k on the original value a_i of cell i. For example, if a cell value a_i is published then $lb_i^k = ub_i^k = a_i$; otherwise lb_i^k and ub_i^k depend on k. Since other information is published, each intruder may reduce the range of potential values defined by lb_p^k and ub_p^k for a sensitive cell p and get a more accurate range of potential values defined by $\underline{y}_p^k$ and $\overline{y}_p^k$. To this end the intruder k solves two optimization problems:

$$\underline{y}_p^k := Minimize\ y_p \quad and \quad \overline{y}_p^k := Maximize\ y_p$$

subject to

$$\sum_{i \in I} m_{ij}\, y_i = b_j \qquad \text{for all } j \in J,$$

$$lb_i^k \le y_i \le ub_i^k \qquad \text{for all } i \in I.$$

For brevity in notation, the set of equations will be denoted by $My=b$ and the set of inequalities by $LB^k \le y \le UB^k$, without k when one attacker is assumed.

If the response variable of the table can assume fractional values, these problems are linear programs. Otherwise, if the values in the cells must be integer (as in frequency tables) these problems are integer linear programs. Solving all these problems is known as the *auditing phase*, and it is the procedure to check the protection of a solution before being released.

Tabular data is protected and can be released when $\underline{y}^k_p$ and $\overline{y}^k_p$ satisfy some constraints for each attacker $k \in K$ and each sensitive cell $p \in P$. To define these constraints, the statistical agency provides three non-negative parameters: a lower protection level LPL^k_p, an upper protection level UPL^k_p, and a sliding protection level SPL^k_p. Then, a publication protects the value in cell p against attacker k if and only if

$$\underline{y}^k_p \le a_p - LPL^k_p \quad, \quad \overline{y}^k_p \ge a_p + UPL^k_p \quad, \text{ and } \quad \overline{y}^k_p - \underline{y}^k_p \ge SPL^k_p.$$

To simplify the definition of these three protection level requirements in practice, there are several rules which are all based on common-sense ideas. For example, for magnitude tables the lower and the upper protection levels for a sensitive cell p could be defined as 20% and 30% of the nominal value a_p, respectively.

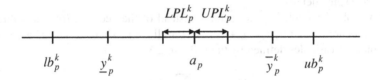

Fig. 1. Diagram of parameters

This definition of protection is known as the interval-disclosure version (see Fig. 1). A particular case, of less interest in practice, is the exact-disclosure version, where the only constraint is that, when the attacker solves the two linear programs, the result should not be a degenerate interval containing only the original value of any sensitive cell. The exact disclosure version only requires $\overline{y}^k_p \ne \underline{y}^k_p$ for all k and p, and it is a particular case of the interval disclosure version where $LPL^k_p = UPL^k_p = 0$ and $SPL^k_p > 0$.

Note that, for each sensitive cell and each attacker, there are three protection levels that the statistical agency needs to decide before classifying a data as protected or not. Typically the protection levels are percentages on the cell values. For instances, the lower protection level may be 50% of the cell value, the upper protection level may be 120% of the cell value and the sliding protection level may be 0%.

Another important concept is the loss of information associated with a publication. The widely used measure is a linear function on the uncertainty that the methodology implies on the output table. The ideal cost is $\overline{y}^k_p - \underline{y}^k_p$, but it leads to a function that depends on the intruder k and which is difficult to minimize. In most cases this function is replaced by a simple estimation, like the difference between the original cell values and the perturbed cell values.

3   Controlled Tabular Adjustment Methods

ECTA is a technique recently introduced in Hernández-García and Salazar-González (2014) and motivated by another approach called Controlled Tabular Adjustment (CTA). This section summarizes both techniques on magnitude tables and address the issue of adapting them to frequency tables and to generated unbiased solutions.

3.1   Standard CTA

CTA is a technique proposed by Dandekar and Cox (2002) as an alternative to cell suppression methodology, and widely analyzed in the last years. The output from CTA is a table v obtained by changing some cell values with a perturbation that is obtained after solving a Mixed Integer Linear Programming (MILP) model. We now summarize some details.

CTA looks for publishing a vector v instead of the vector a (of true values). The two vectors are related by $v_i = a_i + z_i^+ - z_i^-$ for all $i \in I$ where z_i^+ and z_i^- are two set of mathematical variables defined by the following MILP:

$$\text{Minimize } \sum_{i \in I} c_i (z_i^+ + z_i^-) \tag{1}$$

subject to:

$$M(z^+ - z^-) = 0 \tag{2}$$

$$0 \leq z_i^+ \leq UB_i - a_i \quad i \in I \tag{3}$$

$$0 \leq z_i^- \leq a_i - LB_i \quad i \in I \tag{4}$$

$$z_i^+ \geq UPL_i x_i \quad i \in P \tag{5}$$

$$z_i^- \geq LPL_i (1 - x_i) \quad i \in P \tag{6}$$

$$x_i \in \{0,1\} \quad i \in P. \tag{7}$$

The parameters LB_i, UB_i, LPL_i and UPL_i do not have a super index p to represent the intruder because CTA is aimed to protect against a single intruder. CTA cannot guarantee sliding protection levels, which explains why SPL_i is not present in the model.

In addition to the continuous variables z_i^+ and z_i^- for each cell $i \in I$, there is also a binary variable x_i for each sensitive cell $i \in P$. The variables z_i^+ and z_i^- represent the perturbation in the output respect to the true value, while x_i decides if a sensitive value must be perturbed over the upper protection level or bellow the lower protection level.

The vector c represents weights per unit of perturbation on cells, and is defined by the statistical agency to possible encourage perturbing some cells more than others.

The objective function (1) is a weighted function that minimizes the perturbation. It is the L_1-distance considered in Section 3. Equations (2) imply that the perturbation should define an additive table v. Inequalities (3) and (4) enforce the a-priori bounds on the cell values. Inequalities (5) and (6) guarantee that the perturbed value of each sensitive cell satisfies *one* protection level, either the upper *or* the lower. Constraints (7) allow the mathematical model to decide which protection level will be guarantee for each sensitive cell.

Model (1)-(7) can be seen as a linearization of the non-linear model:

$$\text{Minimize} \sum_{i \in I} c_i |v_i - a_i|$$

subject to: $$Mv = b$$

$$LB \leq v \leq UB$$

$$v_i \leq a_i - LPL_i \quad or \quad v_i \geq a_i + ULP_i \qquad i \in P.$$

CTA was original proposed by Dandekar and Cox (2002), and deeply analyzed later in Cox, Kelly, and Patil (2005). An excellent research with optimal and near-optimal approaches to solve the MILP model is given in Glover, Cox, Kelly and Patil (2008). Castro and Giessing (2006) provide extensive experience applying CTA to real-world tables. Although CTA was originally proposed as a technique much simpler to implement than cell suppression, the optimization problem under CTA is also NP-hard and, in practice, the MILP model in CTA is far from trivial to be solved.

3.2 Enhanced CTA

The objective function in CTA is to minimize a distance between the output table v and the original table a. Therefore one could a-priori think that it maximizes the "utility" of the data to a user. However, the user does not know a, hence the user will not know whether a particular perturbed value is near or far from its original value. For that reason, many users do not like data processed with perturbation techniques like CTA.

Further observations regard the "protection" issue. On one side, CTA requires the existence of a table v that must show values outside the required protection range for all sensitive cells at the same time. This differs from the meaning of protection given in Section 1, where it is not required that the same table x must prove protection for all the sensitive cells. Instead, the concept of protection in Section 1 requires that there should be a table for each sensitive cell, and these tables must not necessary coincide for all sensitive cells. On another side, the requirement of ensuring upper *and* lower protection requirements given in Section 1 has been replaced by upper *or* lower protection level in CTA.

These two observations on CTA motivated ECTA. While keeping the main scheme of CTA, it modifies the way of modeling the "utility" and the "protection" in the output information. It generates a table v and two parameters α and β to measure the utility of v to a data user. Assuming the same assumptions as in CTA (i.e. protection against a single attacker and no sliding protecting level requirements), ECTA is an iterative approach, next summarized.

At each iteration, a subset of sensitive cells is randomly selected. Each cell i in this subset is randomly fixed to a value ξ_i in $[\ a_i - LPL_i,\ \ a_i + ULP_i\ ]$. Then the following linear program is solved:

$$\text{Minimize}\ \ \beta \tag{8}$$

$$\text{subject to:}\quad Mv = b \tag{9}$$

$$LB \le v \le UB \tag{10}$$

$$v_i = \xi_i \qquad \text{for all selected } i \in P \tag{11}$$

$$a_i - LPL_i \le v_i \le a_i + UPL_i \quad \text{for all non-selected } i \in P \tag{12}$$

$$(1 - \beta)a_i \le v_i \le (1 + \beta)a_i \quad \text{for all } i \in \backslash P. \tag{13}$$

If this model is feasible, the non-sensitive values have being perturbed in at most β times the true value. Let (v^*, β^*) be an optimal solution. Before releasing this solution we need to find a value α^* to also inform the data user about the maximum perturbation on the sensitive values. To this end ECTA initializes α^* to the maximum percentage ratio of $|v_i^*-a_i^*|/|a_i^*|$ if $a_i^* \ne 0$ and 0.01 otherwise. Still the output (v^*, α^*, β^*) may not be a protected table, thus the auditing phase is necessary. As mentioned in Section 2, this implies solving two optimization problems to compute $\underline{y}_p^k$ and $\overline{y}_p^{k}$ for each intruder k and each sensitive cell p:

$$\underline{y}_p^k := \textit{Minimize } y_p \quad \text{and} \quad \overline{y}_p^{k} := \textit{Maximize } y_p \tag{14}$$

$$\text{subject to:}\quad My = b \tag{15}$$

$$LB^k \le y \le UB^k \tag{16}$$

$$(1 - \alpha^*)v_i \le y_i \le (1 + \alpha^*)v_i \quad i \in P \tag{17}$$

$$(1 - \beta^*)v_i \le y_i \le (1 + \beta^*)v_i \quad i \in \backslash P. \tag{18}$$

When a protection level is not achieved, α^* is increased. See Hernández-García and Salazar-González (2014) for technical details.

3.3   New Implementations of ECTA

It is widely accepted that frequency tables requires solving integer programs, while on magnitude tables one can relax the requirement of Integer Programming tools and use approaches in Continuous Optimization (like Linear Programming). This is not strictly right in practice because, depending on the tabular structure (i.e. $My=b$), the vectors v obtained may have lots of decimals, like for example 5.6785745309870998088876. While in theory this is a valid number for a cell in a magnitude table, in practice statistical agencies do not want to release these numbers with such high precision. A simple rounding or truncation of the decimals leads to a new vector v which may not fit in the tabular structure, or which may loss the protection. For that reason, a sophisticated rounding approach is required. To this end, we scale the original vector a, and assume that the statistical agency wants to publish only integer values. CTA and ECTA can be adapted by requiring the variables z in model (1)-(7), the variables v in model (8)-(13) and the variables y in model (14)-(18) to be all integers.

Another desired feature of a methodology is to ensure unbiased solutions. Cox (1987) addressed this problem when using Controlled Rounding on 2-dimensional tables. We approach the problem in a more general way as follows. In several methodologies the loss of information is measured as the distance between the original table a and the solution v, like (1) in CTA. This objective tends to adjust each cell value to the closest option to the original value, but not with a uniform probability distribution. For example, using Controlled Rounding with base 10, a cell value 12 will go to 20 with a probability smaller than 2/10, and a cell value 18 will go to 20 with a probability higher than 8/10. Figures 2 depicts relations between a continuous number x that must be rounded down to 0 or up to 10 on the horizontal axe and the probability $P(\lceil x \rceil)$ of x being rounded up on the vertical axe. Figure 2 (a) shows the desired (unbiased) probability distribution and Figure 2 (b) shows the (biased) probability distribution when using (1).

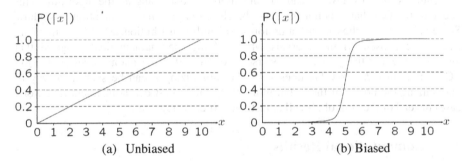

(a) Unbiased   (b) Biased

Fig. 2. Probability distributions of rounding up a cell value

Experimental results using the L_1-distance $\sum_{i \in I} |a_i - v_i|$ as in (1) show the bi-

ased behavior in Fig 2 (b). The biased behavior increases when using the L_2-distance $\sum_{i \in I} (a_i - v_i)^2$, while it reduces when using $\sum_{i \in I} \log(a_i - v_i)$. The last function has the disadvantage of having a non-linear objective function in the mathematical formulation of the problem, which increases the effort to solve it. We now describe a new objective function for CTA to generate unbiased solutions while keeping the objective function in linear form. For each cell $i \in I$, the key idea is to replace the value of a_i when defining $v_i = a_i + z_i^+ - z_i^-$ by a randomly rounded value $R(a_i)$ with a uniform probability distribution. More precisely, let $\lfloor a_i \rfloor$ be the greatest integer not larger than a_i and $\lceil a_i \rceil$ the smallest integer not smaller than a_i. Define $R(a_i)$ equals to a_i when $\lfloor a_i \rfloor = \lceil a_i \rceil$ and, otherwise, equals to $\lfloor a_i \rfloor$ with probability $(\lceil a_i \rceil - a_i)/(\lceil a_i \rceil - \lfloor a_i \rfloor)$ and to $\lceil a_i \rceil$ with probability $(a_i - \lfloor a_i \rfloor)/(\lceil a_i \rceil - \lfloor a_i \rfloor)$. The perturbed table $R(a)$ may be non-protected and non-additive, but is unbiased (i.e. the probability distribution of rounding up the original value follows the distribution depicted in Fig 2 (a)). We have conducted a simulation study on random instances adjusting the nominal values to multiples of 10, and using $R(a)$ instead of a in the objective function of CTA. Fig 3 shows the frequencies of values rounded up in our computational experiments. This figure empirically confirms that the obtained CTA solutions are unbiased.

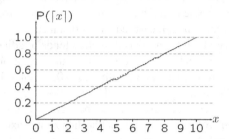

Fig. 3. Observed frequencies in experiments when a is replaced by $R(a)$

Solutions from ECTA, instead, are unbiased without changing the algorithm. This is due to the fact that v_i is not forced to be close to a_i by the optimization procedure. Some values v_i are chosen with a uniform probability distibution, while the others are free to be chosen within intervals when solving the mathematical program that guarantee the additivity of v. It is worse to observe that the main model (8)-(13) in ECTA minimize β. As CTA does with (1), minimizing β can be seen as a way of maximizing the utility of the v, but minimizing the largest cell adjustment (i.e. worst case) instead of the sum of all cell adjustments (i.e. average case).

4   Computational Results

This section analyzes the results of the implementation of ECTA to overcome the drawbacks pointed in Section 3. More precisely, it solves integer programs to ensure the number of digits desired by the statistical agencies, and it uses the new objective function to ensure unbiased solutions. The implementation was done in C++ programming language, using the framework SCIP 3.1.0 (http://scip.zib.de). This is a free-and-open-source software providing routines to solve MILP models. It needs to be linked to a Linear Programming solver, and we considered four options:

- Clp 1.15.6 (https://projects.coin-or.org/Clp),
- SoPlex 2.0.0 (http://soplex. zib.de),
- Cplex 12.6 (http://www-01.ibm.com/software/), and
- Xpress v25.01.05: (http://www.fico.com).

The first two options are free-and-open-source codes to solve Mathematical Programming models. The last two options are commercial solvers. The whole computer code was compiled using the free-and-open-source C/C++ compiler MinGW (Minimalist GNU for Windows), which is a minimalist development environment for native Microsoft Windows applications (http://www.mingw.org/). The code was written and executed on a computer with an Intel Core(TM) Duo CPU at 3.34 GHz running under Microsoft Windows 7, and it is publicly available by request to the authors.

To evaluate the behavior of our implementation linked to the four solvers we have considered ten real-world instances provided by Ramesh Dandekar and public available from CSPlib (webpages.ull.es/users/casc). We have considered these tables as frequency tables, which means that the values are integer and any perturbation must keep them integer. This implies that models (8)-(13) and (14)-(18) are integer programs in our implementation. Table 1 shows the main features (i.e. sizes of the sets I, P and J) of these instances, and Table 2 shows the main results of our experiments using the code with each of the four solvers on these ten instances.

Table 1. Characteristics of 10 benchmark instances from CSPlib

	CSPlib file name	$|I|$	$|P|$	$|J|$
1	Hier13.csp	2020	112	3313
2	hier13x13x13a.csp	2197	108	3549
3	hier13x13x13b.csp	2197	108	3549
4	hier13x13x13c.csp	2197	108	3549
5	hier13x13x13d.csp	2197	108	3549
6	hier13x7x7d.csp	637	50	525
7	hier13x13x7d.csp	1183	75	1443
8	hier16x16x16a.csp	4096	224	5376
9	hier16x16x16b.csp	4096	224	5376
10	hier16x16x16d.csp	4096	224	5376

Columns "Tfind" and "Taudit" give the total time solving models (8)-(13) and (14)-(18), respectively. Column "Infeas" shows the number of models (8)-(13) that finished without solution. Column "Prot" gives the number of models (8)-(13) that finished with an optimal solution that required the auditing phase, i.e. (14)-(18) was solved. Column "Dom" shows the number of models (8)-(13) with the solution discarded because β^* was larger than a previous solution. Column "Abort" is the number of optimal solutions where the auditing started but was aborted because β was increased to guarantee protection. Finally α and β are the percentage values proposed by the ECTA approach for each instance. Note that these values are not unique since the approach has random decisions and therefore different executions produce different values.

The main conclusion from Table 2 is that the ECTA approach, with the requirement that the adjustments must be integer numbers, has similar performances both on commercial and on free-and-open-source solvers. The total time to solve an instance has increased mainly due to the integrality constraints in model (8)-(13). However most of the tables can be protected in less than one hour, which seems to be reasonable in practice for statistical agencies. Protected tables with small loss of information (β under 20%) were obtained for most of the instances after solving ten models (8)-(13), and among their solutions about two of them required solving models (14)-(18).

Table 2. Results of the code with the 4 solvers on the 10 instances

SCIP-CLP	Tfind	Taudit	Infeas	Prot	Dom	Abort	α	β
1	1066	40	2	4	4	0	22	5
2	1112	39	0	3	7	0	10	8
3	1044	52	0	3	7	0	10	8
4	1018	55	0	6	4	0	10	8
5	1175	19	0	1	8	1	31	17
6	68	8	0	3	7	0	14	4
7	242	29	0	1	9	0	15	4
8	2524	340	0	3	7	0	10	8
9	2761	345	0	3	7	0	19	9
10	2322	236	0	2	8	0	20	16
SCIP-CPLEX	**Tfind**	**Taudit**	**Infeas**	**Prot**	**Dom**	**Abort**	**α**	**β**
1	649	15	0	2	8	0	10	4
2	568	22	0	3	6	1	10	8
3	559	37	0	3	2	5	22	8
4	606	14	0	2	8	0	11	16
5	576	11	0	2	8	0	20	16
6	30	5	0	3	7	0	15	4
7	108	10	0	3	7	0	12	4
8	2824	78	0	2	4	4	22	6
9	2676	62	0	2	8	0	10	8
10	2928	72	0	2	4	4	31	10
SCIP-SOPLEX	**Tfind**	**Taudit**	**Infeas**	**Prot**	**Dom**	**Abort**	**α**	**β**
1	646	44	2	3	5	0	10	4
2	1123	49	0	4	6	0	12	8
3	1268	14	0	1	9	0	11	8
4	1076	88	0	6	3	1	12	8
5	1008	31	0	3	7	0	21	16
6	44	5	0	2	8	0	13	4
7	187	72	0	4	6	0	10	4
8	3189	470	0	2	7	1	18	7
9	3516	530	0	2	6	2	22	8
10	2910	635	0	2	6	2	33	10
SCIP-XPRESS	**Tfind**	**Taudit**	**Infeas**	**Prot**	**Dom**	**Abort**	**α**	**β**
1	1371	19	1	2	7	0	10	4
2	1392	28	0	2	6	2	11	8
3	1436	21	0	3	7	0	11	16
4	1440	18	0	2	6	2	12	8
5	1385	17	0	2	7	1	22	22
6	72	6	0	3	7	0	10	4
7	269	8	0	2	8	0	10	4
8	4939	232	0	2	1	7	22	7
9	6094	55	0	1	9	0	20	8
10	5630	119	0	1	5	4	32	11

Acknowledgment. This work was supported by the European Union funded project FP7-INFRASTRUCTURES-2010-1, "DwB - Data without Boundaries", and by the Spanish Government through the research project MTM2012-36163-C06-01, "Optimos 3".

References

Castro, J., Giessing, S.: Testing variants of minimum distance controlled tabular adjustment. In: Monographs of Official Statistics. Work session on Statistical Data Confidentiality, Eurostat-Office for Official Publications of the European Communities, Luxembourg, pp. 333–343 (2006)

Cox, L.H.: A Constructive Procedure for Unbiased Controlled Rounding. Journal of the American Statistical Association 82, 520–524 (1987)

Cox, L.H., Kelly, J.P., Patil, R.: Balancing Quality and Confidentiality for Multivariate Tabular Data. In: Domingo-Ferrer, J., Torra, V. (eds.) PSD 2004. LNCS, vol. 3050, pp. 87–98. Springer, Heidelberg (2004)

Cox, L.H., Kelly, J.P., Patil, R.J.: Computational Aspects of Controlled Tabular Adjustment: Algorithm and Analysis. In: Golden, B., Raghavan, S., Wasil, E. (eds.) The Next Wave in Computer, Optimization and Decision Technologies, pp. 45–59. Kluwer, Boston (2005)

Cox, L.H., Kim, J.J.: Effects of Rounding on the Quality and Confidentiality of Statistical Data. In: Domingo-Ferrer, J., Franconi, L. (eds.) PSD 2006. LNCS, vol. 4302, pp. 48–56. Springer, Heidelberg (2006)

Danderkar, R.A., Cox, L.H.: Synthetic Tabular Data-An Alternative to Complementary Cell Suppression. Manuscript. Energy Information Administration, U.S. Department of Energy (2002)

Duncan, G., Elliot, M., Salazar-González, J.J.: Statistical Confidentiality: Principles and Practice. Springer, Heidelberg (2011)

Glover, F., Cox, L.H., Kelly, J.P., Patil, R.: Exact, heuristic and metaheuristic methods for confidentiality protection by controlled tabular adjustment. International Journal of Operations Research 5(2), 117–128 (2008)

Hernández-García, M.S., Salazar-González, J.J.: Enhanced Controlled Tabular Adjustment. Computers & Operations Research 43, 61–67 (2014)

Salazar-González, J.J.: Statistical confidentiality: Optimization techniques to protect tables. Computers & Operations Research 35, 1638–1651 (2008)

Comparison of Different Sensitivity Rules for Tabular Data and Presenting a New Rule -- The *Interval Rule*

Johan Bring[1] and Qun Wang[2]

[1] Statisticon
johan.bring@statisticon.se
[2] Statistics Sweden
qun.wang@scb.se

Abstract. Statistical disclosure control (SDC) is a set of methods that are used to reduce the risk of disclosing information on individuals, businesses or other organisations. The focus of this paper is on sensitivity rules, which deal with how to define whether a cell in tabular data has the risk of disclosing information or not.

The current popular sensitivity rules include the dominance rule and the $P\%$ rule. There is a weakness with these rules and a new rule - the *interval rule* is presented. The main argument for this new rule is that the rule should only be based on the information that the intruder knows, not on the information that the statistical institution knows.

Based on simulated data, the $P\%$ rule tends to classify a dataset to be "sensitive" when it contains only one observation with a very large value. In this respect, and the dominance rule and the $P\%$ rule share a lot in common. Meanwhile the *interval rule* tends to classify a dataset to be "sensitive" when it contains two observations with large values.

Keywords: Statistical disclosure control, tabular data, sensitivity rules, $P\%$ rule, dominance rule, interval rule.

1   Introduction

National Statistical institutions (NSIs) are supposed to provide the society with trustworthy and detailed statistical information. However, this statistical information may sometimes lead to disclosure of sensitive and confidential information, which might cause harm on both individuals and organisations or on the group level. This paper focuses on macro data, where magnitude tables and frequency tables are two major components.

To protect the confidentiality of survey respondents – not only because of legal and ethical obligation, but because public trust is an important contributor to data quality and response rates (Doyle *et al*, 2001). NSIs have created a set of methods to protect the confidentiality of information provided by respondents. These methods are called statistical disclosure control.

J. Domingo-Ferrer (Ed.): PSD 2014, LNCS 8744, pp. 36–47, 2014.

In statistical disclosure control of tabular data, sensitivity rules are used to decide whether a table cell is sensitive and should therefore not be published. In this paper the characteristics of different sensitivity rules are discussed and compared, and a new rule – the *interval rule* is presented.

2   Sensitivity Rules for Tabular Data

There are different sensitivity rules available for judging which cells are primarily sensitive (unsafe) in a table. Some general assumptions: let $x_1 \geq x_2 \geq \ldots \geq x_N$ be the ordered contribution in a cell by N respondents $1, 2\ldots N$ respectively and let $X = \sum_{i=1}^{N} x_i$ be the sum of all the observations in a cell.

2.1   Dominance Rule

The dominance rule is also called the (n, k) rule. The cell is considered sensitive if the total of the n largest contributions exceeds $k\%$ of the total cell value X:

$$x_1 + x_2 + \cdots + x_n \geq \frac{k}{100} \cdot X \tag{1}$$

2.2 $P\%$ Rule

The $P\%$ rule is based on the following inequality:

$$X - x_j - x_i \leq \frac{p}{100} \cdot x_i \tag{2}$$

The worst case of this inequality is supposing x_i is the value of the largest contributor — respondent 1 —, and x_j is the value for the second largest contributor — respondent 2 —, where x_1 is estimated by respondent 2. The assumption for the "worst case" is therefore: respondent 2, knowing that it is the second largest contributor and its own value x_2, is trying to estimate x_1. As long as this condition is safe, the cell is safe for all other conditions. Therefore for the $P\%$ rule, a cell is considered sensitive if the cell total minus the value of the 2 largest contributions is smaller than a certain percentage of x_1, namely:

$$X - x_2 - x_1 \leq \frac{p}{100} \cdot x_1 \tag{3}$$

The assumption for both dominance rule and $P\%$ rule is that there is no prior knowledge about the contribution for respondent x_i. More detailed information is found in (Loeve, 2001).

2.3   Comparison between Dominance Rule and $P\%$ Rule

The dominance rule with $n = 2$ is sometimes compared with the $P\%$ rule, and when $n = 2$ the dominance rule looks very similar to formulation of the $P\%$ rule.

The $(2,k)$ rule classifies a cell as sensitive if

$$x_1 + x_2 \geq \frac{k}{100} \cdot X \leftrightarrow X - x_2 - x_1 \leq \left(1 - \frac{k}{100}\right) \cdot X \qquad (4)$$

Comparing (3) and (4), it is seen that in both cases a cell is sensitive if $(X - x_2) - x_1$, i.e. the difference between the estimation of x_1 made by second respondent and x_1, is less than a certain percentage of either the first respondent value x_1 in (3) or the cell value X in (4). Indeed, for p and k such that $k = 100 * \frac{100}{100+p}$, every non-sensitive cell for the rule $(2,k)$ is also a non-sensitive cell for the rule $P\%$; but the reverse implication does not hold. It is believed in many articles that in general, the $P\%$ rule is preferred to the dominance rule, see e.g. Hundepool $et\ al$ (2012) or Castro J. (2010).

Comparing these two rules by setting $k = 100 * \frac{100}{100+p}$ is just one specific combination of k and p that could be compared. When this equation doesn't hold, these two rules are not comparable any more. Each rule can be equally restrictive by changing the value of parameters and it is hence hard to tell which rule is more conservative. A more detailed comparison based on simulation is presented in chapter 3.

2.4   Drawback with $P\%$ Rule

Suppose a cell is the sum of three respondents A, B and C. Assume B has the value 40 and the total sum is 100. B could calculate the interval for the largest value (either A, C or B itself) to be (40, 60). Hence, B knows that the largest value is in the interval (40, 60).

According to the $P\%$ rule with e.g. $p = 10$, the cell is identified as sensitive if the values of A, B and C are (59, 40, 1) but safe if the values are (41, 40, 19). Hence, when the largest value is closer to the upper bound (which is 60 in this example) the cell is considered as sensitive. On the contrary, when the largest value lies near to the lower bound of the interval (which is 40 in this example) the cell is considered as safe. This is problematic because the value of the B and the sum has stayed unchanged and hence, the information that B has is exactly the same in these two situations. There is no additional knowledge about the other respondents in case of (59, 40, 1) than (41, 40, 19). It can be argued that it is unreasonable that the former is sensitive but the latter is safe. The following figure illustrates this problem.

It is clearly shown in the figure that when either A or C is closer to the upper bound (which is 60 in this example), the cell is sensitive and otherwise the cell is safe. However, the only information B knows is that the largest value is between 40 and 60. The actual position of the largest value within the interval should not affect the decision whether the cell is safe or not. Moreover, 59 and 41 have the same distance to the limits of the interval. It does not seem rational that when A is 59 the cell is sensitive but safe when A is 41.

The $P\%$ rule seems to be based on the assumption that the intruder should estimate the value for the largest observation as its maximum possible value, $\widehat{x_1} = X - x_2$. But there is no statistical logic behind this estimation. With the information that B

has, a plausible estimate of the value of the largest observation would be 50 (in the middle of 40-60). Hence, from this point of view the cell could be considered sensitive if the true value is close to 50, not the upper bound 60.

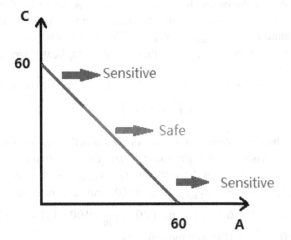

Fig. 1. whether a cell is sensitive or safe depending on the distribution of A and C. Assuming $A+B+C = 100$ and $B = 40$.

2.5   The Interval Rule

In this section a suggestion of a new rule – the *interval rule*- is presented. A basic principle of this rule is that the decision about whether a cell is safe or sensitive should only be based on the information known to the intruder. It is what the intruder can know that is relevant. If an intruder j is trying to estimate the value of another respondent i: based on the information that the intruder knows, it is possible to calculate an interval I, where i may lie in, i.e. $I_{x_i} = x_{i\,max} - x_{i\,min}$. If this interval is narrow, there is risk for disclosure, since the intruder has good information about respondent i. If the interval is wide the intruder has only limited information about the true value for i. An analogy could be a confidence interval; a narrow interval implies good precision and good knowledge about the true parameter value while a wide confidence interval implies uncertainty and lack of precise knowledge. Hence, a cell is classified as sensitive when this interval is narrow, e.g. smaller than $s\%$ of the total value X:

$$I_{x_1} < \frac{s}{100} \cdot X \tag{5}$$

In (5) the right hand side of the equation depends on the total value X. It could be argued that the total value is not relevant for the decision of when the interval is too small or not. With 'substance knowledge' of the variable in question, it should be possible to set an absolute value that could serve as a limit for deciding when the interval is too small (sensitive) or not. For example, if the data concerns a company's spending on Research and Development, the interval could be specified in absolute dollars (or other currency).

The "worst case" here is again when supposing x_i is the value for the largest respondent and x_j is the value for the second largest, and where x_1 is estimated by respondent 2. The assumption for the "worst case" is therefore: respondent 2 knows it is the second largest contributor and is trying to estimate the value for the largest contributor x_1. As long as this condition is safe, the cell is safe for all other conditions.

How to calculate $I_{x_1} = x_{1\,max} - x_{1\,min}$? The maximum value is estimated as $x_{1\,max} = X - x_2$, and for $x_{1\,min}$ is a little bit more complicated (see Appendix I):

$$x_{1\,min} = \begin{cases} X - (N-1) \cdot x_2 & \text{when } X - (N-1) \cdot x_2 > x_2, \text{ namely } x_2 < \frac{X}{N} \\ x_2 & \text{when } x_2 \geq \frac{X}{N} \end{cases} \quad (6)$$

Let us review the example in 2.4 again: suppose a cell is the sum of three respondents A, B and C. Assume B has the value 40 and the total sum is 100. Now B is in the position of x_2 and trying to estimate x_1. $x_{1\,max} = X - x_2 = 100 - 40 = 60$ And since $40 > \frac{100}{3}$ ➔ $x_{1\,min} = x_2 = 40$ and the interval $I_{x_1} = x_{1\,max} - x_{1\,min} = 60 - 40 = 20$. If $s = 25$, then $20 < \frac{25}{100} * 100$, and the cell is sensitive; if $s = 15$, then $20 > \frac{15}{100} * 100$, and the cell is safe.

Different from the $P\%$ rule, the *interval rule* classifies a cell to be sensitive only on the interval of x_1 that the second largest respondent could calculate and different values of parameter s. It does not matter whether the combination of the values for A, B and C is (59, 40, 1) or (41, 40, 19), because the information that B knows has not changed.

3   Comparisons between Sensitivity Rules Based on Simulation

To compare the different sensitivity rules a simulation study is done.

3.1   Simulation Setup

The exponential distribution with $\lambda = 1$ is used since it is likely to generate outliers which is typical for sensitive observations. The sample size per cell is varied from 3-20.

E.g. with $n = 4$, *dataset 1*: [1.87, 0.22, 0.91, 1.63], *dataset 2*: [0.40, 1.05, 0.68, 4.42] etc. There are in total 1000 such datasets generated for each setup. The question is if the total value of the observations in a dataset can be published without risk for disclosure.

Sensitivity Rules
For the sake of simplicity, all the sensitivity rules are denoted with an abbreviation.

D = *Dominance rule*
P = *P% rule*
S = *interval rule*

The parameters used for these three rules are given as k, p and s (each ranging from 1-100).

For each combination of dataset, rule and parameter value, it is determined if the cell is safe or not. For example, *dataset* 2 [0.40, 1.05, 0.68, 4.42] is not safe for all parameter values of k up to 83 and safe for all values of k between [84, 100]. For the $P\%$ rule this cell is safe for all values of p up to 24 but sensitive if the value of p is set to 25 or higher.

3.2   Pairwise Comparison between Sensitivity Rules

Pairwise Comparison between P and S

Each sensitivity rule can be more or less restrictive by adjusting the value for the parameters. Hence, by changing the value it is easy to make one rule more restrictive than another. To achieve a sensible comparison between the different rules, parameter values that make the three rules approximately equally restrictive are found, i.e. the values for p, k and s that make roughly the same proportion of datasets classified as safe.

In the simulations a parameter setup has been used so that makes approximately 20% of the datasets to be classified as sensitive by each rule. The following values are obtained $k = 89$, $p = 18$, and $s = 27$. Applying the different rules and these parameter values on the 1000 datasets used in the simulation, each dataset is classified as safe or sensitive by each rule respectively. In table 1 the classification of 1000 datasets is presented according to P and S.

Table 1. The distribution of 1000 datasets classified by P and S ($s = 27, p = 18$)

	$S \rightarrow$ Sensitive	$S \rightarrow$ Safe	Total
$P \rightarrow$ sensitive	75	124	199
$P \rightarrow$ safe	112	689	801
Total	187	813	1000

There are only 75 datasets that are classified as sensitive by both rules. 112 datasets are classified as sensitive by S but not by P, and 124 datasets are classified as sensitive by P but not by S. To analyse the differences between the rules, firstly each value in the dataset is transformed into percent, i.e. the ordered observations x_1, x_2, x_3 and x_4 are divided by the cell sum X and hence are presented as percentages of the sum X. In figure 2 the 124 datasets that are sensitive according to P but safe according to the S are presented (each row is a dataset with $n = 4$). In the second graph the 112 datasets that are sensitive according to S but safe according to P are presented.

In the datasets that are classified as sensitive by P but safe by S, the value of x_1 is much greater than all the other respondents in the same dataset, meanwhile where the datasets are classified as safe by P but sensitive by S, the value of x_1 and x_2 are both quite large compared with the other two respondents in the same dataset.

P% sensitive S safe

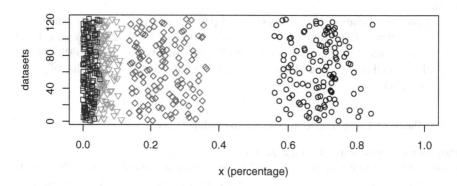

x (percentage)

P% safe S sensitive

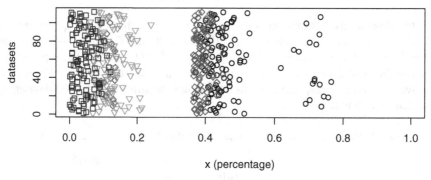

x (percentage)

Fig. 2. Plot of all datasets where P=sensitive and S=safe (graph 1) and when P=safe and S=sensitive (graph 2). Each row is a dataset; x_1, x_2, x_3 and x_4 are illustrated with different symbols within each dataset.

The first dataset in the upper graph (the top row) is [0.02, 0.09, 0.31, 0.58]. According to the *P%* rule this is a sensitive cell while the according to the *interval rule* this cell is safe since the interval for x_1 is (0.31 to 0.69) and the width of this interval 0.38 is larger than the chosen parameter-value for $s = 0.27$.

The first dataset in the lower graph (the top row) is [0.07, 0.08, 0.39, 0.46]. According to the *P%* rule this is a safe cell while according to the *interval rule* this cell is sensitive since the interval for x_1 is (0.39 to 0.61) and the width of this interval 0.22 is smaller than the chosen parameter value for $s = 0.27$.

Pairwise Comparison between D and S

The same procedure is repeated for comparing D and S as well as P and D. And the results are as following:

Table 2. The distribution of 1000 datasets classified by D and S (k=89, s= 27)

	$S \rightarrow$ Sensitive	$S \rightarrow$ Safe	Total
$D \rightarrow$ sensitive	78	118	196
$D \rightarrow$ safe	109	695	804
Total	187	813	1000

The distribution of the sensitive datasets for D and S is quite similar with P and S in Table 2: there are only 78 datasets that classified to be sensitive by both rules. 118 datasets are classified as sensitive by D but not by S, and 109 datasets are classified as sensitive by S but not by D.

Pairwise comparison between P and D

The same procedure is repeated once again to compare P and D, and the results are as following:

Table 3. The distribution of 1000 datasets classified by P and D (p=18, k= 89)

	$D \rightarrow$ Sensitive	$D \rightarrow$ Safe	Total
$P \rightarrow$ sensitive	177	22	199
$P \rightarrow$ safe	19	782	801
Total	196	804	1000

There are 177 datasets that classified to be sensitive by both rules. Only 22 datasets are classified as sensitive by P but not by D and only 19 datasets are classified as sensitive by D but not by P. Unlike the comparison between P and S, these two rules are equivalent at most of the times, and in total there are only 41 datasets that are classified differently. In figure 3 the datasets that are considered as safe by only one of the rules are illustrated.

Even though there are only a few datasets that are classified differently by P and D, the pattern is quite obvious. P tends to classify a dataset to be sensitive when it has one observation with extremely large value, and D tends to classify a dataset to be sensitive when it has two observations with large values.

The same pattern is observed when n is increased. As an illustration, some results for $n = 10$ are presented in appendix 2.

D sensitive P safe

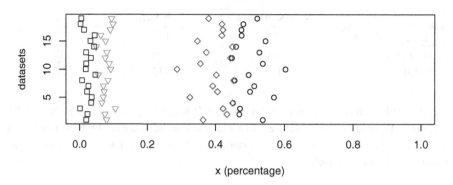

D safe P sensitive

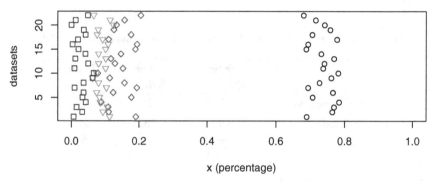

Fig. 3. Plot of x_1, x_2, x_3 and x_4 for all datasets where the D and P rule gives different decisions

4   Discussion

When comparing different rules, it is not sensible to say that one rule is more conservative than another. By changing the value of the parameters, each rule can be adjusted so that it becomes more or less conservative. The decision regarding which rule to use should be based on other arguments. One approach is to study datasets where two rules give different decisions and try to evaluate which decision that seems to be the best. But more importantly there can be significant differences between the different rules with respect to what information that is used in the decision process (calculations).

The most important distinction between the different rules is that the *interval rule* only depends on the information known to the intruder, while the other rules depend on the distribution of the observations, which is not known to the intruder. The purpose of sensitivity rules is to ensure that the intruder could not get too much information about another respondent according to the published data. By publishing a total value for all objects in a cell, the intruder gets new information and can narrow the limit of the possible values for other respondents. Under some assumptions these possible values can be described by an interval. It is the width of this interval that that describes the information known to the intruder. The position where the true value happens within this interval should not affect the decision when considering if a cell is safe or not.

References

1. Castro, J.: Statistical disclosure control in tabular data. In: Privacy and Anonymity in Information Management Systems: New Techniques for New Practical Problem, pp. 113–131. Springer (2010)
2. Doyle, P., Lane, J.I., Theeuwes, J.J.M., Zayatz, L.V. (eds.): Confidentiality, disclosure, and data access: Theory and practical applications for statistical agencies, p. 1. Elsevier, Amsterdam (2001)
3. Hundepool, A., Domingo-Ferrer, J., Franconi, L., Giessing, S., Schulte Nordholt, E., Spicer, K., de Wolf, P.P.: Statistical Disclosure Control. Wiley (2012)
4. Loeve, J.A.: Notes on sensitivity measures and protection levels. Project number: TMO-102966, Statistics Netherlands (2001)

Appendix I

Let $X = \sum_{i=1}^{N} x_i$, $x_1 \geq x_2 \geq x_3 \geq \cdots \geq x_N$ and $x_{rest} = x_2 + x_3 + \cdots + x_N$. In order to obtain $x_{1\ min}$, different situations are supposed to be discussed.

When x_1 achieves its minimum value, x_{rest} achieves its maximum value, and this is when $x_3, x_4, \ldots x_N$ are all close to x_2, i.e. when $x_{rest} = (N-1)\ x_2$, i.e. when $x_1 = X - (N-1) \cdot x_2$; or when x_1 is very close to x_2 that is when $x_1 = x_2$. Hence,

$$x_{1\ min} = \begin{cases} X - (N-1) \cdot x_2 & \text{when } X - (N-1) \cdot x_2 > x_2, \text{ namely } x_2 < \frac{X}{N} \\ x_2 & \text{when } x_2 \geq \frac{X}{N} \end{cases}$$

Appendix II: Pairwise Comparison When $x \sim \exp (\lambda=1)$ and $n=10$

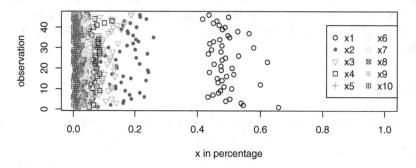

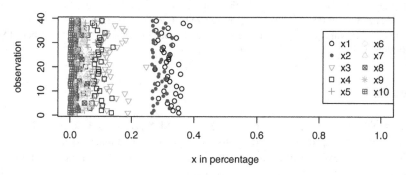

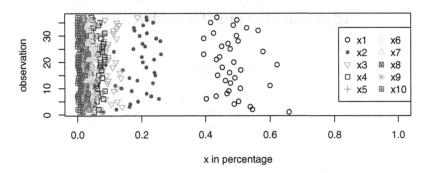

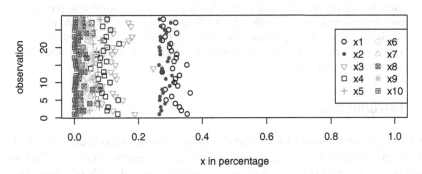

Pre-tabular Perturbation with Controlled Tabular Adjustment: Some Considerations[*]

Sarah Giessing

Federal Statistical Office of Germany,
65180 Wiesbaden, Germany
Sarah.Giessing@destatis.de

Abstract. Controlled Tabular Adjustment (CTA) has been developed as SDC method for tabular data. It aims at finding the closest additive table to a given original table ensuring that adjusted values of all confidential cells are safely away from their original value. In practice, it is usually not possible to process an entire publication as a *single* CTA application. This paper looks into possibilities of designing a sequential application of CTA yielding a protected micro-data set while controlling for the quality of estimates that would be derived from the protected data.

1   Introduction

There is a growing demand for tabular disclosure control methods and tools that are likely to be suitable for practical use in 3rd party research situations. Data users should be free to request (or even generate on their own) all kinds of tables. Disclosure risk limitation should be carried out 'on the fly', i.e. the process of table generation and protection should become automated and self-auditing regarding privacy preservation. "Traditional" protection methods like cell suppression are often not suitable: controlling the disclosure by differencing risks in large sets of multiple tables designed by user demand can become virtually impossible.

Post-tabular methods relying on micro-data seed based stochastic noise applied to the data on the table level, as proposed f.i. in [8],[16],[14], or [9], have proven to be promising[1]. But implementing them requires a major IT investment into a suitable tabulation package[2].

From the IT point of view, pre-tabular SDC methods (as proposed for example in [7]) seem to be attractive, because the SDC process can be organized as separate step, before actual table production. For the latter purpose, the standard tabulation packages will do then.

---

[*] Supported by the FP7-INFRASTRUCTURES-2010-1 project "DwB-Data without Boundaries", number 262608.
[1] ...or are even in regular use (c.f. [16]).
[2] The methodology can guarantee certain desirable properties of the protected results, but only, if these results are generated by specialized tools incorporating the methodology. Such a tool should therefore be as convenient as any standard tabulation package, useable for "anybody".

J. Domingo-Ferrer (Ed.): PSD 2014, LNCS 8744, pp. 48–61, 2014.

Controlled Tabular Adjustment (CTA) ([5, 1]) has been developed as SDC method for tabular data, i.e. as post-tabular method. Several variants have been discussed in the literature [2-4, 6, 10]. CTA aims at finding the closest additive table to a given original table ensuring that adjusted values of all confidential cells are safely away from their original value and that the adjusted values are within a certain range of the real values. The basic methodology will be briefly recalled in section 2 below.

In the context of noise masking (c.f. [7]), [12] introduce a balanced noise masking method as a variant. [13] prove the reduction of cell level noise variance from using the balancing mechanism.

The idea outlined in sec. 3 of the present paper can be regarded as a way to employ CTA as such a mechanism for balancing perturbation: Given a set of "control-tables", after a number of sequentially organized CTA steps, the routine should finally yield a protected (i.e. perturbed) micro-data set. When reproducing a cell of a control-table by summing the respective perturbed micro-data, the perturbation of that cell will tend to be identical to the one that would have resulted from applying CTA directly to that control table.

The paper reports from an early, experimental phase of developing such a routine. Section 4 presents some preliminary findings obtained for an example used for illustration and experimentation. This example was generated as small extract from the huge German Income Tax Statistics database. As conclusion from the lessons learnt in the experiment and as an outlook, section 5 identifies major issues to be solved within a potential future research project addressing the protection of this database with the proposed methodology. The paper ends with a summary section.

2   CTA Method

The sequential procedure to be outlined in section 3 below is designed to work with the CTA package [4]. In this section we briefly summarize the methodology and some important options implemented in the package:

In the denotation of [4], a CTA instance is represented by (i) a set of cells y_i; $i = 1,...,n$, that satisfy m linear relations $Ay = b$ (y being the vector of y_i's; matrix A and vector b imposing the tabular constraints, expressing for example that the cell values of some set of cells must be identical to the cell value of another (marginal) cell); (ii) a set $P = \{i_1, i_2, ..., i_p\} \subseteq \{1,...,n\}$ of indices of sensitive cells; (iii) a lower and upper protection level for each sensitive cell $i \in P$, respectively lpl_i and upl_i, such that the adjusted values satisfy either $x_i \geq y_i + upl_i$ or $x_i \leq y_i - lpl_i$, and (iv) a lower and upper a priori bound for each cell $i = 1,...,n$, respectively l_i and u_i, which can be used to impose that the adjusted values of non-sensitive cells are still "similar" to the original data.

Given these settings of the CTA instance, the purpose of CTA is to find the set of closest feasible adjusted values x_i; $i = 1,...,n$ satisfying the conditions stated in (i), and (iv), that make the adjusted table safe (i.e. satisfy (iii)). This is expressed as the following optimization problem (in terms of the deviations $z_i =: x_i\text{-}y_i$ and w_i being a vector of cell weights)[3]:

$$\min_z \sum_{i=1}^{n} w_i \,|\, z_i \,|$$

$$s.t. \quad Az = 0 \tag{1}$$

$$l_i \leq z_i \leq u_i \quad , i = 1,...,n$$

$$z_i \leq -lpl_i \; or \; z_i \geq upl_i, \quad i \in P$$

A challenge comes from the last line of this statement, because of the "or" condition. The exact formal mathematical expression of this condition requires the introduction of a vector of binary variables into the problem, associated to the direction of the deviation of each sensitive cell. An optimal solution requires an optimal allocation of these "directions" to the binary variables and makes the CTA problem a computationally "difficult" mixed integer linear programming problem (MILP). It can be relaxed significantly by turning it into a continuous (convex) optimization problem which is computationally much easier to solve. To achieve this, the binary variables must be removed. One way accomplish this is to fix the deviation senses of the sensitive cells in advance, which is particularly supported by the current version of the CTA package, see also [3]. Another alternative would be to pre-perturb the sensitive cells by some other method and flag them as non-sensitive for CTA. We will refer to the latter in sec. 5. For more information on the package, in particular "tricks" offered to handle infeasibility see [4].

3   Outline of a Sequential Procedure

The aim of the masking procedure that shall be drafted in this section should be to keep the perturbation of non-sensitive, statistically "relevant" aggregates "low". For those aggregates, the perturbations of the respective unit level data should, more or less, balance each other. It will be up to the users of the method to define which tables or cells to consider as "relevant". In the following, we assume the set of "relevant cells" to be defined as a set of – perhaps linked – tables in a way that can be transformed into a set of CTA instances as outlined in section 2. Such a set of tables is referred to as the "set of control tables". The procedure will consist of at least two stages, outlined below. Appendix A.1 presents a small toy example involving just a few data lines with only one control table, for illustration of the denotation used in the following description. Grey shaded lines of the toy example refer to stage 1.

Stage 1: Apply the CTA method to the set of control tables. For now, we assume this to be a single CTA instance, to be achieved within a single CTA step. It is not unlikely that in practice larger (sets of) control tables have to be defined. It may turn out then that special strategies will be required to break this (so far single) step on stage 1

---

[3]   For the exact mathematical statement see [4].

into a sequence of CTA steps to be performed on subsets. This issue will not be addressed in this paper.

Stage 2: Stage 2 is basically composed of the following three steps:

1. Use the spanning variables of the control tables[4] for clustering the survey units into groups. Select from those n variables a "suitable" one, say, variable i. Define a hierarchical structure (variable i^*) at three levels[5]. The top-level categories (i.e. levels 0 and 1) of variable i^* correspond to the categories of variable i . Each bottom level (i.e. level 2) category refers to a unit identity (ID) of a unit belonging to the respective level 1 category of variable i^* for a given combination k ($k=1,..,K$) of the categories[6] of the other n-1 control table variables. See also sec. 4.1 for illustration.
2. Set up a separate CTA input table for each of the K cross combination categories. All cells of such a table where variable i^* is at level 2 refer to a single unit. They are considered sensitive. For all cells where variable i^* is at level 1 (these cells are identical to a respective control table cell) replace their true cell value by the adjusted value this cell received at stage 1 of the procedure. Declare those cells as non-sensitive (because they received protection already at stage 1). In the CTA input format, assign weights and bounds (see sec. 3.1) in such a way as to achieve that those cells will not be subject to further adjustment, or to at most a "slight" further adjustment. The objective here is to maintain as far as possible the data of the CTA solution of stage 1. Note that this CTA input table is not additive, the table constraints do not hold.
3. Process each of those K tables separately with CTA to (a) restore additivity and to (b) obtain an "optimally" perturbed version of the level 2 data.

3.1 Preserving Data Quality

Basically, there are two options for influencing the behavior of a CTA procedure: cell bounds (c.f. (iv) in sec. 3) and cell weights (e.g. the variables w_i in the mathematical CTA statement (1) in sec. 3). Choice of these "parameters" should be based on some idea of how one wants the program to balance perturbations introduced into the data in order to protect the sensitive cells. A good solution should perhaps introduce rather "small" perturbations into the majority of cells – small enough for the disseminator to claim that these perturbed cell values are still "fit for use". Cases where the perturbation is beyond some threshold might be flagged "less reliable". An analysis of the perturbation might be based on the Hellinger distance, as proposed for example in [15]. Considering for a set of cells the ratios of the (interior) cell values to their mar-

---

4   Spanning variables where the same unit can contribute to more than one category (like f.i. a variable composed of income categories, when the units are tax cases) to be ignored in this step. In the toy instance, spanning variables are MUN and CL.
5   To keep it simple, we assume here for variable i to be without hierarchical substructure.
6   In case of a hierarchical variable: consider categories at the bottom of the hierarchy only. In the toy instance, variable i is CL, the "other" control table-variables are only one, e.g. MUN, with K=3 categories.

ginal sum as discrete probability distribution, the Hellinger distance can be used for measuring the distance between the original distribution, P, and the distribution after adjustment, Q . The distance is computed as the Euclidean norm of the difference of the square root vectors P and Q divided by $\sqrt{2}$. For a formal statement c.f. formula A.1 in appendix A.3 (see also denotations introduced in corollary 1 and its proof).

As starting point for further investigation this paper proposes the following strategy: For all non-sensitive cells define *a priori* bounds on the deviations proportional to a root-function of the cell value, e.g.

(3.1) $-c\ y_i^q \le z_i \le c\ y_i^q$, $0 \le q \le 1$. In principle, for the choice of constants c and q we should say: the smaller, the better. But if they are chosen too small, the CTA problem turns infeasible.

Notably for $q = 0.5$, e.g. for bounds that are about proportional to the square root of the cell values, the Hellinger distance of any feasible CTA solution is below $\dfrac{c}{\sqrt{2\bar{Y}}}$,

where $\bar{Y}$ denote the mean cell value. See Corollary 1 and its proof in appendix A.3.

If it turns out the bounds are too tight, making the CTA problem infeasible, they must be relaxed.

For the two-stage procedure outlined here, all these considerations apply to stage 1 where the goal should be an "optimal" distribution of the perturbations. Whereas at stage 2, one wants to preserve for the cells with a variable i^* category of level 1 to preserve the perturbations they received at stage 1, to the extent possible. At stage 2, cell bounds of those cells will be centered on their adjusted values (received in the CTA step of stage 1, c.f. item 2 of the description of stage 2). They should be considerably tighter as those from stage 1.

Another means for influencing the quality of a CTA-solution are the cell weights. [2] propose weights of the form $y_i^{-\gamma}$, $0 \le \gamma \le 1$. The larger the choice of γ, the lower the probability for smaller cells to be subject to adjustment. A special option described in [2] is to choose γ in a flexible way, depending on the hierarchical level h of a cell, according to the function $\gamma(h) = \dfrac{h_{max} - h}{h_{max}}$, where h_{max} denote the highest level. In a multidimensional table, h is computed for a cell by taking for each spanning variable the hierarchical level of the respective category (0 for bottom level) and summing across the spanning variables. Sec. 4.2 reports test results for several cost functions.

4   Test Application

We test this approach at the example of the German Income Tax Statistics. The data are from an administrative source, the database consists of about 40 million records. For each of those 40 m. tax cases, the database offers about 1500 variables. About 100 of those - mostly quantitative – variables are used for analyses and publications.

The most "important" categorical variable of the file is geography. Many income tax statistics results are published down to the level of municipalities. There are a few other categorical variables, and of course it is always possible to derive more categorical variables, like for example size classes of a quantitative variable, or binary variables indicating f.i. whether a unit has a certain type of income. The most prominent derived variable in the German Income Tax Statistics is an income size class variable with 14 categories, used for classification in several tables of the regular publication.

As for the quantitative variables, there are some with an exact linear interdependence between them (like f.i. "total income = positive income + negative income"). When such a relation is stated in the setup of a CTA problem, it will also hold in the CTA solution.

Income Tax Statistics is far less skewed compared to business (turnover) tax statistics. There are hardly any sensitive cells at the higher levels of geography, and even at the municipality level they are relatively rare. So there is some hope that the perturbations needed to protect them can be "balanced" without causing much harm to the analytical validity of the non-sensitive cells.

4.1   Illustrative Example

As starting point for the testing and first illustrative example for the methodology, we selected a district with relatively small municipalities, in order to get some sensitive cases in the municipality tables. To keep things simple in the beginning, we select for the testing only the data of this district (about 50 000 tax cases), and settle on only one control table. The control table is defined by three variables: geography (15 municipalities), size class (on income, 14 categories) and a hierarchical income-relations variable that defines total income as sum of positive and negative income (plus some rest-position), and with some sub-positions for the positive income sources (like, from agriculture, from employment, from self-employment, etc.). This table has 2640 cells (including zero-cells), 821 table relations and 303 sensitive cells identified by a p%-rule.

In this application, stage 1 consists of applying CTA to this table. Section 4.2 reports some results. At stage 2, we include the unit level data: Here, we process the data of each of the 15 municipalities separately. For municipality 1, for instance, there are about 4500 tax cases. We create a hierarchical variable at two levels. On level 1, we put the 14 size-class categories (thus, in the denotation of sec. 3, the size-class variable takes the role of variable i). For the new variable $i*$, the level 2 categories are generated by concatenating size-class category and unit ID key (for the tax case units falling into the respective size class). The longest table relation (or constraint), i.e. the constraint with the largest number of coefficients determined by this structure is that for size class 2: there are more than 900 tax cases in size class 2, and hence more than 900 coefficients in each of the respective table constraints. On the other hand, there are also rather short constraints, in particular two with only two coefficients each, because two of the size classes consist of only a single tax case. This makes those relations so called "identity relations", literally saying "cell j = cell k".

4.2   Details and Test Results for the Illustrative Example

Testing at Stage 1
The first exercise is figuring out the "tightest", feasible *a priori* bounds (in the form of statement (3.1)) for the control table. For the experiment this was done simply through "trial and error", reducing step by step first the parameter q and then c (after fixing q), until the problem became reported infeasible by the CTA routine[7]. Execution of those test-steps requires just a few seconds for our test table. In a real application, when perhaps hundreds of tables have to be processed, it would of course be necessary to automate this preparation step, utilizing the error return-code of the software. In the experiment the best *a priori* bound parameters were $q=0.6$, $c=3$.[8] For illustration, table A.1 in appendix A.2 shows the maximum feasible deviation obtained by formula (3.1) with these parameters for some typical order of magnitude for the cell values of our instance.

With *a priori* bounds computed with these parameters, four different options for a weighting scheme were tried: we assigned $w_i := y_i^{-\gamma}$ choosing γ from $\{0.1, 0.5, 0.7\}$ and in the 4th variant γ was chosen flexibly ($\gamma = \gamma(h_i)$, where γ is determined by the hierarchical situation of cell i), (c.f. 3.1). For sensitive cells the weighting scheme was rescaled as $w_i := \dfrac{y_i^{-\gamma}}{10\,000}$. The idea was that sensitive cells should be much more likely as non-sensitive cells to be picked for adjustment.

Table 2 shows Hellinger distances between original and adjusted distributions, for four distributions of the total income, i.e. for the 3-way distribution (MSI) by municipality (M), income size class (S) and income source (I), for two 2-way distributions (MI and SI) by M and I and by S and I and for the univariate distribution only by I. It shows the distances obtained for the four tested γ parameters, computed separately for the subsets of the sensitive and the non-sensitive cells[9].

The distances in the last column of table 2 ("Random") can be regarded as a kind of benchmark. They relate to a very simple form of random perturbation (not adjusted by CTA) that introduces about the same order of magnitude of perturbation as CTA (with the parameters of our setting): variable j of unit i was perturbed by multiplication with $(1 + d_{ij}\,p)$, where $d_{ij} \epsilon \{1; -1\}$ denote a (symmetrically distributed) binary random variable that determines the sense of the deviation, and p the parameter of the p%-rule.

Because the number of sensitive cells is much smaller than the number of non-sensitive cells, for the sensitive cells a comparatively small number of individual distances $\left(\left(\sqrt{p_i} - \sqrt{q_i}\right)^2\right.$, c.f. formula A.1 in the appendix) is summed for the Hellinger

---

[7]   In this phase it makes sense to make use of an option offered by the CTA package to stop after the first feasible solution has been obtained.

[8]   Note that in the experiment, these bounds were not applied to the sensitive cells. The idea was that sensitive cells should not be kept close to their original values. For sake of simplicity, we gave them rather wide bounds (+/- 200% of the cell value). Of course, in a real situation, cells that take positive vales only by definition (like "positive income"), or take negative values only ("negative income") must be forced to change by at most +/- 100%.

[9]   The number of sensitive *vs.* non-sensitive cell is 257 *vs.* 1250 (MSI); 10 *vs.* 108 (SI); 1 *vs.* 134 (MI); 1 *vs.* 8 (I).

distances presented in table 2. In spite of this, table 2 shows that for the CTA results the distance is generally much larger for the subset of sensitive cells, except when S is not in the set of spanning variables (because in those distributions there is only one sensitive cell in the instance). This is not the case for the random noise variant. So obviously, sensitive cells receive more perturbation in the CTA variants. For the non-sensitive cells, it is the other way round: here all CTA variants perform better compared to random noise. As expected, the weighting scheme with flexible γ clearly outperforms the other variants in the case of the univariate (and thus highly aggregated) distribution "I". It performs well also on the bivariate distributions ("SI", "MI"). In the 3-dimensional case ("MSI"), results are better with γ of 0.5 or 0.7.

Table 1. Hellinger distances between original and adjusted / perturbed distributions

Inc. by	Sens.	γ-parameter				Random
		0.1	0.5	0.7	$\gamma(h_i)$	
MSI	non-s.	9.60E-07	4.34E-07	4.31E-07	2.04E-06	1.73E-05
	sensitive	1.45E-04	1.07E-04	1.11E-04	1.91E-04	1.23E-05
SI	non-s.	1.29E-07	1.41E-07	1.10E-07	1.18E-07	2.51E-06
	sensitive	3.51E-06	4.49E-06	5.69E-06	1.01E-06	1.65E-06
MI	non-s.	2.80E-07	4.58E-07	4.73E-07	8.87E-08	4.00E-06
	sensitive	1.02E-09	1.09E-09	1.09E-09	1.02E-09	9.88E-10
I	non-s.	1.67E-08	1.80E-08	2.20E-08	2.18E-15	1.29E-07
	sensitive	1.06E-09	1.11E-09	1.11E-09	1.02E-09	9.88E-10

The testing on stage 2 of the procedure was carried out with the result from stage 1 obtained at $\gamma = 0.5$.

Testing at stage 2:
In our instance, stage 2 consists of 15 separate CTA applications (one for each municipality). Until now, only a selection of three of those has been processed. In all three cases, it was possible to preserve on stage 2 the result of stage 1: the adjusted values of the cells on level 1 of the variable generated by concatenating size-class and unit ID could be preserved successfully. *A priori* intervals defining only minor tolerances turned out to be feasible. The ratios of perturbed and original values are almost always near $1 \pm p$ where p denote the parameter of the p%-rule used to define the protection requirement. Only about 70 of the ca. 20600 individual income source data of municipality 1, for instance, were perturbed by more than $(p + 1)$ %.

5   Future Research Issues

As conclusion from the lessons learnt in the experiment this section raises some main issues of future research.

Computing time
So far, we have tested only with data from one of the about 400 districts in Germany. Stage 2 of the method has been carried out for only 3 municipalities. Assume we spend 3 CPU minutes for running CTA[10] on each municipality. Then processing our test district takes 15*3 minutes (not considering the CPU time spent in stage 1). Assuming same CPU times for each of the 400 districts in Germany, we end up with about 18000 minutes (=12.5 days) of CPU time. Even though the actual time spent on the computations can certainly be reduced by some parallel execution, etc., it is obvious that CPU time is a most critical issue. This must be born in mind when considering the other research issues mentioned below.

Sensitivity rule at stage 2
According to the approach presented in sec. 3, all the individual unit data are perturbed by the CTA method and all these cells are flagged as sensitive, because they relate to a single unit. However, this concept from tabular data protection does not make so much sense at stage 2: After all, we deal with large groups of units with identical categories of the control table spanning variables (in our instance for example, about 900 units for size class 2 of municipality 1). Assuming these are the "identifying variables", the units of a sufficiently large group are not identifiable. One might therefore argue to consider them non-confidential. Perturbing them by at least p% as we did in the experiment is likely to overprotect the data. Here one should rather consider concepts of micro-data disclosure risk assessment.

Revision of the procedure for stage 2
In our instance we had at most ca. 900 units contributing to a single cell at level 1 of the hierarchical relation defined for stage 2 and hence at most ca. 900 cells in a single table relation of the tables to be processed at stage 2. While this approach was tested successfully for the very moderate sized municipalities of the test instance, it cannot work for large cities, because table relations become too long. In such cases, one should either use more variables in the definition of the control tables (this will reduce the number of units contributing to the same cell).

Alternatively, considering the remarks above on cell sensitivity at stage 2, the following might be more adequate: if "too many" units contribute to a single cell at level 1, split them (randomly) into two subgroups. Replace the data of one (say, the first one) of the two groups by a version pre-perturbed with some computationally "cheap" micro-data protection method, like multiplicative noise or record swapping (or even leave them unchanged, when they can actually be regarded as "not identifiable"). Then sum the data of the units in this group, subtract the results from the respective level 1 cell values and drop the corresponding categories from the variable $i*$ hierarchy (and list of categories), before setting up the CTA problem. This way, the CTA method is not applied to the unit level data of the first group anymore. The total change of the random perturbation applied to the first group of units must be balanced

---

[10] Test results obtained so far are based on the computationally "difficult" MILP CTA formulation (see sec. 2).

(along with the stage 1 adjustment of the respective level 1 cells) through adjustment of the data of the second group of units, which should therefore not be too small. This way, applying CTA to the data of big cities may not take more time than to apply it to small municipalities.

The idea could even be extended: Do also replace the data of the second group of units (still to be processed by CTA) by a pre-perturbed version first, before setting up the CTA problem. Afterwards, in the input data for the CTA procedure, flag the respective cells 'non-sensitive'. Then stage 2 does not involve any sensitive cells anymore. This makes the CTA problem a continuous LP problem, much "cheaper" in terms of CPU time requirement.

Reduce the perturbation of sensitive cells
As mentioned in the introduction, the CTA methodology has been developed to protect tabular data. In that context, large deviations in sensitive cells are usually not considered as problem. They may even be regarded as desirable. In our context, however, those large deviations may reduce the usability of the data. After all, as explained in the introduction, the basic idea is to enable flexible tabulation. Extreme perturbation in some units may be "balanced" in the control tables, so the information in the control table is "preserved". Nevertheless, it is possible that such units with extreme perturbation contribute to other (for instance user requested) results. Here the deviations may happen not to be balanced (by deviations of other units) and cause major deviations of - perhaps not even sensitive -results.

Sec. 4.2 reports that for the illustrative example a feasible solution for the control table was obtained with *a priori* bounds on the deviations according to $-c\ y_i^q \le z_i \le c\ y_i^q$ with $q=0.6$ (and $c=3$) for non-sensitive cells and with $q=1$ (and $c=2$) for sensitive cells. This is quite a large gap. In future testing one should seek to reduce it. Sec. 4.2 also mentions that for sensitive cells the cell weights were computed according to the same formula as for non-sensitive cells, but afterwards they got divided by 10^5, e.g. put on quite a different scale. Here it might also be better to reduce the rescaling.

Preserve relations between variables
As mentioned above, income tax statistics involves about 100 quantitative variables analyzed in the official publications. In our instance, we have considered only ten of them. It will be an important issue of future research to compare different approaches for how to involve them in the CTA processing. One way to proceed could be as follows:

Apply the sequential procedure of sec. 3 separately for each variable, or set of variables with additive relationship between them similar to the income-relation of the introductive example. Processing variables jointly may even make sense for cases, when the relationship between the variables in that set is not "exact" but "statistical", i.e. from within a linear model involving the set of variables. When "modeling" a CTA problem for such a case, residuals of the linear model should be used to constitute an extra variable.

Control tables may have to be defined differently for each set of variables. They should be 'typical' for the respective variable(s).

However, protecting all the variables in a number of separate or joint CTA processes can become rather computer intensive. Recalling the CPU estimates from above, it might turn out "way too expensive". Other complications might be that the same variable appears in different variable relations. Then one should in principle process all those relations in a single "linked" application. But this might consume even more CPU time. A way out could be the definition of a suitable sequence to process the relations and to allow no further adjustment in variables processed in an earlier step of the sequence.

6   Summary and Final Conclusions

The paper has outlined an idea for a two stage procedure employing CTA as mechanism for balancing perturbations introduced into a database because of disclosure risk concerns. Test results from early experiments derived with a small test data set to investigate the performance of certain parameter settings were compared using Hellinger distances.

While those preliminary experiments gave satisfactory results, they can only be regarded as a starting point of a major research effort necessary to establish practicability and efficiency of the proposed methodology.

For such a future research effort, the paper has identified a number of issues and ideas for revision that should be addressed, like, e.g. CPU time requirement, avoidance of unit-level data overprotection, pre-processing of unit level data with a computationally cheap SDC method, reduction of the size and computational complexity of the CTA problems at stage 2 and, finally, issues of preserving relations between quantitative variables of the dataset.

Acknowledgements. Thanks to Ms. Katrin Schmidt for her help with the integration of the CTA package into the SAS-environment.

References

1. Castro, J.: Minimum-distance controlled perturbation methods for large-scale tabular data protection. European Journal of Operational Research 171, 39–52 (2006)
2. Castro, J., Giessing, S.: Quality issues of minimum distance controlled tabular adjustment. paper presented at the European Conference on Quality in Survey Statistics (Q 2006), Cardiff, April 24-26 (2006)
3. Castro, J., Gonzalez, J.A.: A fast CTA method without thecomplicating binary deci-sions. Joint UNECE/Eurostat Work Session on Statistical Data Confidentiality (2013), http://www.unece.org/fileadmin/DAM/stats/documents/ece/ces/g e.46/2013/Topic_1_Castro-Gonzalez.pdf

4. Castro, J., Gonzalez, J.A., Baena, D., Jimenez, X.: User's and programmer's manual of the RCTA package (v.2), Technical Report DR 2013-06 (2013), http://www-eio.upc.es/~jcastro
5. Cox, L., Dandekar, R.H.: 'Synthetic Tabular Data – an Alternative to Complementary Cell Suppression (2002) (unpublished manuscript)
6. Cox, L.H., Kelly, J.P., Patil, R.: Balancing quality and confidentiality for multivariate tabular data. In: Domingo-Ferrer, J., Torra, V. (eds.) PSD 2004. LNCS, vol. 3050, pp. 87–98. Springer, Heidelberg (2004)
7. Evans, B.T., Zayatz, L., Slanta, J.: Using noise for disclosure limitation for establishment tabular data. Journal of Official Statistics (14), S. 537–552 (1998)
8. Fraser, B., Wooton, J.: A proposed method for confidentialising tabular output to protect against differencing. Monographs of Official Statistics. Work session on Statistical Data Confidentiality, pp. 299–302. Eurostat-Office for Official Publications of the European Communities, Luxembourg (2006)
9. Giessing, S.: Flexible rounding based on consistent post-tabular stochastic noise. In: Domingo-Ferrer, J., Tinnirello, I. (eds.) PSD 2012. LNCS, vol. 7556, pp. 22–34. Springer, Heidelberg (2012)
10. Hernández García, S., Salazar González, J.J.: Enhanced controlled tabular adjustment, Joint UNECE/Eurostat Work Session on Statistical Data Confidentiality, http://www.unece.org/fileadmin/DAM/stats/documents/ece/ces/ge.46/2011/28_Salazar.pdf
11. Höhne, J.: Verfahren zur Anonymisierung von Einzeldaten. Statistik und Wirtschaft, Bd. 16, Statistisches Bundesamt, Wiesbaden (2010), https://www.destatis.de/DE/Publikationen/StatistikWissenschaft/Band16_Anonymisierung Einzeldaten_1030816109004.pdf?__blob=publicationFile
12. Massell, P., Funk, J.: Recent Developments in the Use of Noise for Protecting Magnitude Data Tables: Balancing to Improve Data Quality and Rounding that Preserves Protection. In: Proceedings of the Research Conference of the Federal Committee on Statistical Methodology, Arlington, Virginia (2007)
13. Nayak, T.K., Sinha, B., Zayatz, L.: Statistical Properties of Multiplicative Noise Masking for Confidentiality Protection. Statistical Research Division Research Report Series (Statistics #2010-05). U.S. Census Bureau (2010), http://www.census.gov/srd/papers/pdf/rrs2010-05.pdf
14. Shlomo, N.: Statistical Disclosure Control Methods for Census Frequency Tables. International Statistical Review 75(2), 199–217 (2007)
15. Shlomo, N., Young, C.: Statistical disclosure control methods through a risk-utility framework. In: Domingo-Ferrer, J., Franconi, L. (eds.) PSD 2006. LNCS, vol. 4302, pp. 68–81. Springer, Heidelberg (2006)
16. Thompson, G., Broadfoot, S., Elazar, D.: Methodology for the Automatic Confidentialisation of Statistical Outputs from Remote Servers at the Australian Bureau of Statistics. Joint UNECE/Eurostat Work Session on Statistical Data Confidentiality (2013), http://www.unece.org/fileadmin/DAM/stats/documents/ece/ces/ge.46/2013/Topic_1_ABS.pdf

Appendix A.1   Toy Example for Illustration of the 2-Stage Procedure of Sec. 3

ID	MUN	CL (= var i)	var i*	level var i*	Income (original)	Stage 1 Income (adjusted)	Stage 2 Table k	Stage 2 Income (adjusted)
	Total	Total			410	410		
	A	Total		0	80	65	1	65
	A	01		1	30	25	1	25
1	A	01	01_1	2	10		1	8
2	A	01	01_2	2	20		1	17
	A	02		1	50	40	1	40
3	A	02	02_3	2	50		1	40
	B	Total		0	120	135	2	135
	B	01		1	20	15	2	15
4	B	01	01_4	2	20		2	15
	B	05		1	100	120	2	120
5	B	05	05_5	2	100		2	120
	C	Total		0	210	210	3	210
	C	03		1	210	210	3	210
6	C	03	03_6	2	70		3	70
7	C	03	03_7	2	70		3	70
8	C	03	03_8	2	70		3	70

Appendix A.2

Table A.1. Maximum feasible deviations for typical cell value order of magnitudes

Cell value	Maximum deviation
50,000	198
500,000	788
5,000,000	3,137
50,000,000	12,488
500,000,000	49,717
5,000,000,000	197,926

Appendix A.3

Corollary 1: Let y_i, $i=1,...,n$ a vector of original, non-zero cell values with a total value of $Y := \sum_{i=1}^{n} y_i$. Let c be a positive constant. Let x_i, $i=1,...,n$ the vector of the perturbed cell values and $z_i = x_i - y_i$, $i=1,...,n$ the vector of deviations. If the deviations are bounded by $\left(2c \sqrt{y_i} - c^2\right)$ (i.e. they are about proportional to the square root of the original cell values) and the grand total is preserved, then the Hellinger distance of any feasible CTA solution is below $\frac{c}{\sqrt{2\bar{Y}}}$, where $\bar{Y}$ denote the mean cell value.

Proof: Consider the ratios of the cell values to the grand total as discrete probability distribution. The Hellinger distance is a measure of the distance of the original distribution P (given by $p_i := \frac{y_i}{Y}$ $(i=1,..,n)$) and the distribution after adjustment Q (given by $q_i := \frac{x_i}{X}$ $(i=1,..,n)$), defined as $H(P,Q) = \frac{1}{\sqrt{2}} \sqrt{\sum_{i=1}^{n}\left(\sqrt{p_i} - \sqrt{q_i}\right)^2}$ (A.1).

Obviously

$$\left(2c \sqrt{y_i} - c^2\right) = y_i \left(\frac{2c}{\sqrt{y_i}} - \frac{c^2}{y_i}\right) = y_i \left(1 - \left(1 - \frac{2c}{\sqrt{y_i}} + \frac{c^2}{y_i}\right)\right) = y_i \left(1 - \left(1 - \frac{c}{\sqrt{y_i}}\right)^2\right).$$

Hence from $z_i < \left(2c \sqrt{y_i} - c^2\right)$ it follows $\frac{z_i}{y_i} < 1 - \left(1 - \frac{c}{\sqrt{y_i}}\right)^2$. Thus we have $\left(1 - \frac{c}{\sqrt{y_i}}\right)^2 < 1 - \frac{z_i}{y_i}$, from which follows $1 - \frac{c}{\sqrt{y_i}} < \sqrt{1 - \frac{z_i}{y_i}}$ and then $\left(1 - \sqrt{1 - \frac{z_i}{y_i}}\right)^2 < \frac{c^2}{y_i}$. After multiplying both sides by $\frac{y_i}{Y}$, we see

$$\frac{y_i}{Y}\left(1 - \sqrt{1 - \frac{z_i}{y_i}}\right)^2 < \frac{y_i}{Y}\frac{c^2}{y_i}. \tag{A.2}$$

The left hand side of (A.2) can be written as $\left(\sqrt{\frac{y_i}{Y}} - \sqrt{\frac{y_i}{Y} - \frac{y_i}{Y}\frac{z_i}{y_i}}\right)^2 = \left(\sqrt{\frac{y_i}{Y}} - \sqrt{\frac{y_i - z_i}{Y}}\right)^2 = \left(\sqrt{\frac{y_i}{Y}} - \sqrt{\frac{y_i - (y_i - x_i)}{Y}}\right)^2 = \left(\sqrt{p_i} - \sqrt{q_i}\right)^2$, because we assume the grand total to be preserved, e.g. $X=Y$ and hence $\frac{x_i}{Y} = \frac{x_i}{X} = q_i$.

So (A.2) is equivalent to $\left(\sqrt{p_i} - \sqrt{q_i}\right)^2 < \frac{c^2}{Y}$. After summation across the table cells, we get $\sum_{i=1}^{n}\left(\sqrt{p_i} - \sqrt{q_i}\right)^2 < \frac{n}{Y}c^2$. (A.3)-

$H(P,Q)$ is defined as the square root of the left hand side of (A.2) devided by 2, so obviously from (A.3) it follows $H(P,Q) < \frac{c}{\sqrt{2\bar{Y}}}$ which completes the proof.

Measuring Disclosure Risk with Entropy in Population Based Frequency Tables

Laszlo Antal, Natalie Shlomo, and Mark Elliot

University of Manchester, UK
laszlo.antal@postgrad.manchester.ac.uk,
{natalie.shlomo,mark.elliot}@manchester.ac.uk

Abstract. Statistical agencies assess the risk of disclosure before releasing data. Unacceptably high disclosure risk will prevent a statistical
agency from disseminating the data. The application of statistical disclosure control (SDC) methods aims to provide sufficient protection and
make the data release possible. The disclosure risk of tabular data is
typically quantified at the level of table cells. However, the evaluation
of disclosure risk can require the assessment of the table as a whole,
for example in the case of online flexible table generators. In this paper we use information theory to develop a disclosure risk measure for
population-based frequency tables. The proposed disclosure risk measure
quantifies the risk of attribute disclosure before and after an SDC method
is applied. The new measure is compared to alternative disclosure risk
measures developed at the Office for National Statistics.

Keywords: Information theory, attribute disclosure, conditional entropy.

1 Introduction

Statistical agencies follow strict confidentiality rules since releasing data always
increases the risk of disclosure. They measure the risk of disclosure and apply
statistical disclosure control (SDC) methods if the risk is unacceptably high.
The subject of this paper is disclosure risk measurement in population-based
frequency counts of tabular form.

Dislosure risk measures of tabular data usually express the risk at cell level.
A regularly used disclosure risk measure for frequency counts is the so-called
threshold rule. A cell is of high risk if the count does not exceed a certain value,
for example 2.

The main objective of this paper is to measure the risk of attribute disclosure.
Attribute disclosure happens if confidential information about an individual can
be retrieved from the data. We use information theory to quantify the disclosure
risk of population based frequency tables. The disclosure risk is expressed for
the entire frequency table and for rows and columns of the frequency table.
Single cells in themselves are not considered here. Information theory has been
investigated in [5] to measure the disclosure risk of individual cells of magnitude
tables. However, there has been no attempt to quantify the disclosure risk of an

J. Domingo-Ferrer (Ed.): PSD 2014, LNCS 8744, pp. 62–78, 2014.

entire (either frequency or magnitude) table by information theory. This paper provides a novel disclosure risk measure, which makes relatively quick disclosure risk assessment possible. The bases of the measure are entropy and conditional entropy.

Our aim is to develop a disclosure risk measure around the following properties.

Property 1A If only one cell is populated in the table, then the disclosure risk is high.

Property 1B Uniformly distributed frequencies imply low risk.

Property 2 Small cell values (i.e. ones and twos) are more disclosive than higher values. In general, the greater the cells, the lower the disclosure risk.

Property 3 Assume that two tables are given and there is only one cell populated in each table. The frequencies of the non-zero cells are equal. In this case we deem the table that has more cells (and therefore more zeroes) to be of higher disclosure risk.

Property 4 We would like the disclosure risk measure to be bounded by 0 and 1.

The motivation behind the properties is as follows. The risk of attribute disclosure is normally high if the population is concentrated in one cell, see [7]. It explains Property 1A. On the other hand, attribute disclosure is unlikely to occur if the frequencies are uniformly distributed, which drives Property 1B. The ground of Property 2 is the fact that revealing new information about a respondent becomes more difficult as the cell frequencies increase. The rationale behind Property 3 is that a table may be a more detailed version of another table, e.g. the breakdown of a table-spanning variable might be different in two tables. For example, if we replace super output area with output area, then the table will contain more detailed information. An intruder may obtain more information from more detailed tables. Property 4 is driven by the desire of comparing the disclosure risk of different tables.

Besides disclosure risk, information loss is also a crucial concept in statistical disclosure control. We use another information theory-related expression, Hellinger distance to measure the loss of information.

Although SDC methods provide protection to the data, a statistical agency might not be certain about the adequacy of the protection. Therefore, we assess the disclosure risk not just before but also after perturbation. The disclosure risk measures before and after perturbation are described in Section 2. Perturbation methods used for this study are outlined in Section 3. Section 4 discusses alternative disclosure measures that were used by the Office for National Statistics (ONS). Application of the theoretical results can be found in Section 5. A discussion closes our investigation in Section 6.

2   Disclosure Risk Measures and a Utility Measure

2.1   Before SDC Methods Are Applied

The most important information theoretical definition we use is entropy. Information theory is covered comprehensively in [2]. If X is a random variable with distribution $P = (p_1, p_2, \ldots, p_K)$, then the entropy of X is defined as

$$H(X) = -\sum_{i=1}^{K} p_i \cdot \log p_i .\tag{1}$$

Here log is the natural logarithm. If $p_i = 0$ for a certain i, then the respective term in the sum is considered 0.

Entropy is ideal to capture Properties 1A and 1B listed above since the value of entropy is 0 if and only if the P distribution can be written as $(0, \ldots, 0, 1, 0, \ldots, 0)$, and the value of entropy is maximal $(\log K)$ if and only if P is uniform. Therefore, the expression $[1 - H(X)/\log K]$ exactly reflects Properties 1A, 1B and 4. However, entropy does not capture Properties 2 and 3 properly. The reason for this is given below.

The table of frequencies we investigate is denoted $F = (F_1, F_2, \ldots, F_K)$. The population size is $N = \sum_{i=1}^{K} F_i$. Consequently, the distribution of the table is

$$P = \left(\frac{F_1}{N}, \frac{F_2}{N}, \ldots, \frac{F_K}{N} \right) .\tag{2}$$

If we apply (1) to this distribution, we obtain

$$H(X) = \frac{N \cdot \log N - \sum_{i=1}^{K} F_i \cdot \log F_i}{N} .$$

Consider, for example, an $F = (F_1, F_2, F_3) = (0, 2, 4)$ frequency table. Then $P = \left(0, \frac{2}{6}, \frac{4}{6}\right)$ and $H(X) = \frac{6 \cdot \log 6 - 2 \cdot \log 2 - 4 \cdot \log 4}{6} = 0.6365$.

It can be seen from (1) and (2) that $H(X)$ depends only on the F_i/N, $i = 1, 2, \ldots, K$ ratios. Therefore, $[1 - H(X)/\log K]$ does not meet the expectations outlined in Properties 2 and 3. The entropy of F is the same as the entropy of $c \cdot F$, where $c > 1$ is a constant, contradicting Property 2. On the other hand, (1) shows that zeroes do not contribute to the value of entropy, therefore it does not reflect Property 3.

In order to compensate for Properties 2 and 3, the proportion of zeroes in the frequency table and an additional expression, based on N will be included in the disclosure risk measure. Denote the set of zeroes in the F table by D. The disclosure risk measure we define is a weighted average of three terms as follows. The weights are $\mathbf{w} = (w_1, w_2, w_3)$, where $w_1, w_2, w_3 \geq 0$ and $w_1 + w_2 + w_3 = 1$.

$$R_1(F, \mathbf{w}) = w_1 \cdot \frac{|D|}{K} + w_2 \cdot \left(1 - \frac{H(X)}{\log K} \right) - w_3 \cdot \frac{1}{\sqrt{N}} \cdot \log \frac{1}{e \cdot \sqrt{N}} .\tag{3}$$

Here e is the base of the natural logarithm. Each term is bounded by 0 and 1, and therefore so is the overall disclosure risk measure. The third term is a monotonically decreasing function of N, which reflects Property 2.

Considering the above example with $F = (0, 2, 4)$, we will obtain that $\frac{|D|}{K} = 0.3333$, $1 - \frac{H(X)}{\log K} = 1 - \frac{0.6365}{\log 3} = 0.4206$ and $-\frac{1}{\sqrt{N}} \cdot \log \frac{1}{e \cdot \sqrt{N}} = -\frac{1}{\sqrt{6}} \cdot \log \frac{1}{e \cdot \sqrt{6}} = 0.7740$.

If a frequency table consists of 1s only, that is, $F = (1, 1, \ldots, 1)$, then only the third term of (3) differs from 0. In this case the chance of attribute disclosure is low, since the number of zeroes is 0. The disclosure risk of $F = (1, 1, \ldots, 1)$ is also lower than that of $F = (10, 10, \ldots, 10)$, therefore monotonicity is maintained.

2.2 After SDC Methods Are Applied

The disclosure risk after SDC methods are applied to the table must also be assessed. The perturbed frequencies are denoted by $G = (G_1, G_2, \ldots, G_K)$ and their sum by $M = \sum_{j=1}^{K} G_j$. We assume that a statistical agency intends to release the G frequencies and withhold F. Therefore, we assume that $F \neq G$.

The disclosure risk after perturbation should be lower than that before perturbation, since an intruder has to encounter more uncertainty in G than in F. We adjust (3) in order to assess the disclosure risk after perturbation. The first and second terms of (3) are reduced in the new measure.

Denote the set of zeroes in G by E. The first term of (3) will be changed to

$$w_1 \cdot \left(\frac{|D|}{K} \right)^{\frac{|D \cup E|}{|D \cap E|}} .$$

If $D = \emptyset$ or $E = \emptyset$, then this term will be considered 0. This expression is not greater than $|D|/K$ and is still bounded by 0 and 1.

The second term of (3) will be multiplied by a factor, which depends on the conditional entropy. Assume that X and Y are two random variables with a common domain (I) and a common range $(C = \{c_1, c_2, \ldots, c_K\})$.

$$X : I \rightarrow C .$$

$$Y : I \rightarrow C .$$

The definition of the conditional entropy of X and Y is as follows.

$$H(X|Y) = -\sum_{j=1}^{K} Pr(Y = c_j) \cdot \sum_{i=1}^{K} Pr(X = c_i | Y = c_j) \cdot \log Pr(X = c_i | Y = c_j) .$$

In our case I is the set of individuals and C is the set of table cells (or categories). (Note that c_i is not the frequency of the cell.) X provides the categories where the individuals fall originally. Since we are dealing with the perturbation of frequency tables, the individuals and their categories might not be exactly followed after perturbation. Y should provide a similar categorisation to X after perturbation. More details about the Y variable can be found below.

It is well-known that $H(X|Y) \leq H(X)$. Roughly speaking, in our case X represents the original data and Y the perturbed data. $H(X|Y)$ expresses the uncertainty the X variable has if Y is known. Therefore we choose the second term of the disclosure risk measure after perturbation to be

$$ w_2 \cdot \left(1 - \frac{H(X)}{\log K} \right) \cdot \frac{H(X|Y)}{H(X)} . $$

If $H(X) = 0$, then the second term of the disclosure risk measure is considered 0.

The conditional entropy can be rewritten using the $Pr(Y = c_j | X = c_i)$ probabilities, as it can be found in [8].

$$ H(X|Y) = - \sum_{i=1}^{K} \sum_{j=1}^{K} Pr(X = c_i) \cdot Pr(Y = c_j | X = c_i) \cdot \log \frac{Pr(X = c_i) \cdot Pr(Y = c_j | X = c_i)}{\sum_{k=1}^{K} Pr(X = c_k) \cdot Pr(Y = c_j | X = c_k)} . $$

$Pr(X = c_i)$ in the above formula provides the probability that an individual falls in cell c_i in the original frequency table. It can be easily estimated by F_i/N.

The $Pr(Y = c_j | X = c_i)$ conditional probabilities will be expressed by $F = (F_1, F_2, \ldots, F_K)$ and $G = (G_1, G_2, \ldots, G_K)$. The formula we use is as follows.

$$ Pr(Y = c_j | X = c_i) = $$
$$ = \begin{cases} \dfrac{\min(M \cdot F_i, N \cdot G_i)}{M \cdot F_i} & \text{if } i = j \text{ and } F_i > 0 , \\[2ex] \dfrac{(M \cdot F_i - \min(M \cdot F_i, N \cdot G_i)) \cdot (N \cdot G_j - \min(M \cdot F_j, N \cdot G_j))}{M \cdot F_i \cdot (N \cdot M - \sum_{k=1}^{K} \min(M \cdot F_k, N \cdot G_k))} & \text{if } i \neq j \text{ and } F_i > 0 , \\[2ex] 0 & \text{if } F_i = 0 . \end{cases} $$
$$ \tag{4} $$

The complete justification for the (4) formula can be found in [1], we only outline the proof here.

The X random variable determines the cells where each individual falls in the original frequency table. Assume temporarily that $N = M$. The Y variable should provide the counterpart of X for the perturbed frequency table. It means that the individuals are recategorised in the perturbed table. However, the only requirement for Y is given by the $G = (G_1, G_2, \ldots, G_K)$ frequencies, the cell where a certain individual falls in the perturbed frequency table is not determined unambiguously. In case of a post-tabular SDC method, such as random rounding, Y is not (necessarily) uniquely defined. Different Y variables lead to different values of $Pr(Y = c_j | X = c_i)$. Instead of choosing one of the possible variables, we select a set of Y variables and calculate the average of the $Pr(Y = c_j | X = c_i)$ conditional probabilities in the set. If we took the average of the conditional probabilities over the entire set of possible Y variables, then the $H(X|Y)$ conditional entropy would not differ from $H(X)$. Consequently, the second term of the disclosure risk measure would not be lowered. Therefore, we take the average conditional probability of a narrower set of possible Y variables. In statistical disclosure control a general aim is to cause the least possible distortion to the data, therefore we select the Y variables that are as similar to X as possible. It means that an individual should fall in the same cell by X and Y, provided that the $G = (G_1, G_2, \ldots, G_K)$ frequencies allow that.

Table 1. Example: the X variable and possible Y variables

	Individuals (I)
	1 2 3 4 5 6
X variable	c_2 c_2 c_3 c_3 c_3 c_3
First possible Y variable	c_2 c_2 c_2 c_3 c_3 c_3
Second possible Y variable	c_2 c_2 c_3 c_2 c_3 c_3
Third possible Y variable	c_2 c_2 c_3 c_3 c_2 c_3
Fourth possible Y variable	c_2 c_2 c_3 c_3 c_3 c_2
A Y variable not taken into account	c_3 c_2 c_2 c_2 c_3 c_3

Continuing with our example, where $F = (0, 2, 4)$, we can see that there are six individuals and three categories, that is, $C = \{c_1, c_2, c_3\}$. Assume that $G = (0, 3, 3)$. An X variable and possible Y variables are given in Table 1.

The variable in the last row of Table 1 is not taken into account when calculating the average conditional probability because the category of the first individual changes. It causes more distortion than necessary.

If $N \neq M$, then we can apply the same reasoning to the $M \cdot F = (M \cdot F_1, M \cdot F_2, \ldots, M \cdot F_K)$ and $N \cdot G = (N \cdot G_1, N \cdot G_2, \ldots, N \cdot G_K)$ frequency tables. The entropy of $M \cdot F$ is the same as that of F. The average conditional probability is given under (4).

To summarize, the disclosure risk measure after perturbation is

$$R_2(F, G, \mathbf{w}) = w_1 \cdot \left(\frac{|D|}{K} \right)^{\frac{|D \cup E|}{|D \cap E|}} + w_2 \cdot \left(1 - \frac{H(X)}{\log K} \right) \cdot \frac{H(X|Y)}{H(X)} - w_3 \cdot \frac{1}{\sqrt{N}} \cdot \log \frac{1}{e \cdot \sqrt{N}} \cdot \tag{5}$$

2.3   A Utility Measure

Besides disclosure risk, information loss is also an important aspect of SDC. We measure that by a modified Hellinger distance, which is also related to information theory. Hellinger distance measures the divergence between two probability distributions, $P = (p_1, p_2, \ldots, p_K)$ and $Q = (q_1, q_2, \ldots, q_K)$. The definition of Hellinger distance is as follows.

$$HD(P, Q) = \frac{1}{\sqrt{2}} \cdot \sqrt{\sum_{i=1}^{K} (\sqrt{p_i} - \sqrt{q_i})^2} .$$

This expression is bounded by 0 and 1. We substitute P and Q for F and G respectively.

$$HD(F, G) = \frac{1}{\sqrt{2}} \cdot \sqrt{\sum_{i=1}^{K} (\sqrt{F_i} - \sqrt{G_i})^2} .$$

$HD(F, G)$ is the L_2-norm of the difference of $\sqrt{F} = (\sqrt{F_1}, \sqrt{F_2}, \ldots, \sqrt{F_K})$ and $\sqrt{G} = (\sqrt{G_1}, \sqrt{G_2}, \ldots, \sqrt{G_K})$ and therefore it is a metric. Hellinger distance shows the magnitude of the cells since the difference between the square roots of two 'large' numbers are higher than in case of two 'small' numbers, even if these pairs have the same absolute difference. The lower bound of $HD(F, G)$ is 0, while the upper bound is $\sqrt{\frac{N+M}{2}}$.

In our example, where $F = (0, 2, 4)$ and $G = (0, 3, 3)$, the modified Hellinger distance is $HD(F, G) = \frac{1}{\sqrt{2}} \cdot \sqrt{(\sqrt{2} - \sqrt{3})^2 + (\sqrt{4} - \sqrt{3})^2} = 0.2940$.

3 Perturbation Methods

We place ourselves in the statistical agency's point of view and compare two perturbation methods. The perturbation methods we consider are random rounding to base 3 and record swapping.

Random rounding moves the frequencies to one of the multiples of 3 with certain probability structure. If a cell value is a multiple of 3, it remains unaltered. If the remainder is 1 or 2 when dividing the cell value by 3, then we round it to the closest or second closest multiple of 3 with probability 2/3 or 1/3 respectively. Different cells in the table, including marginal cells, are rounded independently. Random rounding may not result in additive tables, that is, the internal cells may not add up to the marginal total. In this paper we deal with internal cells only.

Record swapping is a pre-tabular method and as such, it is applied to the microdata. It selects some pairs of records and exchanges the values of a variable (or more variables) between paired records. Frequency tables may be generated from the perturbed microdata. However, if the table-spanning variables do not include at least one perturbed variable, then the frequency table generated from the perturbed microdata is the same as that generated from the original microdata. More details about record swapping can be found in [7]. In Section 5, we always include a perturbed variable in the table-spanning variables and consider the resulting $G = (G_1, G_2, \ldots, G_K)$ table as the perturbed frequency table. Although record swapping is a pre-tabular method and the Y variable and the $Pr(Y = c_j | X = c_i)$ conditional probabilities can be determined exactly, we use the (4) and (5) formulae to quantify the disclosure risk after perturbation. The reason for this is ease of computation since (4) and (5), and therefore the $H(X|Y)$ conditional entropy can be calculated on the F and G frequencies directly. There is no need to calculate the exact $Pr(Y = c_j | X = c_i)$ values, which can be computationally challenging since there are $K \times K$ such probabilities.

4 Alternative Disclosure Risk Measures

The Office for National Statistics (ONS) applied alternative disclosure risk measures to the 2001 UK census data in order to determine the best perturbation methods for tabular outputs of the 2011 UK census. The disclosure risk measures below were developed specifically for record swapping. The measure to express the degree of group attribute disclosure risk for rows was

$$GAD_1(F,G) = \frac{\sum I(\text{rows where all respondents fall into same category in the } F \text{ and } G \text{ tables})}{\sum I(\text{rows where all respondents fall into same category in the } F \text{ table})}.$$

Here $I(\cdot)$ is the indicator function. If a row in F has only one populated category, then it is counted as 1 in the numerator of $GAD_1(F,G)$ if the same category is the only populated cell in that row of G and the same individuals contribute to the category before and after perturbation.

The within group attribute disclosure for rows was measured by

$$WGAD_1(F,G) = \frac{\sum I\left(\begin{array}{c}\text{rows where all respondents fall into}\\ \text{same 2 categories in } F \text{ and } G \text{ (only 1 respondent in one)}\end{array}\right)}{\sum I\left(\begin{array}{c}\text{rows where all respondents fall into 2}\\ \text{categories in } F \text{ (only 1 respondent in one)}\end{array}\right)}.$$

The same features can be repeated as for $GAD_1(F,G)$.

The measures above may also be evaluated columnwise to obtain $GAD_2(F,G)$ and $WGAD_2(F,G)$.

$GAD_1(F,G)$ and $WGAD_1(F,G)$ express the proportion of rows where an intruder may correctly reveal a new attribute of an individual or more individuals. In case of $WGAD_1(F,G)$ the data protector assumes that the intruder may be the person who contributes to a cell with frequency 1.

Denote the set of cells having frequency 1 by D_1 and frequency 2 by D_2 in the original table, that is, $D_1 \cup D_2$ is the set of small cells in the table. The counterparts of these sets in the perturbed table are denoted E_1 and E_2 respectively. A third measure, which was also used by the ONS, is as follows.

$$DR(F,G) = \frac{|D_1 \cap E_1| + |D_2 \cap E_2|}{|E_1 \cup E_2|}.$$

The numerator is the number of small cells unchanged in the perturbed table, while the denominator is the number of small cells in the perturbed table. Therefore $DR(F,G)$ measures the proportion of small cells where the original and perturbed frequencies are equal.

The disclosure risk measures above were developed for the pre-tabular method of record swapping. In order to adapt them to post-tabular random rounding in our numerical study, we need to change the definitions slightly. In case of random rounding the individuals cannot be followed through in the microdata, therefore we cannot garantee that the same individuals contribute to a certain category before and after perturbation. Therefore, GAD will be changed as follows.

$$GAD_1^*(F,G) = \frac{\sum I(\text{rows where only one frequency is higher than 0 in the } F \text{ and } G \text{ tables})}{\sum I(\text{rows where only one frequency is higher than 0 in the } F \text{ table})}.$$

In the numerator the non-zero frequencies before and after perturbation are in the same category.

Similarly,

$$WGAD_1^*(F,G) = \frac{\sum I \left(\begin{array}{c} \text{rows where exactly two frequencies are higher} \\ \text{than 0 in the } F \text{ and } G \text{ tables and at least one of them is 1} \end{array} \right)}{\sum I \left(\begin{array}{c} \text{rows where exactly two frequencies are higher} \\ \text{than 0 in the } F \text{ table and at least one of them is 1} \end{array} \right)}.$$

The non-zero categories are the same in F and G if the row is counted in the numerator of $WGAD_1^*(F,G)$.

These measures can also be evaluated columnwise and we obtain $GAD_2^*(F,G)$ and $WGAD_2^*(F,G)$ respectively.

The idea behind $GAD_1^*(F,G)$ and $WGAD_1^*(F,G)$ is similar to $GAD_1(F,G)$ and $WGAD_1(F,G)$. An intruder might correctly reveal a new attribute of an individual or more individuals if the same (one or two) cells are populated in the original and perturbed tables.

5   Numerical Results

5.1   Numerical Results for $R_1(F, \mathbf{w})$ and $R_2(F, G, \mathbf{w})$

The data we use is an extract from the 2001 UK census tables. The table-spanning variables for various tables include age, sex, output area, country of birth, mode of travel, religion. In this paper only two-dimensional tables are considered.

We investigate the output area × country of birth, output area × mode of travel, output area × sex and output area × religion tables, where only 10 output areas are taken into account. The population size is $N = 2449$. In case of the output area × mode of travel table the population is restricted to individuals between 16 and 74 years of age. As can be seen, each table includes output area as a table-spanning variable. It coincides with the practice followed by the ONS, since the geographical variable in their frequency tables is normally output area and is the swapping variable for record swapping.

The entropy-based term is the core of the diclosure risk measure, therefore we assign high weight to that term in $R_1(F, \mathbf{w})$. We use $\mathbf{w} = (w_1, w_2, w_3) = (0.1, 0.8, 0.1)$.

The $R_2(F, G, \mathbf{w})$ disclosure risk depends on the G perturbed frequency table, therefore different perturbed tables provide different values of disclosure risk. In order to avoid an extreme value, we carry out the perturbation 1,000 times and take the average disclosure risk. This also reflects the perturbation method since more possible perturbed tables and their respective chance of being the outcome of the perturbation are taken into account. Random rounding and record swapping were carried out. Random rounding was applied to the frequency table, while record swapping to the output area variable of the microdata. 5% percent of the individuals were selected and paired with other individuals from distinct output areas, resulting in a total of 10% swapped individuals. The G frequency table was generated on the perturbed microdata. The weights of $R_2(F, G, \mathbf{w})$ are unaltered compared to those before perturbation, $\mathbf{w} = (0.1, 0.8, 0.1)$.

An individual's attribute might be revealed using the rows or columns of a frequency table. Since the main point of this paper is measuring attribute disclosure, $R_1(F, \mathbf{w})$ and $R_2(F, G, \mathbf{w})$ are evaluated for each row, for each column and for the entire table. The F frequency tables, $R_1(F, \mathbf{w})$, $R_2(F, G, \mathbf{w})$ and $HD(F, G)$ for random rounding and record swapping can be found in the Appendix, see Tables 2, 3, 4 and 5.

The values of $R_1(F, \mathbf{w})$ reflect the Properties listed in Section 1 reasonably well. It can be observed that longer rows have higher disclosure risk. It might be attributed to the potentially higher number of zeroes in longer rows.

It can be seen that $R_2(F, G, \mathbf{w})$ is always substantially lower than $R_1(F, \mathbf{w})$.

The $R_2(F, G, \mathbf{w})$ disclosure risk measure of rows and columns for record swapping often shows slightly smaller values than for random rounding. This is attributed to the different methods of perturbation. While random rounding completely removes small cell values and frequencies that are not multiples of 3, and therefore it might change the distribution significantly, record swapping results in similar distribution to that of the original table. Record swapping also provides better information loss in numerous cases, especially in rows/columns where the majority of the counts is not higher than 10. Note that the disclosure risk of such rows/columns should not be low. Therefore, for rows and columns record swapping seems to be preferable to random rounding. However, the values of $R_2(F, G, \mathbf{w})$ for entire frequency tables are lower for random rounding compared to record swapping. On the other hand, the Hellinger distance is higher for random rounding compared to record swapping, reflecting higher information loss. The statistical agency must balance the disclosure risk against information loss.

5.2 Alternative Disclosure Risk Measures

For the alternative disclosure risk measures discussed in Section 4, random rounding and record swapping were carried out as described in the previous section. The frequency tables were perturbed 1,000 times and the average disclosure risk measures are shown in Table 6.

The value of $GAD^*(F, G)$ for random rounding is zero with one exception. The non-zero value is the result of column 5 of the output area × country of birth table. The value of $GAD^*(F, G)$ for that column is either 0 or 1 for each iteration.

In case of record swapping, $GAD(F, G)$ and $WGAD(F, G)$ are also zero with two exceptions. Each individual contributes to the same column before and after perturbation since only the output area variable is perturbed. (Consequently, each column has the same total before and after perturbation.) Therefore, columns 5 and 7 in the output area × country of birth table can be accounted for the two non-zero disclosure risk measures.

As it can be seen, $GAD(F, G)$ and $WGAD(F, G)$ are either 0 or 1 for each iteration. This fact might overestimate or underestimate the true risk. The disclosure risk measures defined under (3) and (5) provide more realistic measures.

6 Discussion

In this paper we have presented a new disclosure risk measure for population-based frequency tables. Information theoretical expressions, such as entropy and conditional entropy, are the focus of our investigation. We have demonstrated that they are able to quantify the risk of attribute disclosure both before and after the application of an SDC method.

The proposed disclosure risk measure can be applied to the entire frequency table and to rows and columns of the table. A statistical agency may set a threshold in order to decide whether a frequency table is safe to release or the application of an SDC method is required. We have used the Hellinger distance to measure the loss of information.

The entropy, the conditional entropy and therefore the whole disclosure risk measure can be expressed by the $F = (F_1, F_2, \ldots, F_K)$ original and $G = (G_1, G_2, \ldots, G_K)$ perturbed frequencies. This feature is particularly advantageous for post-tabular perturbation methods, where the category of a certain individual is not determined in the perturbed frequency table.

We compared our new disclosure risk measure with alternative disclosure risk measures. While $R_1(F, \mathbf{w})$ and $R_2(F, G, \mathbf{w})$ provide a disclosure risk measure for each row and column of the original and perturbed tables, $GAD(F, G)$ and $WGAD(F, G)$ use both F and G to evaluate the disclosure risk for entire tables. By applying $GAD(F, G)$ and $WGAD(F, G)$ the statistical agency automatically assumes that an SDC method should be applied to the frequency table. However, it is not always necessary. If $R_1(F, \mathbf{w})$ shows low disclosure risk, then the table might be released without perturbation. As we have seen, $GAD(F, G)$ and $WAGD(F, G)$ can show high disclosure risk if one row or column is of high risk and do not distinguish well between disclosure risk of different tables.

Although we have shown that $R_1(F, \mathbf{w})$ and $R_2(F, G, \mathbf{w})$ are preferable to $GAD(F, G)$ and $WGAD(F, G)$, further research is needed to reveal further properties of $R_1(F, \mathbf{w})$ and $R_2(F, G, \mathbf{w})$.

Acknowledgments. This work was funded by the ONS-ESRC PhD studentship (Ref. ES/J500161/1).

References

1. Antal, L., Shlomo, N., Elliot, M.: Measuring Disclosure Risk and Information Loss in Population Based Frequency Tables, http://www.ccsr.ac.uk/publications/Measuring_Disclosure_Risk
2. Cover, T.M., Thomas, J.A.: Elements of Information Theory, 2nd edn. Wiley, Hoboken (2006)
3. Domingo-Ferrer, J., Oganian, A., Torra, V.: Information-Theoretic Disclosure Risk Measures in Statistical Disclosure Control of Tabular Data. In: Proceedings of the 14th International Conference on Scientific and Statistical Database Management, Washington, pp. 227–231 (2002)

4. Duncan, G., Keller-McNulty, S., Stokes, S.: Disclosure Risk vs. Data Utility: the R-U Confidentiality Map. Technical Report LA-UR-01-6428, Statistical Sciences Group. Los Alamos National Laboratory, Los Alamos, N.M (2001)

5. Oganian, A., Domingo-Ferrer, J.: A Posteriori Disclosure Risk Measure for Tabular Data Based on Conditional Entropy. SORT-Statistics and Operations Research Transactions 27, 175–190 (2003)

6. Oganian, A., Domingo-Ferrer, J., Torra, V.: Internal Intrusion Scenarios in Inference Control of Tabular Databases. In: Information Processing and Management of Uncertainty in Knowledge-Based Systems (2004)

7. Shlomo, N.: Statistical Disclosure Control Methods for Census Frequency Tables. International Statistical Review 75, 199–217 (2007)

8. Willenborg, L., de Waal, T.: Elements of Statistical Disclosure Control. Lecture Notes in Statistics. Springer (2001)

Appendix

Table 2. Frequency table (F) and disclosure risk and utility measures: output area (10 output areas) × country of birth. The right lower corner shows the measures for the entire table, while the other measures are calculated rowwise/columnwise. 'Ran. Rou.' and 'Rec. Sw.' denote random rounding and record swapping respectively.

	1	2	3	4	5	6	7	8	9	10	11	12	13	14	15	16	17	$R_1(F,w)$	Ran. Rou. $R_2(F,G,w)$	Rec. Sw. $R_2(F,G,w)$	Ran. Rou. $HD(F,G)$	Rec. Sw. $HD(F,G)$
1	230	5	7	3	0	0	0	1	19	0	3	13	19	4	0	0	0	0.5847	0.1383	0.1183	1.0169	0.9030
2	154	1	2	8	0	5	0	1	5	0	3	1	11	1	4	3	0	0.5584	0.1720	0.1138	1.5053	0.7302
3	188	9	6	2	0	5	0	2	1	0	2	10	18	6	0	3	6	0.5125	0.0940	0.0981	1.2258	0.7001
4	278	3	1	1	0	1	0	1	8	1	0	3	8	8	0	0	0	0.7085	0.2142	0.1999	1.3384	0.9348
5	173	4	8	0	0	8	0	2	4	1	0	6	14	5	0	4	0	0.5472	0.1570	0.1094	1.2188	0.7532
6	161	10	1	2	0	1	1	1	9	1	1	7	13	0	7	3	1	0.5092	0.1497	0.0862	1.8428	0.8235
7	151	8	1	4	0	1	0	1	7	1	0	8	27	5	3	0	0	0.5422	0.1495	0.1133	1.3765	0.7425
8	208	7	1	3	1	9	1	0	2	6	1	5	29	3	1	2	1	0.5178	0.1249	0.0844	1.8226	0.7743
9	174	12	0	4	0	3	0	0	5	1	0	3	3	3	0	2	2	0.6095	0.1478	0.1326	1.2813	0.7545
10	171	5	1	0	4	0	1	8	0	1	6	10	8	2	2	3	1	0.5558	0.1538	0.1107	1.1956	0.7002
$R_1(F,w)$	0.0175	0.0874	0.2714	0.1435	0.9900	0.1744	0.7344	0.1844	0.1158	0.4915	0.3273	0.0930	0.0756	0.1309	0.5151	0.2185	0.3928	0.3242	-	-	-	-
Ran. Rou. $R_2(F,G,w)$	0.0110	0.0463	0.1295	0.0742	0.1893	0.0791	0.4139	0.1347	0.0538	0.3911	0.2192	0.0463	0.0322	0.0619	0.2747	0.1065	0.2733	-	0.0459	-	-	-
Rec. Sw. $R_2(F,G,w)$	0.0111	0.0440	0.0907	0.0660	0.1898	0.0671	0.1932	0.0879	0.0478	0.1687	0.1227	0.0454	0.0332	0.0592	0.1866	0.0916	0.1360	-	-	0.0469	-	-
Ran. Rou. $HD(F,G)$	0.1031	0.8224	1.4450	1.1257	0.6416	1.2123	0.9152	1.7978	1.0099	1.2946	1.4278	1.7659	0.3677	0.8118	0.9048	0.7980	1.4238	-	-	-	4.4800	-
Rec. Sw. $HD(F,G)$	0.2530	0.5382	0.6842	0.6123	0.1010	0.6995	0.2029	0.5109	0.5824	0.5384	0.5127	0.5483	0.5616	0.6330	0.6520	0.6166	0.5762	-	-	-	-	2.6307

Table 3. Frequency table (F) and disclosure risk and utility measures: output area (10 output areas) × mode of travel (age: 16-74). The right lower corner shows the measures for the entire table, while the other measures are calculated rowwise/columnwise. 'Ran. Rou.' and 'Rec. Sw.' denote random rounding and record swapping respectively.

	1	2	3	4	5	6	7	8	9	10	11	$R_1(F,\mathbf{w})$	Ran. Rou. $R_2(F,G,\mathbf{w})$	Rec. Sw. $R_2(F,G,\mathbf{w})$	Ran. Rou. $HD(F,G)$	Rec. Sw. $HD(F,G)$
1	8	11	7	1	44	5	3	3	47	0	126	0.3291	0.0533	0.0587	0.7576	0.5397
2	5	4	2	0	50	2	0	7	15	1	70	0.3670	0.0829	0.0792	1.1139	0.5386
3	3	1	8	0	18	5	0	8	26	0	122	0.4417	0.0916	0.1034	0.7442	0.5942
4	7	1	10	0	18	4	0	5	24	0	135	0.4536	0.0922	0.1064	0.7665	0.5979
5	3	2	4	1	17	6	0	2	26	0	107	0.3157	0.1000	0.1091	0.8289	0.5539
6	8	2	7	0	97	9	0	8	28	1	54	0.4563	0.0573	0.0674	1.1356	0.6101
7	5	0	8	0	29	2	1	3	14	0	88	0.4252	0.1019	0.0937	0.9364	0.5844
8	14	1	22	1	30	4	0	4	30	0	93	0.3214	0.0615	0.0674	0.9884	0.5623
9	10	0	8	1	23	2	0	0	17	2	78	0.3946	0.0996	0.0865	1.0818	0.6571
10	17	9	5	1	96	3	1	2	17	4	52	0.3003	0.0579	0.0617	1.1450	0.6392
$R_1(F,\mathbf{w})$	0.0850	0.2862	0.0944	0.3715	0.0927	0.0847	0.6206	0.1335	0.0474	0.5107	0.0309	0.2016				
Ran. Rou. $R_2(F,G,\mathbf{w})$	0.0425	0.1363	0.0464	0.2868	0.0219	0.0536	0.4924	0.0655	0.0252	0.3283	0.0147		0.0295			
Rec. Sw. $R_2(F,G,\mathbf{w})$	0.0415	0.0936	0.0427	0.1372	0.0262	0.0490	0.1996	0.0608	0.0258	0.1763	0.0153			0.0372		
Ran. Rou. $HD(F,G)$	0.5190	1.4289	0.7948	1.4492	0.2165	1.1111	0.9151	0.9035	0.2844	1.1103	0.1221				3.1133	
Rec. Sw. $HD(F,G)$	0.5292	0.6876	0.5249	0.3668	0.6663	0.4934	0.3480	0.5969	0.4666	0.4902	0.5434					1.9920

Table 4. Frequency table (F) and disclosure risk and utility measures: output area (10 output areas) $\times$ sex. The right lower corner shows the measures for the entire table, while the other measures are calculated rowwise/columnwise. 'Ran. Rou.' and 'Rec. Sw.' denote random rounding and record swapping respectively.

	1	2	$R_1(F,\mathbf{w})$	Ran. Rou. $R_2(F,G,\mathbf{w})$	Rec. Sw. $R_2(F,G,\mathbf{w})$	Ran. Rou. $HD(F,G)$	Rec. Sw. $HD(F,G)$
1	161	141	0.0247	0.0222	0.0223	0.0376	0.1165
2	105	94	0.0276	0.0259	0.0260	0.0486	0.1259
3	142	116	0.0294	0.0237	0.0239	0.0612	0.1202
4	158	154	0.0220	0.0219	0.0219	0.0539	0.1213
5	139	90	0.0512	0.0252	0.0269	0.0398	0.1445
6	129	90	0.0434	0.0250	0.0265	0.0000	0.1292
7	107	107	0.0252	0.0252	0.0252	0.0660	0.1274
8	133	147	0.0243	0.0228	0.0229	0.0402	0.1343
9	98	115	0.0289	0.0253	0.0255	0.0666	0.1396
10	136	87	0.0529	0.0254	0.0273	0.0409	0.1432
$R_1(F,\mathbf{w})$	0.0170	0.0209	0.0150	-	-	-	-
Ran. Rou. $R_2(F,G,\mathbf{w})$	0.0127	0.0135	-	0.0100	-	-	-
Rec. Sw. $R_2(F,G,\mathbf{w})$	0.0128	0.0136	-	-	0.0100	-	-
Ran. Rou. $HD(F,G)$	0.1227	0.1032	-	-	-	0.1611	-
Rec. Sw. $HD(F,G)$	0.3452	0.3720	-	-	-	-	0.5076

Table 5. Frequency table (F) and disclosure risk and utility measures: output area (10 output areas) × religion. The right lower corner shows the measures for the entire table, while the other measures are calculated rowwise/columnwise. 'Ran. Rou.' and 'Rec. Sw.' denote random rounding and record swapping respectively.

	1	2	3	4	5	6	7	8	9	$R_1(F,\mathbf{w})$	Ran. Rou. $R_2(F,G,\mathbf{w})$	Rec. Sw. $R_2(F,G,\mathbf{w})$	Ran. Rou. $HD(F,G)$	Rec. Sw. $HD(F,G)$
1	181	0	0	1	17	1	1	83	18	0.4626	0.0634	0.0743	1.1356	0.5507
2	138	2	4	2	0	0	1	36	16	0.4973	0.1028	0.0906	1.0752	0.8832
3	130	0	0	0	22	4	1	61	40	0.3939	0.0742	0.0799	0.7054	0.4893
4	173	0	0	1	14	4	1	97	22	0.4403	0.0669	0.0710	0.9668	0.5323
5	142	2	5	0	15	6	1	37	21	0.3869	0.0568	0.0680	0.8948	0.4443
6	129	0	0	0	0	0	1	69	20	0.5460	0.1011	0.1195	0.6535	0.9705
7	118	2	0	2	24	9	1	38	20	0.3456	0.0562	0.0627	1.0288	0.4715
8	130	0	0	0	34	1	1	82	32	0.3974	0.0673	0.0808	0.9218	0.5466
9	148	3	0	0	0	2	1	38	21	0.5243	0.0894	0.1048	0.8468	0.8918
10	136	1	2	0	13	0	0	55	16	0.4692	0.0917	0.0908	0.8783	0.5312
$R_1(F,\mathbf{w})$	0.0152	0.3770	0.5763	0.4754	0.2029	0.2892	0.1166	0.0393	0.0404	0.2315	-	-	-	-
Ran. Rou. $R_2(F,G,\mathbf{w})$	0.0123	0.2235	0.2944	0.3282	0.0690	0.1304	0.0986	0.0178	0.0255	-	0.0327	-	-	-
Rec. Sw. $R_2(F,G,\mathbf{w})$	0.0124	0.1362	0.2085	0.1621	0.0508	0.1012	0.0766	0.0184	0.0259	-	-	0.0377	-	-
Ran. Rou. $HD(F,G)$	0.1176	1.1877	0.6261	1.2280	0.2664	1.1223	1.9488	0.1920	0.2832	-	-	-	2.9751	-
Rec. Sw. $HD(F,G)$	0.3553	0.4995	0.5804	0.3839	1.4187	0.5697	0.4779	0.4832		-	-	-	-	2.2708

Table 6. Disclosure risk measures, $GAD(F,G)$, $WGAD(F,G)$ and $DR(F,G)$

Frequency table		Random rounding			Record swapping		
		$GAD^*(F,G)$	$WGAD^*(F,G)$	$DR(F,G)$	$GAD(F,G)$	$WGAD(F,G)$	$DR(F,G)$
output area	Rows	0	0	-	0	0	-
×	Columns	0.329	0	-	0.902	0.796	-
country of birth	Table	-	-	0	-	-	0.7009
output area	Rows	0	0	-	0	0	-
×	Columns	0	0	-	0	0	-
mode of travel	Table	-	-	0	-	-	0.7444
output area	Rows	0	0	-	0	0	-
×	Columns	0	0	-	0	0	-
sex	Table	-	-	0	-	-	0
output area	Rows	0	0	-	0	0	-
×	Columns	0	0	-	0	0	-
religion	Table	-	-	0	-	-	0.7004

A CTA Model Based on the Huber Function[*]

Jordi Castro

Department of Statistics and Operations Research,
Universitat Politècnica de Catalunya,
Jordi Girona 1-3, 08034 Barcelona, Catalonia
jordi.castro@upc.edu

Abstract. Minimum distance controlled tabular adjustment (CTA) is an emerging perturbative method of statistical disclosure control for tabular data. The goal of CTA is to find the closest safe table to some original tabular data with sensitive information. Closeness is usually measured by ℓ_1 or ℓ_2 distances. Distance ℓ_1 provides solutions with a smaller ℓ_0 norm than ℓ_2 (i.e., with a lesser number of changes with respect to the original table). However the optimization problem formulated with ℓ_2 requires half the number of variables than that for ℓ_1, and it is more efficiently solved. In this work a pseudo-Huber function (which is a continuous nonlinear approximation of the Huber function) is considered to measure the distance between the original and protected tables. This pseudo-Huber function approximates ℓ_1 but can be formulated with the same number of variables than ℓ_2. It results in a nonlinear convex optimization problem which, theoretically, can be solved in polynomial time. Some preliminary results using the Huber-CTA model are reported.

Keywords: Statistical disclosure control, controlled tabular adjustment, nonlinear optimization, convex optimization, interior-point methods, Huber loss function, pseudo-Huber loss function.

1 Introduction

The statistical disclosure control field aims at protecting sensitive information when releasing statistical microdata or tabular data. A description of the state-of-the-art in this field can be found in the monograph [17] and—only for tabular data—in the survey [5].

Minimum-distance controlled tabular adjustment (CTA), introduced in [3,14], is one of the available post-tabular perturbation approaches for tabular data. The purpose of CTA is, given a table with sensitive cells, to compute the closest safe table (i.e., sensitive cells are modified to avoid re-computation, the remaining cells are minimally adjusted to satisfy the table equations) through the solution of an optimization problem using some particular distance in its objective

[*] Supported by grants MTM2012-31440 of the Spanish Ministry of Economy and Competitiveness, SGR-2014-542 of the Government of Catalonia, and DwB INFRA-2010-262608 of the FP7 European Union Program.

J. Domingo-Ferrer (Ed.): PSD 2014, LNCS 8744, pp. 79–88, 2014.
© Springer International Publishing Switzerland 2014

function. CTA is considered an emerging technology for tabular data [17]. It has been empirically shown that CTA in general exhibits a low disclosure risk [6] and, at the same time, a high data utility [10,11].

CTA was originally formulated as a mixed integer linear programming (MILP) problem [14], while the minimum distance formulation of [3] was continuous (either a linear programming (LP) or a quadratic programming (QP) problem). Continuous formulations, which can be obtained by a priori fixing the value of the binary variables, provide faster optimizations, at the expense of reducing the quality of the solution. A wrong assignment of binary variables may result in an infeasible problem. The approach of [12,13] solves this situation by allowing small changes in three different type of CTA constraints. Together with the original objective, this results in a four-objective problem, which can be solved by multiobjective optimization methods [12,13].

In this work we focus on the continuous formulation of CTA. Using ℓ_1 as the distance in the objective function we obtain a LP whose number of variables is twice the number of cells of the table. For ℓ_2 we obtain a QP with a number of variables equal to the number of cells, which is in general more efficiently solved than the LP of ℓ_1-CTA [3]. (This does not hold if binary variables are considered: the MIQP ℓ_2-CTA is significantly harder than the MILP ℓ_1-CTA, as noted in [9].) On the other hand, ℓ_1-CTA solutions have a lesser ℓ_0 norm (where $\|x\|_{\ell_0}$ is the number of nonzero elements of x), i.e., the number of changes in cell values with respect to the original table is smaller. The purpose of this work is to present a new CTA model using a different objective function, whose optimization problem is of the same dimension than the one formulated by ℓ_2-CTA, but with a solution similar to that obtained with ℓ_1-CTA. We will see that the pseudo-Huber function guarantees both properties.

The paper is organized as follows. Section 2 reviews the CTA formulation without binary variables for ℓ_1 and ℓ_2. Section 3 presents a CTA variant based on a pseudo-Huber function, and provides some of its properties. Section 4 discusses the solution of the convex optimization problem formulated by the Huber-CTA model by an interior-point polynomial time algorithm. Finally, Section 5 reports very preliminary computational results with some midsize three-dimensional tables.

2   The CTA Formulation

Any CTA instance can be formulated from the following parameters: (i) a set of cells $a_i, i \in \mathcal{N} = \{1, \ldots, n\}$, that satisfy some linear relations $Aa = b$ (a being the vector of a_i's); (ii) a lower and upper bound for each cell $i \in \mathcal{N}$, respectively l_{a_i} and u_{a_i}, which are considered to be known by any attacker; (iii) nonnegative cell weights $w_i, i \in \mathcal{N}$, used for the distance between the original and the perturbed released cell values; (iv) a set $\mathcal{S} = \{i_1, i_2, \ldots, i_s\} \subseteq \mathcal{N}$ of indices of sensitive cells; (v) and a lower and upper protection level for each sensitive cell $i \in \mathcal{S}$, respectively lpl_i and upl_i, such that the released values must be out of the interval$(a_i - lpl_i, a_i + upl_i)$.

CTA attempts to find the closest values $z_i, i \in \mathcal{N}$ —according to some distance $\ell(w)$, weighted by w— that make the released table safe. This involves the solution of the following optimization problem:

$$\min_z \quad ||z - a||_{\ell(w)} \tag{1a}$$

$$\text{s. to} \quad Az = b \tag{1b}$$

$$l_{a_i} \leq z_i \leq u_{a_i} \quad i \in \mathcal{N} \tag{1c}$$

$$z_i \; i \in \mathcal{S} \text{ are safe values.} \tag{1d}$$

The formulation of (1d) depends on the particular controlled adjustment variant considered. For instance, in the standard CTA approach, this constraint is

$$(z_i \leq a_i - lpl_i) \text{ or } (z_i \geq a_i + upl_i) \quad i \in \mathcal{S}, \tag{2}$$

which, by introducing a vector of binary variables $y \in \mathbb{R}^s$ can be written as

$$\begin{aligned}
z_i &\geq -M(1 - y_i) + (a_i + upl_i)y_i \; i \in \mathcal{S}, \\
z_i &\leq My_i + (a_i - lpl_i)(1 - y_i) \quad i \in \mathcal{S}, \\
y_i &\in \{0,1\} \quad\quad\quad\quad\quad\quad\quad i \in \mathcal{S},
\end{aligned} \tag{3}$$

$0 \ll M \in \mathbb{R}$ being a large positive value. Constraints (3) impose either "upper protection sense" $z_i \geq a_i + upl_i$, when $y_i = 1$, or "lower protection sense" $z_i \leq a_i - lpl_i$ when $y_i = 0$. The CTA problem (1a)–(1c), (3) is a (in general difficult) MILP, but it provides solutions with a high data utility [11].

Formulating problem (1) in terms of cell deviations $x = z - a$, $x \in \mathbb{R}^n$, and fixing the binary variables, the resulting continuous CTA problem can be formulated as the general convex optimization problem

$$\min_x \quad ||x||_{\ell(w)}$$
$$\text{s. to} \quad Ax = 0 \tag{4}$$
$$l \leq x \leq u,$$

where

$$l_i = \begin{cases} upl_i & \text{if } i \in \mathcal{S} \text{ and } y_i = 1 \\ l_{a_i} - a_i & \text{if } (i \in \mathcal{N} \setminus \mathcal{S}) \text{ or } (i \in \mathcal{S} \text{ and } y_i = 0) \end{cases}$$

$$\tag{5}$$

$$u_i = \begin{cases} -lpl_i & \text{if } i \in \mathcal{S} \text{ and } y_i = 0 \\ u_{a_i} - a_i & \text{if } (i \in \mathcal{N} \setminus \mathcal{S}) \text{ or } (i \in \mathcal{S} \text{ and } y_i = 1), \end{cases}$$

for $i \in \mathcal{N}$.

Problem (4) can be specialized for several norms, ℓ_1 and ℓ_2 being the two most relevant. For ℓ_1, defining $x = x^+ - x^-$, we obtain the following LP:

$$\min_{x^+, x^-} \quad \sum_{i=1}^{n} w_i(x_i^+ + x_i^-)$$
$$\text{s. to} \quad A(x^+ - x^-) = 0 \tag{6}$$
$$l^+ \leq x^+ \leq u^+$$
$$l^- \leq x^- \leq u^-,$$

$x^+ \in \mathbb{R}^n$ and $x^- \in \mathbb{R}^n$ being the vectors of positive and negative deviations in absolute value, and $l^+, l^-, u^+, u^- \in \mathbb{R}^n$ lower and upper bounds for the positive and negative deviations defined as

$$
l_i^+ = \begin{cases} upl_i & \text{if } i \in \mathcal{S} \text{ and } y_i = 1 \\ 0 & \text{if } (i \in \mathcal{N} \setminus \mathcal{S}) \text{ or } (i \in \mathcal{S} \text{ and } y_i = 0) \end{cases}
$$

$$
u_i^+ = \begin{cases} 0 & \text{if } i \in \mathcal{S} \text{ and } y_i = 0 \\ u_{a_i} - a_i & \text{if } (i \in \mathcal{N} \setminus \mathcal{S}) \text{ or } (i \in \mathcal{S} \text{ and } y_i = 1) \end{cases}
$$
$$(7)$$
$$
l_i^- = \begin{cases} lpl_i & \text{if } i \in \mathcal{S} \text{ and } y_i = 0 \\ 0 & \text{if } (i \in \mathcal{N} \setminus \mathcal{S}) \text{ or } (i \in \mathcal{S} \text{ and } y_i = 1) \end{cases}
$$

$$
u_i^- = \begin{cases} 0 & \text{if } i \in \mathcal{S} \text{ and } y_i = 1 \\ a_i - l_{a_i} & \text{if } (i \in \mathcal{N} \setminus \mathcal{S}) \text{ or } (i \in \mathcal{S} \text{ and } y_i = 0), \end{cases}
$$

for $i \in \mathcal{N}$. For ℓ_2, problem (4) can be directly recast as the following QP without introducing additional variables:

$$
\begin{aligned}
\min_x \quad & \sum_{i=1}^n w_i x_i^2 \\
\text{s. to} \quad & Ax = 0 \\
& l \leq x \leq u.
\end{aligned}
$$
$$(8)$$

Infeasibilities in continuous models (6), (8) due to pre-fixing the binary variables can be dealt as in [12,13]. Problem (8) requires half the number of variables than (6). In addition, the splitting of variables $x = x^+ - x^-$ may create difficulties to some optimization methods. On the other hand the ℓ_1 solutions are known to change fewer cells than ℓ_2 solutions. The next Section introduces a new nonlinear CTA model with the same number of variables that (8) and similar solutions to those of (6).

3   Using a Pseudo-Huber Function as Objective Function

The Huber function [16] $\varphi_\delta : \mathbb{R} \to \mathbb{R}$, defined as

$$
\varphi_\delta(x_i) = \begin{cases} \frac{x_i^2}{2\delta} & |x_i| \leq \delta \\ |x_i| - \frac{\delta}{2} & |x_i| \geq \delta \end{cases}
$$
$$(9)$$

approximates $|x_i|$ for small values of $\delta > 0$ (the smaller δ the better the approximation). φ_δ is a continuous and first-order differentiable function; but second derivatives are not continuous at points $|x_i| = \delta$.

To avoid this discontinuity in second derivatives, we may consider the pseudo-Huber function $\phi_\delta : \mathbb{R} \to \mathbb{R}$:

$$
\phi_\delta(x_i) = \sqrt{\delta^2 + x_i^2} - \delta.
$$
$$(10)$$

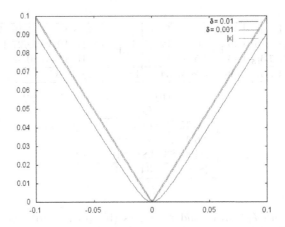

Fig. 1. Pseudo-Huber function for some δ, and $|x|$

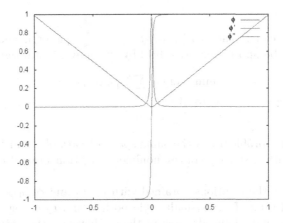

Fig. 2. Graph of ϕ_δ, ϕ'_δ and ϕ''_δ for $\delta = 0.01$

This function has been recently successfully used in other ℓ_1-regularization problems [15]. $\phi_\delta \in \mathcal{C}^2$, with first and second derivatives

$$\phi'_\delta(x_i) = \frac{x_i}{\sqrt{\delta^2 + x_i^2}} \qquad \phi''_\delta(x_i) = \frac{\delta^2}{(\delta^2 + x_i^2)^{3/2}}. \tag{11}$$

As shown in Figure 1, ϕ_δ is a better approximation of $|x_i|$ as δ approaches 0. Figure 2 plots the graph of ϕ_δ, ϕ'_δ and ϕ''_δ for $\delta = 0.01$. As shown in [15], the first and second derivatives are bounded and Lipschitz continuous.

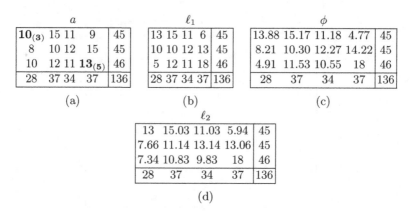

a				
10(3)	15	11	9	45
8	10	12	15	45
10	12	11	**13**(5)	46
28	37	34	37	136

(a)

ℓ_1				
13	15	11	6	45
10	10	12	13	45
5	12	11	18	46
28	37	34	37	136

(b)

ϕ				
13.88	15.17	11.18	4.77	45
8.21	10.30	12.27	14.22	45
4.91	11.53	10.55	18	46
28	37	34	37	136

(c)

ℓ_2				
13	15.03	11.03	5.94	45
7.66	11.14	13.14	13.06	45
7.34	10.83	9.83	18	46
28	37	34	37	136

(d)

Fig. 3. Results with ℓ_1, $\phi_{0.001}$, and ℓ_2 (tables (b), (c) and (d)) for the small two-dimensional small table (a) (rounded to two decimal positions). The optimal value of $||x||_1$ for ℓ_1 and $\phi_{0.001}$ is 20, while for ℓ_2 is 20.69.

Therefore we can replace $||x||_{\ell_1}$ by $f(x) = \sum_{i=1}^{n} \phi_\delta(x_i)$, and the ℓ_1-CTA problem (6) can be approximately solved by the convex optimization problem

$$\min_{x} \ f(x) = \sum_{i=1}^{n} \phi_\delta(x_i)$$
$$\text{s. to } \ Ax = 0 \tag{12}$$
$$l \leq x \leq u.$$

This optimization problem has the same space of variables and feasible region than (8), but with a strictly convex nonlinear function instead of a quadratic one.

Figure 3 shows the solutions obtained with ℓ_1, ℓ_2 and $\phi_{\delta=0.001}$ with a small two-dimensional table. In this small table both ϕ and ℓ_2 changed most of the cells, whereas ℓ_1 only changed a few of them. However, the optimal objective functions with ℓ_1 and $\phi_{\delta=0.001}$ were exactly the same ($||x||_1 = 20$), whereas $||x||_1 = 20.69$ for ℓ_2. The ϕ_δ function thus provided the same objective function that ℓ_1, but cell deviations were distributed among more cells. This is explained by the different optimization algorithms used for the solution of ℓ_1 and ϕ_δ (which needs a nonlinear optimization method, as discussed in next Section). A more extensive study with larger and more complex tables is out of the scope of this work.

4   Solution of the Huber-CTA Model

The Huber-CTA model (12) is a nonlinear convex optimization problem. In theory, this kind of problems are polynomially solved with interior-point methods [18,19], with a best bound of $O(\sqrt{n} \log 1/\epsilon)$, n being the number of variables and ϵ the optimality tolerance (discussed below). The complexity of CTA with ℓ_1 or ϕ_δ is thus the same if solved by an interior-point algorithm.

Broadly speaking, interior-point methods attempt to solve a perturbation of the first-order optimality conditions (named Karush-Kuhn-Tucker or KKT conditions) of (12):

$$
\begin{aligned}
Ax &= b \\
A^\top \lambda + \lambda_l - \lambda_u - \nabla f(x) &= 0 \\
(X - L)\Lambda_l e &= \mu e \\
(U - X)\Lambda_u e &= \mu e \\
u \geq x \geq l, \quad (\lambda_l, \lambda_u) &\geq 0,
\end{aligned}
\tag{13}
$$

where $\lambda \in \mathbb{R}^m$, $\lambda_l, \lambda_u \in \mathbb{R}^n$ are the Lagrange multipliers of respectively the equality constraints and lower and upper bounds, $e \in \mathbb{R}^n$ is a vector of 1's, and matrices $X, \Lambda_l, \Lambda_u, L, U \in \mathbb{R}^{n \times n}$ are diagonal matrices made from vectors $x, \lambda_l, \lambda_u, l, u$. The set of unique solutions of (13) for each μ value is known as the central path, and when $\mu \to 0$ these solutions converge to those of (12). The nonlinear system (13) is usually solved by a damped version of Newton's method, reducing the μ parameter at each iteration, until $\mu \leq \epsilon$, ϵ being the required optimality tolerance. This procedure is known as the path-following interior-point algorithm. An excellent discussion about the theoretical and practical properties of this interior-point algorithm can be found in [20].

Although theoretically the same interior-point path-following algorithm should be as efficient for ℓ_1 than for ϕ_δ, in practice the Huber function requires a more robust solver. Some early tests with general tables using the convex interior-point algorithm of [2] show that even small instances can be difficult with ϕ_δ if the solver is not appropriately tuned. In this sense, reformulations of the model as a second order conic optimization problem could be preferable [1].

However, for some interior-point methods specialized to particular structures, such as block-angular problems, ϕ_δ may be more efficiently solved than ℓ_1: the technical explanation is that, since the Hessian of ϕ is nonzero, unlike for the LP formulated by ℓ_1, the internal linear systems of equations may require less iterations of the preconditioned conjugate gradient [7]. For instance, this may happen for three-dimensional tables, whose constraints exhibit a block-angular structure [8]. Next Section shows a few preliminary computational results with some three-dimensional tables using such a specialized interior-point solver.

5   Computational Results

Preliminary results have been obtained for a set of eight three-dimensional tables of r rows, c columns and l levels (where rows, columns and levels refer to each of the table dimensions). Table 1 shows the problem dimensions for each instance; n and m denote the number of variables and constraints of problems (12) and (8) for ϕ and ℓ_2 (which are of the same size), and (6) for ℓ_1. Tables were obtained with the same generator used in [8].

These eight instances have been solved with an efficient implementation of the specialized interior-point method described in [4] including the quadratic

Table 1. Dimensions of some 3D CTA optimization problems for pseudo-Huber, ℓ_1 and ℓ_2

			ϕ, ℓ_2		ℓ_1	
r	c	l	n	m	n	m
25	25	25	16250	1875	31875	1875
25	25	50	31875	3125	63125	3125
25	50	25	32500	3125	63750	3125
25	50	50	63750	5000	126250	5000
50	25	25	32500	3125	63750	3125
50	25	50	63750	5000	126250	5000
50	50	25	65000	5000	127500	5000
50	50	50	127500	7500	252500	7500

Table 2. Results for 3D CTA using pseudo-Huber, ℓ_1 and ℓ_2

			ϕ		ℓ_1		ℓ_2	
r	c	l	obj.	CPU	obj.	CPU	obj.	CPU
25	25	25	101096	1.68	101572	4.37	4161290	0.09
25	25	50	104706	4.59	105409	10.94	3915100	0.19
25	50	25	104030	4.54	104720	13.87	3969550	0.27
25	50	50	110537	8.71	111679	9.72	3915150	0.55
50	25	25	107138	4.87	107832	23.9	4107990	0.26
50	25	50	109068	7.67	110199	5.54	3832800	0.54
50	50	25	106173	8.17	107309	4.15	3666090	0.9
50	50	50	113858	15.68	116279	67.91	3678810	1.84

regularization strategy of [7]. Table 2 reports for each of the three CTA variants—using ϕ, ℓ_1 and ℓ_2—, the optimal objective function achieved and the CPU time. All runs were carried out on a Fujitsu Primergy RX300 server with 3.33 GHz Intel Xeon X5680 CPUs, under a GNU/Linux operating system (Suse 11.4), without exploitation of parallelism capabilities. It is clearly seen that ℓ_2 provides the fastest executions; this is consistent with the results of [3] obtained with a generic solver. However, the objective function with ℓ_2 naturally differs from that obtained with ℓ_1. On the other hand both ϕ and ℓ_1 provide very similar objective function values, ϕ being more efficiently solved in six of the eight instances. In particular the largest instance required 67.91 seconds with ℓ_1 and only 15.68 with ϕ.

6   Conclusions

We have presented a CTA model which replaces the usual ℓ_1 distance in the objective by the pseudo-Huber function. Although the resulting problem is convex and nonlinear, it requires half the number of variables than the ℓ_1-CTA LP. It has been observed that for certain classes of tables (i.e., some three-dimensional tables) the Huber-CTA model can be more efficiently solved than ℓ_1-CTA using and appropriate interior-point solver.

The preliminary results reported in this work are non-conclusive, but just a first step in the solution of the Huber-CTA model. Among the future tasks to be done in this direction we mention: (i) the application of the Huber-CTA model to other classes of structured tables (real-world linked or hierarchical tables); (ii) a more detailed analysis of the disclosure risk and data utility of tables protected by the Huber function, comparing them with tables protected with ℓ_1- and ℓ_2-CTA; (iii) an efficient implementation for general tables, not just three-dimensional ones; (iv) and the tuning or implementation of second-order interior-point solvers for the highly efficient solution of the Huber-CTA problem.

References

1. Andersen, E.D.: Personal communication (2014)
2. Andersen, E.D., Andersen, K.D.: The MOSEK interior point optimizer for linear programming: an implementation of the homogeneous algorithm. In: Frenk, H., Roos, K., Terlaky, T., Zhang, S. (eds.) High Performance Optimization, pp. 197–232. Kluwer (2000)
3. Castro, J.: Minimum-distance controlled perturbation methods for large-scale tabular data protection. European Journal of Operational Research 171, 39–52 (2006)
4. Castro, J.: An interior-point approach for primal block-angular problems. Computational Optimization and Applications 36, 195–219 (2007)
5. Castro, J.: Recent advances in optimization techniques for statistical tabular data protection. European Journal of Operational Research 216, 257–269 (2012)
6. Castro, J.: On assessing the disclosure risk of controlled adjustment methods for statistical tabular data. International Journal of Uncertainty, Fuzziness and Knowledge-Based Systems 20, 921–941 (2012)
7. Castro, J., Cuesta, J.: Quadratic regularizations in an interior-point method for primal block-angular problems. Mathematical Programming 130, 415–445 (2011)
8. Castro, J., Cuesta, J.: Solving L_1-CTA in 3D tables by an interior-point method for primal block-angular problems. TOP 21, 25–47 (2013)
9. Castro, J., Frangioni, A., Gentile, C.: Perspective reformulations of the CTA problem with L_2 distances. Operations Research (in press, 2014)
10. Castro, J., Giessing, S.: Testing variants of minimum distance controlled tabular adjustment. Monographs of Official Statistics, pp. 333–343. Eurostat-Office for Official Publications of the European Communities, Luxembourg (2006)
11. Castro, J., González, J.A.: Assessing the information loss of controlled adjustment methods in two-way tables. Lecture Notes in Computer Science: Privacy in Statistical Databases (2014) (Submitted)
12. Castro, J., González, J.A.: A fast CTA method without the complicating binary decisions. Documents of the Joint UNECE/Eurostat Work Session on Statistical Data Confidentiality, Statistics Canada, Ottawa, pp. 1–7 (2013)
13. Castro, J., González, J.A.: A multiobjective LP approach for controlled tabular adjustment in statistical disclosure control. Working paper, Dept. of Statistics and Operations Research, Universitat Politècnica de Catalunya (2014)

14. Dandekar, R.A., Cox, L.H.: Synthetic tabular Data: an alternative to complementary cell suppression, manuscript, Energy Information Administration, U.S. (2002)
15. Fountoulakis, K., Gondzio, J.: A second-order method for strongly convex L1-regularization problems. Technical Report ERGO-14-005, School of Mathematics, The University of Edinburgh (2014)
16. Huber, P.J.: Robust estimation of a location parameter. Annals of Statistics 53, 73–101 (1964)
17. Hundepool, A., Domingo-Ferrer, J., Franconi, L., Giessing, S., Schulte-Nordholt, E., Spicer, K., de Wolf, P.P.: Statistical Disclosure Control. Wiley, Chichester (2012)
18. Nesterov, Y.: Introductory Lectures on Convex Optimization: A Basic Course. Kluwer, Boston (2004)
19. Nesterov, Y., Nemirovskii, A.: Interior-Point Polynomial Algorithms in Convex Programming. SIAM, Philadelphia (1994)
20. Wright, S.J.: Primal-Dual Interior-Point Methods. SIAM, Philadelphia (1996)

Density Approximant
Based on Noise Multiplied Data

Yan-Xia Lin

National Institute for Applied Statistics Research Australia,
School of Mathematics and Applied Statistics,
University of Wollongong, Australia

Abstract. Using noise multiplied data to protect confidential data has recently drawn some attention. Understanding the probability property of the underlying confidential data based on their masked data is of interest in confidential data analysis. This paper proposes the approach of sample-moment-based density approximant based on noise multiplied data and provides a new manner for approximating the density function of the underlying confidential data without accessing the original data.

The approach of sample-moment-based density approximant is an extension of the approach of moment-based density approximant, which is mathematically equivalent to traditional orthogonal polynomials approaches to the probability density function (Provost, 2005). This paper shows that, regardless of a negligible probability, a moment-based density approximant can be well approximated by its sample-moment-based approximant if the size of the sample used in the evaluation is reasonable large. Consequently, a density function can be reasonably approximated by its sample-moment-based density approximant.

This paper focuses on the properties and the performance of the approach of the sample-moment-based density approximant based on noise multiplied data. Due to the restriction on the number of pages, some technical issues on implementing the approach proposed in practice will be discussed in another paper.

Keywords: Confidential data, Masked data, Multiplicative noise, Moment-based density approximant.

1 Introduction

Many government institutions and statistical agencies collect survey data from individuals and businesses. Publishing these data with certain level of protection is necessary. Many different protection methods, including microaggregation of sensitive data, local suppression of unique data cells, top and bottom coding of continuous variables, rank swapping, rounding, adding noise, imputation and multiplicative noise, have been introduced and used in practice. More information on data protection can be found in Duncan and Lambert (1986 and 1989), Willenborg and De Waal (2001), Oganian (2010), Shlomo (2010), and the references therein.

J. Domingo-Ferrer (Ed.): PSD 2014, LNCS 8744, pp. 89–104, 2014.

The aim of government institutions and data agencies publishing the masked data sets is to provide end-users an opportunity to work out the statistical information on the underlying data without breaching confidentiality. As mentioned in Nayak *et al.* (2011), data perturbation may destroy unbiasedness and other properties of estimators. Methods and formulas for analysing an original data set may not be appropriate for analysing a masked version of it.

Describing and estimating the probability density function of a random variable are the basic tenets in statistical data analysis.

Provost (2005) introduced the moment-based density approximant method for probability density approximation. He proved and demonstrated that using the moment-based density approximant to approach the density function is mathematically equivalent to using those orthogonal polynomials, such as the Legendre, Laguerre, Jacobi, and Hermite polynomials.

The multiplicative noise method is one type of noise addition used to perturb and protect confidential data. Kim and Jeong (2008) classified the multiplicative noise scheme into two schemes, Multiplicative Noise Scheme I and Multiplicative Noise Scheme II. The multiplicative noise scheme considered in this paper is Multiplicative Noise Scheme I. It is briefly defined as follows. Let Y be a sensitive random variable with observations $y_1, y_2, \cdots, y_N$ (original data). Let C be a positive random variable, independent of Y. When we say the original data $y_1, y_2, \cdots, y_N$ are masked by C, it means the masked data have the form $y_i^* = y_i \times c_i$ where $\{c_i\}$ is a sample from C. In literature, sometimes it imposes $E(C) = 1$. With this restriction, y^* is an unbiased estimator of y given y. This restriction does not apply to the method proposed in this paper. Therefore, the unbiased estimator of y will be $y^*/E(C)$, given y. Without further explanation, the term "masked data" used in this paper is for "noise multiplied data".

For noise multiplied data, developing appropriate data analysis methods and formulas for different inference purposes is necessary (see Kim and Jeong (2008) for domain estimation, Sinha, *et al.* (2011) for quantile estimation, and Lin and Wise (2012) for linear regression parameters estimation). This paper proposes a method to obtain the density approximant of a sensitive random variable Y based on its masked data.

Many properties of the multiplicative noise method, including evaluation of disclosure risk, confidential protection, moment estimation, linear regression parameter estimation, properties of balanced noise distribution and effects on data quality and privacy protection in context of tabular magnitude data, have been deeply discussed and investigated in literature (Evans, 1996; Evans *et al.*, 1998; Hwang, 1998; Kim and Winkler, 2003; Kim and Jeong, 2008; Oganian, 2010; Krsinich and Piesse, 2002; Nayak, et al., 2011; Sinha, et al., 2011; Lin and Wise, 2012 and Klein and Sinha, 2013). One of the important properties is the moments of Y can be evaluated through the moments of its masked variable Y^* and the moments of the noise C used to mask Y.

With the well developed numerical result of the density approximant provided by Provost (2005) and the nice relationship among the moments of Y, masked variable Y^* and noise C, respectively, the density function of Y can be theoretically well approximated by the density approximant based on the moments given by Y^* and C. By noting that, only masked data $\{y_i^*\}$ and, in the best scenario, noise information are available in practice, the motivation of this paper is to investigate the properties of the moment-based density approximant of Y if the $E[(Y^*)^k]$ and $E(C^k)$ in the moment-based density approximant are replaced by their corresponding sample moments estimators. The moment-based density approximant with moments replaced by sample moments is called the sample-moment-based density approximant.

This paper derives the formula for the approximant of a density function based on masked data and demonstrates that the density function of a random variable can be well approximated by its sample-moment-based density approximant. Due to the restriction on the number of pages, this paper only shows how the sample-moment-based density approximant $f_{Y,K|\{y_i^*,c_i\}_1^N}$ is built based on masked data $\{y_i^*\}$ and noise sample $\{c_i\}$. Then, carries out relevant simulation studies and a real data application of the approach of the sample-moment-based density approximant. The details of the technique treatment to implement the approach proposed in practice and the issue of risk of disclosure related to the approach will appear in another paper along with a built R package.

The remainder of this paper is organized as follows. From Section 2 to Section 4, we step by step extend the approach of moment-based density approximant with bounded domain to the approach of sample-moment-based density approaximant based on noise multiplied data for a general situation. The formula and properties of the sample-moment-based density approaximant are presented. Simulation studies and a real life data application are given in Sections 5 and 6.

2 Moment-Based Density Approximant: Density Function with a Finite Domain $[a, b]$

Provost (2005) provided useful formulas of moment-based density approximant. The formulas and notation are adopted in this paper.

The probability density function of a continuous random variable X, taking values on interval $[-1, 1]$, can be expressed as follows:

$$f_X(x) = \sum_{k=0}^{\infty} \lambda_k P_k(x), \tag{1}$$

where

$$\lambda_k = \frac{2k+1}{2} \sum_{i=0}^{Floor[k/2]} (-1)^i 2^{-k} \frac{(2k-2i)!}{i!(k-i)!(k-2i)!} \mu_X(k-2i)$$

with the $(k - 2i)$th moment of X

$$\mu_X(k-2i) = E(X^{k-2i}) = \int_{-1}^{1} x^{k-2i} f_X(x) dx;$$

$$P_k(x) = \sum_{i=0}^{Floor[k/2]} (-1)^i 2^{-k} \frac{(2k-2i)!}{i!(k-i)!(k-2i)!} x^{k-2i} \tag{2}$$

is a Legendre polynomial of degree k in x and $Floor[k/2]$ denotes the largest integer less than or equal to $k/2$.

Denote

$$f_{X,K}(x) = \sum_{k=0}^{K} \lambda_k P_k(x) \tag{3}$$

the polynomial approximation of $f_X(x)$ with order K.

Let Y be a random variable with density function defined on a finite interval $[a, b]$. Its density function and kth moment are denoted by $f_Y(y)$ and

$$\mu_Y(k) = E(Y^k) = \int_a^b y^k f_Y(y) dy, \quad k = 0, 1, \cdots,$$

respectively. Let

$$X = \frac{2Y - (a+b)}{b-a}.$$

The domain of the density function of X is bounded by $[-1, 1]$ and the jth moment of X is

$$\mu_X(j) = \frac{1}{(b-a)^j} \sum_{k=0}^{j} \binom{j}{k} 2^k \mu_Y(k)(-1)^{j-k}(a+b)^{j-k}, \quad j = 0, 1, \cdots.$$

After transformation, by using (3), the approximant of f_Y with order K is given by

$$f_{Y,K}(y) = \frac{2}{b-a} \sum_{k=0}^{K} \lambda_k P_k\left(\frac{2y - (a+b)}{b-a}\right). \tag{4}$$

Let Y be masked by a noise C and yield Y^*. By noting that, for $k = 1, 2, \cdots$,

$$\mu_Y(k) = \frac{E[(Y^*)^k]}{E(C^k)} = \frac{\mu_{Y^*}(k)}{\mu_C(k)}$$

and λ_k is a linear functions of $E(Y^i)$, $i \leq k$, the approximant of f_Y with order K can be expressed in terms of the moments of Y^* and C as follows

$$f_{Y,K}(y) = \frac{2}{b-a} \sum_{k=0}^{K} \lambda_k P_k\left(\frac{2y - (a+b)}{b-a}\right) = \sum_{k=0}^{K} a_k(y) \frac{\mu_{Y^*}(k)}{\mu_C(k)}, \tag{5}$$

where $a_k(y)$ is a continuous function of y, $k = 0, 1, \cdots, K$.

Provost (2005) pointed out that "the density approximants so obtained may be negative on certain subranges of the support of their distributions having low density. This will likely occur if an insufficient number of moments are being used. However, by mere inspection of the approximate density plot, we should be able to determine whether a higher degree polynomial ought to be used." It means that it is possible to determine an appropriate order K such that the plot of $f_{Y,K}$ is close to or mimics to the plot of the density function of Y by inspecting the plot of the density function of Y.

3 Sample-Moment-Based Density Approximant: Density Function with a Finite Domain $[a, b]$

Assume that Y is bounded between the real numbers a and b. Let $\{y_i\}_1^N$ be a sample of size N drawn from Y and $\{y_i^*\}_1^N$ be the masked data of $\{y_i\}_1^N$, masked by the noise C. Let $\{c_j\}_1^N$ be an independent sample drawn from C, which is not the same sample used to yield $\{y_i^*\}_1^N$.

In this section, the relationship between

$$f_{Y,K|\{y_i^*,c_i\}_1^N}(y) = \sum_{k=0}^{K} a_k(y) \frac{\overline{(Y^*)^k}}{\overline{C^k}} \tag{6}$$

and

$$f_{Y,K}(y) = \sum_{k=0}^{K} a_k(y) \frac{\mu_{Y^*}(k)}{\mu_C(k)}, \tag{7}$$

is evaluated, where $\overline{(Y^*)^k} = \sum_{i=1}^{N}(y_i^*)^k/N$ and $\overline{C^k} = \sum_{i=1}^{N} c_i^k/N$, $k = 0, 1, 2, \cdots$, K.

We have the following results:

1. $f_{Y,K|\{y_i^*,c_i\}_1^N}$ *uniformly converges to* $f_{Y,K}$ *almost surely.*

   From the Strong Law of Large Numbers (SLLN), $\overline{(Y^*)^k} \overset{a.s.}{\to} E[(Y^*)^k]$ and $\overline{C^k} \overset{a.s.}{\to} E(C^k)$, as $N \to \infty$. Since $a_k(y)$ is a continuous function of y on $[a, b]$, for each $k = 1, 2, \cdots$, $a_k(y)$ is uniformly continuous on $[a, b]$. Thus, given K fixed,

   $$f_{Y,K|\{y_i^*,c_i\}_1^N}(y) = \sum_{k=0}^{K} a_k(y) \frac{\overline{(Y^*)^k}}{\overline{C^k}} \overset{a.s.}{\to} \sum_{k=0}^{K} a_k(y) \frac{\mu_{Y^*}(k)}{\mu_C(k)} = f_{Y,K}(y),$$

   uniformly for $y \in [a, b]$ as $N \to \infty$.

   Since $f_{Y,K|\{y_i^*,c_i\}_1^N}$ uniformly converges to $f_{Y,K}$, the curve of the function $f_{Y,K|\{y_i^*,c_i\}_1^N}$ will be close to the curve of $f_{Y,K}$, so is to the curve of the density function of f_Y, subject to appropriate K and sample size N.

2. $f_{Y,K|\{y_i^*,c_i\}_1^N}(y)$ *is an approximately unbiased estimator of* $f_{Y,K}(y)$ *for each* $y \in [a, b]$.

   Mood *et al.* (1963) showed that an approximate expression for the expectation of a function $g(W_1, W_2)$ of random variables W_1 and W_2 using a Taylor's series expansion around their means (μ_{W_1}, μ_{W_2}) is given by

   $$E[g(W_1, W_2)] \approx g(\mu_{W_1}, \mu_{W_2}) + \frac{1}{2} \frac{\partial^2}{\partial w_2^2} g(W_1, W_2)|_{\mu_{W_1}, \mu_{W_2}} Var(W_2)$$

   $$+ \frac{1}{2} \frac{\partial^2}{\partial w_1^2} g(W_1, W_2)|_{\mu_{W_1}, \mu_{W_2}} Var(W_1)$$

   $$+ \frac{\partial^2}{\partial w_1 \partial w_2} g(W_1, W_2)|_{\mu_{W_1}, \mu_{W_2}} cov(W_1, W_2). \tag{8}$$

Applying (8) to $E(\overline{(Y^*)^k}/\overline{C^k})$ and noting that $\overline{(Y^*)^k}$ and $\overline{C^k}$ are independent, we obtain

$$E\left[\frac{\overline{(Y^*)^k}}{\overline{C^k}}\right] \approx \frac{E[\overline{(Y^*)^k}]}{E(\overline{C^k})} + \frac{E[\overline{(Y^*)^k}]}{(E(\overline{C^k}))^3}Var(\overline{C^k})$$

$$= E(Y^k) + \frac{1}{N}var(C^k)\frac{E(Y^k)}{[E(C^k)]^3} = E(Y^k) + o(1).$$

Therefore, when N is sufficiently large, we will have

$$E\left[\frac{\overline{(Y^*)^k}}{\overline{C^k}}\right] \approx E(Y^k), \quad k = 1, 2, \cdots, K,$$

and $f_{Y,K|\{y_i^*,c_i\}_1^N}(y)$ is an approximately unbiased estimator of $f_{Y,K}(y)$ for each $y \in [a, b]$.

4   Sample-Moment-Based Density Approximant: Non-restriction on the Domain of the Density Function

Let $\{y_i\}_{0<i\leq N}$ be a sample drawn from a random variable Y. In this section, we point out the facts that (i) the probability of Y taking values beyond the interval $(\min_{1\leq i\leq N}\{y_i\}, \max_{1\leq i\leq N}\{y_i\})$ can be negligible if the sample size N is reasonable large; (ii) $f_{Y,K|\{y_i^*,c_i\}_1^N}$ could be a good candidate for $f_{Y,K}$ regardless of Y bounded or not, as long as the sample size N is reasonable large.

Lemma 1. *Let* $Y_1, \cdots, Y_N$ *be i.i.d. random variables, defined on some probability space* $(\Omega, \mathcal{F}, P)$, *and have the probability distribution of* Y. *For* $\omega \in \Omega$, *define*

$$g_{min}^{(N)}(\omega) = g_{min}(Y_1(\omega), \cdots, Y_N(\omega)) = P(Y \leq min_{1\leq i\leq N}\{Y_i(\omega)\})$$

and

$$g_{max}^{(N)}(\omega) = g_{max}(Y_1(\omega), \cdots, Y_N(\omega)) = P(Y \leq max_{1\leq i\leq N}\{Y_i(\omega)\}).$$

Then, for any real number $0 \leq a \leq 1$,

$$P(g_{min}^{(N)} \leq a) = 1 - (1 - a)^N \quad and \quad P(g_{max}^{(N)} \leq a) = a^N.$$

Lemma 2. *For* $p \in (0, 1)$ *and* $0 < \alpha < 1$, *if* $N \geq \log(1 - p)/\log(1 - \alpha/2)$, *then*

$$P(g_{min}^{(N)} \leq \alpha/2) > p \quad and \quad P(g_{max}^{(N)} > 1 - \alpha/2) > p.$$

The proofs of Lemmas 1 and 2 are in the Appendix.

From Lemma 2, given $\alpha = 0.05$, if we wish to have at least $p = 0.975$ probability to ensure $g_{min}^{(N)} \leq \alpha/2$ and $1 - g_{max}^{(N)} < \alpha/2$, the sufficient condition for N

will be $N \geq \log(0.025)/\log(0.975) = 145.703$; for $\alpha = 0.05$ and $p = 0.9975$, the sufficient condition will be $N \geq 237$; for $\alpha = 0.005$ and $p = 0.975$, the sufficient condition will be $N \geq 1474$.

No matter Y is bounded or not, once the sample $\{y_i\}_{i \leq N}$ was drawn from Y, $\{y_i\}_{i \leq N}$ will be bounded. It is of interest that, for a pre-set real number $0 < \alpha < 1$, what size N will ensure that we have a sufficient confidence to claim that the probability $P(\min_{1 \leq i \leq N}\{y_i\} \leq Y \leq \max_{1 \leq i \leq N}\{y_i\})$ is at least $1 - \alpha$.

From Lemma 2, if $N \geq \log(1-p)/\log(1-\alpha/2)$,

$$P[(g_{min}^{(N)} \leq \alpha/2) \bigcap (g_{max}^{(N)} > 1 - \alpha/2)] \geq 1 - (1-p) - (1-p) = 2p - 1.$$

For $\omega \in (g_{min}^{(N)} \leq \alpha/2) \bigcap (g_{max}^{(N)} > 1 - \alpha/2)$, we have

$$P(min_{1 \leq i \leq N}\{Y_i(\omega)\} \leq Y \leq max_{1 \leq i \leq N}\{Y_i(\omega)\}) = 1 - g_{min}^{(N)}(\omega) - g_{max}^{(N)}(\omega) \geq 1 - \alpha.$$

Therefore, we have at least $2p - 1$ confidence to claim that, for sample $\{y_i\}_1^N$,

$$P(min_{1 \leq i \leq N}\{y_i\} \leq Y \leq max_{1 \leq i \leq N}\{y_i\}) \geq 1 - \alpha,$$

if $N \geq \log(1-p)/\log(1-\alpha/2)$.

Example 1. If we wish to have $0.95 = 2 \times 0.975 - 1$ confidence to claim that more than $0.995 = 1 - 0.005$ chance the values of Y will drop between $\min_{1 \leq i \leq N}\{y_i\}$ and $\max_{1 \leq i \leq N}\{y_i\}$, the sufficient condition for N is $N \geq 1474 \geq log(1 - 0.975)/log(1 - 0.0025)$.

Now, we are at the position of extending the result in Section 3 to sample-moment-based density approximant without the restriction on the domain of the density function.

Assume that Y is a random variable on some probability space $(\Omega, \mathcal{F}, P)$ and $\{y_i\}_{1 \leq i \leq N}$ is a sample from Y. Define a random variable $\tilde{Y}$ from Y. Let $\tilde{Y}(\omega) = Y(\omega)$ if $\min_{i \leq i \leq N}\{y_i\} \leq Y(\omega) \leq \max_{i \leq i \leq N}\{y_i\}$; $= 0$ otherwise, where $\omega \in \Omega$. $\tilde{Y}$ is called a truncated random variable of Y.

Following Example 1, if $N > 1474$, with odds of 0.95, the difference between the cumulative distribution functions of Y and $\tilde{Y}$ can be evaluated as following: if $y \leq \min_{i \leq i \leq N}\{y_i\}$,

$$|F_Y(y) - F_{\tilde{Y}}(y)| = F_Y(y) \leq 0.0025;$$

if $\min_{i \leq i \leq N}\{y_i\} < y < \max_{i \leq i \leq N}\{y_i\}$,

$$|F_Y(y) - F_{\tilde{Y}}(y)| = \left| P(\min_{i \leq i \leq N}\{y_i\} < Y < y) + P(Y \leq \min_{i \leq i \leq N}\{y_i\}) \right.$$

$$\left. - \frac{P(min_{i \leq i \leq N}\{y_i\} < Y < y)}{P(min_{i \leq i \leq N}\{y_i\} < Y < max_{i \leq i \leq N}\{y_i\})} \right|$$

$$\leq P(\min_{i \leq i \leq N}\{y_i\} < Y < y)\frac{1 - P(min_{i \leq i \leq N}\{y_i\} < Y < max_{i \leq i \leq N}\{y_i\})}{P(min_{i \leq i \leq N}\{y_i\} < Y < max_{i \leq i \leq N}\{y_i\})} + 0.0025$$

$$\leq (1 - 0.995) + 0.0025 = 0.0075;$$

if $y > \max_{i \leq i \leq N}\{y_i\}$,

$$|F_Y(y) - F_{\tilde{Y}}(y)| = |1 - P(Y > y) - 1| < 0.0025.$$

Thus, with odds of 0.95, $\max_y\{|F_Y(y) - F_{\tilde{Y}}(y)|\} < 0.0075$ if $N \geq 1474$.

In summary, the larger the N is, the more confidence we can ignore the difference between F_Y and $F_{\tilde{Y}}$. Therefore, with a sufficiently large N, the probability density function f_Y can be well approximated by the probability density function of $f_{\tilde{Y}}$, where $\tilde{Y}$ is bounded subject to $\{y_i\}_1^N$.

By ignoring the difference between F_Y and $F_{\tilde{Y}}$, the sample $\{y_i\}_1^N$ can be considered as a sample from $\tilde{Y}$. Regardless of whether or not Y is bounded, its truncated random variable $\tilde{Y}$ is always bounded. Following the discussion in Section 3, given the masked data $\{y_i^*\}$ of $\{y_i\}$ and an independent sample $\{c_i\}$ from C, where $\{y_i\}$ were masked by C, the probability density function $f_{\tilde{Y}}$ of $\tilde{Y}$ can be well approximated by $f_{\tilde{Y},K|\{y_i^*,c_i\}_1^N}$ subject to appropriate K and N.

Therefore, the **normalized $f_{\tilde{Y},K|\{y_i^*,c_i\}_1^N}$ can be used to approximate the density function of Y subject to appropriate K and N, regardless of Y bounded or not.** From now on, without further explanation, $f_{Y,K|\{y_i^*,c_i\}_1^N}$ means $f_{\tilde{Y},K|\{y_i^*,c_i\}_1^N}$ and "density approximant" means "sample-moment-based density approximant".

5   Simulation Studies on Density Approximant Based on Noise Multiplied Data

In this section, we use simulation examples to demonstrate the performance of the density approximant based on noise multiplied data.

Example 2. Let $Y = I_{(w=0)}Y_1 + I_{(w=1)}Y_2$, where $Y_1 \sim N(30, 4^2)$, $Y_2 \sim N(50, 2^2)$ and w is a Bernoulli distributed random variable with $P(w = 0) = 0.3$. Let $C = I_{(v=0)}C_1 + I_{(v=1)}C_2$ be the multiplicative noise used to mask Y, where v has Bernoulli distribution with $P(v = 0) = 0.6$; $C_1 \sim N(80, 5^2)$ and $C_2 \sim N(100, 3^2)$.

In this example, three issues are investigated/demonstrated. The first issue is the determination of K, such that $f_{Y,K|\{y_i^*,c_i\}_1^N}$ best presents f_Y. For the sake of convenience, this K is called the (optimal) upper order. The second issue is about the fact that the upper order K is related to the sample $\{y_i\}$ and the sample of noise used to yield $\{y_i^*\}$. The last issue is about the impact of the variance of noise on the density approximant.

For the first issue, a sample $\{y_i\}_1^{10000}$ were simulated from Y. Then, use an independent sample from C to mask $\{y_i\}_1^{10000}$ and yield $\{y_i^*\}_1^{10000}$. In Figure 1, to save space, we only report the plots of $f_{Y,K|\{y_i^*,c_i\}_1^N}$ for $K = 5, 10, 11$ and 15. With the reference of the true density function of Y (in solid line), it shows that the plot of the density approximant is improved as K increases up to 10 or 11, then gradually run away from the plot of f_Y. We also evaluated the correlation between f_Y and $f_{Y,K|\{y_i^*,c_i\}_1^N}$ for each K. The correlations corresponding to $K = 5, 10, 11$ and 15 are reported in Table 1. The first row of summary statistics in the table is given by Y. When $K = 10$ or 11 was used in $f_{Y,K|\{y_i^*,c_i\}_1^N}$, the correlation of between $f_{Y,K|\{y_i^*,c_i\}_1^N}$ and f_Y is higher than those when other Ks were used.

The upper order K can be determined by inspecting the plot of f_Y or the correlation between $f_{Y,K|\{y_i^*,c_i\}_1^N}$ and f_Y, given f_Y is available. Using correlation to determine K is more convenient and easy to program.

Although for $K = 5$ and 15, the performance of $f_{Y,K|\{y_i^*,c_i\}_1^N}$ is not as good as those with $K = 10$ and 11, interestedly, the summaries statistics given by those $f_{Y,K|\{y_i^*,c_i\}_1^N}$ in this example are not different too much from the summary statistics given by Y.

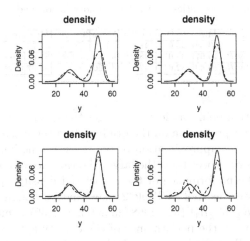

Fig. 1. Left top is for $K = 5$. Right top is for $K = 10$. Left bottom is for $K = 11$ and right bottom is for $K = 15$. The plot of the true density function is in solid line.

Table 1. The summary of statistics and the values of correlation

data source	Min.	1st Qu.	Median	Mean	3rd Qu.	Max.	cor.
y	16.34	33.63	48.83	43.90	50.74	57.70	
$(y^*, K = 5)$	16.34	35.36	47.99	44.00	51.46	55.67	0.9890
$(y^*, K = 10)$	17.80	34.39	48.23	43.88	50.84	57.61	0.9979
$(y^*, K = 11)$	16.51	34.79	48.55	43.94	50.90	56.56	0.9978
$(y^*, K = 15)$	17.07	32.99	47.42	41.72	50.41	57.70	0.9660

For the second issue, two independent samples $\{y_i\}_1^{10000}$ and $\{y_i'\}_1^{10000}$ were simulated from Y. They were independently masked by the noise C. The upper order Ks determined by the two sets of masked data are 10 and 14, respectively (corresponding cor. are 0.9975 and 0.9989, respectively). The plots of the density approximants determined by $\{y_i^*\}_1^{10000}$ and $\{y_i'^*\}_1^{10000}$ based on their own upper order K are given in Figure 3 (in the Appendix B). Both of them well present f_Y. This study shows the upper order K is sample related.

For the third issue, a sample $\{y_i\}_1^{10000}$ were simulated from Y. Two multiplicative noises, $|R_1|$ and $|R_2|$, are considered. $R_1 = I_{(v_1=0)}R_{1,1} + I_{(v1=1)}R_{1,2}$ and $R_2 = I_{(v_2=0)}R_{2,1} + I_{(v2=1)}R_{2,2}$ where v_1 and v_2 are independent and have Bernoulli distributions Bernoulli(0.7) and Bernoulli(0.3), respectively; $R_{1,1}, R_{1,2}$, $R_{2,1}$ and $R_{2,2}$ are independent and have normal distributions $N(100, 5^2)$, $N(150, 3^2)$, $N(100, 25^2)$ and $N(150, 18^2)$, respectively. The standard errors given by the samples from $|R_1|$ and $|R_2|$ are 23.36032 and 32.54968, respectively. The summary statistics and the correlations between f_Y and the density approximant based on their own upper order K are reported in Table 2. The plots of density approximants based on their own upper order K are presented in Figure 4 (in the Appendix B).

Table 2. The summary of statistics, the values of correlation and the upper order K

data source	Min.	1st Qu.	Median	Mean	3rd Qu.	Max.	cor.	K
y	16.34	33.63	48.83	43.90	50.74	57.70		
y masked by R_1	16.67	34.07	48.23	43.84	50.98	57.61	0.9974	8
y masked by R_2	16.43	32.61	47.90	43.66	51.14	55.67	0.9950	7

From data protection point of view, the larger the variance of the multiplicative noise is, the better protection on the original data the noise will provide. In terms of having a better approximation of the density function of the original data, we might guess or expect that, the larger the variance of the multiplicative noise is, the poor the performance of the associated density approximant will have. However, Figure 4 as well as Table 2 show that, although the ratio of the standard errors of $|R_2|$ to $|R_1|$ (32.54968/23.36032 = 1.39) is much larger than 1, the difference between the performance of the density approximant given by the data masked by $|R_1|$ and $|R_2|$, respectively, is not significant. It means that, sometimes, the impact of the variance of noise on the performance of the density approximant might not be significant. It is good in terms of data protection.

6   Real Data Application

In this section, an example of the density approximant based on real life data is presented.

Example 3. A real life data set taken from the United States Energy Information Authority is considered. This data set can be found in the R package *sdcMicro*, and also available from the United States Energy Information Authority website http://www. eia.doe.govcneaf/electricity/page/eia826.html under year 1996. The data set consists 15 variables generally concerning income and sales data and each of them has 4092 observations.

The smoothing density function given by the data of "othrevenue" is skewed to the right. The majority observations of "othrevenue" are less than 10000 and outliers on the right tail are beyond 60000. There are few observations between values 10000 and 60000. To approximate the smoothing density function of "othrevenue" by the approach of density approximant, the density approximant has to take care the outliers on the right tail as well as a few observations in the interval [10000, 60000]. Therefore, the density approximant will shift to the right. If those outliers are removed from the original data set (the number of observations (> 10000) is 96), the density approximant will be more close to the smooting density function given by the original data.

To see the performance of the density approximant, we use two types of noises, a mixture normal noise $C \sim 1/2N(170, 1) + 1/2N(120, 1)$ and an identity noise $C \equiv 1$, respectively, to mask the observations of "othrevenue" and yield two sets of masked data for "othrevenue". The set of masked data given by $C \equiv 1$ is the same as the original data set. We evaluate the density approximants given by the two sets of masked data, respectively. Two scenarios of the sets of original data "othrevenue" are considered. One is the full set of data of "othrevenue" and the other is the subset of data with values > 10000 removed. For each scenario, the plots of density approximant given by the two sets of noise multiplied data are presented in Figure 2, respectively.

When $C \equiv 1$, the data used to evaluate the density approximant of "othrevenue" are the unmasked data of "othrevenue". The plot of the density approximant based on the unmasked data is used as a benchmark as it is the density approximant of the density function of the "othrevenue" without any impacts from additional noise perturbation.

From Figure 2, we find the plot of the density approximant given by the data masked by the mixture normal noise is similar to the one given by $C \equiv 1$. The plot related to the mixture normal noise catched as much information on the

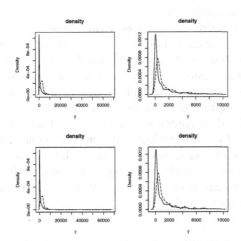

Fig. 2. The density approximants given by data masked by mixture normal distribution and $C \equiv 1$ are shown in the top panels and bottom panels, respectively. For each scenario, the left panel is given by the full data and right one is for data values $\leq$ 10000. The plots of the smoothing density function of "othrevenue" is in solid line.

density function of "othrevenue" as the plot related to $C \equiv 1$ did. Both density approximants shifted to right a bit and showed a fatter tail comparing to the smoothing density function of the original data. The density approximant gives a better approximation to the smoothing density function of the true data after the 96 outliers were removed from the original data set.

The summary statistics given by the density approximants are listed in Table 3 (in the Appendix B). Both of them, with or without noise perturbation, have successfully show the skewness and the main characteristic in the distribution of the data, though the elements of the summaries are not close to those of the summary statistics given by the data of "othrevenue".

7   Discussion

This paper extends the well developed moments-based density approximant approach to the sample-moment-based density approaximant approach based on noised multiplied data.

The motivation of this paper is to develop a fundamental framework for estimating the density function of a sensitive random variable without accessing the original observations of the variable. This work has direct applications to confidential data analysis.

The aim of this paper is to prove and demonstrate that, regardless of a negligible probability, the sample-moment-based density approaximant is able to well present its associated density function if the size of the sample from the underlying variable is reasonably large.

The method proposed is developed for univariate density functions. It can be developed for multivariate density functions if the approach of high dimension Legendre polynomial is considered.

With the density function of the underlying variable Y as a reference, we demonstrated that an (optimal) upper order K can be determined such that the sample-moment-based density approaximant is close to the density function f_Y. However, if Y is a sensitive variable and it observations are confidential, the information of f_Y will be unavailable in practice. It is of interest how the upper order K can be determined. We have developed a statistical computation searching technique for determining upper order K without the reference of the true density function of the underlying confidential variable. The technique and applications will be discussed in another paper. The method proposed in this paper is developed based on and applies to continuous random variables. The technique can apply to categorical data for approximating mass function and will be presented in another paper.

Acknowledgments. I would like to thank my colleague Dr Gulati for the carefully reading and helpful comments on the early version of this manuscript.

References

1. Duncan, G.T., Lambert, D.: Disclosure limited data dissemination (with comment). Journal of the American Statistical Association 81, 1–28 (1986)
2. Duncan, G.T., Lambert, D.: The risk of disclosure for microdata. Journal of Business and Economic Statistics 7, 207–217 (1989)
3. Evans, T.: Effects on Trend Statistics of the Use of Multiplicative Noise for Disclosure Limitation, US Bureau of the Census (1996), http://www.census.gov/srd/sdc/papers.html (accessed December 5, 2008)
4. Evans, T., Zayatz, L., Slanta, J.: Using Noise for Disclosure Limitation of Establishment Tabular Data. Journal of Official Statistics 14, 537–551 (1998)
5. Hwang, J.T.: Multiplicative errors-in-variables models with applications to recent data released by the U.S. Department of Energy. Journal of the American Statistical Association 81, 680–688 (1986)
6. Kim, J.J., Winkler, W.E.: Multiplicative Noise for Masking Continuous Data, Research Report Series (Statistics ♯2003-01), Statistical Research Division, U.S. Bureau of the Census, Washington D.C. 20233 (2003)
7. Kim, J.J., Jeong, D.M.: Truncated triangular distribution for multiplicative noise and domain estimation, Section on Government Statistics - JSM 2008, pp. 1023–1030 (2008)
8. Klein, M., Sinha, B.: Statistical analysis of noise-multiplied data using multiple imputation. Journal of Official Statistics 29, 425–465 (2013)
9. Krisinich, F., Piesse, A.: Multiplicative Microdata Noise for Confidentialising Tables of Business Data: Application to AES99, Data with a Comparison to Cell Suppression, Research and Analytical Report 2002 #19, Statistics New Zealand (2002)
10. Lin, Y.-X., Wise, P.: Estimation of regression parameters from noise multiplied data. Journal of Privacy and Confidentiality 4, 55–88 (2012)
11. Mood, A.M., Graybill, F.A., Boes, D.C.: Introduction to the Theory of Statistics. McGraw-Hill, Singapore (1963)
12. Nayak, T.K., Sinha, B., Zayatz, L.: Statistical properties of multiplicative noise masking for confidentiality protection. Journal of Official Statistics 27, 527–544 (2011)
13. Oganian, A.: Multiplicative noise protocols. In: Domingo-Ferrer, J., Magkos, E. (eds.) PSD 2010. LNCS, vol. 6344, pp. 107–117. Springer, Heidelberg (2010)
14. Provost, S.B.: Moment-Based Density Approximants. The Mathematica Journal 9, 728–756 (2005)
15. Shlomo, N.: Releasing Microdata: Disclosure Risk Estimation, Data Masking and Assessing Utility. Journal of Privacy and Confidentiality 2, 73–91 (2010)
16. Sinha, B., Nayak, T.K., Zayatz, L.: Privacy protection and quantile estimation from noise multiplied data. Sankhya B 73, 297–315 (2011)
17. Willenborg, L., de Waal, T.: Elements of Statistical Disclosure Control. Lecture Notes in Statistics, vol. 155. Springer, New York (2001)

Appendix A: The proof of Lemmas 1 and 2

The proof of Lemma 1

Let $Y_1, \cdots, Y_N$ be i.i.d random variables on $(\Omega, \mathcal{F}, \mathcal{P})$ and have the same probability distribution as Y.

For each $\omega \in \Omega$, define $g_i(\omega) = P(Y \leq Y_i(\omega))$. Random variables $\{g_i\}$ are i.i.d. and have uniform distribution $U(0,1)$.

For each $\omega \in \Omega$,

$$g_{max}(Y_1(\omega), \cdots, Y_N(\omega)) = P(Y < \max_{1 \leq i \leq N} \{Y_i(\omega)\})$$

$$= \max_{1 \leq i \leq N} P(Y \leq Y_i(\omega)) = \max_{1 \leq i \leq N} g_i(\omega).$$

Therefore, $g_{max}(Y_1, Y2, \cdots, Y_N) = g_{(N)}$ the Nth order statistics of $\{g_i\}$, and

$$P(g_{max}(Y_1, \cdots, Y_N) \leq a) = P(g_{(N)} \leq a) = a^N.$$

Following the similar argument, we have

$$P(g_{min}(Y_1, \cdots, Y_N) \leq a) = P(g_{(1)} \leq a) = 1 - (1 - a)^N,$$

where $g_{(1)}$ is the 1st order statistics of $\{g_i\}$.

The proof of Lemma 2

If we wish to have probability at least p to ensure $P(Y \leq \min_{1 \leq i \leq N} \{y_i\}) \leq \alpha/2$ (probability at least p to ensure $P(Y > \max_{1 \leq i \leq N} \{y_i\}) < \alpha/2)$), i.e. $P(g_{min}^{(N)} \leq \alpha/2) \geq p$ (i.e. $P(g_{max}^{(N)} > 1 - \alpha/2) > p$), the sufficient condition is that the sample size N meets the following inequality

$$\int_0^{\alpha/2} N(1-a)^{N-1} da = (1 - (1 - \alpha/2)^N) \geq p,$$

$$\left(\int_{1-\alpha/2}^1 Na^{N-1} da = (1 - (1 - \alpha/2)^N \geq p \right)$$

i.e.

$$N \geq \log(1-p)/\log(1 - \alpha/2).$$

Appendix B: Figures

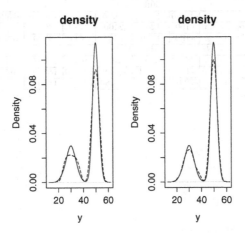

Fig. 3. The left panel is for sample one with $K = 10$ and the right one is for sample two with $K = 14$. The plots of f_Y and density approximant are in solid line and dashed lines, respectively.

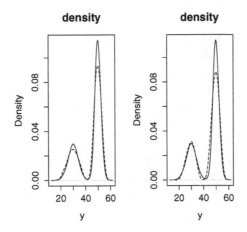

Fig. 4. The density approximant based on the data masked by R_1 is in the left panel and the other one is in the right panel. The plots of f_Y and density approximant are in solid line and dashed lines, respectively.

Table 3. Real data study: the summary of statistics, the values of correlation and the optimal order K

data source	Min.	1st Qu.	Median	Mean	3rd Qu.	Max.	cor.	K
Full Data								
y	-190.0	55.0	255.5	1647.0	1365.0	67520.0		
y masked by mixture normal	-190	1267	2460	3789	3520	64730	0.9583	24
y masked by $C \equiv 1$	-190	1400	2460	3611	3520	67380	0.9810	17
Subset Data								
y	-190.0	53.0	239	995	1187	9853		
y masked by mixture normal	-190	360.3	674.8	1458.0	1874.0	9853	0.9941	48
y masked by $C \equiv 1$	-72.08	380	674.80	1460.0	1834.0	9853	0.9941	22

Reverse Mapping to Preserve the Marginal Distributions of Attributes in Masked Microdata

Krishnamurty Muralidhar[1], Rathindra Sarathy[2], and Josep Domingo-Ferrer[3]

[1] Visiting Professor, Price College of Business, University of Oklahoma, Norman, OK, USA
krishm@OU.edu
[2] Ardmore Chair and Professor of Information Systems, Spears College of Business,
Oklahoma State University, Stillwater, OK, USA
rathin.sarathy@okstate.edu
[3] UNESCO Chair in Data Privacy, Dept. of Computer Engineering and Maths,
Universitat Rovira i Virgili, Tarragona, Catalonia
josep.domingo@urv.cat

Abstract. In this paper we describe a new procedure that is capable of ensuring that the marginal distributions of attributes in microdata masked with a masking mechanism end up being the same as the marginal distributions of attributes in the original data. We illustrate the application of the new procedure using several commonly used masking mechanisms.

Keywords: Data masking, marginal distribution, reverse mapping.

1   Introduction

Releasing masked microdata in place of sensitive data for the purposes of aggregate analysis has received considerable attention in the literature. Hundepool et al [8] provide a comprehensive discussion of the different masking mechanisms that can be used for generating the masked microdata. The masking mechanisms can be classified based on many criteria. For the purposes of this study, we consider in particular classification, namely, whether the marginal distribution of the output (the masked microdata) is exactly the same as the marginal distribution of the input (the original data). Most of the masking mechanisms currently available (such as additive noise, multiplicative noise, and microaggregation) modify the marginal distribution of the attributes they mask. There are only a few mechanisms (data swapping, data shuffling, and log-linear models) capable of preserving the marginal distributions of the masked attributes to be exactly the same as those of the original attributes.

The modification in the marginal distributions of the masked attributes is, in most cases, caused by the masking mechanism modifying the values of attributes in the original data. With some masking procedures, the masked attributes have a completely different marginal distribution compared to the original attributes. Other masking procedures are capable of asymptotically (but not exactly) preserving the marginal distributions of the original attributes. For the purposes of this study, we do not

J. Domingo-Ferrer (Ed.): PSD 2014, LNCS 8744, pp. 105–116, 2014.

distinguish between the two, because our objective is that the marginal distribution of the masked data be exactly the same as that of the original data.

The above requirement may seem extremely stringent, but there is a good reason for it. In many cases, users are reluctant to use data that has been modified. When discussing noise addition, a Census Bureau researcher made the observation that "users have found this extremely irritating and unacceptable" [14]. Raghunathan et al [12] describe the reaction of the users in the following manner: "Could we seriously propose spending time analyzing completely 'fake' data?" Privacy experts often argue that such users are misinformed and that the data is not fake; it has been modified to protect the sensitive information and preserves many of the statistical properties of the original data. With very knowledgeable users, this argument is convincing. However, for a vast majority of the users, this argument carries little weight. In their opinion, modifying the data is the equivalent of fake data. It is of little consequence whether the users are right or wrong. If users perceive the modified data as fake and are reluctant to use it, then the very purpose of providing masked microdata becomes pointless.

Data administrators have the option to not inform users that the data has been modified. This may not be possible if the data administrator is required to provide users with information about the fact that the released data is not the true data. This is particularly true for government agencies that release data; they may be required, legally, to inform users that the data has been masked even if they do not provide the details of the masking. Even if not telling users that the data has been masked was allowed, it presents several practical problems. With many masking mechanisms, in order to reach valid inferences using the masked data, it may be necessary to perform additional processing to compensate the bias of the results obtained from analyzing the masked data as if it were the original data [12]. If the users are not informed about the modification, they will not be able to reach proper statistical inferences. In addition, there is a real danger that the fact that the data has been modified becomes known, hence resulting in users distrusting all data from this source.

It is interesting to note that users do not react in the same manner to all masking mechanisms. Users *seem* to be less reluctant to use the data when agencies use data swapping, even though data swapping is perturbative (that is, it involves the modification of the original values of a particular record) [4]. However, while data swapping is simple and offers the ability to maintain the marginal distribution, it may not satisfy other analytical validity and/or disclosure risk requirements [5, 9, 10]. Hence, there is a need to develop new procedures that are capable of maintaining the marginal distribution while providing the data administrator with the flexibility to choose the appropriate masking mechanism. The objective of this study is to describe a simple, general post-masking procedure that maps the masked values to a permutation of the original values, regardless of the underlying masking mechanism adopted.

2   Data Swapping

Data swapping involves exchanging values of the original attribute between records that lie within the proximity specified by the data administrator [9, 10, 11]. For numerical attributes, the proximity is usually represented by the rank of the value for a particular record. Experience seems to suggest that data swapping is more palatable to users than other forms of masking. So how can we explain the difference in the responses to data swapping and other methods?

We believe that the primary reason is that even though the attribute values of records have been exchanged, the actual values themselves are unmodified.[1] In other words, data swapping does not involve the modifying the actual values that existed in the original data. Hence, the collection of values of each original attribute remains unmodified, even it may have been permuted among records, that is, data swapping ensures that the marginal distribution of the masked attribute is exactly the same as that of the original attribute. It also allows the data administrator to provide a simple explanation of the masking mechanism as follows:

> In order to protect privacy, the values of some records may have been exchanged with other records.

This is a simple explanation that is understood by most users, which is in contrast to other procedures. We believe that these are keys to user acceptance of data swapping and reluctance (and in some cases, outright rejection) of other masking mechanisms.

Based on the above argument, the solution seems relatively straightforward and simple ... always use data swapping. It is true that this is likely to result in high user acceptance and probably explains the popularity of data swapping as a masking mechanism. This is an acceptable solution if user acceptance is the only criterion. This is not the case. When releasing microdata, data administrators have to consider multiple criteria. In addition to user acceptance, data administrators must also ensure that the released masked microdata provides high analytical validity and low disclosure risk.

The relative importance of these three criteria (analytical validity, disclosure risk, and user acceptance) may vary depending on the context. But it is unlikely that analytical validity and disclosure risk can be completely ignored. After all, if disclosure risk is irrelevant, then the data administrator can simply release the original data; and if analytical validity is irrelevant, then the data administrator can simply release randomly sorted data (or encrypted data or no data at all). Either of these situations is extremely unlikely in practice. In most real life situations, the data administrator would have to select a masking mechanism that ensures an adequate level of analytical validity, disclosure risk prevention, and user acceptance.

Unfortunately, while data swapping may promote user acceptance, it does not always provide the desired levels of analytical validity and disclosure risk prevention. Prior research indicates that data swapping always results in attenuating the relationship between attributes [5, 9, 10]. This attenuation is directly related to the proximity of the swapped data; as the distance between the swapped records increases, the attenuation of the relationship between the attributes also increases. The situation is the opposite if we consider disclosure risk. When the swapped records are in close proximity, there is a very high risk of disclosure. In order to provide adequate disclosure

---

[1] Data swapping is one of the earliest masking mechanisms and has been frequently implemented by agencies over the years. One of the reviewers suggested that data swapping is accepted because users have become accustomed to data swapping. We agree that this is also a viable explanation.

risk prevention, it may be necessary to increase the proximity of the swapped records, which results in poor analytical validity. In evaluating a select group of masking mechanisms, Domingo-Ferrer and Torra [5] found that the information loss characteristics of data swapping fell in the lower half of the 100+ alternative mechanisms evaluated. And in terms of disclosure risk prevention, there is considerable evidence to suggest data swapping performs poorly [10, 11]. Nin et al [11] also point to the disturbing possibility that complete disclosure of a masked record is also possible, which Domingo-Ferrer and Torra [5] also acknowledge. Thus, while data swapping may have a higher level of user acceptance, compared to other masking mechanisms, it may also have lower analytical validity and/or higher disclosure risk.

The above discussion indicates the need for a masking mechanism that provides superior analytical validity and/or lower disclosure risk but also provides the intuitively appealing characteristic of data swapping: an unmodified marginal distribution. In this study, we describe a simple, general approach by which the values of each attribute of the masked data can be reverse-mapped to a permutation of the original attribute values; in this way, the masked data has the same marginal distributions as the original data. It is important to note that we are not proposing a new masking method. We wish to provide the data administrator with the flexibility to choose a data masking mechanism that suits the particular context.

3   Post-masking Reverse Mapping

The statement of the problem is straightforward. The data administrator chooses a masking mechanism and uses it to obtain a masked version of the original sensitive data set. Masking can operate on the quasi-identifier attributes to prevent identity disclosure (which would happen if quasi-identifiers allowed an intruder to link a record with an identified record in an external data source), or it can operate on sensitive attributes to prevent attribute disclosure (records linkage is not prevented, but the sensitive attributes are masked) or it can operate on all attributes.

The data administrator now seeks a transformation of the masked data such that each attribute in the transformed masked data (which will be released to the public) has exactly the same marginal distribution as the corresponding attribute in the original data. The data administrator can attempt statistical transformations [13] but such transformations do not guarantee that the transformed data will have exactly the same marginal distributions as the original data.

In this study we propose a simple transformation of the masked attribute values to a permutation of the original attribute values using rank-based reverse mapping. The advantage of this approach is that it maintains the masking (which is necessary to prevent disclosure risk) but also allows preserving the marginal distributions (which facilitates user acceptance). Let $X = \{x_1, x_2, ..., x_n\}$ be the values taken by attribute X in the original data set. Let $Y = \{y_1, y_2, ..., y_n\}$ represent the masked version of X. We make no assumptions about the masking mechanism used to generate Y except that it must be possible to link a single record in Y to a single record in X.

The post-masking reverse mapping is performed as follows:

$For\ i\ =\ 1\ to\ n$
$Compute\ j\ =\ Rank(y_i)$
     $Set\ z_i\ =\ x_{(j)}\ (where\ x_{(j)}\ is\ the\ value\ of\ X\ of\ rank\ j)$
$Repeat$
$Release\ Z\ =\ \{z_1, z_2, ..., z_n\}$

It is easy to see that Z has exactly the same values and hence the same marginal distribution as X, but values have been permuted according to the (rank) order of the masked values Y. The extension of the reverse mapping to the multivariate case does not present a problem – simply repeat the process for every masked attribute. Since the objective is to maintain the marginal distribution of the individual attributes, application of the procedure on an attribute-by-attribute basis has no effect on the outcome.

From a statistical perspective, the reverse mapping procedure can be described as the rank based mapping of the cumulative distribution function of the masked values Y back to the cumulative distribution function of the confidential values X. The concept of copulas in statistical analysis is based on a similar transformation [15]. However, copulas are often used to model the joint distribution of attributes with different marginal distributions. The reverse mapping procedure we describe is a univariate one (where each attribute is reverse-mapped individually) and no effort is made to model the joint distribution of the attributes. Hence, the only property that is maintained is that the rank of Z is the same as that of Y and, unlike copulas, no claims regarding the joint distribution of the attributes can be made. The reverse mapping procedure is also similar to the "Normal to Anything" procedure used to generate related random attributes with different marginal distributions [1, 2].

The extent to which the data administrator wishes to provide information additional to Z would depend on the context. The data administrator may also provide information on the process used to mask the data and extent of the changes. The release of this information would depend, however, on the extent to which the release of this information would affect disclosure risk. Note, for example, that if the masking method deterministically generates Y from X, e.g. $Y = f(X)$, and the administrator publishes Y and the (parameterized) masking method $f()$, then any intruder can compute $Y_{permuted} = f(Z)$; since the permutation that transforms $Y_{permuted}$ into Y is the same that transforms Z into X, the intruder can recover the original X (if there are ties in Y, though, the intruder might not be able to unequivocally determine all values $x_1, x_2, ..., x_n$).

We now illustrate the application of this procedure using a small data set consisting of 25 observations and two attributes: a non-sensitive attribute S and a sensitive attribute X that is to be masked. As mentioned above, we make no assumptions about the masking mechanism other than that the *data protector* must be able to link records in X and Y.

Table 1 shows that the marginal distribution of Z is the same as that of X, because Z has the same set of values as X, but re-ordered according to the ranks of Y.. As discussed earlier, the specific masking mechanism used to generate Y is irrelevant for the purposes of reverse mapping. Consider the first observation. In this observation, the original attribute X takes value 780, the masked attribute Y takes value 817.53, and the reverse mapping yields a value of 819. The large change between the values of X and Y is reflected in a large change in the corresponding ranks (from 23 in X to 13 in Y). For some observations (ID = 3, 6, 9, 24, 25) the ranks of X and Y are the same.

Table 1. Example illustrating the implementation of reverse mapping

ID	S	Rank of S	X	Rank of X	Y	Rank of Y	Z
1	72	1	780	1	817.5	2	819
2	73	2	819	2	786.8	1	780
3	90	7	889	3	856.1	3	889
4	89	6	906	4	960.6	7	921
5	80	3	908	5	881.3	4	906
6	95	9	912	6	958.1	6	912
7	110	18	921	7	993.1	12	1003
8	94	8	934	8	974.8	11	979
9	100	13	963	9	970.1	9	963
10	97	11	974	10	939.4	5	908
11	114	20	979	11	969.5	8	934
12	96	10	1003	12	1107.9	20	1091
13	87	5	1015	13	1111.0	21	1096
14	98	12	1018	14	971.8	10	974
15	84	4	1032	15	1069.5	17	1065
16	112	19	1035	16	1068.1	16	1035
17	133	25	1065	17	1053.4	15	1032
18	109	17	1070	18	1102.8	19	1073
19	108	16	1073	19	1111.9	22	1110
20	121	23	1091	20	1027.4	14	1018
21	102	14	1096	21	1074.1	18	1070
22	131	24	1110	22	1190.9	23	1122
23	104	15	1122	23	1023.6	13	1015
24	116	21	1144	24	1215.2	24	1144
25	119	22	1177	25	1253.9	25	1177

One potential issue that could pose a problem is observations that have tied ranks, particularly when X is a discrete attribute. Tied ranks could also arise in the masked values Y as a result of the masking mechanism. For example, applying univariate microaggregation or generalization could result in tied masked values. There is a simple solution to this situation. Any ties in the original data and/or the masked data are broken randomly. With large data sets, breaking ties randomly will have little or no impact on the procedure, as long as the number of records sharing a certain value is small compared to the number of records in the data set.

In some cases, releasing a permutation of the original attribute values may still be disclosive: e.g., in a data set on a town's population, releasing the highest value of

"Income" reveals the income of the wealthiest person in town, whose identity is easy to guess regardless of the permutation. Hence, statistical agencies may need further measures to prevent disclosure. These include top and bottom coding, rounding, and other similar procedures. These procedures can be implemented on the reverse-mapped attributes exactly as they would for the original attributes.

Finally, the reverse mapping procedure could also be adopted for categorical attributes. Recently, Domingo-Ferrer et al [6] proposed a procedure for numerical mapping of nominal attributes that captures and quantifies their underlying structure (specifically, the hierarchical structure that is often present in nominal classification schemes). This procedure provides the ability to quantify any nominal attribute and, once quantified, the reverse mapping procedure can be applied to such data.

4   Assessing Disclosure Risk and Information Loss

Apart from the fact that the reverse mapping procedure results in the marginal distributions of the original and masked attributes being identical, it also offers another important advantage for data administrators. In Table 1, we have presented the values (Y) resulting from masking the sensitive values (X). Assume that the data administrator wishes to compare the results of this masking procedure with an alternative procedure and assume that the alternative procedure results in a different set of values (Y^*). In most cases, the distribution of Y is different from the distribution of Y^*. This makes evaluation of information loss and disclosure risk difficult, since the data administrator is comparing two different sets of values. However, assume that the values of Y, Y^* have also been reverse-mapped to yield Z, Z^*, respectively. The distributions of Z and Z^* are identical, which allows the data administrator to make a more meaningful comparison of the performance of the two methods.

Consider r_{xz} the rank order correlation between (X, Z). For the purposes of this analysis, and without loss of generality, we will assume r_{xz} to be non-negative and hence $0 \leq r_{xz} \leq 1$. Having $r_{xz} = 0$ implies that Z and X are completely unrelated. For large data sets, the situation $r_{xz} = 0$ can be reached by randomly sorting the values in X to obtain Z. This setting offers the highest level of protection against disclosure risk. Similarly, $r_{xz} = 1$ implies that knowledge of Z results in complete disclosure of X. Thus, r_{xz} represents a simple measure of disclosure risk – the higher the value of r_{xz}, the greater the disclosure risk. It is important to note that the rank order correlation is a superior measure compared to product moment correlation since rank order correlation measures all monotonic relationships (including linear ones), but product moment correlation measures only linear relationships.

Similar to disclosure risk, we can assess the information loss in the relationship between attributes by considering the rank order correlation of the attributes in the released data set compared to the rank order correlation in the original data set. For the illustration provided in Table 1, let r_{sx} and r_{sz} represent the rank order correlation between (S, X) and (S, Z), respectively. The difference between the two rank order correlations represents a simple measure of the information loss resulting from masking the data. When there are multiple non-masked and/or masked attributes in the released data set, the data administrator will consider the pair-wise rank order correlation (1) between all pairs composed of non-masked and a masked attribute, and

(2) between all pairs of masked attributes. Such correlations will be compared with the rank order correlations between the corresponding pairs of attributes in the original data set. This provides a simple versatile approach for assessing the information loss in the relationship among attributes.

It should be noted that we do not preclude the use of alternative measures of disclosure risk and information loss measures. Since the reverse-mapped values are the same across all mechanisms, we are comparing "apples versus apples" rather than "apples versus pears."

5   Comparison of Masking Mechanisms

In this section, we apply reverse mapping to the output of several masking mechanisms to illustrate the procedure as well as to provide a simple comparison of releasing the masked data versus releasing data that is reverse-mapped after masking, using the data in Table 1. We consider four alternative approaches for masking the data: (1) Additive noise (ADD) with noise from a normal distribution with mean zero and variance equal to 25% of the variance of X, (2) A partially synthetic data (SYN) procedure suggested by Drechsler et al. [7], generating the masked values Y using the posterior predictive distribution $f(X|S)$, (3) Microaggregation (MIC) with $k = 5$, and (4) Data swapping (SWP) with rank proximity = 5.

Table 2 provides the original data, reverse-mapped data for all four methods, and the masked data Y for the first three masking procedures (since swapping directly results in Z). The idea of masking mechanisms providing different permutations of the original values is illustrated by the X column and the Z columns of the four different masking mechanisms. The only difference between the four Z columns is the way values are permuted. Evaluation of the masking mechanism can be performed (as we illustrate below) by evaluating only the output (Z) and without any consideration of the parameters of the masking mechanism.

Prior to discussing the performance characteristics of the different masking mechanisms, we briefly address the results of the reverse-mapped microaggregation procedure. In the traditional univariate microaggregation, the values of all records within a single aggregated group are set to the mean of their values. For instance, records {1-5} form one aggregated group. The mean value of X in this group is 860.4 and hence the value of all five of these records is set to 860.4 (see last column MIC Y in Table 2). This presents a problem since there are only five unique values in the entire data set instead of the original 25. This aggregation also results in variance attenuation, that is, the variance of Y (9246.06) is much smaller than the variance of X (10223.51).

When reverse mapping is performed, ties are broken randomly, and the values of X are reverse-mapped based on the values of Y. This is the equivalent of *randomly permuting* the values within each of the aggregated groups and releasing the result. The reverse mapping eliminates the presence of k records with the same values and the subsequent variance attenuation; in fact, it is an alternative to other variance restoration approaches for microaggregation, like [3] (which uses synthetic values rather than a permutation of original values). We believe that the reverse mapping procedure is consistent with the original intent of microaggregation – that values within the aggregated groups should be indistinguishable. Since the values within any aggregated group are completely random, the reverse mapping procedure achieves this objective. This is consistent with the notion of probabilistic k-anonymity [16], which can be attained when multivariate microaggregation with group size k is applied to the set of quasi-identifier attributes and reverse mapping is then used on the microaggregated values of each quasi-identifier attribute.

Table 2. Results of masking and reverse mapping for all masking mechanisms

ID	S	X	ADD Z	SYN Z	MIC Z	SWP Z	ADD Y	SYN Y	MIC Y
1	72	780	780	819	908	908	688.7	826.6	860.4
2	73	819	912	912	906	906	928.7	930.3	860.4
3	90	889	819	934	819	921	863.6	940.5	860.4
4	89	906	889	1035	889	819	875.4	1015.2	860.4
5	80	908	906	906	780	780	886.0	882.3	860.4
6	95	912	934	1018	963	974	953.6	1005.5	940.8
7	110	921	908	1015	921	889	908.6	986.2	940.8
8	94	934	979	780	934	963	991.3	789.4	940.8
9	100	963	1032	1096	974	934	1031.1	1035.2	940.8
10	97	974	1015	908	912	912	1018.4	886.7	940.8
11	114	979	1035	1065	979	1018	1031.9	1019.5	1009.4
12	96	1003	963	963	1003	1035	976.3	944.6	1009.4
13	87	1015	921	974	1032	1065	940.2	970.9	1009.4
14	98	1018	1018	889	1018	979	1027.9	879.1	1009.4
15	84	1032	974	1032	1015	1070	982.2	1007.6	1009.4
16	112	1035	1110	979	1070	1003	1103.8	978.1	1066.8
17	133	1065	1065	1144	1035	1015	1046.0	1214.2	1066.8
18	109	1070	1122	1003	1073	1032	1105.3	985.0	1066.8
19	108	1073	1144	1070	1091	1110	1119.2	1026.0	1066.8
20	121	1091	1003	1122	1065	1177	1017.2	1104.3	1066.8
21	102	1096	1070	1091	1177	1122	1051.9	1033.7	1129.8
22	131	1110	1073	1177	1122	1073	1074.1	1251.9	1129.8
23	104	1122	1096	921	1144	1096	1086.0	935.3	1129.8
24	116	1144	1091	1073	1110	1144	1081.9	1031.5	1129.8
25	119	1177	1177	1110	1096	1091	1174.4	1071.5	1129.8

Table 3. Disclosure risk measures for the four masking mechanisms

	ADD Z	SYN Z	MIC Z	SWP Z
Rank order correlation between X and	0.860	0.577	0.952	0.892

Table 3 provides a disclosure risk assessment based on the correlation between X and Z for each of the masking methods. Of the four mechanisms, SYN has the lowest correlation with the original attribute and hence provides the lowest disclosure risk. Microaggregated values have the highest correlation with the original attribute and hence, the highest disclosure risk (this is consistent with Domingo-Ferrer and Torra pointing out in [5] that *univariate* microaggregation offers little disclosure protection). Additive noise and swapping have lower correlation (and lower disclosure risk) than microaggregation. The disclosure risk of the synthetic sample is significantly lower than that of the other three methods. It is important to note that we made no effort to fine tune the parameters of the masking mechanisms so that they provide comparable disclosure risk. The information in Table 3 allows the data administrator to perform such an analysis (such as increasing the value of k so that the disclosure risk resulting from microaggregation is comparable to the others).

Table 4. Information loss for the four masking mechanisms

	X	ADD Z	SYN Z	MIC Z	SWP Z
Rank order correlation between S and	0.742	0.738	0.710	0.682	0.568

Table 4 provides an assessment of information loss, the rank order correlation between the non-sensitive attribute S and X compared to that between S and each of the masked data. Of the four approaches, additive noise is best at preserving the correlation with the non-masked attribute followed by synthetic data, microaggregation, and swapping. It is important to note that this is only an illustration and it is possible that a different set of pseudorandom numbers could produce different results. The performance of swapping is rather poor – it results in the highest information loss and also results in high disclosure risk. By contrast, the synthetic data easily yields the best performance – extremely low disclosure risk *and* information loss, which is essentially guaranteed by the underlying model used to generate the masked values. Comparing the results of the masked values and the reverse-mapped values indicates that the reverse mapping process does not have a meaningful impact on information loss. Given that this is a small data set, this result is encouraging.

Table 5 presents the actual change in ranks between the original and masked data. As expected, for both swapping (rank proximity = 5) and microaggregation ($k = 5$), the change in rank is less than or equal to 5. Synthetic data results in the highest change in ranks – in one case as high as 16 (record ID = 2). And only the synthetic data has (four) records whose change in ranks is higher than 10. But the results for the synthetic data should not be surprising; the specific purpose of generating the masked value from the posterior predictive distribution is to minimize disclosure risk. The large change in the ranks ensures low disclosure risk. Finally, the objective of this analysis is not to highlight the merits or any particular masking mechanism, but to show that the reverse mapping procedure performs effectively and facilitates an easy comparison of the masking mechanisms.

Table 5. Change in rank for each of the masking mechanisms

Change In Rank	ADD	SYN	MIC	SWP
0	4	1	5	1
1	3	4	8	2
2	3	0	5	4
3	5	5	2	6
4	2	1	5	10
5	4	4	0	2
6 – 10	4	6	0	0
11 – 15	0	3	0	0
16 – 20	0	1	0	0

6   Conclusions and Future Work

The objective of this study was to investigate a new procedure that ensures that the marginal distributions of the masked attributes are the same as those of the corresponding original attributes. We present a post-masking method based on mapping the cumulative distribution function of each masked attribute back to the cumulative distribution function of the corresponding original attribute based on ranks. We refer to this post-masking method as reverse mapping and we have illustrated it using simple examples.

Reverse mapping also allows viewing microdata masking mechanisms in a new framework, namely, one in which the output from *any* masking mechanism applied to an original attribute is simply regarded as a particular permutation of the values of the original attribute. By providing a common ground for all masking mechanisms, we improve the data administrator's ability to perform more meaningful comparisons of masking mechanisms. We also hope that this framework will allow researchers to find potential links between masking mechanisms that may have been considered disparate thus far.

The results presented in this study are illustrative and preliminary. A comprehensive investigation of the impact of reverse mapping on masking is currently being conducted by these authors. Specifically, there are many issues that require further investigation, including : (1) Impact of the size of the data set; (2) Impact of the characteristics of the data set; (3) Incremental disclosure risk (if any) resulting from the reverse mapping; (4) More extensive general analysis of disclosure risk and information loss; (5) Use of reverse mapping with masking methods (e.g. synthetic methods) in which the number of output masked values differs from the number of input original values; and (6) Impact of reverse mapping on privacy models, that is, what privacy models can be satisfied by reverse-mapped masked data (we have already indicated that reverse-mapped microaggregated data can satisfy probabilistic k-anonymity).

References

1. Cario, M.C., Nelson, B.L.: Modeling and Generating Random Vectors with arbitrary Marginal Distributions and Correlation Matrix. Department of Industrial Engineering and Management Sciences, Northwestern University, Evanston, IL (1997)
2. Chen, H.: Initialization for NORTA: Generation of Random Vectors with Specified Marginals and Correlations. INFORMS Journal on Computing 13, 312–331 (2001)
3. Domingo-Ferrer, J.: Non-Perturbative Masking Methods. In: Liu, L., Ozsu, M.T. (eds.) Encyclopedia of Database Systems, pp. 1912–1913. Springer, US (2009)
4. Domingo-Ferrer, J., González-Nicolás, U.: Hybrid Microdata Using Microaggregation. Information Science 180, 2834–2844 (2010)
5. Domingo-Ferrer, J., Torra, V.: A Quantitative Comparison of Disclosure Control Methods for Microdata. In: Doyle, P., Lane, J.I., Theeuwes, J.J.M., Zayatz, L.V. (eds.) Confidentiality, Disclosure, and Data Access: Theory and Practical Applications for Statistical Agencies, pp. 111–133. Elsevier, Amsterdam (2001)
6. Domingo-Ferrer, J., Sanchez, D., Rufian-Torrell, G.: Anonymization of Nominal Data Based on Semantic Marginality. Information Science 242, 35–48 (2013)
7. Drechsler, J., Bender, S., Rassler, S.: Comparing Fully and Partially Synthetic Datasets for Statistical Disclosure Control in the German IAB Establishment Panel. Transactions on Data Privacy 1, 105–130 (2008)
8. Hundepool, A., Domingo-Ferrer, J., Franconi, L., Giessing, S., Nordholt, E.S., Spicer, K., de Wolf, P.-P.: Statistical Disclosure Control. John Wiley & Sons, West Sussex (2012)
9. Moore, R.A.: Controlled Data Swapping for Masking Public Use Microdata Sets. Washington DC: Research report series (RR96/04), Statistical Research Division, US Census Bureau (1996)
10. Muralidhar, K., Sarathy, R.: Data Shuffling: A New Masking Approach for Numerical Data. Management Scienc 52, 658–670 (2006)
11. Nin, J., Herranz, J., Torra, V.: Rethinking Rank Swapping to Decrease Disclosure Risk. Data & Knowledge Engineering 64, 346–364 (2008)
12. Raghunathan, T.E., Reiter, J.P., Rubin, D.B.: Multiple Imputation for Statistical Disclosure Limitation. Journal of Official Statistics 19, 1–16 (2003)
13. Sebé, F., Domingo-Ferrer, J., Mateo-Sanz, J.M., Torra, V.: Post-Masking Optimization of the Tradeoff between Information Loss and Disclosure Risk in Masked Microdata. In: Domingo-Ferrer, J. (ed.) Inference Control in Statistical Databases, pp. 163–171. Springer, Heidelberg (2002)
14. Simpson, G.R.: The 2000 Count: Bureau Blurs Data to Keep Names Confidential. Wall Street Journal 14, B1–B2 (2001)
15. Sklar, A.: Fonctions de répartition à n dimensions et leurs marges. Publications de l'Institut de Statistique de L'Université de Paris 8, 229–231 (1959)
16. Soria-Comas, J., Domingo-Ferrer, J.: Probabilistic k-anonymity through microaggregation and data swapping. In: IEEE International Conference on Fuzzy Systems, pp. 1–8. IEEE, Brisbane (2012)

JPEG-Based Microdata Protection

Javier Jiménez[1], Guillermo Navarro-Arribas[2], and Vicenç Torra[1]

[1] IIIA-CSIC, Artificial Intelligence Research Institute,
Spanish National Research Council, Spain
[2] DEIC-UAB, Dep. of Information Engineering and Communications,
Universitat Autònoma de Barcelona, Spain

Abstract. JPEG-based protections can be obtained by regarding microdata as an image that is transformed by means of a lossy JPEG compression-decompression process. Here we propose a general model that decouples JPEG-based methods into two parts. First part encompasses transformations between data and image spaces. Second part consists in the image transformation itself. Under this general model, we first explore different maps between data and image spaces. In our experiments, quantization using histogram equalization, in combination with JPEG-based methods, outperform other approaches. Secondly, image transformations other than JPEG can be utilized. We illustrate this point by introducing JPEG 2000 as a valid alternative to JPEG. Finally, we experimentally analyze the effectiveness of the generalized JPEG-based method, comparing it with well-known state-of-the-art protection methods such as rank swapping, microaggregation and noise addition.

1 Introduction

In this paper we propose a general protection method based on the JPEG lossy compression algorithms. Our proposal decouples JPEG-based methods into two parts. The first part encompasses transformations between data and image spaces. The second part consists in the image transformation itself. Under this general model, we will explore different maps between data and image spaces and we will also introduce JPEG 2000 as a valid alternative to JPEG image transformations.

The idea of using the JPEG compression standard [14] for microdata protection was introduced by Domingo-Ferrer *et alter* [7, 8, 17]. Basically, it consists in regarding the original microdata file as an image where rows are records and columns are attributes. Then a JPEG lossy compression algorithm is utilized to perturb the data. Once data is recovered from the compression-decompression process, it is reinterpreted as a masked version of the original microdata file. Different values of the JPEG quality parameter are used to attain different levels of protection with a variable trade-off between information loss and disclosure risk. This approach allows us to use current implementations (software and hardware) of JPEG to mask the data, which has benefits both in easy of implementation and performance. Besides these works the idea of using quantization has also been explored for instance to provide k-anonymity [29, 30]

J. Domingo-Ferrer (Ed.): PSD 2014, LNCS 8744, pp. 117–129, 2014.

This paper departs from previous work and introduces a generic JPEG-based protection method, that can be parameterized with both JPEG and JPEG 2000. We also provide a comprehensive evaluation of the methods in terms of disclosure risk and information loss, as compared to traditional SDC methods such as microaggregation [6], rank swapping [22], or randomization [18].

The rest of the paper is organized as follows. We propose our general model of JPEG-based methods in Section 2. This model subsumes both types of *lossy* transformations, JPEG and JPEG-2000, and provides certain flexibility to choose between different quantization methods. The evaluation of our method as compared to existing ones is given in Section 3. Finally we present some conclusions and possible future work in Sect. 4.

2 JPEG-Based Microdata Protection Methods

The interested reader can find descriptions of JPEG and JPEG 2000 in review papers such as [1, 4, 28, 31, 32, 35], which complement the technical standards themselves [14, 15].

Our JPEG-based microdata protection method considers the original microdata file as an image where each record is a file and each variable or attribute is a column of the image. Then a JPEG (or JPEG 2000) lossy compression algorithm is utilized to perturb the data. Once data is recovered from the compression-decompression process, it is reinterpreted as a masked version of the original microdata file. The quality parameters of the compression algorithm are used to attain different levels of protection with a variable trade-off between information loss and disclosure risk.

Table 1. Example of a JPEG protection with q=85%. Original data.

4173	4621	4527	1428	27	27	3480	4550
2639	6045	4208	1902	1008	808	3136	4100
3315	4765	5645	1903	485	485	4284	5600
1619	3932	2380	1177	700	700	1750	2288
4604	4349	2151	1219	751	1	1606	2100
3433	2463	3217	830	167	50	2448	3200
824	372	8730	186	1030	22	589	7700
4145	629	2500	693	1	1	1912	2500

For illustrative purposes, we provide a small example in Tables 1 and 2. Table 1 shows an original microdata with eight attributes and eight records. Table 2 represents a JPEG masked protection of the original dataset at Table 1. The steps to obtain a masked protection of the original dataset are as follows. First, original values are projected onto the image space, as integers in the interval $[0, 255]$, which represent pixel graylevel values. Second, a JPEG compression-decompression process, with a quality of 85%, is applied to the image. Finally, the masked dataset is retrieved after *undoing* the scaling transformation of the first step. The following sections describe our approach.

Table 2. Example of a JPEG protection with q=85%. Masked data.

4108	4759	4245	1746	0	103	3389	4553
2602	5717	4451	1678	1061	993	2842	4348
3424	4930	5854	1712	411	479	4382	5546
1575	4006	2020	1369	685	582	1506	2260
4382	4622	2191	1472	582	0	2123	2054
3595	2294	3150	753	171	0	2362	3047
548	719	8490	274	1267	68	342	8011
4142	650	2568	514	34	34	1951	2362

2.1 General JPEG-Based Perturbative Masking Method

In Alg. 1 we introduce our general schema for JPEG-based protections that we will refer from now on as QJ. The QJ algorithm depends on three parameters, denoted as Q, J_q and Q^*, so the name of the algorithm. These three parameters are detailed below.

Algorithm 1. General JPEG-Based Perturbative Masking Method QJ

Input: X - Original master file
Parameters: J_q, Q, and Q^*
Output: X' - Protected masked file
begin

    $Y \leftarrow Q(X)$;
    $Y_q \leftarrow J_q(Y)$;
    $X' \leftarrow Q^*(Y_q)$;
    return X' ;

The first step of the QJ algorithm consists in a forward processing quantization (or normalization) Q that projects the original data onto the image space. This transformation is particularly necessary when the original values cannot be directly interpreted as pixel values. As in the previous example of Table 1, the JPEG compression-decompression process requires integer values in the range $[0, 255]$. Notwithstanding, with some particular datasets where data values are within the range $[0, 255]$ it may be perfectly valid to consider Q as the identity transformation. The Q transformation establishes a one to one correspondence between data entries and pixel points, so that if the original data set has N records and M attributes, then its associated image also has N rows and M columns.

The second step in the algorithm consists in the lossy compression-decompression of the input image. This transformation is denoted as J_q, where the subscript q denotes the parametrization used to tune different degrees of quality (or distortion) for the compressed image.

Finally, the decompressed image is returned back to the microdata space by means of a dequantization transformation Q^* associated to the forward transformation Q of Stage 1. There may not exist an inverse Q^{-1} such that the composition with Q equals the identity, $Q^{-1}Q = I$. Nevertheless, it seems natural to consider $Q^* = Q^{-1}$ whenever Q is invertible.

The QJ algorithm decouples the transformation between data and image spaces Q from the image transformation J_q. These two components alone are discussed separately in the following two subsections. The discussion describes and justifies the options we have used in our experiments described later in Section 3.2.

2.2   Image Transformations J_q

The QJ method can accommodate both JPEG and JPEG 2000 compression algorithms as the transformation J_q. Both JPEG and JPEG 2000 standards face a difficult trade-off between compression ratio (low size) and quality (low distortion). In order to find an acceptable balance, current implementations offer to end users a quality parameter q in the range $[0, 100]$. Lower values of q are associated with higher compression ratios, but also with lower quality images. Reciprocally, higher values of q are associated with lower reductions in size but also with images of higher quality.

In practice, a default value around 75 is satisfactory for many end-users, that consider it provides an acceptable trade-off between compression ratio and quality. For our purposes, different values of the quality parameter q allow to achieve different levels of protection. In our experiments, we consider a sequence of quality values from 5 to 100, in increments of size 5. But, in order to appreciate better what happens with high-quality compressions, increments are of size 1 for higher quality values. As we will see below, in general, points with quality level 100 depart near the value obtained from simple quantization, from which any increase in the quantization loss is perceived by the disclosure risk and information loss measures (see Section 3.1) as an increase in information loss and a certain decrease in disclosure risk.

Some parameter values may be specific of one of the transformations J_q. This is the case of the image bit depth B, that represents the *quantity of information* each pixel can support, with up to 2^B different values for each pixel. In our experiments, a bit depth $B = 8$ is considered for both JPEG and JPEG 2000, which means that each pixel is able to represent $2^8 = 256$ different values, coded in the range $[0, 255]$. A bit depth $B = 16$ is considered only for JPEG 2000. With this bit depth, each pixel is able to represent a broader range, with up to $2^{16} = 65536$ different values, coded in the range $[0, 65535]$.

2.3   Quantization Q and Dequantization Q^*

Beyond J_q parameters, such as quality q and bit depth B, the selection of a particular quantization Q has a significant impact on overall protections

Let us formulate the quantization process more explicitly. A quantization map Q establishes a projection from the original data space X to the image space Y. If x_{ij} denotes the attribute j of record i in X, let $y_{ij} = Q(x_{ij})$ denote its projection onto the image space. As we have seen before, our image space is constrained by a fixed bit depth B so $0 \leq y_{ij} < 2^B$, which is usually a nominal range with fewer levels than in the original domain. If this is the case, then distinct values of X can be projected by Q to the same value of Y. In other words, the inverse of Q represents a map from Y points to *parts of* X. Usually some criteria is established to select a value, $x' = Q^*(y) \in Q^{-1}(y)$, to *unmap* the projection $y = Q(x)$. For example, a criteria may be to minimize the expected error $D(Q) = E(d(x, Q^*(Q(x))))$. When d is the square error, then $D(Q)$ becomes the mean square error (MSE).

We start considering a global scalar quantizer Q based on an uniform partition of scalar values into consecutive intervals $I_\nu = [\gamma_\nu, \gamma_{\nu+1}]$ such that $Q(x) = \nu$ iff $x \in I_\nu$ for $0 \leq \nu < 2^B$. If the range of scalar values of X data is $[m, M] \subseteq [0, M]$, consider Q as the composition of a rounding operation with a linear transformation of equation $X' = aX$ such that $Q(M) = 2^B - 1$. The result is given explicitly by Eq. 1. We denote this quantizer as Q_E; more concretely as Q_{E8} if $B = 8$ or as Q_{E16} if $B = 16$.

$$Q_E(x) = \text{round}\left(\frac{x \cdot (2^B - 1)}{M}\right) \tag{1}$$

The scaling transformation Q_{E8} was used for the illustrative example of Table 2 above. In practice one can apply the same quantization block by block. For example, we have also considered quantizations Q_{AE8} and Q_{AE16} analogously but column by column.

Different scalar quantizers can be obtained in a similar way by considering *characteristic* equations different from $X' = aX$ of Q_E definition above. For example, we have considered quantizations Q_Q given by a similar equation $X' = aX + b$, such that $Q(m) = 0$ and $Q(M) = 2^B - 1$. The result is given explicitly in Eq. 2. Column-by-column counterparts are also possible, denoted as Q_{AQ8} and Q_{AQ16}.

$$Q_Q(x) = \text{round}\left(\frac{(x - m) \cdot (2^B - 1)}{M - m}\right) \tag{2}$$

Although this formulation is slightly more sophisticated, in practice Q_Q may give similar results if original X data values are close to zero ($m \approx 0$). This is not the unique similarity between Q_Q and Q_E. Both quantizers are uniform quantizers, which means that quantization intervals I_ν are equidistant. This becomes a drawback if original X values are not uniformly distributed. For example, let suppose that almost all values are within a sub-interval $[m, m_2]$ but there is an extreme value at M, very far from the other values. As long as input space is uniformly covered by equidistant intervals, it can happen that many of these intervals become empty. To circumvent this drawback one can consider non-uniform quantizers.

A non-uniform scalar quantizer based on *histogram equalization* [27] is defined as follows. Compute the cumulative distribution function (cdf) $F : [m, M] \mapsto [0, 1]$ of original X values. This function F is known to be a monotonous function increasing from 0 to 1. By a simple scaling, consider a normalized version $F' : [m, M] \mapsto [0, 2^B - 1]$ where the $[0, 1]$ co-domain of F is replaced by the $[0, 2^B - 1]$ range of pixel levels, by $F'(x) := F(x) \cdot (2^B - 1)$. Although F' does not, in general, have an inverse, one can define a *pseudo-inverse* F^* by $F^*(\nu) := \inf_x (F'(x) \geq \nu)$. Now F^* applied to the reference levels $\nu \in [0, 2^B - 1]$ provides 2^B quantization values $x_\nu^* := F^*(\nu) \in [m, M]$. Given these quantization values x^*, every data value x is assigned to its nearest x_ν^* so that $Q(x) := Q(x_\nu^*) = \nu$. We denote this quantization transformation as Q_H; or more specifically as Q_{H8} if $B = 8$ or as Q_{H16} if $B = 16$. Block counterparts are also possible, denoted as Q_{AH8} and Q_{AH16}.

3   Evaluation and Experiments

To evaluate our proposal we use the Census dataset from the European CASC project [3], which contains 1080 records and 13 variables, and has been extensively used in other works [7, 11, 12, 19, 24, 36].

We evaluate the effectiveness of the generalized JPEG-based method QJ, comparing it with well-known state-of-the-art protection methods such as rank swapping, microaggregation, and randomization (or additive noise). The methods are denoted as follows (see references for a detailed description):

- Microaggregation (*MICRO*) [5, 11, 33, 34].
- Rank Swapping (*SWAP*) [22]
- Randomization (*NOISE*) [2, 18]

During the evaluation these methods are parameterized with common values to give a broad comparison of the methods with our proposal. We omit the details of these parameters to avoid digging into the description of the specific methods which will overextend the paper.

3.1   Information Loss and Disclosure Risk

To evaluate our QJ algorithm we use standard and widely accepted measures of information loss (IL) and disclosure risk (DR). Information loss is based in the well known probabilistic information loss measure presented in [20], and disclosure risk is measured using record linkage as introduced in [9].

Information Loss. The probabilistic information loss measure gives a percentage of information loss, where 100% means that all information is lost, and 0% that there is no information lost.

The main idea is based on considering a given statistic or population parameter θ on X (the original dataset), with its corresponding sample statistic on X'

Table 3. Population and sample statistics

Population parameters on X	Sample statistics on X'
r-th moment about zero of the j-th attribute:	
$\mu_r^0(j) = \frac{\sum_{i=1}^{n} x_{ij}^r}{n}$	$; m_r^0(j) = \frac{\sum_{i=1}^{n'} x'^{r}_{ij}}{n'}$
r-th central moment of the j-th attribute:	
$\mu_r(j) = \frac{\sum_{i=1}^{n}(x_{ij}-\mu_1^0(j))^r}{n}$	$; m_r(j) = \frac{\sum_{i=1}^{n'}(x'_{ij}-m_1^0(j))^r}{n'}$
(r,s)-th central moment of the j-th and j'-th attributes:	
$\mu_{r,s}(j,j') = \frac{1}{n}\sum_{i=1}^{n}(x_{ij}-\mu_1^0(j))^r(x_{ij'}-$ $\mu_1^0(j'))^s$	$; m_{r,s}(j,j') = \frac{1}{n'}\sum_{i=1}^{n'}(x'_{ij}-m_1^0(j))^r(x'_{ij'}-$ $m_1^0(j'))^s$
Correlation coefficient between attributes j and j':	
$\rho(j,j') = \frac{\mu_{11}(j,j')}{(\mu_{02}(j,j')\mu_{20}(j,j'))^{1/2}}$	$; r(j,j') = \frac{m_{11}(j,j')}{(m_{02}(j,j')m_{20}(j,j'))^{1/2}}$

(the protected dataset) with value denoted as θ'. Then, the probabilistic information loss can be measured as the standardized sample discrepancy, that is:

$$pil(\theta) = 1 \cdot P_Z(0 \le Z \le \frac{|\theta - \theta'|}{\sqrt{Var(\theta')}}) \qquad (3)$$

Considering the original data set X of size n and the protected dataset X' of size n', and the notation from [20] about population parameters and sample statistics, as shown in Table 3, this measure uses the following statistics, which are assumed to be normally distributed, and obtained by averaging the various attributes j:

- Variance of the sample data: $Var(m_i^0) = \frac{\mu_2}{n'}$
- Variance of the sample variance: $Var(m_2) = \frac{\mu_4 - \mu_2^2}{n'}$
- Variance of the sample covariance: $Var(m_{11}) = \frac{\mu_{22} - \mu_{11}^2}{n'}$
- Variance of the sample Pearson's correlation coefficient:
  $Var(r) = \frac{\rho^2}{n'}\left(\frac{\mu_{22}}{\mu_{11}^2} + \frac{1}{4}\left(\frac{\mu_{40}}{\mu_{20}^2} + \frac{\mu_{04}}{\mu_{02}^2} + \frac{2\mu_{20}}{\mu_{20}\mu_{02}}\right) + \left(\frac{\mu_{31}}{\mu_{11}\mu_{20}} + \frac{\mu_{13}}{\mu_{11}\mu_{02}}\right)\right)$
- Variance of the sample q-quantile: $Q_q = \frac{q(1-q)}{n'f_{Q_q}^2}$, where f_{Q_q} is the value of the attribute density function for the abscissa Q_q.

Then, an information loss measure for each statistic can be obtained with Eq. (3) giving $PIL(m_1^0)$, $PIL(m_2)$, $PIL(m_{11})$, $PIL(r)$, and $PIL(Q_q)$, which are combined to get the general information loss measure as:

$$IL = 100 \cdot \frac{PIL(Q) + PIL(m_1^0) + PIL(m_2) + PIL(m_{11} + PIL(r)}{5} \qquad (4)$$

Disclosure Risk. Disclosure risk is measured in terms of individual (or record) re-identification. That is, the risk an individual is re-identified from the protected dataset. This is a very common and used measure in SDC, which uses record linkage techniques to model a possible attack scenario. We attempt to link records from the protected dataset to the original one. The number of re-identifiable records gives an estimation of the possibility of re-identification by an attacker.

To that end disclosure risk is measured with three values:

- Distance-Based Record Linkage (DRL) [10, 26]: computes distances among records between the original and the masked file. Records in the original file X are labeled as *linked* when one of its nearest records in the masked file X' turns out to be originated from the original record in X. Considering that we do not know the number of variables an intruder may get to know, a partial DRL is computed for the first variable, then for the first two variables, and so on, up to considering the first seven variables; afterward the seven partial DRL values are averaged to compute the final DRL.
- Probabilistic-Based Record Linkage (PRL) [13, 16, 21]: is the average percent of correctly paired records using probabilistic linkage. The matching algorithm uses the linear sum assignment model to choose which pairs of the original and protected records must be matched. In order to compute this model, the EM (Expectation - Maximization) algorithm is normally used.
- Interval Disclosure (ID) [9]: computes rank intervals for a record in the masked dataset as follows. Each variable is ranked separately and a rank interval is defined around the value it takes on each record. For each record in the masked data set, a rank interval is centered on the values of that record. The ranks of values within the interval for a variable around a record r should differ less than p percent of the total number of records, while the rank in the center of the interval should correspond to the value of the variable in the record r. Then the ID measure is the proportion of original values falling into the intervals around their corresponding masked values. A high value means that an intruder may rightly assume that the original values lie within the interval around the masked values.

These three measures are aggregated as a final DR measure as:

$$DR = \frac{1}{4}PRL + \frac{1}{4}DRL + \frac{1}{2}ID \tag{5}$$

An advantage of this DR measure is that it may be interpreted as a probabilistic measure, bounded between zero and one (or between 0 and 100 when using the equivalent percentages).

These measures provide a practical estimation of privacy through the disclosure risk. Given the specific protection methods we use we cannot guarantee for instance the k-anonymity principle. We do not think this is an important limitation since most privacy protection methods suffer the same issue such as noise addition or rank swapping.

3.2   Results

We consider a collection of QJ protections, using both JPEG and JPEG 2000 transformations, 32 levels of quality (as pointed out at Sect. 2.2), 2 bit depths

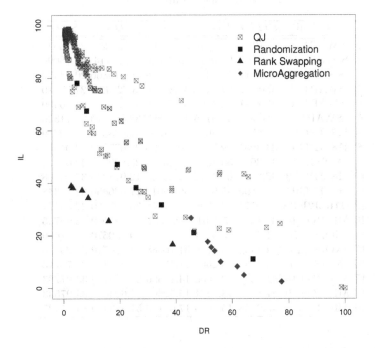

Fig. 1. Disclosure Risk (DR) and Information Loss (IL) of QJ protections for the Census dataset

for JPEG 2000, $B = 8$ and $B = 16$, and a set of transformations between data and image spaces as described in Sections. 2.2 and 2.3.

Fig. 1 summarizes the risk and utility of above mentioned QJ protections for the Census dataset, together with the other protections obtained by rank swapping, microaggregation, and randomization. It shows an R-U map, which uses the IL utility measure from Section 3.1 in combination with the DR from Section 3.1.

Each point in this map represents a different protection. Points near the bottom-right side represent masking methods with low information loss but high risk of disclosure. Points near the top-left corner represent methods with low risk of disclosure but high information loss. Both situations are undesirable for different causes. In between these two extreme situations, there may be some points with an acceptable trade-off between information loss and disclosure risk. In [9] the authors suggest to use a score, defined as the mean average of IL and DR, to easily rank different protections. That is:

$$Score = \frac{IL + DR}{2} \qquad (6)$$

Recall that points incident in a line of slope -1 at the R-U map share the same score. Best protections have lower score and are closer to the bottom-left

Table 4. Desaggregated Scores

	Method	$PIL(Q)$	$PIL(r)$	IL	DR	Score
1	SWAP4_50	1.1031	93.8815	38.13664	3.234286	20.68546
2	SWAP4_100	1.9585	92.0871	38.86240	2.657714	20.76006
3	SWAP4_10	0.0000	70.6411	25.61658	16.070860	20.84372
4	SWAP4_15	0.0000	87.8172	34.35778	8.722429	21.54010
5	SWAP4_20	0.0000	93.4505	37.20440	6.525571	21.86499
6	SWAP4_5	0.0000	48.9185	16.61896	38.807570	27.71326
7	**H8_JPG95**	32.0005	29.8624	27.41602	32.638570	30.02729
8	**H8_JPG92**	34.3931	49.7744	40.93226	23.077860	32.00506
9	NOISE_20	48.3014	50.2242	38.25670	25.820710	32.03871
10	**H8_JPG89**	36.3009	67.4812	51.35706	12.918290	32.13768
11	**H8_JPG94**	31.7896	45.0678	36.79010	27.536860	32.16348
12	**H16_J2K98**	28.0574	40.0830	34.57656	30.105860	32.34121
13	MICRO0_10	30.1033	7.9361	9.99170	55.923000	32.95735
14	NOISE_25	51.3775	65.3011	47.17142	19.180570	33.17600
15	NOISE_15	44.1452	45.0740	31.70588	34.876710	33.29130
16	NOISE_10	40.4505	25.2609	21.15612	46.368140	33.76213
17	MICRO0_15	41.4344	10.5908	14.14696	53.808710	33.97783
18	MICRO0_20	41.8546	13.8271	15.52666	52.624000	34.07533
19	MICRO0_25	46.9738	15.7629	17.64106	51.383430	34.51225

corner of the R-U map. As we said before, a major challenge for perturbative masking methods is to find better protections. The closer is a point to the origin at the bottom-left, the best is the protection.

Our experiments have shown that Q_H quantizations can provide better results than other quantizations. In these experiments, $Q_{H8}JPG$ transformations with quantization levels 95, 92, 89 and 94 offered an acceptable trade-off between disclosure risk and information loss, with scores from 30.03 to 32.16. The fifth score with QJ protections was 32.34 obtained by $Q_{H16}J2K98$.

Table 4 shows different protections sorted by its score. As we said previously, the score is defined as the mean average of IL and DR measures. These two measures are aggregated values of some partial measures focusing on particular aspects of data utility and risk. The tables include, besides of IL, DR and the score, the measures[17] $PIL(Q)$ and $PIL(r)$ (see Section 3.1).

First six rows correspond to protections obtained by rank swapping [22], then JPEG-based protections followed by some parametrization of Microaggregation and Randomization. Thus, QJ is comparable to, or slightly better, than Microaggregation, one of the most recognized approaches for data protection. At the same time, the scores also show that the performance of QJ is behind rank swapping, another recognized approach for data protection. The comparison of unaggregated data utility show that QJ behaves much better with respect to the correlation coefficients than rank swapping. This bad performance of rank swapping with respect to correlations is the reason why other methods are also of interest (there is no method universally valid for all data users). Besides of that, specific attacks[23–25] have been developed for data protected using rank swapping and Microaggregation. It seems more difficult to extend these attacks for JPEG-based methods. For all of this, the proposed approach can be considered a valid alternative to currently well-established methods, such as rank swapping, randomization or microaggregation.

4   Conclusions and Future Work

In this paper we have described a general JPEG-based perturbative protection method for masking continuous microdata, exploring variations in the compression methods and in the quantization maps between microdata and image spaces. In our experiments, results with a quantization based on histogram equalization outperform other quantization methods. Obtained protections are also comparable with other well known methods in terms of disclosure risk and information loss, such as microaggregation or randomization. Other transformations, such as non-scalar quantizations, are to be explored in the future. Furthermore implications of concrete distribution of values can also be explored. For example a given pre-ordering of records could affect both the information loss and disclosure risk.

Acknowledgment. Partial support by the Spanish MEC projects ARES (CONSOLIDER INGENIO 2010 CSD2007-00004), N-KHRONOUS (TIN2010-15764), and COPRIVACY (TIN2011-27076-C03-03) is acknowledged. Partial support of the European Project DwB (Grant Agreement Number 262608) is also acknowledged.

References

1. Antonini, M., Barlaud, M., Mathieu, P., Daubechies, I.: Image coding using wavelet transform. IEEE Transactions on Image Processing 1(2), 205–220 (1992)
2. Brand, R.: Microdata protection through noise addition. In: Domingo-Ferrer, J. (ed.) Inference Control in Statistical Databases. LNCS, vol. 2316, pp. 97–116. Springer, Heidelberg (2002)
3. Brand, R., Domingo-Ferrer, J., Mateo-Sanz, J.M.: Reference data sets to test and compare SDC methods for protection of numerical microdata. Unscheduled Deliverable, European Project IST–2000–25069 CASC (April 2002)
4. Christopoulos, C., Skodras, A., Ebrahimi, T.: The JPEG2000 still image coding system: An overview. IEEE Transactions on Consumer Electronics 16(4), 1103–1127 (2000)
5. Defays, D., Nanopoulos, P.: Panels of enterprises and confidentiality: The small aggregates method. In: Proc. of the 1992 Symposium on Design and Analysis of Longitudinal Surveys, Statistics Canada, pp. 195–204 (1993)
6. Domingo-Ferrer, J., Mateo-Sanz, J.M.: Practical data-oriented microaggregation for statistical disclosure control. IEEE Transactions on Knowledge and Data Engineering 14(1), 189–201 (2002)
7. Domingo-Ferrer, J., Mateo-Sanz, J.M., Torra, V.: Comparing SDC methods for microdata on the basis of information loss and disclosure risk. In: New Techniques and Technologies for Statistics: Exchange of Technology and Know-How, ETK-NTTS 2001, Creta, Hersonissos, pp. 807–826 (2001)

8. Domingo-Ferrer, J., Torra, V.: Disclosure control methods and information loss for microdata. In: Doyle, P., Lane, J.I., Theuwes, J.J.M., Vatz, L. (eds.) Confidentiality, Disclosure and Data Access: Theory and Practical Applications for Statistical Agencies, ch. 5, pp. 91–110. Elsevier (2001)

9. Domingo-Ferrer, J., Torra, V.: A quantitative comparison of disclosure control methods for microdata. In: Doyle, P., Lane, J.I., Theeuwes, J.J.M., Zayatz, L.V. (eds.) Confidentiality, Disclosure and Data Access: Theory and Practical Applications for Statistical Agencies, ch. 6, pp. 111–133. Elsevier (2001)

10. Domingo-Ferrer, J., Torra, V.: Disclosure risk assessment in statistical microdata protection via advanced record linkage. Statistics and Computing 13(4), 343–354 (2003)

11. Domingo-Ferrer, J., Torra, V.: Ordinal, continuous and heterogeneous k-anonymity through microaggregation. Data Mining and Knowledge Discovery 11(2), 195–212 (2005)

12. Domingo-Ferrer, J., Torra, V., Mateo-Sanz, J., Sebe, F.: Empirical disclosure risk assessment of the ipso synthetic data generators. Monographs in Official Statistics – Work Session on Statistical Data Confidentiality, Eurostat (2006)

13. Hartley, H.O.: Maximum likelihood estimation from incomplete data. Biometrics 14(2), 174–194 (1958)

14. ISO/IEC JTC1/SC29/WG1. 10918-1:1994: Information technology — Digital compression and coding of continuous-tone still images: Requirements and guidelines. International Standard, International Organization for Standardization, ITU-T Recommendation T.81 (1994)

15. ISO/IEC JTC1/SC29/WG1. 15444-1: Information technology — JPEG 2000 Image Coding System Part 1: Core Coding System. International Standard, International Organization for Standardization, 2004. ITU-T Recommendation T.803 (2002)

16. Jaro, M.: Advances in record-linkage methodology as applied to matching the 1985 census of Tampa, Florida. Journal of the American Statistical Association 84(406), 414–420 (1989)

17. Jimenez, J., Torra, V.: Utility and risk of JPEG–based continuous microdata protection methods. In: IEEE Proc. of the 4th Int. Conf. on Availability, Reliability and Security, ARES (2009)

18. Kim, J.J.: A method for limiting disclosure in microdata based on random noise and transformation. In: Proc. of the Section on Survey Research Methods, American Statistical Association, Alexandra, VA, pp. 370–374 (1986)

19. Laszlo, M., Mukherjee, S.: Minimum spanning tree partitioning algorithm for microaggregation. IEEE Transactions on Knowledge and Data Engineering 17(7), 902–911 (2005)

20. Mateo-Sanz, J.M., Domingo-Ferrer, J., Sebé, F.: Probabilistic information loss measures in confidentiality protection of continuous microdata. Data Min. Knowl. Discov. 11(2), 181–193 (2005)

21. McLachlan, G., Krishnan, T.: The EM Algorithm and Extensions, 2nd edn. Wiley Series in Probability and Statistics. Wiley-Interscience (March 2008)

22. Moore Jr., R.A.: Controlled data-swapping techniques for masking public use microdata sets. Research report, RR 96-04, Statistical Research Division Report Series, U.S. Bureau of the Census (1996)

23. Nin, J., Herranz, J., Torra, V.: On the disclosure risk of multivariate microaggregation. Data and Knnowledge Engineering 67(3), 399–412 (2008)

24. Nin, J., Herranz, J., Torra, V.: Rethinking rank swapping to decrease disclosure risk. Data and Knowledge Engineering 64(1), 346–364 (2008)

25. Nin, J., Torra, V.: Analysis of the univariate microaggregation disclosure risk. New Generation Computing 27, 177–194 (2009)

26. Pagliuca, D., Seri, G.: Some results of individual ranking method on the system of enterprise accounts annual survey. Esprit SDC Project, Delivrable MI-3/D2 (1999)

27. Parker, J.R.: Practical computer vision using C. John Wiley & Sons (1994)

28. Rabbani, M., Joshi, R.: An overview of the JPEG 2000 still image compression standard. Signal Processing: Image Communication 17(1), 3–48 (2000); Special Issue on JPEG2000

29. Rebollo-Monedero, D., Forn, J., Pallars, E., Parra-Arnau, J.: A modification of the lloyd algorithm for k-anonymous quantization. Information Sciences 222, 185–202 (2013)

30. Rebollo-Monedero, D., Forn, J., Soriano, M.: An algorithm for k-anonymous microaggregation and clustering inspired by the design of distortion-optimized quantizers. Data & Knowledge Engineering 70(10), 892–921 (2011)

31. Skodras, A., Christopoulos, C., Ebrahimi, T.: The JPEG 2000 still image compression standard. IEEE Signal Processing Magazine 18(5), 36–58 (2001)

32. Taubman, D.S., Marcellin, M.W.: JPEG2000: Image Compression Fundamentals, Standards and Practice. Kluwer Academic (2002)

33. Torra, V.: Microaggregation for categorical variables: A median based approach. In: Domingo-Ferrer, J., Torra, V. (eds.) PSD 2004. LNCS, vol. 3050, pp. 162–174. Springer, Heidelberg (2004)

34. Torra, V.: Constrained microaggregation: Adding constraints for data editing. Transactions on Data Privacy 1(2), 86–104 (2008)

35. Wallace, G.K.: The JPEG still picture compression standard. IEEE Transactions on Consumer Electronics 38(1), xviii–xxxiv (1992)

36. Yancey, W.E., Winkler, W.E., Creecy, R.H.: Disclosure risk assessment in perturbative microdata protection. In: Domingo-Ferrer, J. (ed.) Inference Control in Statistical Databases. LNCS, vol. 2316, pp. 135–152. Springer, Heidelberg (2002)

Improving the Utility of Differential Privacy via Univariate Microaggregation

David Sánchez, Josep Domingo-Ferrer, and Sergio Martínez

UNESCO Chair in Data Privacy,
Department of Computer Engineering and Mathematics,
Universitat Rovira i Virgili,
Av. Països Catalans 26, E-43007 Tarragona, Catalonia

Abstract. Differential privacy is a privacy model for anonymization that offers more robust privacy guarantees than previous models, such as k-anonymity and its extensions. However, it is often disregarded that the utility of differentially private outputs is quite limited, either because of the amount of noise that needs to be added to obtain them or because utility is only preserved for a restricted type of queries. On the contrary, k-anonymity-like anonymization offers general purpose data releases that make no assumption on the uses of the protected data. This paper proposes a mechanism to offer general purpose differentially private data releases with a specific focus on the preservation of the utility of the protected data. Our proposal relies on univariate microaggregation to reduce the amount of noise needed to satisfy differential privacy. The theoretical benefits of the proposal are illustrated and in a practical setting.

Keywords: Privacy-preserving data publishing, Differential privacy, Microaggregation, Data utility.

1 Introduction

Data publication often faces privacy threats due to the confidentiality of the information that is released for secondary use.

To tackle this problem, privacy models proposed in recent years within the computer science community [13] seek to attain a predefined notion of privacy, thus offering *a priori* privacy guarantees. Among such models, k-anonymity and the more recent ε-differential privacy have received a lot of attention.

k-Anonymity [28] seeks to make each record in the input data set indistinguishable from, at least, $k-1$ other records, so that the probability of re-identification of individuals is, at most, $1/k$. Different anonymization methods have been proposed to achieve that goal, such as removal of outlying records, generalization of values to a common abstraction [27,30,1,17] or microaggregation [9,8]. The latter method partitions a data set into groups at least k similar records and replaces the records in each group by a prototypical record (*e.g.* the centroid record, that is, the average record). Microaggregation stands out as particularly utility-preserving among the methods for k-anonymization. Indeed, microaggregation does not suffer from the loss of granularity inherent to

J. Domingo-Ferrer (Ed.): PSD 2014, LNCS 8744, pp. 130–142, 2014.

value generalizations and can be adapted to the structure of data [10]. While k-anonymity has been shown to provide reasonably useful anonymized results, especially for small k, it is also vulnerable to attacks based on the possible lack of diversity of the non-anonymized confidential attributes or on additional background knowledge available to the attacker [22,31,20,7].

Unlike k-anonymity, the more recent ε-differential privacy [14] method does not make any assumption on the background knowledge available to potential attackers. ε-Differential privacy guarantees that the anonymized output is insensitive (up to a factor dependent on ε) to modification, deletion or addition of any single input record in the original data set. In this way, the privacy of any individual is not compromised by the publication of the anonymized output, which is a much more robust guarantee than the one offered by k-anonymity. The enforcement of ε-differential privacy requires adding noise to attribute values that depends on the *sensitivity* of such attributes to modification of input records. This sensitivity does not depend on the specific input values, but on the attributes domains, which satisfies the privacy guarantee but may severely distort values, thus compromising the utility of the anonymized outputs. Because of this, ε-differential privacy was originally proposed for the *interactive* scenario, in which the anonymizer returns noise-added answers to interactive queries. In this scenario, the accuracy/utility of the response to a query depends on the sensitivity of the query, which is usually lower than the sensitivity of the attribute. However, the interactive setting of ε-differential privacy limits the number and type of queries that can be performed. Most extensions of ε-differential privacy to the non-interactive setting (data set anonymization) overcome the limitation on the number of queries, but not on the type of queries for which some utility is guaranteed (see Section 2 below). In contrast, k-anonymized data sets offer more flexible utility.

1.1   Contribution and Plan of This Paper

In this paper, we present a procedure to improve the utility of general-purpose ε-differentially private data releases by means of a specific kind of data microaggregation. The rationale is that the microaggregation of input data helps reducing its sensitivity versus modifications of individual records; hence, it helps reducing the amount of noise to be added to achieve ε-differential privacy. As a result, data utility can be improved without renouncing the strong privacy guarantee of ε-differential privacy. Experiments reported on a reference data set show a significant improvement of data utility with respect to plain Laplace noise addition.

The rest of this paper is organized as follows. Section 2 details the background on ε-differential privacy and Section 3 discusses related works on ε-differentially private data releases. Section 4 proposes a new method to generate ε-differentially private data sets that uses a special type of microaggregation to reduce that amount of required noise. Section 5 reports an empirical evaluation of the proposed method, based on a reference data set. The final section gathers the conclusions and details some lines of future research.

2   Background on Differential Privacy

Differential privacy was originally proposed by [14] as a privacy model in the interactive setting. The assumption is that an anonymization mechanism sits between the user submitting queries and the database answering them.

Definition 1. *(ε-Differential privacy) A randomized function κ gives ε-differential privacy if, for all data sets X_1, X_2 such that one can be obtained from the other by modifying a single record, and all $S \subset Range(\kappa)$, it holds*

$$P(\kappa(X_1) \in S) \le \exp(\varepsilon) \times P(\kappa(X_2) \in S). \tag{1}$$

The computational mechanism to attain ε-differential privacy is often called ε-differentially private *sanitizer*. A usual sanitization approach is noise addition: first, the real value $f(X)$ of the response to a certain user query f is computed, and then a random noise, say $Y(X)$, is added to mask $f(X)$, that is, a randomized response $\kappa(X) = f(X) + Y(X)$ is returned. To generate $Y(X)$, a common choice is to use a Laplace distribution with zero mean and $\Delta(f)/\varepsilon$ scale parameter, where:

– ε is the differential privacy parameter;
– $\Delta(f)$ is the L_1-sensitivity of f, that is, the maximum variation of the query function between data sets differing in at most one record.

Specifically, the density function of the Laplace noise is

$$p(x) = \frac{\varepsilon}{2\Delta(f)} e^{-|x|\varepsilon/\Delta(f)}.$$

Notice that, for fixed ε, the higher the sensitivity $\Delta(f)$ of the query function f, the more Laplace noise is added.

3   Related Work on Differentially Private Data Releases

Differential privacy was also proposed for the non-interactive setting. Even though a non-interactive data release can be used to answer an arbitrarily large number of queries, in most cases, this is obtained at the cost of offering utility guarantees only for a restricted class of queries [2], typically count queries. We next review such non-interactive approaches, which are the focus of this paper.

The usual approach to releasing differentially private data sets is based on histogram queries [33,34], that is, on approximating the data distribution by partitioning the data domain and counting the number of records in each partition set. To prevent the counts from leaking too much information they are computed in a differentially private manner. Apart from the counts, partitioning can also reveal information. One way to prevent partitioning from leaking information consists in using a predefined partition that is independent of the actual data under consideration (*e.g.* by using a grid [23]). Several strategies have been proposed to improve the accuracy of differentially private count (histogram) queries. In [18] consistency constraints between a set of queries are exploited to increase accuracy. In [32] a wavelet transform is applied to the data and noise is added in the frequency domain. In [34,21] the histogram bins are adjusted to the actual data. In [5], the authors consider differential privacy of attributes whose domain is ordered and has moderate to large cardinality; the attribute domain is represented as a tree, which is decomposed in order to increase the accuracy of answers to count queries (multi-dimensional range queries). In [26], the authors generalize similar records by using coarser categories for the classification attributes; this results in higher counts for the data partitions, which are much larger than the noise that needs to be added to reach differential privacy.

Our work differs from all previous ones in that it is not limited to histogram queries. In [29] we presented an approach that combines k-anonymity and ε-differential privacy to improve the utility of the output. In that work, we first defined the notion of insensitive microaggregation, which is a multivariate microaggregation procedure that partitions data in groups of k records with a criterion that does not depend on the input data, but just on the domain of attributes. Insensitive microaggregation ensures that, for every pair of data sets X and X' differing in a single record, the resulting clusters will differ at most in a single record. Hence, the centroids used to replace records of each cluster will have low sensitivity to changes of one input record. Specifically, when centroids are computed as the arithmetic average of the elements of the cluster, the sensitivity is as low as $\Delta(X)/k$, where $\Delta(X)$ is the distance between the most distant records of the joint domains of the input data and k is the size of the clusters. Finally, since we were finally releasing n/k centroids, each one computed on a cluster of cardinality k and having sensitivity $\Delta(X)/k$, the sensitivity of the whole data set to be released is $n/k \times \Delta(X)/k$. Thus, for numerical data sets, Laplacian noise with scale parameter $(n/k \times \Delta(X)/k)/\varepsilon$ must be added to each centroid to obtain a ε-differentially private output.

Even though this previous work effectively reduces the amount of Laplace noise to be added to achieve general-purpose ε-differentially private data releases, the fact that it requires using a microaggregation parameter k that depends on the number of records n of the input data set may be problematic for large data sets. To tackle this limitation, in this paper we present an alternative procedure that offers utility gains with respect to standard differential privacy mechanisms regardless of the number of records of the input data set.

4   Differential Privacy via Individual Ranking

In this section we present a method to obtain differentially private data releases which can reduce noise even more than the above-mentioned prior k-anonymity approach based on multivariate microaggregation. For simplicity, we assume data sets with numerical attributes to which an amount of Laplacian noise is added to satisfy differential privacy.

In our previous approach [29] the utility gain was limited by the insensitive multivariate microaggregation used to reach k-anonymity. The sensitivity of the set of n/k centroids obtained from the multivariate microaggregation was $n/k \times \Delta(X)/k$ because, in the worst case,

- Changing a single record in the input data set can cause all n/k clusters to change by one record;
- The record changed within each cluster can alter the value of the cluster centroid by up to $\Delta(X)/k$, where $\Delta(X)$ is the maximum distance between elements in the domain of the input data (we are assuming that centroids are computed as the arithmetic average of record values in the cluster).

The above worst-case scenario overestimates the actual sensitivity of the output and, thus, the noise to be added to the centroids to achieve ε-differential privacy.

Intuitively, the aggregation of the centroid variations would seem to be upperbounded by $\Delta(X)/k$. However, given the multivariate microaggregation used in [29], this is only true if a total order for the domain of X exists for which the triangular inequality is satisfied with equality; that is, when $d(r_1, r_2) + d(r_2, r_3) \geq d(r_1, r_3)$ holds for any records r_1, r_2 and r_3 in X. The goal is to distribute the variation due to the modification of one record among the clusters, but making sure that the sum of variations of centroids is not greater than the original variation over k. Unfortunately, this is generally not the case for multivariate data because a natural total order does not always exist. Artificial total orders defined for multivariate data (as done in [29]), do not fulfill the triangular inequality and, as discussed above, the sensitivity of individual centroids should be multiplied by the number of released centroids to satisfy differential privacy (that is, $n/k \times \Delta(X)/k$).

On the contrary, in univariate numerical data sets, a natural total order (the usual numerical order) can be easily defined with respect to the minimum or maximum value of the domain of values of the attribute so that the triangular inequality holds. In these conditions, it is shown in [8] that clusters in the optimal microaggregation partition contain consecutive values. The next lemma shows that the sensitivity of the set of centroids is indeed $\Delta(X)/k$.

Lemma 1. *Let $x_1, \cdots, x_n$ be a totally ordered set of values that has been microaggregated into $\lfloor n/k \rfloor$ clusters of k consecutive values each, except perhaps one cluster that contains up to $2k - 1$ consecutive values. Let the centroids of these clusters be $\bar{x}_1, \cdots, \bar{x}_{\lfloor n/k \rfloor}$, respectively. Now if, for any single i, x_i is replaced by x_i' such that $|x_i' - x_i| \leq \Delta$ and new clusters and centroids $\bar{x}'_1, \cdots, \bar{x}'_{\lfloor n/k \rfloor}$ are computed, it holds that*

$$\sum_{j=1}^{\lfloor n/k \rfloor} |\bar{x}'_j - \bar{x}_j| \leq \Delta/k$$

Proof. Assume without loss of generality that $x_i' > x_i$ (the proof for $x_i' < x_i$ is symmetric). Assume, for the sake of simplicity, that n is a multiple of k (we will later relax this assumption). Hence, exactly n/k clusters are obtained, with cluster j containing consecutive values from $x_{(j-1)k+1}$ to x_{jk}. Let j_i be the cluster to which x_i belongs. We can distinguish two cases, namely $x'_i \leq x_{j_i k+1}$ and $x'_i > x_{j_i k+1}$.

Case 1. When $x'_i \leq x_{j_i k+1}$, x'_i stays in j_i. Thus, the centroids of all clusters other than j_i stay unchanged and the centroid of cluster j_i increases by Δ/k, because $x'_i + \Delta$. So the lemma follows in this case.

Case 2. When $x'_i > x_{j_i k+1}$, two or more clusters change as a result of replacing x_i by x'_i: cluster j_i loses x_i and another cluster j'_i (for $j'_i > j_i$) acquires x'_i. To maintain its cardinality k, after losing x_i, cluster j_i acquires $x_{j_i k+1}$. In turn, cluster $j_i + 1$ loses $x_{j_i k+1}$ and acquires $x_{(j_i+1)k+1}$, and so on, until cluster j'_i, which transfers its smallest value $x_{(j'_i-1)k+1}$ to cluster j'_i-1 and acquires x'_i. From cluster $j'_i + 1$ upwards, nothing changes. Hence the overall impact on centroids is

$$\sum_{j=1}^{n/k} |\bar{x}'_j - \bar{x}_j| = \sum_{j=j_i}^{j'_i} |\bar{x}'_j - \bar{x}_j|$$

$$= \frac{x_{j_i k+1} - x_i}{k} + \frac{x_{(j_i+1)k+1} - x_{j_i k+1}}{k} + \cdots + \frac{x'_i - x_{(j'_i-1)k+1}}{k}$$

$$= \frac{x'_i - x_i}{k} = \frac{\Delta}{k}. \qquad (2)$$

Hence, the lemma follows also in this case.

Now consider the general situation in which n is not a multiple of k. In this situation there are $\lfloor n/k \rfloor$ clusters and one of them contains between $k + 1$ and $2k - 1$ values. If we are in Case 1 above and this larger cluster is cluster j_i, the centroid of j_i changes by less than Δ/k, so the lemma also holds; of course if the larger cluster is one of the other clusters, it is unaffected and the lemma also holds. If we are in Case 2 above and the larger cluster is one the clusters that change, one of the fractions in the third term of Expression (2) above has denominator greater than k and hence the overall sum is less than Δ/k, so the lemma also holds; if the larger cluster is one of the unaffected ones, the lemma also holds.   □

From the previous lema, it turns out that, for univariate data sets, the amount of noise needed to fulfill differential privacy after the microaggregation step is significantly lower than with the method in [29] (*i.e.* sensitivity $\Delta(X)/k$ vs. $n/k \times \Delta(X)/k$). Moreover, this noise is exactly $1/k$-th of the noise required by the standard differential privacy approach, in which the sensitivity is $\Delta(X)$ because *any* output record may change by $\Delta(X)$ following a modification of any record in the input. To benefit from such a noise reduction in the case of multivariate data sets, we rely on the following two composition properties of differential privacy.

Lemma 2 (Sequential composition [25]). *Let each sanitizing algorithm Ag_i in a set of sanitizers provide ε_i-differential privacy. Then a sequence of sanitizers Ag_i applied to a data set D provides $(\sum_i \varepsilon_i)$-differential privacy.*

Lemma 3 (Parallel composition [25]). *Let each sanitizing algorithm Ag_i in a set of sanitizers provide ε-differential privacy. Then a sequence of Ag_i each applied to a disjoint data set D_i provides ε-differential privacy.*

In the context of differentially private data publishing, we can think of a data release as the collected answers to successive queries for each attribute value in each record of the data set. Let $I_{ra}(X)$ be the query function that returns the value of attribute a (from a total of m attributes) in record r (from a total of n records) in data set X. Then if, for a fixed attribute a, we independently randomize each query $I_{ra}(X)$ for $r = 1, \cdots, n$ to attain ε-differential privacy, by parallel composition the set of n answers obtained are an ε-differentially private version of attribute a (records are disjoint from each other, so parallel composition is applicable). Now, if we publish the differentially private versions of all m attributes, by sequential composition the data set is $m\varepsilon$-differentially private (attributes are considered not disjoint from each other, since they are usually correlated; hence, sequential composition applies here).

To reduce sensitivity and hence the amount of noise needed to attain differential privacy via microaggregation, while exploiting the benefits of the natural orders available on attribute basis, we can use an univariate microaggregation: *individual ranking* [6]. Individual ranking deals with multi-attribute data sets by microaggregating one attribute at a time. Input records are sorted by the first attribute, then groups of successive k values of the first attribute are created and all values within that group are replaced by the group representative (*e.g.* centroid). The same procedure is repeated for the rest of attributes. The attribute-independent microaggregation of individual ranking fits with our goal: to independently attain differential privacy on each microaggregated attribute and then use sequential composition to obtain a differentially private data set.

As discussed in above, each numerical attribute is already equipped with a natural total order that fulfills the triangular inequality. Thus, Lemma 1 guarantees that the centroids output by individual ranking for each attribute A_i have total sensitivity $\Delta(A_i)/k$, where $\Delta(A_i)$ is the maximum distance between two values in the domain of A_i. Hence, we propose the following algorithm to obtain a differentially private version X^D of a numerical original data set X with attributes $A_1, \cdots, A_m$.

Algorithm 1

1. *Use individual ranking microaggregation independently on each attribute A_i, for $i = 1$ to m. Within each cluster, all attribute values are replaced by the cluster centroid value, so each microaggregated cluster consists of k repeated centroid values. Let the resulting microaggregated data set be X^M.*
2. *Add Laplace noise independently to each attribute A_i^M of X^M, where the scale parameter for attribute A_i^M is*

$$\Delta(A_i^M)/\varepsilon = \Delta(A_i)/(k \times \varepsilon).$$

The same noise perturbation is applied to all repeated centroid values within each cluster.

Now we can state:

Lemma 4. *The output of Algorithm 1 is $m\varepsilon$-differentially private.*

Proof. In Step 1 of Algorithm 1, if attribute A_i (with $i = 1, \cdots, m$) has sensitivity $\Delta(A_i)$ in X, by Lemma 1 its microaggregated version A_i^M has sensitivity $\Delta(A_i)/k$. In Step 2, an ε-differentially private version of A_i^M is obtained. By sequential composition, the noise-added data set X^D is $m\varepsilon$-differentially private. Note that sequential composition needs to be applied, because attributes of an individual are not disjoint from each other.   □

Note. In Step 2 of Algorithm 1, it is critically important to apply exactly the same noise perturbation to all repeated values within a microaggregated cluster. If we used different random perturbations for each repeated value, the resulting noise-added cluster would be equivalent to the answers to k independent queries. This would multiply times k the sensitivity of the centroid, which would cancel the sensitivity reduction brought by microaggregation in Step 1.

5   Empirical Evaluation

This section details the empirical evaluation of the proposed method regarding data utility preservation.

As evaluation data we used the "Adult" data set from the UCI repository [16]. We took two numerical attributes AGE and (working) HOURS-PER-WEEK of the training corpus, which consists of 30,162 records after removing records with missing values. Since the two attributes represent non-negative numerical magnitudes, we defined their domains as $[0 \ldots (1.5 \times max\_attr\_value\_in\_dataset)]$, as done in [29]. The difference between the bounds of the domain of each attribute A_i determines the sensitivity of that attribute ($\Delta(A_i)$) and, as detailed above, determines the amount of Laplace noise to be added to microaggregated outputs. Since the Laplace distribution takes values in the range $(-\infty, +\infty)$, for consistency, we bound noise-added outputs to the domain ranges define above.

As done in the literature on statistical disclosure control, we evaluated the utility of the anonymized output in terms of *information loss*[19].

To do so, we used the Sum of Squared Errors (SSE), which is a well-known information loss measure. SSE is defined as the sum of squares of attribute distances between records in the original data set X and their versions in the anonymized data set, that is

$$SSE = \sum_{x_j \in X} \sum_{a_j^i \in x_j} (dist(a_j^i, (a_j^i)'))^2,$$

where a_j^i is the value of the i-th attribute for the j-th original record, $(a_j^i)'$ represents its anonymized version and $dist(\cdot, \cdot)$ corresponds to the standard Euclidean distance. In our experiments, the SSE value was normalized by the number of attributes considered in each test (m).

The ε parameter for differential privacy was set to $\varepsilon = \{0.1, 1.0, 10.0\}$, which covers the usual range of differential privacy levels observed in the literature [15,3,4,23]. Since record attributes are not disjoint, the sequential composition should be applied. Thus, as discussed in Section 4, to obtain ε-differentially private records we need (ε/m)-differentially private attribute values. Hence, Laplace noise addition with scale parameter $\Delta(A_i)/(k \times (\varepsilon/m))$ needs to be added to each attribute A_i, where k is the level of prior microaggregation (which we set between 2 and 100) and m the number of attributes to protect (2).

As baseline methods to compare our proposal with, we considered:

- Plain Laplace noise addition for ε-differential privacy. Since attributes are not disjoint, the sequential composition should be also applied. Thus, to obtain an ε-differentially private record we need (ε/m)-differentially private attribute values. Hence, Laplace noise addition with scale parameter $\Delta(A_i)/(\varepsilon/m) = m\Delta(A_i)/\varepsilon$ needs to be added to each attribute A_i.
- Plain individual ranking, with no subsequent Laplace noise addition. Although this method does not lead to ε-differential privacy by itself, we want to show the contribution of individual ranking to the information loss caused by our method.

Figure 1 shows the comparison between the SSE obtained with plain Laplace noise addition, plain individual ranking and our approach. Due to the broad ranges of the SSE values, a $\log_{10}$ scale is used for the Y-axes. The plain Laplace noise addition baselines are displayed as horizontal lines, because they do not depend on the value of k. Each test involving Laplace noise shows the average results of 5 runs, for the sake of stability.

Regarding plain individual ranking we observe that it causes an information loss that grows with k, but which is shown to be negligible in comparison with the information loss caused by Laplace noise addition for most values of ε (remember that the scale of Y-axes is logarithmic).

Regarding differentially private methods, we observe that, already for $k > 1$, our approach significantly reduces the noise required to attain ε-differential privacy vs. plain Laplace noise addition. The relative improvement of SSE depends on the value of ε. For the smallest ε (that is, 0.1) the amount of noise involved is so high that even with the noise reduction achieved by our method, the output's utility would be severely hampered. However, for $k = 100$ the reduction of information loss almost equals that of 1.0-differential privacy with plain Laplacian noise. This is very relevant because the more robust privacy guarantee offered by the 0.1-differentially private outputs of our method is achieved with an information loss equivalent to that of 1.0-differential privacy for the standard mechanism. For the highest ε (that is, 10.0) there is a substantial decline of SSE for low k and, for larger k, SSE stays more constant and almost as low as the SSE achieved by the individual ranking alone. In this case, the noise added by individual ranking in larger clusters dominates and limits the benefits of the noise reduction at the ε-differential privacy stage due to the decreased sensitivity with larger k. Finally, for $\varepsilon = 1.0$, a more linear decrease is achieved as the k values grow, because the

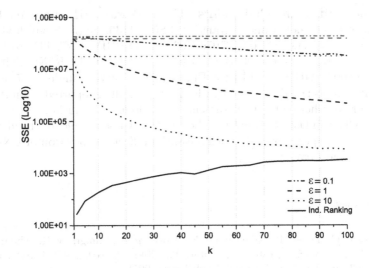

Fig. 1. SSE for the proposed method for different ε values (black non-horizontal lines, as SSE depends on the microaggregation parameter k) vs. plain Laplace noise addition (gray horizontal lines, because SSE does not depend on k) and plain individual ranking microaggregation. Y-axes are in $\log_{10}$ scale.

information loss improvement is less limited by the lower bound of the individual ranking microaggregation.

6   Conclusions

In this paper, we have presented an anonymization method that combines the low information loss incurred by individual ranking microaggregation and its lack of assumptions on data uses and the robust privacy guarantees offered by ε-differential privacy. As a result, our method is able to effectively reduce the scale parameter of noise needed to fulfill differential privacy, and thus improve the utility of anonymized outputs. The method proposed here is easy to implement, because the individual ranking algorithm only relies on the natural order of individual attributes.

As future work, we plan to further evaluate our method with other data sets and compare the results with those of related works on differentially private data publishing, even if that means restricting the utility to specific tasks (*e.g.* counting queries). Finally, we also plan to adapt the proposed procedure to work with categorical data. Unlike for numerical attributes, categorical attributes take values from a finite set of, usually, non-ordinal categories. Hence, appropriate operators to compare, sort, microaggregate and randomize the outputs should be defined [11,24].

Disclaimer and Acknowledgments. This work was partly supported by the Government of Catalonia under grant 2009 SGR 1135, by the Spanish Government through projects TIN2011-27076-C03-01 "CO-PRIVACY", TIN2012-32757 "ICWT", IPT2012-0603-430000 "BallotNext" and CONSOLIDER INGENIO 2010 CSD2007-00004 "ARES", and by the European Commission under FP7 projects "DwB" and "Inter-Trust". J. Domingo-Ferrer is partially supported as an ICREA Acadèmia researcher by the Government of Catalonia. The authors are with the UNESCO Chair in Data Privacy, but they are solely responsible for the views expressed in this paper, which do not necessarily reflect the position of UNESCO nor commit that organization.

References

1. Aggarwal, G., Feder, T., Kenthapadi, K., Motwani, R., Panigrahy, R., Thomas, D., Zhu, A.: Anonymizing tables. In: Eiter, T., Libkin, L. (eds.) ICDT 2005. LNCS, vol. 3363, pp. 246–258. Springer, Heidelberg (2005)
2. Blum, A., Ligett, K., Roth, A.: A learning theory approach to non-interactive database privacy. In: The 40th Annual Symposium on the Theory of Computing-STOC 2008, pp. 609–618 (2008)
3. Charest, A.-S.: How can we analyze differentially-private synthetic data sets? Journal of Privacy and Confidentiality 2(2), 21–33 (2010)
4. Charest, A.-S.: Empirical evaluation of statistical inference from differentially-private contingency tables. In: Domingo-Ferrer, J., Tinnirello, I. (eds.) PSD 2012. LNCS, vol. 7556, pp. 257–272. Springer, Heidelberg (2012)
5. Cormode, G., Procopiuc, C.M., Shen, E., Srivastava, D., Yu, T.: Differentially private spatial decompositions. In: IEEE International Conference on Data Engineering (ICDE 2012), pp. 20–31 (2012)
6. Defays, D., Nanopoulos, P.: Panels of enterprises and confidentiality: the small aggregated method. In: The 1992 Symposium on Design and Analysis of Longitudinal Surveys, pp. 195–204 (1993)
7. Domingo-Ferrer, J.: A critique of k-anonymity and some of its enhancements. In: ARES/PSAI 2008, pp. 990–993. IEEE Computer Society (2008)
8. Domingo-Ferrer, J., Mateo-Sanz, J.M.: Practical data-oriented microaggregation for statistical disclosure control. IEEE Transactions on Knowledge and Data Engineering 14(1), 189–201 (2002)
9. Domingo-Ferrer, J., Torra, V.: Ordinal, continuous and heterogeneous k-anonymity through microaggregation. Data Mining and Knowledge Discovery 11(2), 195–212 (2005)
10. Domingo-Ferrer, J., Mateo-Sanz, J.M., Oganian, A., Torra, V., Torres, A.: On the Security of Microaggregation with Individual Ranking: Analytical Attacks. International Journal of Uncertainty, Fuzziness, and Knowledge-Based Systems 18(5), 477–492 (2002)
11. Domingo-Ferrer, J., Sánchez, D., Rufian-Torrell, G.: Anonymization of nominal data based on semantic marginality. Information Sciences 242, 35–48 (2013)
12. Domingo-Ferrer, J., Sebé, F., Solanas, A.: A polynomial-time approximation to optimal multivariate microaggregation. Computing & Mathematics with Applications 55(4), 714–732 (2008)

13. Drechsler, J.: My understanding of the differences between the CS and the statistical approach to data confidentiality. In: The 4th IAB Wokshop on Confidentiality and Disclosure. Institute for Employment Research (2011)
14. Dwork, C.: Differential privacy. In: Bugliesi, M., Preneel, B., Sassone, V., Wegener, I. (eds.) ICALP 2006. LNCS, vol. 4052, pp. 1–12. Springer, Heidelberg (2006)
15. Dwork, C.: A firm foundation for private data analysis. Communications of the ACM 54(1), 86–95 (2011)
16. Frank, A., Asuncion, A.: UCI Machine Learning Repository. University of California, School of Information and Computer Science, Irvine, CA (2010), http://archive.ics.uci.edu/ml/datasets/Adult
17. Goldberger, J., Tassa, T.: Efficient anonymizations with enhanced utility. Transactions on Data Privacy 3, 149–175 (2010)
18. Hay, M., Rastogi, V., Miklau, G., Suciu, D.: Boosting the accuracy of differentially private histograms through consistency. PVLDB 3(1), 1021–1032 (2010)
19. Hundepool, A., Domingo-Ferrer, J., Franconi, L., Giessing, S., Schulte Nordholt, E., Spicer, K., de Wolf, P.-P.: Statistical Disclosure Control. Wiley (2012)
20. Li, N., Li, T., Venkatasubramanian, S.: t-Closeness: privacy beyond k-anonymity and l-diversity. In: IEEE International Conference on Data Engineering (ICDE 2007), pp. 106–115 (2007)
21. Li, N., Yang, W., Qardaji, W.: Differentially private grids for geospatial data. In: IEEE International Conference on Data Engineering (ICDE 2013), pp. 757–768 (2013)
22. Machanavajjhala, A., Gehrke, J., Kifer, D., Venkitasubramaniam, M.: l-Diversity: privacy beyond k-anonymity. In: IEEE International Conference on Data Engineering (ICDE 2006), p. 24 (2006)
23. Machanavajjhala, A., Kifer, D., Abowd, J., Gehrke, J., Vilhuber, L.: Privacy: theory meets practice on the map. In: IEEE International Conference on Data Engineering (ICDE 2008), pp. 277–286 (2008)
24. Martínez, S., Sánchez, D., Valls, A.: A semantic framework to protect the privacy of electronic health records with non-numerical attributes. Journal of Biomedical Informatics 46(2), 294–303 (2013)
25. McSherry, F.: Privacy integrated queries: an extensible platform for privacy-preserving data analysis. In: The 2009 ACM SIGMOD International Conference on Management of Data, pp. 19–30. ACM (2009)
26. Mohammed, N., Chen, R., Fung, B.C.M., Yu, P.S.: Differentially private data release for data mining. In: The 17th ACM SIGKDD Intl. Conf. on Knowledge Discovery and Data Mining-KDD 2011, pp. 493–501. ACM (2011)
27. Samarati, P.: Protecting respondents' identities in microdata release. IEEE Transactions on Knowledge and Data Engineering 13(6), 1010–1027 (2001)
28. Samarati, P., Sweeney, L.: Protecting privacy when disclosing information: k-anonymity and its enforcement through generalization and suppression. SRI International Report (1998)
29. Soria-Comas, J., Domingo-Ferrer, J., Sánchez, D., Martínez, S.: Enhancing Data Utility in Differential Privacy via Microaggregation-based k-Anonymity. VLDB Journal (to appear)
30. Sweeney, L.: k-Anonymity: a model for protecting privacy. International Journal of Uncertainty, Fuzziness and Knowledge-based Systems 10(5), 557–570 (2002)

31. Wong, R., Li, J., Fu, A., Wang, K.: (α, k)-Anonymity: an enhanced k-anonymity model for privacy preserving data publishing. In: ACM SIGKDD International Conference on Knowledge Discovery and Data Mining (KDD 2006), pp. 754–759 (2006)
32. Xiao, X., Wang, G., Gehrke, J.: Differential Privacy via Wavelet Transforms. IEEE Transactions on Knowledge and Data Engineering 23(8), 1200–1214 (2010)
33. Xiao, Y., Xiong, L., Yuan, C.: Differentially private data release through multidimensional partitioning. In: The 7th VLDB Conference on Secure Data Management (SDM 2010), pp. 150–168 (2010)
34. Xu, J., Zhang, Z., Xiao, X., Yang, Y., Yu, G.: Differentially Private Histogram Publication. In: IEEE International Conference on Data Engineering (ICDE 2012), pp. 32–43 (2012)

Differentially Private Exponential Random Graphs

Vishesh Karwa[1], Aleksandra B. Slavković[1], and Pavel Krivitsky[2]

[1] Department of Statistics, The Pennsylvania State University, USA
[2] School of Mathematics and Applied Statistics of University of Wollongong, Australia
{vishesh,sesa}@psu.edu, pavel@uow.edu.au

Abstract. We propose methods to release and analyze synthetic graphs in order to protect privacy of individual relationships captured by the social network. Proposed techniques aim at fitting and estimating a wide class of exponential random graph models (ERGMs) in a differentially private manner, and thus offer rigorous privacy guarantees. More specifically, we use the randomized response mechanism to release networks under ϵ-edge differential privacy. To maintain utility for statistical inference, treating the original graph as missing, we propose a way to use likelihood based inference and Markov chain Monte Carlo (MCMC) techniques to fit ERGMs to the produced synthetic networks. We demonstrate the usefulness of the proposed techniques on a real data example.

Keywords: Exponential random graphs, edge differential privacy, missing data, synthetic graphs.

1 Introduction

Social networks are a prominent source of data for researchers in economics, epidemiology, sociology and many other disciplines and have sparked a flurry of research in statistical methodology for network analysis. In particular, the exponential random graph models (ERGMs) are a very popular modeling framework for analyzing social network data, e.g., see [16], [32], [15]. While the social benefits of analyzing these data are significant, their release can be devastating to the privacy of individuals and organizations. For example in a famous study by [3], researchers analyzed a social network of high school students to study their romantic relationships, and more broadly to understand the structure of human sexual networks. However, such network data are typically only protected via naive anonymization schemes (e.g., by removing the basic identifiers such as name, social security number, etc.), which have been shown to fail and can lead to disclosure of individual relationships or characteristics associated with the released network (for more specific examples, see [28] and [1]).

In this paper, we develop techniques to provide protection to relationship information while allowing for a valid statistical analysis of the data. We use *edge differential privacy* as a model for measuring privacy risks, and develop inference procedures for analyzing networks using the exponential random graph models.

J. Domingo-Ferrer (Ed.): PSD 2014, LNCS 8744, pp. 143–155, 2014.

2   Past Work on Privately Estimating ERGMs

Our work is the first to develop techniques for actually fitting and estimating a wide class of ERGMs in a differentially private manner. Previous studies on inferring ERGMs in a private manner have only focused on releasing summary statistics that correspond to sufficient statistics of ERGMs. For example, Karwa et al. [23] use the smooth sensitivity framework of [8] to add noise and release subgraph counts such as number of k-triangles and k-stars. These subgraph counts are sufficient statistics for a wide class of exponential random graph models, see for example [21]. Hay et al. [19] propose an algorithm for releasing the degree partition of a graph using the Laplace mechanism. They use post-processing techniques to reduces the L_2 error between the true and the released degree distribution.

Most of the previous studies dealing with private release of network data fall short of demonstrating how to perform valid statistical inference using the noisy statistics, which is a non-trivial task. They typically advocate using the noisy statistics as is for inference, sometimes followed by some form of post-processing, ignoring the noise addition process. It has been well established in statistical literature that ignoring the noise addition process can lead to inconsistent and biased estimates, see for example, [5] and [12]. Moreover, even if we are to proceed naively by ignoring the noise addition process and pretend that the noisy statistics are the true sufficient statistics, we often cannot perform inference using existing estimation procedures. This is because many estimation procedures may fail to converge or may give meaningless results.

Fienberg et al. [10], for example, show that maximum likelihood estimators (MLEs) for log-linear models of contingency tables do not exist when sufficient statistics are released using a generalization of mechanism proposed by Barack et al. [2]. Karwa and Slavkovic [24,25], demonstrate that the MLE may not exist when one uses Laplace mechanism and naive post-processing techniques for releasing degree sequences of random graphs, and present new algorithms to release graphical degree sequences which ensure that the MLE of the β model exists; degree sequences are sufficient statistics of a class of ERGMs known as β model. Furthermore, building on the work of [23], Karwa and Slavkovic [24,25] construct an asymptotically consistent and differentially private estimator of the β model. The main technique relies on projecting the noisy sufficient statistics onto the lattice points of the marginal polytope corresponding to the β model. Marginal polytopes are polytopes of sufficient statistics and existence of MLE is directly tied to the structure of these polytopes. However, approach of [24,25] does not scale to more general ERGMs as the corresponding marginal polytopes are not well understood [9].

In this paper, we take a principled approach, rooted in likelihood theory, to perform inference from data released by privacy preserving mechanisms. Our key idea is to release network data using a differentially private mechanism and estimate the parameters of ERGMs by taking into account the privacy mechanism. Thus, let $X = x$ be the data that requires protection and let $P(X; \theta)$ be a model one is interested in fitting. Privacy preserving mechanisms can be modeled as

$P(Y|X = x, \gamma)$, i.e., the released data y is a sample from $P(Y|X = x, \gamma)$ whose parameters γ of the privacy mechanism are publicly known. Most of the current work advocates on using $P(y; \theta)$ for inference, ignoring the privacy mechanism. In some cases, y is post-processed to minimize some form of distance from x. As noted earlier, using y directly can lead to invalid inferences. Declaring the original data x as missing, we develop methods that take the privacy mechanism into account. Thus we use the likelihood $P(Y; \theta, \gamma) = \sum_x P(Y|X, \gamma)P(X; \theta)$ for inference. This approach offers both the improved accuracy in estimation of θ and meaningful estimates of standard errors.

The rest of the paper is organized as follows. In Section 3, we introduce the key definitions of differential privacy and the randomized response mechanism used to release the networks. In Section 4, we develop the inference procedures to analyze networks released by the differentially private mechanism. Section 5 presents the experimental results, and is followed by conclusions in Section 6.

3   Differential Privacy for Graphs and Randomized Response

This section introduces the privacy model and the notation used throughout the paper. Let X be an undirected simple graph on n nodes with m edges. A simple undirected graph is a graph with no directed edges, and with no self loops and multiple edges. All the graphs considered in this paper are simple and undirected. Let $\mathcal{X}$ denote the set of all simple graphs on n nodes. The distance between two graphs X and X', is defined as the number of edges on which the graphs differ and is denoted by $\Delta(X, X')$. Each node can have a set of attributes associated with it. We will assume that these attributes are known and public. Thus, we are interested in protecting the relationship information in a graph, which is captured by *edge differential privacy*.

3.1   Edge Differential Privacy

Edge differential privacy is defined to protect edges in a graph (or relationships between nodes), as the following definition illustrates.

Definition 1 (Edge Differential Privacy). *Let* $\epsilon > 0$. *A randomized algorithm* $\mathcal{A}$ *is* ϵ*-edge differentially private if for any two graphs* X *and* X' *such that* $\Delta(X, X') = 1$ *and for any subset* S *of possible outputs of* $\mathcal{A}$,

$$P(\mathcal{A}(X) \in S) \le e^\epsilon P(\mathcal{A}(X') \in S).$$

Edge differential privacy (EDP) requires that the distribution of outputs obtained from the algorithm $\mathcal{A}$ on two neighboring graphs (i.e., they differ by one edge) should be close to each other. The parameter ϵ controls the amount of information leakage. Smaller ϵ leads to lower information leakage and hence provide stronger privacy protection.

One nice property of differential privacy is that any function of the differentially private algorithm is also differentially private as the following lemma illustrates.

Lemma 1 (Post-processing [7,29]). *Let f be an output of a differentially private algorithm applied to a graph X and g be any function whose domain is range of f. Then $g(f(X))$ is also differentially private.*

3.2   Randomized Response for Edges

Most differentially private mechanisms perturb the output of a function f applied to a dataset. A basic algorithm for releasing the output of any function f under EDP uses the Laplace Mechanism (e.g., see [8]). This mechanism adds Laplace noise to $f(X)$ proportional to its *global sensitivity*, which is the maximum change in f over neighboring graphs. However, this mechanism is not suitable for releasing synthetic graphs for estimating a large class of ERGMs. This is because in order to use the Laplace Mechanism, we need to fix a set of models apriori and release the corresponding sufficient statistics by estimating their sensitivity.

An alternative way is to perturb the network directly. We call such algorithms input perturbation algorithms. Randomized response is the simplest example of an input perturbation algorithm where random variables are perturbed by a known probability mechanism. Such designs have been extensively used and studied in the context of surveys when eliciting answers to sensitive questions, e.g., see the monograph by [6]. It has also been used for statistical disclosure control when releasing data in the form of contingency tables, e.g., see [20]. We will use a randomized response mechanism to release dyads of a graph, that is subgraphs of size 2, and generate a synthetic graph.

Let X be a random graph with n nodes, presented by its adjacency matrix. In our setting, the adjacency matrix is a symmetric $(0,1)$- $n \times n$ matrix with zeros on its diagonal, and it captures if there is an edge or not between the nodes in the graph. We will apply randomized response to each entry of the adjacency matrix of X. Algorithm 1 shows how to release a random graph Y from X that is ϵ-edge differentially private. Note that for an undirected graph, we need to release $\frac{n(n-1)}{2}$ binary entries. Let p_{11} be the probability of the same edge appearing in both the graphs x and y, and p_{00} if there is no edge in both the graphs.

Proposition 1 (see for e.g., [13]). *Algorithm 1 is ϵ-edge differentially private with*

$$\epsilon = \log \, max \left\{ \frac{p_{00}}{1 - p_{11}}, \frac{1 - p_{11}}{p_{00}}, \frac{1 - p_{00}}{p_{11}}, \frac{p_{11}}{1 - p_{00}} \right\}.$$

Proposition 1 shows that Algorithm 1 is differentially private. Note that when any of p_{00} and p_{11} are equal to 0.5, we get $\epsilon = 0$, which provides no information about the original graph and hence offers the strongest possible privacy possible. When either of them are 1, we get $\epsilon = \infty$. When both p_{00} and p_{11} are 1, the

---

Algorithm 1.

1. Let $x = \{x_{ij}\}$ be the vector representation of the adjacency matrix of X
2. **for** each dyad x_{ij} **do**
3.   if $x_{ij} = 1$, then $y_{ij} = 1$ with prob p_{11}, else $y_{ij} = 0$ with prob $1 - p_{11}$.
4.   If $x_{ij} = 0$, then $y_{ij} = 1$ with prob $1 - p_{00}$, else $y_{ij} = 0$ with prob p_{00}.
5.   Let $Y = \{y_{ij}\}$.
6. **end for**
7. **return** Y

---

algorithm releases the original graph and offers no privacy. When $p_{11} = 1$, the algorithm releases the edges exactly, and when $p_{00} = 1$, the algorithm releases the non-edges exactly. We get a range of ϵ from 0 to ∞ for intermediate values of p_{00} and p_{11}. We will assume that the parameters of this algorithm are public, i.e., p_{00} and p_{11} are known, otherwise there are identifiability issues, that is the parameters of the model are not identifiable.

Let $1 - p_{00} = 1 - p_{11} = \pi$, where π is the probability of perturbing a dyad. This is a special case of the randomized response mechanism, where we flip the state of each dyad with probability π. In this case, we get $\epsilon = \log \max \left\{ \frac{\pi}{1-\pi}, \frac{1-\pi}{\pi} \right\}$. Let X be the input graph and Y be the output of the randomized response mechanism. We can think of Y as the output from a noisy sampling mechanism applied to X. More precisely, if $p_{00} = p_{11} = \pi$ in Algorithm 1, then the output has the following conditional distribution:

$$P_\pi(Y|X = x) = \prod_{ij} \pi^{\mathbb{I}_{y_{ij} \neq x_{ij}}} (1 - \pi)^{\mathbb{I}_{y_{ij} = x_{ij}}},$$

where $\mathbb{I}_{y_{ij} = x_{ij}}$ takes value 1 if there is the same edge in graphs x and y and zero otherwise. Note that if $\pi = 0.5$, we cannot perform any inference on a model for X as all information in the original data is lost. Moreover, if $\pi > 0.5$, the structure of graph "reverses", i.e., edges become non-edges and vice-versa. Hence to provide non-trivial utility, we set $\pi \in \left(0, \frac{1}{2}\right)$. In this case, Algorithm 1 is ϵ-edge differentially private with $\epsilon = -\log \frac{\pi}{1-\pi}$. Note that for conservative values of ϵ, the algorithm may not provide any utility. For instance, for a target $\epsilon = 1$, $\pi \approx 0.27$, meaning with probability 0.27 an edge will be flipped. With $\epsilon = 0.1$, $\pi \approx 0.47$, approaching 0.5. As π approaches 0.5, the "utility" in the perturbed network approaches 0. The question of what is the correct value of ϵ remains open, but in our case in order to maintain utility for inference, we do need larger values of ϵ.

4   Likelihood Based Inference of ERGMs from Randomized Response

Exponential random graph models (ERGMs) for a multivariate distribution of X can be parametrized in the following form according to [4,11]:

$$P(X = x; \theta) = \frac{\exp\{\theta \cdot g(x)\}}{c(\theta, \mathcal{X})}, \quad x \in \mathcal{X}. \tag{1}$$

Here $\theta \in \Theta \subset \mathbb{R}^q$ are a vector of parameters, $g(x)$ is a vector of sufficient statistics, and $c(\theta, \mathcal{X})$ is the normalizing constant given by

$$c(\theta, \mathcal{X}) = \sum_{x \in \mathcal{X}} \exp\{\theta \cdot g(x)\}. \tag{2}$$

In absence of any privacy mechanism, x is a fully observed random sample from the model given by equation 1. One of the main challenges in finding the maximum likelihood estimate (MLE) of θ is that the normalizing constant $c(\theta, \mathcal{X})$ given by equation 2 is intractable due to the sum over all possible graphs in $\mathcal{X}$. A lot of work has been done in estimating the normalizing constant and maximizing the likelihood for estimating ERGMs. For example, Geyer and Thompson [14] use a stochastic algorithm to compute the MLE for a large class of models that includes ERGMs. They approximate the normalizing constant using a Markov chain Monte Carlo (MCMC) algorithm, and compute the MLE by maximizing the stochastic approximation of the likelihood. More precisely, let $\theta_0 \in \Theta$ be a fixed constant. The ratio of two normalizing constants can be approximated as follows:

$$\frac{c(\theta)}{c(\theta_0)} = \sum_{x' \in \mathcal{X}} \frac{\exp\{\theta \cdot g(x')\}}{c(\theta_0)}$$

$$\approx \frac{1}{M} \sum_{i=1}^{M} \exp\{(\theta_0 - \theta) \cdot g(X_i)\},$$

where $X_1, X_2, \ldots, X_M \overset{\text{i.i.d.}}{\sim} P(X = x, \theta_0)$ for some initial guess θ_0. Here M is the number of random graphs sampled. Generally, it is difficult to simulate directly from $P(X = x, \theta_0)$ and we need to resort to MCMC methods to generate the sample. For more details on how to construct Markov chains on the space $\mathcal{X}$ and to sample from ERGMs, see [34,17,27].

The above algorithm used to approximate the likelihood can be extended to infer θ from a private sample y. Such extensions were also considered in [18] in the context of so called *ignorable* sampling mechanisms for network data, i.e. when y is a sample of the original network x. Roughly, ignorable designs are those where the sampling mechanism does not depend on the missing data. Our setting is different because in general, differential privacy mechanisms are not ignorable and depend on the original data. However, as we will see, the MCMC approach of [14] can be extended to estimate parameters from data released by privacy mechanisms since the parameters of the privacy mechanism are public.

The following discussion is general and applies to a generic privacy mechanism $P_\gamma(Y|X)$ with known γ. Recall that we wish to estimate θ using a private sample y obtained from $P_\gamma(Y|X = x)$. A naive approach is to ignore the privacy mechanism and estimate the parameters using the naive likelihood $P(X = y, \theta)$. The correct approach is to include the privacy mechanism in the model and use the full likelihood of Y. We can formulate this likelihood by treating the original data x as missing, and summing over all possible values of x. Thus, if we let $\hat{\theta}_{mle}(y)$ be the maximum likelihood estimator of θ obtained from y, then

$$\hat{\theta}_{mle}(y) = \underset{\theta \in \Theta}{\text{argmax}}\ L(\theta; y) \qquad (3)$$

$$= \underset{\theta \in \Theta}{\text{argmax}} \sum_{x \in \mathcal{X}} P_\gamma(Y = y | X = x) P(X = x; \theta). \qquad (4)$$

For our purposes, $P(X = x; \theta)$ is the ERGM we are interested in fitting. $P_\gamma(Y = y | X = x)$ is the privacy mechanism with parameters γ. In case of the randomized response mechanism of Algorithm 1, $\gamma = \pi$.

With a bit of algebra, we can re-write the likelihood based on y as follows:

$$L(\theta; Y = y, \pi) = \frac{c(\theta | y)}{c(\theta)}$$

$$\text{where } c(\theta | y) = \sum_{x \in \mathcal{X}} e^{\theta \cdot g(x)} P_\gamma(Y = y | X = x).$$

Thus, we need to estimate two intractable constants $c(\theta|y)$ and $c(\theta)$. They can be approximated by using the MCMC technique of [14] described previously. We need two Markov chains, one for the estimating $c(\theta)$ and the other for estimating $c(\theta|y)$. To estimate the latter constant, the MCMC sample needs to be weighted by the privacy weights $P_\gamma(Y|X)$, which are known. Thus, if $X_1, \ldots X_M \overset{\text{i.i.d.}}{\sim} P(X = x, \theta_0)$

$$\frac{c(\theta|y)}{c(\theta_0)} = \sum_{x' \in \mathcal{X}} \frac{\exp\{\theta \cdot g(x')\} P_\gamma(y | X_i)}{c(\theta_0)}$$

$$\approx \frac{1}{M} \sum_{i=1}^{M} \exp\left\{(\theta_0 - \theta) \cdot g(X_i)\right\} P_\gamma(y | X_i),$$

where M is the number of sampled graphs.

Note the key in being able to estimate $c(\theta|y)$ is that the weights $P_\gamma(y|X_i)$ can be computed because the parameters of the privacy mechanism are known. A similar weighting based approach but with the EM-algorithm was proposed by [35] for estimating logistic regression from variables subject to another privacy mechanism known as the Post Randomization Method (PRAM). The standard errors and confidence interval of the parameters can be derived in the usual manner; for details see [27].

5   Experiments

In this section, we evaluate the proposed differentially private randomized response algorithm to release synthetic networks and estimate the parameters of ERGM using the missing data likelihood. Specifically, we consider a subset of a friendship network collected in the Teenage Friends and Lifestyle Study; see [30] and [26]. The study records a network of friendships and substance use for a cohort of students in a school in Scotland. In the current study, we used an excerpt of 50 adolescent girls made available online in the *Siena* package [33]. The network consists of 50 nodes and 39 edges. There are four covariates associated with each node: *Drug usage* (yes or no), *Smoking status* (yes or no), *Alcohol usage*, (regular or irregular) and *Sport activity* (regular or irregular).

As mentioned earlier, we assume that the covariates associated with each node are available publicly. Our goal is to protect the relationship information in the network x. Thus, we release the adjacency matrix of x using the randomized response mechanism of Algorithm 1 for varying values of π. For each value of π, we release 10 synthetic networks. For each released network y, we fit an ERGM, using two different likelihoods: One that takes the privacy mechanism into account, called the *missing data likelihood*, and the other that ignores the privacy mechanism, called the *naive likelihood*. We fit the following ERGM to the network:

$$P(X; \theta) \propto \exp\{\theta_1 edges + \theta_2 gwesp + \theta_3 popularity + \theta_4 drug + \theta_5 sport + \theta_6 smoke\}.$$
(5)

The first three terms in equation 5 capture the network structure of the graph, and the last three terms represent the homophily effect of covariates. The term *edges* measures the number of edges in the network. The term *gwesp* measures the transitive effects in the network, in a weighted manner, and the term *popularity* captures the degree distribution of the network. For more details on these terms, see [27]. We use the *ergm* package [22] in R [31] to fit the models.

We evaluate these methods by measuring the Kullback-Leibler (KL) divergence between the distributions implied by estimates obtained from the private network and the true network. Let θ_x and θ_y be two parameter estimates obtained by using the original network x and the private network y, respectively. Recall that the KL divergence between the two distributions is given by the following equation:

$$
\begin{aligned}
KL(\theta_x, \theta_y) &= E_{\theta_x}\left[\log \frac{P(x, \theta_x)}{P(x, \theta_y)}\right] \\
&= \sum_{x \in \mathcal{X}} \log\left(\frac{P(x, \theta_x)}{P(x, \theta_y)}\right) P(x, \theta_x) \\
&= (\theta_x - \theta_y)g(x) + \log \frac{c(\theta_y)}{c(\theta_x)}.
\end{aligned}
$$

The KL divergence can be easily computed using the MCMC techniques described in Section 4; see also [18] for more details. Figure 1 shows the plot of the KL divergence between the private and non-private network on the y-axis and the perturbation probability π on the x-axis, for different releases of the

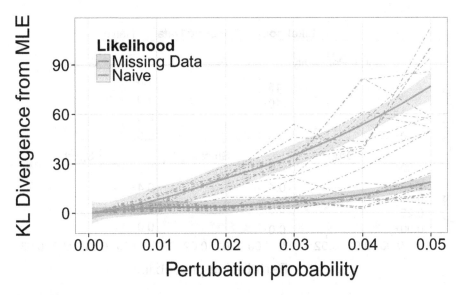

Fig. 1. Comparison of the private ERGM models in the Friendship dataset estimated using the missing data likelihood and the naive likelihood. The red line (lower value of KL) represents the KL divergence between the estimates based on the missing data likelihood and the MLE from the original data. The cyan line (higher value of KL) represents the KL divergence between the estimates based on the naive likelihood and the MLE. The x-axis represents the perturbation probability π used in to release the synthetic network.

synthetic network. The solid line represents the mean KL divergence and the shaded region represents the 99 percent confidence region. The dotted lines show the value of KL divergence for each released dataset. Note that $\epsilon = -\log \frac{\pi}{1-\pi}$, so larger values of π imply stronger privacy.

Figure 1 shows that the KL divergence between the private estimate and the non-private estimate increases as π increases, thus stronger privacy leads to reduced utility. However, the KL divergence of the naive likelihood increases at a much faster rate when compared to the missing data likelihood. This is true especially for larger values of π. Thus for strong privacy protection, the missing data likelihood provides estimates that are closer to the non-private estimates when compared to the naive likelihood.

For a more detailed evaluation of our method, we will look at the relative mean squared error (MSE) of individual parameter estimates. The error is calculated as the mean squared difference between the estimates obtained by the private network and the estimates from the true network. Figure 2 shows a plot of MSE for each parameter in the ERGM model. Note that the first three parameters capture the relational structure of the network and the last three parameters measure the main effects of the nodal covariates *Drug*, *Smoke* and *Sport*.

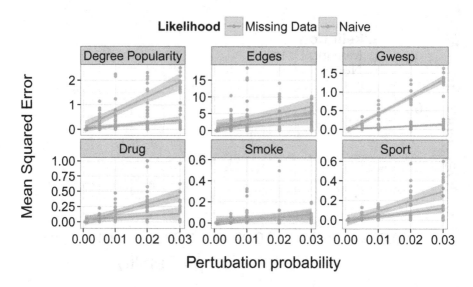

Fig. 2. MSE of parameter estimates of the private ERGM models in the Friendship dataset estimated using the missing data likelihood and the naive likelihood. The red line (lower values) represents the MSE of the estimates based on the missing data likelihood. The cyan line (higher value) represents the MSE of the estimates based on the naive likelihood and the MLE. The x-axis represents the perturbation probability π used in to release the synthetic network.

Table 1 shows the estimate of mean percentage relative efficiency of the parameters, i.e., it shows the ratio $\frac{MSE[Missing]}{MSE[Naive]}$ in form of percentage. In the table, values less than 100 favor the proposed missing data estimator.

Figure 2 and Table 1 show that for structural parameters, the MSE of estimates based on missing data likelihood are much smaller when compared to those based on the naive likelihood. This is true specially for larger values of π. For the parameters related to the homophily effects, the missing data estimates also have lower MSE when compared to the naive estimates. However, the difference is not as drastic as for the structural parameters, especially in case of the node covariate *smoke*. This is due to the fact that the nodal characteristics are assumed to be public, hence the parameter estimates are effected only by the changes in the total number of edges between nodes of the same covariate value. In fact, for the *smoke* parameter, in some cases, as seen in Table 1, the naive estimator seems to do better in terms of MSE. For the structural parameter *gwesp*, the improvement in efficiency is quite substantial when using the missing data likelihood.

Table 1. Table of Relative efficiency of the estimators, $\frac{MSE[Missing]}{MSE[Naive]}$ for different values π of perturbing a dyad

		Parameter				
π	Popularity	edges	GWESP	Drug	Smoke	Sport
0.005	16.5	38.1	9.8	43.4	59.2	37.7
0.01	26.1	80.4	15.8	74.4	69.4	31.8
0.02	17.6	51.7	7.9	58.8	105.3	24.6
0.03	19.9	49.3	10.2	13.2	124.3	49.4

6   Conclusion

In this paper, we present an ϵ-edge differentially private algorithm to release and estimate exponential random graph models. We release synthetic networks using a randomized response mechanism. By treating the original data as missing, we incorporate the privacy mechanism into the likelihood for estimating the parameters. We show that missing data methodology and MCMC techniques can be directly extended to maximize the likelihood of data released by a differentially private mechanism and more generally any privacy preserving mechanisms.

Simulation studies show that our proposed approach leads to estimates with much lower mean squared errors when compared to those obtained by ignoring the privacy mechanism. Although we advocate the use of missing data and MCMC techniques by analysts who use data obtained from a differentially private mechanism, or more general privacy-preserving mechanisms, they can also be used by data curators to release synthetic graphs for performing preliminary analysis of other models. Indeed, using our techniques, the data curator can fit an ERGM to the data and release synthetic graphs from the ERGM. The utility of the synthetic graphs may depend on the goodness-of-fit of the ERGM chosen by the data curator, and this requires further careful investigation.

In this paper, we assumed that the covariate information is available publicly, which may not always be the case. We are currently working on relaxing this assumption and releasing synthetic graphs that protect both nodal and structural information in a graph. Future investigations will also include evaluating the usefulness of this approach for different sizes and sparsity of networks and other ERGM specifications.

Acknowledgments. This work was supported in part by NSF grant BCS-0941553 to the Department of Statistics, Pennsylvania State University. The authors would like to thank the reviewers for their helpful suggestions.

References

1. Backstrom, L., Dwork, C., Kleinberg, J.: Wherefore art thou r3579x?: anonymized social networks, hidden patterns, and structural steganography. In: Proceedings of the 16th International Conference on World Wide Web, pp. 181–190. ACM (2007)

2. Barak, B., Chaudhuri, K., Dwork, C., Kale, S., McSherry, F., Talwar, K.: Privacy, accuracy, and consistency too: a holistic solution to contingency table release. In: Proceedings of the Twenty-sixth ACM SIGMOD SIGACT-SIGART Symposium on Principles of Database Systems, pp. 273–282. ACM (2007)

3. Bearman, P.S., Moody, J., Stovel, K.: Chains of affection: The structure of adolescent romantic and sexual networks. American Journal of Sociology 110(1), 44–91 (2004)

4. Besag, J.: Spatial interaction and the statistical analysis of lattice systems. Journal of the Royal Statistical Society. Series B (Methodological), 192–236 (1974)

5. Carroll, R.J., Ruppert, D., Stefanski, L.A., Crainiceanu, C.M.: Measurement error in nonlinear models: a modern perspective. CRC Press (2012)

6. Chaudhuri: Randomized Response: Theory and Techniques (Statistics: A Series of Textbooks and Monographs). CRC Press (September 1987)

7. Dwork, C., Kenthapadi, K., McSherry, F., Mironov, I., Naor, M.: Our data, ourselves: Privacy via distributed noise generation. In: Vaudenay, S. (ed.) EUROCRYPT 2006. LNCS, vol. 4004, pp. 486–503. Springer, Heidelberg (2006)

8. Dwork, C., McSherry, F., Nissim, K., Smith, A.: Calibrating noise to sensitivity in private data analysis. In: Halevi, S., Rabin, T. (eds.) TCC 2006. LNCS, vol. 3876, pp. 265–284. Springer, Heidelberg (2006)

9. Engström, A., Norén, P.: Polytopes from subgraph statistics. arXiv preprint arXiv:1011.3552 (2010)

10. Fienberg, S.E., Slavković, A.B.: Data Privacy and Confidentiality. International Encyclopedia of Statistical Science, pp. 342–345. Springer (2010)

11. Frank, O., Strauss, D.: Markov graphs. Journal of the American Statistical Association 81(395), 832–842 (1986)

12. Fuller, W.A.: Measurement error models, vol. 305. John Wiley & Sons (2009)

13. Ganta, S.R., Kasiviswanathan, S.P., Smith, A.: Composition attacks and auxiliary information in data privacy. In: Proceedings of the 14th ACM SIGKDD International Conference on Knowledge Discovery and Data Mining, pp. 265–273. ACM (2008)

14. Geyer, C.J., Thompson, E.A.: Constrained monte carlo maximum likelihood for dependent data (with discussion). Journal of the Royal Statistical Society. Series B. Methodological 54(3), 657–699 (1992)

15. Goldenberg, A., Zheng, A.X., Fienberg, S.E., Airoldi, E.M.: A survey of statistical network models. Foundations and Trends® in Machine Learning 2(2), 129–233 (2010)

16. Goodreau, S.M., Kitts, J.A., Morris, M.: Birds of a feather, or friend of a friend? using exponential random graph models to investigate adolescent social networks. Demography 46(1), 103–125 (2009)

17. Handcock, M.S.: Statistical models for social networks: Inference and degeneracy. Dynamic Social Network Modeling and Analysis 126, 229–252 (2003)

18. Handcock, M.S., Gile, K.J., et al.: Modeling social networks from sampled data. The Annals of Applied Statistics 4(1), 5–25 (2010)

19. Hay, M., Li, C., Miklau, G., Jensen, D.: Accurate estimation of the degree distribution of private networks. In: Ninth IEEE International Conference on Data Mining, ICDM 2009, pp. 169–178. IEEE (2009)

20. Hout, A., Heijden, P.G.M.: Randomized response, statistical disclosure control and misclassificatio: a review. International Statistical Review 70(2), 269–288 (2002)

21. Hunter, D.R., Goodreau, S.M., Handcock, M.S.: Goodness of fit of social network models. Journal of the American Statistical Association 103(481), 248–258 (2008)

22. Hunter, D.R., Handcock, M.S., Butts, C.T., Goodreau, S.M., Morris, M.: ergm: A package to fit, simulate and diagnose exponential-family models for networks. Journal of Statistical Software 24(3), nihpa54860 (2008)
23. Karwa, V., Raskhodnikova, S., Smith, A., Yaroslavtsev, G.: Private analysis of graph structure. Proceedings of the VLDB Endowment 4(11) (2011)
24. Karwa, V., Slavkovic, A.: Differentially private synthetic graphs. arXiv preprint arXiv:1205.4697 (2012)
25. Karwa, V., Slavković, A.B.: Differentially private graphical degree sequences and synthetic graphs. In: Domingo-Ferrer, J., Tinnirello, I. (eds.) PSD 2012. LNCS, vol. 7556, pp. 273–285. Springer, Heidelberg (2012)
26. Michell, L., Amos, A.: Girls, pecking order and smoking. Social Science & Medicine 44(12), 1861–1869 (1997)
27. Morris, M., Handcock, M.S., Hunter, D.R.: Specification of exponential-family random graph models: terms and computational aspects. Journal of Statistical Software 24(4), 1548 (2008)
28. Narayanan, A., Shmatikov, V.: De-anonymizing social networks. In: 2009 30th IEEE Symposium on Security and Privacy, pp. 173–187. IEEE (2009)
29. Nissim, K., Raskhodnikova, S., Smith, A.: Smooth sensitivity and sampling in private data analysis. In: STOC, pp. 75–84. ACM (2007)
30. Pearson, M., Michell, L.: Smoke rings: social network analysis of friendship groups, smoking and drug-taking. Drugs: Education, Prevention and Policy 7(1), 21–37 (2000)
31. R Core Team: R: A Language and Environment for Statistical Computing. R Foundation for Statistical Computing, Vienna, Austria (2014)
32. Robins, G., Pattison, P., Kalish, Y., Lusher, D.: An introduction to exponential random graph models for social networks. Social Networks 29(2), 173–191 (2007)
33. Siena. Description excerpt of 50 girls from "teenage friends and lifestyle study" data, http://www.stats.ox.ac.uk/~snijders/siena/s50_data.htm/ (May 2014)
34. Snijders, T.A.B.: Markov chain monte carlo estimation of exponential random graph models. Journal of Social Structure 3(2), 1–40 (2002)
35. Woo, Y.M.J., Slavković, A.B.: Logistic regression with variables subject to post randomization method. In: Domingo-Ferrer, J., Tinnirello, I. (eds.) PSD 2012. LNCS, vol. 7556, pp. 116–130. Springer, Heidelberg (2012)

k^m-Anonymity for Continuous Data Using Dynamic Hierarchies

Olga Gkountouna[1,2], Sotiris Angeli[1], Athanasios Zigomitros[3,2], Manolis Terrovitis[2], and Yannis Vassiliou[1]

[1] National Technical University of Athens, Greece
gkountouna@imis.athena-innovation.gr, el08626@mail.ntua.gr,
yv@ece.ntua.gr
[2] Institute for the Management of Information Systems (IMIS), Athens, Greece
mterrovitis@imis.athena-innovation.gr
[3] University of Piraeus, Greece
azigomit@imis.athena-innovation.gr

Abstract. Many organizations, enterprises or public services collect and manage personal data of individuals. These data contain knowledge that is of substantial value for scientists and market experts, but carelessly disseminating them can lead to significant privacy breaches, as they might reveal financial, medical or other personal information. Several anonymization methods have been proposed to allow the privacy preserving sharing of datasets with personal information. Anonymization techniques provide a trade-off between the strength of the privacy guarantee and the quality of the anonymized dataset. In this work we focus on the anonymization of sets of values from continuous domains, e.g., numerical data, and we provide a method for protecting the anonymized data from attacks against identity disclosure. The main novelty of our approach is that instead of using a fixed, given generalization hierarchy, we let the anonymization algorithm decide how different values will be generalized. The benefit of our approach is twofold: a) we are able to generalize datasets without requiring an expert to define the hierarchy and b) we limit the information loss, since the proposed algorithm is able to limit the scope of the generalization. We provide a series of experiments that demonstrate the gains in terms of information quality of our algorithm compared to the state-of-the-art.

Keywords: Privacy-Preserving Data Publishing, Privacy, k^m-anonymity, Continuous data.

1 Introduction

Datasets that contain sets of numerical data are frequent in various domains. They might describe readings from sensors or from human observation, they might represent health indicators, e.g., measurements of blood pressure, or financial data, e.g., payments.

Consider the example of Table 1, which depicts payments performed by different users for a service, e.g., recharges of a transport card. If this dataset is published, then an attacker who has partial knowledge of a record might be able to identify the record in the published dataset. For example, Alice may know that John has made a payment

J. Domingo-Ferrer (Ed.): PSD 2014, LNCS 8744, pp. 156–169, 2014.

Table 1. Original Payment data

Name	Payments
John	{11000, 11000, 20000, 40000, 40000}
Mary	{11000, 30500, 40000}
Nick	{11000, 11000, 40000, 40000}
Sandy	{11000}
Mark	{20000}

of 11,000 and another one between 18,000 and 22,000. Even if names and unique identifiers are removed from the published Table 1, Alice will be be able to identify John's record in the dataset.

In this work we aim at providing protection against identity disclosure, i.e., to prevent attackers from associating a record in the published dataset with a real person. We ensure the preservation of user privacy in the published data, by guaranteeing k^m-anonymity [1]. k^m-anonymity ensures that any attacker who knows up to m items of a target record cannot use that knowledge to identify more than k individuals in the dataset. This guarantee is a relaxation of the classic k-anonymity [2]. Consider the 2^2-anonymous Table 2 which is an anonymization of Table 1. Any attacker with partial knowledge of up to 2 values of a target, will not be able to identify less than 2 records. To achieve this level of privacy in our dataset, using the data hierarchy of Figure 1, all values had to be generalized because values {20,000} and {30,500} were rare. However, the same privacy can be ensured in Table 3 where values {20,000} and {30,500} are generalized to the range [20,000-30,500]. As we can observe, less values are generalized and a smaller information loss is achieved.

The basic novelty of our method is that we do not assume a fixed generalization hierarchy, i.e., an a priori defined hierarchical mapping of the initial domain values to generalized values, but the anonymization algorithm dynamically explores different possible ways to anonymized the original domain. It relies on clustering values that lie closely together and replacing them by the smallest possible range. The benefits of our approach are twofold: a) the anonymization process does not need a clearly defined hierarchy, which can be a burden for the data publisher and b) by exploring a greater solution space, e.g., many different generalization hierarchies, it manages to significantly limit the information loss due to the anonymization.

Our work differs from existing algorithms for k^m-anonymity [1, 3, 4] because a) it focuses on continuous values, and not categorical ones as previous approaches, b) it

Table 2. 2^2-anonymous table using a data generalization hierarchy

Id	Payments
1	(10000-20000], (10000-20000], (30000-40000], (30000-40000], (30000-40000]
2	(10000-20000], (30000-40000], (30000-40000]
3	(10000-20000], (10000-20000], (30000-40000], (30000-40000]
4	(10000-20000]
5	(10000-20000]

Table 3. 2^2-anonymous table using a dynamic hierarchy

Id	Payments
1	11000, 11000, [20000-30500], 40000, 40000
2	11000, [20000-30500], 40000
3	11000, 11000, 40000, 40000
4	11000
5	[20000-30500]

allows for duplicates in records, i.e., records have bag instead of set semantics and c) it does not consider a given hierarchy.

Our main contributions include the following:

- We extend the problem of anonymizing set-valued data [1] to collections of itemsets with continuous values;
- We present the main differences and challenges of applying k^m-anonymity guarantee to our data scenario;
- We propose a utility-preserving k^m-anonymization algorithm for continuous data that does not use a fixed generalization hierarchy;
- We evaluate our methods with real-world data and compare our results to the apriori algorithm of [1], a k^m-anonymity algorithm using pre-defined data generalization hierarchies for set-valued data.

The rest of the paper is organized as follows: Section 2 describes the problem and presents the attack models. In Section 3 we describe our algorithm and the data structures we use. Section 4 presents the experimental evaluation. Section 5 describes related work and in Section 6 we express our conclusions and possible future directions of this work.

2   Problem Definition

Let dataset D be a collection of records t, where each record is a collection of values v from a continuous domain $\mathscr{I}$. We assume that each record describes a different real world entity (person).

We assume attackers that only have partial knowledge of a record, i.e., m values that are associated with a real person, and want to identify the whole record in the published

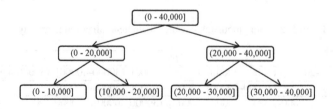

Fig. 1. Data Generalization Hierarchy of the data in Table 1

data. We do not make the distinction between sensitive attributes and quasi-identifiers. Every value is a potential quasi-identifier, and all values are equally sensitive as well. The k^m-anonymity [1] guarantee is defined as follows:

Definition 1. *(k^m-anonymity guarantee [1]) A dataset D is considered k^m-anonymous if any attacker knowing up to m values of a record $t \in D$, is not able to use this knowledge to identify less than k records in D.*

k^m-anonymity requires that each record in the dataset is indistinguishable from at least $k - 1$ others with reference to every possible m-sized combination of its values. In other words, any attacker who knows of m values that are associated with a person will always find k records in the published dataset that match her background knowledge. Unlike traditional k-anonymity, we do not require that records are identical. In the context of sparse multidimensional data, this would introduce great information loss, but it would also be less significant; it would protect from attackers who know a complete or almost complete record, which is unnecessary, and it would also protect against attackers who have negative knowledge, i.e., those who know that a value does not appear in a record. Negative knowledge is a weak quasi identifier in the case of sparse data and it is not covered by k^m-anonymity to increase the quality of the anonymized dataset.

A dataset D which is not k^m-anonymous, can be transformed to k^m-anonymous dataset $D^\star$, by recoding the values so that $D^\star$ satisfies the k^m-*anonymity* guarantee. To achieve this, we generalize only those values that are necessary to make every m-sized combination appear in at least k records, as in Table 3. A generalization is a set of rules in the form $v \rightarrow [a, b]$, which map a value v of the original data to a range that includes it. In this work we use global recoding, i.e., when a value a is generalized to a value A, then *all* appearances of value a in the dataset are replaced by A.

There may be many possible anonymizations of a dataset that satisfy k^m-anonymity for a given attacker's knowledge limit m, as shown in Tables 3 and 2. The worst-case scenario would be to anonymize all values to the maximum domain range $\mathscr{I}$. Such a solution is possible, but it would introduce the highest information loss and the released data would practically have no utility.

The problem of finding the optimal k^m-anonymization is to find the set of generalizations that satisfy k^m-anonymity and produce the least information loss.

3 Anonymization Algorithm

3.1 Solution Space

The solution space is the set of all possible generalizations. These are all the possible substitutions of any data value v with a range that contains it. The range can be any subrange of the domain $\mathscr{I}$. The accepted solutions are those who do not violate k^m-anonymity. The problem of optimal multidimensional k-anonymity was proven to be NP-hard [5]. As we mentioned earlier, our dataset can be represented as a sparse multidimensional table, while the solution space is much larger than that of k-anonymity. There are two reasons for this; (i) k^m-anonymity does not need to form equivalence classes where all records have identical attribute values and (ii) we do not use a generalization hierarchy, therefore the set of possible generalizations is significantly larger.

To deal with the complexity of the optimal anonymization problem we have opted for a heuristic solution. We take advantage of the *apriori* principle, and perform global-recoding generalization on the infrequent values at each step of our algorithm, as we explain below.

3.2 Dynamic Count Tree

According to the a priori principle, given a frequency threshold k, any itemset of size n cannot have frequency higher than k if any of its subsets is infrequent. Equivalently, if an itemset of size n has frequency lower than k, then all its supersets of sizes $n+1, n+2$, etc. are also infrequent.

To exploit this property, our algorithm uses a tree structure similar to the FP-tree of [6]. Every node corresponds to a data value; either original or a generalized range of values. Nodes at the first level of the tree trace the *support* of the values, i.e. the number of tuples that contain the value. A path from the root to a node with depth i, corresponds to an itemset combination of values of size i. Every node n_i in an intermediate level i holds the *support* of the combination of values that appear in the path from the root to n_i.

Definition 2. (support) *The support of a combination of values in a dataset is the number of records that contain this combination.*

Sibling nodes are sorted by their support in descending order, i.e. more frequent nodes appear first. At the first step, a node for every value that appears in the dataset is added to the first level of the tree, as shown in Figure 2(a). At the next step, a new level of nodes is introduced to the count tree. These are the itemsets of size 2. Itemsets are also sorted by their support. Therefore, if the value v_1 of node n_1 is more frequent than v_2 of n_2, we expect to find the 2-itemset $\{v_1, v_2\}$ in the path $n_1 \to n_2$. At each step i of our algorithm, a new level of nodes is introduced to the count tree. Combinations with common prefixes share a common sub-path in the tree. For instance, itemsets $\{5, 10, 2\}$ and $\{5, 10, 1\}$ will share the path $5 \to 10$ in the tree. Note that since we allow for duplicate values in a record, nodes with the same value can appear in the same path.

The goal is for every m-sized combination of values to have support at least k. To achieve this, following the *apriori* principle, we progressively examine itemsets of sizes $i=1, 2, ..., m$. At each step i, we ensure that the supports of every i-itemset is at least k, before we proceed to step $i+1$.

3.3 Information Loss

To estimate the loss of utility introduced by the value generalizations we use the Normalized Certainty Penalty (NCP) metric [7]. Let v be a value in original domain $\mathscr{I}$. Then:

$$NCP(v) = \begin{cases} 0, & v \text{ is not generalized} \\ |g_{max} - g_{min}|/|\mathscr{I}|, & otherwise \end{cases}$$

where $[g_{min}, g_{max}]$ is the range to which v is generalized.

Algorithm 1. Incremental Creation of the Dynamic Count Tree **UpdateDCTree**

Require: D {Original Dataset}, T_{i-1} {tree of size $i-1$}, G {current generalizations}
Ensure: T_i is the count tree of height i.
1. **for** every record $t \in D$ **do**
2.   **for** every value $v \in t$ **do**
3.   **if** $\exists$ generalization range $g \in G$, such that $v \in g$ **then**
4.   replace v with g.
5.   **for** every combination cmb_i of i values in t **do**
6.   find path p_{i-1} that contains (i-1)-subset of cmb_i (prefix)
7.   **if** the ith value exists as a leaf **then**
8.   increase its support by 1.
9.   **else**
10.   add the remaining i^{th} value as a leaf under p_{i-1}
11. **return** D^*

The total information loss of an anonymous dataset D^* with $|D^*|$ records, is the average NCP of all its values:

$$NCP(D^*) = \frac{\sum_{t_i \in D^*} \{\sum_{v_{i,j} \in t_i} NCP(v_{i,j})\}}{\sum_{t_i \in D^*} |t_i|}$$

where $v_{i,j}$ is the jth value in the ith record and $|t_i|$ is the size of record the ith record.

3.4 Algorithm

We propose a heuristic global-recoding generalization algorithm. As shown in the pseudo-code of Algorithm 2, our method has m basic steps. At each step $i = 1, ..., m$, our algorithm, ACD, checks for privacy violations of itemsets of size i. To check every possible i-sized combination of values, we use the count tree created by Algorithm 1.

Each path from the root to a leaf corresponds to an itemset whose support is equal to the support of that leaf. If a leaf has support less than k, then this value combination is rare and is considered vulnerable. To protect individuals whose records contain this itemset, one or more values need to be generalized. The goal is to increase the paths' support. The only way to achieve this is by generalizing a value enough, so that its generalization range will include other values belonging to sibling nodes, thus merging the node with one of its siblings and combining their supports. If the siblings' values

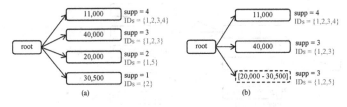

Fig. 2. (a) Count tree T_1 for the dataset of Table1. (b) T_1 after the necessary generalization 30,500→[20,000-30,500].

Algorithm 2. k^m-Anonymization of Continuous Data algorithm **ACD**

Require: D {Original Dataset}, m {maximum size of attacker's knowledge},
         k {privacy parameter}, d {NCP threshold}
Ensure: D^* is a k^m-anonymous Dataset.

1. sort tuples' values with reference to their support.
2. $G = \emptyset$
3. $T_0 = null$
4. **for** $i = 1, 2, ..., m$ **do**
5. $T_i = UpdateDCTree(D, T_{i-1}, G)$
6.   **for** every leaf node f in T_i **do**
7.   **if** $support(f) < k$ **then**
8. $G_f = findGeneralizations(T_i, f, k, d)$
9.   add generalization rules: $G = G \cup G_f$.
10.   parse T_i in a breadth-first traversal
11.   **if** there exist sibling nodes with values $v_1, ..., v_n \in g$, where $g \in G_f$ **then**
12.   replace values $v_1, ..., v_n$ with g
13.   merge them into a single node n
14.   update n's support
15. **return** D^*

---

appear in different records, then the support of the merged node will be higher than the supports of the initial nodes. The merged node's value will be the minimum range that includes the initial values.

Since we opt for global-recoding, once a generalization rule $v \rightarrow [v_{min}, v_{max}]$ is decided by the algorithm for a value v, then every other value v', such that $v' \in [v_{min}, v_{max}]$, will also be generalized to the same range in the dynamic count tree, as shown in lines 10-14 of Algorithm 2. This causes siblings whose values fall in the same generalization range to be merged together. This happens for nodes in all levels of the tree as well, thus reducing the tree's size. Every generalization that has been decided in the previous steps 1,...,i-1, is kept in a generalization rules set G (line 9) so that they will also be considered when building the new level i of the dynamic count tree.

The process we follow to find the generalization rules that will cause the least information loss in the data, is described in Algorithm 3. When a leaf node has a support lower than k, its siblings are the first to be considered for merging. This is because they share a common prefix (the path from the root to their common parent), which

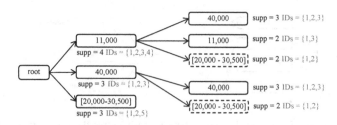

Fig. 3. Count tree T_2 for the dataset of Table1

is an itemset of size i-1, and its support is ensured to be $\geq k$ at the previous step of ACD. Therefore only two values need to be generalized, the values of the leaves. The function $range(v_1, v_2)$ in line 11 returns the range between two values. If $v_1 < v_2$ then $range(v_1, v_2) = [v_1, v_2]$, else $range(v_1, v_2) = [v_2, v_1]$. If the combined support of the two paths is $\geq k$ then it is a candidate solution of this problematic itemset. For every candidate solution we measure the NCP that it would cause and choose the one that introduces the least distortion to the data. If the candidate solution with the lowest information loss gives $NCP < d$, we apply this generalization to the data. Otherwise, we parse the problematic path upwards to the root. At the next set of candidate generalizations we are looking for merges of both the leaves and their parent nodes, and so on, as shown in line 20 of Algorithm 3.

Note that in the worst-case scenario all values will be generalized to the maximum possible range, i.e., the data domain. Therefore, ACD will always find a k^m-anonymous solution to our problem.

Example 1. Consider the dataset of Table 1, let k=2, m=2. Figure 2 a) shows the count tree T_1, of height 1. Value 11,000 appears in records 1, 2, 3 and 4, so its support is 4, while 30,500 has support 1 as it appears only in record 2. Given k=2, this value must be generalized. The best generalization range is [20,000-30,500] as it affects less values in the dataset and thus gives lower NCP than the other options. This generalization is applied to both node 30,500 and 20,000 that fall in the chosen range. The two nodes are merged and their combined support is 3>k, as shown in Figure 2(b). In the next step, we add itemsets of size 2 to the count tree. T_2 is shown in Figure 3 where all leaves have supports at least k. The output of the algorithm is the k^m-anonymous Table 3.

4   Experimental Evaluation

We evaluated experimentally the performance of our algorithm on real datasets from the UCI repository [8]. The implementation was done in C++ and the experiments were performed on an Intel Core 2 Duo CPU at 2.53GHz with 4GB RAM, running Mac OS.

Algorithms. We compare our algorithm to Apriori algorithm (AA) algorithm from [1]. The AA is the state-of-the-art algorithm for creating k^m-anonymous datasets using generalization. It uses a fixed hierarchy and follows the a priori principle: first it creates a k^1-anonymous dataset, then a k^2-anonymous, up to k^m-anonymous. We had to slightly modify it to accommodate duplicate values in records. We also implemented AA in the same platform as our main algorithm ACD.

Data. We use the US Census Data 1990 Data Set [9] from UCI data mining repository. We selected 8 numerical attributes which refer to different types of income. We treated zeros as nulls and removed them from each record. The active domain ranges from 0-197297. The dataset contains approximately 2.5M records, but after eliminating the records that have zero values in all the selected attributes, we are left with approximately 1M records. The average record size was 2.27.

Parameters. We study the behavior of our algorithm with respect to the following parameters: a) k parameter of anonymity, b) the limit on attacker's knowledge m c) NCP

Algorithm 3. Finds a Generalization that fixes a rare itemset **findGeneralizations**

Require: T_i {Count Tree}, f {leaf of a vulnerable itemset path},
$\qquad$ k {privacy parameter}, d {NCP threshold}
Ensure: generalized path of f will have a support $\geq k$.
1. $n = f$
2. $S = \emptyset$
3. $G_f = \emptyset$ {Generalization rules}
4. **for** every s_j sibling of node n **do**
5. $\quad$ $S = S \cup \{s_j\}$ {merge candidates}
6. **for** every node $s_j \in S$ **do**
7. $\quad$ **if** the combined support of s_j and n is $\geq k$ **then**
8. $\qquad$ $NCP_j = NCP(\{v_n, v_{s_j} \rightarrow range(v_n, v_{s_j})\})$
9. $\qquad$ **if** n is not a leaf **then**
10. $\qquad\quad$ **for** every node nc in the path from n to leaf f **do**
11. $\qquad\qquad$ $NCP_j = NCP_j + NCP(\{v_{nc}, v_{sc_j} \rightarrow range(v_{nc}, v_{sc_j})\})$ {node sc_j is descendant of s_j, and it is at the same level as nc.}
12. find $s_j \in S$ such that NCP_j is minimum
13. **if** $NCP_j < d$ **then**
14. $\quad$ $g = range(v_n, v_{s_j})$
15. $\quad$ $G_f = G_f \cup g$
16. $\quad$ **for** every node nc in the path from n to leaf f **do**
17. $\qquad$ $g = range(v_{nc}, v_{sc_j})$ {sc_j is descendant of s_j, and at the same level as nc.}
18. $\qquad$ $G_f = G_f \cup g$
19. **else**
20. $\quad$ let node n be f's parent
21. $\quad$ goto 2
22. **return** G_f

---

threshold d, and d) the dataset size $|D|$. In every experiment we vary one of these parameters keeping others fixed. The default setting of our parameters is $k = 10$, $m = 2$, $d = 0.001$ and $|D| = 100000$. To provide a fair comparison with AA we created a very detailed hierarchy which splits the active domain of 0-197297 to ranges of 100 and then creates a hierarchy with fanout of 2 that is used by AA.

Evaluation Metrics. We evaluate our method with respect to the execution time of our algorithm in seconds and the information loss in terms of NCP.

Anonymization Quality. In Figure 4 we depict the performance of the algorithms in terms of information loss. As k increases, the NCP in both algorithms increases sublinearly, but ACD causes a loss equal to half to 1/3 of that of AA. As the maximum size of the attacker's knowledge m increases, NCP increases superlinearly for both algorithms. However, for ACD it scales a lot better; the cost of AA rises to triple of that of ACD as m grows.

The behavior of NCP threshold as d changes is shown in the first graph of Figure 5. AA is not affected by d, thus we only depict the NCP of AA for the standard parameter setting (k=10, m=2) for reference. When d is small, ACD offers significantly more utility to the released data. Even when d is close to 1 (i.e., the maximum NCP value) our algorithm produces similar information loss as AA.

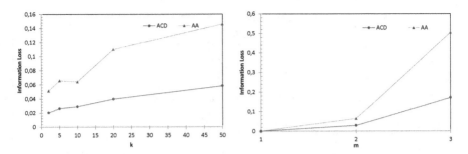

Fig. 4. Information Loss vs. k and m

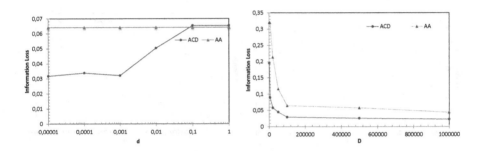

Fig. 5. Information Loss vs. d and $|D|$

In the next graph of Figure 5, we vary the dataset size $|D|$. To perform this experiment we created seven random samples of our dataset of sizes 500,000, 100,000, 50,000, 25,000, 10,000, 5,000, 1,000 records. Each was randomly sampled from the previous one. Information loss of both algorithms decreases with the dataset size, with ACD outperforming AA in every dataset.

Execution Time. Figures 6 and 7 demonstrate the computational cost of our algorithm. Execution time is larger for small k values, and decreases monotonically as k increases. AA is faster than ACD, however the time difference is limited (around 25%) and insensitive to k.

Execution time grows sublinearly with reference to m for both algorithms, as for lager m, more itemsets of bigger sizes need to be considered and more levels of the count trees are needed.

In the next graph we depict the impact of d to running time. While ACD is slow for very small d, it approximates and slightly outperforms AA for $d = 0.0001$ and larger.

Finally, the scalability of our algorithm is shown in the second graph of Figure 7. The curve grows linearly with the dataset size $|D|$ for both algorithms.

In summary, ACD manages to greatly reduce the information loss, with the NCP of datasets anonymized with ACD being half or one third of the those that are anonymized with AA in most settings. This comes at the cost of increased CPU cost, but the overhead is limited to around 20%-40% in most cases.

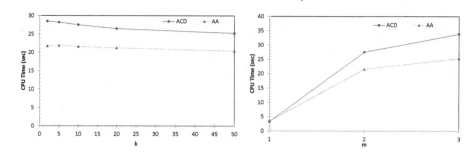

Fig. 6. Execution Time vs. k and m

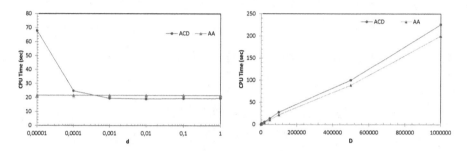

Fig. 7. Execution Time vs. d and $|D|$

5 Related Work

The k-anonymity guarantee [2, 10, 11] was first proposed to protect individuals from identity disclosure, by demanding that each record in a published dataset should be indistinguishable from at least $k - 1$ others, with respect to the quasi-identifiers. Most k-anonymization algorithms transform the data through generalization and suppression [12–21]. Other methods have also been proposed, such as permutation [22], perturbation [23, 24], microaggregation [25–27] and bucketization [4, 28, 29]. In general, k-anonymity is applied in Privacy-Preserving Data Publishing (PPDP) and Privacy-Preserving Data Mining (PPDM) scenarios. Nevertheless, it can be applied in other domains such as Privacy-Preserving Collaborative Filtering (PPCF) [30, 31].

A major difference between k-anonymity and our approach is the distinction between sensitive and non-sensitive values, as well as the assumption that the full set of QI is known. In our setting the problem is different, since any combination of m items can be used by an adversary as QIs. Our proposal extends the k^m-anonymity [1] and performs generalization without hierarchy on numerical attributes. Mondrian [17] also generalizes numerical attributes without the use of a hierarchy, however it applies classic k-anonymity, thus introducing more information loss to the released data.

k-anonymity was proven to be insufficient in preventing attribute disclosure. The ℓ-diversity guarantee proposed by Machanavajjhala et al. [32] demands that each EC have at least ℓ "well-represented" sensitive attribute (SA) values. The ℓ^+-diversity [33] extension sets a different privacy threshold to each SA value in order to reduce information loss. Li et al. [34] proposed t-closeness which requires the distance between a sensitive attribute distribution in an EC and the global distribution of that attribute to be no greater than a threshold t. However, t-closeness lacks the flexibility of specifying different protection levels for different sensitive values and uses the Earth Mover Distance metric that is not suitable for measuring relative loss on individual sensitive attributes. To address these issues Cao and Karras proposed β-likeness [35].

These extensions of k-anonymity have a negative impact on the utility of the released data, as they introduce significant distortion. Relaxations of k-anonymity have been proposed [1, 36–40] aiming to provide a better trade-off between privacy and data utility. The pioneering work of Ghinita et al. [41] for sparse multidimensional data proposed a permutation method which first performs a grouping on transactions and then associates each group to a set of diversified sensitive values. In these data scenarios, it is very unlikely that the adversary has background knowledge of all QIs of his target [42]. Xu et al. [43] assume that the adversary has a limited knowledge of at most p non-sensitive attributes, while performing suppression on items that cause privacy leaks, but they still make the limiting distinction between sensitive and non-sensitive attributes.

6 Conclusions

In this work we studied the problem of k^m-anonymizing continuous data without the use of pre-defined data generalization hierarchies. We proposed ACD, a utility-preserving global-recoding heuristic algorithm. It greedily selects the best generalization ranges at each step, ensuring all itemsets of a particular size, at most m, appear at least k times in the dataset, thus satisfying the k^m-anonymity guarantee. We evaluated our method using real world datasets and compared our algorithm to AA [1] which uses generalization hierarchies for k^m-anonymization. Results show ACD preserves significantly more utility, at a small additional computational cost.

As future work, we plan to extend our solution to more complex attack models which will include both a partial and an aggregate knowledge [44] on the data values. We also wish to study k^m-anonymity under different data models.

Acknowledgements. This work was supported by the MEDA project within GSRT's KRIPIS action, funded by Greece and the European Regional Development Fund of the European Union under the O.P. Competitiveness and Entrepreneurship, NSRF 2007-2013 and by the National Strategic Reference Framework (NSRF) - Research Funding Program: Heracleitus II, which is co-financed by the European Union (European Social Fund - ESF) and Greek national funds through the Operational Program "Education and Lifelong Learning".

References

1. Terrovitis, M., Mamoulis, N., Kalnis, P.: Privacy-preserving Anonymization of Set-valued Data. PVLDB 1(1) (2008)
2. Sweeney, L.: k-Anonymity: A Model for Protecting Privacy. IJUFKS 10(5) (2002)
3. Terrovitis, M., Mamoulis, N., Kalnis, P.: Local and global recoding methods for anonymizing set-valued data. The VLDB Journal 20(1), 83–106 (2011)
4. Terrovitis, M., Mamoulis, N., Liagouris, J., Skiadopoulos, S.: Privacy preservation by disassociation. Proceedings of the VLDB Endowment 5(10), 944–955 (2012)
5. Meyerson, A., Williams, R.: On the Complexity of Optimal K-anonymity. In: PODS, pp. 223–228 (2004)
6. Han, J., Pei, J., Yin, Y.: Mining frequent patterns without candidate generation. In: SIGMOD, pp. 1–12 (2000)
7. Xu, J., Wang, W., Pei, J., Wang, X., Shi, B., Fu, A.: Utility-Based Anonymization Using Local Recoding. In: KDD, pp. 785–790 (2006)
8. Uci repository, http://archive.ics.uci.edu/ml/datasets.html
9. Uci repository us census data 1990 data set (1990), http://archive.ics.uci.edu/ml/datasets/US+Census+Data+%281990%29
10. Samarati, P., Sweeney, L.: Generalizing Data to Provide Anonymity when Disclosing Information (abstract). In: PODS (see also Technical Report SRI-CSL-98-04) (1998)
11. Samarati, P.: Protecting respondents identities in microdata release. TKDE 13(6), 1010–1027 (2001)
12. Sweeney, L.: Datafly: A system for providing anonymity in medical data. In: Proc. of the International Conference on Database Security, pp. 356–381 (1998)
13. Iyengar, V.S.: Transforming data to satisfy privacy constraints. In: SIGKDD, pp. 279–288. ACM (2002)
14. Sweeney, L.: Achieving k-anonymity privacy protection using generalization and suppression. International Journal of Uncertainty, Fuzziness and Knowledge-Based Systems 10(05), 571–588 (2002)
15. Wang, K., Yu, P.S., Chakraborty, S.: Bottom-up generalization: A data mining solution to privacy protection. In: ICDM, pp. 249–256. IEEE (2004)
16. LeFevre, K., DeWitt, D.J., Ramakrishnan, R.: Incognito: Efficient full-domain k-anonymity. In: SIGMOD, pp. 49–60. ACM (2005)
17. LeFevre, K., DeWitt, D.-J., Ramakrishnan, R.: Mondrian multidimensional k-anonymity. In: ICDE, p. 25. IEEE (2006)
18. Fung, B.C., Wang, K., Yu, P.S.: Top-down specialization for information and privacy preservation. In: ICDE, pp. 205–216. IEEE (2005)
19. Bayardo, R.J., Agrawal, R.: Data privacy through optimal k-anonymization. In: ICDE, pp. 217–228. IEEE (2005)
20. El Emam, K., Dankar, F.K., Issa, R., Jonker, E., Amyot, D., Cogo, E., Corriveau, J.-P., Walker, M., Chowdhury, S., Vaillancourt, R., et al.: A globally optimal k-anonymity method for the de-identification of health data. Journal of the American Medical Informatics Association 16(5), 670–682 (2009)
21. Kohlmayer, F., Prasser, F., Eckert, C., Kemper, A., Kuhn, K.A.: Flash: efficient, stable and optimal k-anonymity. In: PASSAT, SocialCom, pp. 708–717. IEEE (2012)
22. Zhang, Q., Koudas, N., Srivastava, D., Yu, T.: Aggregate query answering on anonymized tables. In: ICDE, pp. 116–125. IEEE (2007)
23. Evfimievski, A., Gehrke, J., Srikant, R.: Limiting privacy breaches in privacy preserving data mining. In: ACM SIGMOD-SIGACT-SIGART Symposium on Principles of Database Systems, pp. 211–222. ACM (2003)

24. Verykios, V.S., Elmagarmid, A.K., Bertino, E., Saygin, Y., Dasseni, E.: Association rule hiding. TKDE 16(4), 434–447 (2004)
25. Domingo-Ferrer, J., Torra, V.: Ordinal, continuous and heterogeneous k-anonymity through microaggregation. Data Mining and Knowledge Discovery 11(2), 195–212 (2005)
26. Domingo-Ferrer, J., Solanas, A., Martinez-Balleste, A.: Privacy in statistical databases: k-anonymity through microaggregation. In: GrC, pp. 774–777 (2006)
27. Domingo-Ferrer, J.: Microaggregation: achieving k-anonymity with quasi-optimal data quality. In: European Conference on Quality in Survey Statistics (2006)
28. Xiao, X., Tao, Y.: Anatomy: Simple and effective privacy preservation. In: VLDB, pp. 139–150. VLDB Endowment (2006)
29. Li, T., Li, N., Zhang, J., Molloy, I.: Slicing: A new approach for privacy preserving data publishing. TKDE 24(3), 561–574 (2012)
30. Casino, F., Patsakis, C., Puig, D., Solanas, A.: On privacy preserving collaborative filtering: Current trends, open problems, and new issues. In: e-Business Engineering (ICEBE), pp. 244–249. IEEE (2013)
31. Casino, F., Domingo-Ferrer, J., Patsakis, C., Puig, D., Solanas, A.: Privacy preserving collaborative filtering with k-anonymity through microaggregation. In: e-Business Engineering (ICEBE), pp. 490–497. IEEE (2013)
32. Machanavajjhala, A., Kifer, D., Gehrke, J., Venkitasubramaniam, M.: l-diversity: Privacy beyond k-anonymity. TKDD 1(1), 3 (2007)
33. Liu, J., Wang, K.: On optimal anonymization for l^+-diversity. In: ICDE, pp. 213–224. IEEE (2010)
34. Li, N., Li, T., Venkatasubramanian, S.: t-closeness: Privacy beyond k-anonymity and l-diversity. In: ICDE, pp. 106–115. IEEE (2007)
35. Cao, J., Karras, P.: Publishing microdata with a robust privacy guarantee. Proceedings of the VLDB Endowment 5(11), 1388–1399 (2012)
36. Wang, K., Fung, B.: Anonymizing sequential releases. In: SIGKDD, pp. 414–423. ACM (2006)
37. Gionis, A., Mazza, A., Tassa, T.: k-anonymization revisited. In: ICDE, pp. 744–753. IEEE (2008)
38. Wong, W.K., Mamoulis, N., Cheung, D.W.L.: Non-homogeneous generalization in privacy preserving data publishing. In: SIGMOD, pp. 747–758. ACM (2010)
39. Tassa, T., Mazza, A., Gionis, A.: k-concealment: An alternative model of k-type anonymity. Transactions on Data Privacy 5(1), 189–222 (2012)
40. Stokes, K., Torra, V.: n-confusion: a generalization of k-anonymity. In: EDBT/ICDT Workshops, pp. 211–215. ACM (2012)
41. Ghinita, G., Tao, Y., Kalnis, P.: On the Anonymization of Sparse High-Dimensional Data. In: ICDE (2008)
42. Zigomitros, A., Solanas, A., Patsakis, C.: The role of inference in the anonymization of medical records. In: Computer-Based Medical Systems, CBMS (2014)
43. Xu, Y., Wang, K., Fu, A.W.-C., Yu, P.S.: Anonymizing transaction databases for publication. In: ACM SIGKDD, pp. 767–775. ACM (2008)
44. Gkountouna, O., Lepenioti, K., Terrovitis, M.: Privacy against aggregate knowledge attacks. In: PrivDB, Data Engineering Workshops (ICDEW), pp. 99–103. IEEE (2013)

Differentially-Private Logistic Regression for Detecting Multiple-SNP Association in GWAS Databases

Fei Yu[1,*], Michal Rybar[2], Caroline Uhler[2,**], and Stephen E. Fienberg[1]

[1] Carnegie Mellon University, Pittsburgh, PA 15213, USA
{feiy,fienberg}@stat.cmu.edu
[2] Institute of Science and Technology Austria, Am Campus 1,
3400 Klosterneuburg, Austria
{michal.rybar,caroline.uhler}@ist.ac.at

Abstract. Following the publication of an attack on genome-wide association studies (GWAS) data proposed by Homer et al., considerable attention has been given to developing methods for releasing GWAS data in a privacy-preserving way. Here, we develop an end-to-end differentially private method for solving regression problems with convex penalty functions and selecting the penalty parameters by cross-validation. In particular, we focus on penalized logistic regression with elastic-net regularization, a method widely used to in GWAS analyses to identify disease-causing genes. We show how a differentially private procedure for penalized logistic regression with elastic-net regularization can be applied to the analysis of GWAS data and evaluate our method's performance.

Keywords: Differential privacy, genome-wide association studies (GWAS), logistic regression, elastic-net, ridge regression, lasso, cross-validation, single nucleotide polymorphism (SNP).

1 Introduction

1.1 Genetic Data Privacy Background

The goal of a genome-wide association study (GWAS) is to identify genetic variations associated with a disease. Typical GWAS databases contain information on hundreds of thousands of single nucleotide polymorphisms (SNPs) from thousands of individuals. The aim of GWAS is to find associations between SNPs and a certain phenotype, such as a disease. A particular phenotype is usually the result of complex relationships between multiple SNPs, making GWAS a very high-dimensional problem.

---

* This research was partially supported by NSF Awards EMSW21-RTG and BCS-0941518 to the Department of Statistics at Carnegie Mellon University.
** This research was partially performed while visiting the Simons Institute for the Theory of Computing.

J. Domingo-Ferrer (Ed.): PSD 2014, LNCS 8744, pp. 170–184, 2014.

Recently, penalized regression approaches have been applied to GWAS to overcome the challenges caused by the high-dimensional nature of the data. A popular approach consists of a two-step procedure. In the first step, all SNPs are screened and a subset is selected based on a simple χ^2-test for association between each single SNP and the phenotype. In the second step, the selected subset of SNPs is tested for multiple-SNP association using penalized logistic regression. Elastic-net regularization, which imposes a combination of ℓ_1 and ridge penalties, has been shown to be a competitive method for GWAS (e.g. [1, 2]).

For many years, researchers believed that releasing statistics of SNPs aggregated from thousands of individuals would not compromise the participants' privacy. Such a belief came under challenge with the publication of an attack proposed by Homer et al. [3]. This publication drew widespread attention. As a consequence, NIH removed all aggregate SNP data from open-access databases [4, 5] and instituted an elaborate approval process for gaining access to aggregate genetic data. This NIH action in turn spurred interest in the development of methods for confidentiality protection of GWAS databases.

1.2 Differentially Private Methods for Solving Regression Problems

The approach of differential privacy, introduced by the cryptographic community (e.g. Dwork et al. [6]), provides privacy guarantees that protect GWAS databases against arbitrary external information. Building on such notion, Uhler et al. [7], Johnson and Shmatikov [8], and Yu et al. [9] proposed new methods for selecting a subset of SNPs in a differentially-private manner. These approaches enable us to perform the first step in the two-step procedure for identifying the relevant SNPs in a GWAS without compromising the study participants' privacy. The second step of the two-step procedure would involve performing penalized logistic regression with elastic-net regularization (l_1 and l_2 penalties) on the selected subset of SNPs in a differentially private manner. Kifer et al. [10] proposed an objective function perturbation mechanism that releases the coefficients of a convex risk minimization problem with convex penalties and satisfies differential privacy. We can use this method to perform logistic regression with elastic-net regularization in a differentially private way.

The performance of penalized logistic regression approaches depends heavily on the choice of regularization parameters. Selection of these regularization parameters is usually done via cross-validation. Chaudhuri and Vinterbo [11] proposed a differentially-private procedure for choosing the regularization parameters based on a stability argument. However, the method proposed by Chaudhuri and Vinterbo [11] only works on differentiable penalty functions, such as the ℓ_2 penalty, and it cannot be applied to elastic-net regularization or lasso.

In Section 2, we extend the stability-based method for selecting the regularization parameters developed by Chaudhuri and Vinterbo [11] so that it is applicable to any convex penalty function, including the elastic-net penalty. By combining this new result and the objective function perturbation mechanism proposed by Kifer et al. [10], we are able to carry out a privacy-preserving penalized logistic regression analysis. In Section 3, we demonstrate how to implement the full objective function perturbation mechanism with cross-validation based on the results by Chaudhuri et al. [12] and Kifer et al. [10]. In particular, we provide the exact form of the random noise used in the objective function perturbation mechanism. Furthermore, we show that, under a slightly stronger condition, we can perturb the objective function by an alternative form of noise—the multivariate Laplace noise—and thereby obtain more accurate results. In Section 4, we show how to apply our results to develop an end-to-end differentially private penalized logistic regression method with elastic-net penalty and cross-validation for the selection of the penalty parameters. Finally, in Section 5, we demonstrate how well this end-to-end differentially private method performs on a GWAS data set.

2   Differentially-Private Penalized Regression

We start by reviewing the concept of differential privacy. Let $\mathcal{D}$ denote the set of all data sets. Let $D, D' \in \mathcal{D}$ denote two data sets that differ in one individual only. We denote this by $D \sim D'$.

Definition 1 (differential privacy). *A randomized mechanism $\mathcal{K}$ is ϵ-differentially private if, for all $D \sim D'$ and for any measurable set $S \subset \mathbb{R}$,*

$$\frac{\mathbb{P}(\mathcal{K}(D) \in S)}{\mathbb{P}(\mathcal{K}(D') \in S)} \leq e^{\epsilon}.$$

$\mathcal{K}$ is (ϵ, δ)-differentially private if, for all $D \sim D'$ and for any measurable set $S \subset \mathbb{R}$,

$$\mathbb{P}(\mathcal{K}(D) \in S) \leq e^{\epsilon}\mathbb{P}(\mathcal{K}(D') \in S) + \delta.$$

Let $l : \mathbb{R}^s \times \mathcal{D} \to \mathbb{R}$ denote the loss function, $r : \mathbb{R}^s \to \mathbb{R}$ a regularization function, and $h : \mathbb{R}^s \times \mathcal{D} \to \mathbb{R}$ the validation function. Let $T \in \mathcal{D}^n$ be a training data set of size n drawn from $\mathcal{D}$ and $V \in \mathcal{D}^m$ a validation data set of size m also drawn from $\mathcal{D}$. Let $b \in \mathbb{R}^s$ denote the noise used to perturb the regularized loss function. Then we denote by $\mathcal{T}(\lambda, \epsilon; T, l, r, b)$ the differentially private procedure to produce parameter estimates from the training data T given the regularization parameter λ, the privacy budget $\epsilon > 0$, the loss function l, the regularization function r, and the random noise b. We score a vector of regression coefficients resulting from the random procedure $\mathcal{T}(\lambda, \epsilon; T, l, r, b)$ using the validation data V and the validation score function $q(\theta, V) = -\frac{1}{m}\sum_{d \in V} h(\theta; d)$.

Definition 2 ($(\beta_1, \beta_2, \delta)$-stability. Chaudhuri and Vinterbo [11]). *A validation score function q is said to be $(\beta_1, \beta_2, \delta)$-stable with respect to a training procedure $\mathcal{T}$, the candidate regularization parameters Λ, and the privacy budget ϵ, if there exists $E \subset \mathbb{R}^s$ such that $\mathbb{P}(b \in E) \geq 1 - \delta$, and when $b \in E$, the following conditions hold:*

1. **Training stability:** *for all $\lambda \in \Lambda$, for all validation data sets $V \in \mathcal{D}^m$, and all training dataset $T, T' \in \mathcal{D}^n$ with $T \sim T'$,*

$$| \, q(\mathcal{T}(\lambda, \epsilon; T, l, r, b), V) - q(\mathcal{T}(\lambda, \epsilon; T', l, r, b), V) \, | \leq \frac{\beta_1}{n}.$$

2. **Validation stability:** *for all $\lambda \in \Lambda$, for all training data sets $T \in \mathcal{D}^n$, and all validation data sets $V, V' \in \mathcal{D}^m$ with $V \sim V'$,*

$$| \, q(\mathcal{T}(\lambda, \epsilon; T, l, r, b), V) - q(\mathcal{T}(\lambda, \epsilon; T, l, r, b), V') \, | \leq \frac{\beta_2}{m}.$$

Chaudhuri and Vinterbo [11] gave conditions under which a validation score function is $(\beta_1, \beta_2, \delta)$-stable when the regularization function is differentiable and showed that as long as the validation score function q is $(\beta_1, \beta_2, \delta)$-stable for some $\beta_1, \beta_2, \delta > 0$ with respect to the procedure $\mathcal{T}$, candidate regularization parameters Λ, and privacy budget ϵ, we can choose the best regularization parameter in a differentially private manner using Algorithm 1 and Algorithm 2 in Chaudhuri and Vinterbo [11]. In Theorem 3, we specify the conditions under which a validation score function is $(\beta_1, \beta_2, \delta)$-stable for a general convex regularization function.

In the following, we combine the regularization function and the regularization parameters to form a vector of candidate regularization functions $r = (r_1, \ldots, r_t)$. Then, selecting the regularization parameters is equivalent to selecting a linear combination of r_i's in r.

Theorem 3. *Let $r = (r_1, \ldots, r_t)$ be a vector of convex regularization functions with $r_i : \mathbb{R}^s \to \mathbb{R}$ that are minimized at 0. Let $\Lambda = \{\lambda_1, \ldots, \lambda_k\}$ be a collection of regularization vectors, where λ_i is a t-dimensional vector of 0's and 1's. We denote by $c_{min} := \sup_c \{\forall \lambda \in \Lambda, \lambda^T r$ is c-strong convex$\}$. Let $h(\theta; d)$ be a validation score that is non-negative and κ-Lipschitz in θ. We denote $\max_{d \in \mathcal{D}, \theta \in \mathbb{R}^s} h(\theta; d)$ by h^*. In addition, let $l(\theta; d)$ be a convex loss function that is γ-Lipschitz in θ. Finally, let $\xi \in \mathbb{R}$ such that $\mathbb{P}(\|b\|_2 > \xi) \leq \delta/k$ for some $\delta \in (0, 1)$. Then the validation score $q(\theta, V) = -\frac{1}{m} \sum_{d \in V} h(\theta; d)$ is $(\beta_1, \beta_2, \delta/k)$-stable with respect to $\mathcal{T}$, ϵ and Λ, where*

$$\mathcal{T}(\lambda, \epsilon; T, l, r, b) := \arg\min_\theta L(\theta; \lambda, \epsilon),$$

with

$$L(\theta; \lambda, \epsilon) = \frac{1}{n} \sum_{d \in T} l(\theta; d) + \lambda^T r(\theta) + \frac{\max\{0, \, c^* - c_{min}\}}{2} \|\theta\|_2^2 + \frac{\varphi}{\epsilon n} b^T \theta,$$

$$\beta_1 = \frac{2\gamma\kappa}{\max\{c^*, c_{min}\}}, \qquad \beta_2 = \min\left\{ h^*, \frac{\kappa}{\max\{c^*, c_{min}\}} \left(\gamma + \frac{\varphi\xi}{\epsilon n} \right) \right\}.$$

Proof. See A.1. $\qquad\qquad\qquad\qquad\qquad\qquad\qquad\qquad\qquad\qquad\qquad\qquad\qquad\qquad\qquad\quad$ $\square$

Note that choosing $r(\theta) = \left(\frac{\lambda_1}{2} \|\theta\|_2^2, \ldots, \frac{\lambda_k}{2} \|\theta\|_2^2 \right)$, with $\Lambda = \{e_1, \ldots, e_k\}$, where e_i is a k-dimensional vector that is 1 in the ith entry and 0 everywhere else, results in Theorem 4 in Chaudhuri and Vinterbo [11]. Thus, Theorem 3 generalizes Theorem 4 in Chaudhuri and Vinterbo [11].

The term $\frac{\max\{0, \, c^* - c_{\min}\}}{2} \|\theta\|_2^2$ in Theorem 3 ensures that $L(\theta; \lambda, \epsilon)$ is at least c^*-strongly convex. This is an essential condition for ensuring that our objective function perturbation algorithm (Algortihm 1) is differentially private. The value of ξ in Theorem 3 depends on the distribution of the perturbation noise b. In Section 3, we analyze two different distributions for the perturbation noise.

3   Distributions for the Perturbation Noise

Chaudhuri et al. [12] and Kifer et al. [10] showed that using perturbation noise B_2 with density function

$$f_{B_2}(b) \propto \exp\left(-\frac{\|b\|_2}{2}\right)$$

in the procedure $\mathcal{T}(\lambda, \epsilon; T, l, r, B_2)$ produces ϵ-differentially private parameter estimates. In this section, we describe an efficient method for generating such perturbation noise. Furthermore, we show that under slightly stronger conditions the procedure $\mathcal{T}(\lambda, \epsilon; T, l, r, B_1)$ is differentially private when we use perturbation noise B_1 with density function

$$f_{B_1}(b) \propto \exp\left(-\frac{\|b\|_1}{2}\right),$$

which is simpler to generate than perturbation noise of the form B_2.

Proposition 4. *The random variable $X = \frac{W}{\|W\|_2} Y$, where $W \sim \mathcal{N}(0, I_s)$ and $Y \sim \chi^2(2s)$, has density function $f_X(x) \propto \exp\left(-\frac{\|x\|_2}{2}\right)$.*

Proof. See Appendix A.3.   □

This result shows that $B_2 \sim \frac{W_s}{\|W_s\|_2} Y_{2s}$, with $W_s \sim \mathcal{N}(0, I_s)$ and $Y_{2s} \sim \chi^2(2s)$. On the other hand, B_1 can be viewed as the joint distribution of s independent Laplace random variables with mean $= 0$ and scale $= 2$. In order to specify the stability parameter β_2 in Theorem 3, we need to find $\xi \in \mathbb{R}$ such that $P(\|b\|_2 \geq \xi) \leq \delta/k$. The following propositions enable us to find ξ for the perturbation noise B_1 and B_2.

Proposition 5. $\mathbb{P}\left(\|B_1\|_1 \geq 2s\log(sk/\delta)\right) \leq \delta/k.$

Proof. See Lemma 17 in Chaudhuri and Vinterbo [11].   □

Proposition 6. $\mathbb{P}\left(\|B_2\|_2 \geq \left(\sqrt{s} + \sqrt{\log(k/\delta)}\right)^2 + \log(k/\delta)\right) \leq \delta/k.$

Proof. Note that $\|B_2\|_2 = \left\|\frac{W_s}{\|W_s\|_2} Y_{2s}\right\|_2 = Y_{2s}$, where $Y_{2s} \sim \chi^2(2s)$. The proof is completed by invoking Lemma 1 in Laurent and Massart [13].   □

Because $P(\|B_1\|_1 \geq \xi) \geq P(\|B_1\|_2 \geq \xi)$, Proposition 5 and Proposition 6 enable us to find $\xi \in \mathbb{R}$ such that $P(\|b\|_2 \geq \xi) \leq \delta/k$. When the density function of b is $f(b) \propto \exp\left(\frac{\|b\|_1}{2}\right)$, then by Proposition 5, $\xi = 2s\log(sk/\delta)$. When the density function of b is $f(b) \propto \exp\left(\frac{\|b\|_2}{2}\right)$, then by Proposition 6, $\xi = \left(\sqrt{s} + \sqrt{\log(k/\delta)}\right)^2 + \log(k/\delta)$.

Algorithm 1 below is a reformulation of Algorithm 1 in Kifer et al. [10], i.e., the differentially private objective function optimization algorithm, and it incorporates the alternative perturbation noise. The objective function is formulated in such a way that it is compatible with the regularization parameter selection procedure described in Theorem 3.

Algorithm 1. Generalized Objective Perturbation Mechanism

Input: Dataset $D = \{d_1, \ldots, d_n\}$; a convex domain $\Theta \subset \mathbb{R}^s$; privacy parameter ϵ; λ-strongly convex regularizer r; convex loss function $l(\theta; d)$ with rank-1 continuous Hessian $\nabla^2 l(\theta; d)$, an upper bound c on the maximal singular value of $\nabla^2 l(\theta; d)$ and upper bounds κ_j on $\|\nabla l(\theta; d)\|_j$ for $j \in \{1, 2\}$ that hold for all $d \in D$ and all $\theta \in \Theta$. It is also required that $\varphi \geq 2\kappa_j$ and $\lambda \geq \frac{c}{n(e^{\epsilon/4}-1)}$.

Output: A differentially-private parameter vector θ^*.

1. Sample $b \in \mathbb{R}^s$ according to noise distribution B_j, $j \in \{1, 2\}$.
2. **return** $\theta^* = \arg\min_\theta L(\theta; D, \lambda, b)$, where

$$L(\theta; D, \lambda, b) = \frac{1}{n} \sum_{d \in D} l(\theta; d) + r(\theta) + \frac{\varphi}{\epsilon n} b^T \theta.$$

Theorem 7. *Algorithm 1 is ϵ-differentially private.*

Proof. See A.2. □

3.1 Comparison of the Performance of Algorithm 1 under Different Noise Distributions

Note that we can always upper bound $\|\nabla l(\theta; d)\|_2$ by $\|\nabla l(\theta; d)\|_1$ and hence $\kappa_2 \leq \kappa_1$ in Algorithm 1. However, as we show in this section, results from Algorithm 1 are more accurate when sampling noise from B_1 compared to B_2. To compare the performance of Algorithm 1 under noise sampled from B_1 and B_2, we follow the algorithm performance analysis in Chaudhuri et al. [12] and analyze $\mathbb{P}(J(\theta_b) - J(\theta^*) > c)$, where

$$J(\theta) = \frac{1}{n} \sum_{d \in D} l(\theta; d) + r(\theta)$$

with l and r as defined in Algorithm 1, $\theta^* = \arg\min_\theta J(\theta)$, and $\theta_b = \arg\min_\theta \left[J(\theta) + \frac{\varphi}{\epsilon n} b^T \theta\right] = \arg\min_\theta L(\theta; b)$. That is, $J(\theta_b) - J(\theta^*)$ measures how much the objective function deviates from the optimum due to the added noise. Given random noise $b \in \mathbb{R}^s$, $J(\theta_b) + \frac{\varphi}{\epsilon n} b^T \theta_b \le J(\theta^*) + \frac{\varphi}{\epsilon n} b^T \theta^*$. Hence, $J(\theta_b) - J(\theta^*) \le \frac{\varphi}{\epsilon n} b^T (\theta^* - \theta_b) \le \frac{\varphi}{\epsilon n} \|b\|_2 \|\theta^* - \theta_b\|_2$. Let E denote the event that $\{\|b\|_2 \le \xi\}$, where $\xi = \frac{\epsilon n}{\varphi} \sqrt{\lambda c}$. When E holds, then $\frac{\varphi}{\epsilon n} b^T \theta$ is $\frac{\varphi \xi}{\epsilon n}$-Lipschitz. Hence, with $G(\theta) = J(\theta)$ λ-strongly convex, $g_1(\theta) = \frac{\varphi}{\epsilon n} b^T \theta$ and $g_2 = 0$, we can invoke Lemma 8 to obtain $\|\theta^* - \theta_b\|_2 \le \frac{\varphi \xi}{\lambda \epsilon n}$. Therefore, when E holds, then

$$J(\theta_b) - J(\theta^*) \le \frac{\varphi}{\epsilon n} \|b\|_2 \|\theta^* - \theta_b\|_2 \le \frac{\varphi}{\epsilon n} \xi \frac{\varphi \xi}{\lambda \epsilon n} = c.$$

Thus $\mathbb{P}(J(\theta_b) - J(\theta^*) > c) \le 1 - \mathbb{P}(E) = \mathbb{P}(\|b\|_2 > \xi)$ when the random noise b is sampled from B_1 or B_2. $\|B_1\|_1$ is the sum of s independent exponential random variables with mean $= 2$ and thus $\|B_1\|_1 \sim Gamma(s, 2)$. On the other hand, $\|B_2\|_2 \sim \chi^2(2s)$. But in fact $\chi^2(2s) \sim Gamma(s, 2)$. Therefore, $\mathbb{P}(\|B_1\|_1 > \xi) \le \mathbb{P}(\|B_1\|_1 > \xi) = \mathbb{P}(\|B_2\|_2 > \xi)$. Thus, sampling the noise from B_1 in Algorithm 1 produces more accurate results.

4   Application to Logistic Regression with Elastic-Net Regularization

In this section we show how to apply the results from the previous section to penalized logistic regression. The logistic loss function $l(\theta; x, y)$ is given by

$$l(\theta; x, y) = \log\left(1 + \exp(-y\,\theta^T x)\right),$$

where $y \in \{-1, 1\}$. The first and second derivatives with respect to θ are

$$\nabla l(\theta; x, y) = -\frac{1}{1 + \exp(y\,\theta^T x)} yx$$

$$\nabla^2 l(\theta; x, y) = \frac{1}{1 + \exp(-y\,\theta^T x)} \frac{1}{1 + \exp(y\,\theta^T x)} xx^T.$$

It can easily be seen that the logistic loss function satisfies the following properties: (i) $l(\theta; x, y)$ is convex; (ii) $\nabla^2 l(\theta; x, y)$ is continuous; and (iii) $\nabla^2 l(\theta; x, y)$ is a rank-1 matrix.

We denote by $\|M\|_1$ the nuclear norm of the matrix M and we choose κ such that $\|x\|_j \le \kappa$ for all x, where $j \in \{1, 2\}$. Then

$$\left\|\nabla^2 l(\theta; x, y)\right\|_1 \le \left\|xx^T\right\|_1 = \|x\|_2^2 \le \|x\|_j^2 \le \kappa^2, \quad \text{for } j \in \{1, 2\},$$

$$\|\nabla l(\theta; x, y)\|_j \le \|x\|_j \le \kappa,$$

Thus we can apply Algorithm 1 to output differentially private coefficients for logistic regression with elastic-net regularization. Moreover, the logistic loss function satisfies the conditions in Theorem 3 because $l(\theta; x, y)$ is Lipschitz: There exists a parameter θ such that

$$|l(\theta_1; x, y) - l(\theta_2; x, y)| \le \|\nabla l(\theta; x, y)\|_2 \|\theta_1 - \theta_2\|_2 \le \kappa \|\theta_1 - \theta_2\|_2.$$

Thus we can apply the stability argument in Theorem 3 to select the best regularization parameters in a differentially private way. In Section 5 we show how well this method performs on a GWAS data set.

5 Application to GWAS Data

We now evaluate the performance of the proposed method based on a GWAS data set. We analyze a binary phenotype such as a disease. Each SNP can take the values 0, 1, or 2. This represents the number of minor alleles at that site. A large SNP data set is freely available from the HapMap project[1]. It consists of SNP data from 4 populations of 45 to 90 individuals each, but does not contain any phenotypic information about the individuals. HAP-SAMPLE [14] can be used to generate SNP genotypes for cases and controls by resampling from HapMap. This ensures that the simulated data show linkage disequilibrium (i.e., correlations among SNPs) and minor allele frequencies similar to real data.

For our analysis we use the simulations from Malaspinas and Uhler [15]. The simulated data sets consist of 400 cases and 400 controls each with about 10,000 SNPs per individual (SNPs were typed with the Affymetrix CHIP on chromosome 9 and chromosome 13 of the Phase I/II HapMap data). For each data set two SNPs with a given minor allele frequency (MAF) were chosen to be causative. We will analyze the results for minor allele frequency (MAF) = 0.25. The simulations were performed under the multiplicative effects model: Denoting the two causative SNPs by X and Y and the disease status by D (i.e., $X, Y \in \{0, 1, 2\}$ and $D \in \{-1, 1\}$, where 1 describes the diseased state), then the multiplicative effects model can be defined through the odds of having a disease:

$$\frac{\mathbb{P}(D = 1 \mid X, Y)}{\mathbb{P}(D = -1 \mid X, Y)} = \epsilon \alpha^X \beta^Y \delta^{XY}.$$

This model corresponds to a log-linear model with interaction between the two SNPs. For our simulations we chose $\epsilon = 0.64$, $\alpha = \beta = 0.91$ and $\delta = 2.73$. This results in a sample disease prevalence of 0.5 and effect size of 1, which are typical values for association studies. See Malaspinas and Uhler [15] for more details.

In the first step, we screen all SNPs and select a subset of SNPs with the highest χ^2-scores based on a simple χ^2-test for association between each single SNP and the phenotype. Various approaches for performing the screening in a differentially private manner were discussed and analyzed in Uhler et al. [7], Johnson and Shmatikov [8], and Yu et al. [9]; We concentrated on the second step and did not employ the differentially private screening approaches in this paper. The second step of the two-step procedure consists of performing penalized logistic regression with elastic-net regularization on the selected subset of SNPs and choosing the best regularization parameters in a differentially private manner. In the following, we analyze the statistical utility of the second step and show how accurately our end-to-end differentially private penalized logistic regression method is able to detect the causative SNPs and their interaction.

---

[1] http://hapmap.ncbi.nlm.nih.gov/

The elastic-net penalty function has the form $\frac{1}{2}\lambda(1-\alpha)\ell_2 + \lambda\alpha\ell_1$, where α controls the sparsity of the resulting model and λ controls the extent to which the elastic-net penalty affects the loss function. In the simulation, we apply a threshold criterion to the terms in the model so that we exclude from the model the ith term if its regression coefficient, θ_i, satisfies $|\theta_i|/\max_i\{|\theta_i|\} < r$, where $\max_i\{|\theta_i|\}$ is the largest coefficient in absolute value and r is a thresholding ratio, which we set to 0.01.

In our experiments, we selected $M = 5$ SNPs with the highest χ^2-scores, which include the two causative SNPs, for further analysis. We denote by ϵ the privacy budget, by α the sparsity parameter in the elastic-net penalty function, and by "*convex_min*" the condition of strong convexity imposed on the objective function (see Theorem 3). Note that *convex_min* is a function of M and ϵ. For elastic-net with α fixed, we need the smallest candidate parameter $\lambda_{min} \geq convex\_min/(1-\alpha)$.

In Figure 1, we analyze the sensitivity of our method. For different sparsity parameters α and different privacy budgets ϵ, which determine *convex_min* given a fixed M, we show how often, out of 100 simulations each, our algorithm recovered the interaction term (leftmost bar in red), the main effects scaled by a factor of $1/2$ to account for the two main effects (middle bar in green) and all effects, i.e. the interaction effect and the two main effects (rightmost bar in blue). As the privacy budget ϵ increases, the amount of noise added to the regression problem decreases, and hence the frequency of selecting the correct effects in the regression analysis increases. The plots also show that as the sparsity parameter α increases, the frequency of selecting the correct terms decreases.

In Figure 2 we analyze the specificity of our method. For different sparsity parameters α and different strong convexity conditions *convex_min*, we show how

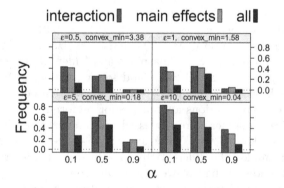

Fig. 1. Sensitivity analysis for different sparsity parameters α, privacy budgets ϵ, and strong convexity conditions *convex_min* when the top 5 SNPs are used for the analysis: the red (leftmost) bar shows how often, out of 100 simulations each, the algorithm recovered the interaction term, the green (middle) bar corresponds to the main effects scaled by a factor of $1/2$ and the rightmost (blue) bar corresponds to all effects, i.e. 2 main effects and 1 interaction effect

often, out of 100 simulations each, our algorithm did not include any additional effects in the selected model. As α increases, the selected model becomes sparser and the algorithm is hence less likely to wrongly include additional effects. We also observe that as *convex_min* decreases, the specificity increases. This can be explained by how we choose the candidate parameters λ, namely as multiples of the smallest allowed value for λ, which is $convex\_min/(1-\alpha)$. When λ is smalll, the effect of the penalty terms diminishes, and we are essentially performing a regular logistic regression, which does not produce sparse models.

In Figure 3, we plotted the results of non-private penalized logistic regression with elastic-net penalty to contrast Figure 1 and Figure 2. The results of the non-private penalized logisitc regression is indirectly related to ϵ because the choice of the smallest regularization parameter λ is bounded below by $convex\_min/(1-\alpha)$ and *convex_min* is a function of ϵ. We can observe from Figure 3 that when the regularization parameter λ is large (i.e., $convex\_min \geq 1.58$), the regression analysis screens out all effects. Hence, the sensitivity is 0 and the specificity is 1. When λ is small (i.e., $convex\_min \leq 0.18$), the amount of regularization

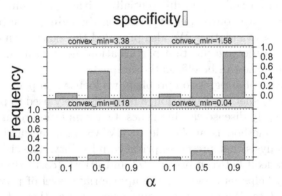

Fig. 2. Specificity analysis for different sparsity parameters α and strong convexity conditions *convex_min*: the plot shows how often, out of 100 simulations each, our algorithm did not include any additional effects in the selected model

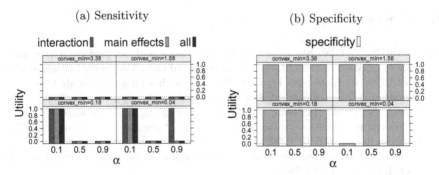

Fig. 3. Results of non-private logistic regression with elastic-net penalty. Figure 3a and Figure 3b would be compared with Figure 1 and Figure 2, respectively.

also becomes marginal, and we begin to see that the sensitivity increases but the specificity decreases. Figure 3 shows that we can identify the correct model when $\alpha = 0.1$ and $convex\_min = 0.18$. In contrast, when we use the same α and $convex\_min$ for differentially private regressions, Figure 1 shows that we can obtain a good sensitivity result, but Figure 2 shows that the specificity result for this choice is poor.

6   Conclusions

Various papers have argued that it is possible to use aggregate genomic data to compromise the privacy of individual-level information collected in GWAS databases. In this paper, we respond to these attacks by proposing a new method to release regression coefficients from association studies that satisfy differential privacy and hence come with privacy guarantees against arbitrary external information.

By extending the approaches in Chaudhuri and Vinterbo [11] and Kifer et al. [10] we developed an end-to-end differentially private procedure for solving regression problems with convex penalty functions including selecting the penalty parameters by cross-validation. We also provided the exact form of the random noise used in the objective function perturbation mechanism and showed that the perturbation noise can be efficiently sampled.

As a special case of a regression problem, we focused on penalized logistic regression with elastic-net regularization, a method widely used to perform GWAS analyses and identify disease-causing genes. Our simulation results in Section 5 showed that our method is applicable to GWAS data sets and enables us to perform data analysis that preserves privacy and utility. The risk-utility analysis about the tradeoff between privacy (ϵ) and utility (correctly identifying the causative SNPs) helps us decide on the appropriate level of privacy guarantee for the released data. We hope that approaches such as those described in this paper will allow the release of more information from GWAS going forward and allay the privacy concerns that others have voiced over the past decade.

References

[1] Austin, E., Pan, W., Shen, X.: Penalized regression and risk prediction in genome-wide association studies. Statistical Analysis and Data Mining 6(4) (August 2013)

[2] Cho, S., et al.: Elastic-net regularization approaches for genome-wide association studies of rheumatoid arthritis. BMC Proceedings 3(suppl. 7), S25 (2009)

[3] Homer, N., et al.: Resolving individuals contributing trace amounts of DNA to highly complex mixtures using high-density SNP geno-typing microarrays. PLoS Genetics 4(8), e1000167 (2008)

[4] Couzin, J.: Whole-genome data not anonymous, challenging assumptions. Science 321(5894), 1278 (2008)

[5] Zerhouni, E.A., Nabel, E.G.: Protecting aggregate genomic data. Science 322(5898), 44 (2008)

[6] Dwork, C., McSherry, F., Nissim, K., Smith, A.: Calibrating noise to sensitivity in private data analysis. In: Halevi, S., Rabin, T. (eds.) TCC 2006. LNCS, vol. 3876, pp. 265–284. Springer, Heidelberg (2006)

[7] Uhler, C., Slavkovic, A.B., Fienberg, S.E.: Privacy-preserving data sharing for genome-wide association studies. Journal of Privacy and Confidentiality 5(1), 137–166 (2013)

[8] Johnson, A., Shmatikov, V.: Privacy-preserving data exploration in genome-wide association studies. In: Proceedings of the 19th ACM SIGKDD International Conference on Knowledge Discovery and Data Mining, pp. 1079–1087 (2013)

[9] Yu, F., et al.: Scalable Privacy-Preserving Data Sharing Methodology for Genome-Wide Association Studies. Journal of Biomedical Informatics (February 2014)

[10] Kifer, D., Smith, A., Thakurta, A.: Private convex empirical risk minimization and high-dimensional regression. Proceedings of Journal of Machine Learning Research - Proceedings Track 23, 25.1–25.40 (2012)

[11] Chaudhuri, K., Vinterbo, S.A.: A stability-based validation procedure for differentially private machine learning. In: Advances in Neural Information Processing Systems, pp. 1–19 (2013)

[12] Chaudhuri, K., Monteleoni, C., Sarwate, A.D.: Differentially private empirical risk minimization. JMLR 12(7), 1069–1109 (2011)

[13] Laurent, B., Massart, P.: Adaptive estimation of a quadratic functional by model selection. Annals of Statistics 28(5), 1302–1338 (2000)

[14] Wright, F.A., et al.: Simulating association studies: a data-based resampling method for candidate regions or whole genome scans. Bioinformatics 23(19), 2581–2588 (2007)

[15] Malaspinas, A.S., Uhler, C.: Detecting epistasis via Markov bases. Journal of Algebraic Statistics 2(1), 36–53 (2010)

[16] Gómez, E., Gomez-Viilegas, M.A., Marín, J.M.: A multivariate generalization of the power exponential family of distributions. Communications in Statistics - Theory and Methods 27(3), 589–600 (1998)

A   Proofs

A.1   Proof of Theorem 3

Lemma 8. *Let G, g_1, and g_2 be vector-valued continuous functions. Suppose that G is λ-strongly convex, g_1 is convex and γ_1-Lipschitz, and g_2 is convex and γ_2-Lipschitz. If $f_1 = \arg\min_f (G+g_1)(f)$ and $f_2 = \arg\min_f (G+g_2)(f)$, then $\|f_1 - f_2\|_2 \leq (\gamma_1+\gamma_2)/\lambda$.*

Proof (of Lemma 8). $G + g_1$ and $G + g_2$ are λ-strongly convex because G is λ-strongly convex and g_1 and g_2 are convex. Then for $j, k, w \in \{1, 2\}$, $j \neq k$,

$$(G + g_w)(f_j) \geq (G + g_w)(f_k) + \partial(G + g_w)(f_k)^T (f_j - f_k) + \frac{\lambda}{2}\|f_j - f_k\|^2$$

where $\partial(G + g_w)$ denotes the subgradient. We know that $0 \in \partial(G + g_w)(f_w)$ because f_w minimizes $G + g_w$. Hence,

$$(G + g_2)(f_1) \geq (G + g_2)(f_2) + \frac{\lambda}{2}\|f_1 - f_2\|_2^2,$$

$$(G + g_1)(f_2) \geq (G + g_1)(f_1) + \frac{\lambda}{2}\|f_1 - f_2\|_2^2.$$

By summing these two inequalities we obtain

$$(G + g_2)(f_1) + (G + g_1)(f_2) \geq (G + g_2)(f_2) + (G + g_1)(f_1) + \lambda \|f_1 - f_2\|_2^2$$

and hence $[g_2(f_1) - g_2(f_2)] + [g_1(f_2) - g_2(f_1)] \geq \lambda \|f_1 - f_2\|_2^2$. The fact that g_w is γ_w-Lipschitz implies that $\left| g_2(f_1) - g_2(f_2) \right| + \left| g_1(f_2) - g_2(f_1) \right| \leq (\gamma_1 + \gamma_2) \|f_1 - f_2\|_2$ and hence

$$\lambda \|f_1 - f_2\|_2^2 \leq [g_2(f_1) - g_2(f_2)] + [g_1(f_2) - g_2(f_1)]$$
$$\leq \left| g_2(f_1) - g_2(f_2) \right| + \left| g_1(f_2) - g_2(f_1) \right| \leq (\gamma_1 + \gamma_2)\|f_1 - f_2\|_2.$$

Therefore $\|f_1 - f_2\|_2 \leq (\gamma_1 + \gamma_2)/\lambda$. □

Proof (of Theorem 3). For notational convenience we assume that $c_{\min} \geq c^*$ so that

$$L(\theta; T) = \frac{1}{n} \sum_{d \in T} l(\theta; d) + \lambda^T r(\theta) + \frac{\varphi}{\varepsilon n} b^T \theta.$$

If $c_{\min} < c^*$, we can extend r to include $r_{t+1}(\theta) = \frac{\max\{0, c^* - c_{\min}\}}{2} \|\theta\|_2^2$ and extend each $\lambda \in \Lambda$ such that $\lambda_{t+1} = 1$. First, we show that $|q(\theta^*(T), V) - q(\theta^*(T'), V)| \leq \beta_1/n$ for training sets T and T' that differ only by one record. Here, $\theta^*(T) = \arg\min_\theta L(\theta; T)$. Let $d = T \backslash T'$, $d' = T' \backslash T$,

$$G(\theta; T, T') = \frac{1}{n} \sum_{d \in T \cap T'} l(\theta; d) + \lambda^T r(\theta) + \frac{\varphi}{\varepsilon n} b^T \theta,$$

$$g_1(\theta; T, T') = \frac{1}{n} l(\theta; d) \qquad \text{and} \qquad g_2(\theta; T, T') = \frac{1}{n} l(\theta; d').$$

Then G is $c_{\min}$-strongly convex, and g_1 and g_2 are convex and γ/n-Lipschitz. By Lemma 8, $\|\theta^*(T) - \theta^*(T')\|_2 \leq \frac{2\gamma}{n c_{\min}}$. Since h is κ-Lipschitz we obtain for any validation set V, $|q(\theta^*(T), V) - q(\theta^*(T'), V)| \leq \frac{2\gamma\kappa}{n c_{\min}}$.

Second, we show that for all $\lambda \in \Lambda$ and for all validation sets V and V' that differ in a single record, $|q(\theta^*(T), V) - q(\theta^*(T'), V')| \leq \beta_2/m$. Since h is non-negative, $|q(\theta^*(T), V) - q(\theta^*(T'), V')| \leq h_{\max}/m$, where $h_{\max} = \sup_d h(\theta^*(T); d)$. By definition, $h_{\max} \leq h^*$. Moreover, because h is κ-Lipschitz, $h_{\max} \leq \kappa \|\theta^*(T)\|_2$. So $h_{\max} \leq \min\{h^*, \kappa \|\theta^*(T)\|_2\}$. Now let E be the event that $\|b\|_2 \leq \xi$. Provided that E holds, we have $|b^T \theta_1 - b^T \theta_2| \leq \|b\|_2 \|\theta_1 - \theta_2\|_2 \leq \xi \|\theta_1 - \theta_2\|_2$. Let $G(\theta) = \lambda^T r(\theta)$, $g_1(\theta; T) = \frac{1}{n} \sum_{d \in T} l(\theta; d) + \frac{\varphi}{\varepsilon n} b^T \theta$, and $g_2(\theta) = 0$. Then G is $c_{\min}$-strongly convex, g_1 is $(\gamma + \frac{\varphi\xi}{\varepsilon n})$-Lipschitz, and g_2 is 0-Lipschitz. Since $G + g_2$ is minimized when $\theta = 0$, we obtain by invoking Lemma 8 that $\|\theta^*(T)\|_2 = \|\theta^*(T) - 0\|_2 \leq \frac{1}{c_{\min}} (\gamma + \frac{\varphi\xi}{\varepsilon n})$.
Therefore, $|q(\theta^*(T), V) - q(\theta^*(T), V')| \leq \frac{1}{m} \min \left\{ h^*, \frac{\kappa}{c_{\min}} (\gamma + \frac{\varphi\xi}{\varepsilon n}) \right\}$. □

A.2   Proof of Theorem 7

Lemma 9. *If A is of full rank and E has rank at most 2, then*

$$\frac{\det(A + E) - \det(A)}{\det(A)} = \lambda_1(A^{-1}E) + \lambda_2(A^{-1}E) + \lambda_1(A^{-1}E)\lambda_2(A^{-1}E),$$

where $\lambda_j(Z)$ denotes the j-th eigenvalue of matrix Z.

Proof (of Lemma 9). See Lemma 10 in Chaudhuri et al. [12].

Proof (of Theorem 7). Similar to the proof by Chaudhuri et al. [12], we show that if r is infinitely differentiable, then Algorithm 1 is ϵ-differentially private. It then follows from the successive approximation method by Kifer et al. [10] that Algorithm 1 is still ϵ-differentially private even if r is convex but not necessarily differentiable.

Let g denote the probability density function of the algorithm's output θ^*. Our goal is to show that $e^{-\epsilon} \leq \frac{g(\theta|D)}{g(\theta|D')} \leq e^{\epsilon}$. Suppose that the Hessian of r is continuous. Because $0 = \nabla L(\theta; D)$, we have

$$T_D(\theta) := b = -\frac{\epsilon}{\varphi}\left[\sum_{d \in D} \nabla l(\theta; d) + n\nabla r(\theta)\right] \quad \text{and} \quad \nabla T_D(\theta) = -\frac{\epsilon}{\varphi}\left[\sum_{d \in D} \nabla^2 l(\theta; d) + n\nabla^2 r(\theta)\right].$$

T_D is injective because $L(\theta; D)$ is strongly convex. Also, T_D is continuously differentiable. Therefore,

$$\frac{g(\theta|D)}{g(\theta|D')} = \frac{f(T_D(\theta))}{f(T_{D'}(\theta))}\frac{|\det(\nabla T_D)(\theta)|}{|\det(\nabla T_{D'})(\theta)|},$$

where f is the density function of b.

We first consider $\frac{|\det(\nabla T_D)(\theta)|}{|\det(\nabla T_{D'})(\theta)|}$. Let $A = -\frac{\varphi}{\epsilon}\nabla T_{D'}$, $E = \nabla^2 l(\theta; D\backslash D') - \nabla^2 l(\theta; D'\backslash D)$. Because l is convex and r is strongly convex, $\nabla T_D(\theta)$ is positive definite. Hence, A has full rank. Also, E has rank at most 2 because $\nabla^2 l(\theta; d)$ is a rank 1 matrix by assumption. By Lemma 9,

$$\frac{|\det(\nabla T_D(\theta))|}{|\det(\nabla T_{D'}(\theta))|} = \left|\frac{\det(A+E)}{\det(A)}\right| \leq 1 + s_1(A^{-1}E) + s_2(A^{-1}E) + s_1(A^{-1}E)s_2(A^{-1}E),$$

where $s_i(M)$ denotes the ith largest singular value of M. Because r is λ-strongly convex, the smallest eigenvalue of A is at least $n\lambda$. So $s_i(A^{-1}E) \leq \frac{s_i(E)}{n\lambda}$. Because $\|\nabla l(\theta; d)\|_j \leq \kappa$ for $j \in \{1, 2\}$, applying the triangle inequality to the nuclear norm yields $s_1(E) + s_2(E) \leq \|\nabla^2 l(\theta; D\backslash D')\|_1 + \|\nabla^2 l(\theta; D'\backslash D)\|_1 \leq 2c$. Therefore, $s_1(A^{-1}E) s_2(A^{-1}E) \leq \left(\frac{c}{n\lambda}\right)^2$, and

$$\frac{|\det(\nabla T_D)(\theta)|}{|\det(\nabla T_{D'})(\theta)|} = \frac{|\det(A+E)|}{|\det(A)|} \leq \left(1 + \frac{c}{n\lambda}\right)^2.$$

Now we consider $\frac{f(T_D(\theta))}{f(T_{D'}(\theta))}$. Since

$$\|T_D(\theta) - T_{D'}(\theta)\|_j = \left(\frac{\epsilon}{\varphi}\right)\|\nabla l(\theta; D\backslash D') - \nabla l(\theta; D'\backslash D)\|_j$$

$$\leq \left(\frac{\epsilon}{\varphi}\right)\left(\|\nabla l(\theta; D\backslash D')\|_j + \|\nabla l(\theta; D'\backslash D)\|_j\right) \leq \frac{2\kappa\epsilon}{\varphi},$$

we obtain $\frac{f(T_D(\theta))}{f(T_{D'}(\theta))} = \exp\left(-\frac{\|T_D(\theta)\|_j}{2}\right) \Big/ \exp\left(\frac{-\|T_{D'}(\theta)\|_j}{2}\right) \leq \exp\left(\frac{\kappa\epsilon}{\varphi}\right)$, and therefore,

$$\frac{f(T_D(\theta))}{f(T_{D'}(\theta))}\frac{|\det(\nabla T_D)(\theta)|}{|\det(\nabla T_{D'})(\theta)|} \leq \exp\left(\frac{\kappa\epsilon}{\varphi} + 2\log\left(1 + \frac{c}{n\lambda}\right)\right) \leq e^{\epsilon}.$$

A.3   Proof of Proposition 4

Proof (of Proposition 4). The distribution of X is a special case of an s-dimensional *power exponential distribution* as defined by Gómez et al. [16], namely $X \sim PE_s(\mu, \Sigma, \beta)$ with $\mu = (0, \ldots, 0)^T$, $\Sigma = \mathrm{Id}_s$ and $\beta = \frac{1}{2}$. Gómez et al. [16] proved that if $T \sim PE_s(\mu, \Sigma, \beta)$, then T has the same distribution as $\mu + Y A^T Z$, where Z is a random vector with uniform distribution on the unit sphere in $\mathbb{R}^s$, Y is an absolutely continuous non-negative random variable, independent from Z, whose density function is

$$g(y) = \frac{s}{\Gamma\left(1 + \frac{s}{2\beta}\right) 2^{\frac{s}{2\beta}}} y^{s-1} \exp\left(-\frac{1}{2} y^{2\beta}\right) I_{(0,\infty)}(y),$$

and $A \in \mathbb{R}^{s \times s}$ is a square matrix such that $A^T A = \Sigma$.

Note that for $\beta = \frac{1}{2}$, the distribution of Y boils down to a χ^2-distribution with $2s$ degrees of freedom. In addition, if $W \sim \mathcal{N}(0, \mathrm{Id}_s)$, then $W/\|W\|$ is uniformly distributed on the unit s-sphere. Finally, since $\Sigma = \mathrm{Id}_s$ we get that $A = \mathrm{Id}$.   □

Disclosure Risk Evaluation for Fully Synthetic Categorical Data*

Jingchen Hu, Jerome P. Reiter, and Quanli Wang

Duke University, Durham NC 27708, USA

Abstract. We present an approach for evaluating disclosure risks for fully synthetic categorical data. The basic idea is to compute probability distributions of unknown confidential data values given the synthetic data and assumptions about intruder knowledge. We use a "worst-case" scenario of an intruder knowing all but one of the records in the confidential data. To create the synthetic data, we use a Dirichlet process mixture of products of multinomial distributions, which is a Bayesian version of a latent class model. In addition to generating synthetic data with high utility, the likelihood function admits simple and convenient approximations to the disclosure risk probabilities via importance sampling. We illustrate the disclosure risk computations by synthesizing a subset of data from the American Community Survey.

Keywords: Bayesian, confidentiality, Dirichlet process, disclosure, microdata.

1 Introduction

Record-level data, also known as microdata, from the social, behavioral, and economic sciences offer enormous potential benefits to society. When made widely accessible as public use files, these databases facilitate advances in research and policy-making, enable students to develop skills at data analysis, and help ordinary citizens learn about their communities. However, as most stewards of social science data are acutely aware, wide-scale dissemination of microdata can result in unintended disclosures of data subjects' identities and sensitive attributes, thereby violating promises—and in some instances laws—to protect data subjects' privacy and confidentiality.

When microdata are highly sensitive or readily identifiable—as may be the case, for example, for business establishments or in large-scale administrative databases—stewards may not be able to protect confidentiality adequately by suppressing/perturbing only a small fraction of values (which is frequent practice in small-scale probability samples). In such contexts, one approach is to generate and release fully synthetic data (Rubin, 1993; Fienberg, 1994; Reiter, 2002, 2005b, 2009; Raghunathan *et al.*, 2003; Reiter and Raghunathan, 2007). These comprise entirely simulated records generated from statistical models designed to preserve important relationships in the confidential data. A related approach is to release partially synthetic data (Little, 1993; Reiter, 2003, 2004), in which only values deemed sensitive are replaced with simulated values.

The U.S. Census Bureau has adopted synthetic data as a dissemination strategy for several major data products, including the Survey of Income and Program Participation (Abowd *et al.*, 2006) and the Longitudinal Business Database (Kinney *et al.*,

* This research was supported by U.S. National Science Foundation grants CNS-10-12141 and SES-11-31897.

J. Domingo-Ferrer (Ed.): PSD 2014, LNCS 8744, pp. 185–199, 2014.

2011). In both of these products, all but a handful of variables are replaced with values simulated from models estimated on the confidential data. Other examples of synthetic data applications have appeared in the literature as well (e.g., Kennickell, 1997; Abowd and Woodcock, 2001, 2004; Little *et al.*, 2004; Graham and Penny, 2005; An and Little, 2007; Hawala, 2008; Drechsler *et al.*, 2008a,b; Graham *et al.*, 2009; Machanavajjhala *et al.*, 2008; Drechsler and Reiter, 2010, 2012; Slavkovic and Lee, 2010; Wang and Reiter, 2012; Burgette and Reiter, 2013; Paiva *et al.*, 2014).

With fully synthetic data, disclosure risks generally are considered to be low—it is pointless to match fully synthetic records to records in other databases, since each fully synthetic record does not correspond to any particular individual. However, researchers have identified scenarios where full synthesis carries non-trivial disclosure risks (Abowd and Vilhuber, 2008; Charest, 2010; McClure and Reiter, 2012; Reiter *et al.*, 2014). Typically, these illustrative scenarios involve stylized data (e.g., a 2^4 contingency table) with simple synthesizers (e.g., a Dirichlet-multinomial distribution). To our knowledge, the literature does not include examples of quantified disclosure risks in fully synthetic data in realistic contexts.

In this article, we illustrate disclosure risk evaluations for fully synthetic, categorical data. In particular, we compute Bayesian posterior probabilities that intruders can learn confidential values given the released data and assumptions about their prior knowledge (Duncan and Lambert, 1989; Fienberg *et al.*, 1997; Reiter, 2005a; McClure and Reiter, 2012; Reiter, 2012; Abowd *et al.*, 2013; Reiter *et al.*, 2014). We synthesize a subset of data from the American Community Survey using a Dirichlet process mixture of products of multinomial (DPMPM) distributions. The DPMPM model has been shown in other contexts to be effective at capturing complex dependence structure in contingency tables while requiring little tuning by the data steward (Dunson and Xing, 2009; Si and Reiter, 2013; Manrique-Vallier and Reiter, 2014).

Our goal here is to illustrate the risk evaluations with realistic data. Thus, although we present some evaluations of data utility to assure readers that the DPMPM synthesizer is not generating worthless data, we refrain from making conclusions about the merits of using the DPMPM synthesizer, or fully synthetic data in general as compared to other disclosure protection methods.

2 The DPMPM Synthesizer

Let the confidential data D comprise n individuals measured on p categorical variables. For $i = 1, \ldots, n$ and $k = 1, \ldots, p$, let x_{ik} denote the value of variable k for individual i, and let $x_i = (x_{i1}, \ldots, x_{ip})$. Without loss of generality, assume that each x_{ik} takes on values in $\{1, \ldots, d_k\}$, where $d_k \geq 2$ is the total number of categories for variable k. Effectively, the survey variables form a contingency table of $d = d_1 \times d_2 \times \cdots \times d_p$ cells defined by cross-classifications of the p variables. Let X_{ik} and X_i be random variables defined respectively on the sample spaces for x_{ik} and x_i.

We generate synthetic data using a finite number of mixture components in the DPMPM. Paraphrasing from Si and Reiter (2013), the finite DPMPM assumes that each individual i belongs to exactly one of $F < \infty$ latent classes; see Si and Reiter (2013) for advice on determining F. For $i = 1, \ldots, n$, let $\eta_i \in \{1, \ldots, F\}$ indicate the class of individual i, and let $\pi_f = \Pr(\eta_i = f)$. We assume that $\pi = (\pi_1, \ldots, \pi_F)$ is the same for all individuals. Within any class, each of the p variables independently follows a class-specific multinomial distribution, so that individuals in the same latent class have the same cell probabilities. For any value $c \in \{1, \ldots, d_k\}$, let $\phi_{fc}^{(k)} = \Pr(X_{ik} = c \mid \eta_i = f)$ be the probability of $X_{ik} = c$ given that individual i is in class f. Let $\phi = \{\phi_{fc}^{(k)} : c = 1, \ldots, d_k, k = 1, \ldots, p, f = 1, \ldots, F\}$ be the collection of all $\phi_{fc}^{(k)}$. The finite mixture model can be expressed as

$$X_{ik} \mid \eta_i, \phi \overset{ind}{\sim} \text{Multinomial}(\phi_{\eta_i 1}^{(k)}, \ldots, \phi_{\eta_i d_k}^{(k)}) \quad \text{for all } i, k \tag{1}$$

$$\eta_i \mid \pi \sim \text{Multinomial}(\pi_1, \ldots, \pi_F) \quad \text{for all } i, \tag{2}$$

where each multinomial distribution has sample size equal to one and the number of levels is implied by the dimension of the corresponding probability vector.

For prior distributions on π and ϕ, we use the truncated stick breaking representation of Sethuraman (1994). We have

$$\pi_f = V_f \prod_{l < f} (1 - V_l) \quad \text{for } f = 1, \ldots, F \tag{3}$$

$$V_f \overset{iid}{\sim} \text{Beta}(1, \alpha) \quad \text{for } f = 1, \ldots, F - 1, \quad V_F = 1 \tag{4}$$

$$\alpha \sim \text{Gamma}(a_\alpha, b_\alpha) \tag{5}$$

$$\phi_f^{(k)} = (\phi_{f1}^{(k)}, \ldots, \psi_{fd_k}^{(k)}) \sim \text{Dirichlet}(a_{k1}, \ldots, a_{kd_k}). \tag{6}$$

We set $a_{k1} = \cdots = a_{kd_k} = 1$ for all k to correspond to uniform distributions. Following Dunson and Xing (2009) and Si and Reiter (2013), we set $(a_\alpha = .25, b_\alpha = .25)$, which represents a small prior sample size and hence vague specification for the Gamma distribution. In practice, we find these specifications allow the data to dominate the prior distribution. We estimate the posterior distribution of all parameters using a blocked Gibbs sampler (Ishwaran and James, 2001; Si and Reiter, 2013).

We note that this model assumes no structural zeros in the data; that is, all cells in the implied contingency table have non-zero probability. See Manrique-Vallier and Reiter (2014) for variants of DPMPM models that allow structural zeros.

To generate one fully synthetic dataset of size n^*, we first sample a value of (α, π, ϕ) from the posterior distribution. Using the generated π, we sample values of $(\eta_1, \ldots, \eta_{n^*})$ independently from (2). Using the sampled ϕ, for each sampled η_i, where $i = 1, \ldots, n^*$, we then sample the ith synthetic record, $x_i^* = (x_{i1}^*, \ldots, x_{ip}^*)$, from independent multinomial distributions with probabilities $\phi_{\eta_i}^{(k)}$ for each k. When n^* is the original sample size n, the synthesis can be conveniently implemented inside the blocked Gibbs sampler—after each Gibbs updating step, we simply sample and save draws of x_i^* for all n records. To create $m > 1$ synthetic datasets, one repeats this process m times, using approximately independent draws of parameters. Approximately independent draws can be obtained by using iterations that are far apart in the estimated MCMC chain.

Let $Z = (Z^{(1)}, \ldots, Z^{(m)})$ be a set of m synthetic categorical datasets under consideration for release by the data steward. In the remainder of the article, we assume that $n^* = n$, although this is not necessary.

3   Disclosure Risk Measure for the DPMPM

With fully synthetic data, disclosure risk metrics based on matching released and external records are generally not applicable, since there is no unique mapping of the rows in Z to the rows in D. Instead, we consider questions of the form: can intruders accurately infer from the synthetic data that some record with particular data values is in the confidential data? When the combination of values is unique in the population (or possibly just the sample), this question essentially asks if intruders can determine whether or not a specific individual is in the confidential data—this may count as a disclosure under some confidentiality protection laws.

3.1   Disclosure Risk Evaluation Strategy

To describe the disclosure risk evaluations, we follow the presentation of Reiter *et al.* (2014). Let x denote an arbitrary realization from the sample space of the contingency table formed by the p categorical variables; x can take on any of d possible values. We suppose that an intruder seeks to learn if a particular x is in D. Let A represent the information known by the intruder about records in D. Let S represent any information known by the intruder about the process of generating Z, for example meta-data indicating the values of F and (a_α, b_α) for the DPMPM synthesizer. Let X be a random variable representing the intruder's uncertain knowledge of whether or not x is in D, where the sample space of X is all possible values of x in the population. Given (Z, A, S), we assume the intruder seeks the Bayesian posterior distribution,

$$p(X = x \mid Z, A, S) = \frac{p(Z \mid X = x, A, S)p(X = x \mid A, S)}{\sum_{x \in \mathcal{U}} p(Z \mid X = x, A, S)p(X = x \mid A, S)} \tag{7}$$

$$\propto p(Z \mid X = x, A, S)p(X = x \mid A, S), \tag{8}$$

where $\mathcal{U}$ represents the universe of all feasible values of x. Here, $p(Z \mid X = x, A, S)$ is the likelihood of generating the particular set of synthetic data given that x is in the confidential data and whatever else is known by the intruder. The $p(X = x \mid A, S)$ can be considered the intruder's prior distribution on X based on (A, S).

Key to the computation of (7) are the assumptions about A and $p(X = x \mid A, S)$. In general, it is not possible for the data steward to know either. We evaluate risks assuming the intruder has very strong prior knowledge in A. In particular, we assume the intruder knows the values of x for all individuals in D except for some record i, also done by Abowd *et al.* (2013). To represent this version of A, we use $D_{-i} = \{x_j : j \neq i\}$. With $A = D_{-i}$, (7) effectively becomes the probability distribution of X_i, i.e., the intruder's distribution of x for the unknown record. For clarity, from now on we write (8) as

$$p(X_i = x \mid Z, D_{-i}, S) \propto p(Z \mid X_i = x, D_{-i}, S)p(X_i = x \mid D_{-i}, S). \tag{9}$$

In many cases, setting $A = D_{-i}$ is conservative, since in contexts involving random sampling from large populations intruders are unlikely to know D_{-i}. Nonetheless, risks deemed acceptable for $A = D_{-i}$ should be acceptable for a weaker A. We note that assuming the intruder knows all records but one is related to, but quite distinct from, the assumptions used in differential privacy (Dwork, 2006).

Intruders can use $p(X_i = x \mid Z, D_{-i}, S)$ to take guesses at the true value x_i. For example, the intruder can find the x that offers the largest probability, and use that as a guess of x_i. Similarly, data stewards can use $p(X_i = x \mid Z, D_{-i}, S)$ in disclosure risk evaluations. For example, for each $x_i \in D$, they can rank each x by its associated value of $p(X_i = x \mid Z, D_{-i}, S)$, and evaluate the rank at the truth, $x = x_i$. When the rank of x_i is high (close to 1, which we define to be the rank associated with the highest probability), the agency may deem that record to be at risk under the strong intruder knowledge scenario. When the rank of x_i is low (far from 1), the agency may deem the risks for that record to be acceptable.

When d is very large, computing the normalizing constant in (7) is impractical. To facilitate computation, we propose to dramatically reduce the support in (7). For any record i, we consider as feasible candidates only those x that differ from x_i in one variable, along with x_i itself; we call this space $\mathcal{R}_i$. Thus, for example, the restricted support of x for a $3 \times 5 \times 2$ table includes only eight possible cases, namely the original x_i and the $2 + 4 + 1$ cases obtained by changing one of the three variables. One can conceive of this support as mimicking an intruder who is knowledgeable enough to be searching in neighborhoods near x_i.

When the support is $\mathcal{R}_i$, the resulting values of $p(X_i = x \mid Z, D_{-i}, S)$ for any $x \in \mathcal{R}_i$ are larger than when the support is $\mathcal{U}$. Similarly, when the support is $\mathcal{U}$ the rank of any x is no higher than the corresponding rank when the support is $\mathcal{R}_i$. In this way, restricting support to $\mathcal{R}_i$ results in a conservative ranking of the $x \in \mathcal{R}_i$. Thus, if a data steward determines that the rank of x_i (or any value of x) is acceptably low when using $\mathcal{R}_i$, it also will be acceptably low when using $\mathcal{U}$.

3.2 Computational Methods for Risk Assessment with DPMPM

Let $\Theta = \{\pi, \phi\}$ denote parameters from the DPMPM synthesis model. For Z generated from the DPMPM synthesizer, we can write (9) as

$$\rho_i^x = c \left(\int p(Z \mid X_i = x, D_{-i}, S, \Theta) p(\Theta \mid X_i = x, D_{-i}, S) d\Theta \right) p(X_i = x \mid D_{-i}, S),$$

$$(10)$$

where c is a normalizing constant. The form of (10) suggests a Monte Carlo approach to estimate ρ_i. First, acting like an intruder, the data steward creates the plausible confidential dataset, $D_i^x = (X_i = x, D_{-i})$. Second, treating D_i^x as if it were the collected data, the data steward samples m values of Θ, i.e., for $l = 1, \ldots, m$, sample a $\Theta^{(l)}$ that could have generated $Z^{(l)}$. Third, for each $(Z^{(l)}, \Theta^{(l)})$, the data steward computes the probability of generating the released $Z^{(l)}$. Fourth, the data steward multiplies the m probabilities; see (12). The value of ρ_i^x is the average of this probability computed over many plausible draws of Θ.

Conceptually, to draw Θ replicates, the data steward could re-estimate the DPMPM model for each D_i^x. However, this would be computationally prohibitive if the data steward intends to examine many x across many records i. Instead, we suggest using the sampled values of Θ from $p(\Theta \mid D)$ as proposals for an importance sampling algorithm. As a brief review of importance sampling, suppose we seek to estimate the expectation of some function $g(\Theta)$, where Θ has density $f(\Theta)$. Further suppose that we have available a sample $(\Theta^{(1)}, \ldots, \Theta^{(H)})$ from a convenient distribution $f^*(\Theta)$ that slightly differs from $f(\Theta)$. We can estimate $E_f(g(\Theta))$ using

$$E_f(g(\Theta)) \approx \sum_{j=1}^{H} g(\Theta^{(j)}) \frac{f(\Theta^{(j)})/f^*(\Theta^{(j)})}{\sum_{j=1}^{H} f(\Theta^{(j)})/f^*(\Theta^{(j)})}. \tag{11}$$

We note that (11) only requires that $f(\Theta)$ and $f^*(\Theta)$ be known up to constants.

We implement importance sampling algorithms to approximate the integral in (10). By construction, we have

$$P(Z \mid D_i^x, S) = \prod_{l=1}^{m} P(Z^{(l)} \mid D_i^x, S), \tag{12}$$

regardless of the exact values in D_i^x. Thus, for any proposed x, we can use importance sampling to approximate each $P(Z^{(l)} \mid D_i^x, S)$ and substitute the m resulting estimates in the product in (12).

Let $x_i^{*(l)} = (x_{i1}^{*(l)}, \ldots, x_{ip}^{*(l)})$ be the ith record's values in synthetic dataset $Z^{(l)}$, where $i = 1, \ldots, n^*$ and $l = 1, \ldots, m$. For each $Z^{(l)}$ and any proposed x, we define the $g(\Theta)$ in (11) to equal $cP(Z^{(l)} \mid D_i^x, S)$. We approximate the expectation of each $g(\Theta)$ with respect to $f(\Theta) = f(\Theta \mid D_i^x, S)$. In doing so, for any sampled $\Theta^{(j)}$ we use

$$g(\Theta^{(j)}) = P(Z^{(l)} \mid D_i^x, S, \Theta^{(j)}) = \prod_{i=1}^{n} \left(\sum_{f=1}^{F} \pi_f^{(j)} \prod_{k=1}^{p} \phi_{fx_{ik}^{*(l)}}^{(k)(j)} \right). \tag{13}$$

We set $f^*(\Theta) = f(\Theta \mid D, S)$, so that we can use H draws of Θ from its posterior distribution based on D. Let these H draws be $(\Theta^{(1)}, \ldots, \Theta^{(H)})$. We note that one could use any D_i^x to obtain the H draws, so that intruders can use similar importance sampling computations. As evident in (1) and (2), the only differences in the kernels of $f(\Theta)$ and $f^*(\Theta)$ include (i) the components of the likelihood associated with record i and (ii) the normalizing constant for each density. Let $x = (c_1, \ldots, c_p)$, where each $c_k \in (1, \ldots, d_k)$, be a guess at X_i. After computing the normalized ratio in (11) and canceling common terms from the numerator and denominator, we are left with $P(Z^{(l)} \mid D_i^x, S) = \sum_{j=1}^{H} p_j q_j$ where

$$p_j = \prod_{i=1}^{n} (\sum_{f=1}^{F} \pi_f^{(j)} \prod_{k=1}^{p} \phi_{fx_{ik}^{(*l)}}^{(k)(j)}) \tag{14}$$

$$q_j = \frac{\sum_{f=1}^{F} \pi_f^{(j)} \prod_{k=1}^{p} \phi_{fc_k}^{(k)(j)} / \sum_{f=1}^{F} \pi_f^{(j)} \prod_{k=1}^{p} \phi_{fx_{ik}}^{(k)(j)}}{\sum_{h=1}^{H} (\sum_{f=1}^{F} \pi_f^{(h)} \prod_{k=1}^{p} \phi_{fc_k}^{(k)(h)} / \sum_{f=1}^{F} \pi_f^{(h)} \prod_{k=1}^{p} \phi_{fx_{ik}}^{(k)(h)})}. \tag{15}$$

We repeat this computation for each $Z^{(l)}$, plugging the m results into (12).

Finally, to approximate ρ_i^x, we compute (12) for each $x \in \mathcal{R}_i$, multiplying each resulting value by its associated $P(X_i = x \mid D_{-i}, S)$. In what follows, we presume an intruder with a uniform prior distribution over the support $x \in \mathcal{R}_i$. In this case, the prior probabilities cancel from the numerator and denominator of (7), so that risk evaluations are based only on the likelihood function for Z. We discuss evaluation of other prior distributions in the illustrative application, to which we now turn.

4   Illustrative Application

We create and evaluate fully synthetic data for a subset of $n = 10000$ individuals from the 2012 American Community Survey public use microdata sample for the state of North Carolina. The $p = 14$ variables are displayed in Table 1. These 14 variables make a contingency table with $d = 8709120$ cells. The 10000 individuals occupy 3523 of these cells. Of the 3523 observed combinations of x, 2394 appear once, 474 appear twice, and 186 appear three times in the sample. The most frequent combination is repeated 233 times. We note that this table is constructed not to include structural zeros.

Table 1. Variables used in the illustrative application. Data taken from the 2012 American Community Survey public use microdata samples. In the table, PR stands for Puerto Rico.

Variable	Categories
SEX	1 = male, 2 = female
AGEP	age of person: 1 = 18-29, 2 = 30-44, 3 = 45-59, 4 = 60+
RACE1P	1 = White alone, 2 = Black or African American alone, 3 = American Indian alone, 4 = other, 5 = two or more races, 6 = Asian alone
SCHL	1 = less than high school diploma, 2 = high school diploma or GED or alternative credential, 3 = some college, 4 = associate's degree or higher
MAR	1 = married, 2 = widowed, 3 = divorced, 4 = separated, 5 = never married
LANX	1 = speaks another language, 2 = speaks only English
WAOB	born in: 1 = US state, 2 = PR and US island areas, oceania and at sea, 3 = Latin America, 4 = Asia, 5 = Europe, 6 = Africa, 7 = Northern America
MIL	1 = active military duty at some point, 2 = military training for Reserves/National Guard only, 3 = never served in the military
WKL	1 = worked within the past 12 months, 2 = worked 1-5 years ago, 3 = worked over 5 years ago or never worked
DIS	1 = has a disability, 2 = no disability
HICOV	1 = has health insurance coverage, 2 = no coverage
MIG	1 = live in the same house (non movers), 2 = move to outside US and PR, 3 = move to different house in US or PR
SCH	1 = has not attended school in the last 3 months, 2 = in public school or college, 3 = in private school or college or home school
HISP	1 = not Spanish, Hispanic, or Latino, 2 = Spanish, Hispanic, or Latino

4.1   Some Evidence of Utility of the Synthetic Data

We generated $m = 5$ synthetic datasets by estimating and sampling from the DPMPM based on the 10000 cases in D. Before illustrating the disclosure risk evaluations, we present evidence that the DPMPM synthesizer generates useful data for this D. Here, we do not intend to offer an exhaustive investigation of data utility; rather, our purpose is to document that the resulting Z are potentially useful for analysis.

Figure 1 and Figure 2 display the joint distributions of (WKL, SCHL) and (HISP, RACE1P), respectively, using the sample percentages in D and the averages of the corresponding percentages in the $m = 5$ synthetic datasets. The DPMPM synthesizer preserves these two joint distributions quite closely. We found similar patterns for the marginal distributions of all variables and for joint distributions involving most other pairs of variables.

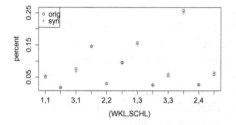
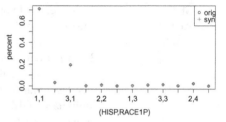

Fig. 1. Estimated joint probabilities for WKL and SCHL across the original and $m = 5$ synthetic datasets

Fig. 2. Estimated joint probabilities for HISP and RACE1P across the original and $m = 5$ synthetic datasets

Table 2. Point estimates and 95% confidence intervals for coefficients in a logistic regression of disability status on several main effects. Results estimated with the original data and the $m = 5$ generated synthetic datasets.

	Original data		Synthetic (m=5)	
Estimand	Estimate	95% CI	$\bar{q}_5$	95% CI
Intercept	2.212		2.108	[1.523,2.692]
SEX	-0.250		-0.221	[-0.361,-0.081]
MIL	0.239		0.205	[0.1255,0.2854]
MIG	0.049		0.060	[-0.0821,0.2014]
SCH	1.090		0.961	[0.6699,1.2521]
RACE1P	-0.078		-0.065	[-0.1147,-0.0145]
LANX	-1.096		-0.970	[-1.401,-0.539]

Table 2 summarizes the results of logistic regressions of DIS on SEX, MIL, MIG, SCH, RACE1P, and LANX. To estimate the coefficients, we use the maximum likelihood estimates (MLE) from D and the averages of the MLEs from the $m = 5$ synthetic datasets. The 95% confidence interval from the synthetic data derives from Raghunathan et al. (2003). Once again, the DPMPM offers reasonable results.

4.2   Disclosure Risk Assessments

Having demonstrated that Z has some analytic validity, we now turn to illustrating the assessment of disclosure risks. To do so, we drop each record in D one at a time. For each i, we compute the resulting ρ_i^x for all x in a reduced support $\mathcal{R}_i$. Here, each $\mathcal{R}_i$ is defined as the union of the true x_i plus the 34 other combinations of x obtained by changing x_i in one variable. For any two records i and j such that $x_i = x_j$ in D, $\rho_i^x = \rho_j^x$ for any possible x. Thus, we need only do computations for each of the 3523 combinations that appeared in the data. To compute each ρ_i^x, we use a uniform prior distribution over all $x \in \mathcal{R}_i$.

Figure 3 displays the distribution of the rank of the true x_i for each of the 3523 combinations. Here, a rank equal to 1 means the true x_i has the highest probability of being the unknown X_i, whereas a rank of 35 means the true x_i has the lowest probability of being the true X_i. Even armed with D_{-i}, the intruder gives the top rank to the true x_i for only two combinations and gives x_i a ranking in the top three for only 31 combinations; these are displayed in Table 3. We note that 2394 combinations were unique in D, yet evidently the DPMPM synthesizer involves enough smoothing that we do not recover the true x_i in the overwhelming majority of cases.

Figure 4 displays a histogram of the corresponding probabilities associated with the true x_i in each of the 3523 combinations. The largest probability is close to 0.2, and only 16 probabilities exceed 0.08. The majority of probabilities are in the 0.03 range. As we assumed a uniform prior distribution over the 35 possibilities in the support, the ratio of the posterior to prior probability is typically one or less, and only a handful of combinations have ratios exceeding two. Thus, compared to random guesses over a reasonably close neighborhood of the true values, Z typically does not provide much additional information about x_i. We note that high probabilities do not automatically result in top rankings.

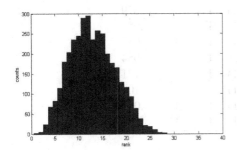
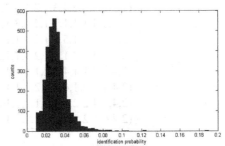

Fig. 3. Histogram of ranks of the probabilities associated with true x_i

Fig. 4. Histogram of probabilities associated with the true x_i

If desired, data stewards can evaluate risk probabilities for intruders possessing additional information about target records in D. For example, suppose the data steward defines each $x_i = (x_{i(1)}, x_{i(2)})$, where $x_{i(1)}$ is a subset of values known to the intruder (e.g., demographic variables) and $x_{i(2)}$ is the remaining subset of values unknown to the intruder (e.g., health variables). To evaluate risks for intruders seeking to estimate

Table 3. The 31 combinations in D with the true x_i ranked in the top three highest posterior probabilities. "Reps." is the number of times x_i is repeated in D.

Combination	Value for true x_i		
	Reps.	Rank	Probability
(1,2,2,2,1,1,1,3,1,2,1,1,1,1)	1	1	.051
(2,4,3,2,2,2,1,3,2,2,2,1,1,1)	1	1	.088
(1,1,1,4,5,1,3,3,1,2,2,1,1,2)	1	2	.086
(1,1,5,3,5,2,1,1,2,2,2,3,2,1)	1	2	.070
(1,3,4,3,3,2,1,1,3,2,2,3,1,2)	2	2	.190
(2,1,5,3,5,1,1,3,1,2,1,1,2,1)	1	2	.076
(2,1,6,3,5,2,1,3,3,2,1,1,2,1)	1	2	.087
(1,1,1,3,1,2,1,3,3,2,2,1,1,1)	1	3	.060
(1,1,4,1,5,1,1,3,1,2,2,1,1,2)	1	3	.065
(1,2,1,4,3,2,1,1,3,2,2,3,2,1)	2	3	.125
(1,3,2,1,5,2,5,3,2,1,1,1,1,2)	1	3	.075
(1,3,2,3,3,2,5,1,2,2,2,1,3,1)	1	3	.069
(1,4,1,1,3,2,1,1,3,2,1,1,1,1)	2	3	.047
(1,4,4,4,1,1,3,3,1,2,1,1,1,2)	1	3	.066
(2,1,1,1,5,1,3,3,2,2,1,1,1,2)	1	3	.081
(2,1,1,2,1,2,1,3,3,2,1,1,1,1)	5	3	.046
(2,1,1,2,5,1,5,3,3,2,1,2,3,1)	1	3	.101
(2,1,1,4,3,2,1,2,3,2,1,3,1,1)	1	3	.085
(2,1,3,1,5,2,1,3,2,1,2,1,1,1)	1	3	.055
(2,1,3,3,5,2,1,3,2,2,2,1,1,1)	1	3	.050
(2,1,5,1,1,2,1,3,2,2,2,1,1,1)	1	3	.059
(2,1,5,3,5,1,1,3,1,1,1,3,2,1)	1	3	.066
(2,2,1,4,1,1,5,3,1,2,2,1,1,1)	1	3	.052
(2,2,2,4,5,2,4,3,1,2,1,3,2,1)	1	3	.079
(2,3,1,4,1,1,1,1,1,2,1,3,1,1)	1	3	.051
(2,3,1,4,1,1,5,3,1,2,1,1,1,1)	1	3	.053
(2,3,1,4,1,2,1,1,1,2,1,1,1,2)	1	3	.054
(2,4,1,3,1,1,4,3,2,1,1,1,1,1)	1	3	.121
(2,4,1,3,2,1,4,3,3,2,1,1,1,1)	1	3	.104
(2,4,1,4,2,2,1,3,2,1,2,1,1,1)	1	3	.065
(2,4,6,1,2,1,4,3,3,2,1,1,1,1)	1	3	.080

the distribution of $x_{i(2)}$, we define $A = (D_{-i} \cup x_{i(1)})$. Using obvious extensions of notation, we then estimate

$$p(X_{2(i)} = x_{(2)} \mid Z, A, S) \propto p(Z \mid X_{i(2)} = x_{(2)}, A, S)p(X_{i(2)} = x_{(2)} \mid A, S). \quad (16)$$

For some $X_{i(2)}$, the implied support may be small enough that one can evaluate the probability over $\mathcal{U}$ rather than $\mathcal{R}_i$, restricting both sets to cases with $x_{(1)} = x_{i(1)}$.

To illustrate these computations, we suppose that $x_{i(2)}$ includes when an individual last worked (WKL), their disability status (DIS), their health insurance coverage status (HICOV), and their mobility status (MIG); and, $x_{i(1)}$ includes all other variables. The sample space for $x_{i(2)}$ comprises $3*2*2*3 = 36$ possible values. We compute the probabilities in (16) for the particular combination $x_i = (2, 4, 1, 3, 1, 1, 4, 3, \mathbf{2}, \mathbf{1}, \mathbf{1}, \mathbf{1}, 1, 1)$, where the boldface indicates $x_{i(2)}$. This record is somewhat arbitrarily selected for illustration, although it is unique on the entire x_i. The true $x_{i(2)} = (2, 1, 1, 1)$ has probability 0.3695, which ranks first among the 36 cases. Evidently, an intruder armed with this much information can guess the true value for this record. For comparison, we repeated these computations for a person with $x_i = (1, 4, 3, 2, 1, 2, 1, 1, \mathbf{3}, \mathbf{1}, \mathbf{1}, \mathbf{1}, 1, 1)$. Here, the probability is 0.0259, which ranks 16 among the 36 cases.

The data steward also may want to evaluate the marginal distribution of $X_{2(i)}$, namely

$$p(X_{i(2)} = x_2 \mid Z, D_{-i}, S) \propto p(Z \mid X_{i(2)} = x_{(2)}, D_{-i}, S)p(X_{i(2)} = x_{(2)} \mid D_{-i}, S). \tag{17}$$

This allows the data steward to compute, for example, the probability associated with particular combinations of age, race, gender, and education for the ith record under the strong intruder knowledge scenario. To compute this efficiently, one approach is to sum the set of probabilities ρ_i^x where $\{x : x \in \mathcal{R}_i, x_{(2)} = x_{i(2)}\}$. Here, using $\mathcal{R}_i$ may be too restrictive, since by construction many of the x in $\mathcal{R}_i$ have $x_{(2)} = x_{i(2)}$. For this article, we did not investigate other approaches to defining $\mathcal{R}_i$ suitable for estimation of (17); this is a topic for future research.

Finally, data stewards need not use uniform distributions on the support of x for the intruder's prior distribution; the computations apply for any prior distribution. Naturally, the choice of prior distribution affects posterior probabilities, although for large m the posterior probabilities can be practically insensitive to specifications of reasonable prior distributions (Reiter et al., 2014). We suggest that data stewards assess the effects of changing the prior distribution by comparing posterior probabilities for selected pairs of candidate x values under different prior distributions, specifically those for x_i and other candidate values of interest, say $x = b$. When $A = D_{-i}$, the ratio of the posterior probabilities for x_i and b is

$$\frac{p(X_i = x_i \mid Z, D_{-i}, S)}{p(X_i = b \mid Z, D_{-i}, S)} = \frac{p(Z \mid X_i = x_i, D_{-i}, S)}{p(Z \mid X_i = b, D_{-i}, S)} \frac{p(X_i = x_i \mid D_{-i}, S)}{p(X_i = b \mid D_{-i}, S)}. \tag{18}$$

Normalizing constants need not be computed in (18), since they cancel from the numerator and denominator. Hence, once the data steward has computed the likelihoods of Z for x_i and b, it can easily compute the ratio of the posterior probabilities for these two values for arbitrary sets of prior probabilities.

The ratios in (18) allow for convenient investigations of the effects of changing the prior probabilities. For example, suppose that the data steward considers records to be at too high risk if the posterior probability of the true x_i is ranked as the top case (or some other minimum ranking). Suppose that some x_i has the tenth highest posterior probability in $\mathcal{R}_i$ under the uniform prior distribution on $x \in \mathcal{R}_i$. Using the likelihoods from the uniform probability case, the data steward can determine the ratio of the prior probabilities that would change the posterior probability of x_i to become the top ranked. For example, our risk evaluations under the uniform prior assumption reveal that $x_i = (1,1,1,1,1,2,1,3,1,2,1,1,1,1)$ has the tenth largest ρ_i^x among $x \in \mathcal{R}_i$, with posterior probability equal to 0.0398. The combination with highest probability in $\mathcal{R}_i$ is $b = (1,1,1,1,1,2,1,3,1,2,2,1,1,1)$, with posterior probability equal to 0.0585. Thus, for an intruder to rank x_i as most likely, the intruder would need to believe *a priori* that $x = x_i$ is 1.46 (0.0585/0.0398) times more likely than $x = b$.

5   Concluding Remarks

When certain x_i have relatively high posterior probabilities, and hence high ranks, data stewards have several options. If the number of cases that are too risky is small, the data steward may decide to release the synthetic data and accept the risks. With this action, the data steward effectively puts low probability on the existence of intruders who know D_{-i} for exactly the records at risk. Alternatively, the data steward could alter the synthesizer, for example by removing risky records from the data used to estimate the synthesis models. It is also prudent for the data steward to examine risks under other assumptions of intruder behavior. For risky cases, data stewards can augment the support of x used to compute posterior probabilities, for example by changing two variables at a time. Implicitly, using a bigger sample space mimics an intruder armed with less precise (but still very substantial) knowledge. The data steward also can use a sensible informative prior distribution to compute risks. For example, the data steward can base prior probabilities for each $x \in \mathcal{R}_i$ on a DPMPM model estimated on D_{-i}. If the resulting posterior probabilities do not differ much from the informative prior probabilities, then arguably releasing Z does not meaningfully increase the disclosure risks for this intruder.

Looking to future research, we see two key next steps in this approach to disclosure risk assessment. First, we would like to develop algorithms for exploring the full support of any X_i. With powerful computing and efficient code—these computations are embarassingly parallel—it may be feasible to compute normalizing constants over much if not all of $\mathcal{U}$. Alternatively, it may be possible to find high probability x via stochastic search algorithms. More complete explorations of $\mathcal{U}$ would allow for more accurate computations of $P(X_{i(2)} \mid Z, D_{-i}, S)$, which helps data stewards assess risks that the intruders learn subsets of key or sensitive variables. Second, we would like to relax the very strong, and perhaps unrealistic, assumption that the intruder knows every case but one. Conceptually, the path to do so is straightforward. If the intruder knows some subset of data D_A, the data steward considers all plausible values in the set $D - D_A$, and identifies sets with high probability of generating Z. Clearly, this approach is computationally very expensive. However, we conjecture that stochastic search algorithms might allow one to identify sets with high probability, and within those sets values of x that appear with regularity.

References

Abowd, J., Stinson, M., Benedetto, G.: Final report to the Social Security Administration on the SIPP/SSA/IRS Public Use File Project. Tech. rep., U.S. Census Bureau Longitudinal Employer-Household Dynamics Program (2006), http://www.census.gov/sipp/synth_data.html

Abowd, J.M., Vilhuber, L.: How protective are synthetic data? In: Domingo-Ferrer, J., Saygın, Y. (eds.) PSD 2008. LNCS, vol. 5262, pp. 239–246. Springer, Heidelberg (2008)

Abowd, J.A., Schneider, M.J., Vilhuber, L.: Differential privacy applications to bayesian and linear mixed model estimation. Journal of Privacy and Confidentiality 5, 73–105 (2013)

Abowd, J.M., Woodcock, S.D.: Disclosure limitation in longitudinal linked data. In: Doyle, P., Lane, J., Zayatz, L., Theeuwes, J. (eds.) Confidentiality, Disclosure, and Data Access: Theory and Practical Applications for Statistical Agencies, pp. 215–277. North-Holland, Amsterdam (2001)

Abowd, J.M., Woodcock, S.D.: Multiply-imputing confidential characteristics and file links in longitudinal linked data. In: Domingo-Ferrer, J., Torra, V. (eds.) PSD 2004. LNCS, vol. 3050, pp. 290–297. Springer, Heidelberg (2004)

An, D., Little, R.: Multiple imputation: an alternative to top coding for statistical disclosure control. Journal of the Royal Statistical Society, Series A 170, 923–940 (2007)

Burgette, L., Reiter, J.P.: Multiple-shrinkage multinomial probit models with applications to simulating geographies in public use data. Bayesian Analysis 8, 453–478 (2013)

Charest, A.S.: How can we analyze differentially private synthetic datasets. Journal of Privacy and Confidentiality 2(2), Article 3 (2010)

Drechsler, J., Bender, S., Rässler, S.: Comparing fully and partially synthetic datasets for statistical disclosure control in the German IAB Establishment Panel. Transactions on Data Privacy 1, 105–130 (2008a)

Drechsler, J., Dundler, A., Bender, S., Rässler, S., Zwick, T.: A new approach for disclosure control in the IAB Establishment Panel–Multiple imputation for a better data access. Advances in Statistical Analysis 92, 439–458 (2008b)

Drechsler, J., Reiter, J.P.: Sampling with synthesis: A new approach for releasing public use census microdata. Journal of the American Statistical Association 105, 1347–1357 (2010)

Drechsler, J., Reiter, J.P.: Combining synthetic data with subsampling to create public use microdata files for large scale surveys. Survey Methodology 38, 73–79 (2012)

Duncan, G.T., Lambert, D.: The risk of disclosure for microdata. Journal of Business and Economic Statistics 7, 207–217 (1989)

Dunson, D.B., Xing, C.: Nonparametric Bayes modeling of multivariate categorical data. Journal of the American Statistical Association 104, 1042–1051 (2009)

Dwork, C.: Differential privacy. In: Bugliesi, M., Preneel, B., Sassone, V., Wegener, I. (eds.) ICALP 2006, Part II. LNCS, vol. 4052, pp. 1–12. Springer, Heidelberg (2006)

Fienberg, S.E.: A radical proposal for the provision of micro-data samples and the preservation of confidentiality. Tech. rep., Department of Statistics, Carnegie-Mellon University (1994)

Fienberg, S.E., Makov, U.E., Sanil, A.P.: A Bayesian approach to data disclosure: Optimal intruder behavior for continuous data. Journal of Official Statistics 13, 75–89 (1997)

Graham, P., Penny, R.: Multiply imputed synthetic data files. Tech. rep., University of Otago (2005), http://www.uoc.otago.ac.nz/departments/pubhealth/pgrahpub.htm

Graham, P., Young, J., Penny, R.: Multiply imputed synthetic data: Evaluation of hierarchical Bayesian imputation models. Journal of Official Statistics 25, 245–268 (2009)

Hawala, S.: Producing partially synthetic data to avoid disclosure. In: Proceedings of the Joint Statistical Meetings. American Statistical Association, Alexandria (2008)

Ishwaran, H., James, L.F.: Gibbs sampling methods for stick-breaking priors. Journal of the American Statistical Association, 161–173 (2001)

Kennickell, A.B.: Multiple imputation and disclosure protection: The case of the 1995 Survey of Consumer Finances. In: Alvey, W., Jamerson, B. (eds.) Record Linkage Techniques, pp. 248–267. National Academy Press, Washington, D.C. (1997)

Kinney, S., Reiter, J.P., Reznek, A.P., Miranda, J., Jarmin, R.S., Abowd, J.M.: Towards unrestricted public use business microdata: The synthetic Longitudinal Business Database. International Statistical Review 79, 363–384 (2011)

Little, R.J.A.: Statistical analysis of masked data. Journal of Official Statistics 9, 407–426 (1993)

Little, R.J.A., Liu, F., Raghunathan, T.E.: Statistical disclosure techniques based on multiple imputation. In: Gelman, A., Meng, X.L. (eds.) Applied Bayesian Modeling and Causal Inference from Incomplete-Data Perspectives, pp. 141–152. John Wiley & Sons, New York (2004)

Machanavajjhala, A., Kifer, D., Abowd, J., Gehrke, J., Vilhuber, L.: Privacy: Theory meets practice on the map. In: IEEE 24th International Conference on Data Engineering, pp. 277–286 (2008)

Manrique-Vallier, D., Reiter, J.P.: Bayesian estimation of discrete multivariate latent structure models with strutural zeros. Journal of Computational and Graphical Statistics (to appear, 2014)

McClure, D., Reiter, J.P.: Differential privacy and statistical disclosure risk measures: An illustration with binary synthetic data. Transactions on Data Privacy 5, 535–552 (2012)

Paiva, T., Chakraborty, A., Reiter, J.P., Gelfand, A.E.: Imputation of confidential data sets with spatial locations using disease mapping models. Statistics in Medicine (to appear, 2014)

Raghunathan, T.E., Reiter, J.P., Rubin, D.B.: Multiple imputation for statistical disclosure limitation. Journal of Official Statistics 19, 1–16 (2003)

Reiter, J.: Using multiple imputation to integrate and disseminate confidential microdata. International Statistical Review 77, 179–195 (2009)

Reiter, J., Raghunathan, T.E.: The multiple adaptations of multiple imputation. Journal of the American Statistical Association 102, 1462–1471 (2007)

Reiter, J.P.: Satisfying disclosure restrictions with synthetic data sets. Journal of Official Statistics 18, 531–544 (2002)

Reiter, J.P.: Inference for partially synthetic, public use microdata sets. Survey Methodology 29, 181–189 (2003)

Reiter, J.P.: Simultaneous use of multiple imputation for missing data and disclosure limitation. Survey Methodology 30, 235–242 (2004)

Reiter, J.P.: Estimating identification risks in microdata. Journal of the American Statistical Association 100, 1103–1113 (2005a)

Reiter, J.P.: Releasing multiply-imputed, synthetic public use microdata: An illustration and empirical study. Journal of the Royal Statistical Society, Series A 168, 185–205 (2005b)

Reiter, J.P.: Discussion: Bayesian perspectives and disclosure risk assessment. International Statistical Review 80, 373–375 (2012)

Reiter, J.P., Wang, Q., Zhang, B.: Bayesian estimation of disclosure risks in multiply imputed, synthetic data. Journal of Privacy and Confidentiality (to appear, 2014)

Rubin, D.B.: Discussion: Statistical disclosure limitation. Journal of Official Statistics 9, 462–468 (1993)

Sethuraman, J.: A constructive definition of Dirichlet priors. Statistica Sinica 4, 639–650 (1994)

Si, Y., Reiter, J.P.: Nonparametric Bayesian multiple imputation for incomplete categorical variables in large-scale assessment surveys. Journal of Educational and Behavioral Statistics 38, 499–521 (2013)

Slavkovic, A.B., Lee, J.: Synthetic two-way contingency tables that preserve conditional frequencies. Statistical Methodology 7, 225–239 (2010)

Wang, H., Reiter, J.P.: Multiple imputation for sharing precise geographies in public use data. Annals of Applied Statistics 6, 229–252 (2012)

v-Dispersed Synthetic Data Based on a Mixture Model with Constraints

Anna Oganian

National Center for Health Statistics,
3311 Toledo Rd,
Hyatsville, MD, 20782, U.S.A.
aoganyan@cdc.gov

Abstract. In this paper a new approach is proposed for the generation of synthetic microdata which reduces attribute disclosure for continuous variables. First, we define a metric of attribute disclosure which is called v-dispersion. This metric quantifies the risk based on the volume of the multidimensional confidence regions for the original data values. Next we describe a method that satisfies the requirements of v-dispersion. This method is based on a mixture model with constraints on parameters of components' spread. Experiments with real data show that the proposed approach compares very favorably with other methods of disclosure limitation for continuous microdata in terms of utility and risk.

Keywords and Phrases: Statistical disclosure limitation (SDL), v-dispersion, mixture models, expectation-maximization (EM) algorithm, constraints.

1 Introduction

National statistical agencies collecting individual information are facing the problem of releasing this data to the public and at the same time have the obligation to protect the confidentiality of data providers.

To protect individuals' data, direct identifiers, such as names, addresses and social security numbers, should be removed. However, some risk of identification still exists, for example, by means of linkage of the released data to external databases. So in addition, released microdata —collections of individual records— are typically modified, in order to make disclosure more difficult. In other words, statistical disclosure limitation (SDL) methods are applied to the data prior to their release. These methods can be divided in two groups: masking methods, that release a modified version of the original microdata, and synthetic methods, that release artificial records generated from the distribution representing the original data.

Examples of masking methods include: data swapping, in which data values are swapped for selected records; noise addition, in which noise is added to numerical data values to reduce the likelihood of exact matching on key variables or to distort the values of sensitive variables; and microaggregation, a technique similar to data binning. See [22,23] for more details.

J. Domingo-Ferrer (Ed.): PSD 2014, LNCS 8744, pp. 200–212, 2014.

Regarding synthetic methods, the crux is to obtain a good data generation model. Often synthetic data are generated using sequential modeling strategies, similar to those used for imputation of missing data [32]. If all the records and all the variables are synthesized then we have a fully synthetic data. The re-identification disclosure risk is considered negligible for fully synthetic data because no synthetic record derives from any specific original record. For partially synthetic data, when only some of the values are synthesized, re-identification risk still exists. However, even fully synthetic data are not risk-free because synthetic records may be too similar to the original ones, so attribute disclosure risk may not be negligible. By attribute disclosure we understand the ability of the intruder to get narrow bounds on the original values of the sensitive attributes. So, attribute disclosure may occur when the model used to generate synthetic data is overfitted. It can also be caused by the particularities of the data, for instance, when the original data closely follows a particular model, for example, a regression model, and the same model is used to generate the synthetic data. If the model is released to the public, the intruder may be able to find confidence regions for the sensitive variables for the target individuals, and if these regions have narrow bounds, for example, the volumes of these regions are very small compared to the volume of the overall data, attribute disclosure occurs.

In this paper we aim to address the problem of attribute disclosure for synthetic continuous data. In particular, we intend to (1) define a criterion which quantifies such a risk and (2) present a method that satisfies the requirements of this criterion with an acceptable level of risk.

To assess the performance of proposed SDL methods, we need to quantify data utility, or the amount of distortion caused by the method. There are different types of utility assessment: analysis-specific utility measures, tailored to specific analyses, and broad measures reflecting global differences between the distributions of original and masked data (see some examples in [10,29,25,41]. In this paper we will use a measure of the latter type, specifically a propensity score measure proposed in [41] and adopted by the US Census Bureau [13].

Regarding attribute disclosure risk assesment several criteria have been proposed in the literature, for example *l*-diversity and *t*-closeness. *l*-diversity requires diversity of the values of the sensitive attribute within each equivalence class, where equivalence class is defined as a group of records that share the same values of quasi-identifiers. So, each equivalence class should have at least *l* "well-represented" sensitive values. This criterion is not very suited for continuous variables as it does not take into account their dispersion, so the values can be different within a group, but still very close in value.

The *t*-closeness criterion [26] was proposed in an attempt to address some of the drawbacks associated with *l*-diversity. *t*-closeness requires that the distance between the distribution of the confidential attribute in the equivalence class and the distribution of the attribute in the whole data set be no more than a threshold *t*. This criterion suffers from several drawbacks as well. One of them is that it is difficult to assess such a distance for multidimensional data when the distribution of the original data is unknown (see [12] for thorough discussion).

Finally we want to note that there is another relevant criterion that originated in computer science and has received a lot of scientific attention, namely ε-differential privacy ([14,16,15]) and some its variants. Differential privacy provides a very strong level of privacy, no matter the intruder's side knowledge, by limiting the influence of any single respondent on the released information. Methods for differentially private data releases aim at preserving utility for a certain class of queries: for example, [21] presents a differentially private algorithm producing a synthetic data set that preserves utility for any set of linear queries (those that apply a function to each record and sum the result, like for example count queries). In other cases strong privacy guarantees of differential privacy may come at a great cost in data utility (see for example [6,7,17])

The focus of this paper is on release of continuous synthetic data with very general utility preservation guarantees. That is why we will not adopt the path of differential privacy in this paper, but rather will use our own attribute disclosure criterion, which has some similarity with t-closeness. This criterion, however, does not have a strict requirement of maintaining the same or close distribution of sensitive variables within the subgroups, because of the decreased utility ([12]) and infeasibility of its implementation for multidimensional data. The details are given in section 2.

1.1 Contribution and Plan of This Paper

The contributions of the paper are two-fold: first we introduce a privacy criterion suitable for continuous variables, which we call v-dispersion. Next, we present a method of disclosure limitation which satisfies this criterion. The proposed approach is predicated on the mixture model with constraints on component covariance matrices. We present empirical comparison of the proposed approach with other SDL methods based on a propensity score utility measure. We show that our method outperforms other methods including fully synthetic data, even though our method is more restrictive than others in the sense that it enforces the requirements of v-dispersion while others do not.

The idea of our method is described in Section 2. The results of a numerical experiment are reported in Section 3. Finally, Section 4 provides a concluding discussion and suggests topics for future work.

2   The v-Dispersion Privacy Criterion and a Method of Disclosure Limitation That Enforces Its Requirements

Ideally to be able to assess attribute disclosure, the data protector must know what information is available to the intruder, which is impossible. However, in the case of releasing synthetic data the risk assessment procedure differs from that of masked data release, because there is no direct correspondence between the records in the original and synthetic file and also because the quality and risk of synthetic records strongly depends on the model used to generate it. The release of synthetic data is sometimes questioned from the point of view "why release synthetic data at all and not just the model?" So, in a sense there is an equivalence between the synthetic data and the model. It seems reasonable to estimate attribute disclosure risk based on the risk associated with releasing the model. This is the focus in this paper. If necessary a follow up analysis can be done when additional intruder's knowledge is taken into account.

Intuitively, attribute disclosure risk corresponds to the ability of the intruder to find low and upper bounds on the values of the original sensitive variable or in the case of multiple sensitive variables - multidimensional regions, such that these bounds are "close enough" or when the volumes are "small enough". Closeness of the bounds and size of the volumes depend on the situation at hand and the standards of the data protector.

We define the criterion for attribute disclosure risk associated with synthetic data release as follows:

Definition 1. *Let X_s be synthetic data to be released instead of the original data X_o. Assume that the model used to generate X_s is released as well and based on the information about the model, an intruder constructs confidence regions for the original values of the sensitive attributes of X_o. If the volumes of these regions are larger or equal to V then the synthetic data is v-dispersed, where v is a parameter of the method specified by the data protector.*

In the next section we will show an example of v-dispersed synthetic data generation based on a mixture model.

2.1   Synthetic Method to Generate v-Dispersed Continuous Data

As mentioned above, our approach for synthetic data generation is based on using a mixture model. There are several reasons for this choice. First, a mixture model is a very flexible and powerful tool which has the ability to accurately represent the first, second, and higher-order observed moments of the continuous attributes if the number of components is sufficiently large. For some types of data, *e.g,* healthcare data, mixture models can be particularly appealing, because in many areas of medical research mixture models are used to classify individuals into disease categories. So, preservation of important distributional characteristics, such as first and second order moments, within these meaningful classes can be considered as a desirable feature for the user.

We want to note that in [30] an SDL method based on the mixture model was presented; however, no attempt was made to assess and limit the risk related to such a data release. In this paper we intend to address this problem and at the same time to obtain synthetic data with good utility properties. To achieve this goal we will incorporate lower bounds on the amount of spread of sensitive attributes within each component of the mixture so that an intruder will not be able to get very narrow confidence regions for the values of the sensitive attributes within each component.

Let us consider the details of the procedure. When a mixture model is used to estimate the density $f(x)$ of the entire original data, it can be written as follows

$$f(x) = \sum_{k=1}^{K} \pi_k f_k(x|\boldsymbol{\theta_k}) \tag{1}$$

where π_k is the probability that an observation belongs to the k-th component ($\pi_k \geq 0$; $\sum_{k=1}^{K} \pi_k = 1$), f_k is the density of the k-th component and θ_k are the parameters of f_k.

A possible choice for f_k is a multivariate normal (MVN) density with $\boldsymbol{\theta_k}$ being the within-cluster mean vector μ_k and the covariance matrix Σ_k. There are several reasons for this choice:

- Density estimation theory guarantees that any distribution can be effectively approximated by the mixture of Gaussians [37,38]. In fact with an adequate number of components Gaussian mixture can reflect skewness and other complex features of the original data;
- Simplicity of the Gaussian mixture makes the whole procedure of model estimation and generation of synthetic data computationally feasible for multidimensional data. It is easy to generate multivariate normal samples, in fact, corresponding functions can be found in any statistical package.
- Using the Gaussian distribution may be advantageous from the point of view of attribute disclosure limitation. The Gaussian model is completely defined by its mean and covariance matrix, so we can directly manipulate the volumes of generated synthetic clusters by embedding constraints on component covariance matrices Σ_k.

Furthermore, cluster covariance matrices Σ_k define the shape, orientation and spread of the data within the cluster. Eigenvalue decomposition of cluster Σ_k can be written as

$$\Sigma_k = Q\Lambda Q' \tag{2}$$

where Q is the orthogonal matrix of eigenvectors, which dictates the orientation of the cluster, and Λ is the diagonal matrix whose diagonal elements are eigenvalues of Σ_k, which define the spread of the cluster. Furthermore, we can construct a prediction ellipsoid for each cluster as

$$Pr\{(\boldsymbol{x} - \boldsymbol{\mu})' \Sigma_k^{-1}(\boldsymbol{x} - \boldsymbol{\mu}) \leq \chi_{d,\alpha}^2\} = 1 - \alpha \tag{3}$$

where $\chi_{d,\alpha}^2$ is the critical value of the chi-square distribution with d degrees of freedom (where d is the dimensionality of the data) at significance level α.

For the synthetic data to satisfy the requirements of v-dispersion we will impose lower bounds on the volume of the ellipsoid (3):

$$V_k = \frac{2\pi^{d/2}}{d\Gamma(d/2)}(\chi_{d,\alpha}^2)^{d/2}|\Sigma_k|^{1/2} \geq V_o \tag{4}$$

where V_k is the volume of the prediction ellipsoid for the cluster k, V_o is some predefined minimal volume and $\Gamma()$ is the gamma function.

From equation (4) we see that the volume of the ellipsoid depends on the determinant of the cluster covariance matrix, which is equal to the product of its eigenvalues. So, by imposing constraints on the eigenvalues we can limit attribute disclosure for the cluster.

To estimate cluster covariance matrices $\boldsymbol{\Sigma}_k$, means μ_k and probabilities p_k, we can use the expectation-maximization (EM) algorithm [28,8]. In EM for mixture models, the "complete data" are considered to be $\boldsymbol{y}_i = (\boldsymbol{x}_i, \boldsymbol{z}_i)$, where $\boldsymbol{z}_i = (z_{i1}, \cdots, z_{iK})$ is the unobserved portion of the data, with $z_{ik} = 1$ if the record $\boldsymbol{x}_i$ belongs to the cluster k and $z_{ik} = 0$ otherwise. The E step is used to compute the probabilities z_{ik}. M step estimates the means, covariance matrices $\hat{\boldsymbol{\Sigma}}_k$ and the probabilities of the cluster memberships. The closed-form expressions for these quantities can be found in the literature (e.g. [28,5]).

To guarantee that the cluster volumes satisfy (4), we will introduce constraints on the eigenvalues of $\boldsymbol{\Sigma}_k$. In particular, on each M step when estimates $\hat{\boldsymbol{\Sigma}}_k$ are computed, we will update $\hat{\boldsymbol{\Sigma}}_k$ according to the following rule

$$\hat{\boldsymbol{\Sigma}}_k^{new} = \boldsymbol{Q} \boldsymbol{\Lambda}^{new} \boldsymbol{Q}' \tag{5}$$

where $\boldsymbol{\Lambda}^{new}$ is the diagonal matrix of the updated eigenvalues of $\hat{\boldsymbol{\Sigma}}_k$ and $\boldsymbol{Q}$ are the eigenvectors of $\hat{\boldsymbol{\Sigma}}_k$. Eigenvalues λ_i^{new} of $\boldsymbol{\Lambda}^{new}$ are computed according to the following rule:

$$\lambda_i^{new} = \lambda_i + \delta, \tag{6}$$

where δ is

$$\delta = \begin{cases} 0, & \text{if } V_k \geq V_0, \\ \delta \text{ is the root of } \prod_{i=1}^{d}(\lambda_i + \delta) = A, & \text{otherwise,} \\ \text{where } A = V_0^2 \frac{(d\Gamma(d/2))^2}{4\pi^d(\chi_{d,\alpha}^2)^d}. \end{cases} \tag{7}$$

This modification of the covariance matrix shifts its eigenvalues by δ with the goal to increase cluster volumes (if they are too small) but preserves the orientation of the cluster. A similar approach of shifting eigenvalues of the covariance matrix is sometimes used in fuzzy clustering (e.g. [2]) with the goal to make the estimation procedure more robust. In fact, when clusters are allowed to have different shapes and orientations, the number of parameters that need to be estimated is $K(d + d(d+1)/2 + 1) - 1$, where d is the dimensionality of the data. With this number of parameters the algorithm can become somewhat less robust as compared to algorithms that only update cluster centers, like k-means. A shift in eigenvalues that leaves eigenvectors unchanged is the basis of the well-known Tikhonov regularization for linear optimization problems (see [2]). Although the update scheme used by [2] is different from ours, shifting eigenvalues in both schemes introduces a tendency towards sphericity and algebraically makes the covariance matrix "less singular" and thus "more regular", which explains the name "regularization" for this modification according to [2].

To find δ we need to find the root of $\prod_{i=1}^{d}(\lambda_i + \delta) = A$. Note that, because A is positive and all λ_i are positive (covariance matrix $\hat{\boldsymbol{\Sigma}}_k$ is positive definite), the function $F(\delta) = \prod_{i=1}^{d}(\lambda_i + \delta)$ is strictly increasing for all $\delta > 0$. Furthermore, $F(0) > 0$ and $F(\delta) = A > F(0)$, so there will be only one positive root of the above equation (uniqueness of the positive root can also be confirmed by Descartes's Rule of signs). This root can be found using numerical methods. R function "uniroot" can be used for that.

Finally, we want to address a question concerning the choice of the number of mixture components. In this regard, we will adopt the approach proposed in the literature (e.g.[19,18]) and use a likelihood-based parsimony criterion such as Bayesian Information Criterion (BIC). The literature on model-based clustering suggests that the model choice based on BIC has given good results from the data utility perspective [3,4,18,39]. As for the number of clusters, we consider from 2 to κ clusters, where κ depends on the number of records in the data set. In our experiments, we set $\kappa = 10$ and computed BIC for each such model. The mixture model which maximizes BIC is chosen.

Also as suggested in the literature [19], we initialized the EM with the result of model-based hierarchical agglomerative clustering, which approximately maximizes the classification likelihood.

After the model parameters are estimated, we generated synthetic data from the mixture using MVN model for each cluster with the parameters set equal to the estimated values.

3   Experimental Results with Genuine Data Sets

The procedure described above was implemented and evaluated on two medical data sets:

- The first data set, called THYROID, was obtained from the UCI Machine Learning Repository [1]. It contains measurements of the following five continuous attributes: AGE (patient's age), TSH (thyroid-stimulating hormone), $T3$ (triiodothyronine), $T4U$ (thyroxine utilization rate), FTI (free thyroxine index). There are 2,800 records in this data set, with some missing values. In our experiments, we used only the complete cases.
- The second data set, called DIABETES ([34] and also available from the R package mclust [20]), contains the following three continuous variables: glucose intolerance, insulin response to oral glucose and insulin resistance (quantified by determining the steady-state plasma glucose (SSPG) concentration in response to an infusion of octreotide, glucose, and insulin). There are 145 individuals in this data set.

We want to note that the fact that these two data sets are public-use files guarantees public-domain reproducibility of the experiments reported here.

Before applying our method to these data sets we had to specify the minimal cluster volume. One possibility is to set the minimal cluster volume to be equal to some fraction of the hypervolume of the entire data set, excluding the outliers. For example, it can be 10%, 20% or 30% of the total volume. In our experiments we computed hypervolumes using built-in function hypvol of the R package mclust and used the aforementioned percentages for the minimal cluster volume. Denote our approach as SCk (Synthetic with Constraints), where $k \in (10\%, 20\%, 30\%)$.

Application of SCk to the data led to the model with six components for the THYROID data and three components for the DIABETES data (these models were chosen by BIC). In the case of DIABETES we note that respondents in this data set can actually be classified as patients with chemical diabetes, patients with overt diabetes and normal subjects. The chosen model was able to identify these meaningful subpopulations. In the case of the THYROID data there is no obvious interpretation for the clusters.

When applying these methods, we also monitored how often the covariance matrices were updated and how much the volumes of the clusters are changed as a result of the imposed constraints. The application of SC10 to the THYROID data didn't require any adjustment of cluster covariance matrices. However, in the case of SC20 three out of six clusters were adjusted, maximal increase in the cluster volume among the adjusted clusters was 1.5 times that of the original cluster volume. And for the SC30 the same three clusters were adjusted and maximal increase in cluster volume was 2.3 times that of the original cluster volume. Similar behavior was observed for the DIABETES data. In the case of SC10, all the clusters satisfied minimal volume requirements, and in the case of SC20 and SC30, one of the three clusters was adjusted.

For the sake of comparison we also generated synthetic data from the MVN mixture but without any constraints on cluster volumes to see how much utility is lost because of the constraints. We denote this method as SNC (Synthetic No Constraints). Another synthetic method that we experimented with was the one based on the multivariate sequential regression approach described in [33,35,27]. A free multiple imputation software IVEware [24] was used for that. We denote this method as SynthReg.

Other methods used for comparison were plain multivariate microaggregation MDAV [11], denoted as Micro, and noise addition Noise, which are perturbation methods. Multivariate microaggregation was done with $k = 10$ for DIABETES and $k = 20$ for THYROID data. The choice of k was made empirically to reach a reasonably fair comparison with the other methods. We used the implementation of MDAV microaggregation available in the R package sdcMicro [40] for our method Micro. Regarding noise addition, we used a version that preserves the mean vector and the covariance matrix. This method was implemented in the following way:

$$X_m = E[X_o] + \frac{(X_o - E[X_o]) + E}{\sqrt{1+c}}, \tag{8}$$

where X_m is the masked data, X_o is the original data, $E[X_o]$ denotes the expectation of X_o, $E \sim N(0, c\Sigma_o)$ is the random noise, Σ_o is the covariance matrix of the original data, and c is the parameter of the method which regulates the amount of the noise added to the data. We used $c = 0.15$, as recommended in the literature [29,31,41]. We call this method Noise.

To compare these methods we chose a measure of data utility which can be suitable for a number of analyses: the propensity score-based measure [41].

This measure is based on discrimination between the original and masked data: masked data that are difficult to distinguish from the original data have relatively high utility.

Propensity-based information loss is computed in two steps. First, the original and masked data sets are merged and an indicator variable T equal to one for masked records, and to zero for original records, is added. Second, for each record in the original and masked data, the propensity score —the probability of being in the masked data set— is computed. It was shown in [41] that, if the propensity scores of all records are close to 0.5, then the original and masked data have the same distributions. The utility measure is computed as

$$\mathbf{Propen} = \frac{1}{N} \sum_{i=1}^{N} [\hat{p}_i - 0.5]^2 , \tag{9}$$

where N is the total number of records in the merged data set and $\hat{p}_i$ is the estimated propensity score for record i.

The propensity score utility measure depends on the specification of the model used to estimate propensity scores (see [41]). The model that we used for the DIABETES data contains all main effects and interactions from the first to the third-order, and for the THYROID data the model contains all main effects and interactions from the first to the fourth-order.

Table 1. Propensity score utility for various methods (lower values mean better utility)

Data set	SC10	SC20	SC30	Synth	SynthReg	Micro	Noise
DIABETES	2.92	3.42	3.45	2.92	16.28	6.11	7.31
THYROID	25.88	29.70	63.39	25.88	565.56	276.11	301.11

The results for the different methods are shown in Table 1. These are average values of data utility for 50 realizations of masked sets obtained from the same original data by the application of SC10, SC20, SC30,Synth, SynthReg and Noise (remember, Micro is a deterministic method).

We can see that SC10, SC20 and SC30 compare very well with the other methods. Their utility is the best compared to the other methods. As the minimal cluster volume increases the propensity score measure increases as well, as expected, however, it is still smaller than the other methods. We want to note also that other methods considered for comparison do not satisfy the requirement of v-dispersion. The only exception is noise addition, which can be considered as a v-dispersed because it is possible to specify a confidence ellipsoid region for the original values X_{oi} given masked values. The volume of this region depends on the parameter c of Noise. In fact, when noise $E \sim N(\mathbf{0}, c\Sigma_o)$ is added to the original observation the corresponding masked observation will be within the ellipsoid region centered at the original observation. The volume of this region is equal to the volume of the original data $\boldsymbol{X_o}$ times $\sqrt{(c^d)}$, where d is the dimensionality of the data. So, by varying the parameter c we can get bigger or smaller confidence regions and thus limit attribute disclosure. In our experiments we set $c = 0.15$ which corresponds to minimal confidence volume equal to $\sqrt{(0.15^3)} = 0.06$ of the total volume for the DIABETES data and $\sqrt{(0.15^5)} = 0.0087$ of the total volume for the THYROID data. Note that these volumes are much smaller than the ones used for the synthetic data SC. So, Noise has higher attribute disclosure and still worse utility than SCk according to the propensity score measure. In addition, there is a possibility of re-identification disclosure for Noise ([29]), which is not the case for SCk, because these are synthetic methods.

We also looked how different distributional characteristics of the original data are preserved. Our experiments showed that the first two moments are very well preserved. The ratio of masked and original means showed only small variation about 1. Similar results were observed for the covariance matrix and third moments, which shows that the mixture model can successfully capture the skewness of the original data (both data sets have skewed distributions with a number of outlying observations). A thorough analysis and comparison of the distributional characteristics is the subject of our future work.

4   Conclusion

In this paper we presented a new method of synthetic data generation that satisfies the attribute disclosure risk criterion defined in the paper. Synthesizing data from the mixture model with constraints on component volumes is a promising and flexible approach for disclosure limitation of continuous data. Data generated from such a model has good utility characteristics and at the same time limits attribute disclosure. In particular we want to note that for both of our data sets, our method was considerably better than the fully synthetic data based on sequential regressions according to the propensity score utility measure. This suggests that global synthesis of data sets with complex structure may not give good results from the point of few of the utility of the resulting synthetic data. In contrast, local synthesis, which is the essence of our method, may be the best option. Using Gaussian distribution to model the components of the mixture model allows us to manage directly the dispersion of synthetic values within a component as was illustrated in this paper.

In general, attribute disclosure depends on the amount of information available to the intruder not only about the disclosure limitation method but also about other sensitive variables. Of course, the data protector cannot know all this information at the moment of data release. However, it seems reasonable to analyze first the risk related to the model. Next step may consist of some follow up analyses when additional information on sensitive variables is taken into account. In the future we intend to work on this question. In particular, we will focus on the following problems:

- Attribute disclosure risk assessment for synthetic data for other scenarios of data release. For example, assume that, in addition to the knowledge about the model the intruder knows the original values of some of the variables which are not publicly available and wants to obtain narrow bounds on a particular subset of sensitive variables.

- Extension of the method to the cases when data have continuous and categorical variables. We plan to experiment with different latent class analysis models with the goal of developing a criterion and a method that would treat categorical and continuous variables jointly while limiting attribute disclosure on both types of variables.

Acknowledgments. The author would like to thank Josep Domingo-Ferrer, Joe Fred Gonzalez, and Vlad Beresovsky for valuable suggestions and help in the preparation of the paper. Any opinions, findings, and conclusions or recommendations expressed in this publication are those of the author only and do not necessarily reflect the views of the Centers for Disease Control and Prevention.

References

1. Bache, K., Lichman, M.: UCI Machine Learning Repository. University of California, School of Information and Computer Science, Irvine, CA (2013), http://archive.ics.uci.edu/ml
2. Borgelt, C., Kruse, R.: Fuzzy and probabilistic clustering with shape and size constraints. In: Proc. 11th Int. Fuzzy Systems Association World Congress (IFSA 2005), Bejing, China, Heidelberg, Germany, pp. 945–950 (2005)
3. Campbell, J.G., Fraley, C., Murtagh, F., Raftery, A.E.: Linear flaw detection in woven textiles using model-based clustering. Pattern Recdognition Letters 18, 1539–1548 (1997)
4. Campbell, J.G., Fraley, C., Stanford, D., Raftery, A.E.: Model-based methods for real-time textile fault detection. International Journal of Imaging Systems and Technology 10, 339–346 (1999)
5. Celeux, G., Govaert, G.: Gaussian parsimonious clustering models. Pattern Recognition 28, 781–793 (1995)
6. Charest, A.S.: Creation and Analysis of Differentially-Private Synthetic Datasets. PhD Thesis, Carnegie-Mellon University (2012)
7. Charest, A.-S.: Empirical evaluation of statistical inference from differentially-private contingency tables. In: Domingo-Ferrer, J., Tinnirello, I. (eds.) PSD 2012. LNCS, vol. 7556, pp. 257–272. Springer, Heidelberg (2012)
8. Dempster, A.P., Laird, N.M., Rubin, D.B.: Maximum likelihood for incomplete data via the em algorithm (with discussion). Journal of the Royal Statistical Society, Ser. B 39, 1–38 (1977)
9. Domingo-Ferrer, J., González-Nicolás, U.: Hybrid microdata using microaggregation. Information Sciences 180, 2834–2844 (2010)
10. Domingo-Ferrer, J., Oganian, A., Torra, V.: Information-theoretic disclosure risk measures in statistical disclosure control of tabular data. In: Proc. of the 14th International Conference on Scientific and Statistical Database Management - SSDBM 2002, pp. 227–231. IEEE Computer Society, Los Alamitos (2002)
11. Domingo-Ferrer, J., Torra, V.: Ordinal, continuous and heterogeneous k-anonimity through microaggregation. Data Mining and Knowledge Discovery 11, 195–212 (2005)

12. Domingo-Ferrer, J., Torra, V.: A critique of k–anonymity and some of its enhancements. In: The Third International Conference on Availability, Reliability and Security, pp. 990–993. IEEE (2008)
13. Drechsler, J.: Synthetic Datasets for Statistical Disclosure Control: Theory and Implementation. Springer (2011)
14. Dwork, C.: Differential privacy. In: Bugliesi, M., Preneel, B., Sassone, V., Wegener, I. (eds.) ICALP 2006. LNCS, vol. 4052, pp. 1–12. Springer, Heidelberg (2006)
15. Dwork, C.: A firm foundation for Private Data Analysis. Communications of the ACM 54(1), 86–95 (2011)
16. Dwork, C., McSherry, F., Nissim, K., Smith, A.: Calibrating noise to sensitivity in private data analysis. In: Halevi, S., Rabin, T. (eds.) TCC 2006. LNCS, vol. 3876, pp. 265–284. Springer, Heidelberg (2006)
17. Fienberg, S.E., Rinaldo, A., Yang, X.: Differential privacy and the risk-utility trade-off for multi-dimensional contingency tables. In: Domingo-Ferrer, J., Magkos, E. (eds.) PSD 2010. LNCS, vol. 6344, pp. 187–199. Springer, Heidelberg (2010)
18. Fraley, C., Raftery, A.E.: How many clusters? which clustering method? answers via model-based cluster analysis. The Computer Journal 41, 578–588 (1998)
19. Fraley, C., Raftery, A.E.: Model-based clustering, discriminant analysis, and density estimation. Journal of the American Statistical Association 97(458), 611–631 (2002)
20. Fraley, C., Raftery, A.E.: MCLUST Version 3 for R: Normal mixture modeling and model-based clustering. Technical Report no. 504, Department of Statistics, University of Washington (September 2006), http://cran.r-project.org/web/packages/mclust/index.html
21. Hardt, M., Ligett, K., McSherry, F.: A simple and practical algorithm for differentially private data release. In: 26th Annual Conference on Neural Information Processing Systems - NIPS 2012, pp. 2348–2356 (2012)
22. Hundepool, A., Domingo-Ferrer, J., Franconi, L., Giessing, S., Lenz, R., Longhurst, J., Schulte-Nordholt, E., Seri, G., DeWolf, P.-P.: Handbook on Statistical Disclosure Control (version 1.2). ESSNET SDC project (2010), http://neon.vb.cbs.nl/casc
23. Hundepool, A., Domingo-Ferrer, J., Franconi, L., Giessing, S., Schulte-Nordholt, E., Spicer, K., DeWolf, P.-P.: Statistical Disclosure Control. Wiley (2012)
24. IVEware. Imputation and Variance Estimation software, http://www.isr.umich.edu/src/smp/ive/ (accessed July 2, 2014)
25. Karr, A.F., Kohnen, C.N., Oganian, A., Reiter, J.P., Sanil, A.P.: A framework for evaluating the utility of data altered to protect confidentiality. The American Statistician 60(3), 224–232 (2006)
26. Li, N., Li, T., Venkatasubramanian, S.: T-closeness: privacy beyond k-anonymity and l-diversity. In: Proceedings of the IEEE ICDE 2007 (2007)
27. Little, R.J., Liu, F., Raghunathan, T.: Statistical disclosure techniques based on multiple imputation. In: Gelman, A., Meng, X.-L. (eds.) Applied Bayesian Modeling and Causal Inference from Incomplete-Data Perspectives, vol. 18, pp. 141–152. Wiley, New York (2004)
28. McLachlan, G.J., Krishnan, T.: EM Algorithm and Extensions. Wiley, New York (1997)
29. Oganian, A.: Security and Information Loss in Statistical Database Protection. PhD thesis, Universitat Politecnica de Catalunya (2003)
30. Oganian, A., Domingo-Ferrer, J.: Hybrid Microdata via Model-Based Clustering. In: Domingo-Ferrer, J., Tinnirello, I. (eds.) PSD 2012. LNCS, vol. 7556, pp. 103–115. Springer, Heidelberg (2012)

31. Oganian, A., Karr, A.F.: Combinations of SDC methods for microdata protection. In: Domingo-Ferrer, J., Franconi, L. (eds.) PSD 2006. LNCS, vol. 4302, pp. 102–113. Springer, Heidelberg (2006)
32. Raghunathan, T.E., Lepkowski, J.M., van Hoewyk, J., Solenberger, P.: A multivariate technique for multiply imputing missing values using a series of regression models. Survey Methodology 27, 85–96 (2001)
33. Raghunathan, T.E., Reiter, J.P., Rubin, D.B.: Multivariate imputation for statistical disclosure limitation. Journal of Official Statistics 19(1), 1–16 (2003)
34. Reaven, G.M., Miller, R.G.: An attempt to define the nature of chemical diabetes using multidimensional analysis. Diabetologica 16(1), 17–24 (1979)
35. Reiter, J.P.: Satisfying disclosure restrictions with synthetic data sets. Journal of Official Statistics 18, 531–544 (2002)
36. Reiter, J.P.: Using CART to generate partially synthetic public use microdata. Journal of Official Statistics 21, 441–462 (2005)
37. Scott, D.W.: Multivariate Density Estimation. John Wiley & Sons, New York (1992)
38. Silverman, B.W.: Density Estimation for Statistics and Data Analysis. Chapman & Hall (1986)
39. Stanford, D., Raftery, A.E.: Principle curve clustering with noise. IEEE Transactions on Pattern Analysis and Machine Inteligence, 601–609 (2000)
40. Templ, M.: Statistical disclosure control for microdata using the R-package sdcMicro. Transactions on Data Privacy 1(2), 67–85 (2008)
41. Woo, M.-J., Reiter, J.P., Oganian, A., Karr, A.F.: Global measures of data utility for microdata masked for disclosure limitation. Journal of Privacy and Confidentiality 1(1), 111–124 (2009)

Nonparametric Generation of Synthetic Data for Small Geographic Areas

Joseph W. Sakshaug[1] and Trivellore E. Raghunathan[2]

[1] Institute for Employment Research, Nuremberg 90478, Germany
[2] University of Michigan, Ann Arbor MI 48104, USA

Abstract. Computing and releasing statistics for small geographic areas is a common task for many statistical agencies, but releasing public-use microdata for these areas is much less common due to data confidentiality concerns. Accessing the restricted microdata is usually only possible within a research data center (RDC). This arrangement is inconvenient for many researchers who must travel large distances and, in some cases, pay a sizeable data usage fee to access the nearest RDC. An alternative data dissemination method that has been explored is to release public-use synthetic data. In general, synthetic data consists of imputed values drawn from a predictive model based on the observed data. Data confidentiality is preserved because no actual data values are released. The imputed values are typically drawn from a standard, parametric distribution, but often key variables of interest do not follow strict parametric forms. In this paper, we apply a nonparametric method for generating synthetic data for continuous variables collected from small geographic areas. The method is evaluated using data from the 2005-2007 American Community Survey. The analytic validity of the synthetic data is assessed by comparing parametric (baseline) and nonparametric inferences obtained from the synthetic data with those obtained from the observed data.

Keywords: data confidentiality, hierarchical Bayesian model, multiple imputation, small area inference.

1 Introduction

One of the primary functions of a statistical agency is to collect high quality survey data and make these data widely available to data users in the public domain. Scientific surveys serve as the principal data sources for many academic researchers, analysts, and policy-makers who use these data to test theories of human behavior and, in turn, inform important policy decisions. The greatest impact of policy decisions and interventions is arguably felt at the local level where people are most likely to be exposed to changes in infrastructure and resource availability. Several studies have shown that neighborhood- and community-level factors are associated with numerous health and behavioral outcomes [1,2,3,4]. These findings underscore the need for high quality survey data which is being demanded by researchers interested in studying how small area effects influence the characteristics and well-being of the population.

J. Domingo-Ferrer (Ed.): PSD 2014, LNCS 8744, pp. 213–231, 2014.

Many statistical agencies release estimates for various levels of geography. For example, the U.S. Census Bureau releases summary tables containing estimates of demographic, social, and economic characteristics of people, households, and housing units for large areas (e.g., national, region, division), small areas (e.g., tracts, block groups), and many intermediate areas (e.g., state, county, census tract). The U.S. Census Bureau also administers specialized programs for producing updated estimates of income and poverty statistics for school districts, counties, and states [5], and health insurance estimates for counties and states [6].

The production of small area estimates can be useful for many research and evaluation purposes, but oftentimes these estimates are not detailed enough for data users who wish to perform their own customizable geographical analyses. Such data is often needed to test complex hypotheses which require analytic estimates and sophisticated modeling procedures. The U.S. Census Bureau and other statistical agencies try to meet this demand by releasing public-use microdata files. However, the usefulness of these files can be limiting as geographic identifiers are typically suppressed for areas that do not meet a predefined population threshold (e.g., 100,000 persons). Disclosure concerns prohibit the release of small area identifiers for areas that do not meet this pre-specified threshold. To overcome this limitation, data users may access the suppressed identifiers in a Research Data Center (RDC). However, working in an RDC is not always ideal for prospective data users for several reasons. First, prospective users are usually required to submit a research proposal that is subject to approval by the agency responsible for granting access to the restricted data. This requirement may be too burdensome for users whose analytic objectives are exploratory in nature and whose research questions are not yet well-defined. Second, there is a significant cost burden associated with using the RDC. Many federal RDCs charge a usage fee upward of $20,000 per year, which can be difficult to cover for data users who lack external funds. Finally, there is no guarantee that small area outputs generated from the RDC will pass disclosure review and be permitted for publication.

1.1 Multiple Imputation for Statistical Disclosure Control

To facilitate data access and maintain strict confidentiality requirements for small geographic areas, this article builds on prior work exploring the use of multiple imputation to generate public-use synthetic data files for small geographic areas [7]. Synthetic data comprises hypothetical (yet plausible) data values that replace some or all of the observed data values. Similar to multiple imputation for nonresponse, the synthetic data values are generated from a predictive model based on the observed data [8]. The main distinction lies in how the "missing data" is defined. In a fully-synthetic data framework [9], the nonsampled portion of the population is treated as missing data to be multiply imputed. After the synthetic populations are created random samples are drawn from each and released as public-use microdata files. Inferences are obtained by using standard combining rules [9]. Statistical agencies have experimented with releasing synthetic data files in practical survey applications [10,11,12], but this approach has not been considered for the purpose of disseminating public-use microdata for small geographic areas.

A necessary prerequisite for creating analytically-valid synthetic data sets for any application is that the imputation model underlying the synthetic data generating process is appropriately specified and reflects all of the key relationships in the observed data. When the imputer's model corresponds to the analyst's model, then the models are said to be "congenial" in the context of multiple imputation for survey nonresponse [13]. The lack of correspondence (or congeniality) between the two models can lead to biased inferences. Incorporating all-possible analytic relationships into the model is one way to minimize bias, but this approach is not always practically feasible. This is an important point of contention among analysts who may be interested in analyzing complex relationships, interactions, and higher-order terms but these uses of the data are usually unbeknownst to the data imputer prior to synthesis [14]. In this case, compromises may need to be chosen that appease the majority of data users with the explicit caveat that more complex analyses may require access to the observed microdata.

A second approach to protecting against bias is to relax the distributional assumptions associated with parametric imputation models to improve model fit and protect against model misspecification. This approach has led to several innovations in the use of semiparametric and nonparametric imputation models for the purpose of generating synthetic data. Raghunathan et al. [9] evaluated a multivariate normal and a nonparametric Bayesian bootstrap procedure to generate synthetic data sets based on the 1994 Consumer Expenditure Survey. Reiter [15] presented a nonparametric imputation method based on classification and regression tree (CART) models to generate synthetic data. Caiola and Reiter [16] considered imputation models based on random forests (RF), which are collections of CARTs based on random subsamples of the original data where each tree is grown using random samples of predictors. Drechsler and Reiter [17] empirically evaluated several synthetic data generators based on nonparametric machine-learning algorithms, including CART, random forests, support-vector machines, and bagging. Woodcock and Benedetto [18] developed an imputation strategy based on kernel density estimation for variables with very skewed and multimodal distributions. These references primarily focus on preserving statistics about the entire sample. Applying nonparametric methods for generating synthetic data for small domains and small geographic areas is an underdeveloped, but potentially worthwhile, area of research.

In this article, we apply a nonparametric simulation procedure for generating synthetic data for continuous variables for small geographic areas. The procedure is based on a Bayesian hierarchical model that accounts for small areas (e.g., counties) nested within larger areas (e.g., states) and is coupled with the parametric procedure described in [7]. The parametric procedure is modified by applying a nonparametric component that is implemented at the final step of the data generation process. The modified procedure is applied and evaluated using public-use microdata from the American Community Survey for years 2005-2007. The synthetic data inferences are compared against the actual data inferences for both descriptive and analytic statistics and both skewed and bimodal variables.

2   Review of Fully Synthetic Data

2.1   Generating Fully Synthetic Data Sets

Procedures for generating and analyzing fully-synthetic data sets are described in [9] and in [19]. The pertinent details are described here. Suppose a sample of size n is drawn from a finite population $\Omega = (X, Y)$ of size N, with $X = (X_i; i = 1, 2, \ldots, N)$ representing auxiliary information available for all N units in the population, and $Y = (Y_i; i = 1, 2, \ldots, N)$ representing the survey variables of interest. It is assumed that there is no confidentiality concern over releasing X and synthesis of these auxiliary variables is not needed. Let $Y_{obs} = (Y_i; i = 1, 2, \ldots, n)$ be the observed portion of Y corresponding to sampled units and $Y_{nobs} = (Y_i; i = n + 1, n + 2, \ldots, N)$ be the unobserved portion of Y corresponding to the nonsampled units. The observed data set is $D = (X, Y_{obs})$. It is assumed that there are no item missing data in the observed data set.

Fully synthetic data sets are constructed in two steps. First, M synthetic populations $P^{(l)} = \{(X, Y^{(l)}); l = 1, 2, \ldots, M\}$ are generated by taking independent draws from the Bayesian posterior predictive distribution of $f(Y_{nobs}|X, Y_{obs})$ conditional on the observed data D. Alternatively, one can generate synthetic values of Y for all N units to ensure that no observed values of Y are released. The number of synthetic populations M is chosen based on the desired accuracy for synthetic data inferences. A modest number of fully synthetic data sets (e.g., 5, 10, or 20) is usually sufficient to ensure valid inferences [9]. In the second step, a random sample of size n_{syn} is drawn from each of the $l = 1, 2, \ldots, M$ synthetic data populations, $D^{(l)} = (x_i, y_i^{(l)}, i = 1, 2, \ldots, n_{syn})$. The corresponding M synthetic samples $D_{syn} = (D^{(l)}; l = 1, 2, \ldots, M)$ comprise the public-use data sets, which are released to data users for analysis.

2.2   Analyzing Fully Synthetic Data Sets

From the publicly-released synthetic data sets, data users can make inferences about a scalar population quantity $Q = Q(X, Y)$, such as the population mean of Y or the population regression coefficients of Y on X. Suppose the analyst is interested in obtaining a point estimate q and an associated measure of uncertainty v of Q from a set of synthetic samples D_{syn} drawn from the synthetic populations $P_{syn} = (P^{(l)}; l = 1, 2, \ldots, M)$ under simple random sampling. The values of q and v computed on the M synthetic data sets are denoted by $(q^{(l)}, v^{(l)}, l = 1, 2, \ldots, M)$.

Consistent with the theory of multiple imputation for item missing data [20,21], combining inferences about $Q = Q(X, Y)$ from a set of synthetic samples D_{syn} is achieved by approximating the posterior distribution of Q conditional on D_{syn}. The approach suggested in [9] is to treat $(q^{(l)}, v^{(l)}; l = 1, 2, \ldots, M)$ as sufficient summaries of the synthetic data sets D_{syn} and approximate the posterior density $f(Q|D_{syn})$ using a normal distribution with the posterior mean Q computed as the average of the estimates,

$$\bar{q}_M = \sum_{l=1}^{M} q^{(l)} / M \tag{1}$$

and the approximate posterior variance is computed as,

$$T_M = (1 + M^{-1})b_M - \bar{v}_m \tag{2}$$

where $\bar{v}_M = \sum_{l=1}^{M} v^{(l)} / M$ is the overall mean of the estimated variances across all synthetic data sets ("within variance") and $b_M = \sum_{l=1}^{M} (q^{(l)} - \bar{q}_M)^2 / (M - 1)$ is the variance of $q^{(l)}$ across all synthetic data sets ("between variance").

Under the conditions specified by [9], $\bar{q}_M$ is an unbiased estimator of Q and $b_M - v_m$ is an unbiased estimator of the variance of Q. The $\frac{1}{M} b_M$ adjusts for using only a finite number of synthetic data sets. It should be noted that the subtraction of the within imputation variance in T_M is due to the additional step of sampling the units that comprise the synthetic samples from each multiply-imputed synthetic population. Because of this additional sampling step, the between imputation variance already reflects the within imputation variability, which is not the case in the usual multiple imputation framework. When n, n_{syn}, and M are large, inferences for scalar Q can be based on normal distributions. For moderate M, inferences can be based on t-distributions with degrees of freedom $\gamma_M = (M - 1)(1 - r_m^{-1})^2$, where $r_m = (1 + M^{-1})b_m / \bar{v}_M$, so that a $(1 - \alpha)\%$ interval for Q is $\bar{q}_M \pm t_{\gamma_M}(\alpha/2)\sqrt{T_M}$ as described in [22].

3   Extension to Small Geographic Areas

In this section, we describe a fully-parametric synthetic data generation procedure presented in [7]. The procedure is based on a hierarchical Bayesian model and involves three steps. In the first step, the joint density of the variables is approximated using the sequential regression procedure described in [23]. In the second step, the sampling distribution of the unknown regression parameters estimated in Step 1 is approximated and the between-area variation is modeled using auxiliary information for larger geographic areas. In the final step, the unknown regression parameters are simulated from the posterior distribution and used to draw synthetic values from the posterior predictive distribution. A modification of the procedure to allow for nonparametric simulation of continuous synthetic data values is then introduced.

3.1   Parametric Approach

Step 1: Approximating the Joint Density via Sequential Regression
For simplicity, we define "small areas" to be counties nested within states, which could also be nested within even larger areas (e.g., regions). Suppose that a sample of size n is drawn from a finite population of size N. Let n_{cs} and N_{cs} denote the respec-

tive sample and population sizes for county $c = (1,2, ..., C_s)$ nested within state $s = (1,2, ..., S)$. Let $Y_{cs} = (Y_{ics,p}; i = 1,2, ..., n_{cs}; p = 1,2, ..., P)$ represent the $n_{cs} \times P$ matrix of continuous survey variables collected from each survey respondent located in county c and state s. Let $X_{cs} = (X_{ics,j}; i = 1,2, ..., n_{cs}, n_{cs} + 1, ..., N_{cs}; j = 1,2,..,J)$ represent the $N_{cs} \times J$ matrix of auxiliary or administrative variables known for every population member in a particular county and state.

A desirable property of synthetic data is that the multivariate relationships among the observed variables are maintained in the synthetic data, i.e., the joint distribution of variables given the auxiliary information $f(Y_{cs,1}, Y_{cs,2}, ..., Y_{cs,P}|X_{cs,j})$ is preserved. Specifying and simulating from the joint conditional distribution can be difficult for complex data structures involving large numbers of variables and different distributional forms. Alternatively, one can approximate the joint density as a product of conditional densities [23]. That is, the joint density $f(Y_{cs,1}, Y_{cs,2}, ..., Y_{cs,P}|X_{cs,j})$ can be factored into the following conditional densities: $f(Y_{cs,1}|X_{cs,j})$, $f(Y_{cs,2}|Y_{cs,1}, X_{cs,j}),...,f(Y_{cs,P}|Y_{cs,1}, ..., Y_{cs,P-1}, X_{cs,j})$. In practice, a sequence of generalized linear models are fit based on the observed county-level data where the variable to be synthesized comprises the outcome variable that is regressed on any auxiliary variables or previously fitted variables, e.g., $Y_{ics,1} = (X_{ics})\beta_{cs,1} + \varepsilon_{ics}$, $Y_{ics,2} = (X_{ics}, Y_{ics,1})\beta_{cs,2} + \varepsilon_{ics}$,..., $Y_{ics,P} = (X_{ics}, Y_{ics,1}, Y_{ics,2}, ..., Y_{ics,P-1})\beta_{cs,P} + \varepsilon_{ics}$. The choice of model (e.g., Gaussian, binomial) is dependent on the type of variable to be synthesized, but only linear models are considered here. It is assumed that any complex survey design features are incorporated into the generalized linear models. After fitting each conditional density, the vector of regression parameter estimates $\hat{\beta}_{cs,p}$, the corresponding covariance matrix $\hat{V}_{cs,p}$, and the residual variance $\hat{\sigma}_{cs,p}^2$ are extracted from each of the P regression models and incorporated into the hierarchical model described below. The reader should note that $p = (1,2, ..., P)$ is used to index the set of parameters associated with the pth synthetic variable of interest and the pth regression model from which the direct estimates are obtained.

Step 2: Sampling Distribution and Between-Area Model
In the second step, the joint sampling distribution of the design-based county-level regression estimates $\hat{\beta}_{cs,p}$ (obtained from each conditional model fitted in Step 1) is approximated by a multivariate normal distribution,

$$\hat{\beta}_{cs,p} \sim MVN(\beta_{cs,p}, \hat{V}_{cs,p}) \tag{3}$$

where $\beta_{cs,p}$ is the $(J + p) \times 1$ matrix of unknown regression parameters and $\hat{V}_{cs,p}$ is the corresponding $(J + p) \times (J + p)$ estimated covariance matrix obtained from Step 1. The unknown county-level regression parameters $\beta_{cs,p}$ are assumed to follow a multivariate normal distribution,

$$\beta_{cs,p} \sim MVN(\beta_p Z_s, \Sigma_p) \tag{4}$$

where $Z_s = (Z_{s,k}; k = 1,2, \ldots, K)$ is a $K \times 1$ matrix of state-level covariates, β_p is a $(J + p) \times K$ matrix of unknown regression parameters, and Σ_p is a $(J + p) \times (J + p)$ covariance matrix. The state-level covariates are included in the hierarchical model to account for variation between and to "borrow strength" across areas. It is assumed that β_p and Σ_p are fixed at their respective maximum likelihood estimates (MLE), a common assumption in hierarchical models for small area estimation [24,25,26]. The procedure for producing the maximum likelihood estimates using the expectation-maximization (EM) algorithm [27] is presented in the Appendix.

Based on standard theory of the normal hierarchical model [28], the unknown regression parameters $\beta_{cs,p}$ can be drawn from the following posterior distribution,

$$\tilde{\beta}_{cs,p} \sim MVN\left[\left(\hat{V}_{cs,p}^{-1} + \hat{\Sigma}_p^{-1}\right)^{-1}\left(\hat{V}_{cs,p}^{-1}\hat{\beta}_{cs,p}\right.\right.$$
$$\left.\left. + \hat{\Sigma}_p^{-1}\hat{\beta}_p Z_s\right), \left(\hat{V}_{cs,p}^{-1} + \hat{\Sigma}_p^{-1}\right)^{-1}\right]$$

(5)

where $\tilde{\beta}_{cs,p}$ is a simulated vector of values for the unknown regression parameters $\beta_{cs,p}$.

Step 3: Simulating Synthetic Data Values from the Posterior Predictive Distribution
Simulating a synthetic variable $\tilde{Y}_{cs} = (\tilde{Y}_{lcs,p}; l = 1,2, \ldots, N_{cs}; p = 1,2, \ldots, P)$ for observed variable Y_{cs} for synthetic population unit $l = (1,2, \ldots, N_{cs})$ is achieved by drawing in sequential fashion from the posterior predictive distributions $f(\tilde{Y}_{cs,1}|X_{cs}, \tilde{\beta}_{cs,1})$, $f(\tilde{Y}_{cs,2}|\tilde{Y}_{cs,1}, X_{cs}, \tilde{\beta}_{cs,1})$, $\ldots$, $f(\tilde{Y}_{cs,P}|\tilde{Y}_{cs,1}, \tilde{Y}_{cs,2}, \ldots, \tilde{Y}_{cs,P-1}, X_{cs}, \tilde{\beta}_{cs,1})$. The first variable to be synthesized $Y_{cs,1}$ is drawn from a normal distribution with location and scale parameters $X_{cs}\tilde{\beta}_{cs,1}$ and $\sigma_{cs,1}^2$, respectively, where $\sigma_{cs,1}^2$ may be drawn from an appropriate posterior predictive distribution $f(\tilde{\sigma}_{cs,1}^2|Y_{cs,1}, X_{cs}, \sigma_{cs,1}^2)$, or fixed at the maximum likelihood estimate $\hat{\sigma}_{cs,1}^2$ (obtainable from Step 1). Once the first synthetic variable $\tilde{Y}_{cs,1}$ is generated, a second (normally distributed) synthetic variable $\tilde{Y}_{cs,2}$ is drawn from the posterior predictive distribution $f(\tilde{Y}_{cs,2}|\tilde{Y}_{cs,1}, X_{cs}, \tilde{\beta}_{cs,2})$, which is achieved by drawing $\tilde{Y}_{cs,2}$ from $N[(X_{cs}, \tilde{Y}_{cs,1})\tilde{\beta}_{cs,2}, \sigma_{cs,2}^2]$, and so on up to $\tilde{Y}_{cs,P} \sim N[(X_{cs}, \tilde{Y}_{cs,1}, \tilde{Y}_{cs,2}, \ldots, \tilde{Y}_{cs,P-1})\tilde{\beta}_{cs,P}, \sigma_{cs,P}^2]$. The iterative process continues until all synthetic variables $(\tilde{Y}_{cs,1}, \tilde{Y}_{cs,2}, \ldots, \tilde{Y}_{cs,P})$ are generated. The procedure is repeated M times to create multiple populations of synthetic variables $(\tilde{Y}_{cs,1}^{(l)}, \tilde{Y}_{cs,2}^{(l)}, \ldots, \tilde{Y}_{cs,P}^{(l)}; l = 1,2, \ldots, M)$.

The synthetic populations can then be released to analysts, or a simple random sample of arbitrary size may be drawn from each population and disseminated. The size of the sample should not affect the final inference result as the total variance of the estimates is a bifurcation of the within- and between-imputation variance components. That is, increasing the sample size will decrease the within-variability, but it will increase the between variability. The converse is also true. However, there is a practical advantage of drawing a large sample from the synthetic populations as statistical software may encounter fewer computational problems (e.g., nonconvergence of multivariate models) if a larger sample is used for the analysis.

Analytic inferences from these data can then be obtained using the combining rules presented in Section 2.2.

3.2 Nonparametric Simulation Procedure

The fully-parametric procedure described above is now modified in such a way that does not require the synthetic data values to be drawn from a normal distribution. Specifically, the final step in the parametric approach (Step 3, Section 3.1) is replaced with a distribution-free simulation procedure while the first two steps remain the same. Note that the method still relies on multivariate normality to model the random effects and to obtain the posterior distribution of $\tilde{\beta}_{cs,p}$ in equation (5).

Recall from Step 3 (Section 3.1) the fully-parametric iterative simulation procedure proceeds as follows. The first continuous and normally distributed observed variable $Y_{cs,1} = (Y_{ics,1}; i = 1,2,...,n_{cs})$ is simulated from a normal distribution with location and scale parameters $X_{cs}\tilde{\beta}_{cs,1}$ and $\sigma^2_{cs,1}$, respectively, i.e.,

$$\tilde{Y}_{cs,1} \sim N[X_{cs}\tilde{\beta}_{cs,1}, \sigma^2_{cs,1}],$$

where X_{cs} is an $N_{cs} \times J$ matrix of auxiliary or administrative variables known for every population member in a particular county and state. The second observed variable to be synthesized $Y_{cs,2}$, is simulated by drawing from a normal distribution with location and scale parameters $(X_{cs}, \tilde{Y}_{cs,1})\tilde{\beta}_{cs,2}$ and $\sigma^2_{cs,2}$, respectively, i.e.,

$$\tilde{Y}_{cs,2} \sim N[(X_{cs}, \tilde{Y}_{cs,1})\tilde{\beta}_{cs,2}, \sigma^2_{cs,2}]$$

where the location parameter $(X_{cs}, \tilde{Y}_{cs,1})\tilde{\beta}_{cs,2}$ conditions on the previously synthesized variable $\tilde{Y}_{cs,1}$. The iterative procedure continues until the final variable $Y_{cs,P}$ is synthesized,

$$\tilde{Y}_{cs,P} \sim N[(X_{cs}, \tilde{Y}_{cs,1}, \tilde{Y}_{cs,2}, ..., \tilde{Y}_{cs,P-1})\tilde{\beta}_{cs,P}, \sigma^2_{cs,P}].$$

The general form of the simulation procedure for the $p^{th} (p = 1,2,...,P)$ synthetic variable can therefore be written as,

$$\tilde{Y}_{cs,p} \sim N[(X_{cs}, \tilde{Y}_{cs,1}, \tilde{Y}_{cs,2}, ..., \tilde{Y}_{cs,p-1})\tilde{\beta}_{cs,p}, \sigma^2_{cs,p}]. \tag{6}$$

The procedural steps for synthesizing the pth variable using the nonparametric procedure are implemented as follows. First, the location parameter from (6) is used to obtain predicted values based on the vector of simulated beta coefficients $\tilde{\beta}_{cs,p}$, any previously synthesized variables $(\tilde{Y}_{cs,1}, \tilde{Y}_{cs,2}, ..., \tilde{Y}_{cs,p-1})$, and any auxiliary information X_{cs} that is known for each population member in county c nested within state s. Specifically, we refer to these synthetically-based predicted values as those obtained from the following equation,

$$\hat{Y}_{cs,p,syn} = \left(X_{cs}, \tilde{Y}_{cs,1}, \tilde{Y}_{cs,2}, \dots, \tilde{Y}_{cs,p-1}\right)\tilde{\beta}_{cs,p} \qquad (7)$$

which is computed for population unit $l = (1,2,\dots,N_{cs})$ located in the small area (or county) of interest.

Second, we modify (7) to obtain another set of predicted values that are based on the set of observed variables Y_{cs} rather than the synthetically-generated ones $\tilde{Y}_{cs}$,

$$\hat{Y}_{cs,p,obs} = \left(X_{cs}, Y_{cs,1}, Y_{cs,2}, \dots, Y_{cs,p-1}\right)\tilde{\beta}_{cs,p} \qquad (8)$$

In the third step, the differences between the observed survey values $Y_{cs,p}$ and the observed predicted values $Y_{cs,p}$ are obtained to create a $n_{cs} \times 1$ vector of deviations,

$$\Delta_{cs,p} = Y_{cs,p} - \hat{Y}_{cs,p,obs} \qquad (9)$$

In the fourth step, we account for the uncertainty associated with the distribution of deviated values by resampling the vector $\Delta_{cs,p}$ using an approximate Bayesian Bootstrap (ABB) procedure [29], which is a more computationally direct procedure than the original Bayesian Bootstrap [30]. The ABB procedure is implemented by drawing the components of an n_{cs}-dimensional vector $\Delta_{cs,p,SRSWR}$ from $\Delta_{cs,p}$ with replacement, i.e., $\Delta_{cs,p,SRSWR} = SRSWR(\Delta_{cs,p})$. The final part of the ABB procedure is to draw the components of a N_{cs}-dimensional vector $\Delta_{cs,p,ABB}$ from $\Delta_{cs,p,SRSWR}$ with replacement, i.e., $\Delta_{cs,p,ABB} = SRSWR(\Delta_{cs,p,SRSWR})$.

The final step of the simulation process involves generating the synthetic variables using the components from the previous steps. Specifically, the pth synthetic variable is generated using the following equation,

$$\begin{aligned} \tilde{Y}_{cs,p} &= \left(X_{cs}, \tilde{Y}_{cs,1}, \tilde{Y}_{cs,2}, \dots, \tilde{Y}_{cs,p-1}\right)\tilde{\beta}_{cs,p} + \Delta_{cs,p,ABB} \\ &= \tilde{Y}_{cs,p,syn} + \Delta_{cs,p,ABB} \end{aligned} \qquad (10)$$

The resulting synthetic data may then be analyzed using the combining rules presented in Section 2.2.

A few general remarks can be made about this simulation method. The idea of using the empirical residuals instead of drawing from a normal distribution has been used in many applications of nonresponse in non-small area applications [20,31]. The procedure is also implemented in the R package Hmisc [32]. The procedure has several advantages in the current application. First, simulating the synthetic values does not rely on any standard distribution as it relaxes the assumption of univariate normality. However, the preceding modeling steps used to construct the hierarchical model still rely on multivariate normality, which may not be an adequate assumption if the random effects follow a non-normal distribution. Second, there is no need to apply a transformation to the variables as the synthetic values are based on deviations from the actual values. This is a useful property of the method as choosing a normalizing transformation can be a difficult task, particularly when the appropriate transformation may vary across geographic areas. The effectiveness of the method for synthesizing non-transformed variables in small areas will be assessed in the next section.

4   Application: American Community Survey

The nonparametric simulation method in 3.2.1 is evaluated using a subset of public-use microdata from the 2005-2007 U.S. American Community Survey (ACS). The ACS is an ongoing national survey that provides yearly estimates regarding income and benefits, health insurance, disabilities, family and relationships, among other topics. The ACS collects information on persons living in housing units and group quarters facilities in 3,142 counties. Data collection is conducted using a mixed-mode design. First, questionnaires are mailed to all sampled household addresses obtained from the Master Address File. Approximately six weeks after the questionnaire is mailed the U.S. Census Bureau attempts to conduct telephone interviews for all addresses that do not respond by mail. Following the telephone operation, a sample is taken from addresses which were not interviewed and these addresses are visited by a field interviewer. Full details of the ACS methodology can be found elsewhere [33].

The smallest geographic unit that is identified in the public-use ACS microdata is a Public-Use Microdata Area (PUMA). PUMAs are non-overlapping census areas that contain at least 100,000 persons that cover the entirety of the United States, Puerto Rico, Guam, and the U.S. Virgin Island. They typically consist of counties, collections of counties, or subsets of counties. For this application, the ACS sample is restricted to the Northeast region, which contains 9 states and 405 PUMAs. ACS data was collected in each of these PUMAs during the 3-year study period. The evaluation is conducted on 5 continuous variables (three household- and two person-level variables) measured on 599,450 households and 1,506,011 persons. The variables, shown in Table 1, include the household- and person-level sampling weights, electricity cost/month, household income, and age of all household residents. The first four variables are right-skewed and the last variable (age) is bimodal. All of these variables are synthesized in the application. The PUMA variable is the only variable that is not synthesized. These variables were suggested by statisticians at the U.S. Census Bureau for this project.

$M=10$ fully synthetic data sets are generated for each "small area" (i.e., PUMA). To ensure that each synthetic data set contains ample numbers of households and/or persons within PUMAs, the synthetic sample sizes are created to be larger than the observed sample sizes, and are approximately equivalent to 20% of the total number of households located in each PUMA based on the 2000 decennial census counts. This yielded a total synthetic sample size of 3,963,715 households and 10,192,987 persons in the Northeast region.

Both parametric and nonparametric synthetic data generation procedures presented in Sections 3.1 and 3.2, respectively, are evaluated and compared in this analysis. For the parametric method, a log transformation is applied to the household- and person-level sampling weight variables and a cube root transformation is applied to the electricity cost and household income variables. The approximate bimodal variable age is left untransformed. All transformed variables are back-transformed in the evaluation and presented in actual units. For the nonparametric method, no transformations are used and the variables are processed in their actual units.

Table 1. List of ACS Variables to be Synthesized

Variable	Range	Distribution
Household variables		
Sampling weight	1 - 201	right-skewed
Electricity bill/mo.	1 – 600+	right-skewed
Income	0 – 2,158,100+	right-skewed
Person variables		
Sampling weight	1 - 341	right-skewed
Age	0 – 95+	bimodal

Note: Some variables are top-coded to prevent disclosure of extreme values.

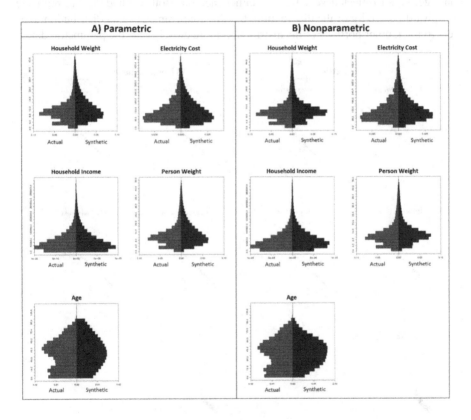

Fig. 1. Back-to-Back Histograms of Actual (Red) and Synthetic (Blue) Distributions Based on the Parametric and Nonparametric Synthetic Data Methods

4.1   Validity of Univariate Estimates

Figure 1 shows back-to-back histograms of the actual (red) and synthetic data (blue) distributions. Panels A and B show the parametrically- and nonparametrically-generated synthetic data variables, respectively. All variables are presented in actual units. The synthetic data distributions generated from both the parametric and nonparametric methods resemble the actual data distributions reasonably well for the right-skewed variables. Both methods preserve the bulk of the distributions. In some cases, the nonparametrically-generated data appears to reflect the distributions more precisely than the parametrically-generated data. For example, the parametric data tends to smooth over the curve between the mode and skewed portion of the distributions, whereas the shape of the nonparametrically-generated data is more closely aligned with the actual shape and curvature of the distribution. The bimodal variable distribution, age, is not reflected very well by either method. Both methods fail to replicate the upward concavity of the distribution, but the nonparametric data distribution does seem to track other portions of the distribution more closely than the parametric data.

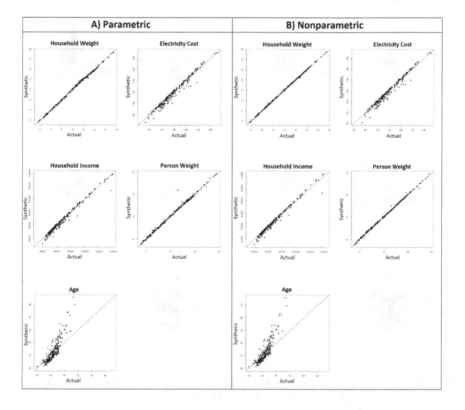

Fig. 2. Scatter Plot of Synthetic (y-axis) and Actual (x-axis) PUMA Means Based on the Parametric and Nonparametric Synthetic Data Methods

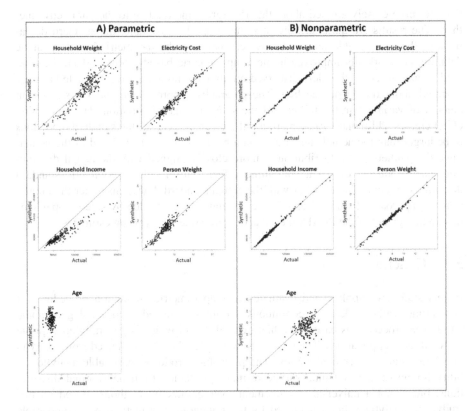

Fig. 3. Scatter Plot of Standard Deviations of Synthetic (y-axis) and Actual (x-axis) PUMA Means Based on the Parametric and Nonparametric Synthetic Data Methods

Although the distributions of the synthetic variables look somewhat reasonable, data users are most interested in the validity of estimates obtained from the synthetic data. Figure 2 shows scatter plots of the actual and synthetic data PUMA means/percentages. Panels A and B correspond to estimates obtained from the parametric and nonparametric synthetic data generation methods, respectively. For the majority of variables, the estimates lie around the 45-degree line, indicating good correspondence between the actual and synthetic data PUMA estimates. This appears to be true for both the parametric- and nonparametric-based estimates as there is little difference between the plots in each of the two panels. Mean estimates of age yield the greatest amount of bias and dispersion around the 45-degree line. PUMAs with the highest average ages tend to be overestimated in the synthetic data. This is not surprising due to the bimodal nature of the age distribution which is poorly modeled with both synthetic data methods.

Scatter plots of synthetic and actual standard deviations of PUMA means are shown in Figure 3. Ideally, each scatter plot point should fall directly on the 45-degree line indicating exact correspondence between the actual and synthetic data standard deviations. In all cases, the nonparametric method yields standard deviations that are more closely aligned about the 45-degree line relative to the parametric method. The results are quite striking in some cases. For example, the standard deviations of the age variable tend to be overestimated in the parametric-based synthetic data, but are markedly improved in the nonparametric-based synthetic data; the standard deviations are still widely dispersed but they are no longer overestimated and are centered about the 45-degree line. The parametric approach produces a significant amount of variation in the tail-end of the synthetic age distribution. The smoothing effect creates additional variation around the mean and causes the standard deviations to be larger than the actual standard deviations. In contrast, the tail-end of the nonparametric synthetic data distribution is more closely aligned with the actual distribution, and produces less of a smoothing effect. This results in synthetic standard deviations that correspond better with the actual standard deviations under the nonparametric approach. Figures 4 and 5 (see appendix) present side-by-side comparisons of standard errors of the PUMA means and simple linear regression estimates.

5   Conclusions

In this study, we applied and evaluated a nonparametric simulation procedure for generating synthetic data for continuous variables collected from small geographic areas. The procedure is based on a hierarchical model which is generally appropriate for small area applications. The procedure was applied to data collected from PUMAs in a large-scale government survey. The procedure produces reasonable analytic validity for univariate and multivariate estimates obtained from non-normal distributions, but is not a universal improvement over parametric methods. Based on this study, the analytic validity achieved by the nonparametric method was comparable and, in some cases, better than the baseline parametric method. Advantages of applying this method in practice include its ability to synthesize continuous, nonnormal variables without the need to apply transformations, which can be a time-consuming and rather subjective process.

Other demonstrated advantages of the applied method include its versatility in terms of handling both skewed and bimodal distributions. Although the nonparametric method did not replicate the bimodal shape or upward concavity of the age distribution in this study, it produced relatively valid PUMA-level estimates, particularly for estimates of regression coefficients. In addition, the method produced synthetic data with moderately high validity for calculating income percentiles recoded from the continuous data.

Limitations of the nonparametric method applied in this application should also be noted. Although simulating the synthetic data values is considered nonparametric, the method itself is preceded by parametric modeling steps that characterize the hierarchical data structure. For example, the linear regression estimates obtained in Step 1 assume that the usual regression assumptions (e.g., normality of the error distribution) hold. In addition, the hierarchical Bayesian model assumes that the random effects are distributed as multivariate normal, which is a common assumption in hierarchical models but not verified in this study. Incorporating the procedure within a fully nonparametric procedure (e.g., CART) may have yielded better analytic properties in this application than the approach considered here.

In conclusion, the nonparametric synthetic data approach applied in this application shows some promise for generating valid synthetic data for small geographic areas, but more evaluations using large-scale survey data are needed before it can be used in a production-type setting or as a supplement to (or replacement of) research data centers. If synthetic data becomes a more common alternative to accessing restricted data from RDCs, then it is likely that nonparametric data generation methods will be preferred in order to address the concerns of data users from data users who are skeptical of the parametric assumptions underlying many synthetic data methods.

Acknowledgements. This research was supported by dissertation grants from the National Science Foundation (SES-0918942), the U.S. Census Bureau (YA132309SE0354), and the Centers for Disease Control and Prevention (1-R36-SH-000016-01), and was partially supported by a grant from the Alexander von Humboldt Foundation.

References

1. Diez Roux, A.V.: Estimating Neighborhood Health Effects: The Challenges of Causal Inference in a Complex World. Soc. Sci. Med. 58, 1953–1960 (2004)
2. Fisher, K.J., Li, M.Y., Cleveland, M.: Neighborhood-Level Influences on Physical Activity Among Older Adults: A Multilevel Analysis. J. Aging. Phys. Activ. 12, 45–63 (2004)
3. Auchincloss, A.H., Roux, A.V., Brown, D., Erdmann, C.A., Bertoni, A.G.: Neighborhood Resources for Physical Activity and Healthy Foods and their Association with Insulin Resistance. Epidemiology 19, 146–157 (2008)
4. Mujahid, M.S., Diez Roux, A.V., Morenoff, J.D., Raghunathan, T.E., Cooper, R.S., Ni, H., Shea, S.: Neighborhood Characteristics and Hypertension. Epidemiology 19, 590–598 (2008)
5. Bell, W., Basel, W., Cruse, C., Dalzell, L., Maples, J., O'Hara, B., Powers, D.: Use of ACS Data to Produce SAIPE Model-Based Estimates of Poverty for Counties. Technical Report, U.S. Bureau of the Census (2007), http://www.census.gov/did/www/saipe/publications/files/report.pdf
6. Fisher, R., Turner, J.: Small Area Estimation of Health Insurance Coverage from the Current Population Survey's Social and Economic Supplement and the Survey of Income and Program Participation. Presented at the American Statistical Association Meetings, Toronto, Canada (2004)
7. Sakshaug, J.W., Raghunathan, T.E.: Synthetic Data for Small Area Estimation. In: Domingo-Ferrer, J., Magkos, E. (eds.) PSD 2010. LNCS, vol. 6344, pp. 162–173. Springer, Heidelberg (2010)
8. Rubin, D.B.: Satisfying Confidentiality Constraints Through the Use of Synthetic Multiply-Imputed Microdata. J. Off. Stat. 9, 461–468 (1993)
9. Raghunathan, T.E., Reiter, J.P., Rubin, D.B.: Multiple Imputation for Statistical Disclosure Limitation. J. Off. Stat. 19, 1–16 (2003)
10. Abowd, J.M., Stinson, M., Benedetto, G.: Final Report to the Social Security Administration on the SIPP/SSA/IRS Public Use File Project. Technical Report, U.S. Census Bureau Longitudinal Employer-Household Dynamics Program (2006), http://www.census.gov/sipp/SSAfinal.pdf

11. Rodriguez, R.: Synthetic Data Disclosure Control for American Community Survey Group Quarters. In: Proceedings of the Joint Statistical Meetings, pp. 1439–1450 (2007)

12. Kinney, S.K., Reiter, J.P., Reznek, A.P., Miranda, J., Jarmin, R.S., Abowd, J.M.: Towards Unrestricted Public Use Microdata: The Synthetic Longitudinal Business Database. Int. Stat. Rev. 79, 362–384 (2011)

13. Meng, X.L.: Multiple Imputation Inference with Uncongenial Sources of Input (with discussion). Stat. Sci. 9, 538–573 (1994)

14. Reiter, J.P.: Using Multiple Imputation to Integrate and Disseminate Confidential Microdata. Int. Stat. Rev. 77, 179–195 (2009)

15. Reiter, J.P.: Using CART to Generate Partially Synthetic Public Use Microdata. J. Off. Stat. 21, 441–462 (2005)

16. Caiola, G., Reiter, J.P.: Random Forests for Generating Partially Synthetic, Categorical Data. Transactions on Data Privacy 3, 27–42 (2010)

17. Drechsler, J., Reiter, J.P.: An Empirical Evaluation of Easily Implemented, Nonparametric Methods for Generating Synthetic Data Sets. Comput. Stat. Data An. 55, 3232–3243 (2011)

18. Woodcock, S.D., Benedetto, G.: Distribution-Preserving Statistical Disclosure Limitation. Comput. Stat. Data An. 53, 4228–4242 (2009)

19. Reiter, J.P.: Releasing Multiply-Imputed, Synthetic Public Use Microdata: An Illustration and Empirical Study. J. Royal Stat. Soc. Series A 168, 185–205 (2005)

20. Rubin, D.B.: Multiple Imputation for Nonresponse in Surveys. Wiley, New York (1987)

21. Little, R.J.A., Rubin, D.B.: Statistical Analysis with Missing Data, 2nd edn. Wiley (2002)

22. Raghunathan, T.E., Rubin, D.B.: Bayesian Multiple Imputation to Preserve Confidentiality in Public-Use Data Sets. In: ISBA 2000: The Sixth World Meeting of the International Society for Bayesian Analysis (2000)

23. Raghunathan, T.E., Lepkowski, J.M., Van Hoewyk, J., Solenberger, P.: A Multivariate Technique for Multiply Imputing Missing Values Using a Sequence of Regression Models. Surv. Methodol. 27, 85–95 (2001)

24. Fay, R.E., Herriot, R.A.: Estimates of Income for Small Places: An Application of James-Stein Procedures to Census Data. J. Am. Stat. Assoc. 74, 269–277 (1979)

25. Datta, G.S., Fay, R.E., Ghosh, M.: Hierarchical and Empirical Bayes Analysis in Small-Area Estimation. In: Proceedings of the Annual Research Conference, U.S. Bureau of the Census, pp. 63–78 (1991)

26. Rao, J.N.K.: Small Area Estimation. Wiley, New York (2003)

27. Dempster, A.P., Laird, N.M., Rubin, D.B.: Maximum Likelihood from Incomplete Data via the EM Algorithm. J. Royal Stat. Soc. Series B 39, 1–38 (1977)

28. Lindley, D.V., Smith, A.F.M.: Bayes Estimates for the Linear Model. J. Royal Stat. Soc. Series B 34, 1–41 (1972)

29. Rubin, D.B., Schenker, N.: Multiple Imputation for Interval Estimation from Simple Random Samples with Ignorable Nonresponse. J. Am. Stat. Assoc. 81, 366–374 (1986)

30. Rubin, D.B.: The Bayesian Bootstrap. Ann. Stat. 9, 130–134 (1981)

31. Schenker, N., Taylor, J.M.G.: Partially Parametric Techniques for Multiple Imputation. Comput. Stat. Data An. 22, 425–446 (1996)

32. Harrell, F.E.: Regression Modeling Strategies with Applications to Linear Models, Logistic Regression and Survival Analysis. Springer, New York (2001)

33. U.S. Census Bureau: American Community Survey: Design and Methodology (2009), http://www.census.gov/acs/www/Downloads/survey_methodology/acs_design_methodology.pdf

6   Appendix

Figure 4 shows scatter plots of the synthetic and actual standard errors of the means under the parametric and nonparametric methods. The synthetic data standard errors tend to be larger, on average, than the actual standard errors for these simple mean estimates. There does not appear to be any striking differences between the parametric and nonparametric methods.

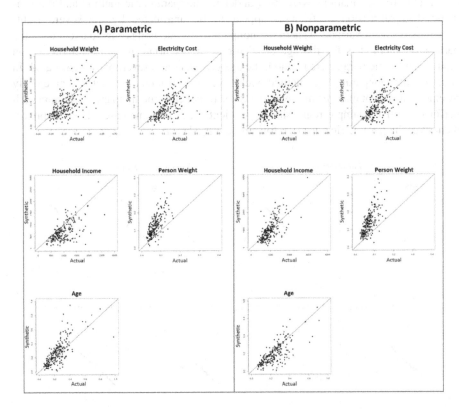

Fig. 4. Scatter Plot of Standard Errors of Synthetic (y-axis) and Actual (x-axis) PUMA Means Based on the Parametric and nonparametric Synthetic Data Methods

6.1   Validity of Multivariate Estimates

The next analysis evaluates the analytic validity of multivariate estimates obtained from the parametric and nonparametric synthetic data methods. Figure 5 shows scatter plots of regression coefficients for simple main effects household- and person-level regression models fit within each PUMA. The dependent variable for the household-level regression model is household income and the independent variables are the sampling weight and monthly electricity amount. For the bivariate person-level regression model the dependent variable is the sampling weight and the independent variable is age. Both variables are log-transformed in the parametric evaluation and are untransformed in the nonparametric evaluation. We acknowledge that these models are not likely to be substantively appealing to analysts. We use them simply for demonstration and evaluation purposes.

Figure 5 shows that the parametric and nonparametric methods yield comparable results as the estimated household-level regression coefficients under both methods tend to be clustered about the 45-degree line. This is remarkable due to the fact that no variable transformations were used under the nonparametric method and the synthetic data regression coefficients appear to be unaffected by the severe right-skewness of the covariates. Where the nonparametric method seems to excel over the parametric method is for the age predictor in the bivariate person-level regression model. Under the parametric method, the age coefficient is severely overestimated. In contrast, the nonparametric method yields valid coefficient estimates that closely resemble those obtained from the actual data. In general, the nonparametric approach performs well for simple regression coefficients and, in some cases, is an improvement over the parametric approach for bimodal predictors.

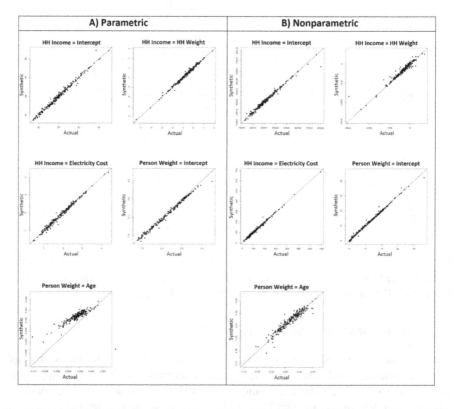

Fig. 5. Scatter Plots of Synthetic (y-axis) and Actual (x-axis) PUMA Regression Coefficients Based on the Parametric and Nonparametric Synthetic Data Methods

6.2   EM Algorithm for Estimating Bayesian Hyperparameters

The EM algorithm is used to estimate the unknown population parameters β_p and Σ_p from the following setup,

$$\hat{\beta}_{cs,p} \sim MVN\left(\beta_{cs,p}, \hat{V}_{cs,p}\right)$$

$$\beta_{cs,p} \sim MVN\left(\beta_p Z_s, \Sigma_p\right)$$

where $p = (1,2, \dots, P)$ is used to index the set of parameters associated with the pth synthetic variable of interest and the pth regression model from which the direct estimates $\hat{\beta}_{cs}$ and $\hat{V}_{cs}$ were obtained in Step 1.

The E step consists of solving the following expectations,

$$\beta^*_{cs,p} = E\left(\beta_{cs,p}\right) = \left[\left(\hat{V}_{cs,p}^{-1} + \Sigma_p^{-1}\right)^{-1}\left(\hat{V}_{cs,p}^{-1}\hat{\beta}_{cs} + \Sigma_p^{-1}\beta_p Z_s\right)\right]$$

$$\left[\beta_{cs,p}\left(\beta_{cs,p}\right)^T\right]^* = E\left[\beta_{cs,p}\beta_{cs,p}^T\right] = \left(\hat{V}_{cs,p}^{-1} + \Sigma_p^{-1}\right)^{-1} + \beta^*_{cs,p}\left(\beta^*_{cs,p}\right)^T$$

Once these expectations are computed they are then incorporated into the maximization (M-step) of the unknown hyperparameters β_p and $\hat{\Sigma}_p$ using the following equations,

$$\hat{\beta}_p = \beta^*_{+s,p} Z_s (Z_s Z_s^T)^{-1} , \text{ where } \beta^*_{+s} = \left(\sum_{c=1}^{C_s} \beta^*_{cs}\right)/C_s, \text{ and}$$

$$\hat{\Sigma}_p = \left[\sum_{s=1}^{S} \left[\sum_{c=1}^{C_s} \left(\beta^*_{cs,p} - \hat{\beta}_p Z_s\right)\left(\beta^*_{cs,p} - \hat{\beta}_p Z_s\right)^T\right]/C_s\right]/S$$

After convergence the maximum likelihood estimates are incorporated into the posterior distribution of $\beta_{cs,p}$ shown in equation (5).

Using Partially Synthetic Data to Replace Suppression in the Business Dynamics Statistics: Early Results

Javier Miranda[1] and Lars Vilhuber[2],⋆

[1] U.S. Bureau of the Census, Washington, DC, USA
javier.miranda@census.gov
[2] Cornell University, Ithaca, NY, USA
lars.vilhuber@cornell.edu

Abstract. The Business Dynamics Statistics is a product of the U.S. Census Bureau that provides measures of business openings and closings, and job creation and destruction, by a variety of cross-classifications (firm and establishment age and size, industrial sector, and geography). Sensitive data are currently protected through suppression. However, as additional tabulations are being developed, at ever more detailed geographic levels, the number of suppressions increases dramatically. This paper explores the option of providing public-use data that are analytically valid and without suppressions, by leveraging synthetic data to replace observations in sensitive cells.

Keywords: synthetic data, statistical disclosure limitation, time-series, local labor markets, gross job flows , confidentiality protection.

1 Introduction

The Business Dynamics Statistics (BDS) were first released in 2008, providing novel statistics on business startups on a comprehensive basis for the U.S. economy [8]. They have been used in a number of recent publications, addressing questions of firm dynamics, who creates jobs, etc. [9].

The BDS are sourced from confidential microdata in the Longitudinal Business Database (LBD). It provides measures of business openings and closings, and job creation and destruction, by a variety of cross-classifications (firm and establishment age and size, industrial sector, and geography). Since the first release, additional cross-tabulations have been added each year: initially provided only based on firm charateristics, tabulations based on establishment characteristics were later added, as were additional geography cross-tabulations (Metropolitan Statistical Area, and Metro/Non-Metro). Sensitive data are currently protected through suppression. However, as additional tabulations are being developed, at ever more detailed geographic levels, the number of suppressions increases dramatically.[1]

⋆ Corresponding author.
[1] The next set of expansions include plans to provide additional industry detail.

J. Domingo-Ferrer (Ed.): PSD 2014, LNCS 8744, pp. 232–242, 2014.

This paper explores the option of providing public-use data that are analytically valid and without suppressions, by leveraging synthetic data to replace observations in sensitive cells. The use of synthetic data in the provision of public-use tabulations has increased in the United States. [16] describe the use of synthetic data in the case of the OnTheMap data visualization, and the use of partially synthetic data in tabulations has been explored by others [1,5,18,17,2]. Few have attempted to provide synthetic data for business data - the cases we are aware of are the Synthetic LBD [15], on which we will rely heavily in this approach, and a synthetic version of the IAB Establishment Panel [3,10,4]. This is, to the best of our knowledge, the first attempt to integrate synthetic data into a public-use data tabulation for businesses.

We leverage the existence of a sophisticated partially synthetic data file the Synthetic LBD [19], henceforth SynLBD – in combination with the techniques first expressed in [7] and [6] to replace sensitive cells with tabulations based on synthetic data. We start by describing the extent of suppressions in the BDS, then lay out the algorithm to combine synthetic and confidential data for the purposes of tabulation. Preliminary results are discussed, and an outlook given on the next steps necessary to achieve a robust public-use tabulation.

2   Item Suppression

BDS processing uses primary and secondary suppressions, derived from a P percent rule, as disclosure avoidance mechanism. All cells of a potential publication table are analyzed to make sure no identifying information about a particular business, household, or individual is released to the public. In the case of the BDS, cells where the top 2 firms account for more than P percent of the total value of the cell are flagged for suppression. The precise P value is not disclosed to minimize the possibility of reidentification by potential attackers. Secondary suppressions are identified so as to minimize the amount of information loss in a given table row or column. To this end, the search algorithm looks for candidate cells that contain the least amount of employment, and suppresses their content. Protecting these secondary cells might require a third round of supressions given the presence of column totals in the tables. Once the tables are analyzed and the necessary cells suppressed, each table row that contains a suppressions is flagged, and the modified table released to the public. Note that individual suppressed cells are not separately flagged, only the row that contains at least one suppressed cell. A necessary feature of this disclosure mechanism is that a large number of secondary suppressions are necessitated by the need to protect the cell that is the primary disclosing cell. The public-use data, of course, doesn't allow the identification of which suppressions are primary or secondary suppressions.

Table 1 describes the extent to which suppressions occur in the published establishment-level BDS, as available at http://www.census.gov/ces/dataproducts/bds/data_estab.html (Table 3 in the appendix also describes the similar pattern in firm-level statistics). The number of cells in each table is indicated, as are the percent of cells with suppression of some variable (d_flag=1), and the percent of cells where "Job Creation by Entrants" is suppressed. Other variables, also present on the establishment-level BDS, are never suppressed.

Table 1. Suppressions in establishment-level BDS

Type	Level	Number of cells	Suppressions (%) Any	Job creation by entrants
Age	e	325	0.3	0.3
Age-Initial Size	e	2925	18.6	14.2
Age-Initial Size-SIC	e	25994	35.9	17.9
Age-SIC	e	2925	3	2.9
Age-State	e	18360	3.4	3.3
Age-Size	e	2925	26.8	16.2
All	e	35	0	0
Initial Size	e	315	0.3	0
Initial Size-SIC	e	2835	19.5	6.5
Initial Size-State	e	17847	26.8	11.2
SIC	e	315	0	0
State	e	1785	0	0
Size	e	315	0.3	0
Size-SIC	e	2834	28.1	11.3
Size-State	e	17848	31.9	14.6

Note: Cells are year x categories, where the number of categories varies by published table.

Clearly, while the usefulness of the data to users would seem to increase for more detailed cross-tabulations, that same detail, under current disclosure avoidance rules, leads to increased suppression, and thus less effective data utility. Suppression is worse for some variables than for others. Establishment and firm counts are never supressed following County Business Patterns and Disclosure Review Board rules. By contrast employment, job creation and destruction are suppressed.

3   Synthetic Data as a Proposed Alternative to Item Suppression

The Synthetic LBD (SynLBD) is a synthetic dataset on establishments with proven analytic validity along several critical dimensions [15]. Additional improvements are currently being developed [13,14]. A growing number of researchers have used the SynLBD, and their continued use contributes to the improvement of the SynLBD.

The use of the SynLBD for the purposes outlined in this paper is particularly appealing, because its analytic validity has been independently established, while maintaining a high level of data privacy. In fact, for many of the cross-tabulations identified in Table 1, no additional disclosure avoidance review would seem necessary. Only tabulations involving state and sub-state geography should require additional review since this variable was removed from the disclosure request that approved the release to the public of the SynLBD.[2]

The available SynLBD is released as a single implicate, and by design, may distort any single analysis by too large an amount. The use of additional implicates for the purposes of BDS table creation may be desirable and will be assessed in later work.

In this paper, we evaluate a simple algorithm to alleviate the problem of large numbers of suppression, while maintaining high, if not equivalent levels of disclosure protection. We then outline a second algorithm that improves on the first. An evaluation of the second algorithm is deferred to later work.

The first algorithm, which we will call the "drop-in algorithm", simply replaces a cell that has been suppressed with its synthetic-data equivalent, i.e., the equivalent table cell from a tabulation based on the SynLBD alone. The second algorithm, called "forward-longitudinal algorithm", is slightly more complicated. At any point in time t, if a (expanded) suppression algorithm identifies a cell that *would* be suppressed, all establishments that contribute to that cell in time period t are replaced by synthetic establishments that match on certain characteristics Z in periods $t - p$ through t, for t and the next n periods. Synthetic and observed values are then tabulated to create the release statistics. If Z describes only the margin characteristics for the table in question (denoted by k below), and for $p = n = 0$, the algorithm reduces to the "drop-in" algorithm.

In this paper, we assess the time-consistency of the first algorithm for a single implicate. Assessing the impact of using multiple implicates is deferred to future work. Identifying acceptable values of Z, p, and n is deferred to a later version of this paper.

3.1   Definitions

The variable of interest is establishment employment e_{jt}, with establishments indexed by j and years indexed by t. All other variables (job creation and destruction from establishment entry, exit, expansion and contraction) are derived from that. For instance, an establishment is born at time t if employment is positive for the first time:

$$birth_{jt} = \begin{cases} 1 \text{ if } e_{jt} > 0 \text{ and } e_{jt-s} = 0 \ \forall s \geq 1 \\ 0 \text{ otherwise} \end{cases} \tag{1}$$

We will denote aggregations using capital letters, so (national) employment is denoted as

$$E_{.t} = \sum_{i=1}^{J} e_{it} \tag{2}$$

---

[2] The Census Disclosure Review Board has not pronounced itself on the disclosure avoidance methodology proposed here as of July 2014.

and (national) births are

$$Birth._t = \sum_{i=1}^{J} birth_{it}. \tag{3}$$

For any establishment j, the synthesized version of variable x_{jt} (from a single implicate) is denoted $\tilde{x}_{jt}$. Furthermore, an establishment j has certain time-varying characteristics $k_t(j)$, such as industry and geographic location, but also derived characteristics, such as establishment or firm age and size. In a slight abuse of notation, $j \in K'_t$ describes the set of firms at time t such that $k_t(j) = k'$. So generically,

$$X_{k't} = \sum_{j \in K'_t} x_{jt} \tag{4}$$

describes the different aggregations across establishments having characteristics k' at time t, for instance aggregations by establishment age or metropolitan areas. Finally, suppression rules for (aggregate) variable X are captured by I_t^X, such that the releasable variable X^o under the current regime can be described by

$$X_{k't}^o = \begin{cases} X_{k't} \text{ if } I_{kt}^X = 1 \\ \text{missing otherwise} \end{cases} \tag{5}$$

For later reference, we denote the tabulations created as per (5) as **BDS**^{o}.

3.2   Algorithm 1: Drop-in

We can now express the "drop-in" algorithm, leading to the released variable $X^{(i)}$, as:

---

if $I_t^X = 1$ **then**
    $X_{k't}^{(i)} = X_{k't}$
else
    $X_{k't}^{(i)} = \tilde{X}_{k't}$
end if

Thus, simply computing a "SynBDS", based on the SynLBD, in parallel to the computation of the BDS (based on the confidential LBD), and replacing suppressed cells with their fully synthetic counterparts, yields a dataset without missing observations. Variations can encompass using the average of multiple implicates as the replacement value. In general, increasing the number of implicates will improve the analytic validity, but reduce the protection provided by the synthesis process.

Because no time-consistency is imposed, this method can lead to seam biases or higher intertemporal variance. We will return to this issue in Section 4. For later reference, we denote the tabulations created by Algorithm 1 as **BDS**$^{(i)}$.

3.3   Algorithm 2: Forward-longitudinal

In part to address the possible time-inconsistencies we propose an alternative algorithm. In order to minimize future seam issues, we remove establishments (or firms) that contribute to sensitive cells of tabulations with characteristics $k't$, for t and the next n periods. These establishments are replaced by synthetic establishments that match on characteristics $k't$, and we simply replace the observed values in the database x_{js} with the synthetic values $\tilde{x}_{js}$ (for all variables), for $s = t, \dots, t + n$.[3] For convenience, denote by $J_{k't}^-$ the set of establishments for which observed values x_{jt} do not contribute to any tabulations at time t. In its simplest form, the algorithm can be expressed as

---

Compute: $X_{k't} = \sum_{j \in K_t'} x_{jt}$

Compute: I_t^X

if $I_t^X = 0$ **then**

    Assign all $j \in K_t'$ to $J_{k't}^-$

    Assign all $j \in J_{k's}^-$ to $J_{k't}^-$ for $t > s > t - n$

end if

Compute:

$$X_{k't}^{(ii)} = \sum_{j \in \{ K_t' \cap J_{k't}^- \}} \tilde{x}_{jt} + \sum_{j \in K_t' \wedge j \notin J_{k't}^-} x_{jt}$$

For $n = \infty$, J_t is an absorbing set, which seems undesirable. For $n = 1$, this reduces to Algorithm 1.[4] For reference, we denote the tabulations created by Algorithm 2 as **BDS**$^{(ii)}$.

4   Analysis

We implemented Algorithm 1 for BDS tabulations by establishment age and size (`bds_e_agesz`). As noted in Table 1, about 26% of all cells have some suppression. For this version of the paper, we analyzed a single variable, "Job Creation by establishment births" (`job_creation_births`). (Additional analyses are pending release).

4.1   Extent of Protection

Protection of the table relies in large part on the fact that the data replacing the suppressions is itself synthetic, and released (in the case of the examples in this paper) or (potentially) releasable (for tabulations with geography) to a broad

---

[3] We thus re-use the index j for both observed and synthetic establishments.

[4] Alternatively to the combining rule described in Algorithm 2, we could also specify a per-establishment weight $w_{jt} \in [0, 1]$ that declines to 0 as s approaches $t - n$. w_{jt} is adjusted as a function of membership in $J_{k't}^-$, and we compute $X_{k't}^{(ii)} = \sum_j w_{jt} \tilde{x}_{jt} + (1 - w_{jt}) x_{jt}$.

audience [2]. No establishment's observed data is released in the SynLBD, and only the industry distribution of establishments is preserved exactly. However, in order to consider a broader notion of disclosure avoidance, we proceed as follows. In cell that would have been suppressed under the current regime **BDS**^{0}, we compute the difference between the confidential values of the establishments contributing to this cell, and each of the values of the synthetic establishments contributing to the cell under **BDS**$^{(i)}$, and assess the distribution of these differences.[5]

4.2   Analytical Validity

In order to assess the analytical validity of each of the methods, we focus on simple time-series properties of the $X_{k't}$. In particular, we estimate a AR(2) process for each of $X_{k't}$, $X^s_{k't}$, and $X^{(i)}_{k't}$. We then assess the number of missing time-series estimates (repeated suppressions in $X^s_{k't}$ may lead to time-series that are too short), the number of significant coefficients for the first lag of the AR(2), estimated from both the confidential data (ρ_1) and the comparison data (ρ^s_1 and $\rho^{(i)}_1$), and finally two measures of utility: *coverage*, the percentage of regressions where the true ρ_1 lies within the confidence band around the coefficient estimated from the comparison ρ^s_1 and $\rho^{(i)}_1$, and the interval overlap measure J_k as suggested by [12]. Table 2 presents these results for job_creation_births.

Table 2. Analytic validity of published data

Variable	Number feasible	Missing		Percent significant			Coverage		Interval overlap	
	$X_{k't}$	$X^s_{k't}$	$X^{(i)}_{k't}$	ρ_1	ρ^s_1	$\rho^{(i)}_1$	ρ^s_1	$\rho^{(i)}_1$	J^s_1	$J^{(i)}_1$
job creation births	89	18	11.2	5.6	6.8	6.3	91.8	93.7	91.6	93.9

(Caveat: different definitions of "job creation births" in the BDS processing and our post-processing lead to incomplete filling in of missing cells. This will be fixed in later work.) For the one variable that has significant suppressions, the number of feasible regressions in the published data increases substantially (reduction in missing $X^{(i)}_{k't}$ relative to missing $X^s_{k't}$). The number of correctly estimated coefficients increases (in terms of assessing statistical significance of the coefficient), and utility increases, in terms of ρ_1 as well as J_1.

5   Concluding Remarks

In this paper, we have described two alternate mechanisms to substitute for suppressions in small-cell tabulations of business microdata, with the goal of improving analytic validity while maintaining a sufficiently high standard of

---

[5] As of June 2014, this distribution had not been released.

disclosure limitation. Neither mechanism fundamentally changes the existing suppression methodology, rather, the mechanisms work to fill in the holes created by the suppression methodology.

Leveraging the availability of a high-quality synthetic datasets (the Synthetic LBD) with proven disclosure limitation efficiency and analytic validity [15], the first method is very simple, but may suffer from seam biases and time-inconsistency. The second method aims to improve on that by "blending in" synthetic establishments, which may slightly reduce analytic validity in time periods where the strict application of the suppression algorithms would no longer impose any constraints, but improving on the time-series properties of the released data.

Several limitations of the research presented here should be highlighted. The examples provided in this article rely on an earlier release of the Synthetic LBD [15]. Recent developments to improve the micro-level analytic validity of the SynLBD [14] should improve the analytic validity of the mechanisms proposed here as well. We also compare our proposed mechanisms to the actual published, but otherwise unmodified BDS. Comparing to post-publication improvements to a table with suppressions [11] will inevitably lead to an apparent reduction in the utility of this particular approach. Finally, the approach relies on continuous availability of synthetic microdata with analytical validity. Other approaches rely on fewer data points, and thus be favored due to lower implementation costs.

Future work for this paper involves assessing the procedure on a wider variety of variables, better synchronisation of the computational algorithms underlying the BDS and the SynBDS, and improved assessment at the microdata level of the protection afforded by Algorithm 1.

Acknowledgments. All authors were affiliated with the U.S. Census Bureau, Center for Economic Studies, when originally contributing to the contents of this paper. This document reports the results of research and analysis undertaken by U.S. Census Bureau staff. It has undergone a Census Bureau review more limited in scope than that given to official Census Bureau publications. This document is released to inform interested parties of ongoing research and to encourage discussion of work in progress. All results have been reviewed to ensure that no confidential information is disclosed. The views expressed herein are attributable only to the authors and do not represent the views of the U.S. Census Bureau. Vilhuber acknowledges support through NSF Grant SES-1042181. This project would not have been feasible without the valuable input from Saki Kinney and Jerry Reiter, and their valuable work on the Synthetic LBD.

References

1. Abowd, J.M., Gittings, K., McKinney, K.L., Stephens, B.E., Vilhuber, L., Wood-cock, S.: Dynamically consistent noise infusion and partially synthetic data as confidentiality protection measures for related time-series. Tech. rep. Federal Committee on Statistical Methodology (January 2012), http://www.fcsm.gov/events/papers2012.html
2. Abowd, J.M., Vilhuber, L.: Synthetic data server (2010), http://www.vrdc.cornell.edu/sds/
3. Drechsler, J.: Synthetische Scientific-use-files der Welle 2007 des IAB-Betriebspanels. FDZ Methodenreport 201101_de, Institute for Employment Research, Nuremberg, Germany (January 2011), http://ideas.repec.org/p/iab/iabfme/201101_de.html
4. Drechsler, J.: New data dissemination approaches in old Europe – synthetic datasets for a German establishment survey. Journal of Applied Statistics 39(2), 243–265 (2012), http://ideas.repec.org/a/taf/japsta/v39y2012i2p243-265.html
5. Drechsler, J., Reiter, J.P.: Disclosure risk and data utility for partially synthetic data: An empirical study using the German IAB Establishment Survey. Journal of Official Statistics 25(12), 589–603 (2009), http://ideas.repec.org/a/eee/csdana/v55y2011i12p3232-3243.html
6. Drechsler, J., Reiter, J.P.: Sampling with synthesis: A new approach for releasing public use census microdata. Journal of the American Statistical Association 105(492), 1347–1357 (2010), http://ideas.repec.org/a/bes/jnlasa/v105i492y2010p1347-1357.html
7. Gittings, R.K.: Essays in labor economics and synthetic data methods. Ph.d., Cornell University (2009)
8. Haltiwanger, J., Jarmin, R., Miranda, J.: Jobs created from business startups in the United States (2008), https://www.census.gov/ces/pdf/BDS_StatBrief1_Jobs_Created.pdf
9. Haltiwanger, J.C., Jarmin, R.S., Miranda, J.: Who creates jobs? small vs. large vs. young. Working Paper 16300, National Bureau of Economic Research (August 2010), http://www.nber.org/papers/w16300
10. Hethey, T., Schmieder, J.F.: Using worker flows in the analysis of establishment turnover: Evidence from German administrative data. FDZ Methodenreport 201006_en, Institute for Employment Research, Nuremberg, Germany (August 2010), http://ideas.repec.org/p/iab/iabfme/201006_en.html
11. Holan, S.H., Toth, D., Ferreira, M.A.R., Karr, A.F.: Bayesian multiscale multiple imputation with implications for data confidentiality. Journal of the American Statistical Association 105(490), 564–577 (2010), http://dx.doi.org/10.1198/jasa.2009.ap08629
12. Karr, A.F., Kohnen, C.N., Oganian, A., Reiter, J.P., Sanil, A.P.: A framework for evaluating the utility of data altered to protect confidentiality 60(3), 1–9 (2006)
13. Kinney, S.K., Reiter, J.: SynLBD: providing firm characteristics on synthetic establishment data. Presentation, World Statistics Conference (2013)
14. Kinney, S.K., Reiter, J., Miranda, J.: Improving the Synthetic Longitudinal Business Database. Working Paper 14-12, U.S. Census Bureau, Center for Economic Studies (2014)

15. Kinney, S.K., Reiter, J.P., Reznek, A.P., Miranda, J., Jarmin, R.S., Abowd, J.M.: Towards unrestricted public use business microdata: The Synthetic Longitudinal Business Database. International Statistical Review 79(3), 362–384 (2011), http://ideas.repec.org/a/bla/istatr/v79y2011i3p362-384.html

16. Machanavajjhala, A., Kifer, D., Abowd, J.M., Gehrke, J., Vilhuber, L.: Privacy: Theory meets practice on the map. In: International Conference on Data Engineering, ICDE (2008)

17. Rodríguez, R.: Synthetic data disclosure control for american community survey group quarters (2007)

18. Sakshaug, J.W., Raghunathan, T.E.: Synthetic Data for Small Area Estimation in the American Community Survey. Working Papers 13-19, Center for Economic Studies, U.S. Census Bureau (April 2013), http://ideas.repec.org/p/cen/wpaper/13-19.html

19. U.S. Census Bureau: Synthetic LBD Beta version 2.0. [computer file], U.S. Census Bureau and Cornell University, Synthetic Data Server [distributor], Washington, DC and Ithaca, NY, USA (2011), http://www2.vrdc.cornell.edu/news/data/lbd-synthetic-data/

Appendix

Acronyms

BDS Business Dynamics Statistics
LBD Longitudinal Business Database
SynLBD Synthetic LBD, a synthetic microdata file at the establishment level

Additional tables

Table 3. Suppressions in firm-level BDS

Type	Level	No. of cells	Percent suppressed
all	f	35	0
metrononmetro	f	70	0
sic	f	315	0
age	f	325	0
agemetrononmetro	f	650	0
st	f	1785	0
agemsa	f	118950	0.3
szmsa	f	153688	1.4
agest	f	18360	1.8
agesic	f	2925	2.8
isz	f	420	9
iszmetrononmetro	f	840	9.8
sz	f	420	10.2
szmetrononmetro	f	840	11.1
iszst	f	23205	16.1
szst	f	23205	16.2
iszsic	f	3780	18.7
szsic	f	3780	19.9
ageisz	f	3874	24.2
agesz	f	3843	26.6
ageiszmetro	f	7647	29.1
ageszmetrononmetro	f	7575	30.8
ageiszsic	f	31500	41.3

Note: Cells are year x categories, where the number of categories varies by published table.

Synthetic Longitudinal Business Databases for International Comparisons

Jörg Drechsler[1] and Lars Vilhuber[2]

[1] Institute for Employment Research, Regensburger Str. 104,
90478 Nuremberg, Germany
joerg.drechsler@iab.de
[2] Cornell University, Ithaca, NY, USA
lars.vilhuber@cornell.edu

Abstract. International comparison studies on economic activity are often hampered by the fact that access to business microdata is very limited on an international level. A recently launched project tries to overcome these limitations by improving access to Business Censuses from multiple countries based on synthetic data. Starting from the synthetic version of the longitudinally edited version of the U.S. Business Register (the Longitudinal Business Database, LBD), the idea is to create similar data products in other countries by applying the synthesis methodology developed for the LBD to generate synthetic replicates that could be distributed without confidentiality concerns. In this paper we present some first results of this project based on German business data collected at the Institute for Employment Research.

Keywords: business data, confidentiality, international comparison, multiple imputation, synthetic.

1 Introduction

Access to microdata has increased greatly in recent years. Many National Statistical Institutes (NSIs) and other data collecting agencies established research data centers, for access to confidential data, and disseminated an ever increasing collection of microdata sets as public use files to facilitate data access. However, accessing confidential data from different countries for comparison studies, in particular for data on businesses, remains difficult if not impossible. Given current statistical disclosure avoidance methods, the current regulatory environment prevents the sharing of confidential business microdata between countries, and often even between agencies within the same country. The absence of useful cross-country data access for business data contrasts with the increasing availability of such datasets for individuals. The IPUMS project at the University of Minnesota (http://www.ipums.org/) provides access to public use microdata samples from population censuses of 74 countries. Recent efforts in Europe within the Data Without Boundaries (DWB) project (http://www.dwbproject.org/),

J. Domingo-Ferrer (Ed.): PSD 2014, LNCS 8744, pp. 243–252, 2014.
© Springer International Publishing Switzerland 2014

funded by the European Union aim at harmonizing access to microdata in Europe and investigate modes of centralized access to research data from European Countries, such as RDC-in-RDC solutions [3]. However, to the best of our knowledge, no publicly accessible micro data sets are available for cross-national comparisons on enterprises or establishments.

The difficulty in providing access to business micro data arises in part due to some of the statistical properties of the data. First, variables such as turnover or establishment size have very skewed distributions that make the identification of single units in the data set very easy. Second, there is a lot of complementary information about businesses already available in the public domain. This information can be used to identify records in any released data set. Third, the benefit from identifying a unit in an establishment survey might be higher for a potential attacker than the benefit of identifying a unit in a household survey. Fourth, in most business surveys the probability of inclusion is very high for large businesses, so no additional privacy protection through sampling is available for these units.

The present project tries to fill this gap by investigating whether synthetic data procedures that have been applied successfully to U.S. business data can be transferred to similar data products from other countries. In the United States, synthetic data procedures were applied to a longitudinally linked version of the U.S. Business Register, called the Longitudinal Business Database (LBD) [13], generating multiple synthetic copies (implicates) of what is called the Synthetic LBD (SynLBD) [12]. One of the implicates was subsequently released to a easily web-accessible computing environment [2]. We report here on efforts to apply the same statistical procedures to German data, thus generating a releasable "German SynLBD." However, the long-term goal is to make these procedures robust enough to be applied in a wider variety of country contexts. As a side product of this project, a confidential but researcher-accessible German dataset is developed that resembles in structure and scope the original U.S. dataset, thus already allowing for comparative studies, albeit with more restrictive access conditions.

The generic setup of the project can be described as a two stage process: In the first stage, suitable data sources are identified and a data product is constructed that resembles the LBD as closely as possible in terms of content and variable definition. In the second stage the synthetic data procedures developed for the LBD are adapted to run on the new data product. In this paper we present some first results based on German establishment data.

The remainder of the paper is organized as follows. In Section 2 we briefly describe the LBD and its publicly accessible synthetic counterpart, the Synthetic Longitudinal Business Database that is already available through the Virtual RDC at Cornell. Section 3 summarizes the steps that were taken to generate a data product that resembles the LBD from the register data of the German Federal Employment Agency. Those sections borrow heavily from an earlier paper [8,9] that mainly focused on the steps that were necessary to construct a German version of the LBD, and the interested reader is referred to this paper for more details on these steps. Section 4 discusses the required adjustments of the synthesis procedures to adapt the code for the German data product. The main message conveyed in this section is that even though the original code developed for the U.S. data was not developed with the goal to apply it in a wide variety of contexts, the adjustments necessary were minimal, and likely declining in the number of countries that utilize the code. Section 5 provides some first results on the analytical validity of the synthetic data. In Section 6 future steps that are still necessary before the data can be made available through the virtual RDC at Cornell are described. The paper concludes with a discussion of possible extensions to other countries.

2   The Synthetic Longitudinal Business Database

The creation of the Longitudinal Business Database (LBD) [14] is described in detail in [13], that of the Synthetic LBD in [12]; we briefly summarize the key characteristics of both here. The LBD is created from the U.S. Census Bureau's Business Register by creating longitudinal links between establishments using name and address matching. The database has information on birth, death, location, industry, and firm affiliation of employer establishments, as well as their employment over time, for nearly all sectors of the economy from 1976 up through the most recent available years (as of this writing, 2011). It is used both as a key file for research applications as well as tabulation input to the U.S. Census Bureau's Business Dynamics Statistics. Other statistics created from the underlying Business Register include the County Business Patterns (CBP).

The Synthetic LBD is derived from the LBD as a partially synthetic database with analytic validity (see [7] for a review of the theory and applications of the synthetic data methodology). The database is generated by synthesizing the lifespan of establishments, as well as the evolution of their employment, conditional on industry. Geography is not synthesized, but is suppressed from the released file. The current version 2.0 is based on the Standard Industrial Classification (SIC) and extends through 2000. Work currently underway using the existing methodology will extend the data through 2010, using NAICS, and newer imputation methodology (Version 3) is under development to improve the analytic validity and extend the imputation to additional variables [10,11]. In this paper, when we refer to the "SynLBD algorithms", we refer to Version 2.

3   Constructing the German Longitudinal Business Database

Except for the IAB Establishment Panel ([6]) and the IAB Job Vacancy Survey ([5]), no data are collected at the business or establishment level at the Institute for Employment Research on a regular basis. Instead, establishment level information is derived by aggregating the information contained in the German

Social Security Data to the establishment level. The German Social Security Data (GSSD) is based on the integrated notification procedure for the health, pension and unemployment insurances, which was introduced in January 1973. Since then each employer is routinely required to provide information on all employees. One of the data products derived from the GSSD is the Establishment History Panel [4, BHP] which provides detailed information on all establishments covered in the GSSD by aggregating the employee level information via the establishment ID. The BHP is the main data source for constructing a German equivalent to the synthetic version of the LBD. The data used for the German SynLBD (GSynLBD) contains information from the years 1975 until 2008 for Western Germany. Information for the former Eastern German States is limited to the years 1992–2008. Unfortunately, although the BHP contains many more variables than the SynLBD requires, including very detailed information on the personnel structure of the establishments, not all the variables contained in the SynLBD are available in the BHP. Since the data are based on employee level information, the information whether the establishment belongs to a multi unit business cannot be obtained. Furthermore, until 1999 the BHP only contains establishments that had at least one employee covered by social security on the reference date June 30 of each year since establishments were only required to report employees covered by social security. Since 1999 all employees must be reported. As a consequence the total number of employees increases substantially between 1998 and 1999 and the same holds for the number of establishments covered in the BHP since establishments that only hired marginal employees are also now included in the dataset. To keep the data consistent, we subtracted the number of employees with marginal employment from the total number of employees and set the total number of employees to missing for all establishments that had zero employment after the subtraction of the marginal employment. We deleted the 967,086 establishments that never had any employees covered by social security. The final dataset consisted of 6,864,676 establishments[1].

Another difference between the LBD and the BHP is that payroll information contained in the BHP is based on the reference date June 30 each year. The SynLBD on the other hand contains the yearly payroll of each establishment. At the current stage of the project we linked yearly payroll information from a data product that was produced for a different project at the IAB. This product contains the yearly payroll for all full time employees. We estimated the yearly payroll for all employees under the simplifying assumption that the average daily wages of full time and part-time employees are equal. This approach implies that no payroll information is available for all establishments that only employed part-time employees in a given year. Exact payroll information for all establishments in the BHP based on all employees from the underlying administrative data could be incorporated in the future.

Further data preparation steps included generating time consistent information on the geographic location and industry code as well as updating the in-

---

[1] This number differs slightly from the 6,916,183 establishments reported in [8,9] since some additional data preparation steps were introduced in the meantime.

Table 1. Variables included in the GLBD

Name	Description
ID	Unique Random Number for Establishment
County	Geographic Information on the County Level
State	Geographic Information on the State Level
WZ73	Industry Code According to 1973 classification (only 3 digit available)
WZ93	Industry Code According to 1993 classification (3 digit and 5 digit)
WZ03	Industry Code According to 2003 classification (3 digit and 5 digit)
WZ08	Industry Code According to 2008 classification (3 digit and 5 digit)
Birth	Birth of Establishment (left-censored at 1975/1991)
Death	Death of Establishment (right-censored at 2008)
Pay_{ft}	Yearly Payroll for All Full-time Employees
Pay_{tot}	Estimated Yearly Payroll for All Employees
$Employment_{ft}$	Number of Full-time Employees on June 30
$Employment_{tot}$	Total Number of Employees on June 30

formation on births and deaths of establishments since the information on the first year and last year an establishment is observed in the BHP is not necessarily equivalent with the birth and the death of the establishment. See [8,9] for further information on the additional data preparation steps. Table 1 lists the variables that form the basis for the German Longitudinal Business Database (GLBD). There are four different industry classification codes ($WZ73$, $WZ93$, $WZ03$, $WZ08$), as the classification changed four times during the reference period 1975–2008. We plan to impute the industry classification whenever it is missing due to the changes in the reporting system. For this we will use a simple probabilistic crosswalk based on the methodology used for the LEHD ECF [1]. The methodology relies on double-coding for at least some periods to estimate transition matrices between the codes, which are used to impute industry codes whenever they are missing. This will give us one consistent industry classification for all years of the GLBD and only this constructed classification will later be used for the synthesis.

4   Adapting the LBD Synthesis Code to the German Data

One of the key goals of this project was a proof-of-concept generalization of the computer code underlying the generation of the SynLBD, as used in the original release documented in [12]. In tight coordination with the original authors of the code, one of us generalized the code in order to work for (i) arbitrary establishment identifiers (ii) arbitrary industry codes (iii) arbitrary geography. The first application of the generalized code was not on German data, but rather on the prototypes of SynLBD for North American Industrial Coding System (NAICS). Subsequently, this code was reviewed for any disclosure risk, and released as non-disclosive code to the authors of this project. The code was then transferred to the German RDC in Nürnberg, where it was run against a prototype of the data described in Section 3.

The computing environment in the German RDC (GRDC) differs substantially from the U.S. Census Bureau's RDC (USRDC). A full description of the differences would warrant a separate article, but for the purposes of this article, the key differences were as follows:

SAS: The original code developed in the USRDC was written for SAS® 9.2 for Linux, run using command line submission (`sas NameOfProg.sas`). In the GRDC, a SAS® enterprise server running on a Windows machine is in use, with submission only available through SAS® Enterprise Guide®. This difference necessitated the largest number of changes.

Job scheduler: In the USRDC, a custom Linux-based job scheduler handled the processing of the 280 (NAICS) to 480 (SIC) independently synthesized industry groups. Adaptation of a similar scheduler, or a simple looping mechanism, is not yet implemented for the GRDC. This is an efficiency constraint, not a functional constraint, since it is feasible to run each industry individually.

Variable differences: As noted earlier, some variables, such as the indicator about multi-unit status are not available in the German data. Other variables may be very relevant for non-U.S. data that were not taken into account in the original synthesis code. For instance, the code assumes that there is a single left-censoring point in the data, but the German data have two (a later one for East German establishments). We are still investigating to what extent creative data construction allows the re-use of the code without modification, for instance by treating the same NACE industry coding in East and West Germany as two different synthesis groups (running the code by region-industry combinations, rather than by industry values alone). Naturally, if such creative data setup solutions fail, code changes will be required.

5   First Results Regarding the Analytical Validity of the GsynLBD

In order to assess the advancement of our project, we have created synthetic data for a single industry and did not condition on geography in the imputation models. Only the variables $Birth$, $Death$, and $Employment_{tot}$ have been synthesized so far. Furthermore, pending implementation of the longitudinal industry edit, we have used only data with valid $WZ03$ codes. This restriction implies that firms in our sample are only observed to have death years in $[2003, 2008]$, or are right-censored at 2008. Thus, the results presented here are not for a representative sample, but are assumed to be representative of the ability of the synthesis process to replicate features of the data.

Figure 1 describes the distribution of start and end years in both the synthetic and the original data. It is apparent that the SynLBD process faithfully replicates the distribution, including any spikes, from the original data.

Number of Establishment Births by Year

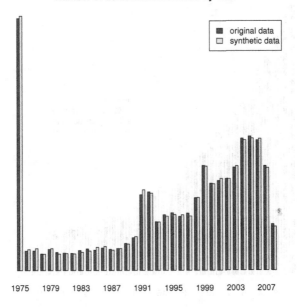

Number of Establishment Deaths by Year

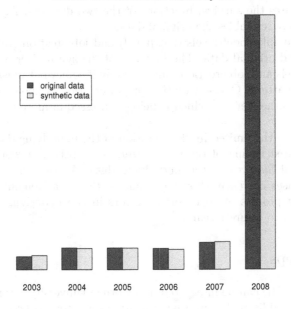

Fig. 1. Distribution of start and end dates

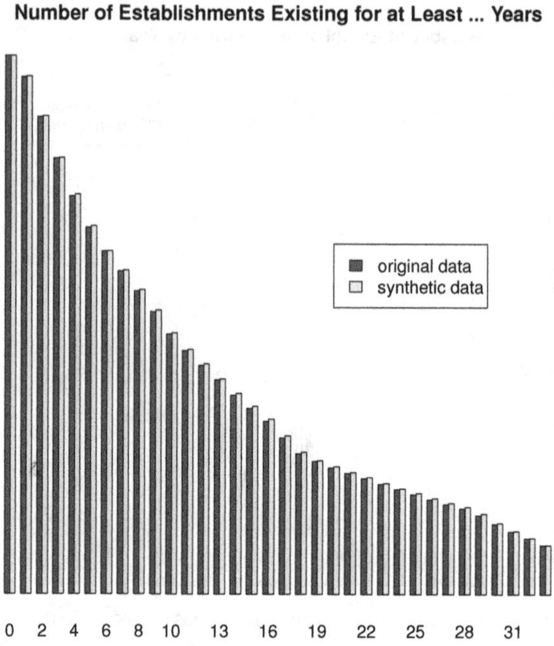
Number of Establishments Existing for at Least ... Years
original data
synthetic data
0
2
4
6
8
10
13
16
19
22
25
28
31

Fig. 2. Survival function

Figure 2 compares the survival functions of the two datasets. Again, the synthetic data closely resembles the original data.
Figure 3 shows employment levels (left panel) and job creation (right panel) in the synthetic and original data. The first run of the synthesizer over-estimates employment levels and job creation, but correctly if somewhat noisily replicates the time-series pattern. Over-estimation of job creation is known shortcoming of the current synthesizer [12] which is being addressed in more recent developments [11,10].

Overall, despite the limited implementation of the underlying data standardization and limited tuning of the synthesizer, the synthesizer works well, and replicates critical features of the underlying data. An overall assessment on whether the biases currently shown in some of the data elements are due to the synthesizing process or to reporting errors in the underlying confidential data are deferred to future research.

6 Next Steps

Before the GsynLBD can be integrated into Cornell University's Synthetic Data Server [2] several additional steps are necessary both in terms of constructing the German LBD as well as in terms of adapting the synthesis code for the peculiarities of the German data. As noted in Section 3 the industry code changed several

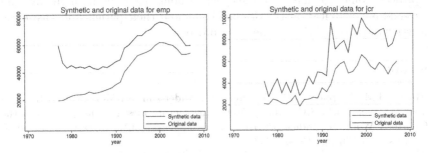

Fig. 3. Employment

times over the reference period of the GLBD and thus consistent industry codes need to be imputed. Furthermore, we will integrate exact payroll information aggregated from the register data of the Federal Employment Agency.

Beyond the straightforward extension of the synthesis to all industry codes we will also ensure that the synthesis models account for data features that are unique to the German data. As noted earlier, it may make sense to use separate models for Eastern and Western Germany, due to (i) differences in data availability (ii) fundamental differences in the behavior of economic variables. The reunification of the two German states in 1990 is an external shock unique to Germany, and may need to be reflected in the synthesis models. Finally, disclosure risk evaluations akin to those performed for the SynLBD will be implemented to ensure that the data could be released without any confidentiality violations.

7 Conclusions

In this paper we illustrated some first steps towards a centralized access to business Census data from the U.S. and Germany. Much remains to be done but the evaluations presented in Section 5 indicate that results obtained from the synthetic data closely resemble results from the original data. It should be noted that we used a brute force approach for these evaluations simply transferring the LBD synthesis code to the German data without any major adjustments. The quality of the results will only improve if the synthesis models will be tailored to the specific features of the German data. We hope that the current project can work as a template for integrating similar data products from other countries in the future. Agencies interested in joining this endeavour are welcome to contact the authors at any time.

Acknowledgments. Vilhuber acknowledges support through NSF Grant SES-1042181. This study uses the Establishment History Panel (years 1975-2008). We thank the German RDC for making available access to the SAS server. Part of the research for this project was performed at the FDZ (Research Data Center) of the German Federal Employment Agency at Cornell University, and while Drechsler was visiting the Labor Dynamics Institute at Cornell University.

This project would not have been feasible without the valuable input by Saki Kinney and Jerry Reiter on the original code, and their patience in answering all questions we had on the synthesizing process.

References

1. Abowd, J.M., Stephens, B.E., Vilhuber, L., Andersson, F., McKinney, K.L., Roemer, M., Woodcock, S.D.: The LEHD infrastructure files and the creation of the Quarterly Workforce Indicators. In: Dunne, T., Jensen, J.B., Roberts, M.J. (eds.), University of Chicago Press (2009)
2. Abowd, J.M., Vilhuber, L.: VirtualRDC - Synthetic Data Server. Online resource (2010), http://www.vrdc.cornell.edu/sds/
3. Bender, S.: The RDC of the Federal Employment Agency as a part of the German RDC movement. In: 2009 Conference on Comparative Analysis of Enterprise Data (2009), http://gcoe.ier.hit-u.ac.jp/CAED/index.html
4. Bundesagentur für Arbeit: Establishment History Panel (BHP). [computer file], Research Data Centre (FDZ) of the German Federal Employment Agency (BA) at the Institute for Employment Research (IAB) [distributor], Nürnberg, Germany (2013)
5. Bundesagentur für Arbeit: German Job Vacancy Survey of the IAB. [computer file], Research Data Centre (FDZ) of the German Federal Employment Agency (BA) at the Institute for Employment Research (IAB) [distributor], Nürnberg, Germany (2013)
6. Bundesagentur für Arbeit: IAB Establishment Panel. [computer file], Research Data Centre (FDZ) of the German Federal Employment Agency (BA) at the Institute for Employment Research (IAB) [distributor], Nürnberg, Germany (2013)
7. Drechsler, J.: Synthetic Datasets for Statistical Disclosure Control–Theory and Implementation. Springer, New York (2011)
8. Drechsler, J., Vilhuber, L.: A First Step Towards a German SynLBD: Constructing a German Longitudinal Business Database. Working Papers 14–13, Center for Economic Studies, U.S. Census Bureau (February 2014), http://ideas.repec.org/p/cen/wpaper/14-13.html
9. Drechsler, J., Vilhuber, L.: A First Step Towards a German SynLBD: Constructing a German Longitudinal Business Database. Statistical Journal of the IAOS 30(2), 137–142 (2014)
10. Kinney, S.K., Reiter, J.P., Miranda, J.: Improving the Synthetic Longitudinal Business Database. Statistical Journal of the IAOS 30(2), 129–135 (2014)
11. Kinney, S.K., Reiter, J.P., Miranda, J.: Improving the Synthetic Longitudinal Business Database. Working Papers 14-12, Center for Economic Studies, U.S. Census Bureau (February 2014), http://ideas.repec.org/p/cen/wpaper/14-12.html
12. Kinney, S.K., Reiter, J.P., Reznek, A.P., Miranda, J., Jarmin, R.S., Abowd, J.M.: Towards unrestricted public use business microdata: The Synthetic Longitudinal Business Database. International Statistical Review 79(3), 362–384 (2011), http://ideas.repec.org/a/bla/istatr/v79y2011i3p362-384.html
13. Miranda, J., Jarmin, R.: The longitudinal business database. Discussion Paper CES-WP-02-17, U.S. Census Bureau, Center for Economic Studies (2002)
14. U.S. Census Bureau: Longitudinal business database (LBD). [computer file], U.S. Census Bureau [distributor], Washington, DC, USA (2012), https://www.census.gov/ces/dataproducts/datasets/lbd.html

A Comparison of Blocking Methods for Record Linkage

Rebecca C. Steorts, Samuel L. Ventura,
Mauricio Sadinle, and Stephen E. Fienberg*

Department of Statistics, Carnegie Mellon University, Pittsburgh, PA 15213
beka@cmu.edu, {sventura,msadinle,fienberg}@stat.cmu.edu

Abstract. Record linkage seeks to merge databases and to remove duplicates when unique identifiers are not available. Most approaches use blocking techniques to reduce the computational complexity associated with record linkage. We review traditional blocking techniques, which typically partition the records according to a set of field attributes, and consider two variants of a method known as locality sensitive hashing, sometimes referred to as "private blocking." We compare these approaches in terms of their recall, reduction ratio, and computational complexity. We evaluate these methods using different synthetic datafiles and conclude with a discussion of privacy-related issues.

1 Introduction

A commonly encountered problem in practice is merging databases containing records collected by different sources, often via dissimilar methods. Different variants of this task are known as record linkage, de-duplication, and entity resolution. Record linkage is inherently a difficult problem [2, 11, 12]. These difficulties are partially due to the noise inherent in the data, which is often hard to accurately model [17, 20]. A more substantial obstacle, however, is the scalability of the approaches [23]. With d databases of n records each, brute-force approaches, using all-to-all comparisons, require $O(n^d)$ comparisons. This is quickly prohibitive for even moderate n or d. To avoid this computational bottleneck, the number of comparisons made must be drastically reduced, without compromising linkage accuracy. Record linkage is made scalable by "blocking," which involves partitioning datafiles into "blocks" of records and treating records in different blocks as non-co-referent *a priori* [2, 11]. Record linkage methods are only applied *within* blocks, reducing the comparisons to $O(Bn_{\max}^d)$, with $n_{\max}$ being the size of the largest of the B blocks.

The most basic method for constructing a blocking partition picks certain fields (e.g. geography, or gender and year of birth) and places records in the same block if and only if they agree on all such fields. This amounts to an *a*

---

* This research was partially supported by the National Science Foundation through grants SES1130706 and DMS1043903 to the Department of Statistics, Carnegie Mellon University.

J. Domingo-Ferrer (Ed.): PSD 2014, LNCS 8744, pp. 253–268, 2014.

priori judgment that these fields are error-free. We call this *traditional blocking* (§2.1).

Other data-dependent blocking methods [2, 23] are highly application-specific or are based on placing similar records into the same block, using techniques of "locality-sensitive hashing" (LSH). LSH uses all of the information contained in each record and can be adjusted to ensure that blocks are manageably small, but then does not allow for further record linkage within blocks. For example, [15] introduced novel data structures for sorting and fast approximate nearest neighbor look-up within blocks produced by LSH. Their approach gave balance between speed and recall, but their technique is very specific to nearest neighbor search with similarity defined by the hash function. Such methods are fast and have high recall, but suffer from low precision, rather, too many false positives. This approach is called *private* if, after the blocking is performed, all candidate records pairs are compared and classified into matches/non-matches using computationally intensive "private" comparison and classification techniques [3].

Some blocking schemes involve clustering techniques to partition the records into clusters of similar records. [16] used canopies, a simple clustering approach to group similar records into overlapping subsets for record linkage. Canopies involves organizing the data into overlapping clusters/canopies using an inexpensive distance measure. Then a more expensive distance measure is used to link records within each canopy, reducing the number of required comparisons of records. [21] used a sorted nearest neighborhood clustering approach, combining k-anonymous clustering and the use of publicly available reference values to privately link records across multiple files.

Such clustering-based blocking schemes motivate our variants of LSH methods for blocking. The first, transitive locality sensitive hashing (TLSH), is based upon the community discovery literature such that *a soft transitivity* (or relaxed transitivity) can be imposed across blocks. The second, k-means locality sensitive hashing (KLSH), is based upon the information retrieval literature and clusters similar records into blocks using a vector-space representation and projections. (KLSH has been used before in information retrieval but never with record linkage [18].)

The organization of this paper is as follows. §2 reviews traditional blocking. We then review other blocking methods in §2.2 stemming from the computer science literature. §2.3 presents two different methods based upon locality sensitive hashing, TLSH and KLSH. We discuss the computational complexity of each approach in §3. We evaluate these methods (§4) on simulated data using recall, reduction ratio, and the empirical computational time as our evaluation criteria, comparing to the other methods discussed above. Finally we discuss privacy protection aspects of TLSH and KLSH, given the description of LSH as a "private" blocking technique.

2   Blocking Methods

Blocking divides records into mutually exclusive and jointly exhaustive "blocks," allowing the linkage to be performed within each block. Thus, only records within the same block can be linked; linkage algorithms may still aggregate information across blocks. Traditional blocking requires domain knowledge to pick out highly reliable, if not error-free, fields for blocking. This methodology has at least two drawbacks. The first is that the resulting blocks may still be so large that linkage within them is computationally impractical. The second is that because blocks *only* consider selected fields, much time may be wasted comparing records that happen to agree on those fields but are otherwise radically different.

We first review some simple alternatives to traditional blocking on fields, and then introduce other blocking approaches that stem from computer science.

2.1   Simple Alternatives to Blocking

Since fields can be unreliable for many applications, blocking may miss large proportions of matches. Nevertheless, we can make use of domain-specific knowledge on the types of errors expected for field attributes. To make decisions about matches/non-matches, we must understand the *kinds of errors* that are unlikely for a certain field or a combination of them. With this information, we can identify a pair as a non-match when it has strong disagreements in a combination of fields. It is crucial that this calculation be scalable since it must be checked for all pairs of records. Some sequence of these steps reduces the set of pairs to a size such that more computationally expensive comparisons can be made. In §4.1, we apply these concepts.

2.2   Cluster-Based Blocking

Others have described blocking as a clustering problem, sometimes with a special emphasis on privacy, e.g., see [7, 13, 14, 21]. The motivation is natural: the records in a cluster should be similar, making good candidate pairs for linkage.

One clustering approach proposed for blocking is nearest neighbor clustering. Threshold nearest neighbor clustering (TNN) begins with a single record as the base of the first cluster, and recursively adds the nearest neighbors of records in the cluster until the distance[1] to the nearest neighbor exceeds some threshold. Then one of the remaining records is picked to be the base for the next cluster, and so forth. K-nearest neighbor clustering (KNN) uses a similar procedure, but ensures that each cluster contains at least k records[2], to help maintain "k-anonymity" [13]. A major drawback of nearest neighbor clustering is that it requires computing a large number of distances between records, $O(n^2)$. Blocking a new record means finding its nearest neighbors, an $O(n)$ operation.

---

[1] The distance metric used can vary depending on the nature of the records.

[2] Privacy-preserving versions of these approaches use "reference values" rather than the records themselves to cluster the records [21].

The cost of calculating distances between records in large, high-dimensional datasets led [16] to propose the method of *canopies*. In this approach, a computationally cheap (if inaccurate) distance metric is used to place records into potentially-overlapping sets (canopies). An initial record is picked randomly to be the base of the first canopy; all records within a distance t_1 of the base are grouped under that canopy. Those within distance $t_2 \leq t_1$ of the base are removed from later consideration. A new record is picked to be the base of the next canopy, and the procedure is repeated until the list of candidate records is empty. More accurate but expensive distance measures are computed only between records that fall under at least one shared canopy. That is, only record-pairs sharing a canopy are candidates to be linked.

Canopies is not strictly a blocking method. They overlap, making the collection of canopies only a covering of the set of records, rather than a partition. We can derive blocks from canopies, either set-theoretically or by setting $t_1 = t_2$. The complexity of building the canopies is $O(nC_n)$, with C_n being the number of canopies, itself a complicated and random function of the data, the thresholds, and the order in which records are chosen as bases. Further, finding fast, rough distance measures for complicated high-dimensional records is non-trivial.

2.3   LSH-Based Approaches

We explore two LSH-based blocking methods. These are based, respectively, on graph partitioning or community discovery, and on combining random projections with classical clustering. The main reason for exploring these two methods is that even with comparatively efficient algorithms for partitioning the similarity graph, doing that is still computationally impractical for hundreds of thousands of records.

2.3.1   Shingling

LSH-based blocking schemes "shingle" [19] records. That is, each record is treated as a string and is replaced by a "bag" (or "multi-set") of length-k contiguous sub-strings that it contains. These are known as "k-grams", "shingles", or "tokens". For example, the string "TORONTO" yields the bag of length-two shingles "TO", "OR", "RO", "ON", "NT", "TO". (N.B., "TO" appears twice.)

As alternative to shingling, we might use a bag-of-words representation, or even to shingle into consecutive pairs (triples, etc.) of words. In our experiments, shingling at the level of letters worked better than dividing by words.

2.3.2   Transitive LSH (TLSH)

We create a graph of the similarity between records. For simplicity, assume that all fields are string-valued. Each record is shingled with a common k, and the bags of shingles for all n records are reduced to an n-column binary-valued matrix M, indicating which shingles occur in which records. M is large, since the number of length-k shingles typically grows exponentially with k. As most shingles are absent from most records, M is sparse. We reduce its dimension by generating a random "minhash" function and applying it to each column. Such functions map columns of M to integers, ensuring that the probability of two columns being mapped to the same value equals the Jaccard similarity between the columns [19]. Generating p different minhash functions, we reduce the large, sparse matrix M to a dense $p \times n$ matrix, M', of integer-valued "signatures," while preserving information. Each row of M' is a random projection of M. Finally, we divide the rows of M' into b non-overlapping "bands," apply a hash function to each band and column, and establish an edge between two records if their columns of M' are mapped to the same value in any band.[3]

These edges define a graph: records are nodes, and edges indicate a certain degree of similarity between them. We form blocks by dividing the graph into its connected components. However, the largest connected components are typically very large, making them unsuitable as blocks. Thus, we sub-divide the connected components into "communities" or "modules" — sub-graphs that are densely connected internally, but sparsely connected to the rest of the graph. This ensures that the blocks produced consist of records that are all highly similar, while having relatively few ties of similarity to records in other blocks [8]. Specifically, we apply the algorithm of [6][4], sub-dividing communities greedily, until even the largest community is smaller than a specified threshold.[5] The end result is a set of blocks that balance false negative errors in linkage (minimized by having a few large blocks) and the speed of linkage (minimized by keeping each block small). We summarize the whole procedure in Algorithm 2.3.2 (see Appendix 5).

TLSH involves many tuning parameters (the length of shingles, the number of random permutations, the maximum size of communities, etc.) We chose the shingle such that we have the highest recall possible for each application. We used a random permutation of 100, since the recall was approximately constant for all permutations higher than 100. Furthermore, we chose a maximum size of the communities of 500, after tuning this specifically for desired speed.

2.3.3 K-Means Locality Sensitive Hashing (KLSH)

The second LSH-based blocking method begins, like TLSH, by shingling the records, treated as strings, but then differs in several ways. First, we do not ignore the number of times each shingle type appears in a record, but rather keep track of these counts, leading to a bag-of-shingles representation for records. Second, we measure similarity between records using the inner product of bag-of-shingles vectors, with inverse-document-frequency (IDF) weighting. Third, we reduce the dimensionality of the bag-of-shingles vectors by random projections, followed by clustering the low-dimensional projected vectors with the k-means algorithm. Hence, we can control the mean number of records per cluster to be n/c, where c is the number of block-clusters. In practice, there is a fairly small dispersion around this mean, leading to blocks that, by construction, have the roughly

---

[3] To be mapped to the same value in a particular band, two columns must either be equal, or a low-probability "collision" occurred for the hash function.

[4] We could use other community-discovery algorithms, e.g. [9].

[5] This maximum size ensures that record linkage is feasible.

the same distribution for all applications.[6] The KLSH algorithm is given in Appendix 5.

3   Computational Complexity

3.1   Computational Complexity of TLSH

The first steps of the algorithm can be done independently across records. Shingling a single record is $O(1)$, so shingling all the records is $O(n)$. Similarly, applying one minhash function to the shingles of one record is $O(1)$, and there are p minhash functions, so minhashing takes $O(np)$ time. Hashing again, with b bands, takes $O(nb)$ time. We assume that p and b are both $O(1)$ as n grows.

We create an edge between every pair of records that get mapped to the same value by the hash function in some band. Rather than iterating over pairs of records, it is faster to iterate over values v in the range of the hash function. If there are $|v|$ records mapped to the value v, creating their edges takes $O(|v|^2)$ time. On average, $|v| = nV^{-1}$, where V is the number of points in the range of the hash function, so creating the edge list takes $O(V(n/V)^2) = O(n^2V^{-1})$ time. [6] shows that creating the communities from the graph is $O(n(\log n)^2)$.

The total complexity of TLSH is $O(n) + O(np) + O(nb) + O(n^2V^{-1}) + O(n(\log n)^2) = O(n^2V^{-1})$, and is dominated by actually building the graph.

3.2   Computational Complexity of KLSH

As with TLSH, the shingling phase of KLSH takes $O(n)$ time. The time required for the random projections, however, is more complicated. Let $w(n)$ be the number of distinct words found across the n records. The time needed to do one random projection of one record is then $O(w(n))$, and the time for the whole random projection phase is $O(npw(n))$. For k-means cluster, with a constant number of iterations I, the time required to form b clusters of n p-dimensional vectors is $O(bnpI)$. Hence, the complexity is $O(npw(n)) + O(bnpI)$.

Heaps's law suggests $w(n) = O(n^\beta)$, where $0 < \beta < 1$.[7] Thus, the complexity is $O(pn^{1+\beta}) + O(bnpI)$. For record linkage to run in linear time, it must run in constant time in each block. Thus, the number of records per block must be constant, i.e., $b = O(n)$. Hence, the time-complexity for blocking is $O(pn^{1+\beta}) + O(n^2pI) = O(n^2pI)$, a quadratic time algorithm dominated by the clustering. Letting $b = O(1)$ yields an over-all time complexity of $O(pn^{1+\beta})$, dominated by the projection step. If we assume $\beta = 0.5$ and let $b = O(\sqrt{n})$, then both the projection and the clustering steps are $O(pn^{1.5})$. Record linkage in each block is $O(n)$, so record linkage is $O(n^{1.5})$, rather than $O(n^2)$ without blocking.

---

[6] This property is not guaranteed for most LSH methods.

[7] For English text, $0.4 < \beta < 0.6$.

3.3 Computational Complexity of Traditional Blocking Approaches

Traditional blocking approaches use attributes of the records to partition records into blocks. As such, calculating the blocks using traditional approaches requires $O(n)$ computations. For example, approaches that block on birth year only require a partition of the records based on these fields. That is, each record is simply mapped to one of the unique birth year values in the dataset, which is an $O(n)$ calculation for a list of size n. Some traditional approaches, however, require $O(n^2)$ computations. For example, in Table 1, we show some effective blocking strategies which require $O(n^2)$ computations, but each operation is so cheap that they can be run in reasonable time for moderately sized files.

4 Results

We test the previously mentioned approaches on data from the RecordLinkage R package.[8] These simulated datasets contain 500 and 10,000 records (denoted RLdata500 and RLdata10000), with exactly 10% duplicates in each list. These datasets contain first and last Germanic name and full date of birth (DOB). Each duplicate contains one error with respect to the original record, and there is maximum of one duplicate per original record. Each record has a unique identifier, allowing us to test the performance of the blocking methods.

We explore the performance of the previously presented methods under other scenarios of measurement error. [1, 4, 5] developed a data generation and corruption tool that creates synthetic datasets containing various field attributes. This tool includes dependencies between fields and permits the generation of different types of errors. We now describe the characteristics of the datafiles used in the simulation. We consider three files having the following field attributes: first and last name, gender, postal code, city, telephone number, credit card number, and age. For each database, we allow either 10, 30, or 50% duplicates per file, and each duplicate has five errors with respect to the original record, where these five errors are allocated at random among the fields. Each original record has maximum of five duplicates. We refer to these files as the "noisy" files.

4.1 Traditional Blocking Approaches

Tables 1 – 2 provide results of traditional blocking when applied to the RLdata10000 and "noisy" files. While field-specific information *can* yield favorable blocking solutions, each blocking criteria is application specific. The overall goal of blocking is to reduce the overall set of candidate pairs, while minimizing the false negatives induced. Thus, we find the *recall* and *reduction ratio* (RR). This corresponds to the proportion of true matches that the blocking criteria preserves, and the proportion of record-pairs discarded by the blocking, respectively.

---

[8] http://www.inside-r.org/packages/cran/RecordLinkage/docs/RLdata

Criteria 1 – 5 (Table 1) and 1 – 6 (Table 2) show that *some* blocking approaches are poor, where the recall is never above 90%. Criteria requiring exact agreement in a single field or on a combination of them are susceptible to field errors. More reliable criteria are constructed using combinations of fields such that multiple disagreements must be met for a pair to be declared as a non-match. (See Criteria 7–10 and 12 in Table 1, and 7 – 8 in Table 2.) We obtain high recall and RR using these, but in general their performance is context-dependent.

Criteria 10 (Table 1) deals with the case when a pair is declared a non-match whenever it disagrees in four or more fields, which is reliable since false-negative pairs are only induced when the datafile contains large amounts of error. For example this criterion does not lead to good results with the noisy files, hence a stronger criteria is needed, such as 7 (Table 2). Using Criteria 12 (Table 1) and 8 (Table 2), we further reduce the set of candidate pairs whenever a pair has a strong disagreement in an important field.[9] These criteria are robust. In order to induce false negatives, the error in the file must be much higher than expected.

Table 1. Criteria for declaring pairs as non-matches, where results correspond to the `RLdata10000` datafile

Declare non-match if disagreement in:	Recall (%)	RR (%)
1. First OR last name	39.20	99.98
2. Day OR month OR year of birth	59.30	99.99
3. Year of birth	84.20	98.75
4. Day of birth	86.10	96.74
5. Month of birth	88.40	91.70
6. Decade of birth	93.20	87.76
7. First AND last name	99.20	97.36
8. {First AND last name} OR {day AND month AND year of birth}	99.20	99.67
9. Day AND month AND year of birth	100.00	87.61
10. More than three fields	100.00	99.26
11. Initial of first OR last name	100.00	99.25
12. {More than three fields} OR {Levenshtein dist. ≥ 4 in first OR last name}	100.00	99.97

Table 2. Criteria for declaring pairs as non-matches, where results correspond to the noisy datafile with 10% duplicates. Similar results obtained for 30 and 50% duplicates.

Declare non-match if disagree in:	Recall (%)	RR (%)
1. Gender	31.96	53.39
2. City	31.53	77.25
3. Postal Code	32.65	94.20
4. First OR last name	1.30	>99.99
5. Initial of first OR last name	78.10	99.52
6. First AND last name	26.97	99.02
7. All fields	93.28	40.63
8. {All fields} OR {Levenshtein dist. ≥ 4 in first OR last name}	92.84	99.92

4.2 Clustering Approaches

Our implementations of [16]'s canopies approach and [21]'s nearest neighbor approach perform poorly on the `RLdata10000` and "noisy" datasets[10]. Figure 1 gives results of these approaches for different threshold parameters (t is the threshold parameter for sorted TNN) for the `RLdata10000` dataset. For all thresholds, both TNN and canopies fail to achieve a balance of high recall and a high reduction ratio.

Turning to the "noisy" dataset with 10% duplicates, we find that TNN fails to achieve a balance of high recall and high reduction ratio, regardless of the

---

[9] We use the Levenshtein distance (LD) of first and last names for pairs passing Criterion 10 of Table 1 or Criteria 7 of Table 2, and declare pairs as non-matches when LD ≥ 4 in either first or last name.

[10] In our implementations, we use the TF-IDF matrix representation of the records and Euclidean distance to compare pairs of records in TNN and canopies. We tried several other distance measures, each of which gave similar results.

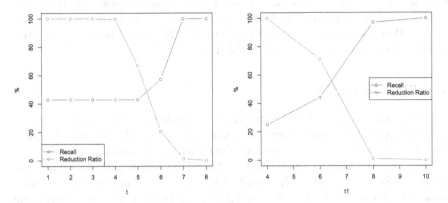

Fig. 1. Performance of threshold nearest neighbors (left) and canopies (right) on the RLdata10000 datafile

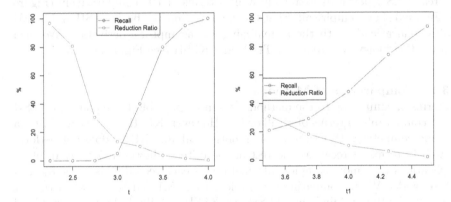

Fig. 2. Performance of TNN (left) and canopies (right) on the "noisy" datafile (10% duplicates). The other "noisy" datafiles exhibited similar behavior as the figures above.

threshold t that is used. Similarly, the canopies approach does not yield a balance of high recall while reducing the number of candidate pairs.

Clearly, both clustering approaches fail to achieve a balance of high recall and RR for any threshold parameters. The inefficacy of these approaches is likely due the limited number of field attributes (five fields) and the Euclidean distance metric used for these datasets. In particular, only three fields in the "noisy" dataset use textual information, which both of these approaches use to identify similar records. Limited field information can make it difficult for clustering approaches to group similar records together, since the resulting term frequency matrices will be very sparse. Thus, we investigate the behavior with the same number of duplicates, but vary the error rate and provide richer information at the field attribute level. Figure 2 illustrates that both methods do not have a good balance between recall and RR, which we investigated for various thresholds. As such, further analysis of these approaches on more information-rich datasets is required in order to make sound conclusions about their efficacy for blocking. (We note that the metrics used in TLSH and KLSH, which shingle the records, were chosen so as to not have such problems.)

4.3   LSH Approaches

Since the performance of KLSH and TLSH depends on tuning parameters, we tune each application appropriately to these. We empirically measure the scalability of these methods, which are consistent with our derivations in §3.

We analyze the RLdata10000 database for TLSH and KLSH. As we increase k under TLSH, we see that the recall peaks at $k = 5$, and does very poorly (below 40% recall) when $k \leq 4$. For KLSH, the highest and most consistent recall is when $k = 2$, since it is always above 80% and it is about the same no matter the total number of blocks chosen (see Figure 4). In terms of RR, we see that TLSH performs extremely poorly as the total number of blocks increases, whereas KLSH performs extremely well in terms of RR comparatively (Figure 5). Figure 3 shows empirically that the running time for both KLSH and TLSH scales quadratically with the n, matching our asymptotic derivation. We then analyze the "noisy" database for TLSH and KLSH (see Figures 6 and 7).

4.3.1   Comparisons of Methods
In terms of comparing to the methods presented in Table 1, we find that TLSH is not comparable in terms of recall or RR. However, KLSH easily beats Criteria 1–2 and competes with Criteria 3–4 on both recall and RR. It does not perform as well in terms of recall as the rest of the criteria, however, it *may* in other applications with more complex information for each record (this is a subject of future work). When comparing the Table 2 to TLSH and KLSH when run for the noisy datafile, we find that TLSH and KLSH usually do better when tuned properly, however not always. Due to the way these files have been constructed, more investigation need to be done in terms of how naive methods work for real work type applications versus LSH-based methods.

Comparing to other blocking methods, both KLSH and TLSH outperform KNN in terms of recall (and RR for the noisy datafiles). We find that for this dataset, canopies do not perform well in terms of recall or RR unless a specific threshold t_1 is chosen. However, given this choice of t_1, this approach yields either high recall and low RR or vice versa, making canopies undesirable according to our criteria.

For the RLdata10000 dataset, the simple yet effective traditional blocking methods and KLSH perform best in terms of balancing both high recall and high RR. As already stated, we expect the performance of these to be heavily application-dependent. Additionally, note that each method relies on high-quality labeled record linkage data to measure the recall and RR and the clustering methods require tuning parameters, which can be quite sensitive. Our studies show that TLSH is the least sensitive in general and further explorations should be done here. Future work should explore the characteristics of the underlying datasets for which one method would be preferred over another.

4.3.2   Sensitivity Analysis on RLdata500 and RLdata10000

A sensitivity analysis is given for KLSH and TLSH. For TLSH, the RLdata500 dataset is not very sensitive to b since the recall is always above 80% whereas the RLdata10000 dataset is quite sensitive to the band, and we recommend the use of a band of 21–22 since the recall for these b is $\approx$ 96%, although this may change for other datasets. We then evaluate TLSH using the "best" choice of the band for shingled values from $k = 1, \ldots 5$. The sensitivity analysis for the "noisy" datafiles was quite similar to that described above, where a band of 22 was deemed the most appropriate for TLSH. For KLSH, we found that we needed to increase the number of permutations slightly to improve the recall and recommend $p = 150$.

For KLSH, we find that when the number of random permutations p is above 100, the recall does not change considerably. We refer back to Figure 4 (right), which illustrates the recall versus number of blocks when $p = 100$. When $k = 4$, the recall is always above 70%. However, we find that when $k = 2$, the recall is always above 80%.

5   Discussion

We have explored two LSH methods for blocking, one of which would naturally fit into the privacy preserving record linkage (PPRL) framework, since the method could be made to be private by creating reference values for each individual in the database. This has been done for many blocking methods in the context of PPRL [7, 13, 14, 22]. KLSH performs just as well or better than commonly used blocking methods, such as some simple traditional blocking methods, nearest neighbor clustering approaches, and canopies [16, 21]. One drawback is that like LSH-based methods, it must be tuned for each application since it is sensitive to the tuning parameters. Thus, some *reliable* training data must be available to evaluate the recall and RR (and tune KLSH or clustering type methods). In many situations, a researcher may be better off by using domain-specific knowledge to reduce the set of comparisons, as shown in §4.1.

LSH-methods have been described elsewhere as "private blocking" due to the hashing step. However, they do not in fact provide any formal privacy guarantees in our setting. The new variant that we have introduced, KLSH, does satisfy the k-anonymity criterion for the de-duplication of a single file. However, the data remain subject to intruder attacks, as the literature on differential privacy makes clear, and the vulnerability is greater the smaller the value of k. Our broader goal, however, is to merge and analyze data from multiple files. Privacy protection in that context is far more complicated. Even if one could provide privacy guarantees for each file separately, it would still be possible to identify specific entities or *sensitive* information regarding entities in the merged database.

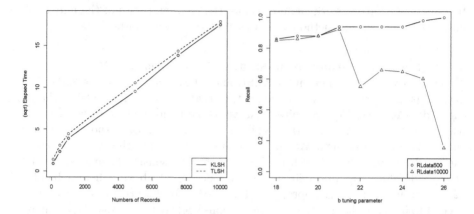

Fig. 3. RLdata10000/RLdata500 datasets. Left: Square Root Elapsed time versus number of records for KLSH and TLSH, illustrating that both methods scale nearly quadratically (matching the computationally complexity findings). We shingle using $k = 5$ for both methods. We use a band of 26 for TLSH. Right: Recall versus b for both RLdata500 and RLdata10000 after running TLSH.

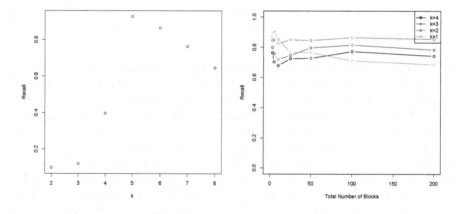

Fig. 4. RLdata10000 dataset. Left: Recall versus number of shingles k for KLSH. The highest recall occurs at $k = 5$. Right: Recall versus the total number of blocks, where we vary the number of shingles k. We find that the highest recall is for $k = 2$.

The approach of PPRL reviewed in [10] sets out to deal with this problem. Merging data from multiple files with the same or similar values without releasing their attributes is what PPRL hopes to achieve. Indeed, one of course needs to go further, since performing statistical analyses on the merged database is the real objective of PPRL. Whether the new "private blocking" approaches discussed offer any progress on this problem, it is unclear at best. Adequately addressing the PPRL goals remains elusive, as do formal privacy guarantees, be they from differential privacy or other methods.

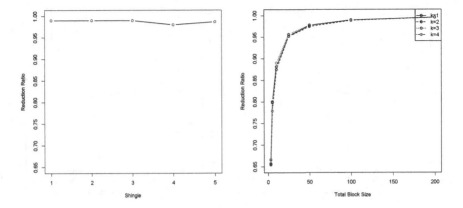

Fig. 5. RLdata10000 dataset. Left: For TLSH, we see the RR versus the number of shingles, where the RR is always very high. We emphasize that TLSH does about as well on the RR as any of the other methods, and certainly does much better than many traditional blocking methods and KNN. (The RR is always above 98% for all shingles with $b = 26$.) Right: For KLSH, we illustrate the RR versus the total number of blocks for various $k = 1, \ldots, 4$ illustrating that as the number of blocks increases, the RR increases dramatically. When the total block size is at least 25, the RR $\geq 95\%$.

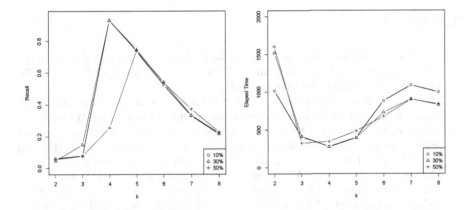

Fig. 6. Left: We run TLSH for 10 percent duplicates, as before, the application is quite sensitive to b, k. Hence, it is quite easy to find values of b, k such that the recall is very low or if tuning is done properly, we can find values of b, k where the recall is acceptable. We note this relies on very good ground truth. The only value of k we recommend is 4 since it is close to 90% recall. The computational time is the same as previously. Right: Elapsed time for 10, 30, and 50 percent duplicates on "noisy" dataset.

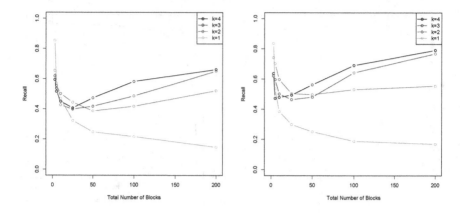

Fig. 7. We run KLSH at 10 percent duplicates with p=100 (left) and p=150 (right). We see as the number of permutations increases (left figure), the recall increases. The behavior is the same for 30 and 50 percent duplicates. This indicates that KLSH needs to be tuned for each application based on p. (We note that KLSH was run here using a bag of words type formulation. Shingling should be explored in future work.)

Acknowledgements. We thank Peter Christen, Patrick Ball, and Cosma Shalizi for thoughtful conversations that led to to early versions of this manuscript. We also thank the reviewers for their suggestions and comments.

References

[1] Christen, P.: Probabilistic Data Generation for Deduplication and Data Linkage. In: Gallagher, M., Hogan, J.P., Maire, F. (eds.) IDEAL 2005. LNCS, vol. 3578, pp. 109–116. Springer, Heidelberg (2005)

[2] Christen, P.: A survey of indexing techniques for scalable record linkage and deduplication. IEEE Transactions on Knowledge and Data Engineering 24 (2012)

[3] Christen, P., Pudjijono, A.: Accurate synthetic generation of realistic personal information. In: Theeramunkong, T., Kijsirikul, B., Cercone, N., Ho, T.-B. (eds.) PAKDD 2009. LNCS, vol. 5476, pp. 507–514. Springer, Heidelberg (2009)

[4] Christen, P., Pudjijono, A.: Accurate Synthetic Generation of Realistic Personal Information. In: Theeramunkong, T., Kijsirikul, B., Cercone, N., Ho, T.-B. (eds.) PAKDD 2009. LNCS, vol. 5476, pp. 507–514. Springer, Heidelberg (2009), http://dx.doi.org/10.1007/978-3-642-01307-2_47

[5] Christen, P., Vatsalan, D.: Flexible and Extensible Generation and Corruption of Personal Data. In: Proceedings of the ACM International Conference on Information and Knowledge Management (CIKM 2013) (2013)

[6] Clauset, A., Newman, M.E., Moore, C.: Finding community structure in very large networks. Physical Review E 70, 066111 (2004)

[7] Durham, E.A.: A framework for accurate, efficient private record linkage. Ph.D. thesis, Vanderbilt University (2012)

[8] Fortunato, S.: Community detection in graphs. Physics Reports 486, 75–174 (2010)

[9] Goldenberg, A., Zheng, A.X., Fienberg, S.E., Airoldi, E.M.: A survey of statistical network models. Foundations and Trends® in Machine Learning 2, 129–233 (2010)

[10] Hall, R., Fienberg, S.: Valid statistical inference on automatically matched files. In: Domingo-Ferrer, J., Tinnirello, I. (eds.) PSD 2012. LNCS, vol. 7556, pp. 131–142. Springer, Heidelberg (2012)

[11] Herzog, T., Scheuren, F., Winkler, W.: Data Quality and Record Linkage Techniques. Springer, New York (2007)

[12] Herzog, T., Scheuren, F., Winkler, W.: Record linkage. Wiley Interdisciplinary Reviews: Computational Statistics 2 (2010), doi:10.1002/wics.108

[13] Karakasidis, A., Verykios, V.S.: Reference table based k-anonymous private blocking. In: Proceedings of the 27th Annual ACM Symposium on Applied Computing, pp. 859–864. ACM (2012)

[14] Kuzu, M., Kantarcioglu, M., Durham, E., Malin, B.: A constraint satisfaction cryptanalysis of bloom filters in private record linkage. In: Fischer-Hübner, S., Hopper, N. (eds.) PETS 2011. LNCS, vol. 6794, pp. 226–245. Springer, Heidelberg (2011)

[15] Liang, H., Wang, Y., Christen, P., Gayler, R.: Noise-tolerant approximate blocking for dynamic real-time entity resolution. In: Tseng, V.S., Ho, T.B., Zhou, Z.-H., Chen, A.L.P., Kao, H.-Y. (eds.) PAKDD 2014, Part II. LNCS, vol. 8444, pp. 449–460. Springer, Heidelberg (2014)

[16] McCallum, A., Nigam, K., Ungar, L.H.: Efficient clustering of high-dimensional data sets with application to reference matching. In: Proceedings of the Sixth ACM SIGKDD International Conference on Knowledge Discovery and Data Mining, pp. 169–178. ACM (2000)

[17] Pasula, H., Marthi, B., Milch, B., Russell, S., Shpitser, I.: Identity uncertainty and citation matching. In: Advances in Neural Information Processing Systems, pp. 1425–1432 (2003)

[18] Paulevé, L., Jégou, H., Amsaleg, L.: Locality sensitive hashing: A comparison of hash function types and querying mechanisms. Pattern Recognition Letters 31, 1348–1358 (2010)

[19] Rajaraman, A., Ullman, J.D.: Mining of massive datasets. Cambridge University Press (2012)

[20] Steorts, R.C., Hall, R., Fienberg, S.: A Bayesian approach to graphical record linkage and de-duplication (2013) (submitted)

[21] Vatsalan, D., Christen, P.: Sorted nearest neighborhood clustering for efficient private blocking. In: Pei, J., Tseng, V.S., Cao, L., Motoda, H., Xu, G. (eds.) PAKDD 2013, Part II. LNCS, vol. 7819, pp. 341–352. Springer, Heidelberg (2013)

[22] Vatsalan, D., Christen, P., Verykios, V.S.: An efficient two-party protocol for approximate matching in private record linkage. In: Proceedings of the Ninth Australasian Data Mining Conference, vol. 121, pp. 125–136. Australian Computer Society, Inc. (2011)

[23] Winkler, W., Yancey, W., Porter, E.: Fast record linkage of very large files in support of decennial and administrative records projects. In: Proceedings of American Statistical Association Section on Survey Research Methods (2010)

Algorithms for KLSH and TLSH

We provide the algorithms for KLSH and TLSH below (see §2.3.2 and 2.3.3):

Algorithm 1. Transitive Locality Sensitive Hashing (TLSH)

Place similar records into blocks and impose transitivity

Data: X_{ij}, tuning parameters b, t, k

Shingle each X_{ij} into length-k strings
Create a binary matrix M indicating which tokens appear in which records
Create an integer-valued matrix M' of minhash signatures from M
Divide the rows of M' into b bands
for *each band* **do**
> Apply a random hash function to the band of M'
> Record an edge between two records if the hash maps them to the same bucket

end
while *the largest community has $> t$ records* **do**
> Cut the edge graph into finer communities using the algorithm of [6]

end
return *the final list of communities*

Algorithm 2. K-Means Locality Sensitive Hashing (KLSH). The number of blocks c is set by $c = n/(\text{desired avg. number of records per block})$.

Place similar records into blocks and using k-means clustering and random projections

Data: X_{ij}, number of desired blocks c, tokenization tuning parameters τ, number of projections p

for *each record X_{ij}* **do**
> Set $v_{ij} = \text{TOKENIZE}(X_{ij}, \tau)$

end
for *each token w* **do**
> Set $N_w =$ number of bags containing w
> Set $IDF_w = \log n/N_w$

end
for *m from 1 to p* **do**
> Set $u_m = $ a random unit vector
> **for** *each bag-of-tokens vector v_{ij}* **do**
> > Set $r_{ijm} = \sum_w u_{iw} v_{ijw} IDF_w$
>
> **end**

end
return KMEANS(r,c)

Probabilistic Record Linkage
for Disclosure Risk Assessment

Natalie Shlomo

Social Statistics, School of Social Sciences, University of Manchester, Oxford Road,
Manchester M13 9PL, United Kingdom
Natalie.Shlomo@manchester.ac.uk

Abstract. Disclosure limitation methods for protecting the confidentiality of respondents in survey microdata often use perturbative techniques which introduce measurement error into the categorical identifying variables. In addition, the data itself will often have measurement errors commonly arising from survey processes. There is a need for valid and practical ways to assess the protection against the risk of identification for survey microdata with measurement errors. A common disclosure risk scenario is when an intruder seeks to match the microdata with an external file. We will examine probabilistic record linkage as a means of assessing disclosure risk and relate it to disclosure risk measures under the probabilistic framework of the Poisson log-linear models.

Keywords: Poisson-log linear model, Misclassification error, Sample unique, Disclosure risk-data utility map.

1   Introduction

Statistical Agencies are obligated to protect the confidentiality of individuals when releasing sample microdata arising from social surveys. The risk assessment is typically based on a disclosure risk scenario where an 'intruder' attempts to link the sample microdata to available public data sources through a set of identifying key variables that are common to both sources. The identification of an individual could then be used to obtain sensitive information and the disclosure of attributes. In order to limit the risk of identification, the statistical agency will implement disclosure limitation methods on the sample microdata, the extent of which depend on the mode of release, such as on-site data labs, data archives or public-use files. Disclosure limitation methods can be non-perturbative where the information content is reduced without altering the data. These include deleting variables, sub-sampling or recoding and collapsing categories of variables. Perturbative disclosure limitation methods alter the data by introducing forms of misclassification. These include data swapping (Dalenius and Reiss, 1982, Gomatam, Karr and Sanil, 2005), noise addition (Kim, 1986, Fuller, 1993, Brand, 2002) and fully synthetic data where the data released is based on a statistical model (Raghunathan, Reiter, and Rubin, 2003). For more

J. Domingo-Ferrer (Ed.): PSD 2014, LNCS 8744, pp. 269–282, 2014.
© Springer International Publishing Switzerland 2014

information on these methods see also: Willenborg and De Waal, 2001, Domingo-Ferrer and Torra, 2001.

Before releasing sample microdata, statistical agencies need to quantify the disclosure risk of identification. One method for assessing this risk is to simulate an 'intruder' attack by using probabilistic record linkage techniques. One of the first examples was carried out in Spruill (1982) who linked perturbed sample microdata back to the original sample using distance based matching. In many studies of this type, a conservative assessment of the risk of identification is obtained since it assumes that the 'intruder' has access to the original dataset and does not take into account the protection afforded by the sampling. More recent examples use the probabilistic record linkage framework of Fellegi and Sunter (F&S) (1969) (see: Yancey, Winkler and Creecy, 2002, Hawala, Stinson and Abowd, 2005 and Torra, Abowd and Domingo-Ferrer, 2006). The identifying key variables used for matching are typically categorical, such as sex, date of birth, marital status and locality. In the F&S framework, each potential pair is assigned a matching weight as described in Section 2. The matching weights are sorted and appropriate cut-offs determined according to pre-specified type I and type II error bounds. Pairs with high matching weights are considered to be correct matches and pairs with low matching weights are considered to be correct non-matches. Pairs with matching weights between the cut-off thresholds undergo clerical review. The matching weights are proxies for the probability of a correct match given an agreement or disagreement. These probabilities can be used as individual record-level measures of disclosure risk. Global measures of disclosure risk include the proportion of correct matches, the proportion of correct matches to false matches, and one minus the estimated false match rate.

In Skinner, 2008, the probabilistic record linkage framework of F&S is linked to the probabilistic modelling framework for quantifying identification risk based on the notion of population uniqueness (see: Skinner and Holmes, 1998, Elamir and Skinner, 2006, Skinner and Shlomo, 2008). The probabilistic modelling framework relies on distributional assumptions to draw inference from the sample and estimate population parameters. The individual disclosure risk measure is the expectation of a correct match given a sample unique on the set of key variables. The global measure of disclosure risk is obtained by summing over the sample uniques to derive the expected number of correct matches. Shlomo and Skinner (2010) expanded the original probabilistic modelling framework to include misclassification errors in the key variables, either arising naturally through stages of data processing or purposely introduced into the data as a perturbative disclosure limitation method. In this paper we provide empirical evidence of the relationship between the probabilistic record linkage framework of F&S and the probabilistic modelling framework based on the notion of population uniqueness taking into account misclassification errors. We also show how a risk-utility assessment might be carried out by a statistical agency for choosing optimal parameters of record swapping.

In section 2 we introduce the notation and theory of the two frameworks for disclosure risk assessment: the F&S probabilistic record linkage framework and the probabilistic modelling framework. We also provide examples that link the two frameworks as set out in Skinner (2008). Section 3 presents an empirical study based on an extract from the UK 2001 Census. We first assume the perspective of the statistical agency where a perturbative method of disclosure limitation has been applied to the data and therefore misclassification probabilities and population parameters are known. We apply both the record linkage and probabilistic modelling framework for assessing the risk of identification and compare results. We also demonstrate how we can estimate population parameters through log-linear modelling in the probabilistic modelling framework when population counts are unknown, or use the EM algorithm to estimate matching parameters in the F&S record linkage framework when the match status is unknown. Section 4 demonstrates a risk-utility assessment using the example of random and targeted data swapping at different perturbation rates. We conclude in Section 5 with a discussion.

2   Notation and Theory

In this section we describe the F&S probabilistic record linkage framework and the probabilistic modelling framework based on the notion of population uniqueness and taking into account misclassification. We demonstrate the relationship between the two frameworks.

2.1   Fellegi and Sunter Probabilistic Record Linkage

Using the notation of Skinner, 2008, let $\tilde{X}_a$ denote the value of the vector of cross-classified identifying key variables for unit a in the microdata ($a \in s_1$) with values labelled $1,2....J$. Let X_b the corresponding value for unit b in the external database ($b \in s_2$). The different notation of X allows for different values of the two vectors due to natural misclassification in the data or an application of a perturbative disclosure limitation method to the sample microdata file. We assume that X_b of the external database is fixed and $\tilde{X}_a$ of the microdata are determined by a $J \times J$ probability misclassification matrix θ, where:

$$P(\tilde{X}_a = k / X_a = j) = \theta_{kj} \tag{1}$$

θ_{jj} on the diagonal of the matrix is the probability of not misclassifying (perturbing) category j. Some examples of probability misclassification matrices when used for the purpose of perturbing microdata are presented in Willenborg and De Waal (2001).

Based on the F&S theory of record linkage, a comparison vector $\gamma(\tilde{X}_a, X_b)$ is calculated for pairs of units $(a,b) \in s_1 \times s_2$ where the function $\gamma(.,.)$ takes values in a finite comparison space Γ. In the simplest case, $\gamma_j(\tilde{X}_a, X_b) = 1$ if there is an agreement on value j of $\tilde{X}_a$ and X_b, and 0 otherwise. For the disclosure risk scenario we assume that the intruder uses the comparison vector to identify pairs of units which contain the same unit $(a,a) \in s_1 \times s_2$. Typically the intruder will use a combination of exact matching and probabilistic matching by considering only pairs that are blocked through an exact match on some subset $\tilde{s} \subset s_1 \times s_2$. The intruder seeks to partition the set of pairs in $\tilde{s}$ into a set of matches: $M = \{(a,b) \in \tilde{s} \mid a \in s_1, b \in s_2, a = b\}$ and non-matches: $U = \{(a,b) \in \tilde{s} \mid a \in s_1, b \in s_2, a \neq b\}$. The approach by F&S is to define the likelihood ratio m/u as the matching weight where m is the probability of an agreement given a match $m = P(\gamma(\tilde{X}_a, X_b)/(a,b) \in M)$ and u is the probability of an agreement given not a match $u = P(\gamma(\tilde{X}_a, X_b)/(a,b) \in NM)$. The higher values of the likelihood ratio are more likely to belong to M and the lower values of the likelihood ratio are more likely to belong to U. In addition, under the assumption of independence the m-probability and the u-probability can be split into individual components for each separate key variable. Let $p = P((a,b) \in M)$ the probability that the pair is in M. The probability of a correct match $p_{M/\gamma} = P((a,b) \in M \mid \gamma(\tilde{X}_a, X_b))$ can be calculated using Bayes Theorem:

$$p_{M/\gamma} = mp/[mp + u(1-p)] . \tag{2}$$

If the match status is unknown, the matching parameters m, u and p can be estimated using the EM algorithm which is an iterative maximum likelihood estimation procedure for incomplete data (not shown here). Based on the estimation of the parameters, the probability of a correct match given an agreement $p_{M/\gamma}$ can be estimated by (2).

2.2   Probabilistic Modelling for Measuring Identification Risk

The probabilistic modelling framework for estimating the risk of identification is based on theory which uses models for categorical key variables. Let $f = \{f_j\}$ denote a multiway frequency table, which is a sample from a population table $F = \{F_j\}$, where $j = 1,2,...,J$ indicates a cell defined by cross-classified categorical key variables and f_j and F_j denote the frequency in the sample and in the population cell j, respectively. Denote by n and N the sample and population size, respectively and the number of cells by J. Disclosure risk arises from small cells, and in particular when $f_j = F_j = 1$ (sample and population uniques). We focus on a global disclosure risk measure based on sample uniques: $\tau = \sum_j I(f_j = 1)1/F_j$. This measure is the expected number of correct matches if each sample unique is matched to a randomly chosen individual from the same population cell. We consider the case that f is known, and F is an unknown parameter and the quantity τ needs to be estimated. An estimate of τ is:

$$\hat{\tau} = \sum_j I(f_j = 1)\hat{E}[1/F_j \mid f_j = 1] \tag{3}$$

where $\hat{E}$ denotes an estimate of the expectation. The formula in (3) is naïve in the sense that it ignores the possibility of misclassification. A common assumption in the frequency table literature is $F_j \sim Poisson(\lambda_j)$, independently, where $\sum_j F_j = N$ is a random parameter. Binomial (or Poisson) sampling from F_j means that $f_j \mid F_j \sim Bin(F_j, \pi_j)$ independently, where π_j is the sampling fraction in cell j. By standard calculations we then have:

$$f_j \sim Poisson\,(\lambda_j \pi_j) \text{ and, } F_j \mid f_j \sim f_j + Poisson(\lambda_j(1-\pi_j)), \tag{4}$$

where $F_j \mid f_j$ are conditionally independent.

We use the approach as developed in Skinner and Holmes, 1998, Elamir and Skinner, 2006 and Skinner and Shlomo, 2008 by introducing log linear models to estimate population parameters and estimating the risk of identification. The sample counts $\{f_j\}$ are used to fit a log-linear model: $\log \mu_j = x'_j \beta$ where $\mu_j = \lambda_j \pi_j$ in order to obtain estimates for the parameters: $\hat{\lambda}_j = \hat{\mu}_j / \pi_j$. Using the second part of (4), the expected individual disclosure risk measure for cell j is defined by:

$$E_{\lambda_j}(1/F_j \mid f_j = 1) = [1 - e^{-\lambda_j(1-\pi)}]/[\lambda_j(1-\pi)]. \tag{5}$$

Plugging $\hat{\lambda}_j$ for λ_j in (5) leads to the desired estimates $\hat{E}_{\lambda_j}[1/F_j \mid f_j = 1]$ and then to $\hat{\tau}$ of (3).

The original probabilistic modelling approach did not consider the case of misclassification naturally arising in surveys or purposely introduced into the data as a disclosure limitation method. Shlomo and Skinner (2010) define disclosure risk measures that take into account misclassification. The individual disclosure risk measures and the aggregated global disclosure risk measure on misclassified sample uniques in this case is defined as:

$$\tilde{\tau}_\theta = \sum_j I(\tilde{f}_j = 1)\{[\theta_{jj}/(1-\pi\theta_{jj})]/[\sum_k F_k \theta_{jk}/(1-\pi\theta_{jk})]\} \tag{6}$$

and it follows that $\tilde{\tau}_\theta \leq \tau = \sum_j I(f_j = 1)1/F_j$ with equality holding if there is no misclassification. The extent to which the left hand side of this inequality is less than the right hand side measures the impact of misclassification on disclosure risk.

If the sampling fraction is small we can approximate (6) by: $\sum_j I(\tilde{f}_j = 1)\theta_{jj}/(\sum_k F_k \theta_{jk})$. Moreover, if the population size is large, we have approximately $\sum_k F_k \theta_{jk} \approx \tilde{F}_j$, where $\tilde{F}_j$ is the number of units in the population which would have $\tilde{X}_j = j$ if they were included in the microdata (with misclassification). Hence a simple approximate expression for the global risk of identification, natural for many social surveys, is:

$$\tilde{\tau}_\theta \approx \sum_j I(\tilde{f}_j = 1)\theta_{jj}/\tilde{F}_j \tag{7}$$

The approximations in (7) does not depend upon θ_{jk} for $j \neq k$ and so knowledge of these probabilities is not required in the estimation of risk if 'acceptable' estimates of θ_{jj} (the diagonal probabilities of not-misclassification) and $\tilde{F}_j$ are available. Similar to the case with no misclassification, the measure in (7) may be interpreted as the expected number of correct matches among sample uniques.

Since the values of F_j or $\tilde{F}_j$ appearing in (6) and (7) are typically unknown, we need to estimate them. We do suppose that the values of θ_{jj} are known, especially in the case that a statistical agency purposely perturbs the data as a disclosure limitation method. Expression (7) provides a simple way to extend the log-linear modelling approach described above. Since the $\tilde{f}_j$, $j = 1,...,J$ represent the available data, all that is required is to ignore the misclassification and estimate $1/\tilde{F}_j$ from the $\tilde{f}_j$, $j = 1,...,J$ by fitting a log-linear model to the $\tilde{f}_j$, $j = 1,...,J$ following the same criteria as before. This results in an estimate for the individual disclosure risk measure $\hat{E}(1/\tilde{F}_j \mid \tilde{f}_j = 1)$ based on the assumptions of the Poisson distribution for the population and sample counts. These estimates should be multiplied by θ_{jj} values and summed if aggregate measures of the form in (7) are needed.

2.3   The Relationship Between the Two Frameworks

Skinner (2008) relates the F&S record linkage framework to the probabilistic modelling framework by providing the following examples:

Example 1:   Assume no misclassification has occurred, i.e. $\tilde{X}_a = X_a$ in both the population (P) and the sample (s) and that the true match status is known by the agency. Assume that sample (s) was drawn by simple random sampling from the population P. We calculate the contingency table in Table 1 for each $X_a = j$ in the realized sample where the rows are a binary agreement/disagreement on the comparison vector: $\gamma(X_a, X_b)$ for pairs $(a,b) \in s \times P$ and the columns the true match status.

From Table 1, we can calculate directly $p_{M|\gamma} = 1/F_j$. We also obtain that the m-probability defined as the probability of an agreement given a match is f_j / n, and the u-probability defined as the probability of an agreement given not a match is $f_j(F_j - 1)/n(N-1)$. The probability of a correct match is $p = 1/N$. Using Bayes formula:

$$p_{M|\gamma} = \frac{1/N \times f_j/n}{1/N \times f_j/n + (1-1/N)f_j(F_j-1)/n(N-1)} = \frac{1}{F_j} \qquad (8)$$

Small F_j therefore results in a high probability of a correct match given an agreement in the comparison vector.

Table 1. Contingency table of binary agreement status and match status for $X_a = j$ with no misclassification

	Non-match	Match	Total
Disagree	$n(N-1) - f_j(F_j - 1)$	$n - f_j$	$Nn - f_j F_j$
Agree	$f_j(F_j - 1)$	f_j	$f_j F_j$
Total	$n(N-1)$	n	Nn

Example 2: In continuation of Example 1, assume now that the microdata has undergone misclassification (either as a result of errors or purposely perturbed for disclosure limitation). Denote $\tilde{f}_j$ the observed misclassified sample counts with $\tilde{X}_a = j$ derived by $\tilde{f}_j = \theta_{jj} f_j + \sum_{k \neq j} \theta_{jk} f_k$. We calculate the contingency table on the realized misclassified sample in Table 2 for $\tilde{X}_a = j$ where the rows are a binary agreement/disagreement on the comparison vector: $\gamma(\tilde{X}_a, X_b)$ for pairs $(a,b) \in s \times P$ and the columns the true match status.

Table 2. Contingency table of binary agreement status and match status for $\tilde{X}_a = j$ with misclassification

	Non-match	Match	Total
Disagree	$Nn - n - \tilde{f}_j F_j + \theta_{jj} f_j$	$n - \theta_{jj} f_j$	$Nn - \tilde{f}_j F_j$
Agree	$\tilde{f}_j F_j - \theta_{jj} f_j$	$\theta_{jj} f_j$	$\tilde{f}_j F_j$
Total	$Nn - n$	n	Nn

From Table 2, we can calculate directly $p_{M|\gamma} = \theta_{jj} f_j / \tilde{f}_j F_j \approx \theta_{jj} / \pi \tilde{f}_j \approx \theta_{jj} / \tilde{F}_j$ where $\tilde{F}_j$ is the number of units in the population (P) with $\tilde{X}_a = j$ (imagining that the misclassification takes place before the sampling). We also obtain the m-probability (the probability of an agreement given a match) of $\theta_{jj} f_j / n$ and the u-probability (the probability of an agreement given not a match) of $(\tilde{f}_j F_j - \theta_{jj} f_j)/ n(N-1)$. The probability of a correct match is $p = 1/N$. Using Bayes formula:

$$p_{M|\gamma} = \frac{1/N \times \theta_{jj} f_j / n}{1/N \times \theta_{jj} f_j / n + (1 - 1/N)(\tilde{f}_j F_j - \theta_{jj} f_j)/ n(N-1)} \approx \frac{\theta_{jj}}{\pi \tilde{f}_j} \approx \frac{\theta_{jj}}{\tilde{F}_j} \quad (9)$$

Expression (9) is similar to the per-record individual risk measures used to define (7). Skinner (2008) also shows that the derivation of the probability of a correct match given an agreement holds for any subset of the population which may be selected arbitrarily.

3   Empirical Study

In this section, we provide empirical evidence based on real data of the connection between probabilistic record linkage according to F&S and the probabilistic modelling framework for calculating the risk of identification. We start from the perspective of the statistical agency where it is assumed that the misclassification matrix is known either because the data was purposely perturbed by the agency for disclosure limitation or a study was carried out to assess error rates in various stages of the data processing. We begin with assuming that population counts are known and hence the agency can calculate the necessary parameters to measure identification risk in both frameworks for this comparison. We also consider the case where population counts are unknown and examine the proximity of estimated individual per-record disclosure risk measures to true disclosure risk measures in both frameworks.

3.1   Preparation of the Data

We use the method of data swapping on an extract of individuals from the 2001 UK Census to compare the F&S framework and the probabilistic modelling framework. The population includes N=1,468,255 individuals and we draw a 1% simple random sample without replacement (n=14,683). There are six key variables for the risk assessment: Local Authority (LAD) (11), sex (2), age group (24), marital status (6), ethnicity (17) and economic activity (10) where the numbers of categories of each variable are in parenthesis (J=538,560). There are 2,873 sample uniques under the cross-classified key variables. We implement a random data swap by drawing a 20% sub-sample in each of the LADs. In each of the sub-samples, half of the individuals are flagged. For each flagged individual, an unflagged individual is randomly chosen within the sub-sample and their LAD variables swapped, on condition that the individual chosen was not previously selected for swapping and that the two individuals do not have the same LAD, i.e. no individual is selected twice for producing a swapping pair.

The misclassification matrix θ for the data swapping design of LAD can be expressed in terms of the 11 by 11 misclassification matrix defined by:

(1)   On the diagonal: $\theta_{jj} = 0.8$

(2)   Off the diagonal: $\theta_{jk} = 0.2[n_k / \sum_{l \neq j} n_l]$ where n_k is the number of records in the sample in LAD k.

The number of sample uniques on the misclassified sample is 2,997.

3.2   Identification Risk Based on Probabilistic Frameworks and Modelling

Since we know the misclassification matrix θ and the true population counts F_j in this study, we can compare the naïve risk measure in (3) and under misclassification in (6) based on the probabilistic modelling framework. Table 3 presents global disclosure risk measures for our sample, which are obtained by summing individual per-record risk measures across sample uniques. The first row of Table 3 shows the true disclosure risk τ in terms of the expected number of correct matches in the data before the misclassification. The second row in Table 3 contains the true disclosure risk $\tilde{\tau}_\theta$ in (6) taking into account the misclassification and the third row the estimated disclosure risk measure under misclassification $\hat{\tilde{\tau}}_\theta$ defined by summing $\theta_{jj}\hat{E}(1/\tilde{F}_j/\tilde{f}_j=1)$ across sample uniques. As can be seen, the estimation of the global disclosure risk measure follows closely the true disclosure risk measure (see Skinner and Shlomo, 2008 for a discussion on model selection and goodness of fit criteria for estimating the risk of identification using log-linear modelling).

The individual per-record risk measures for sample uniques as shown in (6) are more difficult to estimate accurately by estimates: $\theta_{jj}\hat{E}(1/\tilde{F}_j/\tilde{f}_j=1)$. Figure 1 compares the individual per-record estimated risk measures $\theta_{jj}\hat{E}(1/\tilde{F}_j/\tilde{f}_j=1)$ on the X-axis with the individual risk measure from (6) assuming known population counts on the Y-axis. The figure is presented on the logarithmic scale.

Table 3. Global risk measures on sample uniques for the 20% random data swap in the probabilistic modelling framework

Global Risk Measure	Expected correct matches out of sample uniques
True risk measure τ in original sample	363.0
Risk measure (6) under misclassification $\tilde{\tau}_\theta$	298.9
Estimated risk measure under misclassification $\hat{\tilde{\tau}}_\theta$	307.7

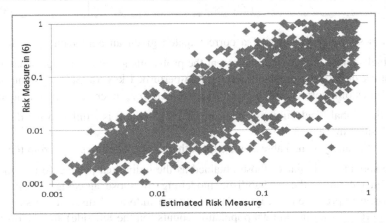

Fig. 1. Individual risk measures for sample uniques shown in (6) and estimated individual risk measure: $\theta_{jj}\hat{E}(1/\tilde{F}_j/\tilde{f}_j=1)$ (logarithmic scale)

Figure 1 confirms that on average, the global disclosure risk measure in (6) is estimated accurately with the graph being symmetrical about the equality diagonal. The individual per-record risk measures however vary and their estimation is less accurate. From the perspective of an intruder who might use log-linear modelling to identify high risk individuals, it would be difficult to ascertain exactly which of the individuals are population uniques.

We turn now to the F&S probabilistic record linkage framework. For our record linkage experiment we block on all key variables that match exactly and calculate the probability of a correct match given an agreement on the perturbed LAD in each block. We focus only on sample uniques in order to compare to the probabilistic modelling framework. All possible pairs between the population dataset and the 2,997 perturbed sample uniques after blocking on all key variables except for LAD results in 1,600,685 possible pairs. Table 4 presents the counts of these pairs under this blocking strategy according to the true match status and the agreement/disagreement indicator on LAD.

From Table 4, the m-probability is 0.78, the u-probability is 0.09   and the probability of a correct match is $p = 0.002$. Note that the m-probability is the same as the overall non-misclassification rate (the diagonal of the misclassification matrix θ). The u-probability represents the proportion of random agreements on LAD (1 out of 11). On average, the probability of a correct match given an agreement on LAD is: $p_{M|\gamma} = 0.016$ or 1.6%.

Table 4. Frequency counts of pairs blocked on agreeing key variables according to agreement/disagreement on LAD and the true match status

	Non-matches	Match	Total
Disagree LAD	1,450,677	659	1,451,336
Agree LAD	147,011	2,338	149,349
Total	1,597,688	2,997	1,600,685

To assess the probability of a correct match given an agreement $p_{M|\gamma}$ for each individual sample unique, we implement the probabilistic record linkage separately in each block defined by cross-classifying non-perturbed key variables. Summing the probabilities of a correct match given an agreement $p_{M|\gamma}$ over the sample uniques, we obtain the global disclosure risk measure of 289.5 which is similar to the disclosure risk measures in Table 3.

From the analysis in Table 2, we expect that the probabilities $p_{M|\gamma}$ from the record linkage should be similar to those obtained as the individual per-record risk measure shown in (6) under the probabilistic modelling for those agreeing on LAD. This comparison is presented in Figure 2 for both the individual disclosure risk measure shown in (6)   assuming known population counts (on the left side) and the estimated disclosure risk measures $\theta_{jj}\hat{E}(1/\tilde{F}_j/\tilde{f}_j = 1)$ (on the right side). The individual disclosure risk measures shown in (6) follow closely the probabilities of a correct match given an agreement $p_{M|\gamma}$ from the F&S framework. In addition, the estimated disclosure risk measures also follow $p_{M|\gamma}$ but with more variance.

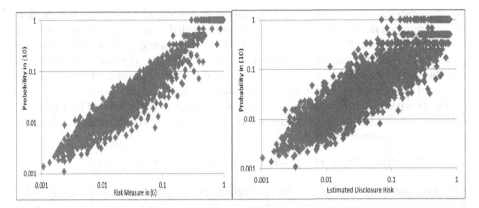

Fig. 2. Plot of $p_{M|\gamma}$ against individual disclosure risk measures shown in (6) (left) and the estimated disclosure risk measure $\theta_{jj}\hat{E}(1/\tilde{F}_j/\tilde{f}_j=1)$ (right) for sample uniques agreeing on LAD (logarithmic scale)

Turning to the estimation of $p_{M|\gamma}$ in the F&S framework, we demonstrate results from the EM algorithm using data from one particular block as shown in Table 5.

Table 5. Frequency counts of pairs within a single block of agreeing key variables according to agreement/disagreement on LAD and true match status

	Non-match	Match	Total
Disagree LAD	916	1	917
Agree LAD	100	3	103
Total	1,016	4	1,020

From Table 5, the true parameters for this particular block are: m-probability is 0.750, u-probability is 0.098, the probability of a correct match is 0.0039 and $\hat{p}_{M|\gamma} = 3/103 = 0.029$. We initiate the EM algorithm with an m-probability of 0.78, u-probability of 0.09 and the probability of a correct match 0.002. Convergence in the EM algorithm means that the sum of the squared change of estimates of the m and u-probabilities between iterations is less than 0.0000001. The estimation of the EM algorithm resulted in: $\hat{m} = 0.798$, $\hat{u} = 0.099$, and $\hat{p} = 0.0022$. From here, we obtain:

$$\hat{p}_{M|\gamma} = \frac{0.0022(0.798)}{0.0022(0.798)+(1-0.0022)(0.099)} = 0.017.$$ As can be seen, it is difficult to estimate the parameters exactly using the EM algorithm. Generally, the EM algorithm will estimate parameters more accurately when there is a large number of pairs and a relatively large number of correct matches (approximately over 5%).

4   Risk-Utility Framework for Assessing Disclosure Limitation Methods

We demonstrate how statistical agencies might assess a disclosure limitation method and its parameters. We focus on random and targeted data swapping with varying rates of perturbation: 2%, 5%, 10% and 20%. Given a measure of information loss, we plot a disclosure risk-data utility map (Duncan, et al. 2001). For disclosure risk, we use the global disclosure risk measure defined in (6). Information loss will be measured by the relative absolute average distance per cell defined as follows:

Let D represent a frequency distribution for a two-way table defined by LAD and Ethnicity and let $D(r,c)$ be the frequency in the cell in row r, $r=1,..R$ and column c, $c=1,...,C$. The distance metric is:

$$RAAD(D_{orig}, D_{pert}) = 1 - \sum_{r,c} |D_{pert}(r,c) - D_{org}(r,c)| / \sum_{r,c} D_{orig}(r,c) \qquad (10)$$

with *pert* and *orig* referring to the perturbed and original table respectively. The *RAAD* provides a measure of the average absolute perturbation per cell compared to the average cell size of the original table.

Figure 3 contains the disclosure risk-data utility map. The points on the map represent different candidate releases of record swapping. The points are denoted by T for targeted or R for random; and 20 for 20%, 10 for 10%, 5 for 5% or 2 for 2%. The points are plotted against the risk measure $\tilde{\tau}_\theta$ in (6) on the Y-Axis and the information loss measure *RAAD* in (10) for LAD*Ethnicity on the X-Axis. We see that for a given level of data utility, we need approximately half of the level of perturbation under the targeted record swapping compared to the random record swapping. Depending on the tolerable risk threshold determined by the agency, the optimal method of record swapping and the swap rate is the one found on the frontier of the disclosure risk-data utility map represented by the connecting line (Gomatam, et al., 2005). This finding could vary in other settings and an agency could use a similar disclosure risk-data utility approach, based on its own data, to determine the preferred disclosure limitation approach.

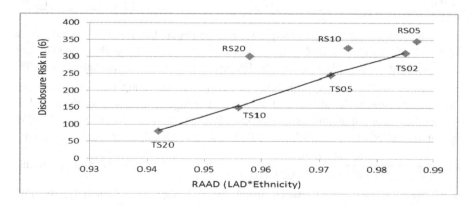

Fig. 3. Disclosure risk-data utility map for record swapping (T – targeted, R – random and 2, 5, 10 and 20 swap rates) for table LAD*Ethnicity

5   Discussion

In this paper, we have provided empirical evidence of the connection between the F&S record linkage framework to the probabilistic modelling framework for estimating the risk of identification based on the notion of population uniqueness as discussed in Skinner (2008). We have seen that statistical agencies are able to estimate accurate global disclosure risk measures that can be used to assess optimal disclosure limitation methods through a disclosure risk-data utility framework assuming that the probability of not being misclassified or perturbed is known, even if there is no population data available.

Individual per-record disclosure risk measures are more difficult to estimate without knowing true population counts in both frameworks. The estimation is carried out through the log linear modelling for the probabilistic modelling framework or the EM algorithm for the F&S record linkage framework. The results show that from the perspective of the 'intruder', it is difficult to identify high risk sample uniques, due to the variability of the estimation of the risk measures.

Acknowlegements. The research leading to these results has received funding from the European Union's Seventh Framework Programme (FP7/2007-2013) under grant agreement n° 262608 (DwB - Data without Boundaries).

References

Brand, R.: Microdata Protection through Noise Addition. In: Domingo-Ferrer, J. (ed.) Inference Control in Statistical Databases. LNCS, vol. 2316, pp. 97–116. Springer, Heidelberg (2002)

Dalenius, T., Reiss, S.P.: Data Swapping: a Technique for Disclosure Control. Journal of Statistical Planning and Inference, 73–85 (1982)

Domingo-Ferrer, J., Torra, V.: A Quantitative Comparison of Disclosure Control Methods for Microdata. In: Doyle, P., Lane, J., Theeuwes, J., Zayatz, L. (eds.) Confidentiality, Disclosure Control and Data Access: Theory and Practical Applications, pp. 111–145. North Holland, Amsterdam (2001)

Duncan, G., Keller-McNulty, S., Stokes, S.: Disclosure Risk vs. Data Utility: the R-U Confidentiality Map. Technical Report LA-UR-01-6428, Statistical Sciences Group. Los Alamos National Laboratory, Los Alamos (2001)

Elamir, E., Skinner, C.J.: Record-Level Measures of Disclosure Risk for Survey Microdata. Journal of Official Statistics 22, 525–539 (2006)

Fellegi, I., Sunter, A.: A Theory for Record Linkage. Journal of the American Statistical Association 64, 1183–1210 (1969)

Fuller, W.: Masking Procedures for Micro-data Disclosure Limitation. Journal of Official Statistics 9, 383–406 (1993)

Gomatam, S., Karr, A., Sanil, A.P.: Data Swapping as a Decision Problem. Journal of Official Statistics 21, 635–655 (2005)

Hawala, S., Stinson, M., Abowd, J.: Disclosure Risk Assessment Through Record Linkage. In: Proceedings of the Joint UNECE/Eurostat Work Session on Statistical Data Confidentiality, Geneva (2005)

Kim, J.J.: A Method for Limiting Disclosure in Micro-data Based on Random Noise and Transformation. In: American Statistical Association, Proceedings of the Section on Survey Research Methods, pp. 370–374 (1986)

Raghunathan, T.E., Reiter, J., Rubin, D.: Multiple Imputation for Statistical Disclosure Limitation. Journal of Official Statistics 19(1), 1–16 (2003)

Skinner, C.: Assessing Disclosure Risk for Record Linkage. In: Domingo-Ferrer, J., Saygın, Y. (eds.) PSD 2008. LNCS, vol. 5262, pp. 166–176. Springer, Heidelberg (2008)

Skinner, C., Holmes, D.: Estimating the Re-identification Risk per Record in Microdata. Journal of Official Statistics 14, 361–372 (1998)

Skinner, C.J., Shlomo, N.: Assessing Identification Risk in Survey Microdata Using Log-linear Models. Journal of the American Statistical Association 103(483), 989–1001 (2008)

Shlomo, N., Skinner, C.J.: Assessing the Protection Provided by Misclassification-Based Disclosure Limitation Methods for Survey Microdata. Annals of Applied Statistics 4(3), 1291–1310 (2010)

Spruill, N.L.: Measures of Confidentiality. In: Proceedings of the Survey Research Methods Section of the American Statistical Association, pp. 260–265 (1982)

Torra, V., Abowd, J.M., Domingo-Ferrer, J.: Using mahalanobis distance-based record linkage for disclosure risk assessment. In: Domingo-Ferrer, J., Franconi, L. (eds.) PSD 2006. LNCS, vol. 4302, pp. 233–242. Springer, Heidelberg (2006)

Willenborg, L.C.R.J., De Waal, T.: Elements of Statistical Disclosure Control in Practice. Lecture Notes in Statistics, vol. 155. Springer, New York (2001)

Yancey, W.E., Winkler, W.E., Creecy, R.H.: Disclosure Risk Assessment in Perturbation Micro-Data Protection. In: Domingo-Ferrer, J. (ed.) Inference Control in Statistical Databases. LNCS, vol. 2316, pp. 135–151. Springer, Heidelberg (2002)

Hierarchical Linkage Clustering with Distributions of Distances for Large-Scale Record Linkage

Samuel L. Ventura and Rebecca Nugent

Carnegie Mellon University, Department of Statistics

Abstract. Distance-based clustering techniques such as hierarchical clustering use a single estimate of distance for each pair of observations; their results then rely on the accuracy of this estimate. However, in many applications, datasets include measurement error or are too large for traditional models, meaning a single estimate of distance between two observations may be subject to error or computationally prohibitive to calculate. For example, in many of today's large-scale record linkage problems, datasets are prohibitively large, making distance estimates computationally infeasible. By using a distribution of distance estimates instead (e.g. from an ensemble of classifiers trained on subsets of record-pairs), these issues may be resolved. We present a large-scale record linkage framework that incorporates classifier ensembles and "distribution linkage" clustering to identify clusters of records corresponding to unique entities. We examine the performance of several different distributional summary measures in hierarchical clustering. We motivate and illustrate this approach with an application of record linkage to the United States Patent and Trademark Office database.

1 Introduction

Hierarchical linkage clustering provides an intuitive solution to identifying clusters of observations given the pairwise distances (or dissimilarities) between all observations in a dataset [11]. Distance measure examples include Euclidean, Manhattan, and Mahalonobis as well as covariate-weighted versions. Although any distance measure between two observations can be used for hierarchical clustering, typically each pair of observations is assigned only one estimate of the distance between them. As such, any clustering results we obtain heavily rely on the accuracy of this single estimate which may be prone to error. For example, humans often round to the nearest 5 pounds or 15 minutes when asked for their weight or the time of day; instruments used to record location may be subject to random or measurement error. By allowing for multiple estimates of the distance between each pair of observations, i.e. a distribution of distances, we may be able to more accurately identify the true clusters.

In the record linkage literature, the need for adapting clustering methodology to distributions of distances is especially important. Briefly, record linkage is the

J. Domingo-Ferrer (Ed.): PSD 2014, LNCS 8744, pp. 283–298, 2014.

process of identifying unique entities across multiple data sources or within a single data source. For example, the United States Patent and Trademark Office (USPTO) maintains a database of all issued patents and their corresponding inventors. However, inventors are not assigned unique identification numbers, making it difficult to track innovation or productivity across patents. Record linkage is often applied to identify each unique inventor's patents [19, 9, 15].

Some authors describe record linkage as a clustering problem [18, 19, 16]. For the USPTO, the observations to be clustered are all records of every inventor on each patent, and the clusters are the sets of patents belonging to the underlying unique inventors. A supervised learning approach assigns a distance to two records by modeling and predicting the probability of two records referring to the same unique individual [18, 19, 16, 10]. The higher the probability of a match, the smaller the distance between records. These techniques recover the unique inventors' clusters of records well when working with problems of computationally tractable size. However, as large-scale record linkage problems become more ubiquitous (e.g. the USPTO has over eight million patents and so 32 trillion pairs of records), it quickly becomes computationally infeasible to train a single model on the entire training dataset [19]. In these cases, a single "best" estimate of the distance between records is unattainable.

While many "divide-and-conquer" strategies might suggest partitioning the data and training a model on each subset, most commonly the set of probabilities/distances from the resulting model ensemble would be averaged. However, this approach inherently assumes that the distribution of estimates is symmetric and centered around the true distance – very often not the case. We propose a formal approach for hierarchical clustering when there exist distributions of distance estimates. Appropriate estimates of the true distance between each pair of observations are adaptively selected based on features of the corresponding distribution of distances. While the specific approach presented here was motivated by a need for computationally tractable large-scale record linkage solutions, the general framework could be used for any similar clustering problem.

After first describing the USPTO record linkage problem (Section 2), we discuss a large-scale classification technique that trains classifiers on partitions of the data (Section 3). Next, we present a hierarchical clustering framework called "distribution linkage" (Section 4). We detail the distribution linkage algorithm (Section 4.2.1) and examine the efficacy of several approaches for summarizing a distribution of distances (Section 4.2.3). We apply these approaches to simulated datasets (Section 4.2.2) and to a labeled subset of the USPTO (Section 5).

2   Record Linkage in the USPTO

Deduplication (or "Disambiguation") refers to the process of identifying records belonging to unique entities in a single database. Like most record linkage methods, approaches to deduplication typically compare the values of shared fields to determine whether or not records should be linked. Perhaps the most well-known large-scale deduplication problems are associated with the United States

Census Bureau, where deduplicating national surveys such as the Decennial Census survey is an ongoing research problem [21]. Deduplication in these large-scale settings requires emphasis on computationally feasible method development. Despite the similarities, standard record linkage methods such as [8], which assumes a one-to-one matching across two databases, cannot be trivially applied to deduplication problems, where duplicated entities occur within the same list.

2.1 Name Disambiguation

A common application of deduplication methods is the identification of unique authors in bibliographic data, or "author name disambiguation." This is an important problem across many disciplines; for example, many bibliographic databases do not include unique identifiers that can link authors across their publications, ensuring appropriate attribution of each author's work. [17] and [18] use semi-supervised and supervised learning methods (respectively) for disambiguating authors in MEDLINE, a database of over 15 million medical journal articles. [10] compare two supervised learning approaches for disambiguating publication lists from researchers' webpages and 300,000 Digital Bibliographic Library Database citations. Although not applied to a bibliographic database, [16] presents a supervised learning approach for duplicate detection of over 1,200 geospatial dictionary and digital gazetteer records.

2.2 Disambiguating USPTO Inventors

The USPTO database contains information from over 8 million patents and is in need of ongoing disambiguation, particularly of its inventors. [6] identify unique inventors using an unsupervised Bayesian approach and evaluate the results with a benchmark dataset of manually disambiguated patents for 445 French scholars. Lee Fleming and his research group first provide a disambiguated version of the USPTO database publicly available for researchers [14, 15]. However, approaches similar to [14] use heuristic decision rules and do not build models using training data; as a result, they can yield systematic false positive and/or false negative errors when matching records [19]. Additionally, [15] can yield inconsistent disambiguation error metrics when applied to different datasets [19]. Our approach takes advantage of a set of labeled USPTO inventor records and employs a supervised learning approach designed to minimize and balance false positive and false negative errors for estimating the distance between pairs of records.

2.3 Labeled USPTO Records

To build our supervised models, we use a set of USPTO inventor records labeled with unique identifiers from [1]. An "inventor record" is a record of an inventor on a particular patent in the USPTO database. Note that a single patent can have multiple inventors (and thus, multiple inventor records). Similarly, a single inventor can have multiple patents (and thus, multiple inventor records that need to be disambiguated). In Table 1, we see examples of common difficulties with deduplication: spelling/typographical errors ("Stanford" vs. "Stanfrod"), name variations ("David A. Miller" vs. "David Andrew Miller"), repetition of common names ("David Miller"), and abbreviations ("UNC").

Table 1. Example of Labeled USPTO Inventor Records

ID	Last	First	Middle	City	St	Assignee	ID
1	Millar	David	A.	Stanford	CA	Stanford University	1001
2	Miller	David	A.	Fair Haven	NJ	UNC	1001
3	Miller	David	A.B.	Stanford	CA	Stanfrod University	1001
4	Miller	David	Andrew	Stanford	CA	Lucent Technologies	1001
5	Miller	David	Andrew	Fair Haven	NJ	Lucent Technologes	1001
6	Miller	David	B.	Los Angeles	CA	Agilent Technologies	1001
7	Miller	David	D.	Billerca	MA	Lucent Technologies	NA

The final hand-disambiguated dataset has 98,762 labeled inventor records; 14,520 are matched to one of 824 unique CV inventors, and 84,242 fail to map to any of our CV inventors [19]. We use these labeled inventor records to (1) train classification models to find predicted probabilities that pairs of records match (Section 3.2) and (2) evaluate deduplication approaches (Section 5).

3   Classification in Large-Scale Training Data Scenarios

We begin by introducing notation for comparing pairs of records. Next, we review decision trees and related approaches and discuss why they are intuitive for comparing pairs of records (Section 3.2). Then, we introduce our ensemble approach to large-scale decision tree classification via subsampling (Section 3) and discuss aggregating a distribution of predicted probabilities (Section 3.4). Finally, note that while other classification techniques exist, previous work has shown decision tree approaches, and random forests in particular, to be the most effective at modeling matches in sets of record-pairs [19, 18, 10, 16]. As such, we focus on random forests here, although any classifier could be used in this ensemble framework.

3.1   Comparing Pairs of Records

In most record linkage and disambiguation algorithms, the operation of interest is the comparison of two records. Each pairwise comparison quantifies the similarity of two records using a set of similarity scores. Similar to [8], we define these similarity scores as follows: Let x_i be the ith record in the database, where $i = 1, 2, ..., n$. Then, γ_{ijm} is the similarity of records x_i, x_j according to field m, where $m = 1, 2, ..., M$. We denote the vector of all M similarities for records x_i, x_j as $\gamma_{ij} = \langle \gamma_{ij1}, ..., \gamma_{ijM} \rangle$.

Similarity scores for deduplication can take several different forms. Depending on the type of field being compared (e.g. long string, short string), similarity scores can be either continuous or binary. We give an overview of the specific set of similarity scores we use for this work in Appendix B. Our similarity scores are motivated by previous work in the USPTO inventor disambiguation [14, 15].

3.2 Classification Trees and Random Forests

Briefly, classification trees build decision trees from a set of covariates by determining cutpoints in the covariates that best separate the classes of a categorical response variable [12]. [5] showed that a random forest, or an ensemble of classification trees trained on bootstrap samples of the training data and covariates, is a powerful method of aggregating classification trees to improve prediction in the decision tree framework.

An advantage of this approach is that the decision tree framework is an intuitive solution to the problem of determining links between pairs of records, since the if-else structure of a decision tree mimics the way a human would make match/non-match decisions. Many heuristic approaches to deduplication and record linkage use "decision trees" with ad hoc, hand-chosen cutpoints [9, 14]. Classification trees and random forests formalize this approach statistically, using training data to choose cutpoints by optimizing according to some criterion rather than some heuristic belief about what constitutes a match.

3.3 Forest of Random Forests

Despite the empirical success of random forests at deduplicating inventors, it is computationally infeasible to train a single random forest on millions of pairwise comparisons. Using multiple random forest classifiers may be more computationally feasible but requires careful consideration of the match probability distributions to have reasonable results without substantially sacrificing accuracy.

Forest of Random Forests (FoRF) is our proposed approach when in the presence of prohibitively large training datasets. We first partition the training data into R random subsets[1] Let F_r be the random forest trained on subset $r = 1, ..., R$, and let $F = \{F_r\}_{r=1}^{R}$ be the FoRF.

3.4 Prediction with FoRF

In a classification tree f_t, the probability of each class g for observation x is equal to the number of training data observations in class g at the terminal node of x divided by $n(x, f_t)$, the total number of training data observations at that terminal node. The predicted class, $\hat{g}_{f_t}(x)$, is the class with the highest

---

[1] We use random partitioning in an effort to generate similar match probability and distance estimates. Alternative sampling methods could be used, e.g. the approach of [13], but any introduced bias would need to be addressed when characterizing the distribution for use in clustering. We can also sample separately from the matches and non-matches to maintain the ratio of matches to non-matches across each subset, e.g. for situations where there are not many matches in the training data.

probability. One potential issue is that some branches may contain very few observations, so the class probabilities may be unreliable. Prediction with random forests mitigates this issue by training T classification trees and aggregating their predictions. For random forest F_r with T trees, the probability that x has class g is equal to the number of trees that predicted class g divided by T. The predicted class of the random forest, $\hat{g}_{F_r}(x)$ is the class with the highest probability.

Prediction with a set of random forests, however, is not quite as straightforward. Since we have potentially RT predicted probabilities, there are many natural aggregation options, such as (1) the class with the highest mean probability across all RT tress, (2) the class with the majority vote across all RT trees, or (3) the class with the majority vote across all R random forests. However, we argue that there is no single best representative measure for each group of predictions. Some distributions of predicted probabilities may be tightly symmetric; others may be skewed or multimodal. In all cases, the end goal is to use the distribution of predicted probabilities to help us determine the true "distance" between records and thereby the true inventor clusters of records.

4   Hierarchical Clustering with Distributions of Distances

Clustering is used commonly in statistics and machine learning to find groups of similar observations within a dataset. Generally, clustering algorithms seek to place observations with high similarity (low dissimilarity or "distance") into the same group, or "cluster," while splitting observations with low similarity (high dissimilarity/distance) into different clusters [11].

As described in Section 1, there are real-world scenarios and datasets where multiple estimates of distance (or distributions of distances) exist. How can we extract the appropriate distances from these distributions? Rather than use the mean, we examine a more adaptive way to summarize the distribution and provide a framework for hierarchical clustering with distributions of distances.

4.1   Hierarchical Linkage Clustering

Hierarchical linkage clustering relies on a distance matrix D. Given a set of n observations, D contains the distance between all $\binom{n}{2}$ pairs of observations. These distances are arranged into the lower triangle of an $n \times n$ matrix D, where $D_{[i,j]} = d_{ij} = dist(x_i, x_j), \forall i, j \in \{1, 2, ..., n\}$ s.t. $1 < j < i < n$. The Euclidean distance, $dist(x_i, x_j) = \sqrt{\sum_{k=1}^{p}(x_{i,k} - x_{j,k})^2}$, is often used to measure the distance between observations in p-dimensional space. With hierarchical clustering, however, any appropriate measure of distance or dissimilarity can be used.

Algorithms for hierarchical clustering can be agglomerative, where each observation starts in its own cluster and subsequently merges with others, or divisive, where all observations start in the same cluster and are subsequently split into separate clusters. Single linkage and complete linkage hierarchical clustering are commonly used types of agglomerative hierarchical clustering.

With any linkage method, hierarchical clustering gives a set of clusterings described by a dendrogram. The dendrogram can be "cut" at a given distance threshold or height τ to extract clusters; any pair of observations with distance lower than τ are considered to be in the same cluster. As τ increases, the number of clusters decreases.

4.2   Distribution Linkage

In our record linkage example, there are R models and so R model-based estimates of the distance between each pair of records. For consistency, we will assume that regardless of the application, there are R estimates of distance between every pair of records. Ultimately, we use features of these sets of distances to recover the cluster structure in the data.

4.2.1   Algorithm
In the context of our supervised learning approach to record linkage, the distribution of distances is obtained directly from the distribution of predicted probabilities of matching from our classifier ensemble (Section 3).

Formally, let $\hat{p}_{ij} = \langle \hat{p}_{ij1}, \hat{p}_{ij2}, ..., \hat{p}_{ijR} \rangle$ be the set of R estimated pairwise probabilities of matching for records x_i, x_j (Section 3.4); let the corresponding set of R estimated distances be $\hat{d}_{ij} = \langle \hat{d}_{ij1}, \hat{d}_{ij2}, ..., \hat{d}_{ijR} \rangle = h(\hat{p}_{ij})$. Note that $0 \le \hat{p}_{ijr} \le 1$, and h is a monotonically decreasing function of the probabilities. Thus, $[h(1) \le \hat{d}_{ijr} \le h(0)]$. Then, let $\hat{f}_{ij}(\hat{d}_{ij})$ refer to this estimated distribution of distances such that $\hat{f}_{ij}$ is also defined on the set $[h(1), h(0)]^2$.

Now, let $\delta(\hat{f}_{ij})$ be some measure on the distribution of distances, $\hat{f}_{ij}$, that returns an approximation, d_{ij}^*, of the "true" distance between records x_i, x_j. For example, different quantiles of $\hat{f}_{ij}$ may better approximate the true distance than the distribution's mean, depending on features of the distribution (e.g. skew). As such, δ may return the distance corresponding to, e.g., a quantile of the distribution, given the distribution's skew. Given some δ, we propose the following algorithm for "distribution linkage" hierarchical clustering[3]:

1. Calculate $\hat{p}_{ij}$ and transform to $\hat{d}_{ij}$ for all pairs x_i, x_j using h (i.e. $\hat{d}_{ij} = h(\hat{p}_{ij})$)
2. Calculate $\hat{f}_{ij}$, the distribution of distances
3. Build D^*, the distance matrix with $D_{[i,j]}^* = d_{ij}^* = \delta(\hat{f}_{ij})$
4. Find the hierarchical clustering solution for D^* corresponding to the choice of linkage function (single, complete, minimax[2], etc)
5. Cut the resulting hierarchical clustering tree at a level τ to find the clusters

---

[2] For example, let $\hat{f}_{ij}(x) = \frac{1}{\omega R} \sum_{r=1}^{R} K(\frac{x - \hat{d}_{ijr}}{\omega})$ be the kernel density estimator for x, where K is some kernel (e.g. the Gaussian kernel). We drop the bandwidth ω for simplicity; choosing a bandwidth is a common problem but not the focus here.

[3] We use the term "distribution linkage" to refer to hierarchical linkage clustering using distributions of distances. "Distribution" refers to the multiple estimates of distance; any linkage type (e.g. single linkage) can be used in this procedure.

For record linkage, we use $h(x) = 1 - x$ so that high probabilities (near 1) map to low distances (near 0), and low probabilities (near 0) map to high distances (near 1). Using single linkage, the hierarchical clustering solution can be found by calculating the minimal spanning tree – a computationally efficient calculation using algorithms such as Prim's or Kruskal's – and breaking the tree into groups of observations at a distance threshold τ [11]. We use single linkage because of it is equivalent to enforcing transitivity of pairwise matches at a distance threshold τ (or a probability threshold $h^{-1}(\tau)$), a useful property for record linkage.

Now, our task is to find a suitable function δ. That is, what measure δ on the distribution of distances should be used to represent d_{ij}^*? Figure 1 shows match probability distributions with differing characteristics for three record-pairs.

For the distribution of match probabilities in Figure 1a, the choice of δ is likely inconsequential, since the distribution has little variance and one large mode near one, a likely match. However, for Figures 1bc, the choice of δ could substantially change the probability (or distance) used for that pair. In Figure 1b, the distribution is right-skewed, with mode at low match probability. However, the right-tail mode occurs above 0.5, indicating a possible matching record-pair. What summary measure δ is most appropriate here? Similarly, in Figure 1c, the distribution of probabilities has two large modes, with mass on either side of the commonly-used 0.5 match threshold. Additionally, the distribution mean occurs in the valley between the two modes. The appropriate decision is not obvious.

4.2.2   Distribution Linkage with Simulated Data

To illustrate, we use an artificial, well-separated two cluster example (Figure 2) and simulate distance distributions with varying features. In doing so, we hope to draw connections between the distributional features and an appropriate measure δ. In particular, we first try summarizing the distributions of distances via quantiles. In our simulations, we find that for distributions with left (right) skew, lower (higher) quantiles are more effective at producing well-separated groups of observations.

For record linkage, recall that the match probabilities and corresponding distances are on $[0,1]$. As such, we simulate from the *Beta* distribution given its appropriate range and to take advantage of its flexibility. For our two cluster data set, we first scale all the distances to be on $[0,1]$. Then for each pair of observations, we might combine the scaled distance with simulated draws from, say, a $Beta(2,8)$ to create a right-skewed distribution (Figure 3) such that the distribution mean is equal to the scaled Euclidean distance between the pair.

We then explore how distribution linkage hierarchical clustering performs when using $\delta(\hat{f}_{ij}) = Q_{0.05}(\hat{f}_{ij})$ (Figure 3a), $\delta(\hat{f}_{ij}) = \mu(\hat{f}_{ij})$ (Figure 3b), and $\delta(\hat{f}_{ij}) = Q_{0.95}(\hat{f}_{ij})$ (Figure 3c), where $Q_q(y)$ returns the qth quantile of a distribution y, and $\mu(y)$ returns the mean. We build a distance matrix D^* for each of the three δ measures above and, for visualization purposes, project these into two-dimensional latent space using multi-dimensional scaling (MDS), colored by the true groups. If the δ measure is appropriate, we should see two well-separated groups. We also plot the corresponding single linkage dendrograms.

The 5th quantile does not separate the groups well for this right-skewed distribution of distances. The 95th quantile yields the best visual separation of the groups, though it appears similar to that of the mean. Although this is just one example, our simulations have shown a general relationship between skew and "best" quantile. For right-skewed distributions, using higher quantiles for δ yields distance matrices that better maintain the structure of the original data than does using lower quantiles. We find an analogous result for left-skewed distributions of distances. However, can we say which is the "optimal" quantile for a given distance distribution? We examine this issue next.

4.2.3   Finding the Optimal Quantile

We repeat the previous simulation 10,000 times, randomly varying the α and β parameters of the *Beta* noise distribution between 1 and 15 to simulate unimodal distributions with different skews. In Figure 4, we show that as right-skew increases (x-axis), the "optimal quantile" (y-axis) increases above the median. (Similarly, as the left-skew increases, the optimal quantile decreases below the median.) Here, we define the optimal quantile as the quantile of the distribution of distances that minimizes the stress coefficient [12] of D^* vs. D, where D^* is the quantile-distance matrix, and D is the "true" distance matrix of the simulated data obtained from the scaled Euclidean distances. We use the method of moments to estimate the α, β, and corresponding skew of the distribution of distances.

Note that this relationship tails off for extreme values of skew, as you might expect, since the quantiles are bounded between 0 and 1. Given this observed relationship, we explore the idea of defining δ to be dependent on the skew of the distribution of distances, $\hat{f}_{ij}$. That is, we choose $\delta(y) = Q_{q^*}(y)$, where the optimal stress-minimizing quantile q^* is obtained by modeling $q^*|skew$ (Figure 4). We model the relationship with a nonparametric regression model using the simulated data and then subsequently predict/choose the optimal quantile given the distributional skew for any pair of observations. Our q_{ij}^* then adapts to the distribution of distances $(\hat{f}_{ij})$ for records x_i, x_j.

5   Results

We illustrate the results of distribution linkage and our FoRF classifier using the labeled USPTO inventor records. We train three models: RF, a random forest trained on 50,000 labeled training pairs; $FoRF_{small}$, a FoRF with $R = 30$, where each of the R random forests is trained on roughly 50,000/30 pairs; and $FoRF_{big}$, a FoRF with $R = 30$, where each of the R random forests is trained on 50,000 pairs. We ensure that the number of terminal nodes in each decision tree is the same (20), so that the underlying decision trees are trained at the same depth regardless of the size of the training data sample.

For the RF and $FoRF_{small}$, we limit the number of pairwise comparisons to ensure computational feasibility and a fair comparison. In practice. the $FoRF_{big}$ is the more common scenario for distribution linkage, and we naturally would expect improved performance with the increased sample size. We examine the agreement rates between FoRF and RF for several different distributional summary measures δ. We also compare results for linking USPTO records with a specific focus on record pairs whose match status is more difficult to predict.

5.1   Agreement Rates between FoRF and Random Forests

Table 2 shows the agreement rates between RF and both $FoRF_{small}$ and $FoRF_{big}$ where $\delta =$ the mean or the optimal quantile. Since FoRF is simply an ensemble variation of random forests and given the large sample size, we expect that the two FoRF models will have high agreement rates with the single random forest.

Table 2. Agreement Rates for FoRF and Random Forest

Model	δ	Agreement Rate (%)
$FoRF_{small}$	$\delta(y) = \mu(y)$	99.92
$FoRF_{small}$	$\delta(y) = Q_{q^*}(y)$	99.86
$FoRF_{big}$	$\delta(y) = \mu(y)$	99.98
$FoRF_{big}$	$\delta(y) = Q_{q^*}(y)$	99.80

In fact, the RF agreement rates are very high for both FoRF models for either δ measure. This behavior is expected, for example, since many record-pairs are easily modeled as matches or non-matches; however, it also gives some evidence that, when faced with a prohibitively large data set, we can rely on the FoRF-distribution linkage combination to give results similar to those of a RF (if an RF were feasible).

We further examine these results in Figure 5 by visualizing example distributions of distances from each FoRF model in comparison to the RF predicted distance. In doing so, we expect that both FoRF models will yield distributions of predicted distances centered near the predicted distance from random forests. We also expect the $FoRF_{small}$ model to have more variability, since its underlying random forests were built using substantially smaller training datasets.

In Figure 5a, the distance distributions from $FoRF_{small}$ and $FoRF_{big}$ are fairly symmetric for the example record-pair. The predicted RF distance is near the center of the distribution of $FoRF_{big}$. The optimal quantile for $FoRF_{big}$ is also very close to the random forests prediction, indicating that the two methods yield similar results. For $FoRF_{small}$, the predicted distances are slightly higher than that of the random forests model, likely because $FoRF_{small}$ had less training data and may be subject to more variability. Note that both $FoRF$s and the RF would suggest possibly a match (recall distance = 1 - match probability).

In Figure 5b, the record pair is not a match. Notice that the $FoRF_{small}$ distance distribution is left-skewed. As such, the optimal quantile approach for δ chooses a lower quantile of the distribution, as expected, but still representative of the true distance between the records. The distribution of distances from the $FoRF_{big}$ model has little variability and is centered near the RF prediction.

5.2   Distribution Linkage and FoRF for USPTO Record Linkage

Table 3 shows the false positive and false negative error rates for USPTO record linkage using a FoRF to obtain distributions of predicted pairwise probabilities of matching and distribution (single) linkage to cluster the records. We compare both FoRF models to the RF model. We expect that each approach will yield similar results, with random forests and $FoRF_{big}$ outperforming $FoRF_{small}$ since these were built using larger training datasets. (Again, note that we are using a computationally feasible subset; in practice, the $FoRF_{big}$ would be used to analyze the entire labeled USPTO data set.)

Table 3. Performance of FoRF and Random Forest for Record Linkage

Model	δ	FNR (%)	FPR (%)
Random Forests	NA	0.93	2.30
$FoRF_{small}$	$\delta(y) = \mu(y)$	1.51	2.23
$FoRF_{small}$	$\delta(y) = Q_{q^*}(y)$	1.61	2.49
$FoRF_{big}$	$\delta(y) = \mu(y)$	1.00	2.30
$FoRF_{big}$	$\delta(y) = Q_{q^*}(y)$	1.81	2.92

RF yields lower false positive and false negative error rates than both FoRF models in this subset example. However, note that $FoRF_{small}$ yields a lower false positive error rate than RF, though this difference is minimal. As expected, $FoRF_{big}$ yields lower overall error rates than $FoRF_{small}$ when δ is chosen to be the mean of the distribution of distances (similar false positive error rate and an improved false negative error rate). Interestingly, $FoRF_{small}$ yields lower error rates than $FoRF_{big}$ when δ is chosen to be the optimal quantile of the distribution of distances according to both error rates.

Finally, note that random forest predictions are subject to error due to the randomly chosen subsets of training data and features for each of the underlying decision trees. As discussed in [12], the variance of a random forest is a function of the sampling variance of any underlying tree and the sampling correlation between pairs of the underlying trees. Additionally, the bias of a random forest is the same as that of the underlying trees. These bias and variance properties will be similar for FoRF, since FoRF is just a combination of R random forests. The exact theoretical bias and variance properties are the subject of future work

5.3   Distribution Linkage for Difficult-to-Link Pairs

In the previous section, our results did not provide strong evidence for using the optimal quantile approach versus aggregating using the mean. The results proved to be similar in performance, but this was not unexpected. The optimal quantile approach is flexible and adapts to the distributions at hand. Many record pairs are obvious matches or non-matches with FoRF distributions near one or zero; in these cases, using either the optimal quantile or the mean will give essentially the same results. Where the optimal approach might gain an advantage is when analyzing record pairs that are less obvious or have asymmetric, multimodal distributions of probabilities (distances).

Here we evaluate using a set of difficult-to-link "coin flip" record-pairs, which includes 987 pairs with probability of matching $0.45 < \hat{p}_{ijr} < 0.55$. Distribution linkage and $FoRF_{big}$ with the optimal quantile δ outperforms the other approaches by a slight margin for this subgroup of difficult-to-link record-pairs, suggesting a possible targeting strategy of focusing the optimal search where needed the most.

Table 4. Performance of FoRF and Random Forest on Difficult-to-Link Pairs

Model	δ	Percent Correct (%)
Random Forests	NA	77.28
$FoRF_{small}$	$\delta(y) = \mu(y)$	76.11
$FoRF_{small}$	$\delta(y) = Q_{q^*}(y)$	76.11
$FoRF_{big}$	$\delta(y) = \mu(y)$	79.04
$FoRF_{big}$	$\delta(y) = Q_{q^*}(y)$	81.26

6   Discussion

Hierarchical linkage clustering relies on the accuracy of a single estimate of distance to link observations and provide a hierarchy of clustering solutions. In practice, a single estimate of distance (e.g. Euclidean distance) may not best represent the true distance between a pair of observations.

We use a large-scale classification framework called "Forest of Random Forests" (FoRF), which allows computationally intensive classifiers like random forests to be built in large-scale training data scenarios. We then provide a framework for applying hierarchical clustering when there exist distributions of distances. We show that the optimal quantile of the distribution of distances can depend on the skew of the distribution. We apply our distribution linkage hierarchical clustering approach for record linkage, using distributions of distances obtained from two FoRF classifiers, to a large-scale record linkage problem in the United States Patent and Trademark Office database. We show that this approach yields false positive and false negative error rates similar to those of common record linkage approaches using hierarchical clustering and a single distance estimate from random forests. We also show that this approach yields lower error rates for "coinflip" record-pairs, which are difficult to disambiguate based on their pairwise probabilities of matching.

In future work, we will examine different choices for δ and include more features of the distribution (e.g. modality, range, etc) in our model that chooses the optimal quantile, in hopes that we can better predict the optimal quantile of a distribution of distances. We will also take into account the distribution of decision tree probabilities/distances within each random forest, since these distributions contain a substantially larger number of underlying distances.

References

[1] Akinsanmi, E., Reagans, R., Fuchs, E.: Economic Downturns, Technology Trajectories, and the Careers of Scientists (2012)

[2] Bien, J., Tibshirani, R.: Hierarchical Clustering With Prototypes via Minimax Linkage. Annals of Eugenics, 1075–1084 (2012)

[3] Bilenko, M., Mooney, R.J.: Adaptive Duplicate Detection Using Learnable String Similarity Metrics. In: Proceedings of ACM Conference on Knowledge Discovery and Data Mining, Washington, DC, pp. 39–48 (2003)

[4] Bilenko, M., Mooney, R., Cohen, W., Ravikumar, P., Fienberg, S.E.: Adaptive Name Matching in Information Integration. IEEE Intelligent Systems 18, 16–23 (2003)

[5] Breiman, L.: Random Forests. Machine Learning 45(1), 5–32 (2001)

[6] Carayol, N., Cassi, L.: Who's Who in Patents: A Bayesian approach (2009)

[7] Christen, P.: A comparison of personal name matching: techniques and practical issues (2006)

[8] Fellegi, I.P., Sunter, A.B.: A Theory for Record Linkage. Journal of the American Statistical Association 64(328) (1969)

[9] Fleming, L., King III, C., Juda, A.: Small Worlds and Regional Innovation. Organizational Science (2007)

[10] Han, H., Giles, L., Zha, H., Li, C., Tsioutsiouliklis, K.: Two Supervised Learning Approaches for Name Disambiguation in Author Citations. In: Joint Conference on Digital Libraries (2004)

[11] Hartigan, J.A.: Clustering Algorithms. John Wiley & Sons, New York (1975)

[12] Hastie, T., Tibshirani, R., Friedman, J.: The Elements of Statistical Learning: Data Mining, Inference, and Prediction, 2nd edn. Springer (2009)

[13] Kleiner, A., Talwalkar, A., Sarkar, P., Jordan, M.I.: A Scalable Bootstrap for Massive Data (2012)

[14] Lai, R., D'Amour, A., Fleming, L.: The careers and co-authorship networks of U.S. patent-holders, since 1975 (2009)

[15] Lai, R., D'Amour, A., Yu, A., Sun, Y., Fleming, L.: Disambiguation and Co-authorship Networks of the U.S. Patent Inventor Database (2014)

[16] Martins, B.: A Supervised Machine Learning Approach for Duplicate Detection over Gazetteer Records. In: Claramunt, C., Levashkin, S., Bertolotto, M. (eds.) GeoS 2011. LNCS, vol. 6631, pp. 34–51. Springer, Heidelberg (2011)

[17] Torvik, V., Smalheiser, N.: Author Name Disambiguation in MEDLINE. ACM Transactions on Knowledge Discovery from Data 3(3) (2009)

[18] Treeratpituk, P., Giles, C.L.: Disambiguating Authors in Academic Publications using Random Forests. In: Joint Conference on Digital Libaries (2009)

[19] Ventura, S.L., Nugent, R., Fuchs, E.: Methods Matter: Rethinking Inventor Disambiguation Algorithms with Classification Models and Labeled Inventor Records (2014)

[20] Winkler, W.E.: String Comparator Metrics and Enhanced Decision Rules in the Fellegi-Sunter Model of Record Linkage. In: Proceedings of the Section on Survey Research Methods (American Statistical Association), pp. 354–359 (1990)

[21] Winkler, W.E.: Matching and Record Linkage. In: Business Survey Methods, pp. 355–384. J. Wiley, New York (1995)

A   Figures

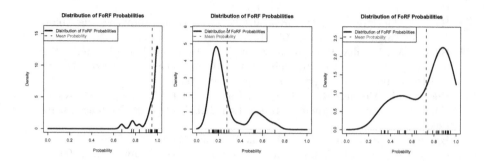

Fig. 1. Distribution of Estimated Probabilities

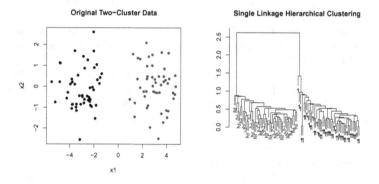

Fig. 2. Simulated Two-Cluster Data and Dendrogram

B   Comparing Two Inventor Records

In disambiguation, we compare pairs of inventor records and determine if each pair is a match (the same unique inventor) or a non-match (two non-unique inventors). Several authors have analyzed the best approaches to comparing different types of fields (names, companies, locations, etc) for record linkage and disambiguation purposes. We direct interested readers to the works of [3], [4], and [7], among several others.

We describe the similarity of each field with a numerical value indicating how closely two records match. For the purposes of this paper, we define all of these "similarity scores" as γ_{ijk}, which represents the similarity score of records x_i and x_j according to field m, where $i, j \in \{1, 2, ..., n\}, m \in \{1, 2, ..., M\}, M =$ the number of unique fields being compared, and $n =$ the number of records in the database. We define similarity scores for long strings, short strings, and lists.

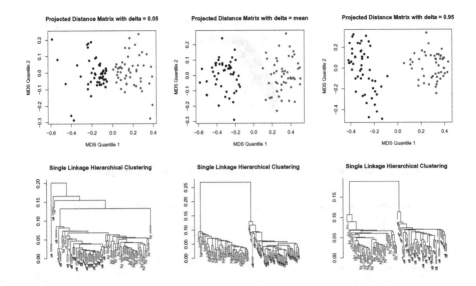

Fig. 3. Distribution Linkage with Right-Skewed Distribution of Distances: Figures 3(a–c) show MDS projections of the distance matrices created using three different δ measures: the 0.05 quantile, the mean, and the 0.95 quantile. Figures 3(d–f) show the resulting hierarchical clustering dendrograms obtained from applying distribution linkage with each of these three δ measures.

B.1   Long Text Strings: Inventor, City, and Assignee Names

Long strings, such as assignee and inventor names, are susceptible to typographical errors and name variations. For example, "David" vs. "Dave" do not match using simple exact matching. More advanced string comparison methods are necessary.

The Jaro-Winkler string comparison (JW) method takes two strings as input and compares the characters and positions of matching characters across two strings [20]. The result is a score between 0 and 1 (inclusive) that indicates how similar two strings are to each other; if two strings are an exact match, their JW score will be 1. The mathematical details of the calculation of JW scores are given in [20]. For our dataset, the long string fields are first name, last name, middle name, assignee name, and inventor city. Several other string comparison metrics exist, such as Token-based similarities, Metaphone, N-grams, Levenshtein, and still several others. Other string comparison metrics were tried, but did not improve our models or results.

B.2   Short Text Strings: State, Country, and Name Suffix

If field m is a short string, we define the similarity score as follows. Given two short strings X_{im} and X_{jm} for inventors i and j and field m, $\gamma_{ijm} = 1$ if $X_{im} = X_{jm}$, and $\gamma_{ijm} = 0$ if $X_{im} \neq X_{jm}$. That is, we check pairs of short strings for exact matches only.

Short string fields include the inventor name suffix, inventor state, and inventor country. We use exact matching for these fields because they are generally not suscep-

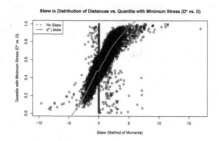

Fig. 4. Distributional Skew vs. Optimal Stress-Reducing Quantile

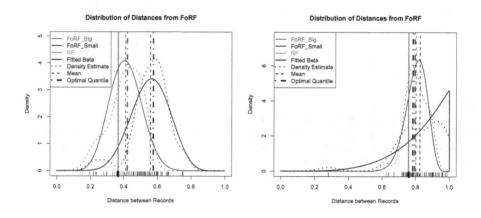

Fig. 5. Distributions of Estimated Distances from each FoRF

tible to typos, and we do not want to give non-identical strings with similar characters a non-zero weight, such as the state abbreviations "MA" and "MN".

B.3   Lists: Co-inventors, Classes, and Subclasses

Each inventor record has two lists associated with it: (1) the list of co-inventors and (2) the list of class-subclass pairs for the corresponding patent. There are several different ways to quantify the similarity of two lists of co-inventors or class-subclass pairs. For our purposes here, we use the following approach when comparing lists of co-inventors or class-subclass pairs. Given two lists X_{im} and X_{jm} for inventors i and j and field m:

$$\gamma_{ijm} = \frac{|X_{im} \cap X_{jm}|}{|X_{im} \cup X_{jm}|}$$

That is, list similarity scores find the ratio of shared elements to unique elements across the two lists. Again, note that other list similarity scores could be substituted here.

Comparison of Two Remote Access Systems Recently Developed and Implemented in Australia

Christine M. O'Keefe[1], Phillip Gould[2], and Tim Churches[3]

[1] CSIRO Computational Informatics
GPO Box 664, Canberra ACT 2601, Australia
Christine.OKeefe@csiro.au
[2] Australian Bureau of Statistics
Locked Bag 10, Belconnen ACT 2616, Australia
phillip.gould@abs.gov.au
[3] Sax Institute
PO Box K617, Haymarket NSW 1240, Australia
Tim.Churches@saxinstitute.org.au

Abstract. National Statistical Agencies and other data custodians are vital sources of data for research and policy analysis. However, external researchers must be provided with access to data in such a way that privacy and confidentiality are protected. We discuss two recently-implemented research data access systems. The first was developed by the Australian Bureau of Statistics for use with certain of its data collections. The second was developed by the Sax Institute, a non-profit health research non-government organisation, for use by population health and health services researchers to analyse complex, linked administrative health and related data sets provided by a range of data custodians. Although these organisations both chose remote access systems, it is interesting that there are significant differences between the two systems. We discuss the drivers for and consequences of the different choices made.

Keywords: Privacy, Confidentiality, Remote Access, Remote Analysis.

1 Introduction

The use of population-level data in research has come to underpin the generation of information for government policy and operations, health services and population health research, as well as advances in many other areas. National statistical agencies and other data custodians make data available to both internal and external researchers under strong confidentiality protections. External researchers are typically located in universities or government agencies, and undertake data analyses ranging from simple descriptive tabulations to the fitting of complex statistical models. In this paper we will discuss approaches taken by two organisations, the Australian Bureau of Statistics (ABS) and the Sax Institute, for making data available for research while protecting confidentiality.

J. Domingo-Ferrer (Ed.): PSD 2014, LNCS 8744, pp. 299–311, 2014.

ABS is Australia's national statistical agency and a major provider of population-level data for research. The Census and Statistics Act 1905, states:

1. The Statistician shall compile and analyse the statistical information collected under this Act and shall publish and disseminate the results of any such compilation and analysis, or abstracts of those results.
2. The results or abstracts referred to in subsection (1) shall not be published or disseminated in a manner that is likely to enable the identification of a particular person or organisation.

The Sax Institute is a non-governmental research institute, providing data access infrastructure to health services and population health researchers. It is a partner in the Population Health Research Network (PHRN), a consortium of research service providers co-funded since 2008 by Australian national, state and territory governments. The PHRN has enabled establishment of record linkage services for population-based administrative health and health-related data across Australia. These linkage services, which use internationally accepted privacy preserving data management and linkage protocols, enable the provision of linked de-identified data for approved research projects. The services which comprise the PHRN operate under Australian national and jurisdictional privacy legislation and regulation, with example provisions including:

- Health information reasonably expected to identify individuals should not be included in a generally available publication.
- The confidentiality of participants and their data should be protected in the dissemination of research results.

Most relevant legislative statements about confidentiality focus on preventing *identity disclosure*, that is, the identification of an individual or organisation represented in the data. Only some include the additional objective of preventing *attribute disclosure*, that is, the disclosure of attributes of an individual or organisation, though this is not always made explicit. In personal data, attribute disclosure is usually only of concern if identity disclosure is a possibility.

1.1   The Changing Research Data Environment in Australia

With regard to the external researcher environment, data custodians are experiencing changing user expectations and differing levels of user sophistication and analytical requirements [15]. In particular, users are increasingly expecting access to richer microdata from an expanded range of collections in a flexible range of access modes or mechanisms. The types of richer microdata include: more detailed, hierarchical, linked, administrative, longitudinal, and business, as well as combinations of some or all of these. Users are also becoming more sophisticated in their adoption of the latest technologies, including online access and sophisticated data analysis and data-mining tools. In addition, researchers are increasingly forming large, multidisciplinary teams and using collaboration platforms and tools for sharing data and results in conducting their research.

These trends are expected to continue, for example, the recent Australian National Commission of Audit [1] recommended that ...*the Government, recognising the need to safeguard privacy concerns, rapidly improve the use of data in policy development, service delivery and fraud reduction by: ... extending and accelerating the publication of anonymised administrative data ...*

At the same time, according to a recent survey of the Australian community's attitudes to privacy [9], the Australian environment has become one of enhanced community understanding of privacy, concern for privacy, knowledge of privacy rights, and willingness to take responsibility and change behaviour because of concerns about the handling of personal information. For government agencies, nearly all Australians (96% of respondents) believe that they should be told how their personal information is stored and protected.

Recently there have been a number of high-profile data breaches in Australia, and the Australian Office of the Information Commissioner handled 61 data breach notifications in 2012-13, a 33% increase since 2011-12 [8]. Although there is little or no evidence of privacy complaints or breaches in research on Australian data [10], the growth in number of data archives, custodian organisations, and researchers, together with the changing external researcher environment, may lead to a growing risk of data breach unless appropriately strong protections are put in place.

1.2   The Evolution of Data Access Mechanisms in the ABS

The ABS has traditionally made ABS census and survey data available via Confidentialised Unit Record Files (CURFs), as follows. CURFs are produced from the original unit-level data by the application of a (manual) confidentialisation process involving removal of name and address information, controlling the amount of detail and changing a small number of values through the application of statistical disclosure control techniques. CURFs are produced in increasing levels of detail, from Basic, through Expanded, to Specialist. Access to a CURF is granted to an organisation at the discretion of the Australian Statistician - then a researcher affiliated with the organisation can apply for registration and access. ABS can also grant access to CURFs to individuals. A precondition of organisational or individual access is the establishment of a legally binding Undertaking setting out the Terms and Conditions under which the access is approved. Basic CURFs are available on CD-ROM for the researcher to analyse on their own computer. Alternatively, a researcher can attend a Data Laboratory on-site at an ABS office in the nearest Australian capital city, in order to access Basic, Expanded or Specialist CURFs. In this case any statistical output derived from Expanded or Specialist CURFs is manually cleared before the researcher can remove it from the on-site Laboratory.

Around ten years ago or so the ABS implemented the Remote Access Data Laboratory (RADL) for access to Basic and Expanded CURFs. The RADL is a secure online data query service that clients can access via the ABS website. Users submit queries written in the SAS, Stata or SPSS statistical programming languages through a web interface, although some commands, functions and procedures are disabled to protect confidentiality, and there are restrictions on the size and nature of allowable outputs. The queries are run against the requested CURF that is kept within the Australian Bureau of Statistics environment. The results of the queries are checked for confidentiality by ABS staff and then made available for download to the users via their web browser.

More recently, the ABS has developed the *TableBuilder* and *DataAnalyser* systems to allow registered users to build their own custom tables and undertake regression analyses on secured ABS microdata, respectively [15].

TableBuilder is an online tool with a menu-driven interface allowing registered users to create confidentialised user-specified tables of count or continuous variables. Requested tables are produced and confidentialised on-the-fly as standalone outputs or as inputs to more sophisticated analyses such as regressions. Under the confidentialisation process, all cell values, subtotals and totals are randomly slightly adjusted to prevent any identifiable data being exposed. The adjustments are done in such a way that consistency of cell values across different tables constructed from the same data set is maintained. TableBuilder has been operating successfully for several years on Australian Census data and is being expanded to include survey data.

DataAnalyser is an online system that allows users to undertake analyses of detailed ABS microdata in real time. It allows users to remotely conduct certain data transformations and manipulations, basic exploratory data analysis, create summary tables and run regression analyses including linear (robust), logistic, probit and multinomial. For the first version of DataAnalyser, a low level of manual confidentialisation is applied to the microdata before loading into the system. The microdata are kept within the ABS secure environment behind a series of firewalls, requests are submitted through a menu-driven interface, and confidentialised outputs can be either viewed on screen or downloaded to the user's own computer. The confidentialisation processes are:

- a menu-driven interface is used to restrict the allowed variables, as well as the range and nature of data manipulations and analyses available
- counts are perturbed
- for regression, a small number of randomly-selected records is removed
- for regression, a model is rejected if it pertains to fewer than a minimum number of records, it has greater than a maximum number of parameters, there are fewer than a minimum number of records for each parameter, any record has a leverage above a given threshold, the sum of the leverages of two records exceed the threshold, or if the summary table constructed with the response variable against any of the categorical explanatory variables contains a zero
- for regression, the score function is perturbed prior to the estimation of the regression parameters
- scatter plots are replaced with hex plots on data where each hexagon with fewer than a minimum number of observations is suppressed

DataAnalyser is planned to be released as a beta product at the end of June 2014. Initially, invited users will be able to access the Australian Census Longitudinal Dataset and Australian Census-Migrants Integrated Dataset. The ABS plans to add additional survey datasets in the future and may consider requests for access to the beta trial from interested users.

The confidentialisation routines applied in TableBuilder and DataAnalyser are applied not at the unit record level, as is the case with CURFs, but at a level of aggregation relevant to the analysis. The level of confidentialisation required is therefore lower, leading to substantially reduced total variances [2].

1.3   The Evolution of Data Access Mechanisms in the PHRN

The PHRN is facilitating the creation of a nationwide data linkage infrastructure in Australia, with nodes servicing States and territories, as well as national linkage capabilities. It includes amongst its nodes the successful Western Australian Data Linkage Branch (established in the mid-1990's) and (NSW and ACT) Centre for Health Record Linkage, established in 2006. The PHRN linkage nodes interface with numerous routinely-collected Australian and State or Territory population-based databases, including Registrations of Births, Deaths and Marriages, Cancer Registries, and Emergency Department and Hospital Admitted Patient Data Collections. Specially-collected data from research studies such as from the 45 and Up study [14] can also be incorporated into the PHRN data linkage infrastructure and operations. All PHRN nodes enable linked, de-identified data to be provided to researchers, using a privacy-enhancing separation protocol involving linkage keys [5]. Under the protocol, the PHRN data linkage units receive *only* demographic information (name, address, sex and date-of-birth) and researchers receive *only* the health or other content data items. Researchers are able to assemble all records for each individual using project-specific de-identified linkage keys provided by the data linkage unit.

Thus, commencing with the Western Australian Data Linkage Branch operations in the mid-1990's, approved researchers in Australia have been provided with de-identified data files for approved population-based studies, after an appropriate user agreement has been signed and compulsory training has been completed. The provisioning of these data has recently been improved using on-line encrypted data transfer technologies.

In the last couple of years, one of the PHRN nodes, the Sax Institute, has developed the Secure Unified Research Environment (SURE) [13] as an alternative to providing linked, de-identified data files directly to researchers. SURE is a remote-access computing environment that allows researchers to access and analyse linked health-related data files for approved studies in Australia. The remote environment is accessible over encrypted internet connections, and effectively replaces a user's local computing environment. For each research study hosted by SURE, a project workspace is established to host virtual computing desktops for the researcher or team of researchers conducting the study. The research datasets are stored on virtual servers also located within the confines of each project or study workspace - thus, an entire virtual network is provided for each study, remotely accessed by researchers who use a facsimile of the screen of their remote virtual computing desktop on their local computer screen to manipulate and analyse the data. A range of standard and optional software is available on each SURE virtual workstation, including statistical packages such as R, SAS, SPSS and Stata, together with add-ons and libraries for each. Users can request other, more specialised software to be installed, if required, subject to cost and licensing conditions.

Although researchers using SURE can directly view microdata, and conduct unrestricted data manipulations and statistical analyses within the SURE remote-access environment, the only way that a file, such as a supplementary data file or a file of analysis outputs, can enter or leave SURE is via a single audited portal called the *Curated Gateway*. It is possible that there are issues of confidentiality associated with analysis outputs which researchers may wish to remove from SURE, for example for publication in the academic literature. Because such outputs cannot be assumed to be free from disclosure risk, outbound files uploaded to the Curated Gateway for use outside of SURE need to be assessed for confidentiality risk and treated with confidentialisation measures if necessary. This is currently the responsibility of the study's chief investigator, though it could also be done by an independent senior investigator or custodian representative as appropriate. Note that the compulsory training provided to all SURE users includes training in privacy and confidentiality regulatory regimes, and in the principles of statistical disclosure control for protecting confidentiality.

Traditionally, it has been the responsibility of the individual researcher and the Curated Gateway reviewer to ensure that analysis outputs removed from the SURE environment do not represent a disclosure risk. A recent project of CSIRO and the Sax Institute has reviewed confidentiality issues associated with public health and health policy research analysis outputs generated in a secure analysis laboratory such as SURE [11]. The outcome of the project has been endorsement of the current two-stage confidentiality protection process for SURE, comprising the existing data preparation and output confidentialisation stages. In the data preparation stage, data custodians and/or SURE administrators apply some basic confidentialisation measures to the dataset before making it available to researchers within each study or project workspace, but this confidentialisation is as lightweight as possible, and typically involves removal of all direct identifiers such as names, street addresses and medical record numbers, as well as removal of data items which substantially increase the risk of re-identification, such as exact date-of-birth, or high resolution spatial attributes of place of residence. These measures are designed to reduce, but not entirely eliminate, the risk of both spontaneous recognition by researchers and disclosure in analysis outputs. The residual risks are managed in the output confidentialisation stage, where the Curated Gateway reviewer ensures that published outputs generated in SURE comply with confidentiality protection requirements. In the CSIRO-Sax Institute project, a checklist was developed to assist reviewer and researchers using SURE to assess confidentiality risks in their analysis outputs, and apply confidentialisation treatments to reduce the risks to acceptable levels. In the future, this step should be able to be at least partially automated, or tools could be provided to enable researchers and reviewers to efficiently carry out such steps as part of a routine workflow.

2 Comparison of ABS DataAnalyser and PHRN SURE

The ABS and the Sax Institute/PHRN are organisations seeking to facilitate the use of routinely-collected data by researchers external to the organisations which collected the data. Both are currently responding to the changing research data environment with the implementation of new data access mechanisms designed to augment their traditional data dissemination channels.

Interestingly, both the ABS and the PHRN, through the Sax Institute, have very recently chosen to develop and implement remote access systems, with several features in common:

- detailed de-identified datasets are held in a secure environment,
- users require registration and/or approval and sign user agreements,
- users access the datasets via a secure channel on the internet, and
- users submit analysis requests and receive analysis outputs

However, the details of the two systems are quite different. Perhaps the major difference is the degree of user access to the dataset. In DataAnalyser, the user has no direct access to the data, in fact, the user cannot even view individual dataset records. This type of remote access system is sometimes called a *remote analysis* system. In contrast, in SURE, the user has unrestricted access to the data and can view every dataset record. This type of remote access system is sometimes called a *virtual data laboratory* or *data enclave*.

Internationally, examples of remote analysis systems include Table Servers developed by the National Institute of Statistical Science (NISS) to disseminate marginal sub-tables of a large contingency table [3,4], and the Microdata Analysis System under development by the U.S. Census Bureau to allow users to receive certain statistical analyses of Census Bureau data, including regression analyses, without ever having access to the data themselves [6]. Examples of virtual data laboratories include the UK Secure Data Service, providing secure remote access to data operated by the Economic and Social Data Service [16] and the US NORC Data Enclave, providing a confidential, protected environment within which authorised social science researchers can access sensitive microdata remotely [17].

In this section we compare the ABS and Sax Institute/PHRN systems and examine the drivers for and consequences of the different choices. In this comparison, we have assumed correct implementation and operation of the the information security functions necessary for the trust characteristics of each solution, including appropriate architecture, firewalls, authentication, monitoring and audit. In practice, this assumption must be carefully verified through independent design reviews and implementation audits.

2.1   Drivers for ABS DataAnalyser and PHRN SURE

In this section we focus on the drivers in the research data environments of the ABS and Sax Institute/PHRN, see Figure 1.

	ABS	PHRN
Mission includes	enable broad use of ABS data and data products	make health and related data available for research
Legislative Requirements	identification should not be likely	identity should not be reasonable to ascertain
Range of data	broad range of census and survey data types	health and social administrative data
Range of users	broad range of users with diverse requirements and statistical sophistication	academic population health and health services research community
Research governance and ethical oversight	data access for statistical purposes	project approved by data providers and Human Research Ethics Committee(s)

Fig. 1. Drivers in the research data environments of ABS and PHRN

The ABS is seeking to deliver on its mission and strategic objective of supporting the informed and increased use of statistics [15]. In response to this driver, the ABS is seeking new data dissemination technologies that minimise actual and perceived barriers to accessing ABS holdings. New data dissemination technologies must therefore deliver infrastructure for real time dissemination of ABS data, increase the detail and the range of collections available, reduce the resources required, and improve timeliness. A broad range of users with a range of levels of sophistication and analytical requirements is contemplated, including: government agency and large corporation employees, individual university researchers, and consultants. The range of data to be made available includes: census, social and business surveys, economic, demographic and land-use data. Since the obligations of the Census and Statistics Act 1905 must be upheld regardless of the type of user, the type of data, or the kind of analysis being undertaken, the ABS needs to implement a one-size-fits-all approach to provide confidentiality protection across a multitude of users and purposes.

The Sax Institute and the PHRN are seeking to deliver on their mission of supporting public health and health services research of national relevance in Australia [12]. In response to this driver, the PHRN is seeking new data dissemination technologies that enable researchers to more efficiently conduct the sort of studies that have been traditional in public health and health services research, although with richer and greatly expanded data collections. Researchers using the PHRN are generally from universities and government health agencies, and the PHRN seeks to grow its user base in these communities. The datasets made available through SURE are predominantly administrative health and social datasets, though research study data can also be included. The PHRN currently enables the provision of linkable, de-identified datasets directly to researchers for use in their own computing environment. The SURE system is designed to be functionally not more restrictive than the current arrangements.

2.2   Summary of Features of ABS DataAnalyser and PHRN SURE

In Figure 2 we summarise the main features of the technological systems implemented by ABS and PHRN, focussing on confidentiality protection.

	ABS DataAnalyser	PHRN SURE
Dataset Preparation	light manual confidentialisation	light manual confidentialisation
User can browse metadata	yes	yes
User can request any data set	within the scope of data sets provided in DataAnalyser	user can only access project datasets with provider and ethics committee approval
User direct access to data including viewing de-identified records	no access	full access
Data manipulations	restricted	unrestricted
Range of queries	restricted	unrestricted
Queries	modified/restricted	unmodified, unrestricted
Software available	only DataAnalyser software	broad range of standard software and some custom
Range of outputs	restricted	unrestricted
Output	confidentialised	reviewed at Curated Gateway

Fig. 2. Features of ABS and PHRN remote access systems

First, and as mentioned in Section 2 above, DataAnalyser prevents the user from viewing any data records, while SURE gives the researcher full access including viewing all (de-identified) data records. In order to provide adequate confidentiality protection in each case, the different levels of direct access to data are balanced by different levels of other measures. In DataAnalyser, researchers can browse and request analysis of any of the data sets which ABS has approved for access via DataAnalyser, while in SURE, researchers must have their project approved by the relevant data providers and by a Human Research Ethics Committee, and can only access the data set and data items approved for that project.

The second major difference is that DataAnalyser applies strong restrictions on the range of data manipulations, range of queries, and range of outputs available to the researcher. DataAnalyser applies modifications to some analyses, for example, it perturbs the score function for a regression, and applies further automatic confidentialisation routines to outputs before returning them to the researcher. In contrast, the researcher using SURE is unrestricted in the data manipulations and analyses they can apply, and there are no restrictions on the types of output they can obtain. Outputs are not modified by SURE, however are subject to review for confidentiality protection at the Curated Gateway. SURE relies on the researchers and/or the Curated Gateway reviewers to confidentialise analysis outputs before publication.

2.3   Comparison of ABS DataAnalyser and PHRN SURE

Types of Users and Data. First, the ABS cannot assume a uniform or even a minimum level of sophistication of its users. Therefore, DataAnalyser is initially targetted to a core group of users with a medium level of sophistication, including: policy analysts and social and economic researchers. The menu-driven system is well suited to these users and makes fully automated confidentiality protection achievable for realistic cost. Future versions of DataAnalyser may have extended capability in order to address the needs of more sophisticated users. The ABS also cannot assume uniformity across its datasets, which are extremely diverse.

The main drawback of the DataAnalyser is that there is significantly reduced flexibility offered to users, for example, DataAnalyser offers users only prescribed data manipulations, methods and outputs. The ABS may never be able to anticipate and provide functionality for the full range of analyses that its very broad user base may wish to perform. If a researcher requires more flexibility or a different analysis, they must use a different ABS data dissemination channel.

SURE can assume a reasonable level of sophistication amongst its researchers, since each project hosted by SURE has been approved by an ethics committee convinced that the outcomes will be of sufficient merit to outweigh any confidentiality risk, and which has thus considered the qualifications and experience of the researchers involved in the project. In addition, normally researchers seeking to use SURE embark in what can be a lengthy negotiation phase to establish whether their proposed study is feasible using available linked data sets. SURE has been set up to enable collaborative team-based storage and workspaces for project teams. SURE is designed for administrative health and social data.

Both ABS and PHRN make use of a user registration process, normally also involving the user's employing organisation. SURE makes use of strong three-factor authentication of users at the web interface.

Scope of Trust. The difference in trust of researchers is also an important drivers for the choices. The level of trust extended depends on the dataset, the custodians, the researcher(s) and the research questions being asked.

DataAnalyser contemplates a broad range of external users of varying levels of sophistication. The appropriate choice has been made to extend a lower level of trust to the users and instead to rely on the automated confidentiality protections built into DataAnalyser technology itself for preventing disclosures.

In contrast, SURE extends a higher level of trust to approved researchers and their computing environments, providing access via a virtual data laboratory mechanism with much lighter automated confidentiality protections. The SURE approach of trusting researchers and/or reviewers to assess confidentiality risk and confidentialise outputs is underpinned by a tighter and more formal research governance practice involving: custodian and Human Research Ethics Committee approvals, targetted training in confidentiality protection, strong user agreements, post-study reporting, and strong sanctions for breaches.

Consistency of Analysis Results. In the case of the ABS, a researcher could analyse the same data via several different data access channels, for example, CURFs, TableBuilder and DataAnalyser. In order to avoid inconsistencies in the application of confidentialisation processes across the range of ABS data dissemination modes, possibly leading to either inconsistent results or unexpected confidentiality risks, the ABS has developed general perturbation algorithms that can be incorporated into a broad range of analysis methods including summary tables, summary statistics and statistical regressions.

In contrast, the nature of the projects hosted by SURE means that it is unlikely that exactly the same data subset is used in more than a handful of studies, so the problem is not so pressing. In cases where the same dataset is used for a number of studies, often it is the same group of researchers and they can ensure consistency as they are applying the confidentialisation methods themselves. More broadly, SURE users are required to actively seek to publish or otherwise disseminate their results, increasing the likelihood that researchers are aware of research outputs published by other groups using the same datasets.

Summary. Marsh et al. [7] noted that a successful disclosure involves first an attempt at disclosure, then success of that attempt. In probabilistic terms, this is: $\mathrm{Pr(disclosure)} = \mathrm{Pr(attempt)} \cdot \mathrm{Pr(disclosure \mid attempt)}$. The ABS environment requires it to assume that $\mathrm{Pr(attempt)}$ is close to 1, and therefore to seek to minimise $\mathrm{Pr(disclosure \mid attempt)}$. The PHRN works to ensure that $\mathrm{Pr(attempt)}$ is negligible, and therefore does not need to minimise $\mathrm{Pr(disclosure \mid attempt)}$.

3 Discussion and Conclusions

We have described the evolution of data access mechanisms in two important Australian organisations providing or enabling data access to researchers, namely, the Australian Bureau of Statistics (ABS) and the Sax Institute node of the Population Health Research Network (PHRN). In the last couple of years, both of these organisations have implemented a new remote access system, however it is interesting that they have chosen different types of remote access. We have analysed the reasons for these differences through a comparison of the context and environment for each system, and the technological responses to them.

In the current international environment of open government and data sharing, organisations are seeking to make more and more data available for research and policy analysis. Both the ABS and the Sax Institute/PHRN are responding to the evolving Australian community environment of increasing concern for privacy and knowledge of privacy rights, by increasing transparency about their data holdings and data access arrangements. Both organisations are responding to growing researcher interest in richer detail across an expanded range of collections by implementing increasingly automated data access technologies. Both organisations make use of appropriately targetted researcher registration and agreements, and have sanctions in place for breaches of the agreements. A stand out observation is that both organisations have chosen types of remote access.

The ABS, in focussing on a broad range of users with varying levels of sophistication, has chosen remote analysis. Under the DataAnalyser approach, the lower trust level implied by providing access to a wide range of users requires a less flexible system and restricted outputs. The Sax Institute, in focussing on a community of more sophisticated users, has chosen a virtual data centre. Under the SURE approach, the higher trust level implied by strongly restricting access allows a more flexible system. A useful way to compare the systems is to note that a disclosure requires first a disclosure attempt, then success of that attempt. The ABS focusses on reducing the likelihood of success of any disclosure attempt, while PHRN focusses on reducing the likelihood of an attempt.

We remark that the U.S. Census Bureau has adopted an automated output confidentialisation approach for its Microdata Analysis System, similar to the ABS DataAnalyser, noting that both are examples of remote analysis systems. In the NORC Enclave, a virtual data centre, any export request from a researcher is scrutinised by a NORC statistician to ensure that it does not contain disclosive data. This is similar but more restrictive than the SURE approach.

Our two detailed examples show that there is no single solution for protecting confidentiality while making data available for research, since differences in context and focus will lead to different requirements and different approaches making use of different combinations of protections. Both of the systems we have discussed have advantages and disadvantages in terms of scope of access and flexibility. In each of our examples there is a combination of individual protections, none of which is sufficient alone but the aggregation of all of which provide strong confidentiality protection for data during research.

One challenge associated with remote access is the need to go through the sometimes lengthly funding application, registration and approval processes before any analysis of the data can be conducted. In some cases, this can be a real problem if it is subsequently found that the data are not suitable for addressing the proposed research question. Both the ABS and Sax Institute/PHRN are seeking to address this question by seeking to make available low risk datasets for initial data exploration and methods development under a lightweight approvals process. The ABS is investigating the use of model-based synthetic datasets, and the Sax Institute is investigating the use of massively perturbed datasets, such as are generated by data swapping with extremely high swapping probabilities.

We conclude with the observation that: ... *recent events in the development of remote analysis servers herald the dawn of a new era in automated confidentiality protection for analysis and we look forward to invigorated research collaborations among NST's and academic institutions to further this research* ... [15].

Acknowledgements. This paper draws on work done while Christine O'Keefe was on secondment to the Australian Bureau of Statistics, and during a collaborative project between CSIRO and the Sax Institute. We thank the Australian

Government Education Investment Fund Super Science Initiative for part funding of the latter project through the Population Health Research Network.

Disclaimer. Views expressed in this paper are those of the authors and do not necessarily represent those of the Australian Bureau of Statistics. Where quoted or used, they should be attributed clearly to the authors.

References

1. Australian Government: National commission of audit. Report, Phase I, http://www.ncoa.gov.au
2. Chipperfield, J., Lucie, S.: Analysis of micro-data: Controlling the risk of disclosure. Research Paper - Methodology Advisory Committee 1352.0.55.110, Australian Bureau of Statistics (2010)
3. Karr, A., Lee, J., Sanil, A., Hernandez, J., Karimi, S., Litwin, K.: Web-based systems that disseminate information but protect confidentiality. In: McIver, W., Elmagarmid, A. (eds.) Advances in Digital Government: Technology, Human Factors and Public Policy, pp. 181–196. Kluwer, Amsterdam (2002)
4. Karr, A.F., Dobra, A., Sanil, A.P.: Table servers protect confidentiality in tabular data releases. Commun. ACM 46(1), 57–58 (2003), http://doi.acm.org/10.1145/602421.602451
5. Kelman, C.W., Bass, A.J., Holman, C.: Research use of linked health data best practice protocol. Australian and New Zealand Journal of Public Health 26(3), 251–255 (2002)
6. Lucero, J., Zayatz, L., Singh, L., You, J., DePersio, M., Freiman, M.: The Current Stage of the Microdata Analysis System at the U.S. Census Bureau. In: Proc. 58th Congress of the International Statistical Institute, ISI 2011 (2011)
7. Marsh, C., Skinner, C., Arber, S., Penhale, B., Openshaw, S., Hobcraft, J., Lievesley, D., Walford, N.: The case for samples of anonymized records from the 1991 census. J. Roy. Stat. Soc. Ser. A 154, 305–340 (1991)
8. Office of the Australian Information Commissioner: Annual report 2012-13
9. Office of the Australian Information Commissioner: Community attitudes to privacy survey (2013)
10. O'Keefe, C., Connolly, C.: Privacy and the use of health data for research. Med. J. Aust. 193, 537–541 (2010)
11. O'Keefe, C., Westcott, M., Ickowicz, A., O'Sullivan, M., Churches, T.: Protecting confidentiality in statistical analysis outputs from a virtual data centre. Working Paper, Joint UNECE/Eurostat Work Session on Statistical Data Confidentiality, Ottawa, Canada, October 29-30, 10 p. (2013), http://www.unece.org/stats/documents/2013.10.confidentiality.html
12. Population Health Research Network: website
13. Sax Institute: Secure Unified Research Environment (SURE). Website, www.sure.org.au
14. Sax Institute: 45 and up (website), https://www.saxinstitute.org.au/our-work/45-up-study/
15. Thompson, G., Broadfoot, S., Elazar, D.: Methodology for automatic confidentialisation of statistical outputs from remote servers at the Australian bureau of statistics. Joint UNECE/Eurostat Work Session on Statistical Data Confidentiality, Ottawa, Canada, October 28-30, 37 p. (2013)
16. UK Data Archive: Secure data service (website), securedata.data-archive.ac.uk
17. University of Chicago: NORC (website), www.norc.org

Towards Secure and Practical Location Privacy through Private Equality Testing

Emmanouil Magkos[1], Panayiotis Kotzanikolaou[2], Marios Magioladitis[1], Spyros Sioutas[1], and Vassilios S. Verykios[3]

[1] Department of Informatics, Ionian University
Plateia Tsirigoti 7, 49100 Kerkyra, Greece
{emagos,mmagiol,sioutas}@ionio.gr
[2] University of Piraeus, Department of Informatics,
80 Karaoli & Dimitriou, 18534 Piraeus, Greece
pkotzani@unipi.gr
[3] Hellenic Open University, School of Science and Technology,
Parodos Aristotelous 18, GR-26335 Patras, Greece
verykios@eap.gr

Abstract. In this paper, we propose a practical, privacy-preserving equality testing primitive which allows two users to learn if they share the same encrypted input data. Our protocol assumes no trust on a third party and/or other peers, and it is specifically suited for low-min entropy data (*i.e.*, data that can be exhaustively searched by an attacker), such as encrypted users locations. We demonstrate that our primitive is secure and efficient: Two public-key exponentiations are required, per each user, for each equality testing. We give implementation results, showing that our primitive is practical in a multiple users scenario. Finally, we describe how we could use our primitive as a building block for a proximity testing buddy-finder service for social networks.

Keywords: Equality testing, Location privacy, Buddy-finder social network, Location-based services, Geo-social applications.

1 Introduction

Privacy is related to a person's ability to control how personal and/or sensitive information is treated by third parties. Controversially, humans as social beings crave for interaction with other people, *i.e.*, thus indirectly or directly divulging such information to others. Today, with the boom of Internet Social Networks Services (SNS), this phenomenon is even more widespread. Furthermore, old and new SNS providers start to deliver location-based services (LBS) to their users (*e.g.*, Meetup, BuddyBeacon, Google Latitude, Facebook Places, Foursquare), thus establishing a mainstream niche market for social LBS applications. Such mixed reality services exacerbate the privacy problem faced by traditional location-based services.

J. Domingo-Ferrer (Ed.): PSD 2014, LNCS 8744, pp. 312–325, 2014.

An LBS provider (LBSP) typically receives a user's current location (among other context) through the Internet in order to answer various query types: Sporadic location-based queries (*e.g.*, "find me the nearest restaurant"), continuous queries (*e.g.*, "continuously report the hotels within one mile of my car"), push services (*e.g.*, "alert me on clothes prices when I pass near a store"), or social queries (*e.g.*, "let me know when my buddies are nearby").

Because of their growing popularity, the privacy risks incurred by uncontrolled LBS applications are high [1,2,3,4]. The main concern is that a user's location data or traces could be used by an adversary for profiling user behavior, targeting the user (*e.g.*, spam, stalking) or make intrusive inferences about user's sensitive data (*e.g.*, lifestyle, state of health, beliefs). For such threats, the role of the threat factor could be played by (a coalition of) a corrupted/compromised LBSP, a network/cellular provider, an external observer, or other system users.

Privacy approaches for location-based services may be categorized depending on whether a trusted party is employed or not [5,6]. Most approaches [7,8,9,10,11,12,13,14,15,16] adhere to a proxy-based model, where a third party (TTP) is fully trusted for user privacy. The problem with such centralized, *full-trust* model is that the TTP becomes a single point of failure and a scalability/performance bottleneck when strong privacy protection is required. Decentralized LBS schemes with privacy preservation [17,18,19,20,21,22,3,23,24,25,26,27] on the other hand adhere to a semi or fully distributed model architecture where trust assumptions are weak or completely removed, leading to *TTP-free* schemes. Recent literature has paved the way for using cryptographic primitives, such as Private Information Retrieval [20,3] or privacy homomorphisms [28,21], in order to support TTP-free schemes and diminish the trust level to third parties in LBS applications.

A Motivating Example. In this paper we deal with private proximity testing in social LBS queries (*i.e.*, Buddy-finder SNSs). Imagine Alice, who subscribes to an SNS that notifies (a subset of) her online friends when they are in proximity with her. This problem is related to testing for equality Alice's and a friend's encrypted locations, which are periodically uploaded to an LBSP [26]. If Alice is in proximity to, say, Bob, she may be allowed to decide whether Bob will become aware of this fact. On the other hand, if Alice and Bob are not in proximity, none of them will learn anything else other than this fact. Furthermore, neither Alice nor Bob a priori trust the LBSP or each other with respect to their location.

Our Contribution. In this paper, we argue on the inadequacy of current state-of-the-art schemes for privacy-preserving equality testing of encrypted low-min entropy data, against untrusted third parties and/or untrusted peers. Then we propose an efficient equality testing primitive with privacy preservation: Our protocol provides unconditional input privacy against external observers; it also provides privacy against other peers, if the Discrete Logarithm Problem (DLP) is hard in the finite cyclic group generated by a user's private input; in addition, if the two inputs are not equal, neither party will learn anything more than this fact; furthermore, any other external party, will not be able to distinguish whether the equality test was successful or not if the Computational Diffie-Hellman (CDH) problem is intractable. Our primitive is specifically suited for low-min entropy data, such as encrypted users locations, and it is also efficient: Two public-key exponentiations are required, at most, per each user, for each testing. We give implementation results, showing that our primitive is practical in a multiple users scenario. Finally, we describe a possible application of our primitive, as a building block for a proximity testing Buddy-Finder SNS.

2   Related Work

The Asymmetric Equality-Testing Scheme of [26]. We describe, in short, the private equality testing scheme of [26], proposed for private proximity testing in LBS applications. Let Z_p be a group of prime order p, g a generator of Z_p, a and b Alice's and Bob's locations, $(x, h = g^x)$ Alice's ElGamal key pair and Alice and Bob communicate through an authenticated channel. Alice first encodes her location as h^a, selects $r \in_R Z_p$, and sends to Bob an ElGamal encryption of her location, with her public key (all operations are modulo p):

$$A \to B: \quad (g_1, g_2) = (g^r, h^{a+r}) \tag{1}$$

Bob selects $s, t \in_R Z_p$ and "hides" his location to Alice's message:

$$B \to A: \quad (u_1, u_2) = (g_1^s g^t, g_2^s h^{(t-sb)}) \tag{2}$$

Finally, Alice decrypts with x by computing $m \leftarrow u_2/u_1^x = h^{s(a-b)}$. If $m = 1$ she concludes that $a = b$, otherwise that $a \neq b$. The protocol is asymmetric since Alice learns whether there is equality while Bob learns nothing. Alice's privacy is based on the DDH assumption [26], while Bob's is unconditional. Concerning performance, the costs are three exponentiations for Alice and four for Bob. Our scheme, presented in Section 3, has better performance, with only two exponentiations per user and it is more scalable, since one of these exponentiations could be used for parallel equality testing sessions with other users.

The authors in [26] noticed a weakness of the above protocol, which in this paper we will call the *deception attack*: Bob sends, maliciously, to Alice, in step (2): (g^s, h^s), and deceives her into believing that $a = b$ while it is not. We believe that, depending on the application, this would constitute a privacy violation for Alice: For example, a deceived Alice could disclose her position to Bob and ask him to meet her, thus revealing her location (thus, also effectively reversing the asymmetry of the protocol). In Section 3 we will present our solution for asymmetric equality testing, where such attacks are not possible.

Other Approaches for Computing with Encrypted Location Data. Towards proximity testing in social LBS applications, we could elaborate on recent developments in the area of privacy-preserving manipulations of stored encrypted data, such as keyword searching, joining / linking encrypted data, computing a function of private client inputs etc. Such protocols consider computing over data encrypted with the same key (symmetric [29,30,31,32,33] or public [34,35,36,37]). We believe that the symmetric key setting is not suitable for proximity testing, since it implies some trust, either among peers or between a peer and a proxy. Similarly, even practical Secure Multi-party Computation (SMC) protocols based on homomorphic encryption (*e.g.*, [38,21]) consider data encrypted with a single public key of an entity which will perform the encrypted computation, and which, usually, cannot be fully trusted. Overall, protocols for TTP-free SMC computations are neither computationally efficient nor practical, in that they assume that clients interact with each other, which is unacceptable in most LBS scenarios.

Admittedly, primitives such as the above could not be directly used for equality/proximity testing in Buddy-finder LBS applications, since capabilities such as keyword search, linking, equality testing etc could be exploited, either by a curious Proxy/LBSP or by curious friends, in order to perform off-line message recovery attacks against location data, which are selected from a low-min entropy set. The entropy argument is also decisive for rejecting solutions that involve deterministic encryption, such as [36].

On Using PKEET for Equality Testing. Recently, the public-key encryption with equality testing (PKEET) primitive [39,40] was proposed to allow an untrusted third party to execute a function $Test(C_i, C_j)$ over two ciphertexts C_i, C_j, probabilistically encrypted with two different public keys $pk_i \neq pk_j$, in order to check whether they contain the same message. The original scheme had the following issues: a) it allowed any entity to perform the equality test between, say ciphertexts of user A and user B (*e.g.*, when such ciphertexts are public information); b) Any entity with access to A's ciphertext $C_a = Enc(pk_a, m)$ and some other public key pk_c, would also be able to choose one or more plaintexts m_j, $j = 1, 2, ...$ and execute $C_j = Enc(pk_j, m_j)$ and $Test(C_a, C_j)$ for testing equality, thus violating standard semantic security. As a consequence, in low min-entropy domains such as the set of users locations in social LBSs, a polynomial adversary can launch an *offline message recovery* attack and violate the privacy of any encrypted message. Such attacks are unavoidable when the equality test functionality, as in PKEET and elsewhere, is outsourced to a third party. In another extension [40], an extra authorization algorithm $\mathsf{Auth}(SK_i, SK_j)$, must be run exactly once between any two users U_i, U_j in order to issue a token that authorizes a designated proxy P to compare their ciphertexts. With that token, the proxy is able to compare the ciphertexts of A and B (and not, for example, of A and another user C). The problem of this approach for low-min entropy messages, is that the Proxy, equipped with the PKEET function and A's, B's public keys, is (again) able to exhaustively select candidate messages, encrypt them with either A's or B's public key and then use the PKEET test function to perform offline message recovery.

3   An Asymmetric PET Protocol

We will first describe a generic Private Equality Testing (PET) protocol, which allows two peers, say Alice and Bob, to securely test the equality of their private, *low-entropy* input data g_A and g_B, respectively, without the involvement of any third party. Our protocol provides unconditional input privacy against external observers, as well as input privacy against other peers if the DLP problem is hard in a cyclic, prime order subgroup generated by g_A and g_B. In addition, if the two inputs are not equal, then neither party will learn anything more than this fact. Furthermore, any external observer will not be able to distinguish whether the equality test was successful or not if the CDH problem is intractable in the same subgroup. Our protocol also establishes *asymmetry*: One party (typically the one who initiates the protocol) learns the answer, while the other party learns nothing. The scheme is depicted in Fig. 1.

Setup. Let $L_n = \{\ell_1, \ell_2, ..., \ell_n\}$ be a discrete, finite input set of order $n < 2^{64}$, *i.e.*, containing low-min entropy data (*e.g.*, GPS coordinates). Let Z_p^* be a multiplicative group[1] of prime order p, where the DLP problem is hard (typically $|p| \geq 1024$ bit) and let S be the set of all generators of the subgroup Z_q of Z_p^*, of sufficiently large prime order q (typically $|q| \geq 160$), where $q|p-1$. In addition, let $\mathcal{L}_n = \{g_1, g_2, ..., g_n\}$ be a random subset[2] of S, of order n. Each value $l_i \in L_n$, $i = 1, 2, ..., n$ is assigned, using a 1-1 mapping[3] $f : L \to \mathcal{L}_n$, to a unique generator $g_i = f(\ell_i)$. The assignment mechanism is (assumingly) transparent to the system users. So, for simplicity's sake, instead of saying that a user U chooses an input $\ell_j \in L_n$, we will directly say that U chooses $g_j \in \mathcal{L}_n$. Note that both sets L_n and $\mathcal{L}_n$ need to be constructed only once by the system authority and can be valid through the lifetime of the system.

Furthermore, Let $H(.)$ denote a cryptographic hash function, of length[4] ℓ and $E_K(.)$ (respectively, $D_K(.)$) denote a symmetric encryption (respectively, decryption) function, of the same length ℓ, with key K. Let $||$ denote concatenation of two messages. Finally, we assume that all communication is authenticated (so that active attacks are thwarted).

Input. Alice has private input $g_A \in \mathcal{L}_n$ and Bob has private input $g_B \in \mathcal{L}_n$.

Output. Alice learns whether $g_A = g_B$ and Bob learns nothing (asymmetry). If Alice chooses to reveal this to Bob, Bob will also learn whether $g_A = g_B$.

Round 1. Alice chooses a random secret value $r_A \in Z_q$, used only once, such that $gcd(r_A, q-1) = 1$. Alice then encodes her private input as: $A \leftarrow g_A^{r_A} \bmod p$ and sends this to Bob.

---

[1] For simplicity we describe our scheme in the setting of Z_p^*, although it can be generalized to work in any finite abelian group G, *e.g.*, the group constructed from the set of points on an elliptic curve over a finite field $\mathbb{F}_q$.

[2] A system authority can construct $\mathcal{L}_n$ as follows: For each $j = 1, 2, ...2^n$, it repeatedly chooses $r_j \in_R Z_p^*$, and sets $g_j \leftarrow r_j^{(p-1)/q} (\bmod\ p)$ until $g_j \neq 1$.

[3] In practice, $f(.)$ need not be a 1-1 mapping: a collision-resistant function, mapping a unique location $l_i \in L_n$ to a unique element $g_i \in \mathcal{L}_n$ would be enough. An efficient implementation of $f(.)$ can be constructed using a cryptographic hash function of suitable length.

[4] We consider one-way cryptographic hash functions with second pre-image resistance, for example $\ell \geq 160$ bit.

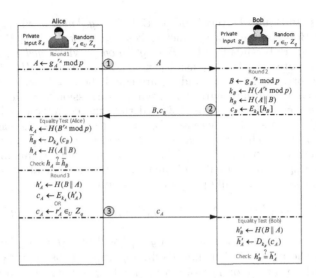

Fig. 1. A private equality testing protocol

Round 2. Bob selects a random secret value $r_B \in Z_q$, used only once, such that $gcd(r_B, q - 1) = 1$. Bob then encodes his private input as: $B \leftarrow g_B^{r_B} \bmod p$. On receiving A from Alice, Bob uses his secret value r_B, and the hash function $H(.)$, to extract a secret key k_B (of an agreed bit length) as: $k_B \leftarrow H(A^{r_B} \bmod p)$. Bob computes $h_B \leftarrow H(A||B)$, then uses the key k_B to encrypt h_B as a "challenge" $c_B \leftarrow E_{k_B}(h_B)$ and sends to Alice: B, c_B.

Equality Testing for Alice. On receiving this, Alice uses the encrypted private input B of Bob, her secret value r_A, and the hash function $H(.)$ to generate a secret key k_A (of the same agreed bit length) as: $k_A \leftarrow H(B^{r_A} \bmod p)$. Then, Alice will use k_A, to decrypt the encrypted challenge c_B received from Bob and compute: $\bar{h}_B \leftarrow D_{k_A}(E_{k_B}(h_B))$. If $\bar{h}_B = H(A||B)$, Alice decides that the private values g_A and g_B are equal. If not, she decides that $g_A \neq g_B$ and nothing else is revealed to Alice about g_B.

Round 3. In case $g_A = g_B$, Alice may optionally decide that she also wants to let Bob know that their inputs are equal[5]. To do that, Alice computes $h'_A \leftarrow H(B||A)$ and sends to Bob $c_A \leftarrow E_{k_A}(h'_A)$. If there is no equality, Alice will send a noise message to Bob, e.g., a random number $c_A \leftarrow r'_A \in_U Z_q$ of length ℓ. This is also useful to preclude any third observers from deducing whether PET between Alice and Bob was successful or not.

Equality Testing for Bob (Optional). After Bob receives an c_A message from Alice, where $c_A \in \{E_{k_A}(h'_A), r'_A\}$ he will compute $h'_B \leftarrow H(B||A)$, and decrypt c_A using key k_B. If $D_{k_B}(c_A) = h'_B$ then Bob decides that $g_B = g_A$.

---

[5] As we will see in Section 4, this could be useful in a Buddy-finder SNS service.

Correctness. In Round 1, Alice sends to Bob $A \leftarrow g_A^{r_A} mod\ p$, where $gcd(r_A, q - 1) = 1$, and Bob computes a symmetric key k_B as: $k_B \leftarrow H(A^{r_B} mod\ p) = H(g^{r_A r_B} mod\ p)$. Bob sends to Alice $B \leftarrow g_B^{r_B} mod\ p$, where $gcd(r_B, q - 1) = 1$, and Alice computes the key k_A as: $k_A = H(B^{r_A} mod\ p) = H(g^{r_B r_A} mod\ p)$. Clearly, if the private inputs g_A and g_B are equal then $k_B = k_A$, meaning that Alice and Bob have mutually agreed on a symmetric session key that will decrypt correctly messages in Rounds 2 and 3, and thus the equality test in the PET protocol will be successful. Otherwise, if $g_A \neq g_B$ then we distinguish two cases: a) $g_A^{r_A r_B} \neq g_B^{r_B r_A}$, which means that $k_B \neq k_A$ and thus the equality test of the PET protocol will fail; b) $g_A^{r_A r_B} \equiv g_B^{r_B r_A}$, which means that a common symmetric key is agreed despite the inequality of the private inputs. The above relation can equivalently be written as (all operations are modulo p):

$$g_A^{r_A r_B} \equiv g_B^{r_A r_B} \Leftrightarrow g_A^{r_A r_B}(g_B^{r_A r_B})^{-1} \equiv 1 \Leftrightarrow g_A^{r_A r_B}(g_B^{-1})^{r_A r_B} \equiv 1 \Leftrightarrow (g_A g_B^{-1})^{r_A r_B} \equiv 1$$

or, equivalently, the order, modulo p, of $g_A g_B^{-1}$ will be $r_A r_B$. By the arithmetic properties of the order of elements, modulo q, this means that $r_A r_B | (q - 1)$, or, equivalently, that r_A or r_B (or both) divide $q - 1$ which contradicts our assumption that r_A and r_B are relatively prime to $q - 1$.

3.1   Security Analysis

Our protocol provides unconditional security of the private inputs of Alice and Bob against external observers who may attempt to learn their private inputs (Theorem 1). The protocol is also secure, under the CDH assumption, against external adversaries that attempt to decide whether the equality test was successful (Theorem 2). Alice and Bob are also secure from each other under the DLP assumption (Theorem 3): The protocol also provides asymmetry *i.e.*, Alice can check whether her input equals Bob's input without disclosing any information about her input to Bob. For the same reason, if $g_A \neq g_B$, no other information is revealed to Alice. An analogous argument stands for Bob. For multiple executions of the protocol, Alice (Bob) needs to use a different r_A (respectively, r_B), or else it will be easy to deduce whether the same input was used. Furthermore, the deception attack against the scheme of [26] (Section 2) is not applicable in our scheme. Bob's difficulty of deceiving Alice is analogous to guessing Alice's input. Of course, in our scheme, as in every such scheme that tests user inputs for equality, nothing can stop a user from lying about its input. In a typical threat model, as the one presented next, we can safely leave such attacks out of scope.

Threat Model. We consider both external and internal adversaries. We assume that all the adversaries are polynomially bounded and do not have the ability to break the computational assumptions of the underlying cryptographic assumptions. An external adversary may eavesdrop the communication between the system entities in order to reveal the private input of the users or learn weather the private input provided by two users is equal or not. We assume that the messages exchanged by the users are authenticated and integrity protected, so that external adversaries will not be able to modify messages or inject fake messages pretending to originate from a legitimate user.

External adversaries are modeled by a distinguish adversary $\mathcal{A}^{dist}$. The goal of $\mathcal{A}^{dist}$ is twofold: First, to learn information about the private input of any of the parties that participate in the protocol. Second, to distinguish whether the private input of two users running the protocol are equal or not, using as input the exchanged messages of a protocol run. Internal adversaries are essentially users running the protocol who may attempt to reveal the private information of the other party, in case of inequality. We assume that users of the protocol adhere to a *honest but curious* (also known as semi-honest) behavior (HBC), in that they abide to the rules of the protocol while trying to learn as much as possible about the private data of the other users of the protocol. Note that most privacy-preserving techniques for fully-distributed LBS protocols, such as the one discussed in Section 4, assume users with HBC behavior [6], as it seems to be a realistic model in the setting of social LBS services where peers are friends, *i.e.*, with no incentive to behave maliciously in an obvious way. It is also important to understand that the HBC model does not prevent collusion between users of the protocol in a multiple-users setting [41].

Theorem 1 (Private input indistinguishability). *An external global passive adversary cannot learn anything about the private input of any of the parties.*

Proof. Here the goal of $\mathcal{A}^{dist}$ is to learn information about the private input of Alice and/or Bob. $\mathcal{A}^{dist}$ will take as input all the messages exchanged in a protocol run, *i.e.*, A, B, c_A and c_B, as well as the low-entropy set $\mathcal{L}_n$ containing all possible private input elements. Since the private input of the users g_A and g_B are hidden with r_A and r_B respectively, which are elements of high entropy, both Alice and Bob have unconditional input privacy. Indeed, consider an external adversary who is not polynomially bounded and is able to break the DLP problem. Since every element of $\mathcal{L}_n$ is a generator of order q, then $\forall\ g_i \in \mathcal{L}_n$, $\exists\ r_i \in Z_q : A = g_i^{r_i}(mod\ p)$. Thus the private input A (respectively B) may contain any element of $\mathcal{L}_n$ with equal probability. $\square$

Concerning the equality test indistinguishability, the goal $\mathcal{A}^{dist}$ is to distinguish whether the equality test between two users running the protocol of Section 3 was successful or not. We formalize $\mathcal{A}^{dist}$ by a security experiment $Exp_A^{PET\text{-}dist}$ where $\mathcal{A}^{dist}$ has access to an oracle $\mathcal{O}^{PET\text{-}dist}$ that takes as input the public system parameters p, q, $\mathcal{L}_n$ and all the messages exchanged in a protocol run, *i.e.*, A, B, c_A and c_B and outputs 1 if the equality test was successful or 0 otherwise.

Definition 1. *The PET protocol of Section 3 achieves equality testing indistinguishability, if every p.p.t. adversary $\mathcal{A}^{dist}$ has negligible advantage:*

$$Adv_A^{dist} = |Pr[(Exp_A^{PET\text{-}dist}(p, q, \mathcal{L}_n, A = g_A^{r_A}, B = g_A^{r_B}, c_A, c_B) = 1) = 1/2] -$$

$$Pr[(Exp_A^{PET\text{-}dist}(p, q, \mathcal{L}_n, A = g_A^{r_A}, B = g_B^{r_B}, c_A, c_B) = 0) = 1/2]|$$

Theorem 2 (Equality test indistinguishability). *The PET protocol of Section 3 is equality test indistinguishable under the Computational Diffie-Hellman assumption, provided that $E(.)$ is a secure encryption function.*

Proof. Assume that $\mathcal{A}^{dist}$ has non-negligible advantage and is able to distinguish a successful equality test from a non-successful one. A successful PET run implies that $g_A = g_B = g$ and thus $k_A = k_B = H(g^{r_A r_B}) = k$. Since $\mathcal{A}^{dist}$ can distinguish, this implies one of the two cases:

Case 1: $\mathcal{A}^{dist}$ **was able to compute the key** k. In that case the adversary would be able to decrypt c_B and c_A and distinguish successful equality tests from non-successful ones. This however contradicts the CDH assumption.

Case 2: $\mathcal{A}^{dist}$ **was able to verify the equality testing phase without learning the key** k. In that case the adversary would be able to verify that c_A is the encryption of the known plaintext h'_A and c_B is the encryption of the known plaintext h_B, encrypted with a common, unknown key k. This however contradicts the assumption that $E_K()$ is a secure encryption function. $\square$

An internal adversary captures a curious user running the protocol of Section 3 trying to reveal the private input of the other party, in case of inequality. Let $\mathcal{A}^{reveal}$ denote such an adversary, whose goal is to reveal the private information g_B of Bob, using the input of a protocol run, as well as the private information of Alice[6].

Theorem 3 (Private input protection from internal attackers). *An internal adversary $\mathcal{A}^{reveal}$ cannot learn anything about the private input of the other party, if the equality test of Section 3 fails, under the DLP assumption.*

Proof. In addition to the external adversary (see Theorem 1), an internal adversary $\mathcal{A}^{reveal}$ will also have access to the secret keys of the corrupted user. For example, if Alice is corrupted, then $\mathcal{A}^{reveal}$ will also have access to g_A, r_A and k_A and the goal of $\mathcal{A}^{reveal}$ is to learn the private input of the other party (say g_B), after the equality test has failed. Since $\mathcal{L}_n$ is a low entropy set, Alice may attempt a brute-force search, in order to find for each element $g_i \in \mathcal{L}_n$, a value $r_i \in Z_q$ such that $B \equiv g_i^{r_i}(mod\ p)$. Then she can verify which is the correct pair by using r_i to compute the key $\widetilde{k}_B = H(A^{r_i})$ and check if this can correctly decrypt c_B. However, under the DLP assumption, $\mathcal{A}^{reveal}$ cannot compute the discrete log of B to any base $g_i \in \mathcal{L}_n$ and thus the protocol provides private input protection from internal attackers. $\square$

4   A Privacy-Preserving Buddy-Finder Service Using PET

We use the Private Equality Testing protocol described in Section 3, in order to design a location privacy-aware, Buddy-Finder SNS service (BFSN), which

---

[6] In the same way, the adversary may attempt to reveal the private information of Alice instead of Bob and take as input the private information of Bob.

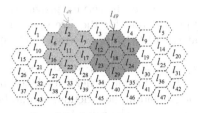

Fig. 2. Mapping locations to proximity testing input. Starting from level-0 cells, higher layer locations can be defined to fine-tune the location privacy level for users

allows users being in the same area (based on a predefined set of location areas) to be aware of this fact, without disclosing location information of the users.

We consider a social network of multiple users, who are subscribed to the BFSN service. Every user can create a personal profile including a group of friends, readable by all friends in the group (*i.e.*, a *bulletin board* public to the users within her/his profile). Thus users who are friends can have access to each others profile. We assume that messages published by a user on his profile area cannot be erased or tampered with. Each user is also able to calculate the coordinates of its current position, *e.g.*, through GPS (Global Positioning System) equipment. We assume that the time is divided into a number of discrete periods (*e.g.*, minutes or hours) T_t, $t \geq 1$, where each period is determined by a common global clock, and that the clocks of all clients are loosely synchronized throughout the whole session.

Preparing Locations for PET. We inherit the setup described in Section 3 and repeat all the assumptions made there. Locations can be described in various ways, including cells, distances of a given range, or circles of a given position and radius. In our system, the location areas are defined based on cells. The service provider (LBSP) defines the cell size and divides the physical map into cells (Fig. 2), which are the minimum (*level-0*) areas that can be used as locations for the proximity testing. Each cell is assigned a unique number l_i from the set L_n. Moreover, the LBSP may also define larger locations as areas consisting of a number of adjacent cells. In our example, we have defined *level-1* areas consisting of the six surrounding cells of each cell. Note that the level-1 areas may be overlapping or not. These areas are also assigned to a unique number in L_n. In our example l_{48} and l_{49} are unique numbers mapped to two adjacent and non-overlapping (disjoint) level-1 areas. The supported levels and the exact mapping of areas to unique numbers is arranged by the LBS provider and announced to all system users.

Setup. The LBSP decides the size of the cell, the size and number of areas of higher level and the mapping of all the locations of all possible levels to a unique number in L_n. The LBSP publishes the system parameters such as: p, q, the set L_n, the mapping of each element $l_i \in L_n$ to a physical location area, the levels of areas that are defined by the LBSP, as well as the mapping function f for assigning each $l_i \in L_n$ to a unique $g_i \in \mathcal{L}_n$. We assume that regardless of the number of levels of areas defined by the service provider, L_n has (polynomially) low entropy (a typical upper bound for the size of L_n is 2^{40}). For simplicity's sake, we will assume that the LBSP supports two levels of areas(Fig. 2).

Proximity Testing. Say that Bob belongs to Alice's friends group. Alice wants to encrypt her location so that if some of her friends are nearby, they can learn this fact. However, no one (including her friends) should be able to find out the location of Alice, if they are not in the same location.

Say that Alice is currently (at time period T_t) located in the cell identified as l_6 (level-0 area). Thus Alice is at the same time located in the level-1 area identified by l_{48}. Then Alice decides the location privacy level(s) she is willing to use. Assume that Alice wants to let her friends find out her location, only if they are at the same level-0 cell (l_6).

Alice computes $g_{A,t} \leftarrow f(l_6)$, runs Round 1 of the PET protocol of section 3 and publishes $A_t \leftarrow g_{A,t}^{r_{A,t}} \bmod p$, on her profile area, as her encrypted level-0 location. This can be seen as sending a probe message for opening a PET session with level-0 location proximity, to any of her friends who may be interested. Let assume a friend of Alice, Bob, who is interested to see if he is in the same level-0 cell with Alice. Bob will accept Alice's probe and establish a PET session by executing Round 2 of the PET protocol. Alice and Bob are able to complete the protocol session in order to find out if they are at the same level-0 cell or not.

Example 1. Say that Bob is currently located in the level-0 cell l_7. Then Bob will compute $g_{B,t} \leftarrow f(l_7)$, both users will run the PET protocol and they will find out that they are not in the same level-0 location. Indeed, if $g_{A,t} = g_{B,t}$ then the location IDs of both users are equal, with overwhelming probability (recall that f may utilize a collision-resistant function H). If not, then neither user will learn nothing about the other's location. More importantly, no other entity, including the LBSP, will learn nothing about the location of the users.

Example 2. Assume Alice and Bob have also decided to use the proximity test for the larger (level-1) areas. Alice also computes $g'_{A,t} \leftarrow f(l_{48})$, runs Round 1 of the PET protocol and also publishes on her profile area $A'_t \leftarrow g'^{r'_{A,t}}_{A,t} \bmod p$ as her encrypted level-1 location. Then, by running PET, Bob and Alice will find out they are in the same level-1 area but not in the same level-0 area.

4.1 Efficiency and Performance

By assuming that symmetric key encryption / decryption and hash evaluation have analogous costs, proximity testing requires, from each user, 2 public key operations (exponentiations modulo p) and at most 5 symmetric key operations. Our protocol is also scalable, since half of the total public key exponentiations per PET session, *i.e.*, the (A_t, B_t) values of Rounds 1, 2, could also be used for parallel equality testing sessions with other users of the group, during period T_t. For example, Alice could also use the $(g_{A,t}, A_t)$ values for establishing a PET session at another friend's profile area, during period T_t.

We measured the CPU time required for Alice, when executing the PET protocol with 100 friends. The processor we used was a Intel Core i5 CPU 650 @ 3.2

GHz x 4. The code was implemented in Python using PyCrypto v2.6.1 routines for selecting a random 1024-bit strong prime, choosing a generator of the cyclic subgroup of prime order q (for a 160-bit q), performing modular exponentiation, and encrypting/decrypting with AES. For hashing we used SHA-512 via Python's hashlib. We considered the worst case scenario where Alice probes for a PET session, and all her friends accept the probe. Execution time was 2.3 seconds $\pm 5\%$. Elliptic Curve Cryptography (ECC) [42] could also offer equivalent security with substantially smaller keys e.g., a 160-bit key is expected to offer comparable security with a 1024-bit key. The ECC-implemention is left for future work.

5   Conclusions

In this paper we described an efficient and secure scheme for PET and argued on its usefulness for establishing location privacy in geo-social applications such as the popular Buddy-Finder SNS. In future work, we intend to elaborate on the specifications of the Buddy-Finder service, implement our protocol using ECC cryptography for smart phones, and use a real social network for managing communication. Furthermore, we intend to explore the application of our private equality testing primitive in other related research areas, such as: Privacy-preserving record linkage (i.e., determining the equality/similarity of encrypted data records in distributed databases), proximity-dependent key agreement (i.e., peers agree on a key only with neighbors), electronic auctions (privately matching bids in multi-item auctions) etc.

Acknowledgement. The authors would like to thank Constantinos Patsakis for indicating an attack in an early version of the PET protocol.

References

1. Duckham, M., Kulik, L.: A formal model of obfuscation and negotiation for location privacy. In: Gellersen, H.-W., Want, R., Schmidt, A. (eds.) PERVASIVE 2005. LNCS, vol. 3468, pp. 152–170. Springer, Heidelberg (2005)
2. Hoh, B., Gruteser, M., Xiong, H., Alrabady, A.: Preserving privacy in gps traces via uncertainty-aware path cloaking. In: Proceedings of the 14th ACM Conference on Computer and Communications Security, pp. 161–171. ACM (2007)
3. Olumofin, F., Tysowski, P.K., Goldberg, I., Hengartner, U.: Achieving efficient query privacy for location based services. In: Atallah, M.J., Hopper, N.J. (eds.) PETS 2010. LNCS, vol. 6205, pp. 93–110. Springer, Heidelberg (2010)
4. Shin, K.G., Ju, X., Chen, Z., Hu, X.: Privacy protection for users of location-based services. IEEE Wireless Communications 19, 30–39 (2012)
5. Chow, C.Y., Mokbel, M.F.: Privacy in location-based services: a system architecture perspective. Sigspatial Special 1, 23–27 (2009)
6. Magkos, E.: Cryptographic approaches for privacy preservation in location-based services: A survey. International Journal of Information Technologies and Systems Approach (IJITSA) 4, 48–69 (2011)
7. Gruteser, M., Grunwald, D.: Anonymous usage of location-based services through spatial and temporal cloaking. In: Proceedings of the 1st International Conference on Mobile Systems, Applications and Services, pp. 31–42. ACM (2003)

8. Gedik, B., Liu, L.: Location privacy in mobile systems: A personalized anonymization model. In: Proceedings of the 25th IEEE International Conference on Distributed Computing Systems, ICDCS 2005, pp. 620–629. IEEE (2005)

9. Bettini, C., Wang, X.S., Jajodia, S.: Protecting privacy against location-based personal identification. In: Jonker, W., Petković, M. (eds.) SDM 2005. LNCS, vol. 3674, pp. 185–199. Springer, Heidelberg (2005)

10. Mokbel, M.F., Chow, C.Y., Aref, W.G.: The new casper: query processing for location services without compromising privacy. In: Proceedings of the 32nd International Conference on Very Large Data Bases, pp. 763–774. VLDB Endowment (2006)

11. Khoshgozaran, A., Shahabi, C.: Blind evaluation of nearest neighbor queries using space transformation to preserve location privacy. In: Papadias, D., Zhang, D., Kollios, G. (eds.) SSTD 2007. LNCS, vol. 4605, pp. 239–257. Springer, Heidelberg (2007)

12. Chow, C.-Y., Mokbel, M.F.: Enabling private continuous queries for revealed user locations. In: Papadias, D., Zhang, D., Kollios, G. (eds.) SSTD 2007. LNCS, vol. 4605, pp. 258–275. Springer, Heidelberg (2007)

13. Xue, M., Kalnis, P., Pung, H.K.: Location diversity: Enhanced privacy protection in location based services. In: Choudhury, T., Quigley, A., Strang, T., Suginuma, K. (eds.) LoCA 2009. LNCS, vol. 5561, pp. 70–87. Springer, Heidelberg (2009)

14. Ku, W.S., Chen, Y., Zimmermann, R.: Privacy protected spatial query processing for advanced location based services. Wireless Personal Communications 51, 53–65 (2009)

15. Xu, J., Tang, X., Hu, H., Du, J.: Privacy-conscious location-based queries in mobile environments. IEEE Transactions on Parallel and Distributed Systems 21, 313–326 (2010)

16. Sioutas, S., Magkos, E., Karydis, I., Verykios, V.S.: Uncertainty for privacy and 2-dimensional range query distortion. Journal of Computing Science and Engineering 5, 210–222 (2011)

17. Chow, C.Y., Mokbel, M.F., Liu, X.: A peer-to-peer spatial cloaking algorithm for anonymous location-based service. In: Proceedings of the 14th Annual ACM International Symposium on Advances in Geographic Information Systems, pp. 171–178. ACM (2006)

18. Ghinita, G., Kalnis, P., Skiadopoulos, S.: Prive: anonymous location-based queries in distributed mobile systems. In: Proceedings of the 16th International Conference on World Wide Web, pp. 371–380. ACM (2007)

19. Ghinita, G., Kalnis, P., Skiadopoulos, S.: MOBIHIDE: A mobilea peer-to-peer system for anonymous location-based queries. In: Papadias, D., Zhang, D., Kollios, G. (eds.) SSTD 2007. LNCS, vol. 4605, pp. 221–238. Springer, Heidelberg (2007)

20. Ghinita, G., Kalnis, P., Khoshgozaran, A., Shahabi, C., Tan, K.L.: Private queries in location based services: anonymizers are not necessary. In: Proceedings of the 2008 ACM SIGMOD International Conference on Management of Data, pp. 121–132. ACM (2008)

21. Solanas, A., Martínez-Ballesté, A.: A ttp-free protocol for location privacy in location-based services. Computer Communications 31, 1181–1191 (2008)

22. Zhong, G., Hengartner, U.: A distributed k-anonymity protocol for location privacy. In: IEEE International Conference on Pervasive Computing and Communications, PerCom 2009, pp. 1–10. IEEE (2009)

23. Jaiswal, S., Nandi, A.: Trust no one: a decentralized matching service for privacy in location based services. In: Proceedings of the Second ACM SIGCOMM Workshop on Networking, Systems, and Applications on Mobile Handhelds, pp. 51–56. ACM (2010)

24. Hashem, T., Kulik, L., Zhang, R.: Privacy preserving group nearest neighbor queries. In: Proceedings of the 13th International Conference on Extending Database Technology, pp. 489–500. ACM (2010)
25. Hashem, T., Kulik, L.: "Don't trust anyone": Privacy protection for location-based services. Pervasive and Mobile Computing 7, 44–59 (2011)
26. Narayanan, A., Thiagarajan, N., Lakhani, M., Hamburg, M., Boneh, D.: Location privacy via private proximity testing. In: NDSS. The Internet Society (2011)
27. Priya, E.M., Mani, G.: Privacy for location based system in mobile p2p environment. Procedia Engineering 38, 2179–2185 (2012)
28. Solanas, A., Martínez-Ballesté, A.: Privacy protection in location-based services through a public-key privacy homomorphism. In: López, J., Samarati, P., Ferrer, J.L. (eds.) EuroPKI 2007. LNCS, vol. 4582, pp. 362–368. Springer, Heidelberg (2007)
29. Song, D.X., Wagner, D., Perrig, A.: Practical techniques for searches on encrypted data. In: Proceedings of the 2000 IEEE Symposium on Security and Privacy, S&P 2000, pp. 44–55. IEEE (2000)
30. Furukawa, J., Isshiki, T.: Controlled joining on encrypted relational database. In: Abdalla, M., Lange, T. (eds.) Pairing 2012. LNCS, vol. 7708, pp. 46–64. Springer, Heidelberg (2013)
31. Chase, M., Kamara, S.: Structured encryption and controlled disclosure. In: Abe, M. (ed.) ASIACRYPT 2010. LNCS, vol. 6477, pp. 577–594. Springer, Heidelberg (2010)
32. Boldyreva, A., Chenette, N., Lee, Y., O'Neill, A.: Order-preserving symmetric encryption. In: Joux, A. (ed.) EUROCRYPT 2009. LNCS, vol. 5479, pp. 224–241. Springer, Heidelberg (2009)
33. Cash, D., Jarecki, S., Jutla, C.S., Krawczyk, H., Rosu, M., Steiner, M.: Highly-scalable searchable symmetric encryption with support for boolean queries. IACR Cryptology ePrint Archive 2013, 169 (2013)
34. Boneh, D., Di Crescenzo, G., Ostrovsky, R., Persiano, G.: Public key encryption with keyword search. In: Cachin, C., Camenisch, J.L. (eds.) EUROCRYPT 2004. LNCS, vol. 3027, pp. 506–522. Springer, Heidelberg (2004)
35. Boneh, D., Waters, B.: Conjunctive, subset, and range queries on encrypted data. In: Vadhan, S.P. (ed.) TCC 2007. LNCS, vol. 4392, pp. 535–554. Springer, Heidelberg (2007)
36. Bellare, M., Boldyreva, A., O'Neill, A.: Deterministic and efficiently searchable encryption. In: Menezes, A. (ed.) CRYPTO 2007. LNCS, vol. 4622, pp. 535–552. Springer, Heidelberg (2007)
37. Canard, S., Fuchsbauer, G., Gouget, A., Laguillaumie, F.: Plaintext-checkable encryption. In: Dunkelman, O. (ed.) CT-RSA 2012. LNCS, vol. 7178, pp. 332–348. Springer, Heidelberg (2012)
38. Cramer, R., Gennaro, R., Schoenmakers, B.: A secure and optimally efficient multi-authority election scheme. European Transactions on Telecommunications 8, 481–490 (1997)
39. Yang, G., Tan, C.H., Huang, Q., Wong, D.S.: Probabilistic public key encryption with equality test. In: Pieprzyk, J. (ed.) CT-RSA 2010. LNCS, vol. 5985, pp. 119–131. Springer, Heidelberg (2010)
40. Tang, Q.: Towards public key encryption scheme supporting equality test with fine-grained authorization. In: Parampalli, U., Hawkes, P. (eds.) ACISP 2011. LNCS, vol. 6812, pp. 389–406. Springer, Heidelberg (2011)
41. Lindell, Y., Pinkas, B.: Secure multiparty computation for privacy-preserving data mining. Journal of Privacy and Confidentiality 1, 5 (2009)
42. SECG: Standards for efficient cryptography group. SEC 1: Elliptic curve cryptography (2005), http://www.secg.org/download/aid-385/sec1_final.pdf

Controlled Shuffling, Statistical Confidentiality and Microdata Utility: A Successful Experiment with a 10% Household Sample of the 2011 Population Census of Ireland for the IPUMS-International Database

Robert McCaa, Krishnamurty Muralidhar, Rathindra Sarathy,
Michael Comerford, and Albert Esteve-Palos

Robert McCaa, Minnesota Population Center, 50 Willey Hall, Minneapolis, MN 55455, USA
rmccaa@umn.edu

Abstract. IPUMS-International disseminates more than two hundred-fifty integrated, confidentialized census microdata samples to thousands of researchers world-wide at no cost. The number of samples is increasing at the rate of several dozen per year, as quickly as the task of integrating metadata and microdata is completed. Protecting the statistical confidentiality and privacy of individuals represented in the microdata is a sine qua non of the IPUMS project. For the 2010 round of censuses, even greater protections are required, while researchers are demanding ever higher precision and utility. This paper describes a tripartite collaborative experiment using a ten percent household sample of the 2011 census of Ireland to estimate risk, mask the microdata using controlled shuffling, and assess analytical utility by comparing the masked data against the unprotected source microdata. Controlled shuffling exploits hierarchically ordered coding schemes to protect privacy and enhance utility. With controlled shuffling, the lesson seems to be the more detail means less risk and greater utility. Overall, despite substantial perturbation of the masked dataset (30% of adults on one or more characteristic), we find that data utility is very high and information loss is slight, even for fairly complex analytical problems.

Keywords: controlled shuffling, population census, microdata sample, data privacy, data utility, statistical disclosure controls, IPUMS-International, Ireland.

1   Introduction

IPUMS-International disseminates integrated, confidentialized census microdata samples to researchers world-wide at no cost[1]. Currently, 259 samples (561 million person records) encompassing 82% of the world's population (79 countries) are available to more than 10,000 registered users, representing over one hundred nationalities. Each year the database expands with the addition of samples for the 2010 round of censuses and for more countries, as the tasks of integrating microdata and metadata are completed.

Protecting the confidentiality and privacy of individuals represented in the microdata is a sine qua non for the IPUMS project. Access is restricted by means of a

J. Domingo-Ferrer (Ed.): PSD 2014, LNCS 8744, pp. 326–337, 2014.

rigorous vetting process. To be granted access, researchers must demonstrate their bona fides, agree to abide by the stringent conditions of the user license, and demonstrate a specific research need. The microdata are further protected by the fact that researchers do not obtain complete copies of samples, but instead must submit an individual ("extract") request, specifying not only the sample or samples but also the precise variables and even sub-populations required. In other words, each extract is unique, and none is complete. This process of dissemination provides additional safeguards against researchers sharing data with unauthorized persons.

Technical measures, such as sampling of households, suppression of variables and codes, and swapping of records, are also used to protect the confidentiality of the microdata. For the 2010 round of censuses, even greater protections are required due to the explosion in available microdata, the development of ingenuous techniques of data mining and matching, and the threat of unethical behavior facilitated by the internet. Honesty, trust and professional responsibility continue to be held in highest esteem by all but the tiniest minority of researchers. Nonetheless, census microdata must be protected such that the slightest allegation of violation of confidentiality may be immediately and credibly debunked.

The threat of de-anonymization in the age of "Big Data" is real. Despite the fact that to gain access to the IPUMS-International database the conditions of use license endorsed by each user expressly prohibits any attempt to identify individuals in the census microdata, before release strong technical measures must be applied to protect the microdata against even the remote likelihood of re-identification. At the same time we must assure researchers that the microdata are of the highest precision and utility.

This paper describes a tripartite collaborative experiment to estimate risk (Comerford), protect the data using controlled shuffling (Muralidhar and Sarathy), and assess the analytical utility (McCaa and Esteve). Thanks to the cooperation of the Central Statistical Office of the Republic of Ireland, a 10% household sample of the 2011 census was used as a test case. The sample is richly detailed with 474,535 person records, 117,945 families, and 79,785 couples described by 43 variables and more than 1,400 unique attributes. Person records include variables for single year of age (0-85+), occupation (number of categories=90), industry (110), country of birth (92), nationality (75), relationship to reference person (12), educational level (7), etc. Before beginning the experiment, we recoded "County of usual residence" (35) into region (8), thereby sacrificing geographical detail to facilitate analysis of social, demographic, cultural and economic attributes.

2   k-Anonymity

A standard approach to the assessment of disclosure risk addresses three key aspects in the literature: the data environment, the sensitivity of the data and the data characteristics. Examples of this type of approach can be seen in [2], [3]. In our analysis we interpreted these three aspects in the following ways. The data environment is an attempt to capture information about the world outside of the data under consideration for release. This information is used to demonstrate the a priori knowledge of a would-be intruder and can be configured in a number of ways to simulate different intruder scenarios. In our experiments we wanted to provide a robust analysis and therefore chose a deliberately conservative re-identification key. This was based on the growing concerns about the amount of information publicly available online through social networking sites, e.g., Facebook and LinkedIn. Searching public profiles on LinkedIn using one of our author's names revealed a number of individuals that share a very detailed personal curriculum vitae, without the need for a 'friend request' style level of security.

Extrapolating the information from social media we constructed our conservative key with the following variables from the census sample: sex, age, marital status, nationality, ethnicity, level of education, occupational group, industry classification, region of usual residence, region of birth, country of usual residence and country of birth. This assumes a high level of knowledge for an intruder and should be seen as a worst case scenario.

In this context, 'data sensitivity' means the extent to which the data's subjects might consider the information held in the dataset to represent a threat to their privacy. This is often considered aside from the legal obligations of the data holders. For example, projects like the Scottish Health Informatics Programme (SHIP) use this aspect of risk assessment to build trust with the data subjects, holding focus groups with patient representatives. For our experiments the data sensitivity contributed to the selection of our test parameters as set out below, taking into account also that we are working with a sample of the population.

The data characteristics take the information gathered from the environment and the data sensitivity and seek to describe the data in an empirical analysis. For this purpose we used k-anonymity, a well-established tool for highlighting re-identification risk. K-anonymity is satisfied if a record is indistinguishable from k-1 other records for a given key. Despite certain criticisms and enhancements k-anonymity still offers a reliable test providing the results are interpreted within the test's definition. For a discussion of k-anonymity see [4]. Given our assessment of the data sensitivity in this case, we set the k-anonymity threshold at 3, and the key as referenced above.[1]

The first pass of the data, using a k-anonymity threshold of three, flagged 78% of records as not meeting the k-anonymity criteria. This high level was to be expected given such a strong key. This allowed us to look at those records that did meet the criteria and unpick their apparent homogeneity. The results showed that at this level young people made up the bulk of our records meeting the k-anonymity criteria because they share a number of values in our key i.e. they tend not to have been married, they do not work, and they are still in school.

For the second pass of the data we experimented by removing variables from the key to see what effect this would have on the k-anonymity rate. After each k-anonymity test we analyzed the remaining risky records to inform the order in which

---

[1] K-anonymity tests were carried out using the NIAH algorithm available from: https://sourceforge.net/projects/niahsdc/

variables could be removed from the key. Once an order was chosen those records that flipped from 'not satisfying' to 'satisfying' k-anonymity were flagged with a dummy variable indicating which variable had affected the change.

We concluded that the variables age, education, occupational group and industry classification followed by the geographical variables should be considered for our later data shuffling experiments.

3   Controlled Data Shuffling to Prevent Disclosure and Preserve Utility

The purpose of disclosure risk assessment is to identify the extent to which the unmodified release of the data could result in potential re-identification of the records and, possibly, the subsequent disclosure of sensitive information regarding individuals. If the risk of such disclosure is deemed low, then it may be appropriate to allow users to analyze the original data resulting in the highest level of analytical utility. When the risk of disclosure is high, then it may be necessary to modify the data prior to dissemination so as to prevent re-identification and disclosure of confidential information. The process of modifying the data prior to allowing access is often referred to as data masking.

There are a wide variety of data masking solutions that are available. At the broadest level, they can be classified as input or output masking. In input masking, the original data is masked and all analyses are performed on the masked data. In output masking, the analyses are performed on the original data and the results of the analyses are masked prior to release. For static data, which includes all the samples integrated into the IPUMS-International database, input masking is generally preferred since it provides the assurance that the results of the same analysis on the same data performed at any point in time will always yield the same results. Maintaining consistency at this basic level is crucial to maintain users trust in the validity of the data. For output masking, unfortunately, it is extremely difficult (if not practically impossible) to ensure consistent results. Hence, in the remainder of this paper, we limit our discussion to input masking.

There are many input masking techniques that are available. Hundepool et al. provide an excellent discussion of these techniques [5]. Given that we have used k-anonymity to identify risky records, it seems reasonable that input masking through aggregation, simple aggregation for categorical data [6] and micro-aggregation for numerical data [7] would be relevant. Unfortunately, given that close to 80% of the records were identified as being at risk, the level of aggregation that is required in order to prevent disclosure is so high the types of analyses that can be performed on the aggregated data would be severely limited. In order to provide users with greater flexibility in analyzing the data, we chose to investigate alternative procedures.

Input masking through data perturbation is one approach that can be used in these situations. There are many data perturbation techniques that are available (see [5]). Most of these techniques rely on modifying the original data through random noise, and the values in the masked data are different from those in the original data. This would be perfectly acceptable for traditional numerical data. The treatment of nominal data is a more difficult problem for data perturbation approaches, and only a few select techniques are capable of perturbing nominal data (see Hundepool et al [5] for a comprehensive discussion).

Recently Domingo-Ferrer et al [8] identified the specific problem of taxonomic data, that is, data whose values are nominal but also have a hierarchical structure such as medical diagnosis coded using the International Classification of Diseases [9]. In the Irish data, there are two variables that fall under the category of taxonomic data (Industry classification with 110 hierarchical categories and Occupation group with 90 hierarchical categories). For example, the 90 3-digit occupation groups are divided into 9 1-digit groups. Group 1, "Managers, Directors and Senior Officials", contains 12 3-digit occupations, while Group 9, "Elementary Occupations", has only 9. By controlling the shuffling to take into account the hierarchical codes, the perturbed data are more likely to preserve associations with other variables, such as education, industry, and even age.

One approach to handling taxonomic data is to convert them to purely nominal data (by representing every unique code within the taxonomy as a nominal variable). The problem with this approach is that it results in a very large number of nominal variables making it extremely difficult to carry out the perturbation. More importantly, this transformation ignores the inherent taxonomy that is an integral part of the variable. Hence, in the presence of taxonomic data, perturbation approaches that "generate new values" for the original values are not appropriate.

Among data perturbation techniques, there are two that differ from all others in the fact they do not replace the original values with newly generated values, but reassign the original values between records. These two techniques are data swapping [10] and data shuffling [11]. In data swapping, the values of a variable are exchanged between two records within a specified proximity. The process will then have to be repeated for every variable that is to be masked. The problem with this approach is that the swapping is performed on a univariate basis and it is difficult to maintain consistent levels of swapping across many variables. Swapping also results in attenuation of the relationship both between the swapped variables and between the swapped and unswapped variables.

Data shuffling, by contrast, is a multivariate procedure where the values of the individual records are reassigned to other records in the data set based on the rank order correlation of the entire data set. One of the key features of data shuffling is that the rank order correlation of the masked data is asymptotically the same as that of the original data. This ensures that all monotonic relationships between the variables are preserved by the shuffling process. When compared to data swapping, data shuffling provides a higher level of utility and lower level of disclosure risk [12]. Data shuffling is capable of handling all types of data. Numerical and ordinal data inherently lend themselves to data shuffling. Nominal data are converted to binary data prior to shuffling. And for taxonomic data, numerical mapping proposed by Domingo-Ferrer et al [8] is used.

Data shuffling can be briefly described as follows. Let X represent the set of confidential variables and let S represent the set of non-confidential variables. Let Y represent the masked confidential variables. Data shuffling models the joint distribution of $\{X, S, Y\}$ as a multivariate normal (Gaussian) copula. Let $\{X^*, S^*\}$ represent the normalized values of the $\{X, S\}$. The perturbed normalized values Y^* are created using the conditional distribution $\{X^*, S^*\}$. Once the values of Y^* have been generated in this manner, the original values of X are reverse mapped to Y^* to result in the perturbed values Y. For a complete description of data shuffling please refer to Muralidhar and Sarathy (2006).

Data shuffling offers the following advantages:

1. The shuffled values Y have the same marginal distribution as the original values X. Hence, the results of all univariate analyses using Y provide exactly the same results as that using X.
2. The rank order correlation matrix of $\{Y, S\}$ is asymptotically the same as the rank order correlation matrix of $\{X, S\}$. Hence, the results of most multivariate analysis using $\{Y, S\}$ should asymptotically provide the same results as using $\{X, S\}$.

One of the key features of data shuffling is that the process is based on joint rank order correlation matrix of *all variables* $\{X, S, Y\}$. This provides the data administrator with the ability to control for disclosure risk by specifying the appropriate relationship between the original (X) and masked (Y) variables. This specification can range anywhere from no protection (no shuffling), to maximum protection (where X and Y are conditionally independent given S), and any level in between. Prior illustrations of data shuffling have used the maximum level of protection. We use the term *controlled data shuffling* to indicate that the desired level of disclosure protection has been specified by the data administrator. This new approach provides a much higher level of flexibility in implementing data shuffling. We now provide the results of implementing data shuffling for the Irish data.

4   Assessing Analytical Utility

The primary purpose of IPUMS-International is to provide researchers access to harmonized census microdata for countries around the globe. Hence, a successful data protection mechanism must ensure not only that the masked microdata are sufficiently confidentialized but also provide results that are similar to those using the original, unharmonized microdata held by the National Statistical Office-owners.

In this section, we assess analytical utility of the 10% household sample for the 2011 census of Ireland entrusted to the IPUMS-International project. One important aspect of this evaluation is that the microdata were masked without knowledge of the subsequent analyses that would be done on the dataset. Hence, this evaluation provides a more genuine assessment of the effectiveness of the masking procedure. As is the universal rule for official census microdata, we agreed to not report details regarding which variables were perturbed or the degree of perturbation. To do so would increase confidentiality risks for the microdata.

We consider confidentiality protection, taken as a whole, to be strong. One or more characteristics were perturbed for 29.9% of adults aged 20 years or more. For couples (excluding same-sex unions, which are too few in number to successfully shuffle as a conditional characteristic), joint attributes were taken into account to maintain husband-wife associations. For individuals, joint characteristics were controlled so as not to attenuate associations between occupation, industry, social class, educational attainment and socio-economic group. Six cycles of experiments were required to produce a "Goldilocks" dataset—one that was neither over- nor under-confidentialized and with utility at the highest possible levels—and therefore acceptable to all parties.

Overall, the results show excellent analytical utility. Consider age, for example. We compared mean age for 34,517 effective subgroups from over ten million permutations of six key variables: sex (2), level of educational attainment (7), industry (110), occupation (90), social class (8), and socio-economic group (11). As expected, differences are inversely proportional to the size of the cell counts. For combinations with counts of equal to or less than ten, the mean difference in age ranges between +/- 0.6 years. With cell counts of 30 or higher, the range shrinks to +/- 0.4

4.1   Log-Linear Models of Cells Counts

We use log-linear models to test whether complex analytical models—original and shuffled—produce the same best fitting models. To illustrate the method consider a four-way cross-classification of Age (20-85+, 66 categories), Sex (2), Marital status (4),and Region of usual residence (8). First we model the original source microdata using seven models. Second, we compute the same models using the shuffled data. Finally we compare the differences in goodness of fit between the two datasets. If the goodness of fit statistics for the original and shuffled data differ substantially, the masking procedure has distorted the results by introducing bias. Our model specification allows for unrestricted associations between all variables.

Our baseline or independent model can be written as follows:

$$\ln(F_{ijklm}) = \mu + \mu_i^A + \mu_j^S + \mu_k^M + \mu_l^R, \tag{1}$$

where $\ln(F_{ijkl})$ is the log of the expected cell frequency of the cases for cell $ijkl$ in the contingency table; $i, j, k, and l$ refer to the categories within the variables Age (A), Sex (S), Marital status (M), and Region (R). μ is the overall mean of the natural log of the expected frequencies; μ_i^A is the effect of age i has on the cell frequencies (the same for μ_j^S, μ_k^M, and μ_l^R).

Table 1 describes each of the models and goodness-of-fit statistics. Model 1 corresponds to the baseline or independent model described above. The modeling strategy consists of adding two level interactions between variables and testing for improvement in the fit of the model. To assess fit, we use the Likelihood Ratio Chi-squared statistic (L^2) and the Bayesian Information Criterion (BIC), which is based on the L^2 statistic [13]. BIC introduces a penalty term for the number of parameters in a model. Thus, it is possible to improve the fit of a model by adding more parameters, but if this adds unnecessary complexity in terms of a reduction in degrees of freedom, BIC will indicate a poorer fit.

Table 1. Log-linear models of original vs. shuffled data show small percentage differences

	Model	df	Goodness of fit				Percentage Difference*	
			Original Data		Shuffled Data			
			L^2	BIC	L^2	BIC	L^2	BIC
1	A, S, M, R	4147	203400.7	150522.8	203226.1	150348.2	0.1	0.1
2	AS, AR, AM	3432	13013.3	-30747.7	13052.5	-30708.5	-0.3	0.1
3	AS, AR, AM, SM	3429	6536.4	-37186.4	6573.5	-37149.3	-0.6	0.1
4	AS, AR, AM, SM, SR	3422	6471.8	-37161.7	6508.8	-37124.7	-0.6	0.1
5	**AS, AR, AM, SM, SR, RM**	**3401**	**5471.0**	**-37894.8**	**5505.7**	**-37860.1**	**-0.6**	**0.1**
6	ASM, ASR	2772	4748.0	-30597.4	4812.6	-30532.9	-1.4	0.2
7	ASM, ASR, SRM	2730	3426.3	-31383.6	3487.8	-31322.1	-1.8	0.2

Note: A (66) Age 20-85+, S (2) Sex, M (4) Marital Status, R (8) Region.
*Percentage difference = ((Original-Shuffled)/Original)*100
Source: Author's calculations from 10% household sample of the 2011 population census of Ireland

Models 2 to 7 include two and three level interactions between age, sex, marital status and region. Comparing goodness of fit statistics of the shuffled data with those from the original source data for each model reveals no significant differences in either L2 or BIC. Model 2 includes all two way interactions between age and sex, marital status and region. Model 2 indicates a substantial improvement over the baseline model in goodness of fit both in terms of L2 and BIC. Model 5 offers the most parsimonious fit for both datasets according to BIC (BIC5 = -37894.8 and -37860.1, respectively). Model five includes all possible two way interactions between age, sex, marital status and region. Three way interactions yield a tighter fit, but the loss in degrees of freedom is proportionally greater than the gains in goodness of fit, so BIC tells us that the additional model complexity is unwarranted.

What is striking from Table 1 is that both the original and shuffled datasets lead to the same best fitting model and the differences in goodness of fit between original and shuffled are trivial, less than 0.3% for BIC. All in all, the results clearly suggest that, with regard to the variables analyzed, there are no statistically significant differences between the shuffled and the original dataset. We conclude that distortions introduced by shuffling have not significantly diminished analytical utility.

4.2   Age Gap between Spouses

For a second test, consider the gap in ages between spouses, a challenging correlation to maintain with masked microdata. A notorious example of perturbation gone wrong is the sample of the 2000 census of the USA, which contains an embarrassing error due to masking of ages for persons 65 years and older. Later, the Census Bureau "corrected" the error, but seemingly worsened the discrepancy (left panel, Figure 1).

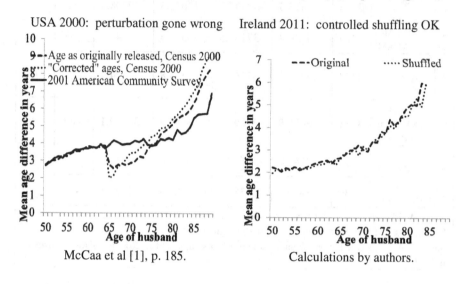

USA 2000: perturbation gone wrong   Ireland 2011: controlled shuffling OK

McCaa et al [1], p. 185.   Calculations by authors.

Fig. 1. Masking effects on age gap between spouses: two examples

In contrast, for the 10% household sample of Ireland (right panel, Figure 1), comparing the unperturbed and shuffled microdata reveals surprisingly minor discrepancies throughout the age range, despite the fact that in 4% of the cases age was masked for both members of the pair and in 20% at least one. The age gap between spouses is a strong test of data utility, a test that the shuffled Irish sample readily passes.

4.3   Own-Child Fertility

As a final test, we focus on fertility. Fertility is fundamental for demographic research, and population censuses offer valuable insights on fertility levels, trends, and differentials. Where the census does not ask questions on fertility, estimates can still be derived indirectly from household samples, using the "own-child method". Children aged 0-14 are matched to their mothers by means of the relationship to reference person variable. Then, a 15 year fertility series is constructed from the ages of mothers and their co-resident children. (The data are adjusted both for children who cannot be matched to mothers and for mortality). A challenging test for masked data is to replicate the age differences between mothers and their children.

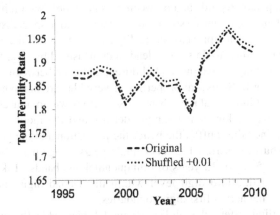

Fig. 2. 15 year series of Total Fertility Rates from shuffled and original microdata[2]

Figure 2 shows that the shuffling strategy yields astonishingly robust results in spite of the fact that the data were masked without any knowledge that it would be tested in this way. Differences in total fertility rates between the original data and the shuffled are at 3 decimal places. They are so imperceptible that for illustration purposes 0.01 was added to the shuffled series in Figure 2 to make the point that there are indeed two sets of data portrayed. Drilling down, we find that both datasets reveal declining fertility for ages 15-29 and rising fertility for ages 30-49. While this is not news to experts on Irish fertility, what is surprising is that the pattern is unmistakable even in the shuffled data.

5   Conclusion

Data shuffling is widely recognized as a robust masking procedure for confidentializing microdata. Controlled shuffling allows the data administrator greater flexibility to protect privacy and enhance utility. The success of this experiment was possible thanks to the close cooperation by the microdata owner/steward, statisticians, data administrators, and researchers. Initially, for the 2011 census sample of Ireland, a reduced set of variables, including age in five year bands, was offered to IPUMS, severely diminishing the utility of the sample. Following further discussion, CSO-Ireland agreed to furnish single year ages and more than a dozen additional variables provided the microdata could be confidentialized satisfactorily.

We were surprised at the difficulty in striking a balance between protection and utility for household samples with a rich array of variables. Six trials were required. The first was deemed acceptable by the CSO and the statistical experts, but not by the data administrators or researchers. With each successive round of experimentation we learned more about how to control the perturbations to retain utility, specifically

---

[2]   Shuffled microdata track the unperturbed source data so closely that to highlight separation its line is shifted +0.01. Otherwise differences are imperceptible.

associations within person records and between person records within households, yet protect the data. One important lesson is that subject matter specialists must be included in the confidentializing process for quality assurance to test the analytical utility of perturbed data. Failure to do so may lead to unmeasured bias, particularly in the associations between couples, parents and children, and even between variables within a single person record. Statistical properties of variables are not synonymous with analytical properties of individual records nor associations within households.

Counter-intuitively, the higher the sample density and the more detailed the variables, the finer grained the shuffle, the better the protection and the greater the utility. For example, shuffling across 1, 2, or 3 single years of age perturbs the data less than shuffling across 5, 10 or 15 years of quinquennial age bands. Likewise, for occupation, shuffling at the third digit level within the second digit distorts the data much less than shuffling across first digit boundaries.

Controlled shuffling offers the ability to model hierarchically ordered coding schemes common to census microdata. The promising results of this experiment may be of interest not only for masking census microdata but for all types of microdata with explicit hierarchical codes, whether based on international standards such as ISCO, ISIC, NACE, NUTS, etc. or ex post facto integrated codes such as those developed by IPUMS. The robustness of the shuffle is enhanced by taking into account associated characteristics—within households and within clusters of variables, such as correlations between occupation, industry, educational attainment, social class, etc.

With the success of this experiment, the CSO entrusted single years of age for the 2002 and 2006 samples which, before release to researchers, were confidentialized using controlled shuffling. Prior to publication of this paper, all three samples were successfully integrated into the IPUMS-International database and released to the research community for dissemination on a restricted access basis. The confidentialized sample of these and eight other censuses of Ireland (1971-2011) along with over 250 other samples for more than 75 countries may be downloaded at: https://international.ipums.org/international/sample_designs/sample_designs_ie.shtml

Researchers must heed the warning that microdata subjected to any masking procedure, including controlled shuffling, introduces bias. Moreover, the smaller the frequency of a combination of characteristics, the greater the proportion of cases perturbed. As indicated by the percentage differences in Table 1, the more complex the statistical analysis, the greater the distortion caused. Nonetheless of the hundreds of models tested (of which only 7 are reported here), the analytical differences are trivial. Compared with the enormous loss occasioned by aggregating age to five year groups and by the suppression of more than a dozen variables due to confidentiality concerns by the data producer, controlled shuffling offers an elegant solution to the conundrum of protecting statistical confidentiality, yet retaining the highest utility in the source microdata.

To assuage concerns regarding analytical validity and disclosure risk, the corresponding author extends an invitation to researchers to conduct analysis on the microdata that can be compared against the original (unmasked) data.

Acknowledgements. The authors greatly appreciate the cooperation of the Central Statistics Office of the Republic of Ireland in providing for this experiment a ten per cent household sample of the 2011 census. The authors alone are solely responsible for the contents of this paper. Funded in part by the National Science Foundation of the United States, Grant Nos. SES-0433654 and 0851414; National Institutes of Health, Grant Nos. R01HD047283 and R01HD044154.

References

1. Cleveland, L., McCaa, R., Ruggles, S., Sobek, M.: When Excessive Perturbation Goes Wrong and Why IPUMS-International Relies Instead on Sampling, Suppression, Swapping, and Other Minimally Harmful Methods to Protect Privacy of Census Microdata. In: Domingo-Ferrer, J., Tinnirello, I. (eds.) PSD 2012. LNCS, vol. 7556, pp. 179–187. Springer, Heidelberg (2012)

2. Elliot, M., Lomax, S., Mackey, E., Purdam, K.: Data Environment Analysis and the Key Variable Mapping System. In: Domingo-Ferrer, J., Magkos, E. (eds.) PSD 2010. LNCS, vol. 6344, pp. 138–147. Springer, Heidelberg (2010), http://www.springerlink.com/index/6KL805434G016U15.pdf (July 13, 2012)

3. Elliot, M., Dale, A.: Scenarios of attack: the data intruder's perspective on statistical disclosure risk. Netherlands Official Statistics 14, 6–10 (1999)

4. Domingo-Ferrer, J., Torra, V.: A critique of k-anonymity and some of its enhancements. In: Third International Conference on Availability, Reliability and Security, ARES 2008, pp. 990–993 (2008), http://ieeexplore.ieee.org/xpls/abs_all.jsp?rnumber=4529451 (accessed July 14, 2012)

5. Hundepool, A., Domingo-Ferrer, J., Franconi, L., Giessing, S., Nordholt, E., Spicer, K., de Wolf, P.-P.: Statistical Disclosure Control. Wiley Series in Survey Methodology. John Wiley & Sons, London (2012)

6. Sweeney, L.: k-anonymity: A model for protecting privacy. International Journal of Uncertainty, Fuzziness and Knowledge Based Systems 10, 557–570 (2001)

7. Domingo-Ferrer, J., Mateo-Sanz, J.M.: Practical data-oriented microaggregation for statistical disclosure control. IEEE Transactions on Knowledge and Data Engineering 14(1), 189–201 (2002)

8. Domingo-Ferrer, J., Muralidhar, K., Ruffian-Torrell, G.: Anonymization Methods for Taxonomic Microdata. In: Domingo-Ferrer, J., Tinnirello, I. (eds.) PSD 2012. LNCS, vol. 7556, pp. 90–102. Springer, Heidelberg (2012)

9. World Health Organization. International Classification of Diseases. Geneva, 9th Revision, Clinical Modification, 6th edn. (2008), http://icd9cm.chrisendres.com/

10. Dalenius, T., Reiss, S.P.: Data-swapping: A Technique for Disclosure Control. Journal of Statistical Planning and Inference 6, 73–85 (1982)

11. Muralidhar, K., Sarathy, R.: Data Shuffling-A New Masking Approach for Numerical Data. Management Science 52(5), 658–670 (2006)

12. Muralidhar, K., Sarathy, R., Dandekar, R.: Why Swap when you can Shuffle? A Comparison of the Proximity Swap and the Data Shuffle for Numeric Data. In: Domingo-Ferrer, J., Franconi, L. (eds.) PSD 2006. LNCS, vol. 4302, pp. 164–176. Springer, Heidelberg (2006)

13. Raftery, A.E.: Choosing models for cross-classifications. American Sociological Review 51(1), 145–146 (1986)

Balancing Confidentiality and Usability

Protecting Sensitive Data in the Case of Inward Foreign AffiliaTes Statistics (FATS)*

Katri Soininvaara[1], Teemu Oinonen[1], and Annu Nissinen[2]

[1] Statistics Finland, Department of Business Statistics
P.O.Box 6 D, FI-00022 Statistics, Finland
katri.soininvaara@gmail.com,
teemu.oinonen@stat.fi
[2] Statistics Finland, Department of Standards and Methods
P.O. Box 3 A, FI-00022 Statistics, Finland
annu.nissinen@stat.fi

Abstract. Statistical institutions are responsible both for protecting confidential information collected from statistical units, and for disseminating information to the public. Adhering to the legislation on confidentiality, the statistical institutions face two contradictory problems: one concerning statistical disclosure control, the other concerning the included level of detail and the usability of the disseminated information for the end users. As an empirical example of balancing the two problems, the paper reports the results of an experiment conducted with case data on the inward Foreign AffiliaTes Statistics (FATS). The results are analysed to support the further decision making on protecting statistical publications against statistical disclosure.

Keywords: Inward Foreign AffiliaTes Statistics, statistical disclosure control, table confidentiality, publication usability, experiment design.

1 Introduction

The paper discusses the issue of producing confidential but useful tables in the case of the inward Foreign AffiliaTes Statistics (FATS). In order to ensure that statistical units cannot be identified from the published tables, tabular data need to be protected by statistical disclosure control methods to prevent possible intruders from disclosing confidential information. However, if protecting the data means that most of the cells in the table cannot be published, there is hardly any sense to publish such tables in the first place. This is the problem of information loss due to the used protection method, currently prominent with the inward FATS.

The paper has three sections. This first section is an introduction, including the descriptions of the inward FATS and the problem of balancing confidentiality

---

* Revised version of a paper published in Statistics Finland's Working Papers series 6.3.2014. Working Papers 3/2014.

J. Domingo-Ferrer (Ed.): PSD 2014, LNCS 8744, pp. 338–349, 2014.

and usability of the inward FATS. The second section describes the experiment design and reports the results of the conducted 18-run experiment. The third section summarises the results and gives recommendations on how to balance the problems related to confidentiality and usability.

The inward FATS are collected from Norway and the European Union member countries to help to determine patterns of internationalisation, as well as to follow the consequences for expanding international business in the European Union. The relevant statistical institutions include Eurostat and the national statistical institutions (NSIs), such as Statistics Finland. The population for the inward FATS are those subsidiaries and branches in the compiling country that are controlled by a foreign entity. The collected data includes the residency of the ultimate controlling institutional unit (uci), industry classification ($nace$) and such characteristics as turnover, total purchases, and the number of persons employed. [2]

The inward FATS comprises two publications, IFATS Series 1 (1G) and IFATS Series 2 (1G2). Both tables 1G and 1G2 have the same two explanatory variables (uci and $nace$) but differ in the terms of included details. For Finland the table 1G includes the aggregated total firms in the compiling country (A1), aggregated compiling country enterprises (A2), aggregated foreign controlled enterprises in the compiling country (Z9), area aggregates V1 (EU-27, excluding Finland) and V2 (extra EU-27), C4 (offshore financial centres), and country level aggregates for the 27 EU countries (excluding Finland) and 14 extra-EU countries. The industry classification variable $nace$ includes three industry levels and the sum of the total business economy (from B to N, excluding K and including S95). The table 1G2 includes all the other countries in the world in addition to the ones displayed in the table 1G but only the sum of the total business economy. More detailed descriptions of the tables are available from the FATS compilation manual. [2]

As described in the beginning, there are two contradictory issues related to protecting tables. One concerns the protection of the identities of the statistical units, while the other relates to maximizing usability. In the inward FATS production the compiling NSIs have settled on using non-perturbative disclosure control methods such as cell suppression and modifying the levels of classification for explanatory variables in the table. The problem for the inward FATS tables is that currently information needs to be suppressed in great amounts to prevent disclosure of sensitive information. Additionally, there may be too much detail included in the classification of the explanatory variables for the IFATS Series 1. This results in an ineffective 1G table, where according to Eurostat's analysis around 64 % of its 6 240 cells are zero values (i.e. the cell value is less than 0.5, or there are no firms, so the cell is empty), further 5 % are missing, 20 % need to be suppressed for confidentiality reasons, and thus only 10 % of the cells display safe non-zero values [3]. The aim of this paper is to find a better solution, if there is one.

The two contradictory problems in the statistics production arise from the inconsistent needs for different stakeholders. The key stakeholders are statistical units, which in the case of the inward FATS are foreign controlled enterprises. Confidential information needs to be protected on account of possible intruders, which can be either internal, such as a foreign controlled unit trying to achieve a competitive edge, or external, such as an outsider investor trying to make a profit. Other interested parties include the end users, which comprise the government, the research community, and the public. Finally, there are the statistics compiling and disseminating institutions: the NSIs such as Statistics Finland, the EU level bodies such as Eurostat, and global organisations such as OECD.

Combining the issues discussed above, the research problem in this paper is to determine how to produce safe but informative inward FATS tables by using cell suppression for disclosure control, including the changes suggested by Eurostat for the classification of the explanatory variables [3]. The idea of the experiment is to analyse the effects of the different levels of classification for the explanatory variables, the use of different safety rule specifications, and the use of different secondary suppression algorithms.

The next section reviews an experiment, which analyses the choices for protection methods available for the statistical institutions compiling inward FATS statistics.

2   Analysis

The idea of the experiment conducted in this paper is to list and compare the different possible inward FATS 1G tables using modified levels of classification, safety rules, and secondary suppression algorithms to protect confidential information. The software used to conduct the experiment is τ-Argus 3.5.0., build 26 [4]. The aim is to find an improvement to the current situation, where most of the cells are either zero values (i.e. the cell value is less than 0.5 or the cell is empty) or need to be suppressed for protection.

The experiment is carried out for one of the response variables according to the specifications of the inward FATS table 1G described in the previous section. The inward FATS includes two series (1G and 1G2), so the protection is completed by linking the two tables. Linking the tables ensures that none of the information published in the other table can be used in disclosing confidential information from the other. In order to keep the experiment as simple as possible, only the table 1G is considered, so further discussion on the use of linked tables is outside the scope of this study.

Table 1 describes the experiment design, which is based on Box [1]. The standard combination $(-)$ shown describes the current situation, whereas the modifications $(+)$ are suggestions for improvements. The different combinations of the factors are run through two different secondary suppression algorithms. Although implicating a 2^5 or a 32-run experiment, the experiment here includes only 18 runs for each algorithm. This is because the factors A and B refer to the same standard specification of the explanatory variable *nace*, making the standard combinations of the factors A and B redundant. The factors differ in their modifications, which are stated as *Mod1* and *Mod2*. Similarly, the factors

Table 1. Experiment design

Factors	−	+
A: *nace*	Std	Mod1
B: *nace*	Std	Mod2
C: *uci*	Std	Mod1
D: *uci*	Std	Mod2
E: safety rule	Std	Mod

C and D refer to the same standard specification for the explanatory variable *uci* but have different modifications. This section presents the results for the first algorithm, while the corresponding tables and figures for the second algorithm can be found from the appendices for comparison.

The factors from A to D represent changes in the levels of classification for the explanatory variables. Changing these factors affects the level of detail included in the *nace* x *uci* table, and consequently adjusts the size of the table. The standard combination refers to the current classifications, which includes three hierarchical industry levels for *nace* and country level detail for *uci*. As discussed in the previous section, Eurostat has suggested that the current classifications may be too detailed, so the function of the experiment factors from A to D is to see what happens to active and confidential cell shares when the levels of classification are modified.

In the first modification to *nace* (factor A), the third level is dropped from examination. The second modification to *nace* (factor B) drops both the second and the third levels, which corresponds to the current Eurostat proposal [3]. In the first modification to *uci* (factor C) the country level is dropped, so that only the large area aggregates V1 (EU-27, excluding Finland) and V2 (extra EU-27) and their total aggregate Z9 (all foreign controlled enterprises in Finland), and the aggregate A2 (all Finnish controlled enterprises in Finland) are retained. In the second modification to *uci* (factor D), continental aggregates are introduced. Additionally, the second *uci* modification includes the aggregates A2 and Z9.

The factor E refers to the used safety rule. Changing the safety rule affects the amount of sensitive cells, and thus changes the level of confidentiality. The reason for modification to the safety rule in the experiment is to test if it is possible to reduce the share of confidential cells by slacking the used safety rule. Statistics Finland's internal guidelines on protection of tabulated enterprise data [5] restrict the safety rule alteration. In practice slacking the safety rule here means keeping the threshold rule for sensitive cells the same but altering the required safety margin. A similar reasoning lays behind the use of two different secondary suppression algorithms offered by the used software. The first algorithm is the hypercube algorithm and the second one is the modular algorithm [4].

The experiment results in four types of cells: active, safe, confidential, and empty. The total cells in the table consist of active and empty cells. Active cells or non-empty cells have firm activity between the particular *nace* x *uci* combination. Active cells are either safe or confidential. Safe refers to the cells that are published. Confidential cells consist of primary confidential cells plus the secondary suppressions determined by the used safety rule and the secondary suppression algorithm.

Empty cells refer to such cells, where there is no firm activity between the particular *nace* x *uci* combination. It should be noted that Eurostat refers to these as zero cells, which include both empty cells (marked as zeros in the inward FATS tables) and additionally such cells, where the cell value is less than 0.5. Thus in the experiment there are a few cells, which are counted as active, where values equal zero (i.e. there is firm activity in the cell but the value of the activity is zero), whereas in the FATS manual these are calculated as zero cells (i.e. there might or might not be any activity in the cell). The difference stems from the used software, which produces empty cells rather than zeros, and the Eurostat practise, described in more detail in the FATS compilation manual [2]. As the count of cells valued zero is negligible in the experiment, the difference does not affect the conclusions.

Table 2 summarises the results of the experiment for the first algorithm. The results for the second algorithm can be found from appendices, Table 5. It can be seen that the first run, where no modifications to the current situation are made, shows that 66 % of the active cells are suppressed. While this is the worst case in terms of confidential cell share, the unmodified table also includes the most detailed information, its active cell count totalling to 1 636, which includes 554 safe cells. The safe cell count is maximized at 597 with the run number two, where the only factor changed to the current situation is the safety rule factor E. In the modified specification, the safety rule has been slacked, and consequently the confidential cell share reduces to 64 %. From the appendix table 5 it can be seen that the second algorithm is more efficient, suppressing only 54 % and 53 % of the active cells in the corresponding cases.

The best case in terms of confidential cell share is the table resulting from the runs numbered 15 and 16, which are otherwise the same but have different modifications to the safety rule factor E. They result in identical tables, indicating

Table 2. The 18 runs and the results of the table redesign experiment

Run number	A *nace*	B *nace*	C *uci*	D *uci*	E safety rule	Total	Total active	Total safe	Safe/ Active	Confidential/ Active
1	−	−	−	−	−	6240	1636	554	0.34	0.66
2	−	−	−	−	+	6240	1636	597	0.36	0.64
3	+	−	−	−	−	3840	1148	438	0.38	0.62
4	+	−	−	−	+	3840	1148	460	0.40	0.60
5	−	+	−	−	−	864	370	183	0.49	0.51
6	−	+	−	−	+	864	370	191	0.52	0.48
7	−	−	+	−	−	650	599	424	0.71	0.29
8	−	−	+	−	+	650	599	430	0.72	0.28
9	−	−	−	+	−	1040	656	406	0.62	0.38
10	−	−	−	+	+	1040	656	414	0.63	0.37
11	+	−	+	−	−	400	381	313	0.82	0.18
12	+	−	+	−	+	400	381	315	0.83	0.17
13	+	−	−	+	−	640	432	298	0.69	0.31
14	+	−	−	+	+	640	432	301	0.70	0.30
15	−	+	+	−	−	90	89	81	0.91	0.09
16	−	+	+	−	+	90	89	81	0.91	0.09
17	−	+	−	+	−	144	112	82	0.73	0.27
18	−	+	−	+	+	144	112	82	0.73	0.27

that changing the chosen safety rule does not affect the results in this case. In these runs, both *nace* and *uci* are modified. Following the Eurostat suggestion, only the first level of *nace* is retained. Additionally, only the large area aggregates are retained from the variable *uci*. The result is a table with only 89 active cells, which is the smallest amount of safe cells from the alternatives presented here. However, the share of the confidential cells is minimized, as only 9 % of the cells need to be suppressed. Comparing with the appendix table 5, it can be seen that in this case the second algorithm results in the same table.

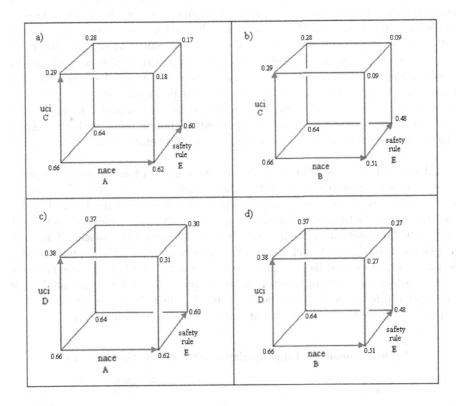

Fig. 1. Cube display of the experiment results

Figure 1, based on Box [1], is a graphical representation of the results for confidential cell share shown in the Table 2. In appendices Figure 2 presents a similar figure for the second algorithm. Each cube represents interactions between different combinations of the classification factors from A to D, and the safety rule factor E. Panel a) is a display of the factors A (*nace* with two levels), C (*uci* with large aggregates) and E (safety rule). Panel b) is a similar display for the factors B (*nace* with one level), C and E, panel c) is a display for the factors A, D (*uci* with continental aggregates) and E, and panel d) displays the factors B, D and E. The current situation, i.e. the run number one in the Table

2, is located in the left hand corner of each cube in the Figure 1. Changing *nace* means moving to the right and modifying *uci* means moving up. As a result, the upper right hand corners represent situations, where both variables are modified. Additionally, changing the safety rule means moving to the back panels of the cubes.

It can be seen from the Figure 1 that changing the safety rule affects the share of the suppressed cells in a minimal way or not at all. The most dramatic reductions in the confidential cell share come from modifying both *nace* and *uci* at the same time. While changing *nace* from three levels to two does not affect the confidential cell share in a significant manner, as seen from the panels a) and c), modifying *nace* further to contain only one level reduces the confidential cell share by 15 percentage points, as shown by the panels b) and d). Modifying *uci* changes the confidential cell share even more drastically, and using any combination of the two explanatory variable modifications results in both smaller tables and lower confidential cell shares as seen by looking at the upper right hand corners of each cube. Comparing with the appendix figure 2, it can be seen that the most results are five to ten percentage points lower with the second algorithm, meaning that the second algorithm is more efficient and results overall in fewer suppressions.

Table 3 displays nine table alternatives derived from the experiment results. As the chosen safety rule modification did not affect the results in a significant manner, the tables are shown only for the standard safety rule. It can be seen that the original situation results in a large 130 x 48 table, which only has 26 % of its cells filled with active cells. Only 9 % of the total cells are safe. The most drastic modification to the classifications leads to a table with dimensions 18 x 5, which only has 90 cells in total. However, a total of 99 % of these cells are active, in fact, only one of the cells is left empty. This highly aggregated table means that almost all, 90 % of the total cells in this table can be published. In appendices Table 6 displays a similar table for the second algorithm.

Table 3. Summary of the experiment with the standard safety rule

Table number	Run (Cf. Table 2)	nace levels	uci	Total	Active	Safe	Active Total	Safe Total	Table size	Size compared to original
1	5	1	countries	864	370	183	0.43	0.21	18 x 48	0.14
2	3	2	countries	3840	1148	438	0.30	0.11	80 x 48	0.62
3	1	3	countries	6240	1636	554	0.26	0.09	130 x 48	1.00
4	15	1	large areas	90	89	81	0.99	0.90	18 x 5	0.01
5	11	2	large areas	400	381	313	0.95	0.78	80 x 5	0.06
6	7	3	large areas	650	599	424	0.92	0.65	130 x 5	0.10
7	17	1	continents	144	112	82	0.78	0.57	18 x 8	0.02
8	13	2	continents	640	432	298	0.68	0.47	80 x 8	0.10
9	9	3	continents	1040	656	406	0.63	0.39	130 x 8	0.17

Removing the third *nace* level results in the table two, which has 80 x 48 cells. It is sized 62 % of the original table. However, only a slightly larger percentage for safe cells out of the total cells is gained, as it increases to 11 % from the original 9 %. Keeping only the first *nace* level, as suggested by Eurostat, the result is the table one, which has 18 x 48 cells. While the size of the table compared to the original shrinks to just 14 % of the size of the original table, the total safe cell share increases only to 21 % from the original 9 %. Additionally, keeping an eye on the absolute counts of the safe cells, it can be seen that the number of safe cells reduces to about a third from the original, from 554 to 183. Compared to the table five, where two of the *nace* levels are retained and *uci* is modified so that only the large aggregates remain, 313 safe cells are available, and the total safe cell share rises to 78 %. However, the size of the table compared to the original shrinks even further, to 6 %. The appendix table 6 shows the summary of the results for the second suppression algorithm.

Table 4 describes the results of an analysis, which aims to help choosing the most useful alternative from the choices considered in the experiment.

Table 4. Analysis of the alternative tables

Table number	Confidential cell share	Safe cell count	Size	Weight 1	Weight 2	Weight 3	Total	Rank
1	0.51	183	864	0	0	15	15	x
2	0.62	438	3840	0	25	25	50	x
3	0.66	554	6240	0	30	30	60	x
4	0.09	81	90	30	0	0	30	x
5	0.18	313	400	25	10	0	35	x
6	0.29	424	650	15	20	10	45	1
7	0.27	82	144	20	0	0	20	x
8	0.31	298	640	10	5	5	20	3
9	0.38	406	1040	5	15	20	40	2

Each table has been given weights based on three criteria. The first criterion states the share of confidential cells. It reflects the need to minimize the information loss due to protection, which implies that the smaller the confidential cell share, the better the usability. The lowest share gains 30 points and the highest three are given zero points. The second criterion is the safe cell count. It stands for the need to maximize usability, and reflects the absolute amount of information gained from the table. The largest number gets 30 points and the smallest three are given zero points. The third criterion is the size of the table measured by the total cell count. It reflects the need for included detail, implying that more detail is preferred to less detail. The largest table gets 30 points and the three smallest tables are given zero points. The total points are calculated as the sum of the three weight columns. Finally, if a table got zero points with any criteria, it is given a rank x, otherwise it is ranked based on the weighted points.

According to the analysis, the usability is maximised with the tables six, eight and nine. Tables six and nine retain the original three *nace* levels, whereas the table eight drops the third *nace* level. Table six includes aggregating the *uci* so that only large area aggregates remain. Tables eight and nine aggregate *uci* so that the countries are grouped under continental aggregates. The Eurostat suggestion [3], table one, gets an x-rank, as it is given zero points in the first and second criteria (confidential cell share and safe cell count). Moreover, it does not rank highly in the final criterion either, and results in the lowest total point score in the analysis.

Table 4 shows that the table six is ranked the highest given the three criteria after the x-ranked alternatives are dropped from the analysis. Thus the most useful table found in this paper as an alternative format for the inward FATS 1G table has a total of 650 cells. 92 % of the total cells are active, and 424 of the cells are safe. Although the size is just 10 % of the original and the reduction in size means also a reduction in the absolute count of safe cells, this is a great improvement from the current situation looking at the confidential cell share, which increases from 9 % to 65 %. However, usability remains a concern, as the alternative table implies large area aggregates, which replace the more detailed country level information. Nonetheless, as long as the need for the level of protection stays the same, this is the most usable version of the 1G table alternatives presented in this experiment given the three utilised criteria.

3   Conclusions

The objective of statistical institutions is both to protect the confidentiality of statistical units and to disseminate data for public use. These contradictory goals manifest as problems with balancing confidentiality and usability. The research problem in this paper set in the first section has been to determine how to produce safe but informative inward FATS tables by using cell suppression for disclosure control, including the changes suggested by Eurostat for the reclassification of the explanatory variables [3].

The second section presented an experiment, where the effects of the different levels of classification for the explanatory variables, the use of different safety rule specifications, and the use of different suppression algorithms were analysed in depth. It was shown that the current 1G table is not very useful to the end users as only 9 % of the total cells are active and safe (cf. table three in the Tables 3 and 4). However, aggregating the classifications too much would result in highly aggregated table, of which most could be published, but none would likely describe any useful information (cf. table four in the Tables 3 and 4). The analysis shown in the Table 4 illustrated that the most usable alternative ranks the highest with three criteria: confidential cell share, the absolute amount of safe cells, and the size of the table.

Eurostat has suggested aggregating the activity breakdown variable *nace* to contain its first level only (cf. table one in the Tables 3 and 4, [3]). The findings from this paper indicate that the size of such table reduces to 14 % of the original, and the absolute amount of safe cells reduces drastically, while the confidential cell share remains relatively high at 51 %. Thus, the findings of this experiment do not support the Eurostat proposal for the table 1G. According to the analysis in this paper, the most usable table has a total of 650 cells (cf. table six in the Tables 3 and 4). With this table, there are three levels for *nace* and large area aggregates for *uci*. 92 % of the total cells are active, and 65 % are safe.

While the results were generally similar for the other suppression algorithm, it was noted that especially for the large tables the second algorithm was more efficient, resulting in five to ten percentage points lower secondary suppression rates. For the most usable table, the total safe cell share increases to 69 %.

The size of the most usable table suggested in this paper is only 10 % of the original 1G table, which indicates that a lot of detail is lost in aggregating *uci* from the country level to the area aggregates. Thus, a concern remains that such aggregation might not be useful to those end users, who have been using the currently available detailed *nace* information on the country level on the EU member countries and the fourteen most important partner countries. On the other hand, it should be noted that the researchers would still have access to the 1G2 table, where all of the world's countries are presented with the sum of the total business economy. As the alternative 1G table presents the aggregated geographical totals (EU and the rest of the world) for the detailed business activity breakdown, the two inward FATS tables would intuitively complement each other to as much detail as possible given the current demand for protection.

Although this paper has shown that using aggregation of the explanatory variables can result in great reductions in the confidential cell share in the case of the inward FATS, there remains other concerns related to the usability of the tables. Alternative ways to publish the inward FATS data could be considered in order to be able to publish more detailed information. One option could be to use the perturbative statistical disclosure control methods. However, as perturbative methods are not currently used in Statistics Finland or in the inward FATS production, more research should be conducted to examine the suitability of such methods in the case of the inward FATS and similar statistics.

This paper has discussed the task of balancing confidentiality and usability in the case of the inward FATS data. If the required level of confidentiality is given by the current legislation, there is not much room to manoeuvre the level of usability either. The demand for detail depends on the uses of the statistics. There may also exist conflicting needs, where different types of end users need different types of information. Therefore the appropriate level of detail is difficult to adjust from the point of view of the NSIs, as acknowledging the needs for specific users is most of the time outside the scope of their capabilities.

Choosing the most efficient variable *uci* for aggregation, the current situation of the inward FATS series 1G can be improved at least to some extent. While it is definitely more useful to have non-suppressed cells rather than suppressed ones, aggregation in itself is a method of reducing information. Consequently, the question remains whether the amount of information increases to any usable degree, even if the confidential cell share reduces. The paper shows that the task of balancing confidentiality and usability by aggregation and secondary suppression algorithms is nearly impossible.

References

1. Box, G.E.P.: Improving almost anything: Ideas and essays. Wiley-Interscience, Hoboken (2006)
2. Eurostat: Foreign AffiliaTes Statistics (FATS) recommendations manual, 3rd edn. Eurostat Methodologies and Working papers (2012)
3. Eurostat: FATS in FRIBS. Draft document for JOINT FATS WG meeting, June 10, 2013, Luxembourg. Internal documentation (2013)
4. Hundepool, A., van de Wetering, A., Ramaswamy, R., de Wolf, P.-P., Giessing, S., Fischetti, M., Salazar-Gonzalez, J.J., Castro, J., Lowthian, P.: τ-ARGUS User's Manual. Version 3.5. ESSnet-project (2011), http://neon.vb.cbs.nl/casc/Software/TauManualV3.5.pdf
5. Statistics Finland: Guidelines on Protection of Tabulated Enterprise Data. Reg. no. TK-00-270-13 (2013)

Appendices

Table 5. Experiment with the second algorithm

Run number	A nace	B nace	C uci	D uci	E safety rule	Total	Total active	Total safe	Safe/ Active	Confidential/ Active
1	−	−	−	−	−	6240	1636	749	0.46	0.54
2	−	−	−	−	+	6240	1636	775	0.47	0.53
3	+	−	−	−	−	3840	1148	560	0.49	0.51
4	+	−	−	−	+	3840	1148	589	0.51	0.49
5	−	+	−	−	−	864	370	212	0.57	0.43
6	−	+	−	−	+	864	370	222	0.60	0.40
7	−	−	+	−	−	650	599	448	0.75	0.25
8	−	−	+	−	+	650	599	451	0.75	0.25
9	−	−	−	+	−	1040	656	438	0.67	0.33
10	−	−	−	+	+	1040	656	442	0.67	0.33
11	+	−	+	−	−	400	381	321	0.84	0.16
12	+	−	+	−	+	400	381	322	0.85	0.15
13	+	−	−	+	−	640	432	308	0.71	0.29
14	+	−	−	+	+	640	432	314	0.73	0.27
15	−	+	+	−	−	90	89	81	0.91	0.09
16	−	+	+	−	+	90	89	81	0.91	0.09
17	−	+	−	+	−	144	112	85	0.76	0.24
18	−	+	−	+	+	144	112	85	0.76	0.24

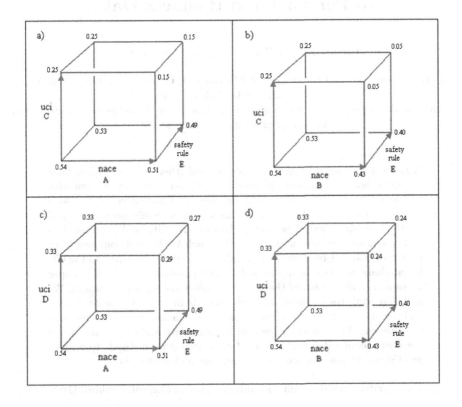

Fig. 2. Cube display for the second algorithm

Table 6. The table choices with the second algorithm

Table number	Run (Cf. Table 5)	nace levels	uci	Total	Active	Safe	Active Total	Safe Total	Table size	Size compared to original
1	5	1	countries	864	370	212	0.43	0.25	18 x 48	0.14
2	3	2	countries	3840	1148	560	0.30	0.15	80 x 48	0.62
3	1	3	countries	6240	1636	749	0.26	0.12	130 x 48	1.00
4	15	1	large areas	90	89	81	0.99	0.90	18 x 5	0.01
5	11	2	large areas	400	381	321	0.95	0.80	80 x 5	0.06
6	7	3	large areas	650	599	448	0.92	0.69	130 x 5	0.10
7	17	1	continents	144	112	85	0.78	0.59	18 x 8	0.02
8	13	2	continents	640	432	308	0.68	0.48	80 x 8	0.10
9	9	3	continents	1040	656	438	0.63	0.42	130 x 8	0.17

Applicability of Confidentiality Methods to Personal and Business Data

Christine M. O'Keefe[1] and Natalie Shlomo[2]

[1] CSIRO Computational Informatics, GPO Box 664, Canberra ACT 2601, Australia
Christine.O'Keefe@csiro.au
[2] School of Social Sciences, The University of Manchester, Manchester, M13 9PL, UK
natalie.shlomo@manchester.ac.uk

Abstract. National Statistical Agencies and other data custodians have a responsibility to protect the confidentiality of commercially sensitive business data as well as personally private social and survey data. However, traditional confidentiality methods have generally been developed for the context of social or survey data about individual persons. Several recent studies have highlighted that such traditional confidentiality measures may not be directly applicable to business data, due to the different characteristics of business data and personal data. In this paper we provide a discussion of these recent studies and their conclusions. We find that while the confidentiality objective is the same for business data and social and survey data, the disclosure scenarios and disclosure risks are different. There is evidence that business data and social and survey data may require different confidentiality protection methods to achieve an effective balance between disclosure risk and data utility.

Keywords: Confidentiality, Privacy, Disclosure Control, Business Data.

1 Introduction

National Statistical Agencies and other data custodians hold a wealth of data vital to informed decision making, research and debate within governments and the community. At the same time, data relevant to issues of public interest, such as health, education or criminal justice, can reveal highly sensitive information about individual persons. People expect that their privacy will be protected, where privacy is understood as the interest a person has in controlling the dissemination of information about themself. Thus data custodians usually give an assurance of confidentiality, which is understood as the expectation on a data custodian not to disseminate information about individual persons. The balance between allowing statistical analysis of sensitive data and assuring confidentiality is often characterised as a trade-off between disclosure risk and data utility [12], where *disclosure risk* attempts to capture the probability of a disclosure of sensitive information, while *data utility* attempts to capture some measure of the usefulness of the released data. *Confidentiality methods* are technical approaches designed to address the balance between disclosure risk and data utility, in addition to governance and information security measures.

J. Domingo-Ferrer (Ed.): PSD 2014, LNCS 8744, pp. 350–363, 2014.

Traditionally, the study of confidentiality methods has assumed a context of data about people. As recently as 2011 confidentiality has been defined as *a status accorded to information about a person* [13, Section 1.1].

National Statistical Agencies and other data custodians also collect business data for reporting and policy analysis of business growth and performance at the microeconomic level. Such data usually contain commercially sensitive information about individual businesses, for example: production, employment, customs, sales, financial and tax data. In addition to the privacy issues which can arise when business data contain personal information about employees, businesses will normally seek to protect their competitive advantage by controlling the dissemination of information about their business operations. Thus, data custodian agencies also operate under an imperative not to disseminate information about individual businesses, although for the different reason of commercial sensitivity rather than personal privacy. Confidentiality assurances given by data custodians to businesses can often also cover publicly available data. This situation is recognised in an alternative recent definition of disclosure: *A disclosure occurs when a person or organisation recognises or learns something that they did not know already about another person or organisation, via released data* [19].

In practice, the confidentiality protection objective for business data is the same as for personal data, that is, not to reveal confidential information. On the other hand, a 2006 survey of OECD countries [2] found that: *Only a limited number of countries permit some form of access to business microdata; illustrating the practical difficulties inherent in preserving confidentiality of individual businesses.* The survey analysts found this to be particularly true in smaller economies where large businesses are more prominent. They concluded that: *The increased difficulty and the risks associated with disclosure of business microdata have so far stopped some countries from moving forward in this domain.*

It is the purpose of this paper to seek to shed light on the increased difficulty and the risks associated with providing access to business microdata, in comparison with social and survey data, through a discussion of recent collaborative studies involving the authors. In the paper we focus on microdata, that is, data where each record is contributed by a single data subject (person or business), so that the record typically comprises values of a number of variables for the corresponding data subject. A data subject may contribute more than one record, for example, if the data are time-stamped hospital event data.

1.1   Characteristics of Personal and Business Data

The table in Figure 1 is intended to highlight the different general characteristics of personal and business data. Personal data are those in which each record corresponds to an individual person, and the data represent information gathered in a population census or survey on a given population sample. Business data are those in which each record corresponds to an individual business, and the data generally represent information gathered in a business survey.

	Personal data	Business data
Number of records	many	few
Each record relates to	person	business
Geographic association	point	point, line or region
Pattern of sample inclusion probabilities for population units	each person has a low probability of inclusion	• large businesses always included • medium size businesses frequently included • each small business has a low probability of inclusion
Number of variables	many	few
Types of variables	mostly categorical	mostly continuous
Variable distributions		highly skewed, strong correlations
Outliers	rare	large businesses are outliers on most variables

Fig. 1. Characteristics of Personal and Business Data

The combination of the small size of business datasets, the certain inclusion of large businesses in surveys, and the fact that their data record values are outliers on most variables, heightens the confidentiality issues for large businesses.

1.2   Types of Disclosure

The literature distinguishes different types of disclosures commonly considered for statistical microdata, see [19, Section 3.3] and its references. These are applicable both for individual persons and individual businesses.

An *identity disclosure* occurs when an individual is identifiable from the data release, because a particular microdata record can be associated with that individual. An example of identity disclosure occurs in personal data when a de-identified record representing a medical procedure is associated with a patient's name, such as could occur if the record of the procedure is compared with records in a database of surgery bookings containing patient names.

An *attribute disclosure* occurs when sensitive information is attributed to a particular individual. In the above example of the medical procedure dataset, the record may include comorbidity details, or the surgery booking may include contact details of next of kin or details of the patient's prior procedures.

The main ways that an identity disclosure can occur are:

- *Release of identifying information* - avoided by de-identification.
- *Spontaneous recognition* - where an individual is sufficiently unusual in a data collection, so that the individual can be recognised from normally non-identifying attributes. This may occur if the attributes have extreme values such as extreme old age or an unusual combination of attributes.
- *Matching* to another data base - where combinations of *key variables* in the data occur in other databases sufficiently rarely. If a match is found to an external dataset containing identifying information, then identification occurs. Otherwise, a match may be found to an external dataset with sufficient

additional characteristics that spontaneous recognition occurs. Dates and locations are unique and therefore are particularly vulnerable to matching.

Attribute disclosure usually follows identity disclosure. An individual is first identified in a dataset, using some variable values, and then disclosure of values of other variables included in the same dataset or the matched dataset follows.

1.3   Confidentiality Protection - Overview

A high level discussion of the problem of balancing allowing statistical analysis of private or sensitive data and maintaining confidentiality typically covers two broad approaches often used in combination [14,22]. The first approach is *restricting access,* where access to data is granted under strong controls including researcher training and registration, supervised secure data laboratories or secure remote access environments with analysis output checking, as well as legal and operational protections and agreements [3,4,25,37,38,39]. The second approach is *restricting or altering data,* where less than the full data set is released or the data altered in some way before release to analysts, in order to provide enhanced confidentiality protection. Recognising that achieving an identification requires first an attempt at an identification, then success of the attempt [23], we see that these two broad approaches correspond to minimising the likelihood of an attempt and the likelihood that an attempt will be successful, respectively.

When datasets are prepared for statistical analysis, identifying attributes such as name and address are almost always removed, as well as other sensitive attributes. Often, this is followed by the application of *statistical disclosure control* methods such as aggregation of geographic classifications, rounding, swapping or deleting values, and adding random noise [1,7,8,9,10,13,26,41].

Motivated by the drawbacks associated with statistical disclosure control, Rubin [33] suggested the alternative of generating and releasing *synthetic data* [22,32]. In this approach, the data custodian fits a model to the original data then repeatedly draws from the model to generate multiple synthetic datasets which are released for analysis.

Under the alternative *remote analysis* approach [18,30,35], a remote analysis system accepts a query from an analyst, runs it on data held in a secure environment, then returns confidentialised results to the analyst. The recently-developed *differential privacy* standard seeks to formalise the notion of confidentiality in the context of the output of algorithms executed on confidential databases, which includes statistical analysis enabled via remote analysis [15,16].

From the above discussion it should be clear that there are a number of different approaches to achieving a balance between allowing statistical analysis of confidential or private data and maintaining standards of confidentiality. Each approach has its own strengths and weaknesses, which means that there is no common approach that is suitable for every situation. It is important in any given situation to select the method which is most suitable for the given dataset, custodian, researcher, research project and regulatory environment.

1.4   Confidentiality Protection - Business Data

In practice, business datasets are not released by agencies unless they are highly perturbed by, for example, removal of all large businesses and application of other statistical disclosure control techniques or by replacement of the entire dataset with a synthetic dataset [29,31]. The risk of identity disclosure is reduced by ensuring that there are no small counts in the cross-classifications of identifying key variables, and the risk of attribute disclosure is often reduced by the addition of random noise to the continuous data variables.

The Australian Bureau of Statistics (ABS) releases business microdata as Confidentialised Unit Record Files (CURFs) on CD-ROM, as well as through its Remote Access Data Laboratory and its On-site Data Laboratory [3]. In these contexts: *It is primarily the impact that the confidentiality policy has on the release of information from ... large businesses that is of concern* [36].

The United Kingdom Office For National Statistics (ONS) Business Data Linking (BDL) Project provides access to business data only via its secure on-site Microdata Lab, where academic researchers can carry out statistical analyses [25]. These data are confidential, therefore access is tightly restricted.

The US Census Bureau Center for Economic Studies (CES) allows research using microdata files under strictly controlled confidentiality rules, at Census Research Data Centers (RDC) [38]. The CES research program also develops public-use business data products by combining and enhancing existing data.

2   Personal and Business Data - Examples and Disclosure Scenarios

A disclosure scenario includes: motivation, target variables, opportunity, means and attack types [13]. In this section, we discuss motivation and target variables in the different contexts of personal and business data.

We assume a common context for opportunity, means and attack types, as follows. First, we suppose an analyst (sometimes called a snooper, intruder or attacker) has *opportunity* provided by having access to a microdata file by one of the approaches described in Section 1.4. The *means* available to them are statistical and computational skills, computational power, as well as knowledge including dataset metadata and other additional information. The main *attack type* that we consider is matching all or part of the released dataset to an external dataset on a selection of *key variables*.

2.1   Example of Personal Data and Disclosure Scenarios

As an example of personal data, consider the public use microdata sample from the 2002 Uganda Population and Housing Census provided by IPUMS International [24] and used in [11]. The microdata file is a 10% systematic sample of the population living in Uganda, comprising 2,497,449 questionnaire records involving more than 100 variables at the household and personal level for each respondent. The variables include: number of persons in the household, ranging 1 to 30; age, ranging from 10 to 95; marital status, with five categories; literacy, with two categories; and employment status, with three categories.

A possible *motivation* for a disclosure attempt would be to discredit or otherwise embarrass a national statistical agency by showing that their assurances of protection of data confidentiality are unfounded. An analyst would use values of demographic variables for matching with records in other databases, in order to achieve identity disclosure and consequent attribute disclosure. In this case it can be enough that a record is re-identified by associating it with a person - it may not be necessary to reveal further sensitive values for the re-identification to have serious consequences for trust in the national statistical agency.

Personal data usually arise from surveys, and the typically low sampling fractions lead to uncertainty about identity of any individual. It is therefore most important to protect against identity disclosure, because once an identification is made, attribute disclosure will almost always follow.

In order to quantify disclosure risk for personal data, it is usually assumed that the analyst would have no knowledge of any attributes in any records. Measures of disclosure risk for personal data focus on estimating the probability of re-identification either probabilistically or by matching to an external dataset such as a telephone directory or electoral register, see for example [34].

2.2 Example of Business Data and Disclosure Scenarios

As a business data set, we discuss the *Sugar Farms* data from a 1982 survey of the sugar cane industry in Queensland, Australia [6]. The data set corresponds to a sample of 338 Queensland sugar farms, where the sample was stratified by cane growing region and size of quota and within each stratum a simple random sample was selected. The data set has one nominal categorical variable: Cane Growing Region (region) and five continuous variables: Sugar Cane Area (area), Sugar Cane Harvest (harvest), Receipts (receipts), Costs (costs) and Profit (profit). The variable profit is calculated as the difference between receipts and costs and is not considered further in this paper. There are no missing values.

Figure 2 shows summary histograms for the variables area and receipts, which are also similar to those for harvest and costs. All four variables area, receipts, harvest and costs are highly correlated as suggested by Figure 3.

In the Sugar Farms data, the variable region is not sensitive. The variable area is considered an identifying variable because of the risk of data matching to public registers of farm size and thereby re-identifying farms in the data. The variables harvest, receipts, costs and profit are commercially sensitive because they reveal information about the farm's production, efficiency and profitability.

In addition to the possible *motivation* of discrediting or otherwise embarrassing a national statistical agency by showing that their assurances of protection of data confidentiality are unfounded, a more likely motivation for a disclosure attempt would be to learn commercially sensitive information in order to gain competitive advantage. The types of disclosures relevant to business data differ from those relevant to microdata arising from social and household surveys.

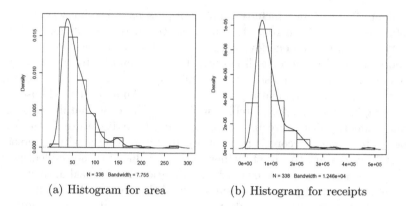

(a) Histogram for area   (b) Histogram for receipts

Fig. 2. Histograms and densities for area and receipts in the Sugar Farms data

	Region2	Region3	Region4	area	log(harvest)	log(costs)
Region2	1	-0.21	-0.21	-0.53	0.16	0.14
Region3		1	-0.35	0.17	0.07	0.02
Region4			1	-0.21	-0.16	-0.22
area				1	0.82	0.82
log(harvest)					1	0.91
log(costs)						1

Fig. 3. Correlations between variables in the Sugar Farms data

First, the identities of the market leading businesses in any industry sector are usually widely known and vulnerable to spontaneous recognition. For these large businesses, therefore, the major concern is attribute disclosure. Also, there are often public registers of business characteristics, such as farm sizes or other enterprise data, which make identity disclosure very easy for many businesses. For these reasons, business data mainly need protection against attribute disclosure.

To quantify disclosure risk for business data, the dataset is treated as a census of a population of known businesses, so that business identities are not afforded any protection by sampling as occurs with personal data. Measures of disclosure risk focus on attribute disclosure and typically quantify the distance between real and estimated attributes, using appropriate distance measures [28].

3 Personal and Business Data Confidentiality Case Studies

In this section we summarise three recent studies involving the authors to provide a discussion of the applicability of traditional confidentiality methods to the challenge of protecting confidentiality of business data.

3.1   Remote Analysis

Business datasets made available for research commonly have the large businesses removed (in addition to other confidentiality protection measures). Full business datasets are not made available for research. The alternative remote analysis paradigm would seem attractive in this application, since large businesses can be included in analyses, and only the results need to be confidentialised. In this case, the analysis results then represent all businesses.

The potential for remote analysis to address the balance between microdata access and confidentiality protection, in the context of business data, has been investigated for exploratory data analysis and linear regression [28]. The remote analysis approach was compared with a traditional statistical disclosure control (SDC) approach on the Sugar Farms business data. The main difference between the approaches was that the five large farms were removed from the dataset under the SDC approach, but left in the dataset under remote analysis. However, remote analysis required some smoothing and trimming of results, including removal of outliers from analysis output and output plots. Note that the outliers removed from the analysis output and plots did not necessarily correspond to the large farms.

The main relevant features of the SDC approach, and their main consequences, were found to be:

- *The deletion of large farms from the dataset* meant that it models only the small and medium farms, resulting in similar medians but reduced means and variances.
- *The addition of noise to variable values* led to significant information loss.
- *The categorisation of area into groups to reduce identity disclosure risk* led to significant information loss.
  - In exploratory data analysis, there was a significant deterioration in the information made available to the analyst.
  - In regression analysis of the sugar farms data, there were incorrect conclusions regarding significance of variables.

The main relevant feature of the remote analysis approach, and its main consequence, is:

- *The smoothing and trimming of displayed results in order not to reveal outliers and individual values* meant that the results presented to the analyst would not exactly correspond to the analysis as it was carried out. The removal of outlying points from residual plots could be indicated, so that the analyst will know that the model has outlying residual values, but will have no information about their magnitude or impact.

The worked example in [28] supports the conclusion that the advantages of remote analysis may outweigh the disadvantages in some cases, including for some analyses of unconfidentialised business data, provided the analyst is aware of the output confidentialisation methods and their potential impact. For example, the remote analysis system may provide analysts with a good way of developing their research strategies and obtaining preliminary indicative results prior to gaining full access to licensed detailed data in an on-site data laboratory. It may also be useful in the context of providing access to research data to support the objective of enabling reproducibility of research.

Remote analysis systems often have restrictions and disadvantages, including inability to import external microdata sets, and potentially restrictions on allowable data transformations, data subsetting and new variable definitions all of which can increase disclosure risk if uncontrolled. There are potentially many useful analyses which would not be possible through a remote analysis system, and the user would need to seek an alternative data access mode.

3.2   Synthetic Data

Drechsler and Reiter [11] conducted a simulation study to compare four data synthesisers based on machine learning algorithms, using the above subset of the 2002 Uganda census public use file. The four synthesisers were based on classification and regression trees, bagging, random forests, and support vector machines. Their evaluation suggested that the synthesisers based on regression trees can give rise to synthetic datasets that provide reliable estimates and low disclosure risks, and can be implemented easily.

In the context of this current study, it is of interest to ask whether Drechsler and Reiter's conclusion also holds for business data, as well as the subsets of census data used in the original evaluation. Lee, Kim and O'Keefe [21] gave a detailed example on the Sugar Farms business data enabling a comparison of the outputs of exploratory data analysis and linear regression under a regression-tree-based synthetic data approach, as well as an evaluation with respect to analysis of the original data. The example showed that univariate exploratory data analysis of the synthetic data provided good information about the distribution of the individual variables. However, this was not always the case for bivariate exploratory data analysis which tended to show more outliers and/or tended to underestimate the correlations between the variable pairs. Perhaps more seriously, the regression analysis of the synthetic dataset did not give the same inferences (in terms of variable significance levels) as regression analysis of the original data. It also had higher residual standard errors and greater spread was observed in the regression residuals.

The authors suggested that the inaccurate results of the statistical analysis of the synthetic dataset were due to the failure of the synthetic data to adequately capture the strong correlation structure structure amongst the variables in the dataset. This situation is made worse by the presence in business data of records corresponding to large enterprises, which are outliers on each of the main variables and would make large contributions to correlation measures.

3.3   Confidentialising Maps

The use of spatial methods and maps is essential in epidemiology and public health surveillance, where the health information of each individual person in the dataset is associated with the home address of the person. The need to protect the confidentiality of individuals' health information is well-recognised, and several approaches for protecting confidentiality of spatial health datasets have been proposed and evaluated in the epidemiology and health research literature [20,40]. These approaches address confidentiality issues regarding a restricted class of spatial datasets, namely those with a large number of records, and where each record is associated with a single geographic location, or point. The main methods for confidentialising spatial point data and maps are: reducing map resolution, suppression, aggregation, transformation and random perturbation.

Geographic Information Systems and related technologies have also long been part of the daily operation of government authorities, whose operations rely on geographical information. However, such applications often involve a more general type of spatial dataset, in which the geographic characteristic associated with each record could be either a point, a line or an area. In addition, there are often fewer records. For example, consider pollutant and emissions datasets, which are growing in importance as society seeks to understand the environment and our impact on it [5,17]. Typically, the records correspond to businesses and industries, which are generally fewer in number than individuals in any given area. Also, each record can be associated with either a spatial point (such as a factory), a spatial line (such as a road) or a spatial area (such as a farm).

The confidentialisation of more general maps of spatial (business) datasets containing a mixture of point, line and area records has been recently considered [27]. We say a record is *diffuse* if it corresponds to a geographic line or area, and call a dataset *mixed* if it contains both point and diffuse records. Any of the approaches of reducing map resolution, suppression, aggregation, transformation or random perturbation could be applied to the point records in a mixed dataset, and in principle most of them can be generalised to line and area records, however each approach has problems, as follows. The approaches of reducing map resolution and suppression are applicable, however the resulting significant information loss is likely to make them undesirable in practice. Aggregation could be applied to line and area records, but the chosen level of geography would need to be sufficiently high that it effectively aggregates the associated lines and areas as well as the points. Transformation and random perturbation may not sufficiently mask lines and regions with distinctive shapes unless they quite radically transform or perturb, which is likely to be undesirable in practical applications.

An additional concern in business data contexts including emissions and pollutant release reporting, is that accurate information must be reported in a transparent process, so that suppression, transformation and random perturbation are not suitable solutions.

The following is suggested as a framework for confidentialising spatial datasets:

1. partition of the map region into disjoint cells,

2. distribution of the data records into grid cells, where diffuse records are distributed over grid cells in proportions suggested by a suitable proxy dataset,
3. confidentialisation of the data in the grid cells, and
4. representation of the data as a heat map in which data in the cells (in ranges) are represented as colours.

The map partition could be, for example, a square or hexagonal grid, or a geographic or political area partition, with data records distributed either directly or apportioned according to a readily accessible proxy database. The use of a heat map effectively "bins" the data values into ranges and reduces the amount of confidentialisation needed in the third step of the framework, however small cells and outliers may still present a confidentiality risk. In some cases aggregation can be used, with care to avoid increasing the total "mass" or "heat" of the map region [27]. An alternative is identification of sensitive cells then redistribution of sensitive cell values to adjacent cells until no sensitive cells remain.

This method is designed to be useful for business data sets. It combines and adapts traditional non-perturbative disclosure control techniques, which would not introduce bias but could cause some information loss.

4   Discussion and Conclusions

National Statistical Agencies and other data custodians have a responsibility to protect the confidentiality of commercially sensitive business data as well as personally private social and survey data. Traditionally the study of confidentiality methods has assumed the context of social or survey data about individual persons. However, business data are quite different in nature from social and survey data. In this paper we have sought to shed light on the question of whether the confidentiality issues are the same, and whether the confidentiality methods developed for personal data are also applicable for business data.

For both business data and personal data, the confidentiality objective of not disclosing confidential information is the same. However, the common disclosure risk channels are different. For personal data typically arising from social surveys, identity disclosure through matching to external databases is the major concern because attribute disclosure almost always follows identity disclosure. For business data, business identities are vulnerable to spontaneous recognition and hence the major concern is attribute disclosure.

Turning to the question of whether the confidentiality methods developed for personal data are also applicable for business data, we have discussed three case studies on business data to highlight potential issues.

The first case study explored the potential of remote analysis servers to overcome the problem of large businesses in business data sets. Under remote analysis, outliers can still be included in statistical analyses (in contrast to traditional statistical disclosure control methods), yielding valid inferences, however statistical analysis outputs are confidentialised before delivery to the analyst. The study supports the conclusion that the advantages of remote analysis may outweigh the disadvantages in the case of the statistical analysis of business data.

The second case study involved using a regression-tree based synthetic business dataset as a confidentialised version of a business data set. The example highlighted the challenge of capturing the high correlations characteristic of business data, and showed the consequences of not meeting this challenge, in terms of incorrect inferences in regression analyses.

The third case study, on confidentialising maps of point and diffuse spatial business data, highlighted the need for non-perturbative confidentialisation methods to ensure that accurate information is presented in a transparent way. Most of the methods developed for epidemiological and public health spatial data and maps are not applicable, with only aggregation being acceptable. A four stage framework is proposed, involving a range of confidentialisation measures introduced at several stages.

These case studies have highlighted several points worth noting. First, since synthetic data need to avoid outliers, variable relationships are distorted unless preserved through the confidentiality model. On the other hand, users are generally unrestricted in their use of the data. Synthetic data are typically not used for producing final results for publication, but are useful during preparation for access to confidential data. There are a range of different remote analysis systems with varying degrees of confidentiality protection, depending on the scenario including the particular type of data involved. For highly sensitive data such as business data, the aim of preventing the identification of a single observation leads to limitations on data transformations, individual analyses (eg requiring robust regression) and results releases. On the other hand, such systems are often designed to avoid the need for expert checking of outputs which can be released for publication. The issue of confidentiality for geography can be addressed with either of the synthetic data or remote analysis approaches. The data represented in maps can be synthetic, aggregated, or confidentialised via remote analysis.

In conclusion, it would seem that while the confidentiality objective is the same for commercially sensitive business data and personally private social and survey data, the disclosure risks are different. Further, there is evidence that personal and business data types require different confidentiality protection methods to achieve an effective balance between disclosure risk and data utility. It would be interesting to further investigate this phenomenon and try to understand which confidentiality methods are best applied to data with which characteristics. The issue of personal data contained within business data also needs further exploration. This issue arises, for example, for employees represented in business data, students represented in school data, and patients represented in hospital data. There is a real need to more closely tailor confidentiality methods according to the characteristics of the data, or possibly to develop new methods.

Acknowledgments. We thank Ray Chambers for the Sugar Farms data.

References

1. Adam, N., Wortmann, J.: Security-control methods for statistical databases: A comparative study. ACM Comput. Surv. 21, 515–556 (1989)
2. Ahmad, N., Backer, K.D., Yoon, Y.: An OECD perspective on microdata access: Trends, opportunities and challenges. Statistical Journal of the IAOS 26, 57–63 (2010)
3. Australian Bureau of Statistics (website), http://www.abs.gov.au
4. Australian Bureau of Statistics: Remote Access Data Laboratory (RADL) (website), http://www.abs.gov.au (accessed January 23, 2013)
5. Australian Government Department of Climate Change and Energy Efficiency: Australian National Greenhouse Accounts National Inventory Report 2010, vol. 1. Tech. Rep., 320 p. (2012), http://climatechange.gov.au
6. Chambers, R., Dunstan, R.: Estimating distribution functions from survey data. Biometrika 73, 597–604 (1986)
7. Domingo-Ferrer, J., Magkos, E. (eds.): PSD 2010. LNCS, vol. 6344. Springer, Heidelberg (2010)
8. Domingo-Ferrer, J., Saygın, Y. (eds.): PSD 2008. LNCS, vol. 5262. Springer, Heidelberg (2008)
9. Domingo-Ferrer, J., Torra, V. (eds.): PSD 2004. LNCS, vol. 3050. Springer, Heidelberg (2004)
10. Doyle, P., Lane, J., Theeuwes, J., Zayatz, L. (eds.): Confidentiality, Disclosure and Data Access: Theory and Practical Applications for Statistical Agencies. North-Holland, Amsterdam (2001)
11. Drechsler, J., Reiter, J.: An empirical evaluation of easily implemented, nonparametric methods for generating synthetic datasets. Comput. Stat. Data An. 55, 3232–3243 (2011)
12. Duncan, G.T., Keller-McNulty, S.A., Stokes, S.L.: Disclosure risk vs data utility: The R-U confidentiality map. Technical Report LA-UR-01-6428, Los Alamos National Laboratory (2001)
13. Duncan, G., Elliot, M., Salazar-Gonzàlez, J.J.: Statistical Confidentiality. Springer, New York (2011)
14. Duncan, G., Pearson, R.: Enhancing access to microdata while protecting confidentiality: prospects for the future. Stat. Sci. 6, 219–239 (1991)
15. Dwork, C., McSherry, F., Nissim, K., Smith, A.: Calibrating noise to sensitivity in private data analysis. In: 3rd IACR Theory of Cryptography Conference, pp. 265–284 (2006)
16. Dwork, C., Smith, A.: Differential privacy for statistics: What we know and what we want to learn. J. Priv. Confid. 1, 135–154 (2009)
17. European Pollutant Release and Transfer Register, http://prtr.ec.europa.eu
18. Gomatam, S., Karr, A., Reiter, J., Sanil, A.: Data dissemination and disclosure limitation in a world without microdata: A risk-utility framework for remote access systems. Stat. Sci. 20, 163–177 (2005)
19. Hundepool, A., Domingo-Ferrer, J., Franconi, L., Giessing, S., Nordholt, E., Spicer, K., de Wolf, P.P.: Statistical Disclosure Control. Wiley series in survey methodology. John Wiley & Sons, United Kingdom (2012)
20. Kamel-Boulos, M., Curtis, A., AbdelMalik, P.: Musings on privacy issues in health research involving disaggregate geographic data about individuals. Int. J. Health Geogr. 8, 46, 8 p. (2009)

21. Lee, J.H., Kim, I.Y., O'Keefe, C.M.: On regression-tree-based synthetic data methods for business data. Journal of Privacy and Confidentiality 5(1), 5 (2013)
22. Little, R.: Statistical analysis of masked data. J. Off. Stat. 9, 407–426 (1993)
23. Marsh, C., Skinner, C., Arber, S., Penhale, B., Openshaw, S., Hobcraft, J., Lievesley, D., Walford, N.: The case for samples of anonymized records from the 1991 census. J. Roy. Stat. Soc. Ser. A 154, 305–340 (1991)
24. Minnesota Population Center: Integrated public use microdata series, international: version 6.0. Tech. rep., University of Minnesota, Minneapolis, technical Report (2010)
25. Office for National Statistics (website), http://statistics.gov.uk
26. Office of Information and Regulatory Affairs: Statistical policy working paper 22 - report on statistical disclosure limitation methodology. Subcommittee on Disclosure Limitation Methodology, Federal Committee on Statistical Methodology, Statistical Policy Office, Office of Information and Regulatory Affairs, Office of Management and Budget (1994)
27. O'Keefe, C.: Confidentialising maps of mixed point and diffuse spatial data. In: Domingo-Ferrer, J., Tinnirello, I. (eds.) PSD 2012. LNCS, vol. 7556, pp. 226–240. Springer, Heidelberg (2012)
28. O'Keefe, C., Shlomo, N.: Comparison of remote analysis with statistical disclosure control for protecting the confidentiality of business data. Trans. Data Privacy 5, 403–432 (2012)
29. Raghunathan, T., Reiter, J., Rubin, D.: Multiple imputation for statistical disclosure limitation. J. Off. Stat. 19, 1–16 (2003)
30. Reiter, J.: Model diagnostics for remote-access regression systems. Stat. Comput. 13, 371–380 (2003)
31. Reiter, J.: Releasing multiply imputed, synthetic public-use microdata: An illustration and empirical study. J. Roy. Stat. Soc. A. Sta. 168, 185–205 (2005)
32. Reiter, J.: Using CART to generate partially synthetic public use microdata. J. Off. Stat. 21, 441–462 (2005)
33. Rubin, D.: Discussion: Statistical disclosure limitation. J. Off. Stat. 9, 462–468 (1993)
34. Skinner, C., Shlomo, N.: Assessing identification risk in survey microdata using log-linear models. J. Am. Stat. Assoc. 103, 989–1001 (2008)
35. Sparks, R., Carter, C., Donnelly, J., O'Keefe, C., Duncan, J., Keighley, T., McAullay, D.: Remote access methods for exploratory data analysis and statistical modelling: Privacy-Preserving Analytics™. Comput. Meth. Prog. Bio. 91, 208–222 (2008)
36. Sutcliffe, P., Caruso, M., Teasdale, H.: Issues associated with producing a longitudinal dataset of businesses. Research Paper, Methodology Advisory Committee 1352.0.55.062, Australian Bureau of Statistics, Statistical Services Branch, Canberra, 32 p. (2004)
37. UK Data Archive: Secure data service (website), http://securedata.data-archive.ac.uk
38. United States Census Bureau (website), http://census.gov
39. University of Chicago: NORC (website), http://www.norc.org
40. VanWey, L., Rindfuss, R., Gutmann, M., Entwisle, B., Balk, D.: Confidentiality and spatially explicit data: Concerns and challenges. P. Natl. A. Sci. USA 102, 15337–15342 (2005)
41. Willenborg, L., de Waal, T.: Elements of Statistical Disclosure Control. Lecture Notes in Statistics, vol. 155. Springer (2001)

Author Index